MISSIONS TO THE GAELS

Missions to the Gaels: Reformation and Counter-Reformation in Ulster and the Highlands and Islands of Scotland

Fiona A. Macdonald

First published in Great Britain in 2006 by
John Donald, an imprint of Birlinn Ltd

West Newington House
10 Newington Road
Edinburgh
EH9 1QS

www.birlinn.co.uk

ISBN 10: 0 85976 618 7
ISBN 13: 978-0-85976-618-0

British Library Cataloguing-in-Publication Data
A catalogue record for this book is available on request from the British Library

Typeset by Carnegie Publishing, Lancaster
Printed and bound by Bell & Bain Ltd, Glasgow

For John

Table of Contents

Acknowledgements

MY SINCERE THANKS go to a number of people and institutions who assisted in the making of this book. It was begun while I was in the Scottish History department at Glasgow University. I should particularly like to thank Professor Allan Macinnes, now of Aberdeen University, for commenting on my chapters at an earlier stage of their evolution, and for sharing his perceptive knowledge of Highland history. Thanks also are due to Professor James Kirk for some general pointers and to Dr John Durkan for some translations from the Latin. The book was finished in the Wellcome Unit for the History of Medicine of Glasgow University, where my colleagues created a most convivial, sociable environment that was so conducive to research. It was a department I very much enjoyed working in. In addition, I wish to thank the late Roy Porter, Professor of the Social History of Medicine at the Wellcome Centre for the History of Medicine at University College, London, for some general comments on the manuscript. I am also grateful to my colleagues in a previous department, the Celtic department at Glasgow University, to the peoples of the islands of Harris, Lewis and South Uist, where I had summer jobs, to the people of Skye, where I spent many vacations, and to the people of Moidart, the homeland of my late paternal grandfather, Sandy Macdonald, whose native knowledge, poetry, music and song or religious devotion imbued in me a love of the Gaelic culture.

Special appreciation on the archival side goes to the Right Rev. Mark Dilworth and Dr Christine Johnston, the staff of the Scottish Catholic Archives, Columba House, during the years in which I visited the archive and who hospitably shared with me copious amounts of tea and biscuits, as well as to the staff of the National Archives of Scotland in Edinburgh, where I consulted most of the presbyterian manuscript material used in this book. I also wish to acknowledge the assistance of the manuscript rooms of the National Library of Scotland in Edinburgh, the British Library in London and the reading room of the Presbyterian Historical Society in Belfast. The Public Record Office of Northern Ireland kindly allowed me to view three boxes of the Papers of the MacDonnells of Antrim, which had not then been catalogued. I am grateful to the Duke of Argyll for permission to consult the Argyll Survey in the National Register of Archives (Scotland) at the National Archives of Scotland, and to Mr Murdo MacDonald, Argyll and Bute District Archivist, who always gives so generously of his archival knowledge. Also fundamental to the ongoing progress of my research were the staff of the Glasgow University Library Document Delivery Unit who dealt with a multitude of inter-library loans over a number of years.

Copyright is acknowledged and I am grateful for permission to reproduce the following maps and figures: Church of Ireland dioceses *c.* 1570, by permission of Ruth Dudley Edwards and Routledge, Taylor and Francis Group Ltd, London; Highland parishes of the eighteenth century and list of parishes referred to by number, by permission of Charles Withers and the School of Scottish Studies, Edinburgh; Parishes of Argyll and Bute in 1689 (a section of 'The Highland Parishes in 1698: An Examination of Sources for the Definition of the Gaidhealtachd' (see Bibliography)), also by permission of Charles Withers and the School of Scottish Studies, Edinburgh; Synods and presbyteries in the 1640s, by permission of David Stevenson and the Royal Historical Society, London; The Catholic *Gaidhealtachd*, 1732, by permission of Charles Withers; and The Scottish *Gaeltachd* in 1698, by permission of Charles Withers and Routledge, Taylor and Francis Group Ltd, London.

I also have to thank a number of people for their more personal contribution in giving time and resources to enable me to undertake my research: my parents, Anne and the late Angus Macdonald, supported me generously with care, time and finance through the long years of education and research which brought me to this stage, and my son, Kaeran MacDonald, lived with his mother's compulsion to research through much of his youth. In particular, I owe a great debt to John Dempster, who made space, literally and temporally, in which I could work and who also digitised the maps. Above all, I would like to thank him for his unqualified friendship over so many decades. And it is in acknowledgement of all that he has done that I dedicate this book to him.

Conventions and Abbreviations

Dates: Dates are given throughout in New Style. Prior to 1600, the new year is taken to begin on 1 January (Scottish usage) rather than 25 March (English usage), and for these months the year is given in its modern form.

Money: Monetary values are generally given as either sterling or Scots, but where unstipulated are Scots prior to 1707 and sterling afterwards.

Quotations: All abbreviations from primary sources have been extended, but the spelling is original. Punctuation is mainly original, but in long, unpunctuated sentences, punctuation has been inserted where this is necessary to assist the sense.

The following abbreviations are used in the text:

A New History of Ireland, II, III, IV	A. Cosgrove (ed.), *A New History of Ireland: II, Medieval Ireland* 1169–1534 (Oxford: 1987); T. W. Moody, F. X. Martin and F. J. Byrne (eds.), *A New History of Ireland: III, Early Modern Ireland, 1534–1691* (Oxford, 1976); T. W. Moody and W. E. Vaughan (eds.), *A New History of Ireland: IV, Eighteenth-Century Ireland, 1691–1800* (Oxford, 1986).
Anson, *Underground Catholicism*	Peter F. Anson, *Underground Catholicism in Scotland 1622–1878* (Montrose, 1970).
CSPI	H. C. Hamilton, E. G. Atkinson *et al.* (eds.), *Calendar of State Papers relating to Ireland, 1509–1670*, 24 vols. (London, 1860–1910).
CSPS	J. Bain *et al.* (eds.), *Calendar of State Papers relating to Scotland and Mary, Queen of Scots, 1547–1603*, 13 vols. (Edinburgh, 1898–1969).
Fasti	Hew Scott *et al.* (eds.), *Fasti Ecclesiae Scoticanae*, 10 vols. (Edinburgh, 1915–1981), I, II, IV, VII.
General Assembly Commission, I, II, III	A. F. Mitchell and J. Christie (eds.), *General Assembly Commission Records: I, Records 1646–47*, SHS, 1st series, 11 (Edinburgh, 1892); Mitchell, A. F. and J. Christie (eds.), General Assembly Commission Records: II, 1648–1649, SHS, 1st series, 25 (Edinburgh, 1896); Christie, James (ed.), General Assembly Commission Records: III, 1650–52, SHS, 1st series, 58 (Edinburgh, 1909).

IFM	Cathaldus Giblin (ed.), *The Irish Franciscan Mission to Scotland, 1619–1646. Documents from Roman Archives* (Dublin, 1964).
Irish Fasti	Rev. James McConnell and Rev. S. G. McConnell, *Fasti of the Irish Presbyterian Church* (Belfast, 1937–50).
Memoirs of Scottish Catholics, I, II	W. Forbes Leith, *Memoirs of Scottish Catholics during the XVII and XVIIIth Centuries*, I, 1627–1649, and II, 1647–1793 (London, 1909).
Minutes of the Synod of Argyll, I, II	Duncan C. Mactavish (ed.), *Minutes of the Synod of Argyll, 1639–1651*, SHS, 3rd series, 37 (Edinburgh, 1943); Mactavish, Duncan C. (ed.), Minutes of the Synod of Argyll, 1652–1661, SHS, 3rd series, 38 (Edinburgh, 1944).
NAS	National Archives of Scotland, Edinburgh (formerly the Scottish Record Office (SRO)).
NLS	National Library of Scotland, Edinburgh.
OFM	Order of Friars Minor (Franciscans).
Presbyterian Church in Ireland, I, II, III	James Seaton Reid, *The History of the Presbyterian Church in Ireland*, 3 vols. (London, Dublin and Belfast, 1st edition, 1837; 2nd edition, 1853), I, II, III.
PRONI	Public Record Office of Northern Ireland, Belfast.
Records of the General Synod of Ulster, I, II	The General Assembly of the Presbyterian Church in Ireland, *Records of the General Synod of Ulster*: I, 1691–1720; II, 1721–1777 (Belfast, 1890, 1897).
RPCS	J. H. Burton, and D. Masson (eds.), *The Register of the Privy Council of Scotland, 1545–1625*, 1st series, 14 vols. (Edinburgh, 1877–1898), 1607–1610, 1616–1619; P. Hume Brown and D. Masson (eds.), *The Register of the Privy Council of Scotland, 1625–1660*, 2nd series, 8 vols. (Edinburgh, 1899–1908), 1625–1627, 1629–1630, 1630–1632.
RSCHS	Records of the Scottish Church History Society.
SCA	Scottish Catholic Archives, Columba House, Edinburgh.
SGS	*Scottish Gaelic Studies*.
SHS	Scottish History Society (Edinburgh, 4 series: 1887–1911, 61 vols.; 1911–1920, 20 vols.; 1921–1964, 55 vols.; 1964–).
SHR	*Scottish Historical Review*.
TGSI	*Transactions of the Gaelic Society of Inverness*.
UJA	*Ulster Journal of Archaeology*

List of Figures

Introduction

WHETHER viewed from an establishment or a traditional Gaelic standpoint, the period from the sixteenth to the eighteenth century was a period of dramatic transformation in Gaelic society. Evocatively described by the Irish poet Dáibhidh Ó Bruadair in 1760 as '*tonnbhriseadh an tseanghnáthaimh*' or the final cataclysm (literally 'wave breaking') of the old order, it was characterised by change at every level of society: political, administrative, ecclesiastical, social, cultural and commercial. As the independent Gaelic chiefdom was drawn increasingly into the sphere of centralised government, Gaelic society suffered irreparable cultural damage as the fabric of its learned institutions – the classical schools which taught bardic verse, harping, piping, *seanchus* (history and genealogy), law, medicine, stonemasonry and military skills – was ripped apart and the foundations of clan-based society were significantly eroded. Politically, this period marked a transition from fairly autonomous Gaelic units – lordships and clans with distinct social and economic frameworks – to the assimilation of the *Gaidhealtachdan* into their respective nation states. Indeed, it would not be an exaggeration to say that during this period the traditional mould of Irish and Scottish Gaelic societies was so totally rent asunder that the Gaels – coerced into an alien political and social system – were henceforth able to retain their distinctiveness in only a linguistic and cultural sense.

In order to appreciate the subtleties of activity in the religious sphere, it is necessary to understand something of the political and social contexts of Gaelic society. Both Irish and Scottish Gaelic societies were essentially militaristic: prowess in arms was a dominant feature of the lives of the ruling classes. A particular fulcrum of interaction between the Gaels, in and around the mid-sixteenth century, was the trade in Highland mercenaries to Ulster and, to a lesser extent, Connacht.[1] This had been encouraged by the settlement of a branch of the MacDonalds of Dunyveg in north-east Ulster in the late fourteenth century, after the marriage of Iain Mhòr, brother of Donald, Lord of the Isles, to Maire Biséd, heiress to the seven lordships of the Glens of Antrim.[2] Dynastic struggles, feuding and inter-clan rivalry resulted in groups constantly branching off and creating new dynasties. A lord or chief 's status was determined, in these patriarchal societies, as much by the number of men he could mobilise (based on the service he was due) and his success in intertribal warfare as by the extent of the land he owned. The Gaels were essentially a seafaring nation, and their main thoroughfares were the sea lanes.[3] Both were essentially pastoral economies in which there was a seasonal population movement associated with the transfer of cattle to the upland summer pastures; and increasingly during the early modern period, a network of drove roads in the Highlands (for the droving of cattle to the Lowland markets) rendered road communications more important.[4] Cattle were an important part of the Gaelic economy; many luxury items could be bought for a certain 'cattle price'. Hence, the successful execution of cattle raids was not only regarded as a legitimate extension of tribal activity but was also seen as a public demonstration of manly courage.

The significance of relationship to the chief and the importance of kinship in Gaelic society can never be underestimated, especially as chiefdoms expanded and acquired new territory, requiring new administrators. Day-to-day living was in extended family groups, underwritten by the system of fosterage. This institution was a major social bond in both Ireland and Scotland, used as a method of cementing recognised alliances. It acted not only as a form of hostageship for the behaviour of its dynasty but was also important – given the fairly flexible nature of Gaelic marriage customs and the lack of distinction between legitimacy and illegitimacy – as a means of separating the sons of different wives and diffusing the tension.[5] A sense of cohesion was additionally supplied by the bards and *seanchaidhean*, as keepers of clan traditions which bought into an idea of descent from a common ancestor – an emotional and social ruse to induce group loyalty, allegiance and a sense of belonging – and by communal feasting.[6]

The traditional order of Gaelic society was just beginning to be seriously threatened in 1560. 'The writing on the wall' did not go unseen by the Gaelic literati, especially the bards, who found their security and status in jeopardy as the entire social structure (and hence their patronage) came under threat. In the late sixteenth century, the Irish poet Tadhg Dall Ó Huiginn warned that

Fir Lonndain, laochruidh Alban,	The men of London, the warriors of Scotland
siad re chéile ag comhardadh,	are contending together,
a cheann shaorshlóigh Shíthe Truim,	thou chief of the noble host of Sioth Trium,
a n-aonbhróin fhíthe umainn.	in one compact mass about us.[7]

The major motive for this assault on the *Gaidhealtachdan* was political: the governments of Elizabeth I in Ireland and James VI in Scotland both pursued policies of reducing the native Gaelic lordships in order to bring these largely autonomous communities under central control. As they gained more power and authority in these regions, the militaristic heart of kin-based Gaelic society was increasingly threatened. The accession of James VI to the crown of England in 1603 simply enabled him to undertake concerted action to pacify the western seaboard, permitting him to work against Highland mercenaries and their native Irish employers at one and the same time. Concerted military action was taken in Ireland which concluded with 'the Flight of the Earls' in 1607 and annexation of land on an enormous scale; in Scotland, on the other hand, a policy of slow but consistent 'daunting of the Isles' was undertaken: political, military and expropriatory offensives were more sporadic there, but they nevertheless effected fundamental change of a similar nature. Irish and Scottish Gael alike was alienated: no fewer than six counties were escheated to make way for the plantation of Ulster, while in Scotland the Clan Donald South in Kintyre and Islay, Clan Leod in Lewis and Clan Iain in Ardnamurchan were expropriated.[8]

The alarm continued to sound in 1623 at the hands of the Scot Cathal MacMhuirich.

Laimh re colbha gach calaidh	Numerous beside your land
iomdha drong do dhanaruibh	are enemies and warmongers,
ag brath ort (a chnú chridhe	they are coming with spite against the Gaelic race
's tú gan locht) dá leófaidhe.	and nobody gets any mercy from them.[9]

In the western Highlands, the kinship ties so fundamental to the operation of traditional Gaelic society were slowly transformed by government policy into relationships which were essentially commercially orientated.[10] The increasing involvement of clan chiefs in central politics encouraged their eventual assimilation into the Scottish landed classes, but the inevitable emasculation of the Gaelic political system resulted in the breakdown of those cultural and social systems which ratified and bolstered Gaelic society. The Gaelic élites were effectively recruited as instruments of their own demise.[11]

The Historical Context

The academic study of interaction between Irish and Scottish Gaels has been opened up in the last two decades, but mainly from fairly isolated historical standpoints. A great deal, for instance, has been written from the cultural and socio-economic angles in work edited by Louis Cullen and T. C. Smout,[12] Tom Devine and David Dickson,[13] Rosalind Mitchison and Peter Roebuck,[14] and more recently by S. J. Conolly, Rab Houston and R. J. Morris,[15] but these studies have tended to concentrate on the English-speaking world where commercial enterprise had its roots. David Stevenson has thoroughly explored the vagaries of the political situation in the seventeenth century,[15] and Jane Ohlemeyer has produced an excellent study of the first Marquess of Antrim, a figure of immense importance in cross-channel Gaelic politics of that century.[17] Similarly, Celtic scholars such as Derick Thomson[18] and Ronald Black,[19] and the historian John Bannerman,[20] have elucidated the world of the hereditary Gaelic learned families in the early modern period – families who often had feet in both the Irish and Scottish camps – some of whom, like the Beatons, were transferring to and infiltrating the ranks of the Kirk as Gaelic society disintegrated. However, a comprehensive study of the Gaels' interaction in religious affairs during this period is conspicuous by its absence.

The standard text for the history of Irish presbyterianism – which puts due emphasis on its close links with Scotland – remains J. S. Reid's *History of the Presbyterian Church in Ireland* (1867). Equally valuable are the unpublished typescripts by A. F. Scott Pearson, 'Puritan and Presbyterian Settlements in Ireland 1560–1660' (1948), I, II; D. Stewart's 'The History of the Presbyterian Settlements in Ireland 1641–1760' (1948); and Peter Brooke's *Ulster Presbyterianism: The Historical Perspective 1610–1970* (1994). The only book which has attempted to sketch a history of Scottish Catholicism since 1560 – P. F. Anson, *Underground Catholicism in Scotland, 1622–1878* (1970) – does not concentrate, by definition, exclusively on the Gaelic contribution. This is also the case with Brian Halloran's *The Scots College, Paris 1603–1792* (1997), which provides a context for Scottish Catholicism in exile. While the transcription and publication of vast amounts of original source material from the archives of the *Congregazione de Propaganda Fide* (Congregation for the Propagation of the Faith)[21] by Cathaldus Giblin has been a major contribution to Gaelic ecclesiastical history,[22] the abundance of material relating to the Highland mission from the late seventeenth century in the Blairs Collection of the Scottish Catholic Archives has as yet been only partially tapped. Similarly, the work of the presbyteries in constantly trying to curtail missionary activity is well enough known, but the Protestant record has not been systematically trawled for links with Irish presbyterianism. And there is still room for a work of historical synthesis and analysis of the specifically Gaelic dimension.

This book is a study of the ecclesiastical ties between the Gaelic peoples of Scotland and Ireland between 1560 and 1760. Throwing historical perspectives onto the origins of the sectarian polarisation in northern Ireland, it discusses both Protestants and Catholics and their interaction with each other rather than dealing with one denomination in isolation. It emphasises a two-way Gaelic missionary activity: of the early Scottish Gaelic-speaking presbyterians who made such a contribution to the Protestant Church in Ulster, and of the various orders of Irish regular and secular priests who kept Catholicism alive in the Highlands and Islands of Scotland. Ecclesiastically, the sixteenth century was the century of the Reformation in Ireland and Scotland. As it swept across Europe, the Protestant Reformation drew immense political and administrative change in its wake, but it was not until the seventeenth century that significant steps were taken to deal with the clerical vacuum brought about in both countries by the removal of the priesthood. This situation was not ameliorated in either country until the mid-eighteenth century. By then, the Protestant Church in Ireland was self-sufficient in supplying its own ministers without recourse to Scotland, while in the Highlands the Kirk had at last established more than a skeleton network of ministers.

The following chapters elucidate the complex ecclesiastical interrelations between Irish and Scottish Gaels. Chapter 1 shows the Established Churches in Scotland and in Ireland in the active creation of a reformed faith. The completion of the Tudor conquest of Ireland and the Union of the English and Scottish Crowns in 1603 not only led to a pool of redundant swordsmen, but also provided an opportunity for James VI and I to extend the Protestant Church into the *Gaidhealtachdan* as an instrument of 'civilisation' and subjugation. Those who abjured the hand of Protestant fellowship effectively set themselves in opposition to the English-speaking central governments. The plantation of Ulster – which opened up both land and 'soul' markets in the north of Ireland – attracted the co-operation of the infant Scots Kirk in supplying a number of Gaelic-speaking ministers to evangelise the native Irish in their own language. Harnessed more potently as a political force in the Gaelic-speaking areas of Ireland, the Counter-Reformation began to stake out a place for Catholicism in the Highlands and Islands of Scotland.

Chapter 2 discusses religion in the *Gaidhealtachdan* during the period of the Irish Franciscan mission to the Highlands and Islands. Inadequate Protestant penetration of the Highland area, exacerbated by a continuing trickle of Gaelic-speaking ministers to Ulster, merely opened a window of opportunity for Irish Franciscans to reclaim parts of it for Catholicism. But the Franciscan mission was able to re-establish the Catholic faith only in territorial pockets due to the immense difficulties under which the mission laboured: underfunding, understaffing and a consistent lack of understanding by their backers in Rome. Harnessing the co-operation of the Ulster and Highland élites was essential when the instruments of central government were controlled by establishments which proscribed Catholicism. The Ulster connection emphasises the significance to the mission of the support of Randal MacDonnell, first Earl of Antrim, through which he hoped to further his own political agenda – the reclamation of the lost MacDonald heritage of Kintyre and Islay. In this way, the Franciscan mission strengthened west Highland links with Gaelic Ireland which had been weakened by the rift between the MacDonalds of the Clan Donald South and the MacDonnells of Antrim, and more seriously by the plantation of Ulster.

As Chapter 3 explains, the new Protestant relationships fostered by the plantation were forged in steel during the ensuing civil war, which resulted in the setting up of the first (army) presbytery in Ulster. The Kirk was concerned to send as much assistance as necessary to bolster the political instability in

Ireland because it was potentially such a threat to the presbyterian establishment in Scotland. This led to the consolidation of a dissenting presbyterian church in Ireland. Furthermore, the service of presbyterian ministers in the Ulster army chaplaincy between 1642 and 1648 had knock-on effects in both countries: Scottish presbyterian probationers and ministers continued to sustain the embryonic Irish church, while in Scotland similar missionary activity into politically disaffected areas of the Highlands and Islands was encouraged, as was the translation of the scriptures into Gaelic. The equally important contribution made by Royalist presbyterian collaborators in Scotland is also examined, a contribution which demonstrates that Royalism was not always synonymous with Catholicism, as has sometimes been mooted. Scottish Gaelic-speaking ministers exhibited a cultural – even political – affinity for the native Irish and Royalist causes, nurtured (in spite of their Calvinism) by a common Gaelic culture.

Chapter 4 charts the inexorable expansion in the Catholic mission and the arrival of missionaries from orders other than the Franciscans, such as the Vincentians and Dominicans. The presence of several Irish priests in Alasdair MacColla MacDonald's expeditionary force to the Highlands resulted in the creation of open-air mass sites with natural stone altars – like the one that survives in Lochaber. However, with the appointment of the first Prefect-Apostolic in 1653 a distinctly secular dimension developed on the mission: where the regulars had no resident superiors, they acted in a quasi-secular capacity as a variety of regular orders were drawn into the mission field. Missionaries did not evangelise any district south of Moidart and Brae Lochaber after 1653. But the missionary legacy of the Franciscans was mirrored in the close connection of the Catholic mission to the political fortunes of the Kintyre and Ulster MacDonalds, a by-product of which was the entrenchment of anti-Campbell attitudes among the missionaries. The territories of MacDonald of Clanranald saw the most sustained Catholic missionary activity during this period and so became the hub of the Counter-Reformation dynamic in the Highlands and Islands. By the Revolution, the present-day areas of Roman Catholicism were more or less codified.

Chapter 5 considers the extent of practical co-operation in missionary activity between the presbyterian communities in the Highlands and Ulster. Unlike the established Church of Ireland, the presbyterians did much in the early eighteenth century to promote an Irish-speaking mission to the native Irish. Appreciating 'the earnest Desire of all true Protestants that the Ghospel [sic] may be propagated in its Purity, and particularly that the Papists may be converted', the synod of Ulster left a significant proportion of its Irish preaching to Highland ministers and probationers. In this, they were undoubtedly following the example of the Kirk's missionary activity to the Highlands and Islands. However, after 1720 the presbyterian church in Ulster came of age. No longer symbiotically dependent on the mother Kirk, and no longer reliant on Scottish ministerial graduates to staff their parishes, its members began to flaunt doctrines divergent from the Church of Scotland. Experiencing a similar consolidation in the eighteenth-century Highlands, the Kirk no longer felt so threatened by the Catholic mission there, and felt able to leave the Catholics more to their own devices.

Chapter 6 evaluates the immense contribution made by Irish priests to the rejuvenation of Catholicism in the Highlands and Islands, summarising the extent and periodisation of Catholic penetration of the region during the two centuries between 1560 and 1760. Their work resulted eventually in the emergence of a native Scottish Gaelic-speaking clergy, which was greatly encouraged by the appointment of Bishop Nicolson as Vicar-Apostolic in 1694. Fairly predictably, this led to an element of rivalry between the Scots and the Irish, as the Scots fought to establish the upper hand and assume control of the mission. From this point, Irish missionaries were often labelled substandard. But arguably the mission was hardest hit during this century by the Jansenist controversy. Having lost his bid in 1731 to become Vicar-Apostolic in the Highlands, and later to become coadjutor in the Lowlands, the politically incorrect Colin Campbell vented his spleen on the mission hierarchy, and on any other missionaries who failed to support him, by accusing them of Jansenism. The periodic outbreak of Jacobite rebellion did little to alleviate the plight of the Irish, whose numbers were gradually eroded by all of the above-mentioned factors. By 1760, the mission field was bereft of Irish regulars, having reverted exclusively to the charge of the native clergy.

Objectivity of Sources

Finally, I should like to say a word about the difficulties inherent in the study of religion in the Highlands during this period. The first is the sheer paucity of indigenous primary source material for all religious denominations before the mid-seventeenth century – especially for the sixteenth century – because of the drastic effect of changes ordered at the Reformation. There is particularly little information about survival of the Catholic faith in the Highlands and Islands in the late sixteenth century. Although the tremendous work of Cathaldus Giblin in translating the Latin documents from the Vatican Archives has provided abundant source material for the Franciscan mission to the Highlands and subsequent Franciscan activity there, there is no record of the missionaries' activity in the Highlands and Islands before 1624.[23]

James Kirk has stated that the 'Gaelic emphasis on oral tradition offers only a partial explanation for this deficiency' of ecclesiastical records in the Highlands.[24] Certainly, the survival of a substantial number of Gaelic medical tracts, bardic poems and genealogies, for example, shows that there was a significant scribal tradition among the educated echelons of Gaelic society. But the oral tradition perhaps engendered a degree of indifference to the value of certain written records. It was really only with the advent of commercialism into the Highlands in the late seventeenth and early eighteenth centuries, and the need to keep accurate fiscal records, that it became increasingly necessary to write down and preserve detailed official documentation in the locale, such as customs or estate ledgers.

However, what clues do survive about the religion of the common people are mainly contained in the substantial body of work called *Carmina Gadelica*, collected from oral tradition by Alexander Carmichael in the mid-nineteenth century, which not only provides information on the mode of life of the Gael, but also of his spiritual beliefs. Although poetic in expression and imagery – a blend of folklore and stories of Christian saints and miracles, invoking St. Bride, Columba, St. Michael, Christ and Mary – Carmichael's collection is none the less indicative of what was revered, in a religious context, within that society.[25] It shows, for instance, that the Marian cult survived after the Reformation in areas which became staunchly Protestant, such as Skye.[26]

In Ireland, too, there is a dearth of parish records for the period just after the Reformation and few surviving sources which give an indication of the state of popular religion.[27] The situation improves for Protestant material in the early seventeenth century because of the documentation which survives relating to the plantation of Ulster. Settler bishops such as George Montgomery, bishop of Raphoe, Clogher and Derry (1605–09) carried out surveys of their Sees which furnish details about the resident clergy.[28] The majority of the early presbytery records subsequently disappeared in the various military and civil upheavals of the following centuries, although copies of a few extant manuscripts were made in the late nineteenth and early twentieth centuries, and these have preserved the little that remained for posterity. Fortunately, given the extent of Scottish migration there, the earliest copy presbytery records are for Antrim between 1654 and 1691.[29] There are also just over two decades of copies for the presbytery of Lagan – where the earliest 'prescopalian' ministers settled under Knox – between 1672 and 1695.[30] In general, however, the Irish presbytery records contain much less social material than the Scottish ones: they concern themselves more with the minutiae of administration and the role of ministers. This is perhaps due to the fact that the Irish congregations and presbyteries were more concerned with fighting for their very survival as non-conformists, and in inducing ministers to come and settle in their midst, than in a detailed record of the flight of fugitives from justice or of general social movement.

Surviving presbytery and synod records for Highland and Island areas date only from the 1630s.[31] The earliest of the relevant minutes date from 1631 for the presbytery of Strathbogie, an area on the periphery of the mainland Highlands, which includes lands under Gordon control. Possibly the most important source for the Highland and Island area as a whole is the *Minutes of the Synod of Argyll*, which begin in 1639 and continue right through to 1760.[32] This synod covered a vast area: the shire of Argyll, the western mainland of Inverness as far north as Glenelg, the islands of Arran and Bute, and the whole of the Inner and Outer Hebrides.[33] The presbytery books of Kintyre – that area of the Scottish Highlands closest to Ulster – are another important source which is extant from 1655.[34] The type of information contained in the Scottish records (which can only occasionally be corroborated in the Irish records) covers most aspects of seventeenth- and eighteenth-century society, from the minor social through to the major political problems of the period, such as the Irish civil war of the 1640s and the Jacobite rebellions, and attempts to circumscribe the forces of the Catholic Counter-Reformation.

The second difficulty inherent in the study of religion in the Highlands (and indeed everywhere) is the virtual impossibility of finding an objective religious source. Most commentators wrote not only with a view to their own salvation, but paranoia generated by such events as the 'Popish Plot' of 1678 was effectively used by the Protestant authorities to re-enforce the penal laws against Catholics and to augment government funding of Protestant missionary work in the Highlands.[35] The Catholics were equally adept at turning the circumstances of persecution to their own financial advantage. Priests clearly had a vested interest in scaling up their stories of persecution and potential capture in an attempt to wheedle more money and additional faculties out of *Propaganda* for their mission work. But the association of Catholicism with papal and other continental powers made this into a political issue which took on a greater magnitude with the birth of Jacobitism. Priests were hunted almost as emissaries of foreign polities, but it was relatively infrequently that severe reprisals were taken on the Highland civil population. The Establishment, like the priests, tended to do its work among the clan élite with the understanding that their conversion represented a strong example to the people. The records of the synod of Argyll, for example, are full of repeated calls for excommunication – supposedly the highest penalty for practising Catholicism, with its implied social ostracism – yet their constant reiteration merely shows the weakness of excommunication exercised as a civil and social sanction.

The inherent credibility of the Catholic mission reports and testimonials is a third difficulty in the interpretation of the source material. The priests spoke of great numbers of conversions, with figures in the region of hundreds converted at one swoop after only a few days in an area. When Fr. Ward visited North Uist in December 1625, for instance, he claimed to have 'won 768 back to the practice of the faith', leaving 'only fourteen who remained loyal to the minister'.[36] Yet, when Fr. Dermit Duggan, an Irish Vincentian working in Barra in the 1650s, wrote to his superior about the work of the Franciscan fathers before him, he said that while they had some knowledge of the Sacraments of

Penance and the Holy Eucharist, 'these people were so little instructed that they did not know how to make the sign of the Cross'.[37] This hardly classifies the huge numbers who flocked to the missionaries as converts, in any meaningful sense. In Giblin's opinion,

> It is difficult to determine what exactly they meant by the word 'conversion'. An examination of their reports leaves the impression that the word was used indiscriminately by them for Calvinists who embraced the catholic faith as a result of their preaching, or for catholics whom they brought back to the practice of their religion, which had been given up through carelessness or ignorance.[38]

A much better word, and one which appears in later primary sources of the period, is 'reconciliations', but priests operating on very limited budgets had a personal interest in claiming large numbers as converts in order to justify their work. Indeed, when in 1633 Cornelius Ward stated that, to date, the missionaries had converted 6,627 souls between them and baptised 3,010, these figures were quite understandably challenged by some Scots priests at Rome. They could almost more aptly be viewed as census figures of the districts in question. The problem was, perhaps, that *Propaganda* itself failed to establish what exactly constituted a conversion for record purposes.

The ensuing chapters deal with this practical work of conversion in the *Gaidhealtachd mòr fada na h'Alba agus Eirinn* (the all-encompassing *Gaidhealtachd* of Ireland and Scotland) by both faiths from the Reformation to the mid-eighteenth century. To the extent that there was ever a master plan for the mission activities of either faith, it was not an overriding geographical strategy for the conversion of particular regions by specific dates; it was more about socio-political control. Broadly, the Protestants aimed at the civilisation and subjugation of the Gaelic race by converting as many of them as they could to Protestantism. In doing this, however, they obviously targeted particular areas of native intransigence for reduction by Protestant plantation, a phenomenon which occurred in Scotland as well as more extensively in Ireland. The Catholics, on the other hand, in quickly becoming a focus for resistance to the foreign and Lowland invaders, and in providing an institutional and ideological framework for that resistance, aimed at the restoration of their pre-Reformation power-base.

ONE

Gaelic Attitudes to Religion, 1560–*c*.1619

> Shakkin aff all feare of god and obedience to His Majesties Lawes ...
> Criminal Letters against Raonull Mac Ailein 'ic Iain MacDonald of Benbecula (1634)

TECHNICALLY earlier than in Scotland, the Reformation in Ireland dated from the Irish parliament's enactment in May 1536 that Henry VIII was 'the only supreme head in earth of the whole church of Ireland', and the consequent breach of the Irish Church with Rome.[1] However, the actual creation of a Protestant Church in Ireland did not begin until about the same time as in Scotland when, shortly after the accession of Elizabeth I, the Act of Supremacy of 1560 provided for an ecclesiastical commission to superintend church reform, while the Act of Uniformity, in the same year, enforced statutory attendance at the parish church. Furthermore, services were to be taken by English-speaking clergy using the Book of Common Prayer and, for those who did not speak English, Latin rather than Irish was to be the preferred second language for conducting the service. This was because the Dublin government equated use of Irish with disloyalty to the crown,[2] but it was a great irony in a reform movement which emphasised use of the vernacular: 'To approach the task of converting Ireland whilst at the same time stressing the use of English was automatically to limit the appeal of Protestantism.'[3] It led to a scarcity of Irish-speaking Protestant clergy, which was partially met from the Scottish *Gaidhealtachd*.

In spite of the generally anti-erastian nature of the reformers, the close working relationship between the Church and the state (then a feature common throughout Protestant Europe) presented further difficulty for the establishment of Protestantism in Ireland, a problem mirrored to a certain extent in the Scottish Highlands and Islands. In Ireland, the power of the Dublin government was not effective over vast tracts of the country, particularly in Connacht and Ulster – precisely those areas where Highland settlement was greatest during the sixteenth century. Indifference and hostility was manifested to the Church of Ireland in Connacht, where the lack of commitment either by the clergy or the civil government resulted in a substantial loss of resources to the Church.

By 1615, for instance, 86 per cent of rectories in the province of Tuam (see Fig. 1.1) were in the hands of laymen, and a great many benefices were not being served. In Ulster, the diocese of Raphoe in Donegal was particularly regarded as being outwith royal control. Elizabeth I nominated no bishop there throughout her reign, while the register and revenues of the See remained firmly under the control of the Catholic bishops until 1606. Thus, James VI and I's appointment of the Scottish Gaelic-speaking Highlander, Denis Campbell, to the See in 1604, and of Andrew Knox, bishop of the Isles, in 1610, must be seen as a concerted attempt to check the autonomy of the Irish *Gaeltacht*. In addition, the Protestant evangelisation of the native Irish community bolstered and underwrote the plantation of Ulster: the Church of Ireland was generously endowed from the escheated lands, and Protestant clergy were often attracted to Ulster through their ties of kinship with Plantation settlers. By 1622 there were 136 ministers in the planted Ulster dioceses.[4] Bishop George Montgomery (incumbent of the Sees of Derry, Raphoe and Clogher between Campbell and Knox) was the sibling of Hugh Montgomery, laird of Braidstone in Ayrshire and pioneering planter in County Down. In his ecclesiastical capacity, he pushed to increase substantially the acreage for plantation in his Sees, which was ultimately far more than the English government had envisaged.[5]

The Reformed Church in Ireland fell heir to the ministry, lands and patronage of the medieval church but, as in the Highlands of Scotland, it was a somewhat dilapidated institution which declined further in the late sixteenth century due to lay appropriation and the generally poor quality of the clergy. But unlike the Highlands, which had many cumbersome parishes, effective ministry in the Church of Ireland was made difficult by the existence of a network of relatively small parishes, some with insufficient income to support a minister. The Established Church was able to put in place little more than a 'skeleton ministry' throughout the country, which was particularly sparse where the native Irish held political control. The situation was exacerbated further by the inadequacy of the clergy. Many of the native or Anglo-Irish who conformed on the accession of Elizabeth were simply 'reading ministers' who read the service book but did not preach; they were often pressurised by Catholic relatives to alienate church lands. As in the Scottish *Gaidhealtachd*, Irish-speaking conformers ensured a degree of continuity and were, at least, able to speak the native tongue when few native Irish were entering the ministry. However, the growth of the Church of Ireland was severely constrained by the strength of the Counter-Reformation in Ireland; Catholic church leaders were able to rely on and kindle 'a basic popular distaste for Protestantism' and the Established Church which was based partly on religious concerns but also on political and racial ones.[6] This is not to say that the failure of the Protestant Reformation in Ireland was a foregone conclusion; on the contrary, the Catholic faith was, as K. Bottigheimer has put it, 'a slender, fragile plant which survived both official proscription and an age of scepticism' to blossom many centuries later. But there is little doubt that the plantation of Ulster did much to render permanent that distinctive polarisation of religion, politics and culture that is characteristic of the region.[7]

Not only were the English resented as Protestant reformers, but they were disliked even more for their political interference in Ireland, which was seen to be in direct conflict with the interests of the Catholic faith. In the 1570s, Catholic intrigue on behalf of the imprisoned Mary Stewart served – in Ireland as in Scotland – to increase the efforts of the Counter-Reformation. The 1579 revolt of James Fitzmaurice Fitzgerald, cousin of the Earl of Desmond, and his international connections with Catholic leaders such as the Pope and Philip II of Spain, alarmed the government, paving the way, after the attainder of the late Earl of Desmond in 1586, for attempts at the reformation of Munster.[8] The political arm of the Counter-Reformation was also to the fore during the Ulster rebellion (1594–1603), when Hugh O'Neill appealed for Spanish support. The Counter-Reformation movement in Ireland was especially invigorated after 1596, when a Jesuit residency was set up, heralding the arrival of substantial numbers of priests from Europe who worked doggedly to sustain the Catholic faith. By 1600, there were already three Vicars-Apostolic or missionary bishops in Ireland. The year 1618 saw the re-establishment of a resident Catholic episcopacy in Ireland which put the faith on a far firmer footing; indeed, by 1623 there were no fewer than 800 secular priests operating in Ireland, as well as 200 Franciscans and 100 regulars from other orders. There was phenomenal Catholic regrouping in Ireland in comparison with what occurred in Scotland. Rome was actively involved in recovering Ireland for Catholicism from the mid-1590s, so that by the outbreak of the native Irish rising in 1641, much of the Irish population, it seems, had implicitly rejected Protestantism.[9]

The hierarchy of the Church of Ireland was undoubtedly perturbed. Although there were some communication difficulties between the Old Irish and native clergy, various financial problems and worries that the Catholic clergy were often substandard as well as insufficient in number, 'the wonder was not that the Roman clergy performed badly, but that they performed at all! There was not supposed to be a clandestine, parallel counter-Church in seventeenth-century Ireland. And yet it was ubiquitous and seemingly ineradicable.'[10] The Dublin government had sought to protect the Established Church after the accession of James VI to the English throne by issuing a proclamation in 1605 banishing priests from the country and enforcing the fine for recusancy. But this had little effect on the most essential task of the Church: the evangelisation of the native Irish. Many remote Irish-speaking parishes were vacant, the livings held by absent pluralists or poverty-stricken Irish curates, and as in many remote Highland parishes, the churches were decayed. That most clergy appointed to Irish parishes in the early seventeenth century came from England, Wales and Scotland simply aggravated the problem.[11] Among these, only a handful of Gaelic-speaking Scots were capable of ministering to the Irish.

In Scotland, with Parliament's acceptance of the Reformed Confession of Faith in August 1560, papal authority there was completely destroyed, and it became punishable to celebrate mass. Within a few years of 1560, the hierarchy of the Catholic Church in Scotland had been removed. Although many people appear to have remained nominally Catholic, there were no longer any bishops to co-ordinate or supervise the work of those priests who remained or, more importantly, to safeguard the recruitment of new priests.[12] What happened to these priests in the Highlands and Islands? While it is in general very difficult to trace the fate of the ordinary priest there, it is clear that some continued to administer the sacraments according to Catholic rites. On the other hand, it is a little easier to trace the path of the higher clergy, where there appears to have been – as might be expected – a period of adjustment. As late as 1565, Patrick Maclean received Queen Mary's nomination to the Pope as bishop-elect of the Isles (a nomination which he had possibly had since 1560), but around January 1565 he transferred his right to the Protestant John Carswell in return for a pension. On Maclean's resignation, Carswell received a crown grant of the revenues of the See, which was subsequently provided by the crown on 24 March 1567. In Argyll and surrounding areas, the fifth Earl of Argyll's support of Protestantism created a framework probably unsurpassed elsewhere in the Highlands, which Carswell was able to exploit to further the Reformed ministry. Donald Munro, author of a *Description of the Western Isles* (1549), was archdeacon of the Isles on 11 September 1553; probably in post earlier, he was still archdeacon on 25 January 1563. Munro later conformed to Protestantism and was appointed Commissioner of Ross by the General Assembly. The Commendator of Ardchattan, John Campbell, was designated bishop-elect of the Isles between 1557 and 1560, by which time he was considered a good Protestant; he was still Commendator of Ardchattan in 1564. Appointed bishop of Argyll in 1553, James Hamilton conformed, and though relatively inactive, he remained in the Protestant heartland until he died on 6 January 1580.[13]

The overall impression is that after 1560 the Catholic structure was crumbling, and some of the higher clergy introduced into the Highlands were Lowlanders. For instance, Henry Sinclair was dean of Glasgow as well as president of the college of justice when he received papal provision to the diocese of Ross, two years before Munro was appointed there as commissioner. Although Sinclair died a Catholic in Paris in 1565, he was, if nothing else, a pragmatist. Whilst still in Glasgow he had agreed to supply bread and wine for Protestant communion in the parish kirk of Glasgow. Once in Ross, he declined to answer the papal envoy and stated that the laws, including the one forbidding the celebration of mass, were to be upheld. Indeed, he even paid £50 a year out of his own income to the Protestant preacher of the kirks of Nigg and Tarbert. The preacher was probably a reader (that is, a man who could read the service but was not qualified to celebrate baptism or communion), because the records of the assignation of stipends indicate that the post of reader in Nigg was vacant by 1574 and that Gavin Dunbar was then 'reidare at Tarbert'. Another Catholic, John Leslie, was subsequently nominated to the diocese of Ross by the crown in 1566. Inducted in January 1567, he was forfeited in the following year but received a new papal provision to the See in April 1575, a month after the Protestant Alexander Hepburn had been provided to the bishopric. Similarly, in Caithness, Robert Stewart, son of the third Earl of Lennox, had been appointed to the bishopric of Caithness as a minor in 1542. He lost the bishopric in 1545 for treason, but having conformed at the Reformation he was then returned to it. Stewart was relatively inactive from 1570 but retained the bishopric until his death in 1586. The next crown nominee, Robert Pont, the provost of Trinity College, Edinburgh, was clearly a Lowlander, but objecting to episcopacy, he was only prepared to be a minister.[14]

The new Protestant regime sought to protect its infant establishment and give it financial security. None the less, this was not done without some thought for the current possessors of benefices. It was ordained in February 1562 that as long as they did not celebrate mass, existing benefice holders could draw two-thirds of their revenues during their lifetimes. The remaining third was to be divided between the crown and the Protestant Kirk.[15] However, significant numbers of pre-Reformation clergy in certain dioceses in the mainland Highlands did conform to Protestantism.[16] At the time of the 1573 Test Act, which sought to obtain the benefices of non-conforming clergy for the Reformed ministry by requiring all benefice holders to subscribe the Protestant Confession of Faith and acknowledge the King's supremacy in ecclesiastical and civil matters, there were only fourteen deprivations in the dioceses of Dunblane, Dunkeld, Aberdeen and Ross, and two in Moray. Significantly, there was none in the exclusively Highland diocese of Argyll and the Isles,[17] though in the Isles at least, this was probably due more to the existence of vacancies than to total conformity on the part of the priests. The 1573 statute removed only 'the very small number of determined recusants', and it is likely that the geographical isolation of the Highlands protected those Catholic priests who still wished to serve there without much fear of detection. None the less, by the 1570s, those Catholic priests still operating in the Highlands and Islands must have been very few.

The Established Church minister, on the other hand, did not exist in some remote parts of the Highlands and Islands until the middle of the seventeenth century, or much later, though there were readers and exhorters in some parishes. Highland benefices were notoriously unpopular, and except in a few cases, it was probably the less able ministers who received them. Even then, the minister's absence was still marked in enclaves such as Moidart, which was reclaimed for Catholicism by the Irish Franciscans during their mission in the 1630s.[18] It was generally not until the early seventeenth century that anything approaching even a basic provision of ministers was made for the Isles. John Lorne Campbell made an interesting claim for this period. 'It is significant that in several cases the earliest recorded appointments of Protestant ministers to Hebridean parishes date from the year of the Statutes of Iona, 1609. But even then few could be found.'[19] The first extensive report on the area, compiled in 1626, lists only ten ministers in Hebridean parishes,[20] but it has since been proven that there were no fewer than nineteen ministers there, as well as two readers, at this time. While the particulars of this report pertain to the next chapter, it must be agreed that 'the conventional claim which assigns the first recorded appointments of ministers in Hebridean parishes to 1609 and the Statutes of Iona cannot be entertained'.[21] However, such meagre provision did little to promote extensive survival of ecclesiastical records, leading rather to the very fragmentary sources with which we are left today.

What exactly was the extent of the Reformed presence in the Highlands and Islands between 1560 and 1619? Though it might be said that the Kirk made an admirable attempt to provide ministers in the early decades after the Reformation, it was working against huge odds, both because of geographical isolation and because there were very few Gaelic speakers among those who had conformed to Protestantism. Its success or failure clearly denied or offered opportunities for the Catholic faith to move in.

Catholic Conformers and Protestant Reformers

Owing to the relative paucity of indigenous Church records for the Highland district, historians have tended to fall into the well-trodden path of assuming that almost all parishes were unattended. However, research conducted by James Kirk on two series of financial records kept by the crown – recording the rentals of ecclesiastical benefices from 1561 to 1595 and the assignment of stipends from 1567 to 1615[22] – has shown that, contrary to previous opinion, the Reformed Church had established a not insignificant presence in many mainland parishes within just a few years of the Reformation. Though this is a valuable revision, the Reformed presence can by no means be regarded as having been extensive in the Isles and certain districts of the western Highlands. Two qualifications must be made here. First, this presence was not necessarily in ministers but sometimes in readers, who could not celebrate the important sacraments of baptism and communion. Second, the financial records do not exist for Argyll and the Isles. The marginal and isolated nature of the Isles and the lack of Gaelic-speaking clergy make it unlikely that the Kirk achieved anything other than the sparsest presence there, and this is confirmed by the little evidence which survives.

On the other hand, it may be a fair assumption that a similar level of provision of Reformed personnel had been made in Argyll as, for example, in Ross. A state report for 1574 indicated that the sixth Earl of Argyll had obtained ministers and readers, with assigned stipends, for every parish in Lorn, central Argyll and Cowal, and that he had made provision for the administration of the sacraments and forms of church discipline 'after the order of Geneva, translated out of the English into the Irish tongue by master John Carswell, late bishop of the Isles'. Certainly, the parishes of Craignish, Glassary, Glenaray and Inveraray, Kilmartin, Knapdale, Dunoon (whose incumbent often held the parish of Kilmun), Inverchaolain, Kilfinan, Ardchattan, Glenorchy and Inishail, Kilchrenan and Dalavich, and Lismore had all been filled either from the Reformation or by the mid-1570s (see Fig. 5.2). Similarly, in Lorn, the parish of Muckairn had a minister by 1578, Kilninver and Kilmelford by 1580, and Kilbrandon and Kilchattan by October 1584. However, Kilmodan or Glendaruel in Cowal had no minister until 1598, nor, surprisingly, did the parish of Lochgoilhead and Kilmorich (next to the Inveraray heartland) until 1601, and Kilmore and Kilbride in Lorn did not have one until 1608. Moreover, the united parish of Strachur and Strathlachlan, in Cowal, did not have a minister (even if it had a reader) until 1652: that is, ninety-two years after the Reformation.[23] Here it is not just a case of lack of record, as these parishes are known to have been vacant until the dates given.

Yet, though the above parishes comprised a substantial part of Argyll, the report's equal emphasis on the existence of readers should not be allowed to create an impression of abundant ministerial coverage. Also, the report still implies a lack of coverage over a broad area – the Isles, Kintyre, Ardnamurchan, the Moidart region and Glenelg – which was more accessible by sea. In short, it leaves out about half the diocese of Argyll and the Isles. Although Argyll and the Isles were separate dioceses before 1560, the Protestant superintendent of Argyll was provided to the bishopric of the Isles in 1565.[24] Furthermore, reference to either the presence or absence of ministers in the reports of the Irish Franciscan missions shows that even by the early seventeenth century the existence of parish ministers had not become general in the rest of the Highlands and Islands. Although inroads had been made into the Isles by the end of the sixteenth century, it was still possible for Farquhar M'Rae, minister of Gairloch in Ross, to say when he undertook a mission to Lewis in 1610 that 'its inhabitants were strangers to the Gospel', and that few under the age of forty had previously been baptised.[25] The Isle of Lewis only had one Protestant minister by 1572,[26] which is hardly a healthy coverage of the four parish kirks mentioned by Munro in his 1549 survey and an indication of the early constraints under which the Reformed Kirk operated in such a vast territory.[27]

From the information uncovered, it appears that some of the pre-Reformation priests happily took on the role of minister in certain Highland areas. The advantages of this were obviously that they knew the district intimately, with all its regional quirks and characteristics, and, no less importantly, they spoke Gaelic. For example, in the diocese of Ross, about half of the ministry on record in the region in 1569 had held office in the pre-Reformation Church. This is one of the main reasons why the Reformation made such good progress in Ross. In this way, the majority of parishes in the diocese had either readers or ministers (though mostly ministers) by the late 1570s. Fearn, in Easter Ross, had no minister until 1590; more significantly, of other parishes on the west coast, Gairloch was unfilled until 1583, Lochcarron until 1587 (although Alexander Fraser alias Moir served as a reader in 1574), and Applecross, which had Murdo Johnston as reader from 1574 and minister from 1579 to 1590, did not have its own minister again until 1731. Until 1607, the parishes of Applecross, Gairloch, Lemlair and Dingwall, stretching across the country from Easter to Wester Ross, were the responsibility of one minister, and in 1614 Applecross was served by the minister of Gairloch. In 1656, an ordinance was made that the minister of Lochcarron, with which the parish was joined by this time, should visit Applecross every five to six weeks, staying for at least three days to catechise the people. This situation goes a long way towards explaining the persistence of the animal sacrifices recorded there by the presbytery of Dingwall in the early eighteenth century. The district was probably eschewed by the Catholic missionaries in the seventeenth century because of its proximity to well-staffed Protestant areas. In the diocese of Moray – part of which was in the *Gaidhealtachd* – twenty pre-Reformation secular priests took office in the Reformed Kirk, as well as around a dozen monks and friars.[28]

On the other hand, the evidence for Caithness indicates that the recruitment of candidates for the Reformed Kirk did not noticably come from the existing beneficed clergy in the diocese. All parishes in Sutherland and Caithness appear to have been filled by the late 1570s, however. By the same token, there was relatively little conformity in the dioceses of Dunkeld and Dunblane (parts of which were in the Highlands), but most parishes in these dioceses also had Reformed staff. Significantly, however, five parishes in the diocese of Dunkeld, which had been filled prior to 1560 but lacked even readers in 1574, lay in Atholl and Breadalbane: all were in the southern Highland rather than the Lowland parts of the diocese. The one exception of a priest who conformed in this diocese is revealed through the action of Colin Campbell of Glenorchy, who paid the stipend of the minister of Kenmore, his former chaplain in Finlarig Castle and curate at Killin.[29]

The degree of post-Reformation conformity in Ross and Moray probably accounts for attested popular support for the Kirk there between 1590 and 1610. When a commission sent to the north by the General Assembly passed through Moray, Inverness and Ross in 1597, 'the visitors found an unexpected avidity for religious instruction and great readiness on the part of the principal proprietors to Make provision for it. Foremost amongst these ... was Lachlan Mor Mackintosh [16th chief] who met the deputation in Inverness and subscribed obligations for payment of stipend in different parishes on his estate.' Similarly, when Robert Bruce of Kinnaird, a powerful preacher and twice Moderator of the General Assembly, was exiled to Inverness in 1605, he conducted a mission there. According to tradition, it was attended by multitudes from the neighbouring parishes, and people were even said to have come from Ross and Sutherland to hear him.[30] But in general the lack of organised town life in the Highlands has been seen as a factor impeding the spread of Protestantism; there was certainly less opportunity for the dissemination of knowledge by preachers at large public assemblies, though Inverness, as one of the few sizeable towns in the Highlands, was an exception to the rule. However, Catholic missionaries were able to centre their work of dissemination and conversion fairly effectively around the *baile*, or township, instead.[31] Like the re-establishment of Catholicism in the Highlands, the Reformed faith was initially concentrated in clearly defined geographical pockets.[32]

The difficulty in making comparisons within the diocese of Argyll – for which the two series of crown financial records do not exist – has already been mentioned, but the Reformed Kirk is known to have had the support of the fifth Earl of Argyll. Yet, although serving as the Protestant Queen Elizabeth's proxy at the baptism of Prince James, the Countess of Argyll was ordered by the General Assembly of 1567 to undergo public repentance in the royal chapel at Stirling for her attendance.[33] The public defection of the seventh Earl of Argyll to Catholicism in 1618 probably had a regressive effect upon the progress of Protestantism in Argyll, though his son, Lord Lorne, continued to support the Protestant religion. This support was by no means insignificant, because after his father's exile Lorne was the head of the family in all but name. However the defection of members of the Campbell kin group – such as Campbell of Cawdor – to Catholicism later during the Franciscan mission was attributed by the missionaries themselves to the influence of the Catholic Earl of Argyll.[34] Moreover, in 1618, when Argyll was ordered to appear before the Privy Council under pain of treason to answer for his conduct, he was also chastised for being 'not secretlie reconceilled bot oppinlie enterrit in verie professed freindschip and suspitious dealing with our proclaimed tratour Sir James McDonald and olde McRonnald'.[35] (After the quelling of the MacDonald rebellion in Islay in 1615, Sir James MacDonald of Knockrinsay had escaped to Ireland with Alasdair MacDonald of Keppoch, and they were concealed in Galway by Valentine and Robert Black – resetters of Jesuits – before escaping to Spain.)[36] Fear engendered by their fraternisation shows the extent to which not only the government but also the clans identified adherence to Catholicism with political protest against the establishment, just as it was so identified contemporaneously in Ireland.

Argyll also had the renowned John Carswell as its superintendent, whose diligent translation of the Book of Common Order into Gaelic in 1567 under the Earl of Argyll's patronage showed practical concern for the people to whom he ministered. Carswell dedicated his translation to the Earl and – significant to the contemporary recognition of a common, cultural *Gaidhealtachd* – to all Christians throughout the world, 'go h'áiridhe d'fhearaibh Alban agus Eireand' (especially to the men of Scotland and Ireland).[37] It was the first book printed in Gaelic in Scotland or Ireland. In the sixteenth-century Highlands, three written languages were commonly in use: Latin and (increasingly throughout the century) Scots, the languages of government, and the common classical Gaelic of the *Gaidhealtachd mòr* of Scotland and Ireland, the literary dialect of Gaelic. There were few schools in the Highlands at this time, and the Statutes of Iona (1609) and their subsequent ratification (1616) promoted the use of vernacular English at the expense of Gaelic. But John Bannerman contends that in a metropolitan region like the former Lordship of the Isles, the supportive role played by the bards and their highly wrought panegyric in the maintenance of traditional kin-based society may infer a higher degree of literacy in Gaelic among the laity than has hitherto been presumed. It is, as he says, inconceivable that bardic verse was intended to be anything other than fully intelligible, and it may indeed be that common classical Gaelic was then more intelligible to the contemporary layman than has previously been thought. There would undoubtedly have been more pressure on lay people to be literate in Gaelic than in Latin or Scots, although (as in most other aspects of social and cultural life) the attitude of the head of the kindred was of paramount importance in determining the incidence of literacy (and certainly in Scots). There is no doubt that Carswell anticipated a congregation for his translation of the Book of Common Order: he expected his book primarily to be of use to the Gaelic-speaking clergy. Most Gaelic speakers who attended university did so as a way into a career in the church, where a degree was an important factor in preferment. The extent of the lay readership which he anticipated can only be surmised, although literacy in Gaelic must have been relatively common among the clan *fine* or *uaislean*.[38]

Carswell was one of an educated Gaelic élite who actively communicated at the cynosure of the three languages, but it was common classical Gaelic that he chose as an instrument to promote the Reformed faith in the Highlands so soon after it had been sanctioned by the Reformation Parliament in 1560.[39] Carswell implied that the ability to write classical Gaelic was extensive enough in his time (although it was obviously beginning its long decline as part of the general assault on Gaelic society), but he was concerned about the lack of printed devotional material in Gaelic: although a certain amount of their history, the tabular staves of the bards and the transcripts of the literati were available in manuscript, none was printed and certainly not the Bible.[40] He therefore produced a book which gave the form of prayers and the holy sacrament in Gaelic two centuries before the Bible was available;[41] it was intended as a service book for worship in the Reformed Kirk.[42] As an exercise in deference to the arrogantly defended status of the bards, he was modest about his translation: there was in it neither excess nor defect, 'acht mura bfuil uireasbhuidh no imarcaidh and do reir dheachtaidh no cheirt na bfileadh ar an nGaoidheilg, an ni ar nach bfuil feidhm no foghnamh ag an sgribhtuir dhiadha air' (unless indeed there is excess or defect therein according to the standard of diction or propriety laid down for Gaelic by the poets, a matter for which the holy scriptures have no need or use). On the contrary, however, his command of the language has been estimated as particularly fine.[43]

Argyll tradition paints Carswell as a keen-fingered money grasper.

Tha droll mar dhruinnein na curra	His rump is like the back of a crane,
's a sgròban lom, gionach farsaing	and his empty maw greedy and rapacious.[44]

He certainly seemed to make the most of the teinds and revenues of his churches, but apparently with more self-interest than was strictly necessary. Nevertheless, he was conscientious in collating to benefices and making visitations within his jurisdiction.[45] Carswell had a sensible commitment towards gradual change: answering criticism of his work in Argyll, he said in 1564, 'latt thaim say quhat thai list, my conscience will nocht latt me use rigour but aganis the sturbborne'.[46] Carswell had held the parsonage of Kilmartin in Argyll since the year 1553; eventually in 1565, he was promoted to the bishopric of the Isles, holding it in conjunction with that of Argyll. His political support of the fifth Earl of Argyll undoubtedly played its part in his early preferment. Although in theory this promotion extended the area of his work as superintendent,[47] it appears that the Isles – by dint of its geographical isolation – remained more immune to the inroads of the Reformed Kirk than areas of the mainland. That the seventeenth-century reformers themselves recognised this is apparent from the records of the synod of Argyll and from the later records of Royal Bounty whose committee was operative from 1728.[48] Ministers were in place in some areas by the end of this period, but their parishes were huge.

In Jura, Alexander MacAllister was incumbent at the time of Andrew Knox's 1626 report of his diocese of Argyll and the Isles, but no one is recorded prior to that. At the same time, Mull had three ministers for one parish – (——) Maclean, 'parson of Kilean', Mr John Campbell and Ninian MacMillan –

presumably Killean in Torosay.[49] For Mull to have been served by three ministers at the beginning of the seventeenth century makes a strong case for some kind of Reformed presence having preceded this: at least one pre-Reformation cleric conformed. Fingon MacMullen was chaplain of St. Mary's Chapel at Tobermory in Mull in 1539, and he was serving the Reformed order as vicar of Iona (or Icolmkill) in 1573, where his immediate successor was Ewen Maclean, who died some time before 26 May 1642. In nearby Islay, Sir Charles Maclean also conformed: he had been presented to the parish of Killarow on 24 August 1538 and was still incumbent there in 1573. In Tiree and Coll, Thomas Knox was already minister when he was made dean of the Isles on 4 August 1617. In the following year, 1618, the two Tiree parishes of Kirkapol and Sorobie were joined with Coll on 31 July. Yet just how effectively was the Protestant Church established in Coll when, during the Commonwealth period, parents who lived in vacant parishes in Argyll and wished their children to be baptised had to bring a certificate of fitness from the session, while those residents of Coll who wished their children to be baptised had to bring a certificate from the island's baillie?[50] This shows either that they wanted Protestant baptism or, less positively, that communications were so uncertain in the joint parish of Coll and Tiree that Coll was really without a ministry.

The Long Island – South and North Uists, Benbecula, Barra, Harris, Bernera, St. Kilda and Lewis – already had some ministers in the first two decades after the Reformation, and more ministers were in place by the early seventeenth century.[51] When in October 1633 criminal letters were taken out against Ranald MacDonald, first of Benbecula, he was accused, amongst other things, that when he came to the Isle of Barra in June 1609, he there 'slew to the death umquhile Johnne Mcniell persone and minister of Bara'.[52] In combination with the ministrations of Irish regular missionaries of various denominations throughout the seventeenth century, the murder appears effectively to have decided the future religious bent of the island as a Catholic community. At the time of Knox's report, Barra was nominally served by the minister of Harris, which tends to imply that there was no Protestant minister in the islands that lay between the two.[53] In the same year as the murder, 1609, Kenneth McKenzie, minister, was presented by Knox to the parish of Sleat, including Trotternish and the Small Isles of Eigg, Muck, Rhum and Canna.[54]

The Hebridean Isles, Skye and Harris had the earliest settlements of Reformed ministers. Skye and Harris both had ministers in 1566, and Lewis by 1572. It was probably because the Reformed Kirk had arrived before them that the various waves of Catholic missionaries in the seventeenth century were able to make only limited headway in these islands. In Skye, as early as 1566, Malcolm MacPherson was granted the parsonage and vicarage of Duirinish for life by Archibald, fifth Earl of Argyll. In the following year the grant was confirmed by Queen Mary, as was his collation by John Carswell, as abbot of

Iona. However, since he was one and the same as the Malcolm MacPherson who was also granted the parsonage and vicarage of St. Bride in Harris during his lifetime, and was confirmed in that grant too in 1567, there is some possibility that he may simply have been drawing the revenues of both as an absentee.[55] This means that the first Reformed minister in the parish of Duirinish may have been Alan O'Colgan, who witnessed a contract between Donald MacDonald of Sleat and Roderick MacLeod of Harris in 1609. The appointment of this minister shows a deliberate attempt at cultural empathy, because he seems to have been of native Irish extraction, although his forename is Scottish rather than Irish, which might indicate second-generation settlement. Similarly, there was a minister in the parish of Bracadale by 1614, which makes a total of two operational Reformed parishes in Skye by this date.[56] However, this represents a coverage of only one-sixth of the twelve parish kirks in Skye mentioned by Munro in 1549, and it appears to have left openings for the survival of at least one Catholic enclave.[57]

Alexander Campbell, parson of 'Killychmynewyr', either held or was simply drawing the revenues of the benefice of Kilmuir in Trotternish, in Skye, when in 1580 he witnessed a bond from Angus MacDonald of Dunyveg, to John, bishop of the Isles.[58] He appears to have been the pre-Reformation incumbent who continued to hold two-thirds of the fruits of the benefice during his lifetime.[59] The fact that he was a Campbell supports this interpretation, for the majority of that name were employed in and around Argyll. Moreover, the eighty-year gap before the next incumbent, Farquhar MacLennan, in 1662 (who is historically recognised as the first Reformed minister) might partially account for Trotternish becoming the most Catholic of all the districts of Skye in the seventeenth century.[60] Further evidence of continuance of the old church in Trotternish is the survival of a medieval Gaelic–Latin *Cisiojanus* – or mnemonic list of feasts – a manuscript which was acquired locally by Donald Macqueen, parish minister of Kilmuir in Trotternish between 1740 and 1785. It is in itself, as an unsophisticated composition, an indication of the esteem in which the saints were held in the area of origin. It derived from the Beaton family in Skye and dates from the sixteenth century.[61]

In 1566 in the parish of Kilbride in Harris, Malcolm MacPherson was granted the parsonage and vicarage of St. Bride in Harris for his lifetime by Archibald, fifth Earl of Argyll. He still held the grant in 1568, but John McPherson was in place in 1626 and may have been there earlier. A minister was also working in the service of MacLeod of Harris at Rodel in 1605: only in Harris was there a Reformed presence as early as in Skye. In North Uist in 1626, Donald MacMillen was said to be 'ane verie auld man'; he had probably been there for some time. Technically, MacMillen also served South Uist, but he lived in North Uist, where the people had taken to Protestantism; in South Uist the people seem to have shown no inclination for Protestantism even prior to the advent of the Irish Franciscans. Fr. Ward allegedly converted Ranald MacDonald to Catholicism, claiming that he was the minister in South Uist.[62] This, however, appears to have been another of MacDonald's many ruses: the first minister of South Uist, rector John MacKinnon, is not recorded until 3 June 1633 and he was probably not resident there.[63] Under any circumstances, MacDonald was to prove a disreputable convert.[64]

In Lewis, two clergymen are mentioned in the two decades after 1560. Sir Patrick McMaster Martin was parson in Barvas in 1566, but his designation as confessor indicates that he was one of the pre-1560 clergy who had retained his benefice. A minister, Ronald Anguson, was also in place in Uig by June 1572, although because of the amalgamation of the parishes of Stornoway, Gress, Ey, Lochs and Uig he was responsible for a vast parish which covered a good three-quarters of the island (see Fig. 5.1). An obligation of 16 April 1573, in which Roderick MacLeod of Lewis pledged his co-operation with John Campbell, bishop of the Isles, designated Anguson 'persoun of Wig', such terminology making it feasible that he was incumbent in the benefice at the Reformation and had simply conformed. The island of Lewis was also briefly served twice by ministers in a missionary capacity. Robert Durie, minister of Anstruther, accompanied the Fife Adventurers[65] to Lewis in October 1598 and again in April 1601, at the behest of the presbytery of St. Andrews, in order 'to plant ane kirk' in Stornoway. When sixty Lowland planters were murdered in December 1601, Durie beat a retreat to his former parish. In 1610 – the final year of the Adventurers' attempts at colonising the island – Farquhar McRae, minister of Gairloch, went as missionary to Lewis, where little had as yet been done to instruct the inhabitants in the Reformed faith.[66]

It is difficult to deny the general receptiveness of the late sixteenth-century Scottish population to the Protestant faith and the relative ease with which the Reformed Kirk was able to establish its superiority in many areas.[67] After the abdication of Queen Mary in 1567, the Reformation was regarded more or less as a political fait accompli.[68] Hence, any Counter-Reformation plot with the least suggestion of foreign involvement had decidedly political overtones. The transition from the Catholic to the Reformed faith was aided and abetted by the apparent inability of the Scots Catholic community resident on the continent to mobilise either the manpower or the finance for a mission. Yet the Protestant Kirk was hardly replacing a fully operational parochial system in the Highlands and Islands. Prior to the Reformation, the Catholic Church had been as guilty of providing absentee appointments there as was the Protestant Kirk, which was similarly unable to fill all its benefices. As elsewhere in Scotland, parochial revenues had been used to endow other religious institutions, although there was some restriction on appropriation in the Highlands and Islands because of the limited number of putative recipients and the inaccessibility of some parishes.[69] Furthermore, the granting of the headships of religious institutions *in commendam* – that is, appointing a caretaker in the absence of the rightful *in titulo* possessor – had been used as a way of circumventing the rules against pluralism, resulting even in the appearance of lay commendators.[70]

The nature of the remaining records makes it very difficult to gauge the extent of the antipathetic reaction to Protestantism in the Highlands and Islands, although the behaviour of Ranald MacDonald of Benbecula was undoubtedly an extreme example of its type. But opposition to Protestantism was often symptomatic of a rejection of Lowland politics and culture in favour of local Gaelic hegemony, as was expressed, for example, when the Fife Adventurers attempted to colonise Lewis. The establishment of the Reformed faith in the Highlands and Islands was used, as in Ireland, as a tool to civilise the natives. In the first decade of the seventeenth century, James VI and I made steps to bring the Highlands under state jurisdiction, which meant, by implication, bringing them within the fold of the Established Church. The very first term of the Statutes of Iona in 1609, by which the main Highland and Islands chiefs were made to subscribe an oath of their future obedience to the King and the laws of Scotland, referred to the chiefs' lack of support of the Reformed Kirk. The registered copy of the Statutes of Iona went as far as to equate the chiefs' ignorant state with lack of the Protestant religion.

> The speciall barronis and gentilmen of the saidis Yllis undirwrittin ... togidder with the maist pairt of thair haill speciall freindis, dependairis and tennentis, compeirand judiciallie, and undirstanding and considering the grite ignorance unto the quhilk not onlie thay for the maist pairt thameselffis, bot also the haill commonalitie inhabitantis of the Illandis, hes bene and are subject to, quhilk is the caus of the neglect of all dewtie to God and of his trew worschip, to the grite grouth of all kynd of vice, proceiding pairtlie of the laik of pasturis plantit and pairtlie of the contempt of these quha ar alreddy plantit.[71]

The proposals made for remedying this state of affairs were that the ministers planted (and to be planted) in the Isles were to be reverently obeyed, their stipends dutifully paid, the ruinous kirks repaired, the sabbath kept, and all sexual misdemeanours as well as handfasting[72] were to be punished 'conforme to the lovable Actis of Parliament of this realme and disciplein of the Reformit Kirk'.

The overall aim of the Statutes of Iona was to encourage the assimilation of the clan *fine* (the élite of the lineage group in the clan) and to make them more like the Lowland gentry. In terms of what the Statutes achieved concerning the Kirk, it does appear that a sustained effort was made to introduce more ministers to the Isles, particularly by the time of Knox's report in 1626. The virtual capitulation of the native Irish in Ulster and the escheating of the six counties would also have served to focus the minds of Highland and Islands chiefs with respect to similar occurrences on the west coast of Scotland. None the less, the reconstitution of the Statutes by the Privy Council seven years later is an indication that not all of the proposals had been fully implemented.[73] So even though more ministers were in place in the Isles following the enactment of the statutes, there was still much room for improvement. By no means all the vacant parishes were occupied, and thus there was an added burden on those ministers *in situ*, who usually had cumbersome parishes in the first place. Even fifty years after the Reformation, there was still only a modicum of occupied benefices in the Isles.

It was apparent, a decade later, that some people in the Highlands adhered to a tenuously remembered Catholic faith. This was perhaps as much a consequence of the uncertainty which the Kirk seemed to bring as of innate conservatism or, alternatively, of defiance of the Clan Campbell. One view of the situation has been put thus:

> The religion the people of the Isles wanted was clearly apparent when the Irish Franciscans came to the Hebrides in 1624, when several of the subscribers to the Statutes and thousands of ordinary Hebrideans were speedily reconciled to the Roman Catholic church – the latter mostly from ignorance, not from Protestantism – in numbers that the Vatican found difficult to believe, having the illusion that Scotland was by then totally Calvinist.[74]

This statement calls for qualification at several levels, not least numerically, because evidence of the early conversion of parts of some islands (such as Skye and Harris) to Protestantism refutes the statement that all the people of the Isles wanted Catholicism. Perhaps some found it flattering that a clergyman of any denomination took an interest in them at all. Many of the areas where people were more receptive to the tradition of Catholicism were especially isolated, and some of them were in the Isles or in mainland areas where there was a strong link with other clan territories in the Isles, like the Moidart territory of the MacDonalds of Clanranald. On the mainland, Glengarry and Lochaber were also more favourably inclined to the Catholic tradition. Geographical, cultural and political isolation forged the attitudes which kept the Protestant Kirk out, as they did in the Isle of Barra in 1609.

There was also a certain pragmatism in the exercise of religion. For instance, although there was an early Reformed presence in Skye, Donald Gorm MacDonald, seventh of Sleat, stressed his Protestantism as much in the hope of gaining lucrative mercenary contracts in Ireland from Elizabeth I of England. In a letter of 1598, he pointed out that he could ascertain for her all the secret actions and intentions of the recently restored Catholic Earls of Huntly, Angus and Errol, 'whoe hes gottin tham selfis (be his Majestie's speciall caire and politique Industrie) resaved agane in the bosome of the Church of Scotland'. He would also be able to find out the intentions of the Spanish and their plots against England 'and that throw the veray speciall credeitt Inteirfreindschipe and familiaritie I have with Mr James Gordoune Jesuit,[75] Mr Walter Lyndesay With divers other Scottis papistis Jesuits and seminarie preistes', whose diabolical, pestiferous and anti-Christian practices he nevertheless professed to hate with all his heart and soul.[76]

Any mainland Highlanders who accepted the discipline of the Kirk must have done so by dint of personal persuasion by their local minister, backed by the increasingly strong arm of the state, because no Kirk Sessions were established to assist ministers in the Highlands until well into the seventeenth century.[77] Adherence to Catholicism, especially in the absence of a resident priest to bring home the immediacy of its practical lifestyle, must have been attractive. In some localities, many were able to use the existing discrepancy in religious observance to achieve aims which ultimately might not have been allowed by either church. Surviving presbytery and synod minutes of a later period document in graphic detail the sins and errors, particularly of adultery and fornication, which the Kirk so readily denounced. The Highlands had its fair share of this type of sin, although it undoubtedly went on before the extant Highland Kirk records began in the 1630s. One of the terms of the Statutes of Iona was that marriages contracted for only a certain number of years were no longer permissible. Much has previously been made of the practice of 'handfasting' – so-called trial marriage in the Highlands – but as A. E. Anton has shown, 'there is no proof, or approach to proof, that handfasting in Skene's sense (trial temporary marriage) or any other peculiar customs of marriage were recognised in medieval Scotland after the introduction of Christianity had given one rule of marriage to the whole Christian world'. After the Reformation, geographical and other difficulties often upgraded the status of the *rèiteach* or formal engagement, which was considered sufficiently binding for cohabitation pending a formal church marriage, especially when the participants did not wish to be married by a Protestant minister.[78] None the less, judging by the extramarital couplings of many of the Irish and Scottish chiefs of the period, cohabitation – whether bound by the *rèiteach* or not – was perfectly socially acceptable, and was probably equally so for the average clansman.[79] Such unions could of course be dissolved later, and frequently were.

It was Denis Campbell, dean of Limerick, the illegitimate son of Archibald, fifth earl of Argyll (1558–73) and a known loyalist in Ireland, who was engaged by the English in their negotiations with the Highland mercenary clans rather than Donald Gorm MacDonald of Sleat. In his report, 'Observations on the Western Isles of Scotland (*c.* 1596)', which was based on an unrivalled knowledge of the political situation in the west of Scotland, he provided a detailed commentary on the genealogical interconnections between the main Highland mercenary families in the late sixteenth century. In it, he noted the apparent abduction of Agnes (or Anne) Campbell by James MacDonald of

Dunyveg and the Glens, sixth chief, who succeeded in 1538. Having been imprisoned by James V for non-payment of feu duties to the Crown, James MacDonald escaped prison after the King's death and took 'a lease of Ilahi [Islay] and letters patent ... of Kintyre, acknowledging a good yearly rent for the same, [which] was, notwithstanding, holden in great jealousy by the house of Argyll'. MacDonald's method of bringing this jealousy in check was to abduct Agnes Campbell, then wife of the sheriff of Bute, 'by whom she was hardly entreated'. Allegedly because of this harsh treatment, she was making her way to Argyll but 'was intercepted by the said James and married', subsequently producing six sons and a daughter.[80] There is no surviving evidence of any ecclesiastical censure of James MacDonald. But by the 1630s, when the Protestant Kirk had made some progress in establishing a network of presbyteries in the Highlands, it did begin to deal retrospectively with such transgressors. For example, another part of the indictment of 5 October 1633 which accused Raonull Mac Ailein 'ic Iain MacDonald of Benbecula of murdering a minister in Barra, also accused that having

> shakkin aff all feare of god and obedience to His Majesties Lawes he in 1603 with out any Lawful devorcement putt away [blank] nyn Rannald Vcdonald his first mareit wyiff and mareit umquhile Margaret nccleoyd sister to umquhile sir Rorie Mccleoyd of Dounvegoune. Efter quhais deceis he mareit Marie Ncconnell sister to Sir Donald McDonald of Sleatt and keepit house with her Ten yeires and thaireftir in ane most godles and Lawles manner without any Decreit of Devorcement patt the said Marie away and mariet Margaret NcConnell sister to Angus McConnell of Dounnavaig with quhome he keipes present companie and societie.[81]

The Protestant Establishment was absolutely scandalised that 'at this present hour he hes thrie mareit wyiffes alive', and MacDonald was charged to appear at Inveraray on 10 January 1634 to answer criminal letters on the complaint of Malcolm Fisher, Procurator Fiscal. He was not only charged with murder, but with polygamy as well.[82]

Effect of the Plantation of Ulster on Religious Connections

Protestantism had been legally established as the state religion in both Ireland and Scotland by the 1560s; James VI and I also sought to convert the Gaels to Protestantism with the idea that it would have a beneficial affect on their behaviour. The beginning of the next century heralded two events with powerful implications for the future of the Gaelic world. The first – the Union of the Crowns of Scotland and England in 1603 – effectively limited the opportunities for Irish and Scottish Gaels to associate with each other politically and militarily. When James VI of Scotland also became King of England and Ireland, he inherited the problems linked with Anglo-Irish condominium and worked to circumscribe the activities of Highland mercenaries in the pay of the native Irish. Second, the defeat and flight of the last truly independent Irish chieftains, O'Neill and O'Donnell, in 1607 led – through the wholesale forfeiture of their lands – to the extensive Protestant plantation of Ulster.

After the Union of the Crowns, James was in a better position to mastermind a concerted policy of subjugation or 'danting' of the Gael. In the second book of his *Basilicon Doron* (1599), written as a kingly instruction manual for his son, he mentioned the Highlanders as internal saboteurs not conducive to the ultimate civilisation of the kingdom: 'As for the Hie-landes, I shortly comprehend them all in two sortes of people: the one, That dwelleth in our maine land that are barbarous, and yet mixed with some shew of civilitie: the other, that dwelleth in the Iles and are alluterlie barbares, without any sorte or shew of civilitie.' The best way of proceeding with the mainland Gaels was to execute the laws already constituted against the chiefs, by which they would be easily suppressed. 'As for the other sorte, thinke no other of them all, then as of Wolves and Wilde Boares'. The nostrum here was to 'followe foorth the course that I have begunne, in planting Colonies among them of aunswerable In-landes subjectes, that within shorte time maye roote them out and plant civilitie in their roomes'. However, James was just as wary of 'vain Puritans', protesting that he 'never founde with anie Hie-land or Bordour thieves so greate ingratitude, and so many lyes & vile perjuries, as I have found with some of them', as he was of 'proud Papall Bishoppes'.[83] The nominal acceptance of Catholicism by many politically non-conforming Irish and Scottish Gaels was regarded as a further embodiment of their cultural differences. Yet James was also a pragmatist: he was quite willing to retain the Catholic MacDonnells of Antrim as major planters in Ulster.

Ireland continued to be furnished with priests sufficient to maintain the old religion, mainly because the people still wanted it but also because the Irish Colleges in France, Italy and Spain were able to supply clergy. Quite why the same did not happen in the Highlands of Scotland is worthy of greater attention than it has been given, although it probably has not a little to do with the fact that all the Scots Colleges were in the hands of Lowlanders (the Reformed faith took off well in the Lowlands). However, by no means all of the Irish missionaries sent to Ireland at this time spoke Irish;[84] some spoke only English, others only Irish and others spoke both, so the lack of the Gaelic tongue can hardly be blamed for a failure to supply priests in Scotland. The irony remains that while Scots made such a contribution to the Protestant effort in Ulster, the Irish were to make a similar commitment to the Catholic effort in the Highlands and Islands of Scotland.

The polarisation of culture and religion seen in Ireland today had already begun to reveal itself as early as 1576 when it was suggested that Gaelic-speaking Scots should be brought to Ireland to preach the true religion to the Irish. On 28 April of that year the Lord Deputy, Sydney, wrote to Elizabeth I concerning the lamentable state of the Church of Ireland. He requested that the Queen write to the Regent of Scotland to send some honest, zealous and learned men who could speak the Irish language.[85] One more eminent than the rest was Denis Campbell (illegitimate son of the fifth Earl of Argyll), who became dean of Limerick in 1587.[86] The state papers refer in 1596 to 'the contention betwixt the bishop of Limerick and him' and how his friends had 'provided that he shall be advanced to the bishopric of the Isles'. Campbell's problem with the bishop would appear to have arisen from a conflict perceived between his ecclesiastical office and his involvement in the mercenary trade, both as an adviser to the government and as go-between for Argyll. On 30 April 1596, Robert Bowes, English agent in Scotland, wrote that the dean had 'covered (as he says) the wrongs done to him by the bishop of Limerick, both in the particular violence against himself and also in offensive words towards Argyll and the house of Campbell, which he called Redshanks to their disgrace[87] and which might stir the house to passion and contempt'. In June, Argyll asked Bowes to suggest that the Queen 'direct the Lord Deputy and Council in Ireland with the better expedition to hear and determine the controversies depending betwixt the bishop of Limerick and the Dean'.[88] In spite of the possibility of advancement to the bishopric of the Isles, Denis Campbell seems to have elected to stay in Ireland. This may have been due in part to his alleged unpopularity in the Highlands. George Nicolson, English agent in Scotland, wrote in 1600 that Campbell was 'a gentleman of good affection to her Majesty's service, but much disliked and crossed here' – especially it seems, by Agnes Douglas, Countess of Argyll, wife of the seventh Earl, which would not have helped his chances of preferment to the bishopric of the Isles.[89] He is noted in Ireland in 1599 and 1601 as one of several preachers to the army, for which he was paid the princely sum of thirty shillings per week. Attending the soldiers in garrison, he stayed in Dublin.[90]

The importation of Gaelic-speaking Scots was put forward again to Cecil in 1604 by Sir John Davies, the Solicitor General. Davies was under no illusion as to the inadequacy of the Irish clergy even after the Protestant Reformation, scoffing that the Irish Protestant churchmen were 'for the most part mere idols and ciphers, that many are serving men and some horseboys, and that many cannot read' – dismissive labels which scarcely differed from those applied to the Catholic clergy in the previous century.[91] Following a visitation of Cashel and Emly (see Fig. 1.1) in 1607, Thomas Jones, archbishop of Dublin (1605–19), similarly remarked that the native Irish clergy there were 'fitter to keep hogs than serve in the church'.[92] This is part of what has been called the 'abundant literature of Protestant dismay' which sought to blame the native Irish population for the many problems experienced by the clergy of the Established

Fig. 1.1. Church of Ireland dioceses, *c.* 1570.

Church in evangelising the country. It was not simply the plantation of Ulster which contributed to the polarisation of Irish society, but the dismissive attitude of the Church of Ireland. The Irish were seen as unregenerate by nature, and therefore that time would be far better spent in the pleasanter task of preaching to the converted.[93]

The Church of Ireland was not only burdened by a deteriorating church fabric, but by the gross abuse of appropriation. Davies highlighted the case of Miler Migrath, Protestant archbishop of Cashel (1571–1622), who in February 1604 held four bishoprics as well as another seventy-seven livings. He suggested that the English government examine the situation: preachers really were in great demand, so Gaelic-speaking ministers should be brought across from Scotland to fill the gap; at least they would be understood by that 'clamorous and whining nation' (the native Irish).[94] Opinion has it that Denis Campbell's elevation to the three Sees of Derry, Raphoe and Clogher in 1604 resulted from Davies' suggestion. Although Campbell died before he could take up his new post, the appointment of Andrew Knox, bishop of the Isles, to the See of Raphoe in the summer of 1610 was undoubtedly a continuation of this same enterprise; both men knew the Highlands and Isles intimately. This strategy ultimately sought to reduce connections between Gaelic Ireland and the Highlands, as a natural extension of James VI and I's civil policies.[95] In effect, the King aimed to tame Gaelic resistance by the conversion of the Gaels to Protestantism. In 1620, James clarified the role that he envisaged the new Protestant Trinity College, Dublin (founded in 1592)[96] would play in fashioning missionaries to evangelise the natives. He stated that

> because our College of Dublin was first founded ... principally for breeding up the natives of that kingdom in civility, learning and religion, we have reason to expect that in all this long time ... some good numbers of the natives should have been trained up in that College, and might have been employed in teaching and reducing those that are ignorant among that people ... and therefore we do require that henceforth special care be had ... and, for the supplying of the present want, that choice be made of some number of towardly young men already fitted with the knowledge of the Irish tongue, and be placed in the university ... for two or three years till they have the grounds of religion and be able to catechize the simple natives and deliver unto them so much as themselves have learned.[97]

It was inordinately difficult, though, to attract native Irish to Trinity College when the official education system was geared towards the English. The few Irish-speaking students who went to Trinity in its early decades rarely served in the native strongholds of Connacht or Ulster, but more often in the more lucrative eastern dioceses which already accommodated large numbers of Protestants. The College certainly never lived up to James's ideal of becoming a seminary for the native Irish.[98]

Inattention, at least in the first few decades after the Reformation, to spreading the gospel in the vernacular (Irish Gaelic) has been held as the root of the failure of the Protestant Reformation in sixteenth-century Ireland. It is a persuasive argument, although Scotland suffered from a similar dearth of Gaelic-speaking clerics. When Archbishop Adam Loftus wrote to the English Council in March 1604, he insisted that during the thirty-six years of his incumbency in the See of Dublin (1567–1605), the city had attracted preachers as distinguished as those in any English city, but regrettably only the English had been able to hear them.[99] In June of the following year, the Scot George Montgomery, dean of Norwich and the King's chaplain, acceded to the combined Sees of Raphoe, Clogher and Derry. Montgomery, unlike Campbell, probably had little or no Gaelic. He remained in England for a further two years before taking up his appointment, but he was interested enough in the meantime to undertake a survey of his three Sees. Montgomery's survey – dated some time before September 1607 (probably around 1605) – is a useful indicator of Highland or Gaelic-speaking penetration into the area, although such visitors were but a minority among Irish indigenes. However, it should be stressed that there is insufficient evidence to support Perceval-Maxwell's claim about the Scots in the survey that: 'Despite these tenuous Scottish connexions, almost certainly all were nominal Roman Catholics.'[100] The survey shows significant movement of Highland Protestant clergy into Ulster over a decade before the first Irish regulars took their Catholic mission to the Highlands.[101] Besides the numerous clergy versed in Latin, many spoke Irish and 'Scots';[102] the survey also confirms, because of its proximity to Ulster, that many of the Irish clergy had studied at Glasgow University;[103] these clergymen, at least, were unlikely to have been Roman Catholic. Until Ulster got its first university in the mid-nineteenth century, studying at the nearest Scottish university was the only alternative to Trinity College, Dublin.[104]

Among the Derry clergy, many are noted as speaking Irish, but at least two spoke Scots as well as Irish. Both had attended Glasgow University.[105] John O'Henney of Banagher knew Scots, Irish and Latin, and had studied at Glasgow University. Hugh MacDonnell ('Donaldeus'), rector of Donaghmore and Ardara in Raphoe, was 'clever in Irish, Latin and Scots tongue, the man in all the bishoprics, in my [Montgomery's] judgement, most learned and most worthy'. Quite an irony, then, that in spite of these linguistic skills, he allegedly found 'difficulty in expressing his opinions'. MacDonnell is placed with the Derry rather than the Raphoe clergy, which tends to confirm that he was an absentee rector.[106]

The Raphoe clergy were replete with similar talents. Donatus Maginnell who worked in a parish 'on this side of the mountains' – probably to the north of the Blue Stack Mountains – was 'learned in Latin, Irish and Scots, studied at Glasgow', but to his eternal credit was further endowed with 'a good disposition'. Nellanus M'Callen (Mac Cailein or Campbell?), alias Groome, located 'beyond the mountains' – or to the south of the Blue Stack Mountains – had also studied at Glasgow and spoke Irish, Latin and Scots. On the other hand, Lodus M'Swine (MacSween?) in Kilcar – referred to as 'honest' and 'guileless' – spoke only Irish and Latin, although he had studied at Glasgow too. Lastly, also 'beyond the mountains', there was Magonius M'Connell, another Glasgow student who spoke Scots.[107] M'Callan, M'Swine and M'Connell definitely sound Scottish in origin; indeed, it is difficult to attribute anything other than this nationality to a man (in the last instance) who is said only to speak Scots. The surprise here, with a name like M'Connell, is that he did not also speak Irish. None of the clergy in the bishopric of Clogher were Scots-speaking or had attended Glasgow University, but at the end of a six-name list of the previous bishops of Clogher is 'Dromitius Campbell'.[108] Though not yet identified, if 'Dromitius' is taken as a misreading of 'Dionicius' (i.e. Dioness),[109] this might easily refer to Denis Campbell, incumbent of the neighbouring ecclesiastical diocese of Raphoe, who died at about the time the survey was made.

George Montgomery is unlikely to have continued a policy of positively encouraging Gaelic speakers into his bishoprics because the plantation was a time for the encouragement of Lowland Scots. He certainly worked assiduously to increase the lands of the Church in Ulster in the early days of the plantation – advertising for tenants in all the ports in the south-west of Scotland and particularly around his brother's Scottish estate of Braidstane near Irvine. Settlers began to arrive in 1607. In effect, the Montgomery brothers worked in tandem as right and left arms – ecclesiastical and temporal – in the same task: the strengthening of royal authority in Ulster. Hugh Montgomery, sixth laird of Braidstone, was planted in Down (in much the same way as was Sir James Hamilton) to block the easy movement of fugitives and malcontents from James VI and I's policies of subjugation in the Isles. He also founded a school at Newtonards which taught Latin, Greek and Logic, and he intended to convert the priory houses into a college for philosophy; several young men there were 'bred for the college' – the University of Glasgow.[110] His brother similarly sought to subdue and impede them with politically correct doctrine. Having extended the land assigned to the Church in his dioceses by 25,000 acres, George Montgomery then translated to the bishopric of Meath in July 1609, becoming more involved with Church affairs in the country as a whole. While he remained bishop of Clogher *in commendam*, the way was opened for new appointments in the other two Sees.[111] The nomination by the King of Andrew Knox to the bishopric of Raphoe on 12 August 1610 is significant not only as a real attempt to appoint somebody who could effectively communicate with the native Irish but, retrospectively, is highly significant for the growth of presbyterianism in Ireland. The King had especially chosen Knox, who had been bishop of the Isles since 1605, because – as he wrote to Chichester, the

Irish Lord Deputy in May 1610 – there had been a good deal of intercourse between Raphoe and the Scottish Isles, where Knox had already shown his worth in negotiating with and attempting to reduce the Islesmen to a state of civil obedience. Though Knox had visited Ulster by April 1611 and began shortly afterwards to operate from Ireland, he was allowed to retain his Scottish See concomitantly until 1616, a state of affairs which could be interpreted as supplying a moveable feast of ministers and tenants.[112]

Initially, Knox had difficulty in persuading Scots tenants to settle in his Donegal See, so that he was obliged to grant more favourable terms of tenure. This was in contravention of his patent, and he was indicted in 1632 for the despoliation of the See. However, in a serious drive for spiritual improvement he implemented a rigorous plan of reform which, for example, dared actually to recommend the residence of bishops in their bishopric. By 1611, Chichester praised him for doing more during his few months in office than Montgomery had done in five years.[113] By 1612 he had already drawn seven ministers across from Scotland to serve in the twenty-eight parishes which constituted the See of Raphoe, three of whom are described as Irish-speaking. The word 'prescopalian' was coined to describe the Scots ministers who came across during this period, because they were presbyterian in attitude but worked within the fold of the episcopal Church of Ireland. But during the period of Arminian ascendancy under Archbishop Laud (1630–40) most were forced to reveal their true presbyterian tendencies; they thus became ministers of presbyterian nonconformist congregations. For although he never set foot on Irish soil, Laud none the less exerted his influence through the various agents whom he chose to implement his reforms there. He worked firstly through Archbishop James Ussher of Armagh (1625–26), Primate of Ireland, with whom he corresponded from 1629, then from 1631 through William Bedell, bishop of Kilmore and Ardagh. Finally in 1633, the year in which Laud was appointed archbishop of Canterbury, he worked through Thomas Wentworth (later first Earl of Strafford), who was appointed Lord Deputy of Ireland in the same year, and his chaplain John Bramhall. Wentworth did his job well, earning himself the epithet 'the Irish Canterbury' from Oliver Cromwell, while 'Bishop Bramble' was universally loathed by Irish presbyterians.[114]

Taughboyne, Raymoghy, Raphoe and Donaghmore, four parishes in the barony of Raphoe, and Conwall, Aughnish and Clondavoddog, three parishes in the nearby barony of Kilmacrenan, were all served by the Scots brought across by Knox; they are regarded as the 'mother-parishes' of Donegal presbyterianism.[115] Although these seven ministers were reputedly despised by the Irish, the policy of Gaelic promotion must have had some effect on the numbers of native Irish claimed for Protestantism, for even to present them with arguments, never mind to convert them, it was necessary to speak their language.[116] Another Scot who appeared in the diocese of Raphoe as a non-conformist to episcopacy was the uncompromising presbyterian, Robert Pont. Though not Gaelic-speaking, he had previous connections with Caithness, in the far north of Scotland.[117] He was one of three Scots who were denizated[118] as 'preachers of the Word of God' on 12 February 1619 and probably ministered to the Donegal Scots about Ramelton.[119]

One of the original 'magnificent seven' was the Gaelic-speaking Dugald Campbell, who probably hailed from Argyll.[120] In all likelihood he was a student of St. Andrews University, although this cannot be stated with any certainty.[121] During his period in Ireland, Campbell was ordained in Raphoe on 1 September 1611 to the rectorship of Conwall, though his church was subsequently removed to Letterkenny, where eighty British families lived. According to A. F. Scott Pearson, 'he was one of the Gaelic or Erse preachers employed by Bishop Knox in his praiseworthy but belated endeavour to teach the Irish Protestantism in the vernacular'. Yet despite the introduction of Gaelic-speaking Scots, which occurred particularly in the diocese of Raphoe, this method of evangelism was ultimately of limited success in Ireland. Scott Pearson was of the opinion that: 'The emphasis placed by the Scottish Bishop upon the teaching mission of the Protestant Church and upon the need to engage the intelligence of the natives, came after the psychological moment had passed, and ... seems to have been insufficient, of itself, to ensure permanently the conversion of the whole of Donegal.'[122] But since the Scots came to Ulster (even before the plantation) as foreigners and expropriators, bringing their own tenants with them, it is hardly surprising that their religion was rejected. Although the use of Irish as a tool in Protestant conversion would probably have been used to greater effect if implemented after Sydney's initial request in 1576, and although the Catholic priests of the Counter-Reformation had the upper hand in using it first, it was because it was the religion of conquest that Protestantism in Ireland really failed to take hold.

The bleeding of ministers west across the North Channel must have had an adverse affect on the Kirk's evangelisation of the Highlands; it lost a small but significant number of its Gaelic-speaking personnel to Ulster, a loss which it could ill afford when there were so many vacant parishes in the Highlands and Islands. But most importantly, the Kirk's inability to provide anything other than a skeleton ministry in the Highlands and Islands opened a window of opportunity for Irish Catholic missionaries to move in during the second decade of the seventeenth century.

The Catholic Counter-Attack

What was left of Catholicism in Scotland seems to have been in difficulty by the end of the 1570s: by then, the older generation of priests still incumbent at the Reformation (who had been allotted two-thirds of their stipends as a retiral pension) were inactive and there was no new blood. Even before the Reformation, the Highland parishes were in many cases so large as to be administratively unwieldy; the diocese of Caithness, for instance, comprised twenty-four very large parishes. After 1560, the problem must have been exacerbated. Many of the benefices in the pre-Reformation Highlands (as in other areas of Scotland) had been vacant or had had their revenues appropriated, further compounding any shortages of revenue. All fifty-nine parsonages of Caithness and Ross, being more accessible on the mainland than in the Isles, had been appropriated to the cathedrals of Dornoch and Fortrose. However, after 1573 when the Test Act was administered – demanding that all benefice-holders subscribe to the Reformed Articles of Faith and to royal supremacy in ecclesiastical and political affairs – benefices came exclusively under Protestant control. In the Highlands, many church lands were in the hands of the chiefs and, following the Reformation, it was probably at their discretion whether the teinds were paid or not. As might be expected, there is evidence in the diocese of Ross between 1559 and 1561 to show that some laymen took the opportunities provided by the Reformation to stop paying teinds altogether to the existing clergy in the parishes of Kilmorack, Suddie and Kilmuir, and Rosemarkie. Similarly, in Kiltearn the vicarage teinds were apparently not to be paid 'be reasoun the paroshineris will not pay quhill farder ordour be put to the kirk of the samin'.[123] Support for priests from the spiritual faithful may have continued for a number of years in some areas, but any effective attempt to restore Catholicism in Scotland probably required political and financial support from abroad.

The Book of Clanranald mentions the construction of an ecclesiastical foundation in the late sixteenth century, which gives some indication of continuing religious devotion. Here, the money was provided by a chief, John Moydartach MacDonald, eighth of Clanranald (1529–84). The Gaelic reads: 'acht do thaobh eoin mhúidéordaigh de chaith deiredh abhetha go diagha trocaireach, do thogaibh tempall a ceillmaoilridhe anárasáig ⁊ tempall a ccill Donnáin anéige ⁊ do fáguibh máoin do chum caibeil do thogmhail an hogmór anuibhisd bhala ar cuiredh achorp san bhliadhnasa daois chriosd 1574'[124] (Concerning John Moydartach, he spent the end of his life godly and mercifully. He erected a church at Kilmarie in Arasaig, and a church at Kildonan in Eigg;[125] and he left funds to erect a chapel at Howmore in Uist, where his body was buried in the year of the age of Christ 1574.)[126] This would seem to indicate, at least in the Clanranald area of Uist, that Catholicism was still practised at the height of the Reformation. This is important and goes part of the way towards explaining Clanranald's subsequent role as arch-protector of Highland Catholics, because even as late as the early eighteenth century the Kirk was prepared to admit that the Reformation had not yet entered Clanranald's bounds;[127] therefore the chapel at Howmore in Uist must have been a Catholic building.

Further examples of the continuity of Catholicism are difficult to find. Certainly, some of the Clan Donald South came into contact with Catholicism in Ireland on their mercenary trips, or lived in surroundings which nurtured their old beliefs. Sir John Perrot wrote to Sir Francis Walsingham on 20 October 1584, sending him an ornamental Iona cross of which he spoke mockingly because of the esteem in which this totem was held by Somhairle Buidhe MacDonald.

> And for a token I have sent you Holy Columkill's cross, a god of great veneration with Surle Boy and all Ulster, for so great was his grace, as happy he thought himself that could get a kiss of the said cross. I send him unto you, that when you have made some sacrifice to him, according to the disposition you bear to idolatry, you may, if you please, bestow him upon my good Lady Walsingham or my Lady Sidney, to wear as a jewel of weight and bigness, and not of price and goodness, upon some solemn feast or triumph day at Court.[128]

Others of the Isles folk took to travelling to Ireland – where strong social links were encouraged during this period by the trade in mercenaries – to revitalise their faith. In 1593, the Barramen were still making the pilgrimage to Cruach Phádruig, County Mayo, in Connacht.[129] Pilgrimages to Ireland, however, did little to provide regular instruction in the faith: when the Vincentian Dermit Duggan visited Barra in the 1650s, he found the people very poorly instructed in the rudiments of faith.[130]

By no means all Highland chiefs continued to support Catholicism. Some took the Reformation as a good opportunity to secularise Church lands, so that the old ecclesiastical lands in the Isles were effectively occupied by the clan chiefs.[131] Secularisation was not simply a product of the Reformation but was the continuation of a process which had been gathering pace throughout the sixteenth century. The exploitation of vacancies within the Scottish monasteries (in addition to crown taxation) had resulted in a deteriorating economic situation which led amongst other things to an increase in feuing of their lands and ultimately alienation thereof into the hands of laymen.[132] A contract of 8 December 1580 between John Carswell, bishop of the Isles, and Lauchlan Maclean of Duart shows that Maclean (designated baillie) had annexed lands in Iona and the Ross of Mull formerly held of the bishop and the abbacy of Iona. The 1561 rental of the bishopric of the Isles and abbacy of Iona lists those lands held of the abbot by MacIain of Ardnamurchan, MacLeod of Harris and MacDonald of Dunyveg and the Glens, as well as by the bishop of the Isles, but shows that Maclean of Duart held no lands.[133] As Nicholas Maclean-Bristol puts it: 'It was a massive grant which probably formally recognised Maclean's *de facto* control of the church's lands in the Inner Hebrides.' It seems to have been granted by Carswell in return for Maclean sanction of his office.[134]

By the 1580 contract, Lauchlan Maclean of Duart promised to assist and maintain the bishop in all his rights and actions, especially in the collection of the fruits, rents and emoluments pertaining to the bishop, the abbacy of Iona and priory of Ardchattan. He also bound himself to go with the bishop's forces and bring in the profits six days after being charged by the bishop 'sua that the said Lauchlane be nocht chergit be the kingis grace or my lord of Ergile service in the meyntyme'. Besides this, he obliged himself

> to causs the said reverend fader joiss and broik the ile of Ycolmkill, the landis and barony of Rosse, the half of Ballifoill, and the grange of Kilmenie in Ylay, als frelie with all males, dewiteis, setting (and) resing of tenentis, removing and dispossessing of fre halderis, according to the ordour of law, use and consuetude of Ycolmkill and barony of Rosse, als frelie as ony bischop or abbot broikit the samine.

The only one of the above lands held by the bishop of the Isles in the 1561 rental was Kilmeny ('Keilvennie in Illa'), which probably indicates that the others were abbacy lands. Maclean also pledged himself to remove Lauchlan MacDonald MacConych and his galley from the lands of Ross and never to place a steward-depute on the said lands during the bishop's lifetime. Only the thirds of court were to pertain to Maclean and his heirs (as baillie), who were not to permit anyone to oppress the lands of Iona and Ross or the tenants in them with 'stenting, conyow,[135] gerig service'[136] or any other kind of exaction. Four men only from the Ross and another four from Iona were to maintain the fort of Carnburgh – in the Treshnish Isles, off the west of Mull – at their own expense, when Maclean was attending a host. In every other respect, the services of the tenants of Iona and the Ross were to pertain to the bishop alone. In 1572, Maclean bound himself to pay 1,000 merks 'in pairt of payment to ane guid compt of the byrun males and dewiteis of the kirklandis, that the said Lauchlane broikis, perteining to the bischopriks of the Ylis and abbacie of Ycolmekyll sen the bischoppis entrie' – a clear acknowledgement that he had been misappropriating the duties of the lands. Finally, Maclean was ordered to produce his feu charter of those lands which he held of the bishopric of the Isles and abbacy of Iona on 28 December; he was also to appear before the Lords of Session to give security to the bishop for the annual payment of the duties pertaining to the bishopric and to Iona. In return, the bishop agreed to renounce and discharge the decreet obtained against Lauchlan for feus belonging to the bishopric of the Isles and abbacy of Iona; Maclean's charter was to have the same force as before the decreet.[137]

The bishop of the Isles' attempt to wrest these lands in Iona and the Ross of Mull from Maclean proved short-lived, as demonstrated by a surviving Precept of a Royal Charter of Novadamus, dated 1587–88, to Hector Maclean (son and heir apparent of Lauchlan Maclean of Duart) of the island of Iona and other lands formerly belonging to the Abbot of Iona.[138] Maclean probably benefited from the passing in 1587 of the Act for the Annexation of the Temporalities of Benefices to the Crown, which declared that all lands and revenues belonging to the clergy and the monasteries were now to be disposed of by the church. One of the many exceptions to the Act was that lands which had been held for life by lay commendators who became heritors before the Act was passed were to remain with those who had infeftments of them. Baronies or lairdships were included within this. Also excepted were all teinds, a peace offering sure to pacify proprietors.[139] Most of the lands conveyed in the 1587–88 charter were in the Ross of Mull, but it also included lands in other parts of Mull, the Isle of Iona, Islay (though not Kilmeny) and Tiree.[140] More importantly, in terms of Gaelic interconnections, a small portion of the land conveyed to Maclean – the five merk lands of Narrabolsadh in Islay – had been held formerly not of the Abbot of Iona, like all the rest, but of the Monastery of Derry.[141]

As the remnants of the old church decayed and the sweeping tide of secularisation advanced, the cogs of Counter-Reformation crept slowly into action in Scotland. In spite of subsequent criticism of the Jesuits' handling of their mission to Scotland, they must none the less be credited with being the first continental order to send ordained priests into Scotland on a regular standing. Though there is some evidence of native Scots regulars making similar trips on an unco-ordinated basis,[142] such unorganised 'missions' into the Highlands at this time were a result of the priests' personal zeal for sustaining their countrymen and their ability to attract the necessary subsidies. None the less, one of the main reasons why the Franciscans were called in to help on the seventeenth-century Scots mission was the marked absence of Highlanders from the Scots Colleges on the continent. Before this, priests came across occasionally from Ireland, but few of their names survive.[143] Given the incessant cross-channel trafficking of the period, such visits probably occurred more frequently than the extant records divulge, especially amongst the MacDonalds and their associates.

Highland mercenaries had ample opportunity to commune with priests on their mercenary forays into Ireland. Sir Francis Walsingham, Elizabeth's principal advisor, was informed from Dublin in July 1579 that: 'Friars practise with O'Rourke, O'Donnell, Turlough Lynagh, and the Scots.'[144] A lengthy discourse on the service of Sir Richard Bingham (governor of Connacht) in County Mayo, in the summer of 1586, reported that on the night of 22 September a vast regiment of Scots was encamped near Ardnarea[145] in the barony of Tireragh. English spies were sent to reconnoitre.

> Here our guide, who was Edmund M'Costello ... found out a priest, who had that day broken from the Scots, who had him prisoner; he brought the said priest to myself, who assured me that they were encamped at Ardnary ... I dealt with this priest to guide me thither, who of himself durst not undertake it.[146]

Caught between two camps, the priest instead requested a couple of horsemen to accompany him to find two O'Haras who, duly unearthed, sent a couple of spies 'to discover the enemy more certainly'.[147] (O'Hara of Leyney held the lordship adjacent to Tireragh.)

The Campbells, of course, had as many mercenary contacts in Ireland as did the MacDonalds, and they must have been equally exposed there to Catholicism even though the house of Argyll fervently championed the Protestant cause back home. Certainly, a one-off mission into Scotland was undertaken by the Capuchin John Campbell, son of Hugh Campbell, Provost of the burgh of Irvine. Although not known to have visited the Highlands, he had a strong family connection with Denis Campbell, dean of Limerick, and his brother, John Campbell, Provost of the collegiate church of Kilmun.[148] Both illegitimate sons of the fifth Earl of Argyll,[149] the siblings appear to have been raised by the Provost, who was a nephew of Colin, sixth Earl of Argyll. It seems likely that the Capuchin fraternised with Highlanders in the Lowlands. His connection with the dean of Limerick comes to light through his arrest in England en route for Scotland in 1599. On his person was a letter for his brother, minister at Westchester – apparently Denis Campbell – as well as one for Anne of Denmark, wife of James VI. Subsequently imprisoned in the Marshalsea, his close relationship to Argyll probably ensured his survival but, unwilling that the popish contagion should spread, the Privy Council gave warrant on 18 March to the keeper of the Marshalsea to deliver the priest to Denis Campbell, Protestant dean of Limerick, who had done such great service to the English government in Ireland. The dean was empowered to transport him overseas immediately. But strong religious conviction was all the brothers shared: Denis was a crypto-presbyterian Protestant in the Church of Ireland and John an expatriate Catholic. John Campbell, born in 1570, was a champion of the Counter-Reformation; he joined the Reformed branch of the Franciscans known as the Capuchins in Lorraine, where he went under the religious name Fr. John Chrysostom. A person of some influence (if not substance), he is credited with founding the houses of the Capuchin order in Pont à Mousson and Nancy.[150]

Fr. Campbell survived to make another attempt on Scotland in 1609, confining his visit to the area around Irvine where he had been brought up. The ecclesiastical foundation of his family was indeed strong: his brother was a minister, as was his half-brother Alexander Campbell, while two of his sisters married ministers. Ironically, the Capuchin was given accommodation and board by no fewer than five members of the presbytery – surely an indicator of the clout wielded by the family of which he was a member, if not of the tolerance extended at a personal level between members of differing convictions. But tongues wagged. Campbell was eventually arrested for a second time, deported, and his resetters reprimanded. He made one more trip to Britain whence he was banished for a final time in 1619.[151]

On the other hand, envy was aroused among Scots priests by proposals made in the first decade of the seventeenth century to send Irish Franciscans to Scotland; the Scots felt that they should have first call on funds. There is a distinct possibility that some bilingual priests amongst the Scots Minims or Scots Jesuits crossed the frontiers into Gaeldom from the north-east of Scotland even earlier than the Irish Jesuits. This would certainly explain MacDonald of Sleat's friendship with the Jesuit James Gordon, which shows links between Gaels on the western seaboard and Catholics in the north-east, though Sleat's connection with the Jesuits more likely came about through the affiliations of both with the Ulster lords.[152]

Though the majority of Scots priests did not speak Gaelic, a possible exception to this generalisation was John Brown, a Scots Minim – probably a native of Moray – who joined the order at Nigeon near Paris in 1595. Distinguished in higher education, he had a doctorate in theology from the universities of Alcalá and Avignon. In Antwerp early in 1615, Brown was in St. Andrews by April of that year, perhaps on his way to the north-east. In September 1617, he set out for England; from this time he made mission work his priority. He was back in Scotland with other Scots Minims – Andrew Baird, John Francis Maitland and Thomas Robertson – in 1621.[153] It is likely that Brown was bilingual: in May 1622 he wrote from Dunkirk to the papal nuncio in Brussels, Giovanni Francesco Guidi di Bagno, that he was attending mercenaries under Argyll en route to serve in the King of Spain's army. The mercenaries' first tongue would have been Gaelic, making it possible that Brown had served Gaels when he visited Scotland before. In June 1623 Brown was in Antwerp again, preparing to depart once more for Scotland. He left for Brussels on 10 June.[154] Although aspects of the Minims' story pertains chronologically to the next chapter, there is a sense in which Brown's whole initiative, i.e. the attempt to establish a house for university-educated Scots Minims on the continent who wanted to be missionaries in Scotland, pre-dates that of the Franciscans, and so it is dealt with here.

Of these Scots Minims, Brown and Maitland were vehemently anti-Jesuit. Di Bagno informed *Propaganda* on 16 July 1622 that Maitland had presented to the Spanish Infanta a brief recommending the Minims' mission. Yet although she was in favour of it, the Infanta objected to Brown as proposed head of the mission, since he and two or three of his disciples had allegedly led the lives of libertines. Further, although Brown had received patents stating that his proposed house in the Low Countries would be directly dependent on the General of the order of Minims and not on the Low Countries provincial, the General had already annulled Brown's appointment as vicar general. Maitland's brief was bitter: the rulers of France and Flanders willingly granted privileges to the English and Irish, but apparently not to these Scots religious; the Infanta too bypassed Scots in favour of the Irish. In 1623, Brown and

Maitland submitted another relation to Rome pointing out that none of the Scots Colleges, including Paris, sent men to the Scottish mission, and that the profligate lifestyle of many Scots in Rome actively discouraged the conversion of Scots visitors. But they were full of praise for the Capuchin John Chrystostom Campbell, mentioned above. The action taken on their relation is symptomatic of a whole area of contention in the seventeenth century, i.e. the rivalry exhibited between the Scots Jesuits and seculars, and between the Irish and Scots canons regular.[155]

Feeling victimised, in June 1623 Brown and Maitland reported the necessity of appointing an exclusively Scottish agent at the Curia to ensure the accurate transmission of information. They also appealed for help with their mission. It had been amply supported by Paul V, whose funds had maintained four fathers, but under Urban VIII they lost favour. To complicate the issue, in September 1623 Maitland and Robertson were imprisoned by the Flanders Minims – regulars of their own order – who feared a revival of past quarrels. There was also suspicion that rival religious – Fr. Robb, Scots Jesuit in Antwerp, and David Chalmers of the Scots College in Paris, to name but two – were hindering Brown and Maitland's attempts. On 30 September, di Bagno appointed Andrew Baird to replace Brown, though some Scots gentlemen petitioned *Propaganda* to allow Brown to return to Scotland with them two years later. In 1626 Brown came to Scotland via Calais; he suffered some persecution in Edinburgh. Almost a decade later, in 1635, he appeared in England asking permission to say the communion prayer in the Scots tongue, although he did not specify for whom.[156]

Contrary to what is usually suggested, there were a few Scots regulars prepared to return to serve the Highlands as part of a more extensive mission to the whole of the north of Scotland. Unfortunately, the Scots' cause was not assisted by the general climate of religious and international rivalry at a time when many groups were vying for the limited resources available from Rome. Proscribed in Scotland, Scottish Catholicism was no longer a powerful voice in the ear of the Vatican. In this position of weakness, some politically adept but short-term decisions were made on behalf of the Scots – the sanctioning of the Irish Franciscan mission to the Highlands and Islands was but one of them. For although many (but by no means all) of the Franciscan missionaries were committed to their task, the introduction of Scots missionaries from the continent would undoubtedly have facilitated the earlier establishment of an indigenous priesthood. But as it was, this had to wait until the eighteenth century.

The Jesuit Missions

The Scots Jesuits were the first organised arm of Catholicism to return to Scotland after the Reformation. According to a history of the mission written by John Thomson (1742–92), they came back to Scotland in 1582.[157] The majority were Scots-speaking and therefore tended to ensconce themselves as chaplains in the houses of Lowland or north-east-coast Catholics. The support given by heads of powerful families to closet Catholicism – notably by the Gordons in the north-east from the sixteenth century and by MacDonald of Clanranald and MacDonell of Glengarry in the Highlands and Islands from the seventeenth century – cannot be overestimated. It was one of the major factors in the survival and regeneration of the Catholic faith in Scotland. In his account of Catholicism in Scotland at the end of the sixteenth century, Sir Walter Lindsay wrote, 'the Scotch especially the nobles, are accustomed to act in concert so that every one sides with his family'.[158] Such was the persistent recusancy of Catholic noblemen in Scotland that in 1601 the General Assembly resorted to placing ministers in the homes of the most renowned, including Huntly, Errol, Angus and Sutherland. This policy of persuasion did not prove very successful.[159] But, it might be partly explained by the presence of two Scottish Jesuits – the Earl of Huntly's uncle and William Maxwell – in the camp of Hugh O'Neill of Tyrone in about April 1601. The English government feared that O'Neill made common cause with the Catholic party in Scotland; certainly, according to an English spy, he intended to use the Jesuits as agents to procure Highland mercenaries from Huntly.[160]

Some Jesuits were operating in the north-east Highlands; others may have made occasional trips into the central Highlands. In the first decade of the seventeenth century, Jesuits and seminary priests, notably William Murdoch, 'were busy in Caithness, north of the Ord, dispersing books and giving public and private discourses', as well as saying mass.[161] At some stage, the Jesuits must have crossed the Highland–Lowland border into the central Highlands: when Montrose's army came to Atholl in the summer of 1644, the forces met up with the Jesuits, one of whom was able to furnish them with a list of local Catholics, which suggests that they had been there for some time.[162] Yet whether it was a question of language or greater financial and political influence and connection, it ultimately fell to the Irish to supply priests to the Highlands and Islands.

Before the Irish Franciscan mission was officially up and running in 1619, there is some evidence that Irish Jesuits had begun to make small inroads into the Highlands and Islands in the first decade of the seventeenth century, and perhaps before that. Furthermore, the Jesuit mission to the Highlands had support among the higher echelons of the Irish clergy. Only a few years after the Jesuits had repaired to Scotland, Fr. Tyrie wrote on 31 September 1585 from

Paris that Edmund MacGuaran – the Catholic archbishop of Armagh (1587–93) maintained by O'Rourke – had been in the north of Scotland with Frs. Edmund Hay and James Gordon, from where he proceeded to France and Spain. In Paris, alleged Tyrie, MacGuaran exulted in having administered the sacrament of confirmation to at least 10,000 people.[163] This was probably the first example of a practice of exaggeration which was to become the stock-in-trade of Catholic missionaries in the Highlands: reports of unbelievably huge numbers of conversions. The Irish regular missionaries who ministered to the Highlands and Islands in the next century used the device with the same intent – to convince Rome of the absolute necessity of their funding. According to intelligence received by the English in January 1587 from Cúchonnacht Maguire in Fermanagh, the Catholic bishop of Derry, Redmond O'Gallagher (1569–1601), had also been in Scotland, France and Spain. Though the location of his Scottish visit is unspecified, it seems likely that he also went to the north-east like MacGuaran, perhaps even as one of the same party.[164]

O'Gallagher – one of three Irish bishops at the Council of Trent – was a particularly influential member of the Catholic hierarchy in Ireland. According to Miler Magrath, Catholic bishop of Down and Connor (1565–80), O'Gallagher's spiritual jurisdiction effectively extended throughout Ulster and was not operational simply within his own diocese.[165] In his 'Observations on the Western Isles of Scotland', the dean of Limerick opined that he was 'the chief practiser between the Spaniards and Tyrone and the pretended catholics of Scotland, who coming to Glasgow six years ago [1590] and remaining there some time the ministers upon information that he was a papist searched his casket for letters and books but his person was not touched or stayed at all'.[166] This particular episode (and the connections on which it was based) has previously gone unnoticed in the history of the Counter-Reformation in Scotland.

O'Gallagher arrived in Dumbarton before 8 March 1590. His mission was 'to drawe a league and confederacie betwixt our iles and hylandes and the rebells of Ireland' – the language anachronistically resonant of fifty years earlier – 'and for that cause, it is thought, he is alreadie to Mull and Tyntire [Kintyre]; but others saye he is over as yet in the north with Huntley and that faction'. The bishop was to acquaint the Catholics and confederates in Scotland with the information that many Irishmen and some Englishmen there were ready to rebel with aid from Spain and the Scottish Isles. So he was promoting a Spanish-funded Catholic rebellion of the Gaels and the Old English. According to the bishop, Turlough Luineach O'Neill of Tyrone was old and weak and not willing to soil his hands in the matter;[167] this attitude had offended his friends. Campbell of Lochnell – 'one of the house of Argyll, having great interest amongst the islands of Scotland' – had therefore been targeted to come across, raise O'Neill's forces and take charge of the action. By 16 March O'Gallagher had met with the Earl of Erroll, but thereafter reports of his whereabouts are conflicting: according to one report he was with Angus MacDonald of Dunyveg on 3 April, while another states that he was still in the north-east on the 5th, apparently 'stricken with suche feare to be apprehended as he will not trust to shew him self to any other then to Mr. James Gorden or suche like'. On 25 April O'Gallagher incontrovertibly crossed the Tweed near Kelso, intending to ride to Durham, from where he aimed either to return to Scotland within ten days or to cross to the west coast and sail for Ireland.[168]

The Jesuits also opportunistically converted Scots when they could in Ireland. A Jesuit father, James Archer, a missioner famous throughout the country during the Earl of Tyrone's rebellion and renowned for his nationalist sympathies, wrote to Rome from Ireland on 29 September 1604 stating that he had converted three Scots, one of whom was a stubborn Puritan.[169]

The enormous potential of the Irish language as a weapon for the cause was not fully realised until the Ulster rebellion, particularly after the Flight of the Earls in 1607 when Irish-speaking Catholics on the continent came into contact with the ideology of the Counter-Reformation. Its latency as a tool for conversion had been recognised even earlier by Protestants but not fully exploited because of ingrained cultural and social prejudices. The Catholics eventually wielded it more effectively. Many of the exiled Irish literati – clergy, poets, *seanchaidhean* and other learned men who fled to the continent in 1607 – took refuge in seminaries there, forging a highly informed, intellectually galvanised atmosphere which thrived at the end of the sixteenth and beginning of the seventeenth centuries, a time when theological and philosophical study in Europe was at its zenith. In the seminaries, native Irish lived alongside Anglo-Irish; united in their zeal for renewal of the Catholic faith in Ireland, both groups shared the conviction that the Irish language should be the vehicle of their missionary activity. Every student took an oath to return to Ireland,[170] because their political aim of encouraging an environment suitable for the consolidation of their religion in their native country was of no less importance to them.[171]

Catholicism in Ireland was, after all, a religion under siege – its practice more than usually devout – so parents felt an innate responsiblity for grounding their children in the faith. For many, the medium of Catholicism was the Irish language. Just as the geographical marginalisation of Highlanders was praised for having shielded significant numbers from Protestantism in the seventeenth century, in Ireland it was rather the lack of English which shielded the Irish from the perverted Protestant doctrines then just beginning to be printed in their own language.[172] But in the late sixteenth century there was little in the way of printed aids to Catholic devotion in Irish. The Spanish catechism of Jeronimo de Ripalda, published in Madrid in 1591, was abridged and translated by Archbishop Conry, but it did not reach Ireland until 1598, and then only less accessibly in manuscript form.[173]

Under the driving thrust of the Counter-Reformation, some devotional aids in Irish were printed in the second decade of the seventeenth century. A basic catechism by Bonabhentura Ó hEodhasa, published in Antwerp in 1611, became available for the general instruction of the people, while books dealing with new liturgical forms and elucidating doctrinal contentions between Protestants and Catholics – such as Séathrún Céitinn's *Tri bior-ghaoithe an bháis* (The Three Shafts of Death), completed in 1631 – were aimed more at informing the clergy.[174] Céitinn's corpus amply illustrates the bifurcation, both political and religious, of the Counter-Reformation dynamic. In addition, he worked hard to provide the native Irish with a glorious past worthy of their traditions. In his *Foras feasa ar Eirinn* (A Basis of Knowledge about Ireland, a narrative history of Ireland which circulated widely in manuscript), he contended that ancient Celtic morality had been very similar to the Christian ethic: hence Christianity had been assimilated easily. But significantly, this was diametrically opposite to the view taken by contemporary critics of Gaelic Ireland, who thus aimed to justify English conquest of the indigenous savage with the purifying sword of Christianity. By implication therefore, and most importantly, Céitinn sanctioned native Irish rebellion against the English.[175] Flaithri Ó Maoil Chonaire's *Desiderius, Otherwise Called sgáthán an chráibhidh* (The Mirror of Faith), published in Louvain in 1616, sought to enrich individual devotion. Significantly, these books were published in vernacular rather than classical Irish – following the direction which Carswell had tended towards in Scotland a few decades before – so that they could be more readily understood. These devotional publications were based on literature popular on the continent but specially adapted to Irish purposes.[176]

Of greater significance was the increasing use made of Gaelic poetry to disseminate fundamental Catholic doctrine to an illiterate Irish-speaking population; poetry also gave form to their prayers. While the technique, which encouraged the use of mnemonics, is thought first to have been used by a Franciscan in Ireland, it was readily adopted by those trained on the continent. Counter-Reformation priests from native Irish backgrounds were now prepared to admit what Catholic clergy from the urban areas, where English was in currency, had long claimed – that the Gaelic Irish were poorly Christianised. Once admitted, and having thrown in their lot with the Old English clergy, the native Irish made plans for a mission in the Irish language targeted at both clusters. The use of poetry as an aide-mémoire among the illiterate was a totally new technique in ecclesiastical terms and was undoubtedly successful. The essence of the more important treatises printed on the continent also appeared in the form of poetic summaries wrought by the seminarians.[177] While the groundwork for the Counter-Reformation movement in Ireland was laid down during this period, it came to fruition in the next century.[178]

Contemporary allusions to the use of Gaelic in the Irish mission also refer to the employment of Irish priests on the Scottish mission. In 1608 an Irish Jesuit in Rome, thought to be one Fr. Wale, made observations about the currency of the Irish language and the work of the order's Irish-speaking missionaries. He reported that Fr. Holywood, then superior of the Irish Jesuit mission, could not go much beyond Dublin because of his lameness as well as his ignorance of Irish, then the universal language in Ulster, Connacht and Munster, and the more common speech of Leinster (since English was used in only one or two counties there). Some Jesuit fathers – 'though learned and prudent and holy' – could not preach in Irish and so could only work in the English-speaking counties. 'Others speak only Irish and can preach all over Ireland, the Highlands and Isles of Scotland, except in these one or two counties.' On the other hand, those who spoke both Irish and English could go everywhere. Fathers Robert Nugent, Moroney, Leinach, O'Kearney, Wale, Wise and Sheyn commonly preached in Irish, but sometimes in English; Holywood and Lenan preached in English.[179]

In November 1611, Fr. Christopher Holywood, Jesuit superior in Ireland (1603–26), wrote in English to Fr. Conway, SJ in Madrid. He alluded in his letter to the Scottish mission.

> As for our neighbour Mission, when Claudius [code for Father General] first acquainted me with his desire, wishing that I should give the Superior thereof two of mine ... I had but six, whereof two could not speak the language, and the other three were spent, or at least broken, weak and sickly, and not able to undergo so difficult an enterprise, a thing the Superior himself, at his being here, saw, and therefore motioned for none of them.

The superior of the Scottish mission referred to here was Archbishop Peter Lombard of Armagh (1601–25),[180] who also claimed primacy over the Highlands of Scotland; he sent Irish priests to Scotland intermittently from the beginning of the seventeenth century. An account of only one of Lombard's adopted Jesuits survives, although there may have been more. In spite of Holywood's protestations, the Father General was insistent that they lend a helping hand. Holywood eventually concluded with Lombard shortly before he departed 'to assist him with the help of others, which I proposed to send for, and came since'. In the meantime, he 'sent to sound the way and see what might be done – of which labour some fruit hath been already gathered, and more will, if it shall please God; but of this matter the less noise the better'.[181]

On at least one occasion, a visit to the Highlands from an Irish Jesuit can be attributed to the persecution of Catholics in Ireland. Just as Scots often escaped to Ireland when they wanted to lie low, there was a counterflow. In 1613, according to Holywood, the Catholics of County Dublin were called before the magistrates on four occasions and by alternate threats and promises were coerced into going to church and taking the oath of supremacy; they would either be robbed of their religion or impoverished by fines. The Jesuits hid themselves, finding shelter where they could. 'One of them from our Meath residence went into the North, and even to the most remote islands of Scotland, where the Catholics had not heard Mass for fifty years. When his presence was felt by the heretics he was tracked and had to return to Ulster. He went through that country doing all the good in his power.'[182]

In all likelihood, the man identified in this report was the young Cork Jesuit, Fr. David Galwey, of whom more below.[183] This particular expedition, like those he undertook later in the decade, was probably to the southern isles (a short sail from Ulster) because he was tracked down relatively quickly. Some of the good which Galwey was able to do in Ulster may have been on the recommendation of Scots to their Ulster relatives – Holywood specifies only that a minister's son was converted, as well as a lady who 'had educated the daughters of a dynast of that country (that is, Ulster)'. The minister's son apparently 'devoted himself to teaching the catechism to little children in order to atone for the harm he had tried to do to grown-up Catholics'.[184]

In his 1617 report, Holywood said that one of the Irish Jesuits 'went to console the Irish Scots who dwell in Ulster'. Again, this may refer to Galwey, while the Irish Scots were probably tenants of the Earl of Antrim or the MacDonnells themselves. Certainly, the first Earl of Antrim was called to Dublin in 1621 where he was indicted for sheltering priests. Admitting the charge, he escaped with a mere warning. But in this particular instance, the steward of the 'Baron of Belfast' and the Marshal of the district suspected the presence of a priest, because the Jesuit went to a Catholic's house instead of staying at the public inn. They planned his capture while they were drinking but, even though he was a Protestant, the steward's wife warned him and the priest stayed where he was, preferring that to the perils of the unknown. 'In the morning, while his two enemies were buried in a drunken sleep, he got his horses and escaped to his Scot, preached every day for three weeks, heard very many confessions, and converted four Protestants!'[185]

From this point (doubtless under the barrage of letters requesting spiritual succour for Scotland which Rome is said to have received) the immediacy of the Scottish problem seems to have been accepted. On 17 November 1618, Cardinal Borghese wrote to Lucio Morra, nuncio at Brussels, mentioning the departure of four Jesuits for the Scottish mission. Considering how difficult it could be for Catholic priests to support themselves there, he expressed his opinion that enough had been sent for the time being. These four missionaries were not destined for the Highlands in particular; later, he said, other Scottish Jesuits would be trained for the mission; Irishmen in the Jesuits would also be of help.[186] But the Vatican clearly envisaged that Irishmen would supply the Highlands. Even though Scots Jesuits may already have penetrated the central and northern Highlands, the kinship ties between Ireland and the West

Highlands and Islands were felt to be even stronger. His later commitment to the Franciscan mission suggests that the Earl of Antrim probably supported these earlier developments too.

None the less, the name of only one Irish Jesuit who laboured on the Scottish mission survives – Fr. David Galwey. The account of his mission to the Isles is therefore all the more valuable. Interesting parallels can be drawn – both in terms of activity and area of labour – between his expedition and the first Franciscan mission.[187] Acting under orders from Rome, Fr. Holywood had sent the Cork Jesuit to visit the Scots in their own territory; he gave an account of Galwey's mission in his 1619 report. 'Tesqua is forty miles from Ireland, it contained only three Irish-Scottish families, and paid rent to the Puritan Laird of Callaton.[188] Its only chapel had been burned by the Puritans in 1615.' The only island which fits this description is Texa, off Islay, which was probably populated by MacDonalds or associates of the Clan Donald South. And though Galwey may have been the mission leader, there were others with him: the report refers to 'priests' and 'two companions', though no others are named. Allegedly nearly dead with hunger and thirst when they arrived, the priests and sailors were well received, fed stirabout and fish, and given milk and water to drink. Their host and his wife apparently repudiated their errors and went to confession, but though the other two families expressed a desire to do the same, they were afraid of the presbyterians ('Puritans'). On Islay, Galwey reconciled forty 'of mature age' to the church and said mass for them – 'an act of religion which they had never witnessed before'. But after seven days there he was denounced, so he went on to Oronsay, where there was a chapel to St. Columba, and afterwards to Colonsay. He reconciled forty of mature years in each place 'who had never seen a priest before' and said Mass for them.

The commander of the place (Colla Ciotach), his wife and children and some soldiers were also converted 'but this gentleman, fearing that the natives would suffer if Galwey remained, gave him a boat and some soldiers to protect him'. In Jura, Galwey reconciled (with truly remarkable standardisation) yet another forty adults, and baptised eight children.[189] Were the numbers of conversions – forty in Islay, and forty each in Oronsay and Colonsay – approximate; were they even contrived to improve on the report, when they appear to be so uniform in each place? The report certainly reads more like a census of the people Galwey encountered on his travels.

When soldiers came to Jura, Galwey had to depart in a frail craft for Gigha, where the natives were amazed that he had ventured out in such a boat in such weather. The chief of the place, being informed of the object of his visit, urged Galwey to go away since there was a price on priests' heads there. But after admitting that he was prepared to risk his head for the salvation of souls, the Jesuit was harboured hospitably for two days; then, having procured a promise from the chief to look better to his soul than he had previously done, Galwey passed on to Kintyre.[190] He found the people better disposed to him there, visited twenty villages, converted over a hundred people – allegedly from atheism and heresy – and baptised sixty. The Isle of Arran, however, was not fertile ground: accompanied by a sixteen-year-old youth, he stayed for a week but converted only a few, as the people were stubborn Calvinists. Thence he went to the island of 'Cuin',[191] four miles off Arran, reconciled all nineteen natives to the church and baptised six grown boys. In Kintyre a minister, finding no one in his church but the sexton, got soldiers armed with swords, pikes and long knives, and went to the place where Father Galwey was hearing confessions, but the priest had time to take shelter in a hut some way off. The converts were frightened by the furious threats of the minister, giving the priest an opportunity to comfort them with his words and remind them of the constancy of the Irish, of which (according to Holywood's account) they were well aware. On another occasion, the Jesuit had to hide in a cave, exposed to wind and rain, and had many other hair-raising escapes by day and night.

Fr. Holywood gave the ultimate sanction to the expedition by implying that it had been divinely prophesied: 'The Irish-Scots of the isles told him that it was prophesied that a servant of Patrick would come from Rome to their help; and that some had a foreboding that he would arrive at that time.'[192]

Referred to elsewhere as Fr. David Galvins, SJ, it appears from Jesuit mission reports in Ireland in the decade between 1641 and 1651 that Galwey made three journeys to Scotland. The first, when he travelled disguised as a merchant, was not very successful, because he could convert none of the islanders to a profession of the Catholic faith, 'such was their terror of the Duke of Argyll, a bitter enemy of the Catholics and lord of that territory'.[193] The Jesuit *Relatio*, which limits his mission to the Argyll area, stresses that Galwey was known throughout the Irish province for his piety and zeal.[194] It was infectious.

> When returning to Ireland, all sad for the bad success of his journey, the Scottish sailors, who themselves were imbued with Calvinism, surprised that, though he styled himself a merchant, yet he had purchased no goods, asked him for what object he had undertaken so long a journey? The good Father replied that he was indeed a merchant, but of merchandise far more precious than all earthly goods, and that he sought for souls redeemed by the most precious blood of Jesus Christ. The sailors, reasoning amongst themselves, declared with one accord that that religion should be true which could inspire such a desire for the salvation of souls, and before the vessel reached the Irish coast he had the consolation of receiving these straying children into the fold of Christ.[195]

On his first trip, Galwey had gone by the simplest crossing to Scotland, probably anticipating a good response from old Clan Donald lands. With the experience gained from his initial reconnoitre, he was better able to define the bounds of friendly territory, so that the labours of his second and third missions were 'crowned with abundant fruit': in some districts whole townships –

parents as well as children – received the Sacrament of Baptism. Holywood's 1619 account must have been based on Galwey's later missions. It was necessary even to endure potentially rampant body odour for the sake of personal salvation: 'on one occasion, so incessant was his toil in instructing the poor mountaineers, that for five months he never changed his garments'. The Jesuit seems to have continued working in those areas close to Ireland (replete with presbyerians), for the text notes: 'Such was the hatred conceived against him by the heretics that they publicly sent round his likeness in order to secure his arrest.' Most missionary priests of the period were consummate in the art of disguise, feigning a second skill or employment to evade possible capture. Sometimes Galwey employed 'the artifice of declaring himself a merchant, and bringing around some sacks in corn, as if they were samples, the better to disguise his true mission'.[196] It seems to have worked.

There is some evidence of lingering Catholicism in the Highlands and Islands – certainly in the first two decades after the Reformation – in places like South Uist and Trotternish in Skye, while the MacNeills of Barra were still heading on pilgrimage to Ireland in the 1590s, though this was doubtless as much a social as a religious occasion. On the other hand, Fr. Holywood's report to the Jesuit superior states that the inhabitants of Islay heard mass for the first time in their lives in 1619. Remote and tiny places like St. Kilda (or Hirta) appear scarcely to have caught up with Catholicism, let alone been affected by the Reformation. Donald Munro, dean of the Isles, said of the island in 1549: 'The inhabitants therof are simple poor people, scarse learnit in aney religion, Bot McCloid of Herray his Stewart or he quhom he deputs in sic office, sailles anes in the Yeir ther at Midsummer with some chaplain to baptize bairns ther, and if they want a Chaplaine they baptise ther barnes themselves.'[197] This seems to document an absence of organised religion, a state matched in other inaccessible Highland areas such as Glengarry prior to the advent of either minister or priest in the seventeenth century. St. Kilda did not have its first visit from a minister for almost another 150 years, when John Campbell went to the island in 1697 in the company of Martin Martin.[198]

None the less, those islands such as Skye, Harris and Lewis, where an effort was made by the Kirk to provide ministers as soon after the Reformation as possible, have remained Protestant to the present day. Even though ecclesiastical provision, in terms of the size and number of parishes on some of the islands, was spread thinly, the evidence indicates that ministers did effect conversions in that part of population which they reached. The same was true of those areas of the mainland Highlands where the Kirk was able to fill a significant number of benefices in the decade after the Reformation. Much as with Catholicism, the Reformed faith was established in clearly defined areas, as families, communities and townships were gradually won over. Moreover, with the expansion of the land and 'soul' market in Ulster at the plantation, the infant Kirk was even able to supply a moderate number of Gaelic-speaking ministers to attempt to convert the Catholic Irish. In Ireland, however, there was formidable opposition to the established church from the forces of Counter-Reformation, which effectively harnessed the vernacular as the vehicle of their missionary activity. Although some Scots regulars from the continent made the odd unco-ordinated attempt in the late sixteenth and early seventeenth centuries to bring the Catholic faith to those in the *Gaidhealtachd*, from the beginning of the new century this work was assisted by Jesuits from Ireland. In Scotland, the Protestant Church fared better than in Ireland. But in those areas where the Kirk did not make a sufficiently swift impact, Irish regulars were able to stake a place for Catholicism through a variety of seventeenth-century missions. On the other hand, almost all of those areas (Kintyre and the nearby southern isles) visited by the Jesuit Fr. Galwey did not remain Catholic because there was already too great a Protestant presence in the early seventeenth century. Where Fr. Galwey simply went to those areas close to Ireland, the missionaries of the first Franciscan mission – with a threefold increase in manpower from 1624, and the patronage of the first Earl of Antrim – were able to visit the more northerly Hebridean islands as well. And there they reaped a far greater harvest.

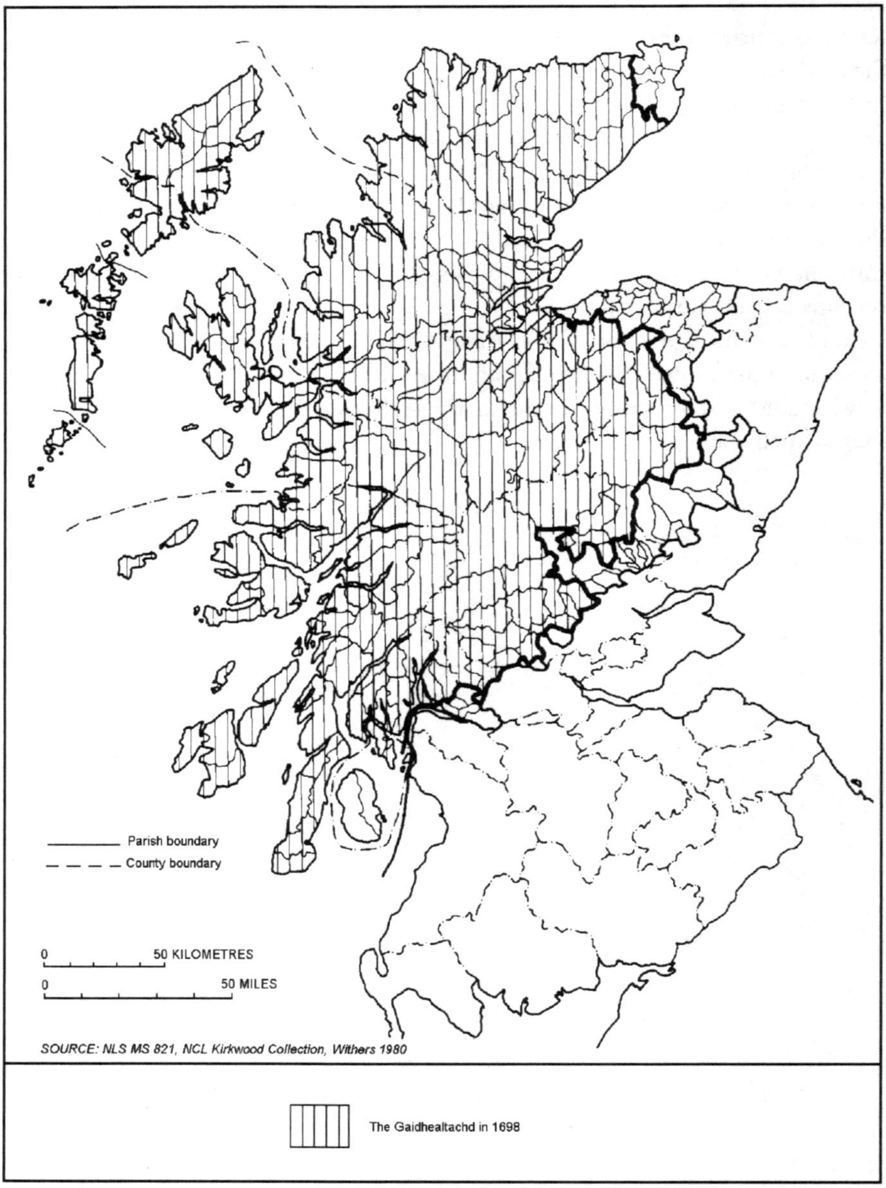

Fig. 2.1. The Scottish *Gaidhealtachd* in 1698.

TWO

The Franciscan Mission to the Highlands and Islands, 1619–1637

They did not know how to make the sign of the cross.
Comment on the legacy of the Franciscan missionaries, by Fr. Duggan (1652)

ALTHOUGH the Reformed Church made a fair stab at providing ministers and readers for Highland and Island parishes in the decades after 1560, many areas were left unattended while vast, composite parishes were created where a minister also served the surrounding vacancies in his area – a practice still well-documented later in the seventeenth century. There were nineteen ministers in the Isles when Bishop Knox reported on his diocese (1626), and there was tremendous scope for improvement.[1] As Knox pointed out, 'the Yle Bara ... is servit be the Minister of Hereis' – hardly a formula conducive to regular religious instruction.[2] Only nineteen ministers meant there were many Hebridean vacancies; they were numerous because the parishes were isolated and therefore unattractive, but also because there was a dearth of Gaelic-speaking ministers. Inasmuch as the record is deficient for Argyll and the Isles, even the lack of evidence from the accounts of the collectors of the thirds of benefices (a series of financial records compiled between 1561 and 1595 recording the rentals of benefices) corroborates this relatively sparse provision in the Hebrides.[3]

The Isles had been eschewed by the Scots (though not Irish) Jesuits – the only organised Catholic force of Counter-Reformation working in Scotland in the late sixteenth century – for similar reasons of isolation and the lack of Gaelic-speaking personnel in the Jesuit heartland of the north-east. In addition, the clan *fine* did not carry sufficient political clout. Missionaries of all denominations realised the value of establishing good contacts with the élite, but powerful patronage was sought by the Jesuits in particular, who tended to live in a state of dependency in the houses of their patrons. As Peter Anson put it, the clan *fine* 'did not mix with court circles. In comparison with most of the nobility and landed gentry in the Lowlands they were uncultured. So perhaps it was better that some other religious order should be found to minister to them and their peoples.'[4] While Highlanders cannot be seen as even comparatively uncultured, it is true that a society based on the mercenary trade and tenant farming was unlikely to have the degree of refinement to which the Jesuits had become accustomed in continental Europe.

Even though much of this assessment of Jesuit motives may be true, their presence in areas bordering on the Highlands probably led to a degree of infiltration of Catholic ideas in these areas. This occurred notably in Perthshire and the north-east, where both the clan élite and the factors for Lowland landlords with Highland estates were usually bilingual.[5] (For the basic geographical division between the Gaelic-speaking Highlands and the English-speaking Lowlands in the seventeenth century, see Fig. 2.1. The earliest date at which the extent of the *Gaidhealtachd* has been calculated is 1698; clearly its extent during the period from 1619 to 1637 would have been greater.) Anson concedes that 'there was a sub-section of the Lowlands made up of the counties of Aberdeen, Banff and Moray, where variants of the so-called Buchan dialect were spoken': it was 'a remote and different world, dominated by the Gordons of Huntly and a number of other Catholic lairds, represented by members of the families of Abercromby, Dunbar, Forbes, Fraser, Hay, Innes, Leslie, and Ogilvie'. It was fairly safe here for all classes to profess their Catholicism, except in times of marked persecution.[6] Particularly pertinent to the present discussion, this area touched on the Gaelic-speaking periphery at several points along its boundary. Although recusancy was not sustained among the clans in Atholl, inroads were made by Catholic priests among the clan élite and factors in Upper Deeside, Strathavon and Strathdon. These provided a foundation for the later work of conversion by Irish priests as well as Scottish priests from the indigenous clans in the neighbouring districts of Braemar, Inveravon and Glenlivet and further north in Strathglass, Strathfarrer and the Aird.[7]

However, the surviving evidence indicates that at least some communities drifted into a state of semi-paganism while retaining a modicum of Catholic traditions, memories of which are embodied in the *Carmina Gadelica*. This state of semi-paganism is certainly borne out by the records of the presbytery of Dingwall, which testify to the pagan practice of animal sacrifice within their bounds.[8] Such practices had undoubtedly survived from a pre-Reformation era, probably because Catholicism had never been thoroughly organised in the Highlands.[9] But where Catholicism had tolerated, assimilated and to a certain degree patronisingly ignored such practices, Protestantism tended to stress their hideousness. Revitalisation of (or reversion to) traditional practices must have been further encouraged in the absence of any religious ministration. Yet it was the very lack of attention to the spiritual needs of the Highlanders that was to provide such fertile ground for the Franciscan missionaries. Indeed, according to John Lorne Campbell, the Irish link – fuelled by a native people who spoke more or less the same language and who had remained staunchly Catholic in spite of an established Protestant church – was the only religious link which remained productive in the Isles.[10] Understandably, as Allan Macinnes puts it, this led to 'the entrenchment of Catholicism as the faith of whole communities'.[11]

But all this was in the future. In 1622, the death-knell effectively tolled for the pre-Reformation Church in Scotland: with the institution of the Congregation for the Propagation of the Faith (*Congregazione de Propaganda Fide*), Rome finally acknowledged that Scotland was a missionary country. *Propaganda*'s task was, as its name implies, primarily to propagate the faith in the newly discovered lands of the period – America, Africa and Asia – and to reconcile schismatic oriental churches; it also took some responsibility for countries such as Scotland which had lapsed totally into heresy. In some Protestant states (like England) where relations were not so hostile, the Pope could station an ambassador or papal nuncio, but because Catholicism had been so utterly rejected in Scotland, Catholic interest in the country operated through the nuncio in Brussels. One of *Propaganda*'s innovations was to send consecrated bishops into missionary countries without the permission of the civic rulers – and very often without their knowledge. The first of these Vicars-Apostolic, William Bishop, appointed for England in 1623,[12] was given jurisdiction over Scotland as well; some Scottish priests stressed the ancient enmity between the two nations in the hope of getting a bishop of their own, but to no avail.[13]

The maintenance of Catholicism in Scotland in the early seventeenth century was in no small part due to those Irish connections originally fostered through an aristocratic marriage in the fourteenth century and subsequently sustained through social, commercial and mercenary contact. Certainly, the MacNeills of Barra kept the faith alive by making occasional religious excursions to Ireland.[14] But whether the territory of the MacDonalds of Kintyre remained Catholic in sentiment in any meaningful sense, or whether its people were reconverted by Irish Jesuits, is more difficult to discern. An account of the 1615 rebellion in Islay states that 'the religioun that the cuntrie pepill hes heir amongst them is Popishe for thair is never a minister in the wholle Ile except wan poore man that the bishop[15] did leave heir'. On the other hand, the report of the Irish Jesuit superior noted that when Fr. Galwey went to Islay in 1619 no one there had received mass in their lifetime,[16] so it seems likely that the people there were just inclined to Catholicism. Though Islay had passed into Campbell hands in 1614, it was subsequently visited on several occasions by Franciscan missionaries; this can in part be accounted for by the conversion of Cawdor, the new landowner. After 1629, however, Islay was largely ignored by the Franciscans. But why they omitted to visit Colonsay or Oronsay after 1629 is much more of an enigma. After all, Colla Ciotach MacDonald still lorded it over these islands in 1633 when Lord Lorne accepted his de facto presence by reconfirming feus of Colonsay and Oronsay made in 1619 and 1624.[17]

There was undoubtedly also a political element in Sir Randal MacDonell, first Earl of Antrim's financial subsidies to the Franciscan mission, for although James VI and I had confirmed Antrim as a substantial landholder in Ulster, the Protestant plantation of Ulster still constituted a major threat (at the hands of suspicious English and Lowland Scots settlers) to his future as a Catholic landowner. Antrim's support for the Catholic mission in Scotland was intimately entwined with plans to maintain his status in Ulster by providing it with a broader power-base in Scotland. He thus tried to assume leadership of the Kintyre MacDonalds after their expropriation. As well as attempting to buy out the house of Argyll from Kintyre in 1635, Antrim supported plans for the appointment of a Catholic bishop of the Isles, which David Stevenson argues was probably linked to his plans for reviving the power of the MacDonalds.[18] During this period the Franciscans frequently called for the restoration of episcopal authority. In 1640, pressurised by the Irish hierarchy, *Propaganda* got as far as discussing the revival of the diocese of Sodor, an ancient jurisdiction which had incorporated the Isle of Man and all the Western Isles of Scotland.[19] With the advent of the National Covenant in 1638, Antrim's status – enthusiastic Royalist that he was – markedly improved; Catholics were more openly tolerated in the shade of problems caused to the Church of Ireland by exiled Scottish presbyterian non-conformists in the 1630s.[20] Antrim then seized a prime opportunity to promote his own ends through Royalist service in Scotland against the Covenanters, coveting the expropriated MacDonald lands in Kintyre as his prize.[21]

The Advancing Tide of Protestantism

Though the Ulster plantation undoubtedly strengthened ties between Scots and Irish Protestants (and there were very few presbyterians in Ulster before the plantation), this book specifically focuses on Gaelic speakers, who were officially excluded from this settlement.[22] While in practice some Highlanders were accepted into it, in much the same way as were the Irish peasants – particularly, perhaps, on the Antrim estates – their inclusion was illegal and therefore disguised.[23] Catholics might even have been listed as nominal Protestants so that they would not show up in the records. Moreover, with relatively few ministers in the Hebrides by 1626, Protestantism had only impressed itself on parts of the Gaelic-speaking population. Matters had made better progress on the mainland in the shires of Argyll, Ross, Caithness and Sutherland (though not in Inverness), but there was sufficient work to retain these Highland ministers on their own doorsteps. Although an abundance of Lowland ministers had followed their congregations to Ulster or had moved there to serve the English-speaking settlers, with the ascendancy of episcopalianism in Scotland in the mid-1630s, most Highland presbyterians were content to stay in the relative safety of their Highland backwaters.

But what kind of impact had presbyterianism made in the Highlands and Islands by 1637? Argyll as a whole appears to have been adequately provided for during this period: many parishes had had fairly consistent ministerial coverage either from the Reformation or from the early 1570s.[24] However, the majority of parishes with ministers were fairly near to the Campbell heartland of Inveraray. The further away they were, so proportionately later did the parish obtain a minister. Thus, most of Kintyre – old Clan Donald South territory – was not provided for until the seventeenth century. At the northern end of Kintyre, only the parish of Kilcalmonell and Kilberry had been filled consistently from 1580. South of this, the united parish of Killean, Kilchenzie and Kilmalrubh, which included the lands of Skipness, did not have a minister until the third decade of the seventeenth century: Murdoch M'Whirrie was in place in August 1629. The adjoining parish of Saddell still had no minister by 1637. The same minister – Murdoch M'Whirrie – eventually left Killean and was subsequently admitted to Saddell in 1639. Similarly, the parish of Kilchiaran (later Campbeltown) also got its first minister in the 1630s. Duncan MacCalman was minister in the parish kirk of Kilchiaran by 1631 which, with the old parishes of Kilchuslan and Kilmichael, comprised the united parish of Kilchiaran (as created by a parliamentary commission for the plantation of kirks in 1617). Finally, the most southerly parish in Kintyre, Southend – opposite the coast of Ireland and comprising the united parishes of Kilcholumkill, Kilblaan, and Kilchievan – was filled in August 1629 by Duncan Omey, of the renowned Gaelic ecclesiastical family of that name.[25]

The parishes further north near Clanranald territory were also filled later, as if in a second wave of appointments by the synod of Argyll once the foundation had been laid in the Campbell heartland. Morvern had a minister by 1611, but the parish of Ardnamurchan and Eilean Finain did not get Donald Omey – who was specially 'plantit and placed' there – until February 1624. In such areas, the Kirk was resented as the arm of an alien authority: this was shown clearly by the intrusion of a young, armed man into the kirk one day, when Omey was preaching, to deliver a letter from Clanranald 'intimating that the minister sould with all convenient diligence reteirr himself from those boundes, and have him hame, utherwayes it sould coast him his lyffe'.[26] Since there is no record of the Franciscan missionaries yet having visited the Moidart region, the initiative to 'retire' the Protestant minister can only have come from Clanranald and his own people.

The very worst provision of ministers in the mainland Highlands was in that area established in the eighteenth century as the presbytery of Abertarff; at this time, it was in the presbytery of Lorn or Kilmore within the jurisdiction of the synod of Argyll, and situated mainly in Inverness-shire. It encompassed the MacDonald enclaves of Morar, Moidart and Arisaig within the joint parish of Ardnamurchan, Eilean Finnan and Arisaig, which was probably served infrequently (if at all) after 1624 from Ardnamurchan. Glenelg, the next parish to the north, had been vacant since the Reformation and continued so throughout this period. The adjacent parish of Kilmallie, covering the area south of Loch Arkaig, as well as the Inverlochy and Fort William region, also remained vacant throughout the whole period; it was first filled in 1651. Within this area, too, was the seemingly impenetrable hinterland of Lochaber, in the parish of Kilmonivaig, a vast parish (see Fig. 5.1) which included Glengarry. It was vacant until 1720, when the first minister was settled there. Only the joint parish of Kilchuimin or Abertarff (now Fort Augustus) and Boleskine had a minister from the sixteenth century. Half the composite parishes in this area had no minister until the early eighteenth century; hardly surprising then that the Catholic Church was able to claim a fair proportion of this region as its own by the end of the seventeenth century.[27]

This area of non-provision also extended, at its southern boundaries, into Perthshire and the jurisdiction of the presbytery of Dunkeld. Although the parish of Kilchonain or Kinloch in Rannoch had a reader as early as 1574 and who remained until his death in 1582, the first appointment exclusively to this parish was not made until 1755. Even then the appointee was not a minister but a catechist – the renowned Gaelic spiritual poet, Dugald Buchanan – who was paid £20 a year by the Annexed Estates Board to continue the job of 'civilising' his Gaelic brethren.[28] Before that, Kilchonain had been served by the minister of Fortingall, a parish united with Glenlyon and Kilchonain in 1585. Fortingal was served by two men named James Ross, father and son, the first admitted before September 1629 and the second three years after his predecessor's death in April 1639. However, the first resident minister was not presented to Kinloch Rannoch until the nineteenth century, some sixty-two years after Buchanan's death. The parishes of Struan, Kilmoveonaig and Lude were filled in name only through their union with Blair Atholl in the early seventeenth century, but in reality the reader in Kilmoveonaig had left in 1580, while those in Struan and Lude had both died in post in 1582.[29]

And how many Protestant ministers were there in the Isles during this period? If there was reasonable provision here, the most marginal area in the Highlands and Islands as a whole, that can only be indicative of fairly adequate Protestant penetration of the entire region. In Skye, Bracadale continued to be served until 1632 by John McColgan, and thereafter by John MacKinnon, a presentee of John Leslie, bishop of the Isles. In Duirinish, Ewen MacQueen had replaced Alan O'Colgan some time after 1613, and continued there until 1643. There was still no minister in Trotternish, which therefore gave the Catholic missionaries carte blanche, though Kenneth MacKenzie – presented to Sleat in 1609 and still there in 1627 – technically had Trotternish and the Small Isles of Eigg, Muck, Rhum and Canna as part of his charge.[30] But given the huge extent of this territory, the ministration in these places can have been little other than infrequent and cursory. When combined with the influence of MacDonald of Clanranald, this goes some way to explaining the inroads made by Catholicism in Canna and Eigg. On the other hand, there was continuity in Sleat with the admittance of Neil MacKinnon in 1633.[31] Prior to his incumbency there, MacKinnon had served from 1627 in Strath, the territory of the MacKinnons – *Strath Mhic Fhiònghainn* or 'MacKinnon's valley' – where he was minister for at least six years. Protestantism thus extended into a third parish in Skye, though to all intents and purposes only two ministries were fully operational (as in the period before 1619) because a replacement was not found for Neil MacKinnon in Strath until 1663. However, it seems likely that he continued to minister to Strath from Sleat, given that the parishes were contiguous, particularly since the last mention of MacKinnon as minister in Sleat occurs in May 1661.[32]

In Barra, there was no minister between 1619 and 1637, allowing Catholicism a free rein on the island, as in other places. None the less, reports by the Irish Franciscans indicate that not all of the Long Islanders were predisposed to Catholicism, either in religious terms or as a particular expression of their political and cultural identity.[33] In Harris, John MacPherson was admitted in about 1625; the benefice had possibly lain vacant at some time between the incumbency of the first minister in 1566 and MacPherson's arrival,[34] although a distinct lack of evidence makes this difficult to prove. There was another gap, perhaps, in North Uist; Donald MacMillan was considered old in 1626, and is not referred to again, but the second minister, Angus MacQueen, is not known to have been in post until May 1642. In South Uist, John MacKinnon was appointed rector on 3 June 1633, the first confirmed Protestant appointee there. It is possible, and quite likely, that this is the same John MacKinnon referred to above – presented to Bracadale in Skye in the previous year – since the parish faced the vacant South Uist. This tends to suggest that he might only have drawn the teinds of the benefice. Barvas in Lewis was filled in the first instance by the pre-Reformation parson who was still incumbent in 1566. The benefice did not have its first Protestant minister until 26 May 1642. Overall, Protestant regression was the order of the day in Lewis at this time; in Uig, the one parish in Lewis which had a minister in 1572, the same incumbent was either a very old man and limited in his activity, or was dead, and the next minister was not appointed there until 1726. The length of time during which the parish lay vacant after his death also tends to suggest that the first minister of Uig was a priest[35] who conformed to Protestantism, perhaps only superficially, though it is just as likely that it shows a profound difficulty in procuring Reformed staff for such an isolated area. Having made a start – and perhaps having done sufficient to ensure the island's long-term inclination to Protestantism – the Protestant Kirk largely failed to sustain its ministry in Lewis before 1637.[36]

Did Protestantism fare any better among the Gaels in Ireland? Many of the Scots presbyterians who crossed to Ireland during this period – which was characterised by the growing deference to prelatical power favoured by James VI and I and his son Charles I – did so as non-conformists to the idea of ecclesiastical hierarchy. They were particularly encouraged after 1615 with the adoption by the Church of Ireland of an independent Irish Confession of Faith; more puritanical in its outlook than the English one, it readily appealed to the Calvinists.[37] The presbyterian presence was apparent in Ulster by 1621 when the archbishop of Armagh complained that on the estates of one of the main Scottish planters in Down there were 'certain factious and irregular puritanes who I have discovered of late to be settled in the lands of Sir Hugh Mountgomerie intertayning the Scottish discipline and litergie so strongelie, that they offer wrong to the Church government here established'.[38]

Though there is no evidence of presbyterian ministers from the Highlands being admitted to Ulster parishes during this period, some who had gone earlier continued in post. This is apparent from a visitation of 1622 undertaken in Raphoe during the primacy of Bishop Andrew Knox (1611–33), ex-bishop of the Isles. Knox was one of a small group of reforming bishops in the north: he took his place with the Scot Robert Echlin of Down and Connor (1613–35) and the Englishman William Bedell of Kilmore (1629–42) who, showing great sensitivity, sought to supply as many Irish-speaking ministers for Irish-speaking parishes as he could and in 1631 had a small catechism printed in Irish. As far as Bedell was concerned, this was the only way of combatting the considerable Counter-Reformation threat in his diocese. Writing to his friend Dr Samuel Ward in Cambridge, he stated:

> the Popish clergy is double to us in number and having the advantage of the tongue, of the love of the people, of our extortions upon them, of the very inborn hatred of subdued people to their conquerors, they hold them still in blindness and superstition, ourselves being the chiefest impediments of the work that we pretend to set forward.[39]

But Knox did more than either Echlin or James Spottiswood, bishop of Clogher (1621–45) – the other Scots-appointed bishops in the reign of James VI and I – to promote the Protestant cause in Ulster. The 1622 Visitation Roll shows the continuation of a Highlander originally admitted into a charge early in the primacy of Bishop Knox; another was admitted in this period as a reader.[40] In addition, it underlines the stringent effort being made by Knox to minister to the Irish in their own language.

The Raphoe Visitation Roll not only gives information about the academic status of the Protestant clergy, but also what provision they had made for evangelising the Irish community. The roll lists fifteen clergymen: fourteen of them have degrees; twelve are definitely Scots. One of the fifteen – the Highlander, Dugald Campbell of Letterkenny – has already been discussed.[41] Of the others, John Aiken of Dunfanaghy was said to know Erse; in addition, he was assisted by one or two Irish curates. William Patton of Ray had two assistants as well, one of them a converted Irish priest. John Hough of Kilmacrenan and Carrigart was helped by an Irish reader in Carrigart.[42] William Cunningham of Tullaghfernan (in Ramelton) and Gartan, Donegal, was assisted by John Ross, who knew Irish. Like Campbell, Ross may have studied at St. Andrews University, though there were also several alumni of Glasgow of that name.[43] Most importantly, Ross was a Gaelic-speaking Scot; he is the only Scottish Gael known to have been brought by Knox into his diocese after 1619, although three were shipped in before 1612.[44] Robert Whyte of Clondavaddog (curate to a non-resident incumbent) was also assisted by an Irish-reading clergyman. Similarly, Claud Knox of Aghanunshen (between Letterkenny and Ramelton) and Inniskeel (north of Killybeggs) was helped by Irishmen.[45] Therefore, in just under half – seven or eight – of the parishes mentioned, Knox had set up ministration in Irish. While it could be said that even this was inadequate, it was a valiant attempt to address the deficiency, especially since the national average in Ireland was then one minister to every six parishes. According to Knox, the native clergy endeavoured 'by all means the conversion of their country people'. But the native Irish ministers were at the bottom of the heap: they held the less lucrative parishes, serving as curates under settler British ministers.[46] This attitude to the native Irish – apparently directed even at those who had converted – has been held partly responsible for the failure of the Protestant mission. According to this argument, the Irish rising of 1641 marks the point at which Protestant belief in the likelihood of achieving a Protestant Ireland evaporated; this loss of hope was a fundamental part of the process of polarisation.[47]

However, in the short term at least, this positive discrimination in favour of Gaelic speakers, both Irish and Scots, meant that Knox's diocese began to reap Irish fruit. The schoolmaster at Donegal, described as 'a very good humanist', converted from Catholicism, while three priests doffed their robes to join the growing band of Irish readers.[48] And although Knox made a concerted attempt to bring Irish Gaels on board, the sixteenth-century policy of importing Gaelic-speaking Scots was perpetuated in the seventeenth through pleas from Ireland to the synod of Argyll for Gaelic-speaking ministers.[49] The Catholics mirrored this initiative: it was precisely their command of the Irish language that so contributed to the popularity of the Irish priests and friars, a few decades later, on the Highland mission. Like George Montgomery, the previous incumbent of Raphoe (1605), Knox can be seen as a sort of Ulster agent who brought many Lowland Scots into his diocese before the start of the official plantation.[50] Yet ultimately, Knox's policy of bringing in Scots, both Lowland and Highland, did not stand him in good stead. With the rise of Archbishop Laud's Arminian influence in Ireland,[51] Knox was soon accused of despoiling his See. His defence before the Lords Justices in April 1632 was that the rents in his diocese were paltry when he first took over.

> I then went to Scotland and, with great difficulty, persuaded a number of Scotch people to come and colonise my see. When they came over I had, owing to the conditions of the land market to give them better terms than I had bargained for, but I made reservations on all the lands, and the result is that this see is now planted with over 300 families of British Protestant settlers.

And who could argue with the fact that he had raised the rents from £30 to between £500 and £600 sterling a year?[52]

After 1634 – with the persecution of non-conformists to episcopacy by the Irish governor Thomas Wentworth, first Earl of Strafford – the clerical tide once again turned in the opposite direction. Seeking to effect doctrinal uniformity with the Established Church in England, the Convocation of 1634 convened by Wentworth drastically changed the status of presbyterians.[53] The most tenacious presbyterians were compelled to return to Scotland because they would not conform. Scots were obvious targets: after all, many of them were crypto-presbyterians. The Laudian Bishop Brahmall of Derry (1634–61) understandably shone the spotlight on the Scots following the Glasgow Assembly of 1638. He complained to Laud:

> But that which troubles me as much as all the rest is that never any Bishop of that (the Scottish) nation prefers any man but his own countrymen, yea, and them many times, with the extrusion of more deserving men. So as in a Bishop's time all the whole clergy of a diocese shall become merely Scottish, which how safe it is either for his Majesty's service or the settlement of the Church and State I leave it to your grace to apprehend.[54]

There is at least an element of truth in his assertion for the dioceses of Down and Connor, Raphoe and Clogher: all these had exclusively Scottish bishops until the Laudian period. In the dioceses of Derry and Dromore, on the other hand, where there were English bishops, Scottish clergy were conspicuous by their absence. So it is as part of an overall movement – mainly of non-conformist Scots into Irish dioceses held by Scottish bishops – that the immigration of Gaelic-speaking ministers must be seen. Only one Highland episcopalian was an exception to this movement. Thomas Mackenzie of Inverlaul, son of John Mackenzie of Inverlaul (minister of Killearnan in Ross), was admitted to the parish of Tarbat in Ross in 1633. But because his parishioners opposed his using a form of the liturgy, he deserted his charge and went to Ireland in 1635, probably hoping to find a more conformist congregation.

A good many lay conformists may also have crossed to Ireland at the same time: when Sir William Brereton (author of *Travels in Holland, the United Provinces, England, Scotland and Ireland, 1634–5*) was at Irvine in 1636, he was told that in the previous two years 'above ten thousand persons ... have left the country wherin they lived, which was betwixt Aberdeen and Ennerness [Inverness], and are gone to Ireland'.[55] This figure is an apparent exaggeration, but a significant number must have gone. Thomas Mackenzie eventually returned to Scotland and was admitted to his father's old parish of Killearnan in 1638. In the same year he was elected to the Glasgow Assembly, where charges were brought against him. On behalf of the presbytery, he protested against the Assembly as constituted, adhering to the declinature by the bishops; he was therefore deposed in 1638 and charged with excommunication.[56]

Episcopalians were equally capable, in their turn, of exerting pressure on Scottish Catholics, some of whom fled to Ireland. One Highland Catholic who made a refuge of Ireland in 1631 was Sir Alexander Gordon. The third surviving son of the eleventh Earl of Sutherland and Lady Jane Gordon, he should not be mistaken for his namesake, Sir Alexander Gordon of Cluny, mentioned later in this chapter. Holding the lands of Navidale and others in the parish of Kildonan, Sutherland, he assisted his brother, Sir Robert, in the management of the Sutherland estate.[57] Raised a Catholic, Gordon remained, like his elder brother and his mother, true to the faith. He suffered much under the court of high commission on account of his religion, doggedly refusing to conform to episcopacy. In the hope of winning freedom to pursue his religion, he went to Ireland in August 1631 with his wife and family.[58] He returned to Scotland the next year on business concerning the redemption of some of his lands by his nephew, the thirteenth Earl,[59] but he obviously intended to stay in Ireland where he had put down roots in County Monaghan. He was back in Dornoch for several months in 1636, but after this nothing more is known of him in Ireland.[60]

Just as surprising is the retention by the Scot, Sir George Hamilton of Greenlaw (son of Lord Claud Hamilton), of a portion of the plantation of Ulster for the Roman Catholic religion. As Michael Perceval-Maxwell remarks, this 'gave rise to one of the most anomalous circumstances in the entire Scottish plantation'. After his brothers died leaving only minors as issue, Sir George eventually controlled five proportions in Strabane. Furthermore, the children of both the Earl of Abercorn and Sir Claud Hamilton of Schawfield were converted to Roman Catholicism through his influence, so that within a generation one of the best success stories of the Scottish plantation was run by Roman Catholics. These lands must surely have been amenable to receiving Highland Catholics. A report on Hamilton's proportion by Sir D. L.[61] in 1622 certainly noted negative discrimination against Protestant settlers in the barony of Strabane. It also reported that Hamilton (understandably) surrounded himself with men of his own religion. Sir George and his kinsman, the Earl of Abercorn, encouraged this movement in the reign of Charles I, attracting Roman Catholic immigrants – including some Jesuit priests – from Scotland.[62]

The bishop of Derry considered the situation so serious in 1630 that he feared rebellion would break out in Strabane if the burgeoning Catholic community in his diocese was not imminently curtailed.

> There was a great meeting of priests last November at 'Ury', in the parish of 'Commye', wherein MacSwyne, Vicar-General for the diocese of Derry, gave up his place to Tirlough O'Kelly, who is now Dean and Vicar-General, and lives with Scottish papists at Strabane. He is generally harboured by James Ferrall, not by the Master of Abercorn, but the master often entertains him, and lodged him when the bishop of Derry and the provost of Strabane thought to arrest him.

Perhaps more pertinent, the depositioner demonstrated that the mass was attended by the Irish.

> There is evidence of the holding of mass on Sunday at Sir George Hamilton's and in other houses where it is attended by the Irish and forty Scotch from about Strabane. Sir George is praised for having made many converts during his residence in Ireland, both at Strabane and at Killybegs.[63]

There had been a Scottish Highland settlement in Strabane, County Tyrone, since Agnes Campbell had brought over a thousand men on her marriage to Turlough Luineach O'Neill in 1569. In 1598 she still 'drew great repair of Scottishmen thither insomuch as at this present there are above 3 or four Score Scottish Families inhabitting there'.[64] This Highland colony is often regarded as one of the few exceptions to the rule of non-settlement by the group which Perceval-Maxwell dubbed the 'New Scots' mercenaries.[65] There were over a hundred families there by 1622.[66] By the same token, in 1624 the native Irish were in possession of 305 out of 608 (or 50 per cent) of the ploughlands in Derry,[67] a significant percentage in an escheated county.

The authorities knew of Hamilton's religious proclivities as early as 1614, when he was ordered either to conform or be expelled from the country, but he retained his faith, continued in residence and waited. Nothing punitive occurred. A similar pattern can be traced in the authorities' dealings with that other arch-Catholic, the Earl of Antrim. The apparent tolerance of the religious waywardness of both is above all a gauge of their status as economically sound planters.

The Franciscan Mission to the Highlands and Islands

Because Protestantism was identified with a government unsympathetic to Gaelic culture, Hebrideans pestered Rome with requests for missionaries for the west coast after similar appeals to Scots in monasteries on the continent had failed. The Vatican received several appeals in 1611.[68] Catholicism was used by certain clan chiefs as a weapon against assimilation into the Scottish state, and in this respect 1611 was a significant date. For it was in May 1611 that the subscribers of the Statutes of Iona – MacLean of Duart, MacDonald of Sleat, MacDonald of Dunyveg, MacLeod of Harris, MacDonald of Clanranald, MacKinnon of Strathordell and Cameron of Lochiel – were compelled to reappear before the Privy Council.[69]

The Irish Franciscan college of St. Anthony of Padua, at Louvain, was chosen to answer the Hebridean call. This was no coincidence, given the history of the college: after the defeat of the Irish at Kinsale in 1601 and the subsequent flight of the Earls of Tyrone and Tyrconnel and their friends in 1607, the college became the cynosure of Gaelic learning in exile. It not only had a vested interest in things Catholic, but also Gaelic, and it was already skilled at matching Irish-speaking missionaries with shepherdless Catholic flocks in the motherland. It has been suggested that Irish speakers could easily be understood in the Hebrides and on the mainland south of Kintail but probably not so readily in Ross-shire or Sutherland,[70] but this reads more like a retrospective attempt to justify those areas in which the Irish missionaries did not find success. The reason that few Catholic converts were won in Ross-shire and Sutherland was undoubtedly less to do with their Irish being understood than with the militancy of the Protestant clergy. If the Hebridean appeals are to be believed, the situation there was dire: not a priest remained in the Highlands and Islands, nor were there any Gaelic-speaking students in the Scots colleges in Rome, Douai or Paris.

Following the acceptance of the call, there was much discussion between the Franciscan college, the papal nuncio at Brussels and the *Congregazione de Propaganda Fide* in Rome about the financial practicalities of the mission. Although a great deal was made of the links of friendship between the two countries – to say nothing of the fervent desire to perform spiritual service in a completely neglected land – the superiors of St. Anthony's were nevertheless unwilling to take on the financial burden of a Scottish mission. Their plea was valid enough: they were scarcely able to meet the demand for missionaries to Ireland, and they doubted whether the Irish benefactors of the college would remain so generous if they learned that their charitable gifts were being purloined to equip a mission to Scotland.[71] In short, a Scottish mission would compete with the extensive missionary work of the Counter-Reformation movement being undertaken by Irish colleges to Ireland in the early seventeenth century.[72] In spite of this, the college deferred to the wishes of Rome, and the Irish Franciscan mission to the Highlands and Islands was officially launched on 4 January 1619.[73] John Stuart, a Scottish lay brother (with distinguished relatives) at St. Anthony's College had been sent to Scotland in the vanguard in 1613. He played a major part in setting up the mission, travelling often between Scotland and Louvain as well as visiting Ireland, England and France.[74] He made for Scotland in January 1619 with two priests, Edmund McCann an Patrick Brady, one of them an Irish secular who had donned the Francisca habit.[75]

On their arrival in March 1619, the mission field was carved up between the two priests. McCann made for the Isles and Brady for the mainland. Stuart went with Brady, probably in the capacity of a general assistant and to explain the rudiments of the catechism. (He was, in effect, the Catholic equivalent of the Reformed Church reader). Claiming instantaneous success in the reconciliation of Islesmen to the Catholic faith, McCann began by baptising 360 people. He expressed himself thankful for vestiges of the old faith and an almost subliminal memory of the Roman Church, although many islanders were married within the forbidden degrees of kindred. McCann's impact on the Islanders made him a threat, so he was forced to flee to Ireland a few times in order to evade capture. He was caught towards the end of 1620, imprisoned for the next two years, and then banished on pain of death.[76] Further appeals sped from the Islanders to Louvain. Once again, the political dimension was weighted, particularly in relation to the Clan Donald South and the possibility of their seeking Catholic aid from the continent to reinstate them. In 1618, the Catholic Earl of Argyll had been declared a traitor; with Argyll safely out of the way, James VI and I felt able to recall Sir James MacDonald (of the expropriated Clan Donald South) and MacDonald of Keppoch (his partner in rebellion) from Spain. Keppoch was returned to possession of his estate, but Sir James was never permitted forth of London.[77] This may have been through fear of MacDonald attempts to regain their expropriated territories, especially since Sir James had been seen fraternising with the exiled Argyll in Spain.[78]

The apparent lack of enthusiasm in the higher echelons of the Franciscan order was not mirrored in the regular priests themselves: no fewer than twenty volunteered to go to the Highland mission, though many were considered ill-experienced. On 4 September 1623, papal approval extended the mission to include three more Franciscans – Paul O'Neill, Patrick Hegarty and Cornelius Ward; Edmund McCann went back again, too. The neophyte missionaries reached Scotland in 1624. Each priest was officially granted an annual allowance of 70 scudi from *Propaganda*, but a plethora of letters pushing for financial assistance attest to its irregular payment throughout the mission period. Stuart was still labouring in Scotland when they arrived but had the misfortune to be captured and imprisoned on a visit to Drogheda in 1624. (See Fig. 2.2.) In the event, King James intervened on his behalf, which surely says something of his tolerance of Catholics; Stuart was returned to Belgium, where he died on 6 September 1625.[79]

O'Neill did not long endure the mission field either. He withdrew from Scotland at the beginning of 1626 with no reason given. Significantly, this

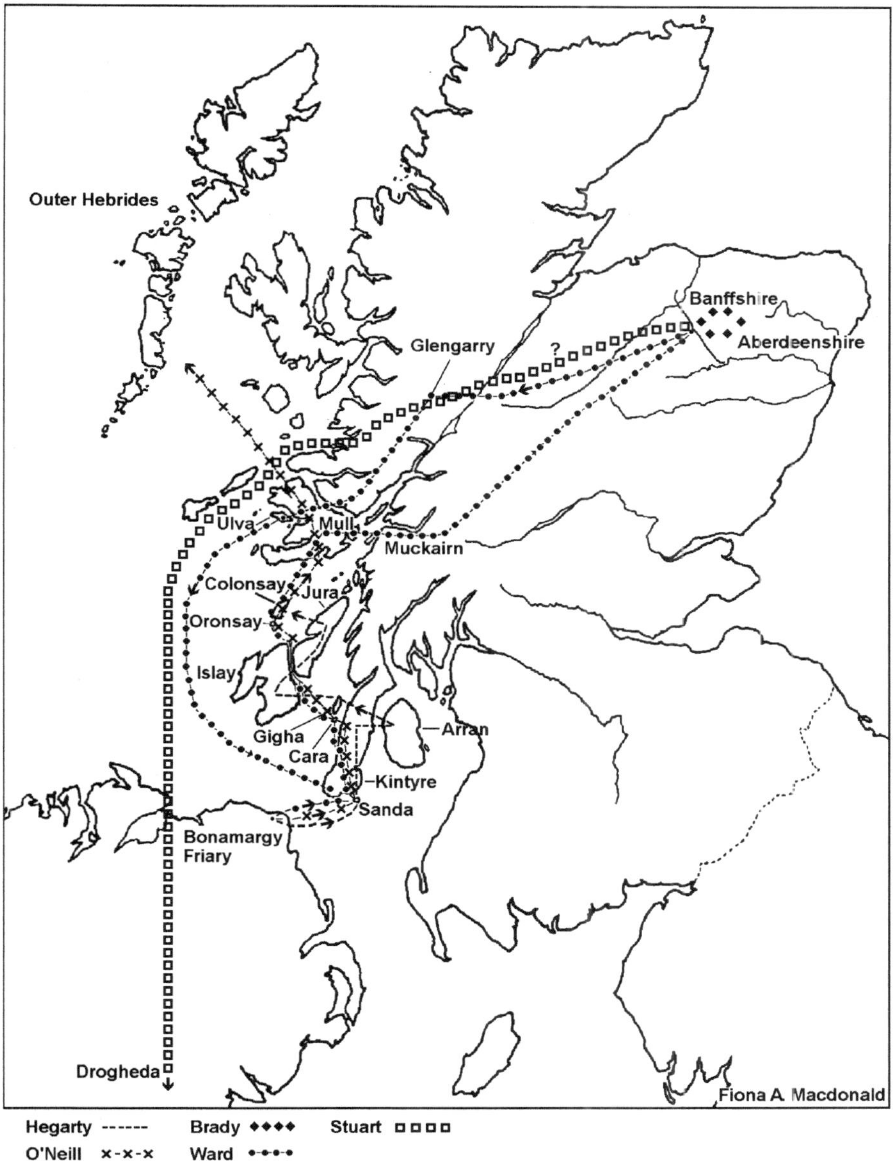

Fig. 2.2. First Franciscan mission, 1624: priests' itineraries.

was also the year when *Propaganda* acceded to a constant barrage of requests from the missionaries that they be granted the friary of the Franciscan Third Order Regular at Bonamargy. Left on the mission were Patrick Brady, who worked somewhere on the Highland peripheries, and Edmund McCann, who had returned after his imprisonment, and two of the second contingent – Patrick Hegarty and Cornelius Ward. Fortunately for the historian, the reports of these last two supply intricate detail of mission activities from 1624 to its demise in 1637. Although other priests were approved for the mission now and again, there is no evidence of any arriving,[80] so in effect the care of the Catholic flock in the Highlands was in the hands of just four individuals who spent another thirteen years on the mission, apart from visits to the continent to rally *Propaganda* and periods spent in Ireland, from where all but Brady operated after 1626.

Cultivating the Scottish *Fine*

In a land where the instruments of state and government were very firmly in the hands of a religion which proscribed Catholicism, it was essential for many reasons to cultivate the friendship of sympathetic clan chiefs and *daoine uaisle*[81] – that is, the clan *fine*. Particularly perfected by the Jesuits, this approach was taken up by most Catholic missionaries who, following the Jesuit guidelines for Counter-Reformation, paid considerable attention to the social hierarchy in the hope of influencing the general populace. A co-operative clan chief exercised both a cohesive and coercive force which was invaluable in converting his followers. Clan chiefs and tacksmen were also in a better position to give physical assistance (like food and maintenance) and to provide guides and bearers, to say nothing of free passage in their boats.[82] Again and again, the missionaries' letters testify to their being kept alive on the hospitality of the Highland nobility.[83] The missionaries' own social backgrounds and contacts were of prime significance here. Two priests in particular, both hailing from privileged social backgrounds, exerted inordinate influence on the mission, as well as being copiously productive in their written reports. Cornelius Ward – or Conchobhair Mac an Bhaird of the famous Connacht family of poets, the Mac an Bhairds – was himself a bard, while Fr. Francis MacDonnell was a natural son of the first Earl of Antrim.

Recognising the importance of such social integration, Hugh de Burgo, guardian of St. Anthony's, Louvain, instructed the missionaries 'to become friendly with the more important people in the mission territory, and, as occasion offers ... to help them in writing histories and in other such ways'.[84] At the start of the mission, a document from *Propaganda* helpfully listed those who could be relied upon to assist the missionaries.

> In Kintyre, at a place called Carskiey, there dwells a laird named Hector MacNeill who is very well disposed towards Catholics; Colla MacDonald, the laird of Colonsay, is a Catholic, and he can provide the missionaries with information, and give them directions as to how to visit the other islands; the missionaries are to take advice from MacDonald as well as from the governor of the island; another leading man in the Hebrides is Roderick MacLeod of Harris, who is a Catholic; the missionaries can find out from the governor of Colonsay how they are to reach the laird of Harris, who, fervent Catholic that he is, will attend to their needs and give them whatever instructions they might want.[85]

Malcolm MacPhee is probably the governor of Colonsay referred to here, although he was not to prove of much help in the long term because he was killed by Colla MacDonald in February 1623.[86] The common thread among those deemed sympathetic to the Franciscans seems to have been mercenary service and settlement in Ireland. Looming large in the early days of the Franciscan mission was connection with the Clan Donald South, which probably cannot be separated from that clan's attempts to regain its lost Hebridean hegemony. Cardinal Borghese wrote from Rome on 24 March 1618, asking the Belgian nuncio to try to persuade the Franciscan superiors in Louvain 'to send priests to Scotland under the guidance of a Scottish laird named MacDonald'.[87]

The role of the clan chiefs during the first Franciscan mission – especially the piratical voyage of Colla Ciotach and his friends in 1616,[88] and the relationship of their political submission to their ecclesiastical compliance – has attracted particular attention. The deposition of Robert Williamson (the main source for the voyage of pillage and plunder) stated that Colla Ciotach's party went island-hopping, which included a stop-off in Canna before eventually sailing with provisions to St. Kilda, where they stayed for a month. From there, the party sailed to inspect the Isle of Boreray, to see if the construction of a fortification there was practicable. John Lorne Campbell has emphasised that 'Coll Ciotach and his friends can hardly have made an extended voyage around the Hebrides in a small hijacked vessel simply for the purpose of visiting St Kilda and inspecting Boreray'. Clearly not. The implication seems to be that they were scouting for a suitable location for a Catholic mission headquarters. This is possible, but pirates have rarely sought excuses to raid isolated communities or sail the seas for plunder at their leisure, especially after the collapse of the Highland mercenary trade.

Campbell continues: 'It is significant, although one cannot prove the connection, that the islands which he visited in 1616, Texa, Islay, Colonsay, Mull, Canna, North Uist, and Iona were all likewise visited by the Irish Franciscans in 1624 and 1625, and possibly earlier – the mission began in 1619, but earlier reports are lost.' (See Figs. 2.2 and 2.3.) This assumption is

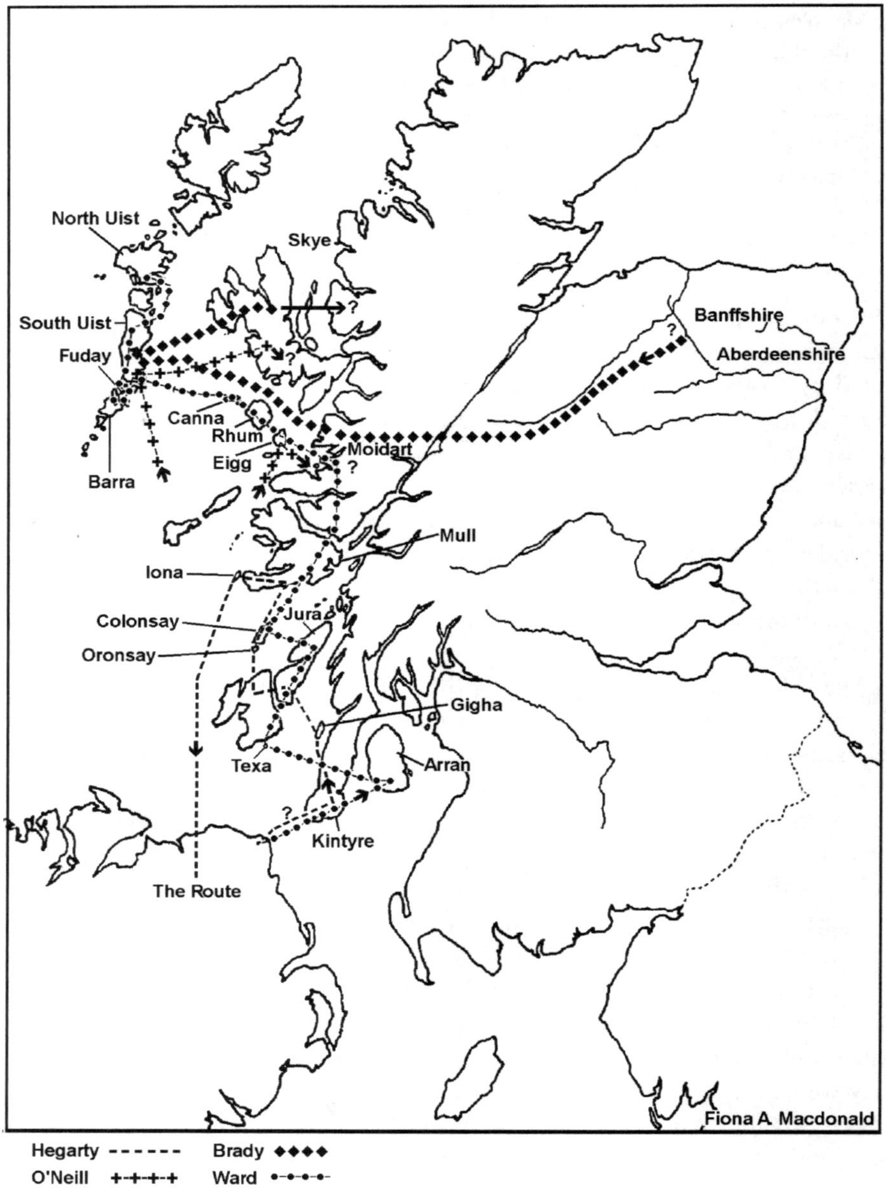

Fig. 2.3. First Franciscan mission, 1625: priests' itineraries.

supported by evidence that before they left for the Highlands in 1623 the second wave of Franciscan missionaries was again informed by the Belgian nuncio that Colla Ciotach MacDonald (by that time well ensconced in Colonsay) was a Catholic leader who could direct them through all the islands.[89] Nor should the political ramifications be forgotten: many of the above-mentioned islands, except Mull, North Uist and Iona, were homelands of the Clan Donald South with its strong Irish connections. None the less, its undisputed Hibernian connection is not sufficient to prove any absolute commitment by the Clan Donald South to an Irish-staffed mission, because when Sir Randal MacDonnell of Dunluce obtained a lease of Islay in 1613, the inhabitants complained of his oppressive Irish exactions. This could be seen as a means of demonstrating their opposition to the Irish branch of the family; more importantly, their discontent is held to have provoked the 1614 MacDonald rebellion. Cawdor eventually took over in Islay, obtaining a feu of the island in November 1614, and although there were still MacDonalds there, in all likelihood Cawdor's conversion to Catholicism in 1624 created more sympathy on the island for Campbells. So while the MacDonald connection was undoubtedly important, it should not be overstated.[90]

Highland tradition has long venerated Colla Ciotach as a hero, but by the same token, though nominally a Catholic, the fervour attributed to him in preparing the way for promoters of the faith hardly tallies with his treatment of men in the field (like Malcolm MacPhee) or with his suspect negotiations in the Islay rebellion. For all the retrospective adulation by his own culture, it is doubtful whether even Colla Ciotach could sustain such a whitewashing. He definitely assisted the missionaries – he probably even admired them – but he certainly did not emulate them; such action as he undertook on their behalf was totally in character with his quasi-brigand-like role. Thus he protected Ward and O'Neill when a minister in Kintyre threatened to attack them for converting a member of the local gentry in the summer of 1624. But he was at least consistent in his protection: in a testimonial of 1 April 1629 to *Propaganda* verifying the achievements of Ward, Hegarty and O'Neill, Colla Ciotach referred to an attempt by ministers and heretics to capture Ward earlier that year, which he had foiled. He was severely injured in doing so.[91]

Attention has also been drawn to a potentially more interesting piece of analysis concerning the polarisation of the traditional clan chiefs. John Lorne Campbell has analysed the stance of the 1609 subscribers of the Statutues of Iona with respect to their support – tacit or otherwise – of the Franciscan mission. 'Angus MacDonald of Dunyveg was dead before the missionaries arrived in Scotland. Clanranald, MacLeod of Harris, and MacLaine of Lochbuie, welcomed them and accepted the Catholic religion. Donald Gorm of Sleat had died in 1617 ... Donald MacPhee of Colonsay's successor Malcolm had been eliminated by Coll Ciotach MacDonald in 1623.' Colla Ciotach, who favoured Catholicism, thereby put himself in de facto control of the island, even though Argyll had technical superiority. So who had disappeared from the list of subscribers when the Franciscan mission was in full swing? Hector Og MacLean, tenth of Duart, and his two brothers, Lachlan and Allan, had signed the Statutes, but by the time Ward landed on Mull in the summer of 1625 (see Fig. 2.3.) Hector Mòr MacLean, eleventh of Duart, was fervently opposed to Catholicism. Also absent from Franciscan reports were the descendants of Gillespie MacQuarrie of Ulva, though Ward did go to Ulva in 1624. Donald Gorm Mòr MacDonald, seventh of Sleat, had been succeeded by his son, Donald Gorm Og who, not wishing to antagonise the Lowland government and doubtless well content with the teinds of kirk lands appropriated by the clan since the Reformation, did not actively welcome the missionaries, although he appears to have done little to hinder them. Likewise, the Statutes had been signed by Rory MacKinnon of Strath (Skye), who does not feature in the missionaries' reports. It would appear, then, that most of the Skye chieftains were keeping a low profile regarding the mission though the island was visited by the Franciscans on a number of occasions. Most inclined to Catholicism was the Trotternish peninsula: acquired by the MacDonalds of Sleat in 1596 after a century of struggle with the MacLeods of Dunvegan, Sleat had occupied it continuously since 1540.[92]

And to what extent did MacLeod of Harris and MacLean of Lochbuie welcome the Franciscans? If they did so, there is little to show that the faith was ultimately sustained in their lands. MacLeod of Harris (probably William, thirteenth chief) had been cited as early as 1590 as a commissioner for punishing adversaries of Protestantism; both Ruaraidh Mòr, fifteenth of MacLeod, and Eachunn Odhar MacLean, ninth of Lochbuie, appeared in person before the Council in Edinburgh in 1622 promising to repair parish churches. But even MacDonald of Clanranald – that inveterate papist – was occasionally cited as a commissioner during the seventeenth century, so such appointments hardly carry much weight.[93] At the very least, Ruaraidh Mòr MacLeod was a pragmatist: MacLeod of Harris was certainly never cited before the Privy Council for recusancy.[94] None the less, the family memorial insists that MacLeod was a Catholic, and he did allow his daughter to marry into the MacDonalds of Clanranald; however, his children were educated as Protestants (in accordance with government direction) and he made quite sure that he did nothing to draw attention to himself.[95] Ultimately, it is difficult to know in which camp MacLeod stood. Murdoch MacLean, tenth of Lochbuie, on the other hand, was cited in 1631 in a complaint to the Council by Mr Martin MacIlvory, minister of Killean and Killenachane. The minister stated that he had been provided to both kirks for several years, but felt his labours were likely to be ineffectual both because of MacLean's hostility to the Kirk and because – as master and landlord of most of the parishioners – he withdrew them from hearing the gospel.[96]

Can any conclusion be drawn from all of this? The caucus of those who signed the Statutes of Iona can be seen as a group intent on achieving political independence within their own clan territories; most of them still thought this way two decades later. In a sense, the government was not so inaccurate in holding adherence to Catholicism as the adoption of a political stance. It was less their recognition of a foreign power – such as the papacy, France or Spain – but rather their firm rejection of the present state which was important. The current status quo was renounced through their association with the religion which had held sway during the golden age of the independent chiefdom. Iain Muideartach, twelfth of Clanranald, for instance, had been somewhat compromised by the rebellion of the Clan Iain of Ardnamurchan in 1624. As a Catholic, he chose on his own behalf and that of his principal relations and clan to write a letter on 5 February 1626 to Pope Urban VIII, by which he probably sought assistance to restore them as a clan.[97] Although Ruaraidh MacLeod of Harris also stood surety for the Clan Iain, he had not been similarly compromised because he did not overtly identify with Catholicism; he was therefore quite happy to assist Lord Lorne in suppressing the clan.[98] In the letter, Clanranald insisted that his people had long been under the tyranny of the Calvinists, who were 'exterminating among our predecessors the holy Catholic faith, the one apostolic Catholic Roman faith'. Dramatically overplaying the ties between the Irish and Scots MacDonalds, he claimed that, acting together, all the Clan Donald septs could easily conquer Scotland, but to do this 'they would need the help of four ships and sufficient arms for 7,000 of their men, and the help of the Catholic Kings to hold it'.[99] The plea for ships in particular bolsters the suggestion that Clanranald may have been seeking to reinstate the Clan Iain.

Having the sense to emphasise the religious dimension with the Pope, Clanranald promised: 'If we receive help of this kind we shall easily reduce the whole of Scotland to obedience to the faith of Christ and of your Holiness.'[100] Yet at root, identification with Catholicism was far more of a political statement of cultural solidarity than of religious commitment, and it had the same implications for polarisation in the Highlands as in the province of Ulster. Clanranald drew on the religious argument in much the same way as post-Revolution Jacobites drew upon the re-establishment theme in their attempt to attract foreign aid when, irony of ironies, the Stewarts had been the main persecutors of Gaels in the previous century. But in both cases the prime consideration was ever the re-establishment of their own autonomy, which came above any other kind of loyalty. Clanranald's plea could also be seen as a Gaelic attempt to reverse the Stewart policy of driving a wedge between the native Irish and the Highlanders, which had caused a decline in the Ulster mercenary trade as well as an immense shortage of money and available arms.

None the less, when Clanranald assured the Pope that 'all the Gaelic-speaking Scots and the greater part of the Irish chieftains joined to us by ties of friendship, from whom we once received the faith (in which we still glory) from whose stock we first sprang, will begin war each in his own district to the glory of God', he was indulging in nothing less than myth-making.[101] The Gaelic-speaking Scots were far too factionalised to fight together: they naturally divided into kinship groups according to territorial affinity and leadership, along the lines of the mercenary alliances of the late sixteenth century. And while the MacDonalds' blood-ties with the Antrim MacDonnells were undisputed and they had also built up other long-term loyalties with septs such as the O'Cahans, difficulties and rivalries reared their heads even in the closest of blood relationships.

On the other hand, the perennial value of befriending eminent men in the mission territory manifests itself in Ward's conversion of John Campbell of Cawdor – highly prized indeed, not only because he was the main Islay landholder, but particularly because he had been a Protestant and a member of the prestigious Clan Campbell. Ward's report for the years 1624 and 1625 emphasised the difficulty of gaining access to Cawdor. Ward therefore used a ruse: knowing that Cawdor held poets in high esteem, Ward, operating under his poetic alter ego, Conchobhair Mac an Bhaird, composed a eulogy for Cawdor. Attired in poet's garb and accompanied by a singer carrying a harp, he then presented himself before Cawdor, by whom he was graciously received. Continuing in the guise of a poet for three days, Ward finally disclosed his real identity to Cawdor, as well as revealing the errors of Cawdor's Protestantism until, after much discussion, Cawdor declared himself convinced. And after the departure from his house of some Protestant lairds, he agreed to receive absolution. At Ward's direction, Patrick Hegarty visited Cawdor a little later, when he became a Catholic.[102]

Hegarty was convinced that 'by his example and his outstanding zeal for the catholic religion he [Cawdor] will draw great numbers of the gentry to catholicism'. It certainly seems to have had some effect, because shortly after Cawdor's conversion another relative of the Earl of Argyll – Archibald Campbell, laird of Barbreck – was apparently reconciled to Catholicism. Ward, at least, put this down to the force of Cawdor's convictions.[103] In the event, it may have been just a temporary (or closet) reconciliation, for there is no mention of Barbreck being persecuted by the synod of Argyll, nor was he cited before the Privy Council.[104] Archibald Campbell's sister-in-law (wife to his elder brother) also converted. In all, Ward netted two of Cawdor's sons and no fewer than fifty of his relatives.[105] A testimonial written from Islay on 17 March 1629 and signed by four Islay Scots and five Irishmen stated that Ward and Hegarty had been so successful in their visits to the island that Cawdor and his brother William had to leave Islay because of the heretics, and that 'the inhabitants of the island are being wiped out by fines and exile'.[106] The conversion of Cawdor's brother, William Campbell, can be corroborated: in

1626 an order was given by the Privy Council charging him to appear before the Lords 'to answeir to suche thingis as sall be demandit of him toucheing his ressett of Jesuites, seminarie and messe preistis, the heiring of messe, and toucheing his apostacie and defectioun fra the true religioun, under the pane of rebellioun'. Yet it was surely the political implications of the Campbells losing an island gained only fifteen years previously from the Clan Donald South which encouraged presbyterian persecution of Catholics on Islay.[107]

Cornelius Ward wrote from Dublin on 20 November 1626 that a severe persecution of the mission's converts had begun in Scotland. He mentioned specifically the Baron of Cawdor, who had been imprisoned for open profession of his Catholic faith.[108] Cawdor's confession before the Privy Council in August 1626 recorded that 'of lait he hes wittinglie and willinglie ressett within his house some Irishe preistis and participat with thame in thair idolatrous worship, and hes thairby maid apostacie and defectioun from the trew religioun'. He was, therefore, to be warded in St. Andrews, there to remain until the Council met with the archbishop and other literati so that he might receive instruction and give satisfaction for his doubts in religion. Henceforth, the non-reset of Catholic priests was an article enforced in the annual bonds taken by the chiefs for their own good behaviour and that of their clans.[109] In March 1629, Cawdor was eventually excommunicated for being 'ane profest and avowed Papist and apostat'. But according to the Privy Council he was still 'suppleed and interteanned amongs his familiars and acquaintance in the countrie as if he wer ane free and lawfull subject'; he also retained possession of 'his place and fortalice of Caddell'.[110]

Ward laboured in Glengarry, Mull, Ulva and Kintyre, according to his 1625 report. (See Fig. 2.2.) He converted a man identified by patronymic as Alexander Mac Iain, but Ward felt constrained to say that he 'was still a catholic' when he wrote his report, which tends to indicate that he did not necessarily have high hopes of his remaining so. The name, combined with Ward's trepidation, probably identifies this alleged convert as the last chief of the MacIains of Ardnamurchan. The clan had been in rebellion since September 1624 – which goes some way to explaining the priest's hesitancy – and by the beginning of 1625 had taken to a piratical life.[111]

In his next report (1626), Ward wrote that he visited South Uist in October 1625 in the company of one of its leading men. This was probably Ranald MacDonald, an uncle of Clanranald, whom Ward was invited to visit; he was joined there by Paul O'Neill and Patrick Brady. 'The gentry whom Ward had invited to come to hear him preaching said it was difficult to embrace catholicism, seeing that no catholic priest had visited them for about one hundred years, and that there was nobody to instruct the ignorant even if the people decided to become catholics.' This was the Church which Clanranald allegedly sought to restore: one which had not visited his territory for at least thirty-five years prior to the Reformation. Ward 'converted' only forty-one on the island; hardly a wholesale reconciliation, although if confined to the clan *fine* (about whom he had generally been speaking), the conversion of forty-one tacksmen would have been a significant slice of the island's gentry. Among his converts were Ranald MacDonald's eldest son and his household. There was a similar lack of enthusiasm initially from another area of subsequent Catholic entrenchment. Ward visited Barra in early 1626, where he converted the rightful heir to the island – Niall Uibhisteach MacNeill (from whom the MacNeills of Vatersay are descended) – but he 'was opposed by the laird and many of his subjects'. Niall Og MacNeill had recently usurped the island from Niall Uibhisteach and, in the short term, probably threw his lot in with Protestantism to secure his title, though Hegarty seems to have converted him on a subsequent visit in 1632.[112]

Indeed, the results of failing to secure undivided support, particularly the physical presence of the chief at open gatherings, are well illustrated by Ward and O'Neill's visit to Eigg in August 1625. Ward had been invited to Clanranald's lands by Iain Muidertach himself, to whose family the sacraments were administered, but the chief was allegedly too busy to receive them personally and did not receive the sacrament until some days afterwards when O'Neill (who had converted Clanranald) arrived. In addition, Ward wrote that 'all the chief men on the island along with their households were won over to the faith, except one, who was a relative of the minister'. But although he claimed that they converted 198 people, they crossed to Rhum with Clanranald's brother and other members of the gentry, 'since Clanranald and his dependants were busy with matters concerning the Scottish court' and therefore 'it was not possible to convert many'.[113] Ward and O'Neill had clearly expected to reconcile more on Eigg; that they did not is probably because Eigg had a minister by this time. His presence accounts for the reported interrogation of the priests by the people (who would doubtless have been well versed in anti-papist controversy) as well as for Clanranald's low profile. Although Clanranald had been a Catholic for a year and had given Ward a letter for the Pope, he would not have been keen to flaunt his Catholicism in front of a Protestant informer. His behaviour also tends to reinforce the opinion that political considerations were indeed paramount in Clanranald's 1626 overture to the Pope, when he asked him to sanction what amounted to a Gaelic crusade.[114] But where the chief did not lend obvious countenance, that of the leading tacksmen could be just as useful. For instance, although the laird of Mull, MacLean of Duart, was a staunch Protestant, Hegarty converted (whatever limitations might be placed on the word) 266 people there by building a base of support among the tacksmen. Gillean MacLean, Duart's brother, was among them: Hegarty converted him in 1625.[115]

Some élite converts opted for the alternative of flight to Ireland. On 31

March 1634 Philip Clery, a clerical student who had spent some time in Ireland, wrote in a testimonial from Rome that he 'spent twenty days in Drogheda with Patrick Hegarty, when Hegarty and three of the gentry, who were converts, had fled from Scotland because of persecution'. This is also a further testament to the protective role supplied by some nobles, because Hegarty, who had been taken prisoner in Scotland, had been rescued by these gentlemen of the house of Clanranald.[116] Others went to Ireland not out of compulsion but simply to promote relationships there with others of their class. Terence Kelly, cleric, wrote in another testimonial of 1634 that in the last year he had seen 'Louis Macallea and thirty-three Scots in County Donegal; these had all been converted by Hegarty, and had come to Ireland to see other Catholic nobles there'. Unfortunately, no clue is given to Louis Macallea's origin, although a connection with Arran might be posited on the basis of the name Louis.[117] Arran would certainly accord with Hegarty's stipulated mission field in 1624 and 1625, which covered most of the southern isles from Arran to Mull but at this time appeared to go no farther north.[118] (See Fig. 2.4.) Similarly, in April 1634, Luke Tully, OFM admitted to hearing that 'Brady spent about nine continuous years on the mission, and brought over to Ireland a nobleman who disposed of his goods and went into exile rather than allow his faith to be undermined at home'. This particular titbit was clearly doing the testimonial rounds: it also appears in Roger Ó Duierma's letter to *Propaganda* of the same date from the Irish College in Rome.[119]

Not only Catholic Gaels but also Lowland Catholics on the periphery of the Highlands were being attracted to Ireland. The pull of both Sir Claud Hamilton's and the Earl of Abercorn's estates in this respect has already been mentioned. In June 1633, Fr. Andrew Leslie also wrote in his report of the Jesuit mission's achievements for 1632 that:

> Some of the highest character, both men and women, have resolved to emigrate to Ireland, and some are already gone, for it is quite evident they could not remain long in England, though that would be nearer. Sir Alexander Gordon has crossed the Sodorian sea, and is living quietly at Derry, among the Irish. He did not expect to find the natives very civilised, but he has found them at any rate good Catholics, and although there are many Calvinists among them, they are accustomed to restrain the rude bitterness of controversy, and are not perpetually giving utterance to it. Others are likely to follow him soon, after they have made their peace with God and the Church by penance, for fear they should be shipwrecked on the voyage.[120]

This convert, who can be identified as Gordon of Cluny, is probably the same nobleman referred to above by Luke Tully.[121] However, Cluny – 'but a mean gentleman whose estate consists only in a wadset[122] of 7000 merks' – may have gone to Ireland as much to escape financial difficulties as religious persecution.[123] Nevertheless, his comment on the deliberate avoidance of

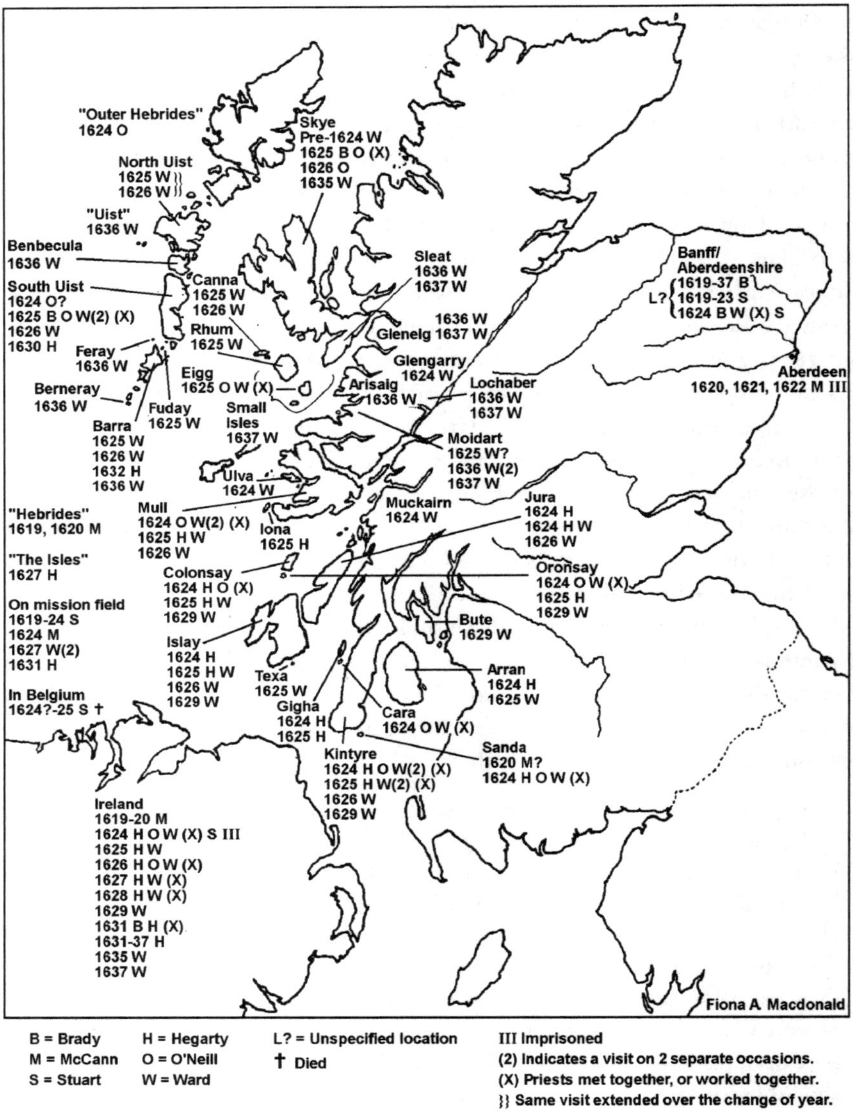

Fig. 2.4. First Franciscan mission, 1619–1637: incidence map.

religious debate by Derry Catholics and presbyterians should be emphasised. Furthermore, if it is Cluny who is referred to here, Giblin's assertion that Brady worked in Sutherland has to be reviewed.[124] Though Cluny held lands in Kildonan, there is no evidence in the mission reports which proves definitively that Brady ever worked in Sutherland. An undated mission report, probably written in 1628, is quite categoric in stating that 'Brady is in a district bordering on the Highlands, and stays there permanently, but he very often spends a few days visiting the Highlands; during the past seven years he has not gone to Ireland or England, but spends all his time winning souls for God on the mission.'[125] Given that Sutherland is in, and not bordering on, the Highlands, it seems far more likely that Brady was actually quartered with Gordon of Cluny in Aberdeenshire, from where he probably made forays into Badenoch or Highland Perthshire. But very little is actually known of Brady's mission, and so it is therefore exceptionally difficult to clarify the matter. The only other mention of his mission field was made earlier in Ward's report for 1624 and 1625, in which Brady was said to labour 'in the northern parts of Scotland', and there is certainly no reason to assume that this applies more to Sutherland than to those areas around Aberdeenshire and Banff; when writing of Huntly's protectorate, contemporary Catholic commentators refer more often to the north than to the north-east.[126] In addition, a list of priests drawn up at the beginning of Charles I's reign shows that there were no fewer than twenty priests in the north-east in 1625. Although they usually laboured within 'the Dyoceis of Aberdene and Murraye', they made frequent incursions into other areas, particularly in the south-west, north and north-west.[127] On balance therefore he was probably most often, if not always, in Aberdeenshire.

In 1637, after the Franciscan mission to the Highlands had technically been terminated, both clan *fine* and ordinary clansmen circled like moths around the candle of Bonamargy. Patrick Hegarty mentioned in December 1640 that if Congregation had received his report for 1639 they would know that 'within the space of four months 1,000 had been received into the church by Hegarty and his companions, and given the sacrament of confirmation by Magennis; notable among these was Alexander MacDonald, laird of Largie, who died one month after his reception, and by his example drew other leading personages to the true faith'. Though he had been dead some seven months by the time of Hegarty's letter, in 1639 Bonaventure Magennis was the Franciscan bishop of Down and Connor (1630–40).[128] Once again, politics and religion worked hand in hand: in the first sixth months of 1639 many MacDonalds fled to Ireland as Argyll tightened his grip on Kintyre and Islay; in June of the same year, the Campbells invaded Colonsay.[129] But even before the last days of the mission, on their visits to Ulster the Franciscans had begun to take their mission into the Irish community, and did so all the more after Bonamargy became theirs in 1626.

Hobnobbing with the Ulster Élite

Access to the élite in Ireland was of prime importance to the missionaries: the ethic of charitable giving was apparently more vital in Ireland than in Scotland, although many Highland chiefs were reputedly sympathetic to the Catholic cause. In April 1626, *Propaganda* granted the missionaries permission to seek aid from rich people in Ireland and to give presents to members of the principal families in order to promote their enthusiasm. The evident implication is that the Irish clan élite would grease the mission wheels more willingly than the Scottish ones.[130] *Propaganda*'s sanction perhaps also suggests that the long-standing argument for the Highlanders' natural inclination towards Catholicism should be tempered. Certainly, when Ward wrote from Louvain on 19 August 1626 to give an account of recent events in the Hebrides, he had been refused lodging at a village in North Uist at three miles' distance from the church of the Most Holy Trinity in Carinish, but a woman whose mother was a native of Ireland took him in instead.[131] While Protestantism had been established in North Uist by this time, this tends to suggest that, at the very least, links forged through the mercenary trade in the late sixteenth century had preserved a veneration of the faith in the Hebrides.[132] Most importantly, the operation of the missionaries from Bonamargy (their base since 1626)[133] was favoured both by financial expediency and because it afforded them the protection of the first Earl of Antrim, a known resetter of priests. In 1621 he had been summoned to Dublin, where he was obliged to admit the charges, although he was released with just a warning.[134]

But the missionaries had been reaping a small harvest in Ulster before their official settlement at Bonamargy. Fr. Hegarty completed a tour of the Hebridean islands in 1625, and on his return to Ireland he converted 'a non-catholic minister' and sixty Scots in the Route. It is unclear whether these Scots were English- or Gaelic-speaking. There were both Lowlanders and Highlanders on the Antrim estates, and the Jesuit reports make it clear that many of the Jesuit missioners to Ireland spoke both languages in the early seventeenth century.[135] As a consequence of the minister's conversion, Hegarty claimed that the missionaries' faculties should extend beyond Scotland to Ireland and England; that is, their official permission to evangelise should not be limited to just one country. By the beginning of 1628 – about a year after the Franciscans had been granted Bonamargy – Ireland was Ward's base.[136]

According to a mission report for 1627 and 1628, Ward had been in Scotland twice in the previous year but had retreated to Bonamargy on the advice of some of the converted Scottish gentry. Clearly attempting to justify his Irish base, the report stated that it was 'easier for him to go to the Isles from Bonamargy than from the Scottish mainland, so he stays at Bonamargy, and when he gets a chance goes to Scotland for a few weeks; because of persecution, he cannot stay too long on the mission at one time'. A report by Ward for the years 1627–29 reiterated that 'because of persecution, he was compelled to flee to Bonamargy on the Irish coast, and there, in 1628, he and Patrick Hegarty administered to the Scots who flocked to them from Ireland and Scotland; Hegarty won back to the faith about 200 Scots from the Hebrides, and Ward twelve'. Ward embarked upon a further tour of the nearby Scottish islands of Islay, Oronsay, Colonsay, Bute and Kintyre in February 1629, which caused another spate of Scottish pilgrim communicants. By August 1629 the missionaries were requesting a privileged altar for the church at Bonamargy because 'great crowds frequent the place'.[137]

Nor was the pilgrimage to Ireland a short-lived phenomenon. In August 1637 Hegarty, in answer to *Propaganda*'s queries about his non-residency on the mission, said that he had been working just as hard in Ireland, since 'the people from the Hebrides flock daily to Bonamargy for spiritual aid, so that the friars resident there are always kept busy'. In March 1634, a trainee cleric spoke of an Irish student, John Cryan, 'who, under Ward's direction, used to attend to the ecclesiastical needs of the Scots who had been converted'. Ironically, then, there was post-conversion back-up for new Catholics in Ireland, but not in their own country.[138] Among a flurry of petitions sent by the missionaries to *Propaganda* in August 1629, they asked:

> If it be necessary that one of the missionaries should remain in Ireland for a time, let him, while he is there, act as penitentiary at St Patrick's Purgatory; a missionary might have to go to Ireland for any of the following reasons: to flee from persecution in Scotland, to procure hosts and wine, to send reports on the mission, or to rest from his labours.[139]

But *Propaganda* was never in favour of an Irish base; it replied in November 1629 that it did not see it as fitting for one of the missionaries to act as penitentiary. Such a move was declared 'outside the scope of the mission'.[140]

Unlike *Propaganda*, the missionaries warmed to the increased stability of their Irish residence. Mission activity continued in Scotland in the summer months, when the weather was more clement. Of all the missionaries, it was Brady in the north-east who least frequently visited Ireland, although he was there in May 1631 'because of persecution in Scotland'.[141] This also tends to support Brady's settlement in the north-east of Scotland rather than in Sutherland, because although the episcopal campaign against recusants was more discretionary in its implementation than draconian, the majority of the thirty-five members of the landed and commercial classes apprehended and brought before the Privy Council from 1629 to 1631 were nevertheless from north-east Scotland.[142]

The most significant product of the missionaries' building of relationships with the Ulster élite was their close connection with Randal MacDonnell, first

Earl of Antrim. One of their main arguments for being granted rights to Bonamargy Friary was that 'the earl of Antrim, on whose land the friary is built, has no objection to the missionaries taking possession of it'. Not only did the MacDonnells of Antrim have a magnificent tomb in its grounds, but there were usually eight or nine priests working in the vicinity. The number of priests is in itself some indication of the generosity of Antrim's patronage of the mission.[143] Moreover, he had a personal interest in this work because his natural son, Francis MacDonnell, OFM was raised to the priesthood on 20 December 1625, the likely fruit of his father's extended patronage of the Catholic faith.[144] Francis MacDonnell volunteered for missionary work in Scotland in 1627. He was by this time at the College of Saint Isidore in Rome. And when Paul O'Neill withdrew from the mission field only two years after entering it, MacDonnell was officially approved by *Propaganda* on 8 May 1628 to replace him. But the appointment of a priest with such eminent connections (if only by dint of illegitimate birth) would inevitably have attracted more attention, some of it politically adverse, to the Scottish mission. So MacDonnell's lofty aspirations went unrealised when the Earl of Antrim refused to allow his son to be a missionary in Scotland. Protective of his own position, Antrim feared that, with his son serving as a priest in Scotland, he would incur disfavour or suspicion with the King.[145] Since the MacDonnells still laid claim to the expropriated MacDonald lands, Antrim undoubtedly worried that his son's presence in Scotland would compromise his political ambition to secure the MacDonald heritage in Kintyre and Islay. Antrim's lease of Islay had been terminated in 1614 after his lack of acceptance there was blamed for inciting the Islay rebellion (at the hands of the sons of Angus MacDonald, late chief of Clan Donald South), which permitted the feu to fall into the hands of Campbell of Cawdor.[146]

Randal had gone no small way towards attracting the favour of the monarch. Having failed in Islay, Antrim later pursued his ambitions through his son Randal, Viscount Dunluce: Randal attempted to secure Kintyre first by purchase from Lord Kintyre in 1635, and second by conquest, as a prize for his staunch support of the Royalist cause from 1638 onwards.[147] Those who sought to contain his popularity and influence – for example Lord Lorne, who had his own interests to protect – continued to level charges of sheltering priests against him. When Antrim tried to buy Kintyre in 1635, Lorne argued that 'the Earle of Antrim would bring in a number of priests, and so make the whole people turn Papistes'.[148]

Francis MacDonnell's understanding of the mission, its needs and difficulties was absolutely unrivalled, certainly in terms of presenting the Highland case to *Propaganda*. His petitions indicate that he had a grasp of the most vital matters. In 1628, for instance, he addressed the issue of giving preference to boys from English-speaking districts of Scotland when allocating places in the

Scots colleges abroad. *Propaganda* should find a way, he insisted, to promote the acceptance of Gaelic speakers at the Scots College in Douai.[149] The missionaries themselves, still anxious to appoint a designated superior of the mission in location, also wished this to be Francis MacDonnell. A good deal of energy was expended on this subject; the missionaries were divided in their allegiance between MacDonnell and Brady. Those preventing MacDonnell's appointment appear to have been members of the Irish congregation at Louvain, but it is likely that they were merely acting under the wishes of the Earl of Antrim.[150] In a land where many of his Catholic countrymen had but recently been deprived of their estates for intriguing with foreign powers, it was imperative that the Earl tread with great care. Heavy fines had to be evaded, too. While it was extremely unfortunate for Francis MacDonnell that he was sacrificed to his father's caution, the circumstances were compelling.[151] And rivalries and jealousies between the religious orders and political sensitivities were not the only difficulties under which the mission laboured.

Problems, Difficulties and Extenuating Circumstances

Due to the immense labours of the Franciscans, Catholicism was eventually established in pockets of the Scottish Highlands and Islands. This containment was due to the manifold difficulties under which the mission struggled.[152] The sheer physical magnitude of the parishes was a problem which continued to be faced wherever a small population scattered itself over a vast geographical area with poor communications. At least it was a problem shared by the Protestant ministers, but this did not mitigate it for either faith. Indeed it was greatly exacerbated for the Catholic mission, which operated with only a handful of priests until the latter part of the seventeenth century – although numbers later expanded as an indigenous Scottish priesthood was revived. It was mainly because of this and the associated difficulties of sustaining the converted that the Catholic faith became entrenched in territorial pockets.[153]

To take their ministrations to as many people as possible, the missionaries kept to a gruelling schedule. Cornelius Ward wrote in August 1626: 'it happens too that every two or three days the missionaries or their attendants have to travel by sea'. While true, the main reason for bringing this to *Propaganda*'s attention, predictably, was that the missionaries 'need money to pay their fares on such occasions'. Three years later they pleaded the necessity of their own boat, 'as the Scots are forbidden to carry missionaries in their boats under penalty of heavy fines'.[154] But such requests only undermine the credibility of the missionaries' reports to Rome, because it is difficult to believe – and there is no response from *Propaganda* on this subject – that most islanders would not have taken them in their boats anyway.[155]

The biggest problem the missionaries had to contend with was the lack of understanding of their task at almost every level by *Propaganda*. At its most absurd, *Propaganda* directed the missionaries to meet every three nights to discuss their progress – and this when they were usually hundreds of miles apart.[156] Again and again, *Propaganda*'s decisions on a variety of issues indicated that they viewed the Highland mission as if it were operating in a country where the Catholic Church was legally established. This presented innumerable problems, particularly regarding functions which could only be executed by a bishop. For instance, while the missionaries could have faculties to bless chapels, cemeteries, vestments and chalices, the water or holy oils used had to have been blessed by a bishop, and there was no Catholic bishop in Scotland.[157] In his August 1629 report, Ward asked that 'a directive be given about the use of faculties on the mission, where there are no prelates, and where the faith has not been practised for ninety or a hundred years'. This, of course, hardly equates with the missionaries' previous arguments that the Highlands had remained Catholic, by default, since the time of the Reformation.[158] And faculties were rarely granted straight away. Ward was still negotiating for extraordinary faculties three years before the official end of the mission in September 1634. Hard-hitting and shrewd, he stated to Cardinal Barberini that

> the ignorance of the Congregation and of the Inquisition about the state of affairs in the Highlands and the Isles is responsible for the restrictions included in the faculties sent to him; they may be well informed, but they forget what has been told them because there is nobody at Rome to keep the affairs and the needs of the Highlands and the Isles before their minds.[159]

In addition to the scarcity of priests to administer the Catholic sacraments, there was an equally restricting lack of basic physical resources; these were almost impossible to replenish in the absence of a bishop.[160] On 29 December 1624, Patrick Hegarty reported that he 'had to send his attendant to Ireland for bread, and wheat can only be got with difficulty from Ireland and the Lowlands of Scotland'. But this could be seen another way: were the missionaries simply seeking excuses for their own inability to make converts? Towards the end of 1624, for instance, Ward reported that he was labouring in Glengarry, Mull, Ulva and Kintyre, where he 'won' 287 for the faith.

> He would have done much more if he had sufficient wine, but he was without wine for two months, and could not procure any to say mass even on Christmas Day, 1624; it was only rarely and with great difficulty that wine could be brought to the Highlands from the towns in the Lowlands of Scotland; there were no towns in the Highlands for contracting business.[161]

It surely stretches the bounds of credibility to believe that a missionary could not make converts simply because he lacked wine (although participation in the mass may have been regarded as tenable evidence in authenticating conversions, and therefore in justifying payment according to results).[162]

Those who had personal contact with the missionaries, on the other hand, were well aware of the enormity of the problems and the need for some flexibility. Hugh de Burgo, guardian and apostolic visitator of the Irish province, wrote to *Propaganda* in 1619:

> They should be given faculties also to dispense in certain matrimonial impediments, and should be allowed to ride horses, use money, and leave off the habit; they should be given jurisdiction to decide in matrimonial disputes; it is necessary also that they have a house on the Irish coast nearest Scotland where things needed for the mission might be had, and to which they could go, at times, to rest from their labours.

Unless these concessions were granted, he insisted, the mission could not continue. Only the most ardent missionaries persevered under such conditions. *Propaganda* did little to help: it took exception to the missionaries taking respite on occasional visits to Ireland, holding the view that they should reside permanently in the mission territory.[163] Almost a decade later, in August 1628, Francis MacDonnell, OFM was still arguing that the missionaries should be allowed to flee to Ireland when under imminent threat of arrest, or they would have little or no chance of saving themselves.[164] And missionaries certainly did retreat to Ireland in spite of wishes to the contrary. As far as horses were concerned, the missionaries used them anyway.[165] What remained intact were the restrictions on dispensing marriage impediments, which the missionaries were probably loath to contravene. Yet the priests were clearly anxious to record as many souls as possible on their lists.[166] The evidence suggests that the marriage impediments which they did feel capable of dispensing with were in cases of divorce or where the union had been ratified by a minister.[167] Limited concessions were granted on 19 March 1626, of which no details are given, and again on 7 April 1626, which sanctioned the shipping-in of secular priests from Ireland; the issue of dismissorial letters (two) to Scots under impediment who wished to become priests; and permission to request funds from laymen in Ireland. The submission of conversion lists in the previous year probably facilitated this gift.[168]

The above-mentioned lack of co-operation among the various religious orders was a major problem for the missionaries, and the internecine strife among the Franciscans themselves did little to improve the situation. Although magnanimous efforts, to some extent successful, were made to soften the differences between the Irish religious on the continent, tensions remained. Mutual vexations were apparent among Old English and Old Irish factions, the Jesuits, who monopolised Irish seminaries in the Iberian Peninsula and were criticised for only recommending students likely to become regulars; and among other regulars who were none the less prepared to open secular colleges, like the Franciscan colleges of Alcalá in Spain and Louvain in the Netherlands, which also trained secular priests. Franciscans looked with particular disdain upon Jesuits, Capuchins and Discalced Carmelites. There was a good deal of provincialism within each order.[169] 'Within the Franciscan order there was a struggle for control of colleges, almost from the time of foundation of their first college at Louvain.' Meath Franciscans, for instance, attempted (without success) to gain control of Louvain, which was in Ulster hands.[170]

The missionaries also experienced difficulty in the supervision of their work from Ireland; naturally enough, they wished to appoint a superior in their own midst. *Propaganda* decided on 7 April 1626 that the head of the mission should have the supervisory status of 'prefect' (administrator). Cornelius Ward asked in his 1626 report 'that the superior of the mission be subject to nobody in the Franciscan order except the minister general and the commissary general; the missionaries state that they cannot easily recur to prelates in the English-speaking parts of Scotland or in Ireland because of the distances separating them and the dangers involved'. Apparently, the situation did not improve. In January 1630, Hugh Ward, the guardian of Louvain, wrote: 'the missionaries asked also that nobody be made superior of Bonamargy unless approved by them, because others wished to take over that friary which had been granted to the missionaries by the pope.' 'Others' can be identified, by a decree of *Propaganda* dated 18 September 1634, as the friars of Carrickfergus. The decree ordained that 'in the future nobody was to be made superior at Bonamargy except one of the missionaries, or a friar chosen by them'; the archbishop of Dublin was entrusted with its execution. The mission was placed under the wing of Bonaventure Magennis, but on his death in April 1640, Patrick Hegarty, who had worked from Ireland since 1631, was appointed prefect.[171]

Particularly difficult for the Franciscans to combat was the jealousy of Lowland Scots on the continent with better contacts in Rome. This stemmed, perhaps, from feelings of inadequacy on the part of Scottish priests because they had not equipped a mission to the Highlands or, more likely, that they were irked at having no control over this mission. The mission field was just another battleground in the general atmosphere of controversy and contention which then existed between Scots and Irish ecclesiastics on the continent. A Scots priest, Thomas Dempster, published some histories which rendered little credit to the Irish missionaries for the tremendous work they were doing in Scotland. By way of reply, the *Hiberniae sive Antiquioris Scotiae vindiciae adversus Thomas Dempsterum* – attributed to an Irish priest, Henry Fitzsimon – was published in 1621. Fitzsimon attempted to shame the Scots into carrying their own cross: he charged the Scots clergy with neglect of the Highlanders' spiritual welfare.[172] Certainly, there appears to have been a distinct lack of co-operation by Lowland Scots in recruiting Highlanders into the priesthood; the acceptance of Scots in the continental colleges who spoke Gaelic was an exception to the rule. The missionaries often mentioned the hostility between

English-speaking Scots and Highlanders at the lay and religious levels; it was most necessary, they emphasised, for their own kind to be trained to lead them. In August 1626, Cornelius Ward wrote from Louvain of the vast cultural divide that he perceived lay between them.

> There is a lasting and mutual enmity between the Anglo-Scots and the Gaelic-speaking Scots; furthermore, the Anglo-Scots do not know Gaelic, and there is only one priest among them who has a knowledge of that language; there is as much difference in mode of life and in outlook between the Scots and the Greeks.

He continued, with the poetic satire of his second profession, 'and indeed, the Anglo-Scots would be about as useful as the Greeks in helping the people in the Highlands and Isles'.[173] Yet it must be said that in Ranald MacDonald, an alleged ex-minister who now wished to become a priest but had been refused admission to a Catholic college, Ward chose a very poor example.[174]

The Scots Colleges also seem to have been responsible for most of the venom fed to *Propaganda* about the mission, frequently resulting in the withdrawal of the missionaries' allowances. Certain decisions about the Scots mission were made by *Propaganda* at a meeting of 6 November 1629. It ordered that the nuncio in Belgium 'be asked to verify what was contained in Ward's reports, as their veracity was questioned by some Scots at Rome'. Attention was also drawn to the testimonials sent in by Ward which were considered inadequate and too general; more than this, 'one of those who had subscribed to a testimonial, on being questioned by a certain Scot, replied that he had given the testimonial in order to please the missionaries'. This might have been so, but was it inaccurate? Similarly, in 1633, someone 'intimated to the congregation that the claim made by Hegarty and his companions of having converted 10,000 in the Hebrides was false'. In Louvain, Hugh Ward was obliged to write to *Propaganda* in January 1630 warning that 'the Congregation should be on its guard lest it be wrongly informed, because the Highland Scots have enemies, even among their own people, who on other occasions showed their ill-will and spite'.[175] Unbelievably, it was even doubted in Rome if the missionaries had actually laboured in Scotland at all. Cornelius Ward was obliged to write – doubtless with all the humility he could muster – refuting this claim.[176] The poison pens were probably Jesuits. They had the greatest vested interest in the Scottish mission: not only had they established an almost exclusive presence on the mission, which they wished to preserve, before the Franciscans came, but the Society also ran three of the four Scots Colleges on the continent: Douai, Rome and Madrid. Only Paris was retained in secular hands.[177] And their doubts about the missionaries' claims to large numbers of converts were, after all, perfectly valid.

But the most enduring difficulty – and perhaps the most pertinent to the success or failure of the whole mission – was the consistent lack of finance. The high-faluting spiritual aims laid down for the missionaries were replete with the expected and necessary platitudes about renunciation, particularly of worldly wealth.[178] Yet the barest essentials were scarcely provided for those who expended so much energy. According to Ward in 1626, 'the people of the Highlands and Isles are poor, but even if they were not, it would not be advisable to quest there, nor would it be possible for the missionaries to do so because of pressure of work and the difficulties of the times'.[179] Only the most circumscribed financial support was available in the mission field, usually from the clan *fine*. None the less, it is doubtful whether Ward's argument (1637) that the ordinary people of Uist were compelled to pay teinds to the minister and therefore could not support the Catholic priest as well carries any weight, because it is unlikely that John MacKinnon, appointed rector there in 1633, was actually resident. Would it necessarily have made any difference if he had been?[180]

One would be hard-pressed to argue that the missionaries had an interest in anything other than stressing the poverty of the mission field. *Propaganda*'s preliminary remarks on the missionaries' reports put it more poetically: more money was needed 'lest the seed which has been sown pine away before it takes root'.[181] In general, *Propaganda* remained more productive of fine poetic expression than pecuniary aid, although it must be conceded that it did have far-reaching priorities, with mission fields all over the globe. A letter written on 28 August 1637 by Dr Bonaventure Magennis to the secretary of *Propaganda* puts the matter in some kind of perspective. Cornelius Ward, wrote Magennis,

> compelled by poverty, which so often stands in the way, returned to his native land, and cannot any longer bear up against the heavy weight. The liberality indeed towards himself of his friends, whom he has lately converted to the faith, if it be not altogether exhausted, is considerably wearied out. On the Scotch he does not wish to be heavy, lest, perhaps, he would frighten the weak by the burthen.[182]

One of the main reasons that the mission began to operate out of Ireland was in all probability because it could command greater patronage there.

Unless it received regular mission reports, *Propaganda* simply refused to forward the next instalments of the missionaries' allowances. That many of the reports eventually got through is evident from the number of them still extant, but often they took some time, travelling with their bearers by circuitous routes, or got through only on the second draft. After May 1626 the missionaries were instructed to send their letters to the archbishop of Dublin and not, as Ward had suggested, to a Franciscan superior. Even when *Propaganda* did send money, the missionaries did not always receive their full entitlement, because the nuncio in Flanders often milked some for other purposes.[183] Complaints about the reports were sometimes surprisingly petty. *Propaganda* objected, for instance, to reports in Irish because none of the Roman dignitaries understood the language themselves. At one level it was simply an inconvenience to them but, according to Francis MacDonnell in 1628, they also feared that they could be more easily duped if the letter was in Irish. MacDonnell stressed that it was a matter of security: reports written in Latin could easily be read if intercepted, whereas few people in Lowland Scotland or England could read and write Irish. He also felt constrained to point out that if the missionaries really wished to send false accounts of their endeavours on the mission, they could do so in Irish as readily as Latin.[184]

On occasion, the necessity of chasing funds could be as much a threat to the missionaries' freedom as the vigilance of the Protestant forces. Fr. Ward, for instance, was captured in London in 1630 en route from Belgium where he had gone to make a case for additional funds and faculties and to give an account of the mission. Capture was no small matter: a priest's imprisonment potentially threatened his converts, Ward was asked to reveal the names of the gentry converted to Catholicism, but he refused. He was also accused of coming to Scotland to incite rebellion. Though this was a stock accusation, it indicates that the authorities chose to interpret Catholicism as a political threat.[185] And although limited progress was made on some issues, the missionaries' constant cries for support and assistance remained essentially the same right to the end of the mission.

Achievements of the Mission

The sheer unmitigated want of support in terms of morale, finances and necessary faculties, especially the failure to supply a bishop for the mission, ultimately dictated its official downfall. The missionaries could endure no more. Cornelius Ward wrote in the report for 1637 that they were 'worn out by excess of work and as they are receiving help from nowhere, there is no alternative but to leave the mission; indeed, all of them have already abandoned it, except Patrick Hegarty, who continues his missionary activities at Bonamargy on the coast of Ireland nearest Scotland'.

But even Hegarty had not been resident on the mission for six years before 1637, the year in which the Franciscan mission to the Highlands and Islands ended. In a letter to *Propaganda* of 26 August 1637, the first reason Hegarty gave for this was that he 'did not receive any money allowance from the Congregation after he had sent them the last report of his work on the mission'. Not entirely plausible, on the other hand, is his assertion that he was impeded from going on the mission because he was definitor of the province and guardian of the friary of Bonamargy.[186] The letter was written a month after the first outbreak of religious opposition to the rule of Charles I, on 23 July

1637, at the reading of the service book in St. Giles in Edinburgh; given that, apart from liturgical innovation, fear of popery was the other major concern in Scottish Lowland society, the missionaries' final retreat may not be entirely coincidental.[187] Hegarty insisted, however, that he had worked hard in promoting the mission's interests from Bonamargy, and emphasised: 'should the pope or the Congregation wish to continue the mission, let the missionaries be given sufficient means to support themselves, as, otherwise, it is impossible for them to reside in Scotland.'[188]

Though the mission proper can be said to have finished in 1637, in a sense it continued to function from Ireland under the momentum established over the previous twenty years. On 31 October 1639, Hegarty wrote in abject mortification from Bonamargy to the secretary of *Propaganda*.

> This year the God of all consolation has deigned, by means of my so vile labour, to convert to the Catholic faith about 700 Scots, very many of whom belong to the principal families of the Islands and Highlands of Scotland. All these, after confession of their sins, and after reception of holy Communion, the Most Rev. the Lord Bishop of Down and Connor fortified in our monastery of Bunamargy with the holy Sacrament of Confirmation.

A certain amount of deception was used to engineer the ceremony. The bishop was allegedly on a visit to see his relative Randal MacDonnell, second Earl of Antrim;[189] the Highlanders, on the other hand, came under the guise of a day at the great fair of Ballycastle – which may well have attracted them just as much. Most importantly, all official suspicion was thus deemed to be allayed.[190]

On 4 December 1640, Hegarty complained that the other four Franciscans labouring in Scotland had withdrawn, leaving him to his own devices. It grieved him deeply that *Propaganda* made no effort to remedy this.[191] He asked that *Propaganda* 'order the superiors of the Irish Franciscans to assign new missionaries to him, or to allow Anthony Hickey and Luke Wadding to name suitable priests for the mission from among the Irish friars at Rome'.[192] Employing the tactics of ultimatum once again, he asked to be relieved of directing the mission unless this was done.

The reasons for the failure of the mission have already been dealt with. But what did the mission actually achieve? The Franciscan mission kept Catholicism alive, if in a limited sense, although the extent of its enduring influence in Highland communities at this time is doubtful. For instance, when Hegarty visited Iona in 1625, although the mission had already been operating for six years, it was apparently the first time mass had been said since the suppression of the Catholic religion there.[193] Money aside, perhaps the main reason that the mission did not achieve more was the sheer lack of missionaries and, related to this, the failure to inspire and produce native missionaries. In a sense, the success of any religious mission can be partially gauged by the number of people it creates who wish to emulate their teachers. In this respect, offering education for the clan *fine* was of vital importance. Even had potential acolytes existed, there was absolutely no provision for the training of young Highlanders. The missionaries attempted to persuade *Propaganda* to fund twelve bursaries, but to no avail.[194]

Although swarms crossed daily to Bonamargy in the late 1630s, when Ward was in Canna in October 1625 the truths he preached apparently 'pleased the people, but having to put them into practice did not, for, children of the earth as they were, they were intent on the crops, not their salvation, and, as it was autumn, they paid more attention to the harvest than to their souls'. The Islanders received only the most cursory of annual visits, yet seeing the tenacity and dedication of these priests, it would have been unusual if some of the people had not come to respect and love them. In his report for 1636, Ward said that he spent a month working in the islands of Barra, Feray and Berneray. He preached every day before and after mass and, 'though the people of the Hebrides may be rough and uninstructed, they have not entirely forgotten the traditions of their fathers, as they always show great affection for the mass, and for the old faith of Rome, as they call it'.[195] Comments like this seem to confirm the survival of a body of oral tradition with a distinct religious flavour, preserved in such collections as the *Carmina Gadelica*, which was 'the common heritage of the whole population, whether Protestant or Roman Catholic'.[196] It would certainly also account for statements like Hegarty's in the 1637 report that he would continue as long as he lived 'to strengthen and preserve what little faith the people have, provided the Congregation gives him an annual allowance'. Indeed, it has been suggested that it was the Franciscans who popularised parts of that body of Gaelic religious lore in the *Carmina Gadelica* which, in verse form, was highly usable in an oral culture.[197] However, seeing a priest once a year, if that, can hardly have been conducive to spiritual growth. Donald MacDonald, a former captain in the Spanish army, stated in a testimonial from Colonsay in March 1629 that 'those converted persevere true to the faith, although they seldom see a priest', but he also added, 'it is true, however, that some few, through fear of the ministers, have strayed a little from the teachings of the church'.[198]

The lack of sustenance from priests settled in one fixed locality should be seen as one of the major deficiencies of the Franciscan mission, because most of the missionaries necessarily covered vast distances in order to take Catholicism to as many people as possible. (See Figs. 2.2 and 2.3.) In 1628, Francis MacDonnell asked *Propaganda* to allow him or other missionaries to appoint parish priests among those who had been converted until such time as there were bishops or Vicars-Apostolic in Scotland. Understandably, this was not granted; there is certainly very little evidence to show that anyone had sufficient knowledge or had reached such a stage of spiritual development in the past nine years' mission to be able to fulfil such a role. Given the limitations on physical and human resources, the missionaries dealt with the immediate needs of the mission as well as they could. Fortunately, the Highlanders were often mesmerised by the sheer physical presence of Catholicism in the spectacle of the mass. In South Uist in October 1625, Cornelius Ward conducted a baptism in the open, surrounded by a great crowd, 'who were so impressed by the ceremony that they all wished to be baptised by him'.[199]

As a result of the Franciscan mission, vibrant pockets of Catholicism were established, many of which have survived to the present century, in South Uist, Barra, Eigg, and Moidart: that is, mainly the lands of MacDonald of Clanranald and its cadets, and of the MacNeill. There is no doubt that Barra was so well served due to its proximity to Clanranald territory. (See Fig. 2.4.) However, the missionaries' initial foothold on the mission, according to the earliest extant reports of 1624, was in the lands of the expropriated Clan Donald South. These reports also hint at earlier activity in that area. When Hegarty preached to the people of the Isle of Sanda (see Fig. 2.2) in July 1624, he stated that 'they had been instructed in the elements of the faith four years before by another Irish Franciscan, but had seen no priest since then'.[200] Most probably this was McCann, the only priest on the mission in 1619 who is known to have worked in the Hebrides. However, although the missionaries laboured from 1624 to 1629 (and probably for a few years before this) on the old Clan Donald South lands of Sanda, Kintyre, Gigha, Texa, Islay, Colonsay, Oronsay and Jura with as much regularity as they did in the Outer Hebrides, Skye, Moidart and the Small Isles, Catholicism took root only in Colonsay and Oronsay. On the other hand, the missionaries' visits to the Ross of Mull from 1624 to 1626 may have had some effect. When Ward and O'Neill visited the island in 1624, moreover, they stayed with a man 'who, though a catholic of long standing, had not seen a priest for twenty years'.[201] This is highly significant if the last priest he had seen was in Mull itself, because it might further extend the boundaries of Irish Jesuit missions to the west coast of Scotland in the early decades of the century. The missionaries probably succeeded in converting MacLean of Lochbuie, his wife and another member of his family, but after this they do not seem to have visited Mull. It is difficult, therefore, to conclude that the faith was sustained there. However, there are later signs of a limited survival of Catholicism in Mull, although the island was apparently not visited by any other missionaries in the seventeenth century.[202]

Kintyre and the surrounding islands of Argyll were extensively visited during the 1620s. However, the last Franciscan activity there can be dated to 1629 when Ward visited Kintyre, Islay, Oronsay and Colonsay, as well as Bute. (See Fig. 2.4.) So why did the missionaries virtually abandon what had once been worthy of their extended attention? Ward was certainly of the opinion that 'the missionaries could hope for greater results if they had sufficient means to enable them to stay on in certain places for a while'. He also inferred that the people in those areas were not so hospitable, which impeded the missionaries' work; he felt that 'there is greater hope of doing fruitful work in the Hebrides'. However, the main reason appears to have been the strong efforts of the Protestant Kirk, using whatever influence it could wield to root out any trace of Catholicism. For instance, Hegarty reported that he visited Gigha during the summer of 1624, 'but because of the opposition of the minister and the smallness of the island, he had no success'. Going on to Islay, he worked in constant danger of capture and of his life, and was saved by a band of thirty Catholics. Hence his labours in this area were not conducted openly. During the eight weeks which he spent in Kintyre, he hid by day in a cave and preached, baptised and administered the sacraments by night. Mass was said at two separate locations, ten miles apart, before the sun rose. Similarly, on Arran he was compelled to live in a cave. Only in Jura and Colonsay did Hegarty evade persecution.[203] The Protestant authorities also used whatever sanctions were in their own power to destroy Catholicism. Excommunication, for instance, though not always fully effective, worked to a limited degree as a social and ecclesiastical sanction. The Kirk certainly followed through on each case of recusancy, making particular examples of the élite, and this in itself is indicative of the pressure that could be brought to bear on the individual.[204]

But it was probably the near capture of Cornelius Ward by the Protestant authorities in 1629, and his rescue by Colla Ciotach MacDonald, that finally dictated the missionaries' abandonment of Kintyre and those islands which, ironically, were most accessible from Bonamargy.[205] Even though Colla Ciotach's de facto occupation of Colonsay was legally recognised in 1633, the co-operation of the Kirk and the house of Argyll effectively banished the missionaries from the southern isles, ensuring that they did not work farther south than Moidart and Morar on the mainland or (off that coastline) the Small Isles in the future. In fact, apart from incursions into Argyll with the Royalist army in 1644–45, and a small Catholic presence in North Lorn, Mull and Ardnamurchan in the early eighteenth century, the Catholic mission to the Highlands and Islands continued to be restricted mainly to those areas until 1760. By the same token, although the missionaries visited Skye on at least four occasions (twice in Sleat) – that is, just as many times as they went to other parts of the western Highlands and Islands during the course of their mission – they failed to convert MacDonald of Sleat or to make anything more than a crypto-Catholic of MacLeod of Harris. This inevitably had consequences inimical to the survival of Catholicism in Skye.

One of the by-products of the Irish Franciscan mission was the restrengthening of west Highland links with Gaelic Ireland which had been weakened by the plantation of Ulster and the destruction of the Clan Donald South. The mission, it has been suggested, was probably under the patronage of the first Earl of Antrim right from the start; it served his end as a means of unifying and boosting the morale of the MacDonalds with a view to reviving their power.[206] More pertinently, he probably saw it as a method of extending his own power base. But in the final analysis, just how much co-operation and interconnection was there between Irish and Scottish Gaels in religious matters between 1619 and 1637? Here the evidence is conclusive. Only two Gaelic-speaking Scots clerics appear to have gone to Ireland during this time: one on the basis of previous acquaintance with Bishop Knox of Raphoe, ex-bishop of Isles, and the other, during the Laudian period, to escape a non-conformist congregation. Further, although both Irish and Scottish Gaelic speakers ministered in Knox's diocese, the Scots were accused of provincialism by the English.

And just how strong were the Scoto-Irish Gaelic bonds in reality when the convent at Louvain had to be coerced by Rome into supplying the Highland mission? The Franciscan missionaries certainly stressed the common historical link between the two peoples established by the mission of Saint Columba, and they were of the opinion therefore that 'it was only fitting that missionaries from Ireland rather than from any other place were chosen to go to Scotland, so that that faith which was first brought to the Scots from Ireland should be revived by men from the same country'.[207] Nevertheless, like the *seanchaidhean*, they felt obliged to fall back on an ancient link rather than a contemporary one to stress their common heritage. In effect, the links of most of the Highland élite to Catholicism were somewhat tenuous, except in a very few cases mainly connected with the MacDonalds. This amply explains the initial focus of the Franciscan missionaries on the lands of the Clan Donald South. However, although some undoubtedly went on regular pilgrimages to Bonamargy and others ultimately settled in Antrim when the Campbells took control of Colonsay in 1639, these links were not sufficiently strong, nor the expropriated clan élite sufficiently powerful, to sustain and protect the growth of Catholicism in those areas. Therefore, the results produced by the dedication of so few missionaries were directly proportional to their immense personal zeal and enthusiasm. That so many of the Highland and Island areas remain Catholic today is a result not only of the labour of the later indigenous ministry, but also of the Irishmen who preceded them.

THREE

The Entrenchment of Gaelic Presbyterianism, 1637–1689

We also exhort yow, dear brethren, to keip good correspondence with the army there, sieing they are scarse of ministers to attend them.

General Assembly Commission (1647)

A PERIOD which endures change from an episcopal form of Protestantism to a presbyterian one in 1638, a further restoration of epicopacy in 1660 and, finally, a reversion to presbyterianism again in 1690, requires a certain definition of terms at its outset. Scottish Protestantism, as introduced at the Reformation, is generally recognised as a moderate form of Calvinism with regard to its theology and ecclesiastical polity.[1] The reformers believed in an autonomous ecclesiastical jurisdiction separate from the state, that is, an anti-erastian one. Present in the Kirk from 1560, presbyterians became far more conspicuous in the 1570s when their anti-erastian beliefs were directly challenged by James VI.[2] Seeking to exercise control over the Kirk – particularly the presbyterians within it – James pursued this end by deliberately strengthening the status of Protestant bishops (who were restored in 1572) and by implementing the 'Black Acts' in 1584. These Acts were aimed at curtailing the independence of the church courts – or 'new pretended presbyteries' – and of the General Assembly which had operated before this without licence from the crown. Although bishops continued to be appointed by James, so they could vote in parliament, they were largely titular and as yet wielded little ecclesiastical power. None the less, the thin end of the episcopal wedge was in position.[3] After a pragmatic early retreat,[4] James doggedly pursued his reconstitution of diocesan episcopacy;[5] achieved by 1610, this was followed by twenty-seven years of episcopal government. Ironically, in Ireland, the Scottish 'prescopalian' faction – presbyterians working within the episcopal Church of Ireland – served to reinforce and keep alive the Calvinist tradition there, but they were under increasing pressure from the mid-1630s.[6] In Scotland, James VI began his reform of liturgical policy – changes enshrined in the Five Articles of Perth which were passed with difficulty at a General Assembly in 1618 and ratified by parliament in 1621, although in practice they were widely disregarded.[7]

Under James' son, Charles I, who succeeded in 1625, ecclesiastical, administrative and economic reform was taken to an extreme. The Act of Revocation, passed in the same year, sought to cancel grants of crown property made since 1455 and rescind sales of ecclesiastical real estate which had been erected into temporal lordships since 1587. Most importantly, by this the crown claimed a right to the disposal of their teinds. When, unsurprisingly, no voluntary surrenders of church property occurred, the threats of reduction and deprivation of those holding such temporal lordships – the lords of erection – led to discontent among Scottish landholders. This was only exacerbated by an unpopular fiscal policy (which introduced heavier taxation), constitutional grievance over the King's manipulation of parliament and, more particularly, Charles' unwise attempts to introduce the English prayer book and liturgy into Scotland, mainly on the strength of his own prerogative. In particular, the rise of the anti-Calvinist trend in Arminianism with its taste for flamboyant ceremonial and the exalted status of bishops caused widespread unease that the King was introducing a distinct Romanising tendency into the Kirk.[8]

July 1637 saw the introduction of the new 'Romish' liturgy into the Church in Edinburgh, which created uproar amongst presbyterians. In turn, this resulted in the formulation of the National Covenant, signed in Edinburgh on 28 February 1638, which ultimately led to the establishment of presbyterianism at the Glasgow Assembly in November and December 1638. Presbyterians, backed by civil authority, turned with renewed vigour upon Catholics, as they did on any individual who refused the compulsory signing of the Covenant in 1640, which embodied a pledge to disregard 'the novations lately introduced in public worship, the corruptions of the public government of the kirk and the civil power and places of churchmen'. Some Scottish episcopalians – including incumbents of a Highland parish and bishopric – fled to Ireland. Hordes of Ulster presbyterians also signed the Covenant during visits to Scotland, so that in May 1639 Thomas Wentworth, Earl of Strafford and Lord Deputy of Ireland, felt compelled to draw up the Black Oath. Imposed by proclamation on all Scots in Ulster over sixteen except Roman Catholics, the signees to the oath not only abjured the Covenant but promised abjectly to defend and maintain royal power and authority. This of course excluded the Antrim MacDonnells, serving only to increase presbyterian bitterness against Wentworth. In 1640, England was invaded by the Covenanters (as it was in 1644, 1648 and 1651), and with the outbreak of the native Irish rising in Ulster in 1641 – to which Scotland sent an army in the spring of 1642 – Covenanting resources were deployed in all three kingdoms. Mainly in recognition of the Royalist threat supported by the Earl of Antrim, in 1643 the alliance with the English parliamentarians was enshrined in the Solemn League and Covenant, which made provision for the continuation of the Reformed faith in Scotland and for the reformation of religion in England and Ireland. Failing to attract any support in England for a new invasion of Scotland, in mid-August 1644 Montrose returned to Scotland in disguise in an attempt to organise a new Scottish Royalist rising, or to join the force which the newly created Marquess of Antrim had sent from Ireland. The Royalist cause was temporarily salvaged by this Irish force (brought across two months earlier by Alasdair MacColla MacDonald), but it ultimately fell to the Covenanters at Philiphaugh on 13 September 1645.[9] The whole decade was one of political, military, religious and economic change, which was characterised by much personal and community upheaval.

When parliamentary forces took Dublin in the summer of 1647, the Directory of Worship – essentially a presbyterian form of church order and discipline – was enforced on the clergy there in place of the Book of Common Prayer and Established Church ceremonial.[10] But although they had sought to limit his prerogative powers, many presbyterians in Ireland and Scotland were nevertheless stunned by Charles' execution on 30 January 1649.[11] With England already in his grip, Cromwell set about reducing the rest of Eire: making for Ireland in 1649, he attacked Royalist and rebel forces in Drogheda and Wexford in September and October, where he succeeded in breaking the severest resistance, although fighting continued for another two years in Ulster and Connacht. At this point, the Long Parliament insisted on the use of the Directory of Worship throughout the country, as well as making plans for the introduction of a presbyterian form of church government as outlined in 'The form of church government to be used in the church of England and Ireland' which had been instituted in England in 1648. Although it was never legally enacted in Ireland, the Church of Ireland was none the less effectively disestablished. On the failure of the Royalist cause in Ireland, Charles II took refuge with the Scots, disowning in 1650 the treaty made earlier by Ormond, lieutenant-general of his Irish army, with the Catholic Confederates. With the King in Scotland, Cromwell was obliged to send an army to defend the Commonwealth; the Scottish army suffered defeat in 1650 at the battle of Dunbar. The Kirk subsequently split into Resolutioners and Protesters (the former Royalists and the latter protesting against participants in the Engagement of 1647–48)[12] fighting a righteous war against Cromwell. Following the battle of Worcester in 1651 and the defeat of Charles II's forces, Cromwell reigned supreme in all three countries. A hindrance to the King's cause, the rift in the Kirk resulted in the association of all presbyterians with subversiveness in the mind of Charles II, and their consequent exclusion from taking part in formulating the ecclesiastical settlement at the Restoration.[13]

Many presbyterians refused to take the Engagement in 1652 – a somewhat ironically styled (in view of the 1647–48 Engagement) oath of loyalty to the

Commonwealth – and so life was difficult for Irish presbyterians in the first years of Cromwellian rule. This, and the actions of the council of war against the ministers, forced substantial numbers of them to leave Ireland in 1653, although apparently none ended up in the Highlands.[14] In Scotland, intelligence of a Royalist conspiracy had come to light by February 1653: Lilburne, acting commander-in-chief of the English army in Scotland, was concerned about the formation of subversive links between Royalists in Ulster and the Western Isles, as was the Council of State, which ordered boats to patrol the sea between them.[15] A plan was even drawn up in May of that year to remove 'all the popular Scotts' from Ulster (which included those known for their Royalist and presbyterian sympathies) to areas of Munster, though it was never executed.

The Royalist standard, tentatively supported by some Resolutioners, was again raised in August 1653 by the Earl of Glencairn, who landed in the west Highlands to mobilise a force of 5,000 men mainly from Atholl and Lochaber; but although the force was in arms for a year, with one major success at Dumbarton, in the absence of continental aid it eventually dispersed.[16] With Cromwellian religious toleration, the number of presbyterian congregations in Ulster grew from twenty-four in 1653 to eighty just a few years later. Acting under commission of the presbytery, by 1659 the meetings of Down, Antrim, the Route, Lagan and Tyrone were additionally constituted to deal with the expansion.[17] In 1655, the lot of Irish presbyterians was assisted by Henry Cromwell's implementation of an arrangement, first proposed under his predecessor, Lord Deputy Fleetwood, for paying ministers' salaries direct from the state. Declining at first, presbyterian ministers insisted that they would rather retain their parish tithes, but ultimately the arrangement seems to have worked well, ushering in a period of presbyterian growth in Ulster. State salaries were accepted by a Highlander in southern Ireland and by another in Ulster.

When it became clear, on the accession of Richard Cromwell as Protector in 1658, that the monarchy must be re-established, ironically it was Scottish Resolutioner ministers who first communicated the idea to George Monck, the commander of the parliamentary army in Scotland, and principal noblemen. Under Monck's protection, many presbyterians returned to parliament, arranging for the erection of a new parliament in April 1660. Faithfully renewing the Solemn League and Covenant, they set about deciding the terms on which the King might be restored. James Sharp (later archbishop of St. Andrews) was sent to plead the Resolutioner cause to Charles II at Breda in Holland. However, mainly due to the machinations of Monck and the Scottish nobles, Charles II was invited to resume the crown as a hereditary right, in the absence of constitutional limitation; it soon became clear that the Covenant would be discarded. In spite of their hand in his restoration, conditions under the King did not prove favourable to presbyterianism.[18]

The new parliament showed itself anti-puritan; the nobility blatantly indicated their support for an episcopal church. In Scotland, the Earl of Middleton, fired both by political ambition and a desire to destroy a presbyterian system by which he had been publicly humiliated, effected the restoration of episcopacy and the erastianism so abhorred by presbyterians. Passed on 28 March 1661, the Act Rescissory withdrew all legal guarantees of presbytery; it was closely followed by the Act Concerning Religion and Church Government, which placed the decision on the form of church government firmly in the King's hands. Furthermore, a series of statutes passed in the summer of 1662 revived lay patronage, declared the Covenants unlawful and proscribed conventicles. Presbyterians in Scotland once again entered the ranks of nonconformists. Isolated areas of the Highlands continued to be used as a repository for politically suspect, substandard or rejected presbyterians.[19] In Ireland, the Church of Ireland was re-established after the Interregnum, and the King began nominating to the bishoprics as early as August 1660. The climate was no longer so favourable to presbyterians. After the hierarchy was restored in January 1661, steps were taken to deal with presbyterianism, by then a powerful force in Ulster.[20] Their separate jurisdictional arrangements intimidated the state which, in January 1661, forbade meetings of presbytery at the same time as the episcopate took action against its ministers for failing to be ordained by bishops. Sixty-one ministers were deposed; only seven conformed.[21]

Scottish ministers who refused the indulgences of 1669 and 1672 (allowing dissenting presybterians to continue in their parishes) fuelled the conventicling movement. A Highland Host was therefore quartered on the disaffected western districts in 1678 as a means of repressing the movement, while fear that the dissenters would rebel led to the alerting of forces in England and Ireland. Rising Covenanting dissent (under a progressively more repressive régime) culminated in the rout at Bothwell Brig in 1679 at the hands of the Duke of Monmouth.[22] In Ireland, the ministers were more or less left alone except when Blood's Plot – a revolutionary attempt in 1663 by some Cromwellians in the south of Ireland – implicated a couple of presbyterian ministers in Ulster with whom their secret had been shared. The ministers' imprisonment and banishment from Ulster brought renewed suspicion upon the faith.[23] However, from October 1672 the presbyterians became recipients of a grant of £600 sterling from the King – the *Regium Donum* – which was paid until 1869; this at least gave some state recognition to the economic and social status of presbyterians in Ulster. But it did not stop the bishops occasionally perpetrating campaigns of persecution, particularly in Donegal, where presbyterianism had been long established in communities with deep-rooted Highland connections (and was therefore a threat on two counts), between 1681 and 1684.[24] At least one Highland minister fled to another charge in Ireland because of this.

In Scotland, attitudes changed markedly during the administration of the Catholic Duke of York, who in 1681 implemented the Act of Succession and the Test Act. These not only required acceptance of the royal supremacy but implied the eventual succession of a Catholic. Refusing to take the Test, the ninth Earl of Argyll rose in rebellion for Monmouth in 1685 and was ultimately executed, resulting in the departure of some of his supporters to enrich the presybterian communities of Ulster. A number of Campbells escaped to Ireland with the assistance of Angus Campbell, a Harris merchant who traded between Ireland, the Clyde and Argyll.[25] James VII and II's burning desire to extend toleration to Catholics on his accession in 1685 effectively meant that in April 1687 presbyterians were also relieved from persecution. But they were as alarmed as the Churches of Scotland and Ireland at the power then being wielded by Catholics. Hence they gave full support to James' daughter Mary, and to her husband, the Protestant William of Orange, when they were invited to ascend the thrones of England and Scotland at the tail end 1688 and in the spring of 1689 respectively.[26]

The Irish in Scotland from Civil War to Restoration

The civil war in Ireland, which began as a rising of the native Irish against the plantation, had a significant effect on the southern Highlands, particularly Argyll: substantial military levies were raised from the lay peoples of Argyll, and numbers of their ministers were removed to act as army chaplains. The Kirk had precious little need of this extra burden while it was still struggling to fill its own vacancies, which demonstrates the immense importance of victory for the Covenanting forces to the Kirk and to the house of Argyll. The fear of Royalist invasion from Ireland was felt keenly in Argyll as early as the summer of 1638 when, on 2 August, Lord Lorne called a meeting of the barons and gentlemen of the shire to arrange musters and wapinshaws; a Campbell-dominated committee of defence emerged. Both the King's encouragement of Antrim's plans for a Royalist alliance in the Western Highlands and the death of Archibald Campbell, seventh Earl of Argyll, in the autumn of 1638 contributed to Lorne (now the eighth Earl of Argyll) declaring for the Covenanters against his clan's traditional enemies. Continuing the fortification of his defences, he bought a fully armed frigate and other weapons in the Netherlands.[27] Irish Royalists were equally perturbed about a Covenanting invasion from Scotland. To that end, the Earl of Strafford, the Irish Lord Deputy, disarmed the Scots (and puritans in general) in 1639 by forbidding powder or arms to be kept in their houses, except what was allowed them from the King's stores in Dublin. By the following year, he was considering the rather extreme action of banishing all Scots from Ulster. On the reassembly of parliament, Strafford planned to recommend the transportation of all Scots lest they join forces with the Covenanters in Scotland, or in case Argyll invaded Ireland, placed himself at the head of the presbyterians there and organised an insurrection – 'and God forbid they should tarry there till the Earl of Argyle brings them armies to cut our throats, to our apparent disturbance, if not certain ruin'.[28]

Neither side's fears proved groundless. The records fully reveal the extent to which traditional MacDonald–Campbell antagonism was a factor in the devastation wrought by Alasdair MacColla's Irish and Highland contingents on the lands of Argyll between 1644 and 1647. Protestant apprehension of Royalist military reprisal is illustrated by a Remonstrance of 22 September 1646 'concerning the oppressed people of Argyle to be presented to the Committee of Estates'. Alluding to the presence of Irish priests and friars in the Isles, it recorded:

> We do easily believe that quhen they (the Romish party) have seen their hopes cut off amongst the more understanding that they have thought best to dryve their designe in these places quhair there is les knowledge and zeale, and from thence by their means to propagat it southward, untill they have made a prey of us quhom they have long hunted for.[29]

Solidarity was also sought from the Ulster presbytery, as shown in a letter to the brethren in Ireland from the Commission of the General Assembly, acquainting them with the proceedings for August and September 1647: 'We also exhort yow, dear brethren, to keip good correspondence with the army there, sieing they are scarse of ministers to attend them. Wherever they have any randevouse, or wher officers meitt for publick consultations, it wer fitt some of your number be present to blesse their meitings, consultations, and proceidings.'[30]

Back-up missionary action was organised in those areas of Scotland thought to be sympathetic to the native Irish. For instance, when the synod of Argyll met in late May 1642, Mr Alan Clerk was 'injoyned to serve in preacheing and celebrating the sacraments and especially in catechising in Knudort', the extant record showing that since it began in 1639 there had been no Protestant evangelising in that area at all . In the following year, 1643, Mr Neill Cameron spent the 'summer season in preaching to the men of Lochabber'.[31] However, there were some presbyterian ministers who were simply naturally inclined to the Royalist cause. Indeed, ministers in Gaelic-speaking congregations were in general more sympathetic to the Royalist cause and likely to be more generously received by the 'rebels'.[32]

Moral support was also exhorted from those who remained at home. Obstacles and social difficulties were regarded by the presbyterians as signals of the wrath of God; fasts were frequently called for to atone for misdeeds and for the related success of their cause in Ireland. In May 1644, the synod of Argyll

> ordained that throw this whole province shall be keept a publict humiliation and fast for the procureing of Gods' blessing and assistance as to all our armies abroad both in England and Ireland, so for a good and happy success to my Lord Marquesse of Argyll in this his expedition against those who made insurrection in the north pairts of his kingdome.[33]

But is it significant that the army presbytery in Ulster did not authorise any fasts between 1645 and 1648? The army there was not blessed with overwhelming success, so this seems somewhat strange in presbyterian terms. It has been suggested that it was because the ministers responsible for setting fast regarded Ireland as peripheral to the Covenanters' concerns.[34] Yet, while the immediacy of invasion from Ireland had receded after the Bishops' Wars, it could scarcely be implied – with the continuation of Royalist resistance under MacColla until the summer of 1647 – that Ireland was a backwater.[35]

Scottish Ministerial Collaborators

The Scottish records are replete with tales of Gaelic ministers who exhibited an obvious cultural, even political, affinity for the native Irish and Royalist cause during the civil war.[36] Their very existence shows that it was not simply Catholic priests who attended the Irish and Gaelic-speaking Royalist populations. Their ranks probably included people of ambiguous religious affiliation who were simply looking for spiritual succour of almost any description; there were clearly numbers of Gaelic-speaking nominal presbyterians in Montrose's army who were less interested in the niceties of religion than in a common cultural heritage and the maintenance and acquisition of territory and political power. This takes on far greater significance considering that the army actually travelled with its own Irish Catholic priests; in addition, it acquired the services of Jesuits already in the north-east of Scotland.[37] Obviously, Protestant ministers were specifically called for. The synod of Argyll addressed itself in 1646 to the excommunication of various Islesmen who had aligned 'themselves in actuall rebellion with these cruell, insolent and barbarous enemies of this Kirk and Kingdom under the command of these bluidy and excommunicat traitors James Graham and Alexander McDonald'.[38] (For the extent of the synod's jurisdiction and location of the few presbyteries operating within it in the 1640s, see Fig. 3.1.)

About half of the culturally sympathetic ministers came from those areas reclaimed for Catholicism by the first Franciscan mission; the rest came from Sutherland and Caithness. The minister of Ardnamurchan and Eilean Finnan, Duncan MacCalman, was deposed in 1644 for complicity with Alasdair MacColla; subsequently excommunicated on 1 May 1650, his sentence was rescinded after 10 July 1672 when he was restored to the parish.[39] But the duration of his excommunication, compared with others who had their

Fig. 3.1. Synods and presbyteries in the 1640s.

sentences rescinded within the same decade, is indicative of the immense suspicion under which he was held. Here, the way in which he conducted himself in his early ministry gives a clue. He initially ingratiated himself with his congregation, none of whom came to his kirk when he first arrived, by joining in with a crowd which had gathered at the side of the church to 'putt the stane'. Capitalising on his athletic build to appeal to traditional Celtic esteem for a strong man, he thereby gained their respect and so filled his church,[40] showing that an attitude of accommodation and cultural integration could succeed where Calvinist austerity had not.

During the gradual demise of the Gaelic learned tradition in the sixteenth and seventeenth centuries, the tendency of some of the hereditary Gaelic literati to redeploy their talents in the clerical area is a feature which must be taken into account in any study of religion in the Highlands and Islands. Hereditary ecclesiastical families during this period included the MacQueens in Skye, the MacLachlans of Kilbride and the MacCalmans in Lorn, the Omeys of Kintyre and Lorn, and the Martins or MacMartins and the MacArthurs, both from Skye, most of whom are on record from the fifteenth century. The Beatons of Skye, latterly a medical family, were also transferring to and infiltrating the Kirk during this period. By the mid-seventeenth century, the MacLachlans were particularly well represented, with six ministers in Argyll and elders in a similar number of congregations. But in the Scoto-Irish Gaelic context, it is the MacCalmans of Lorn who loom large.[41]

Duncan MacCalman's case unravels as follows in the presbyterian record. In May 1650, the presbytery of Lorn drew the synod's attention to a Mr Duncan MacCalman, sometime minister of Ardnamurchan who had been excommunicated when Alasdair MacColla landed from Ireland in July 1644 'for complyance with and preacheing to the rebells'. But this ecclesiastical sanction carried little clout with the people to whom he ministered, where he continued 'dayly in the barbarouse and remote highlands [to] baptize children and mary pairties comeing to him for that effect'.[42] As in most cases in which the synod was unable to do anything to inhibit contrary behaviour, it appealed to the Marquess of Argyll to apprehend and punish him, declaring in passing that any services performed by MacCalman were invalid and that those knowingly resorting to him were to be excommunicated, too. Whether Argyll deliberately stayed his hand (as Mactavish suggests in the introduction to the synod minutes), or whether he simply did not consider the case of much import, MacCalman remained on the run. Indeed, the synod's somewhat puerile insistence that all services performed by him were to be declared invalid only served to store up future difficulties for the synod itself: some couples who had been married by MacCalman and since repented the action were then able to see a perfectly legal redress for their mistakes.[43] An illegal marriage was unratified, not solemnised according to the order of the Kirk,[44] and therefore might conveniently be dissolved. Consequently, the synod had to send visiting ministers to those areas where MacCalman had been working in order to ratify marriages. Their duty fulfilled, they proceeded to minute their abhorrence of MacCalman and of 'his scandalous cariage as being a drunkard and runagat excommunicat non-minister', and called upon the civil authorities to deal with him.[45]

But was MacCalman's main crime not simply that he exercised 'ministeriall dewties in Lochabour, Ardgour, Shunart and Ardnamurchy, and in thes places where the word is not preached'? There is little indication that he went to the Irish army in any other capacity than a minister visiting those in need of spiritual succour. In May 1656, in a report which stated that the clan élite were engaged in recovering those 'perverted' by Vincentian priests, MacCalman was classed along with notorious recusants: 'there are in the Iles severall excommunicat persones, such as Captans Clanrannald elder and younger, and Mr Duncane mc Calman with divers others'.[46] In the same year, MacCalman's ministerial duties were apparently so constrained by his excommunication that he supplicated for relaxation 'from that fearfull sentence', which hardly attests to Catholic sympathies on his part. By way of reparation, and doubtless to engineer his future obedience to their authority in such matters, it was ordained that 'he goe and repaire to the severall ministers of Argyll and Lorn who are to confer with him and bring him to farther lenth of his sence of his horrid guiltenes and sins and to bring along with him ane testimoniall from one minister to another of his cariage and obedience, and to have all thes to be presented to the next synod be himself'.[47]

That MacCalman had the humility to go along with this surely demonstrates the extent of his inner spirituality. He tested his steadfastness to the cause over more than twenty years of trial, which is surely proof enough, were it needed, that he considered himself a Calvinist (though not necessarily a presbyterian), but one who felt comfortable with the traditional values of Gaelic society. Ultimately, it is the synod's arrogance which is least attractive.

Others, too, were deposed for complicity with the rebels. John Darroch, admitted to the parish of Jura or Kilearnadail in 1635, and minister there at the erection of the synod of Argyll on 24 April 1639, was deposed on 1 September 1646 'for preaching to and gross compliance with the rebels'. Darroch remained in Islay for the duration of the rebellion, except for two short spells away. Confessing in the following year, 1649, to contact with the rebels, he also told of an attempt by the Campbells to regain Islay when Matthew Campbell, Captain of Skipness, landed there with Argyll's regiment on its way back to Ireland after the battle of Inverlochy. This attempted invasion can probably be dated to April and May of 1646, but it failed; MacDonald of Clanranald disembarked to drive the Campbells out. Archibald MacAllister, minister of Kilchoman in Islay, was suspended on 11 October 1648 for having conversed with the Royalists. In his favour, it was argued that since he was on an island distant from the mainland, 'he was evidently surprised by the enemies coming, and was forced to converse with them', a course of action that was compounded by the fact 'that his whole congregation turned rebels'.[48] Farquhar Fraser, minister of Tiree, which comprised the three parishes of Kirkapool, Sorobie and Coll, was also debarred from his charge and lost his stipend for becoming a preacher in Sir Lachlan MacLean's regiment in 1645. As a consequence, he was plundered by Campbell of Ardnamurchan.[49]

The Argyll synod, sitting in October 1648, recorded the confession of Mr Martin MacIlvory, found guilty of providing services to MacLean of Duart's regiment, which was undoubtedly as a consequence of connections he had made during previous incumbencies in Mull. Since 1626 he had worked mainly in Gaelic-speaking areas like Tiree and Coll, Killean or Torosay, and Kilfinichen in Mull, and finally transferred to Iona in November 1643. Recapping the events of the previous three years, he confessed that when Sir Lachlan MacLean decided to join Montrose and MacColla, raising his men in arms in April 1645 to march to Lochaber, MacIlvory 'went along with the people, being threatened to go by Sir Lachlan'. The synod added wryly, and probably with no small degree of justification, 'as he alleadges'. Excommunicated at the time for this action, MacIlvory's activities had not been curbed; he confessed 'that he preached and prayed to Sir Lachlan two severall tymes after he was excommunicat, once in Icollumkill and Rodill in the north yles'. Further, Sir Lachlan had compelled him to leave Mull in December 1645 to attend the rebel army when MacColla was in Kilmore in Lorn; he 'remained three nights with them and took Alister be the hand'. Asked 'how it cam to passe that mc Claines and their men, being all on the course of the rebellion against the Covenant, religion and the kingdome, did suffer this deponent peaceably to dwell at home and possesse his goods and lands, whillas they burnt and destroyed their neighbour ministers of that presbyterie and province', MacIlvory answered, somewhat naively, 'that it was God's good providence and the love they had to have the gospell continued within their bounds'.[50]

Still ministering to the forces with Sir Lachlan in the summer of 1647, MacIlvory went with them to the north isles, although he had been 'long before excommunicat, and did eat and drink and said grace to him for the space of fifteine dayes'. Clearly in the confidence of the Royalist forces, he confessed to seeing the 'Earle of Antrom and Alister mc Donald at Dowart after their return from yland Tirim and conversed with them'. Hardly surprising, in the light of such evidence, that MacIlvory's pleas that he did all this under compulsion held little weight; on 11 November 1648, he was deposed from his office and benefice for complying with the rebels.[51] However, his sin cannot have been considered particularly, heinous because his sentence was reponed by the General Assembly in August 1649. Instead, he was simply kept outside the recognised presbyterian pale, returning in 1650 as minister for Ardnamurchan, an unpopular marginal parish.[52] Cases such as MacIlvory's are interesting for the light they throw on the sometimes irreconcilable marriage of religious, political and cultural stances in this period. MacIlvory and his like may have been committed Calvinists, but the presbyterian establishment found the association with their traditionalist Gaelic countrymen untenable, because to them such contact smacked more of politically incorrect Royalism than presbyterian evangelism.

Another cultural collaborator who can also be linked with particular rebels is Mr Murdo MacKenzie, the ministerial agent of the Earl of Seaforth. The postscript of a letter to the General Assembly from the synod of Argyll stated on 21 September 1646 that 'We ar certanly informed from the rebellis quarters, by diverse reports and letters, that there is one Mr. Murdoch M'Keinyie hes latlie come towards Antrum from the North, and, as is reported, is negotiating with him and Alester M'Donald in name of the Earle of Seafort'. Though this does not identify MacKenzie as a minister, the same record refers elsewhere to the deposition of 'Mr. Murdo M'Kenyie, minister at Suddie and Mr. Coline M'Kenyie, minister at Contoun [Contin]', in the presbyteries of Chanonry and Dingwall in Ross, confessing to fraternising with the rebels.[53] The postscript also revealed that the synod had received a missive 'shewing that the rebellis were to remove, if not already removed, towards Ila, quhair ther is a great feast prepared for them, and thence intends for Ardnimurchan; quhairas they make the people that ar joyned with them persuaded that Seafort, M'Laine, Captane of Clan Ronald, and Sir James M'Donald ar to meit them'. The synod singled out MacKenzie for the crime of cajoling: 'and Mr. Murdoch M'Keinyies being with them does confirme the people the more to believe the same, so that many that wer of purpose to come off ar resolved to adhere to them.'[54]

Another minister, Ewen Cameron of Dunoon parish, exemplifies the preferential treatment received by some Gaelic-speaking ministers at the hands of the Royalists. Cameron, who was later, in 1649, one of the translators into Gaelic of the *Shorter Catechism* and *A Brief Sum of Christian Doctrine*, had a promise of protection from Montrose, dated 20 August 1645. Compelled to leave his parish during the rebellion, 'having neither congregation or maintenance', he returned there in October 1648.[55]

Supreme among the collaborators of this period was Ranald MacDonald who, according to the Catholic record, was the ex-minister of South Uist.[56] He first appears in the presbyterian record at the meeting of the provincial synod of Argyll in May 1643, which notes that 'Ronald mcRonald, priest', had been apprehended at the hands of the Marquess of Argyll and brought, at its request, to the General Assembly in Edinburgh. The Assembly found him 'so grossly ignorant that they cannot accept of any acknowledgment and confession from him untill he be bettir informed, And therefore does ordaine him to study diligently to understand the errors of his bygone profession'. Exactly what level of Calvinist knowledge had he attained prior to his 'conversion' by the Franciscans, or was the synod referring merely to the error of his current Catholic conviction? Argyll himself stood caution for MacDonald's next appearance at the synod, when 'he was fund not to be strongly grounded in his profession, neither very able to cleare himselfe to the satisfaction of others that he was resolved of his doubts as he alleadged'.[57] His character is possibly most transparently revealed in the statement of the brethren appointed to assess him, who insisted:

> Neither did they perceive that ever he had any considerable measure of knowledge or affection to the religion he professed formerly, but that the weightiest principle that did allure him from the beginning to the renunceing of his own religion, and embraceing of popery, was the want of maintenance, being out of this countrey and the Colledge of Douai offering him free sustentation, and now he was come to a compunction of heart for that that principall should have prevailed so strongly with him.[58]

If anything, MacDonald was an outright opportunist. That he was supported, according to the Protestant record, by the Scots College at Douai is worth noting, when the Catholic record insists that MacDonald was refused a place there.[59] But he did not attract anything like the respect accorded to the Irish Franciscans. Ward wrote in 1637 that many of the Catholics had had to go without confession until he visited them, because they had no priest of their own except Ranald MacDonald. Rather ironically, in view of his repeated apostacy, MacDonald apparently visited the islanders to strengthen their faith, and he secretly administered the sacraments to them now and again. But he was said to be greatly constrained by his poverty – that old missionary chestnut – since the islanders were unable to support MacDonald as well as the minister, to whom the law compelled them to pay tithes. And surprisingly little came of 'the patrimony of a well-born relative' – MacDonald of Clanranald – which he was supposed to enjoy after his ordination.[60] MacDonald's subsequent conversion to Protestantism for a second time probably masked a desire to secure legal funding.

In 1643, the synod of Argyll allocated a third of the rent of the kirk at Snizort in Skye to MacDonald. But MacDonald clearly had a deep-rooted sympathy for the Royalist cause, and by May 1650 he had incredibly changed his allegiance yet again. MacDonald may indeed have reverted to Catholicism through contact with Montrose's chaplains, but on the other hand the synod may simply have regarded his political position as so untenable that it felt unable to continue supporting him.[61] The Assembly ordained 'Ranald mc Ranald, who hes diverse tymes before jugled in his religion and profession, and now since the late rebellion is become apostate and a preist, to be sumarily excommunicat be the presbyterie of Sky'. The synod summarised his fickle career: not only had he previously renounced papacy, he had even subscribed to the Covenant; he was (in some way) actively involved 'in the late rebellion', possibly only in a ministerial capacity but, considering his most singular character, very possibly bearing arms. However, like many dispossessed ministers he continued his spiritual ministrations, albeit now under a Catholic guise; notwithstanding his excommunication, he was 'still laboureing to pervert poore ignorant people in the pairts where he hants in the yle of Uist and other pairts of the farre yles to the dishonour of God and ruine of poore soules'.[62]

It was not only Irish priests who came to Scotland: there is some evidence of a transfer, if only partly expedited, of Irish-speaking ministers across the North Channel. With the immense social upheaval and reorganisation occasioned by the Irish civil war, ministers found themselves looking for new parishes when they and their parishioners were compelled to flee. On 20 August 1646, the Commissioners of the General Assembly considered a question from the synod of Moray, within whose jurisdiction was a sizeable area of the Highlands. It obediently requested guidance on the influx of ministers from Ireland. 'What sall be done with ministers coming from Ireland, who having the testimoniall of tuo ministers coming from thence at the same time, that they were actuall ministers ther and forced to flie, in regaird of the persecutione, that they could bring no further testimoniall with them?' It asked whether they should be considered expectants or fully fledged ministers. The Assembly wisely advocated caution, lest the upheaval be used by those less scrupulous to gain gratuitous employment. 'The Presbitrie may admitt such to preach as expectants, and therafter according to the order of the Kirk upon lawfull calling and due tryell they may be admitted actually to the ministrie.'[63] There is no indication as to whether those who came were Gaelic-speaking, but there may have been a connection with the vast numbers of Scots said to have left the region between Inverness and Aberdeen in the 1630s.[64]

In October 1649, on the other hand, the synod of Argyll, 'considereing the pitifull condition of thir bounds for want of ministers', had extended a search abroad for those with the Irish language. The list of six ministers and expectants that it came up with included 'Mr Jeremie O Queine' (or O'Queen, Aquin, O'Cronie, O'Quin[n], O'Cahan or Ognitie), the Irish presbyterian minister of Billy. Brought to the attention of the Commission of the General Assembly by the presbytery of Carrickfergus on 1 June 1649, O'Quinn was renowned for his republican (Cromwellian) sympathies.[65] A Gaelic-speaking native Irishman, O'Quinn had studied in Glasgow, from where he graduated in 1644,[66] thereby continuing a tradition established by several Protestant (prescopalian) ministers in the first decade of the seventeenth century.[67] Brought up at Templepatrick in Antrim as the protégé of Mr Upton of Castle Upton, O'Quinn was 'one of the first-fruits of Irish Presbyterianism' and of inestimable value as a convert from Roman Catholicism. He was still an expectant on 31 October 1646, although he had begun preaching in Billy but was not ordained to the charge until late in 1646 or early in 1647.[68] O'Quinn was sufficiently well-established just a few years later as to be known by name in the Gaelic-speaking Highlands.[69]

The synod of Argyll extended its search for Gaelic-speaking ministers far and wide, stipulating in October 1649 that all ministers and expectants be written to and 'invited to this province'; O'Quinn, however, was singled out for special mention: 'in particular that Mr Jeremie O Queen may be pleased to answer the call of Inneraray'.[70] That he was offered the prize of Inveraray is a testament to his bilingualism, but it also shows that the synod, unlike the presbytery of Carrickfergus, was not at all threatened by his political affiliations. Indeed, the knowledge that Mr O'Quinn was unpopular with his own presbytery probably encouraged them. After all, O'Quinn was nominally a presbyterian, and the puritan sectarianism of the Cromwellians was marginally more acceptable than either Roman Catholicism or fully fledged Royalism.

In June 1649, the General Assembly considered letters from the Carrickfergus presbytery and from Mr James Ker, minister of Ballymoney and a graduate of Edinburgh University who had appealed for its support.[71] The presbytery had even sent a representative, Mr Thomas Hall, to Scotland, serving to underline the symbiotic relationship of the Irish presbyterians at this time with the Scottish Kirk.[72] The General Assembly plainly related the presbytery's displeasure at the failure by O'Quinn and Ker to read out a representation from the presbytery of Carrickfergus 'because of severall objections ... against severall things therein contained'. This refers to a petition entitled 'A necessary representation of the present evils and eminent dangers to religion, laws and liberties arising from the late and present practices of the sectarian party in England', which denounced the execution of Charles I and emphasised the strong position presbyterians felt that they were in in Ulster. Betraying Royalist sympathies, it explains why O'Quinn was considered eminently suitable for Inveraray. Although O'Quinn and Kerr also condemned the 'judicial murder' of the King, they objected to the representation's condemnation of the excesses of the English army and the 'purging' of the House of Commons.[73] Upholding the presbytery's censure, the Assembly none the less declared that if they submitted, the ministers were to be permitted to continue their ministry. It also drew attention to the ministers' political responsibility, urging them to pray in order that they 'be enabled to discerne the times', so that 'as faithfull watchmen, yee may give warning of all dangers'.[74] But although suspended by the Carrickfergus presbytery, there is no evidence to suggest that O'Quinn ever took up the position at Inveraray.[75]

However, this uneasy alliance between some Ulster presbyterians and the Stuart king in exile potentially rocked the stability of the three kingdoms.

Colonel Venables, independent governor of Carrickfergus, therefore attempted to coax presbyterian ministers round to the new régime. When he failed either to coax or coerce them into taking the Engagement – the oath of loyalty to the Commonwealth – a plan was cooked up to transplant those ministers and other influential presbyterian families in Ulster to Munster.[76] The following reasons for the prospective removal were proclaimed:

> Whereas the right honourable the commissioners of the commonwealth of England have commissioned us, for the settling and securing of these parts from those disturbances which the council of state did intimate unto them were like to arise here through the designs of the neighbouring highlanders in Scotland, and whereas, many persons here have (to our grief) too much confirmed these fears; in discharge of that trust reposed in us, that the good people here of the English and Scottish nation, who have manifested their good affection towards the present government, might receive all due protection and encouragement; we have thought fit, as the most probable expedient for the peace and settlement of this province, to transplant a certain number of such persons as we judge (by reason of their interest and disaffection) to be therein most dangerous, into the province of Leinster and Munster.

This plan hints at the probable underestimation of the extent of Highland emigration to Ulster during the plantation due to official unwillingness to recognise Highland settlement by denization. A list of the prospective 260 transplantees reveals some Highland names, notably five Campbells (three of whom have military designations), a MacClee, a M'Kerger, a Corporal MacCormick and an Ensign Cormick, a MacColpin, three Fergusons (all with military designations), a Captain Macbride, a Lieutenant MacIlroy, three Donnelsons, two MacDougalls, a M'Clelland, a M'Philip and a M'Ferson, but the list is predominantly Lowland in flavour. However, mainly because of the establishment of the Protectorate in the same year, 1653, the project did not progress beyond sending some leading members of the presbyterian community to stake out the land.[77] In the event, this radical step was to be unnecessary; the Commonwealth negotiated a compromise with the Scottish presbyterian ministers instead, under which (as will be seen below) they received a salary from the government in return for their support.[78]

The usual direction of flight for ministerial refugees during this period was from Scotland to Ireland, but on occasion it went in the opposite direction. On 5 May 1658, the presbytery of Kintyre

> being crediblie informed that Mr Adam Ritchie was deposed at leist suspended by the presbitrie quhairin he lived in Irland, from exercing the ministeriall function, and that because of his scandalous cariage of tipling drinking & otherwayes, and sieing that now constantlie he resideth within yla exercing all the pairts of the ministeriall calling The presbrie therfor appoynteth that the said Mr Adam Ritchie be suspended fra the exercise of the ministrie in yla or

> any other pairt within their bounds, ay and quhill he bring a sufficient testimoniall.[79]

The name Ritchie – in some cases, a curtailment of MacRitchie as is most likely here – is common in the Borders and on the Highland periphery, where it is particularly associated with Perthshire.[80] It is unlikely that Ritchie would have been tolerated in Islay without the Gaelic language. While he probably chose Islay for its appeal as a social backwater, anyone prepared to minister to an island with a large, traditionally inclined Gaelic-speaking population would have received a warm welcome. More colourfully put in relation to the Established Church's attitude to the Highlands as a whole in around 1690, 'the Highland area in general was for the presbyterians something of a *damnosa hereditas*'. And although the presbyterians were back at the helm by this time, there is little to indicate that this had been any less the view of the episcopalians. Indeed, the introduction of low-calibre Gaelic ministers during the episcopal period may have paved the way for the Highland region's emergence as a presbyterian dumping ground both for the Restoration and post-Revolution churches alike. But there is no further evidence during the Restoration period of any incursions into the Highlands by Irish ministers displaced from Ulster. Conversely, there was a noticeable movement to Ireland by Highland ministers during and after the civil war.

Highland Ministers in Ireland

With the establishment of a presbyterian régime in Scotland at the end of 1638 and the implementation of compulsory subscription to the Covenant, it might be asked what happened to those episcopal clerics who did not conform. At least eight fled to the sanctuary of the (episcopal) Church of Ireland.[81] It was almost inevitable that John Maxwell, a presentee of Charles I to the bishopric of Ross in 1633 and a close friend of Archbishop Laud, should be forced to flee to England in March 1639 to seek protection from the King. He did not return to Scotland but was deposed, excommunicated and indicted for treason before parliament. The King, however, promoted him to the Irish bishopric of Killala and Achenry in Connacht in October 1640. But having escaped the Covenanters, providence ultimately caught up with Maxwell, who was attacked by Catholics during the 1641 rebellion and left for dead. He recovered to be appointed archbishop of the adjacent bishopric of Tuam (also in Connacht) in August 1645, where he remained until his death in Dublin in February 1647. John MacKenzie, minister of Urray and Tarradale in the recently formed presbytery of Dingwall was similarly deposed for opposition to the Covenant in 1639. Having fled to England in the first place, he then transferred to Ireland where he remained until the civil war commenced. Ultimately reponed in April 1643 by the synod of Ross, he became minister of Suddie in the following year.[82] But if the effect of ousted Highland clergy on the Church of Ireland was minimal, the impact of Highland ministers on the growth of presbyterianism in Ulster was far more significant.

The revitalisation (if not re-establishment) of presbyterianism in Ulster must be firmly laid at the door of the Covenanting army. For although at least sixteen crypto-presbyterian (prescopalian) ministers conformed and remained in Ulster in the early days of the rising, they were all in Scotland by the spring of 1642. Under the army's auspices, the 'General Eldership' or 'Common Ecclesiastic-Judicatory' – the first (albeit army) presbytery under the jurisdiction of the Scottish General Assembly – was established in Carrickfergus, County Antrim in 1642. The army played an absolutely vital role in protecting presbyterianism, although it exacted heavy tolls in quartering: it created a safe zone for ministers to work in by pressing the Irish into isolated garrisons at a distance from presbyterian parishes in Antrim and Down and, additionally, by quartering outwith those two counties. Further, renewed enthusiasm was brought to the cause by the administering of the Solemn League and Covenant in 1644, and by the apparent repentance of many episcopal ministers and those who had taken the Black Oath in 1639. In 1645, presbyterian authority was officially sanctioned when the presbyterian clergy were allowed the tithes of their parishes by the English parliamentary commissioners; the Carrickfergus army presbytery was also given jurisdiction over all Ulster, including civilians (essentially settlers) in Antrim and Down. Indeed, the Scots clergy's success in using the army presbytery to secure and expand presbyterianism between 1642 and 1649 is unique in the history of early modern Europe.[83]

Nevertheless, there was such a problem in obtaining ministers for Ulster that in 1642 the General Assembly appointed three pairs of itinerant supply ministers.[84] Regular requests for ministers were submitted to the synod of Argyll and the General Assembly from Ulster. Four years later, in August 1646, after considering 'the petitioners from Irland for certaine brethren to repair ther for exercising ministeriall duties in a settled charge of the ministrie in some congregations of that kingdome', the Commissioners of the General Assembly replied, as they had in 1642, that 'in regaird of the present conditione of this Kirk, they cannot at this time advyse any to embrace a settled constant charge ther'.[85] Once again, they ordained it sufficient that two ministers visit for three months each. Fortunately, by 1648 there were enough presbyterian ministers resident in Ulster.[86]

During the First and Second Bishops' Wars in 1639 and 1640, army chaplains often came from the same part of the country as their regiments. For instance, when the Earl of Argyll raised between 800 and 900 men in 1639 to counter the fear of invasion from Ireland, the presbytery of Inveraray supplied fifteen ministers; in 1640, with the threat continuing, it sent five. And from 1642 onwards, it played a prominent role in staffing the Ulster chaplaincy, appointing over a third of the (known) ministers who went there, and sending eighteen ministers to Ireland in all. Given the number of Gaelic-speaking troops who went to Ulster in the Argyll regiments, it was not only politically expedient but a necessity that there were Gaelic-speaking ministers to attend them. But the presbyterian presence in Ireland led to a native Irish fear of 'the Scottismen's frequent brags in the North, that General Leslie wold come over ere long, and make a general reformation', which in turn encouraged reprisals against presbyterians in the ensuing civil war. There were also financial incentives for regimental service, since a remuneration was paid in addition to that for the parochial charge; not least, many had a strong ideological commitment to presbyterianism.[87] (It was also to the synod, as overseer of poor relief, rather than to the civil authorities, that a considerable sum of money was given for the restitution of Argyll following the Montrose raids.)[88] Although a chaplain's tour of duty was officially set at three months, in practice a tour of duty in Ulster often lasted much longer. Indeed, tours of service with the Ulster army were longer than those in any Covenanting army, at five and a half months,[89] whereas most in the other armies served two and a half months, or three at the most.[90] And while ministers were away on legitimate business, neighbouring ministers were always appointed to preach in their churches every second Sunday – although presumably they did not take on the extra burden of pastoral care during the week.[91] In this respect, a few individuals merit particular consideration.

Mr Dugald Campbell

On 26 May 1642, the synod of Argyll approved the departure to Ireland of Mr Dugald Campbell, minister of the parish of Knapdale, who was 'appoynted to serve the regment till the next provinciall'. Synods were being held every five or six months (not every three months, the term allocated to itinerant supply ministers) in Argyll during the early 1640s because of the political situation.[92] At the next synod, in October 1642, Dugald Campbell was told to continue with Argyll's regiment in Ireland for the next six months. In May of the following year, similar relief was supplied for Dugald Campbell's Irish charge, who was appointed to go to Ireland to preach to the Marquess' regiment, by Mr Archibald MacCallum. The appointment was authorised until 1 September 1643, with ministerial locums assigned for Knapdale until that date.[93]

Dugald Campbell was probably ministering to Argyll troops under the command of his great-uncle, Sir Duncan Campbell of Auchinbreck, chief heritor in Knapdale. If so, he can be traced to the Route, where this particular regiment was stationed. Dubbed 'one of the ablest ministers who served in the Knapdale parish', as the eldest son of Patrick Campbell of Stuck and a grandson of Donald Campbell, first of Kilmory, Campbell certainly had every social advantage. His three great-uncles were high in the Campbell hierarchy: they were the fourth laird of Auchinbreck, the above-mentioned Duncan Campbell of Castle Sween (later of Auchinbreck), and Archibald Campbell of Danna; and he was also distantly related to the house of Argyll itself.[94] In his own right, he was proprietor of Barchuil in Glassary.[95] A politically sanitised, well-connected presbyterian, he was just the sort of minister required to boost the morale of the Campbell regiments.[96]

Many Lowland (and probably some Highland) presbyterians had been settled on the good agricultural lands of the Route by the Earl of Antrim in the early seventeenth century, where Scottish presbyterian settlements were strongest in its western parts.[97] But missions undertaken by Highland ministers within the body of the Church of Ireland earlier in the century had concentrated on the diocese of Raphoe.[98] The Route had not become a bastion of radical presbyterianism but it did prove a testing point of the Ulster presbytery's authority. Started around September 1644, the Route meeting was an attempt at the creation of an alternative presbytery. The Route clergy did not have the unqualified support of their congregations because, although they had subscribed the Covenant, they were also conformists to the Church of Ireland; that is, essentially episcopalian. Many therefore felt they had 'generally come in upon these parishes at their own hand, with the consent of a few not well inclined people'. Understandably, the Ulster presbytery did not recognise the meeting's jurisdiction, and in its turn the Route meeting went as far as to complain to the English Commissioners in October 1645 that the Ulster assembly was an illegal and foreign body. But sensible of the army's power, the Commissioners rejected its petition, underlining the extent of the presbytery's monopoly on ecclesiastical power there.[99]

Presbyterianism in the Route seemed to advance in leaps and bounds in 1646, when three presbyterian ministers were admitted to parishes there. But their presbyterianism was called into question when two of these ministers were taken to task by the presbytery for their republican (Commonwealth) sympathies. Presbyterians stood firm against Royalists and Republicans alike. As licentiates,[100] Ker and O'Quinn had been called by the majority of the parishioners of Ballymoney and Billy. Significantly, opposition to their calls came from those of Highland extraction: from the renowned Archibald Stewart of Ballintoy,[101] who had interests in the first parish, and from Donald McNeill in Billy. Both objected to the licentiates' doctrine.[102]

As a regimental chaplain, Mr Dugald Campbell was particularly prized for his experience and his Gaelic tongue. Several years later, in February 1647, the Commission of the General Assembly received a petition from the Marquess of Argyll himself, as a result of which it appointed 'Mr. Dougal Campbell to attend his regiment in Irland for the space of thrie moneths, to performe ministeriall duty unto them, and that his Presbyterie be carefull of supplying his place during his absence'.[103] Once again, Campbell ran over his allotted span; by October 1648, he had been in Ireland for a year and a half, much to the detriment of his home parish. The synod of Argyll ordered him home by New Year's Day 1649, 'otherwayes his kirk shal be declared vacand'.[104]

Knapdale was temporarily supplied by two other ministers in Campbell's absence. Reporting in October 1648, the synod of Argyll thought it expedient – 'In regard that Marteine mc Lachlan was forced to escape with his lyfe out of Yla to the continent,[105] and left all that he had, and hes served for Mr Dugald Campbell, now in Yreland, at the kirk of Kilmichael in Knapdaill' – that he should have twenty bolls of victual for his service at the said kirk until 1 November, and after that time proportionately. On Campbell's return, McLachlan was assigned to Kilberry, then vacant, to uplift whatever teinds the parish could afford.[106] The synod's minute is interesting in that it links attitudes antipathetic to presbyterian ministers in Islay at this time to the clear anti-Campbell stance of the longstanding inhabitants of the island. Islay was traditional Clan Donald South territory, and although it had been in Campbell of Cawdor's hands since 1614 and relations between him and the old MacDonald tenants had probably been improved by Cawdor's conversion to Catholicism in 1624, the attitude of the old MacDonald commonalty was still virulently anti-Campbell.[107] But Catholicism cannot necessarily be equated with a hatred of presbyterianism amongst the Royalist clans, although there would appear to have been a distrust of Protestantism as the religion of Lowlanders.[108] However, it must be agreed that 'an aversion towards Presbyterianism was essentially an important unifying element in Royalist efforts to create a common front among the clans on the western seaboard who were opposed to the influence of the Campbells and fearful of the prominence of the Marquis of Argyle within the Covenanting Movement'.[109] Just as certain Royalist clans used their Catholicism as a political statement, presbyterianism had taken on political dimensions in the Highlands under the patronage of the Earl of Argyll.[110] Though they were in predominantly Campbell regiments, George Campbell of Airds' complaint in July 1642 to his brother Colin of Ardesier, tutor of Cawdor, about the low quality of Islay troops sent to Ireland – 'ther is noe wrong done in Ireland bot onli that quhilk is done be those men that comes out of Illa' – reflects a similar ambivalence on their part towards the Campbell feu holders.[111]

Although active fighting had come to an end in the previous year, the Scottish army was kept in Ireland in 1647, although more as an occupying force.[112] But why did Campbell procrastinate? He probably wished to stay on in Ulster during the birth pangs of presbyterianism there. Latterly, given that the presbytery of the army undertook extensive duties in the civilian sphere, he may even have been administering to the civilian population rather than the military one – an explanation which would certainly explain the synod's ultimatum to him.

It is likely that Campbell either served in the Route, because of his previous connection there, or in the Irish bedrock of early Highland presbyterianism, the Lagan region, comprising west Tyrone, east Donegal and south-west Londonderry in the jurisdiction of the Protestant diocese of Raphoe.[113] But a network of circumstantial evidence favours the Donegal region: in particular, he had family ties with Mr Dugald Campbell, parson of Letterkenny, his cousin, one of the original prescopalian ministers in the Church of Ireland, who had been in Ireland since 1611.[114]

Ties between the two Campbell families were quite close, becoming more so when the parson returned to Scotland around 1653. The parson had an astoundingly large family of nine daughters and twenty-one sons, many of whom married in Scotland, upholding their Scottish Gaelic and Argyll presbyterian connections. There was even a marriage between the minister's third daughter Mary, widow of Archibald Campbell of Ormsary, and William, the parson's second son.[115] This evidence supports the existence of a vibrant Highland community in Donegal, serviced by Scottish Gaelic-speaking ministers and intermarrying with Highlanders. The parson's eldest daughter married John Lindsay, who was successively minister at Clachan Dysart, Lochgoilhead, Glenaray, and Kilchrenan and Dalavich between 1666 and 1692.[116] Giles, the third of the parson's daughters, married Robert Duncanson, who supervised the printing of the Irish metrical version of the psalms in 1658 and was in 1660 allocated the first book of Samuel when the scriptures were translated into Gaelic;[117] initially minister of Dalavich, he transferred to Campbeltown in July 1681. Indeed, there would seem to be some justification in making an addition to the list of hereditary ecclesiastical families in the Highlands and Islands in the seventeenth century, that of the Campbells of Knapdale and Letterkenny.[118]

The parson of Letterkenny was back in Scotland by May 1653 when, hardly surprisingly in view of the size of his family, the synod of Argyll referred to his inability to meet his financial commitments. 'The synod, taking to consideratione the indegent conditione of Mr Dougall Campbell, lait minister at Laterkenzie in Irland, hes appoynted him to get that which rests of the allowence appoynted him by the last synod owt of the vaccansies of Jura and Ila.'[119] One of his sons was mentioned in May 1657, when the synod considered 'the supplicatione of John Campbell, sone to Mr Dougall Campbell, sometyme minister at Letterkenizie in Ireland, intending and promiseing to follow furth his studies according as he hath made a good deall of proficiency alreadie in a short tyme'.[120] He was enrolled among the list of boys selected as probationers.

Capitalising on his experience in Ireland and his knowledge of the Gaelic langauge, his cousin, Dugald Campbell the Knapdale minister, continued the crusade against disaffected Gaels. Visiting Skye, which was then under threat from Vincentian missionaries, in 1655, he spent two months in Ardgour and Lochaber the following year. Finally, he transferred to the presbyterian outpost of Lochaber in 1658 to be minister there. But the region was not yet ready for such a mission: there were severe problems with his maintenance, and the planting was ultimately unsuccessful. Campbell spent the remaining years of his ministry translating religious works into Gaelic during the winter and going on short-term missions into the undermanned Gaelic-speaking areas in the summer. Both of these tasks can be seen as an extension of his work with the Ulster army, i.e. an exercise in civilising the natives. The catechism in Gaelic, which he translated in tandem with Ewen Cameron of Dunoon, was published in 1653. The pair also finished translating the first fifty metrical psalms into Gaelic in May 1658, and these were on sale by 1659; because of the number of psalms, the book was known as the *Caogad*. The last hundred psalms were entrusted to Dugald and his son Duncan Campbell, who had just become minister in Glenorchy.[121]

Although most presbyterian ministers went from Scotland to parishes in Ulster, a few served in the south of Ireland. During the Cromwellian period (more especially under the Lord Deputyship of Henry Cromwell, the Protector's son, who arrived in Ireland in July 1655), their presence can once again be seen as a means of civilising or controlling the Irish. Besides a number of Huguenots, a minister with a Highland name, 'Murdogh McKenzy', appears in a list of state clerical allowances for 1655, employed at a salary of £80 in the precinct of Athy, County Kildare in Leinster 'to preach in Irish'.[122] This is surely none other than Murdo MacKenzie, late minister of Suddie who was deposed in 1646.[123] As a Royalist, having negotiated with Antrim during the civil war, he may simply not have been acceptable to some staunch presbyterians in Ulster, whereas a ministry confined to the south of Ireland did not present the same sort of problems; although, as T. C. Barnard has stated, there were various half-shades 'between the unspotted royalism of Ormond[124] or Lane[125] and the Irish adherents of the Cromwellians'. The ease of passage to Scotland and optimism in Charles II aided the survival of Stuart loyalties in some presbyterians in Ulster, just as there were ministerial collaborators in the Highlands of Scotland.[126]

MacKenzie was first appointed in September 1653 to preach in Irish and English in the precinct of Athy, as part of largely unsuccessful Cromwellian drive to bring Protestantism to the native Irish in the vernacular. Previous attempts had been made by Bishops Knox, Bedell and others, but they were not sufficiently extensive to be of longstanding effect. In the previous year, a book entitled *The Christian Doctrine Gathered into Six Principles Necessary for Every Ignorant Man to Learn* (1652) had been printed in Dublin by William Bladen and translated into Irish by Godfrey Daniel. The two languages appeared side by side in double columns. Some attempt, at least, was being made to provide back-up literature.[127]

By 1654, relations were easing between the Cromwellian government and the Ulster presbyterians. But fear that the tensions in the Scottish Kirk might spread to Ulster led to the passing of the Act of Bangor in 1654, which forbade ministers who came to Ireland of speaking about the divisions and prevented congregations from presenting a call to ministers in Scotland without approval from the presbytery of Belfast, which insisted on recommending candidates approved by both Resolutioners and Protesters. It was not likely to succeed. As Phil Kilroy puts it, 'the strong tradition of dissent within Scottish Presbyterianism, the theological, cultural and social contacts between Presbyterians in Ulster and Scotland, combined with the fact that both countries were as geographically proximate as the shores of a lake, ultimately doomed this legislation to failure'.[128] Nevertheless, in this more tolerant climate, Scots presbyterians began once more to step up their social interaction with Ulster. In September 1654, the presbytery of Dunoon, acknowledging 'that thair is a dor open to irland, and that people may repair thither and returne safe', licensed Mr James Johnestoune to go to Ireland 'for some civill bussiness'.[129] And Mr John Stewart, a minister from the same presbytery, was in Ireland the following year.[130] Nevertheless, the years of persecution had left the presbyterian church with a deficiency of ministers which was, in time-honoured fashion, partially met from Scotland. The Antrim meeting appointed the keeping of a fast on Wednesday 17 December 1656, among the reasons for which were 'the unfruitfullnes of the Gospell', as well as 'the many desolate Congregations through the land being as sheep without a sheepheard, in whose behalf the Lord is more then ordinar to be supplicat'.[131]

The appointment of Scottish probationers and expectants continued to be a marked feature of presbyterian expansion in Ulster well into the eighteenth century. Whether Ulster had been peripheral to the Covenanters' concerns or not, it can definitely be argued that the Kirk allocated far fewer resources to it in the period afterwards.[132] On 27 May 1657, the synod of Argyll heard a report from Mr James Garner (probably a church elder), who had been asked to speak with Mr John Thomson, a student at Glasgow College who by the time the synod met had 'gon to Irland'. The synod wished Thomson to join the ministry and engage in its work, but Thomson was leaving his options open and had given 'no sure answer in reference to that that was required of him'.[133] Shortly afterwards, the period of presbyterian government drew to a close, and although presbyterians were able to worship in relative peace after 1664, since they no longer drew salaries (unless they conformed), there were severe problems in maintaining the ministry. The Antrim meeting alluded, on 2 February 1675, to the stricken state that the church was in.

Whereas the meeting of Downe by their correspondent have overtured to us,

> viz: Consideration being had that the brethren are all under Great Straites for want of maintainance, and that the Gospel Ministry in Ireland is like to cease upon the accompt that there is no way for the maintainance thereof, it is overtured that the Moderator of the Last Comittee write unto the severall meetings, that each of them send foure Commissioners unto the next Comittee, prepared with some effectual overtures for the remedying of the said inconvenience and hazard, and that there may be an harmonious way taken in that affaire.[134]

This very drive for survival perhaps accounts for the influx of another small contingent of Highland ministers to Ulster.

Besides John Campbell, another of the parson of Letterkenny's sons, Duncan Campbell, became a probationer in Scotland.[135] When visiting in Lagan in early 1674, he received a call to Killybegs, Killachli and Inver. On 17 March the Lagan meeting, asking for his response to the call, noted that he

> declareth that he can settle no where, being to return shortly to Scotland; but that while he is in the countrey he is willing to visit such places as the M. doth appoint; and that place particularly about Killibegs, Killachhee, and Inver. The brethren renew their desire to Mr Duncan Campbell, that seeing God hath shutt the door on him to labour in Scotland, and that that people hes given him such an invitation, that he would remain among these people till God open a door to him in Scotland, or whiles he continues in this Countrey: which he condescended unto.

The 'shutting of the door' tends to indicate that Campbell was a nonconformist, but he would still have preferred Scotland to Ireland.[136]

Mr James Tailzeur, First Minister of Enniskillen

One of the more interesting Scottish ministers in Ireland was Mr James Tailzeur, first known minister in Enniskillen, who came not from Argyll like most Highland ministers who went to Ireland during this period but from Morayshire in the mid-1670s. A connection might even be posited here between the complaint made in 1646 by the synod of Moray about the incursion of ministers from Ireland, which may in turn hint at the older connection referred to by Brereton in the 1630s.[137] Throughout most of the seventeenth century, the presbyterian church in Ireland suffered from a lack of personnel. It was in response to just such a deficiency in the bounds of the Lagan presbytery, with its longstanding Scottish connection, that on 10 November 1674 Mr Robert Rule was 'again desired to write to Scotland for some Godly young men of his acquaintance whom he named to the Meeting to come over and supply Fermanagh and other vacancies amongst us'. Consequent on this request, the Lagan meeting referred in February 1675 to one young man having been dissuaded by the Scottish brethren, who hoped that a Mr James Tailzeur, then still a probationer, would come instead. But reluctant to build up expectations, it determined that 'if Mr James Tailzor (who is expected from Scotland) doe come, he shall supply vacant and desolate congregations' until the presbytery met again.[138]

Tailzeur came on the recommendation of Mr Thomas Hogge, the renowned Covenanting minister of Kiltearn, who wrote to Robert Rule in 1675 in support of Tailzeur, indicating that his 'testificats' were coming 'from the North of Scotland'.[139] Tailzeur had perhaps been working in Ross and Cromarty, since Hogg had technically been ejected from Kiltearn in 1662 and was a conventicler.[140] The seriousness of the ministerial dearth in Ulster can be inferred from the veritable profusion of calls presented to this one man. In May 1675, a call was recorded from the people of Letterkenny, while in June there was reference to another two calls from Fermanagh and Urny. But in July 1675 the meeting was ready 'to propose Mr. James Tailzour to the Committee, in reference to Ordination', and asked for any objections against this.[141]

On 17 August 1675, the Lagan meeting, an area of known Highland settlement, recorded the same profusion of calls from commissioners in the above-mentioned three areas. But only the Fermanagh representative was prepared to lay a specific stipend on the table, reporting that in 'Monnae, Iniskilling, & Derryvallan, some considerable share of these parishes ... have engaged to give £30 with a great probability of more yearly Maintenance, if once they had a Minister'. Tailzeur was asked to state his preference in the matter, but showing a degree of pragmatism he left it to the meeting to determine, 'because he knowes not how to doe it'. After much deliberation, it decided on Fermanagh. Being on the losing end of the decision, the commissioners from Urny decided to try for a minister from the same source, desiring 'the concurrence and assistance of the Meeting in naming some Ministers whom they may seek out of Scotland. So also the Elders & Commissioners from Letterkenny'.[142] Even towards the end of the seventeenth century, the presbyterian church in Ulster was still heavily dependent on support from Scotland.

On the following day, 18 August 1675, 'because of his urgent affairs hastening him back to Scotland', the meeting set Tailzeur's ordination for a fortnight hence, ordering the dispatch of a minister to Fermanagh to help and advise them in their preparation for their new minister.[143] By 14 September 1675, Tailzeur had neither been ordained nor left for Scotland, but as an incentive the people of Fermanagh offered him an extra £10, making £40 per annum in total.[144] Satisfied with his trials, the meeting cleared him for ordination on the following day, although there were 'severall things in his case, singular, which require dispatch'.[145] Finally, on 15 September 1675, he was 'with fasting & prayer & imposition of hands Ordained & set apart for the work of the Ministry amongst that people of Fermanagh who called him', in the joint charge of Monea, Enniskillen and Derryvullen.[146]

By 11 January 1676, both James Tailzeur and Robert Rule, ministers, were in Scotland. Tailzeur did not return to Ulster until around 28 November 1676, when he kept an appointment to supply 'Ballick'.[147] In the summer of 1677, he seems to have overheard information about a prospective foreign invasion, information discovered over a year later by Titus Oates, which became known as the Popish Plot. Three ministers from the presbytery of Lagan – John Hart, Robert Craighead and William Traill – wrote a letter dated at Taboin, 10 August 1677, to Sir Arthur Forbes, Viscount Granard, privy councillor in Ireland, drawing his attention to the fact that 'one Mr. James Taylor, a faithful and godly minister in the county of Fermanagh living within two miles of Inniskilling and one of our number, having revealed unto him a matter of very dangerous consequence to his majesty's government, if real, and being but a stranger unacquainted with the law in this country, and not knowing what might be the fittest way to discover the same', none the less divulged the matter to his three brethren. According to them, a gentleman who had been a captain abroad revealed to him nothing less than the 'heading of a party to be furnished with money and ammunition from foreign parts'. Although Tailzeur was rewarded with ten guineas by the Lord Lieutenant, the information was clearly not acted upon at the time.[148] Titus Oates did not make his first revelations until over a year later, in September 1678.[149]

Tailzeur's intelligence came to light during the examination of William Trail, minister of Lifford, before the Privy Council in June 1681. After the battle of Bothwell Brig in June 1679 which had sought to contain Covenanting dissent in Scotland, the government in Ireland was anxious to avoid a similar insurrection there. Although many presbyteries adopted declarations of loyalty, the authorities remained somewhat in awe of public gatherings of presbyterians. For instance, when the Lagan meeting decided to hold a fast and publicly intimated the same a week before it was to be held, the magistrates of the district – 'intolerant prelatists' – pressed the oath of supremacy on the officers and soldiers in the Lagan district.[150] Not recognising the absolute supremacy of the King in ecclesiastical matters, some presbyterians refused this. As a result, four local ministers – William Trail of Lifford, James Alexander of Raphoe, Robert Campbell of Ray and John Hart of Taughboyne – were called before the magistrates in Raphoe, and then in Dublin, where they were closely examined. Indicted for holding the fast, they were found guilty by a packed jury and imprisoned for eight months. After their release from prison, at least two of them decided to cut their losses and return to Scotland.[151] The ministers' departure was the signal for a renewal of persecution against non-conformists which endured for two years, particularly in Derry and Donegal, two areas of the densest Highland presbyterian settlement in Ulster. The ministers of the Lagan meeting even intimated to the other presbyteries their intention to emigrate to America. Furthermore, ten Highland infantry soldiers listed in the muster on the arrival of the Earl of Dunbarton's regiment at Kinsale in April 1679 (which formed a part of the standing army in Ireland) also scrupled to take the oath of supremacy. Probably presbyterians, they were conveniently excused on account of their alleged inability to speak English, report being given 'of the companies to which certain Highlanders do belong who did not take the oaths of supremacy and allegiance, by reason they understand not English'.[152]

James Tailzeur continued on the sederunts of the Lagan meeting through to 27 March 1678, when he offended the ministers in the neighbouring county of Tyrone by preaching beyond his own bounds. The Lagan meeting appointed Mr William Trail, their correspondent, 'to deall effectually with the Meeting of Tyrone for clearing thair brother Mr James Talzor of all these things that they seem to charg him with'. The problem seems to have arisen as a result of Mr Tailzeur's call to a Tyrone parish, executed without the knowledge of the Tyrone meeting. The meeting of Lagan decided that

> the Call presented to them by Thomas Greg and John Pickins Commissioners from McGuiers bridg for the said Mr James Talzor to settle amongst them as their minister should be presented to the Meeting of Tyron by the said Mr William Traill, to show what pains this Meeting hath been att to gett that people supplyed with a settled ministry, & withall to show them that they did deny thair concurrence to so good a work, in as far as they were concerned in it the desolation of (that) Countrysyd would be left at thair door, and that he bring back the said call.

Although the Lagan meeting of 3 July 1678 had received a letter from the Tyrone brethren about the planting of McGuire's bridge, they laid it aside 'and advysed Mr. James Tailzeor to continue as yet where he is'.[153] In August, Tailzeur was even chosen as moderator for the next quarter.

The Lagan meeting declined to release Tailzeur to Tyrone, to reside and preach 'at the Fyvemyltoun [Fivemiletown]' in Fermanagh. He gave his own account of the affair in October 1678, as a result of which Mr Robert Rule wrote in support of his action to the Tyrone brethren, 'desiring them not to hinder Mr Tailzior's preaching there'. In the meantime, Tailzeur was asked 'to forbear any further meddling in this affair, except he have advice from this Meeting'.[154] But in April 1679 he was imprisoned at Enniskillen, and on the pretence of lacking a written certificate stating that he was an ordained minister he was fined £5.[155] The whole justification for the controversy surrounding him and, indeed, of his need to demonstrate his loyalty to the government by feeding them anti-Catholic intelligence was, perhaps, fear of his connection with the conventicling movement.

The controversy concerning Tailzeur's work in Fermanagh continued. In early September 1679, the Lagan meeting commissioned a letter to be written to the Tyrone brethren about Tailzeur's affair '& to show them that he was orderly settled there, in Fermanagh, & that of necessity he came to that place where he now is, & therefore he is not a disorderly walker, & that this aspersion of his being a disorderly walker must either be put out of their books, or that this our Letter must be noted there'.[156] Nevertheless, a barrage of calls continued to come in to Tailzeur. In March 1680, petitioners from Ramullan, Killigarvan and Clandevaddock asked assistance from the Lagan meeting in presenting a call to him, the last two promising £29 per annum jointly for his maintenance. By May, the stake had doubled, with a pledge of £30 per annum maintenance from Ramullan alone. In the same month, a commissioner from Glendermott in County Londonderry, another county that had experienced a high degree of Highland settlement, sought the concurrance of the meeting in a call to Tailzeur, who had preached in Derry in February, while a commissioner from the Muff also came to prosecute a call to him in July. But the meeting could give them no positive answer in Tailzeur's continued absence, although he was appointed to preach in Ramullan one Sunday in April.[157]

When Tailzeur attended the presbytery in April, he was encouraged to speak his mind about his labours in Fermanagh. Sent first to Machrybuy with the concurrance of the presbytery, he had ended up serving Fivemiletown, too. His reply was that 'he sees not how the Gospell shall be settled in that place, if he leave it: & on the other hand, he sayes, he is not able to endure the travell which hitherto he hes had in that countrey, & that he is not able to serve both places, of Fermanagh: & sees he cannot stay there in peace & quietness'. The meeting continued in its former resolution to transport him, but not until it had done what it could, in conjunction with the Tyrone brethren, to settle the gospel in Fermanagh.[158] Asked to consider the calls of Killigarvan and Glendermott two months later, Tailzeur was scarcely more enthusiastic, declaring that 'because of the weakness of his body he cannot close with the Call to KilliGarven: nor can he as yet positively determine himself to close with the Call of Glendermot'.[159] The proliferation of requests for his services continued, with a commissioner from Fivemiletown coming to underline its desire for 'the continuation of Mr James Tailzior's labors amongst them as formarly'. But the meeting declined to answer any of these requests 'till they see what further the people of Machrybuy (by whom he was first & especially called & to whom he was first sent) will doe for retaining him, & whether they will give sufficient security for their performance of their promises'. However, since Fivemiletown had so willingly contributed to Tailzeur's maintenance, the Tyrone meeting was asked 'to take care of that people'.[160]

In July 1680, a month after the remnant of Scottish Covenanting dissent had disowned the King in the Sanquhar Declaration, the presbytery discharged Tailzeur 'from meddling any more with the practice of physic or medicine', due to complaints of his frequent absence.[161] The practice of medicine was often a sideline during this period for those in positions of responsibility in the community such as ministers and priests, or the local élite and their wives.[162] The Lagan meeting found that the people of Fermanagh fell far short of their promises concerning Tailzeur's maintenance; it was therefore confirmed in the necessity of declaring him transportable. Furthermore, the presbytery stated: 'neither do any of that people come to this Meeting to give us any ground of Clearness or encouragements for this stay in Fermanagh: he having no hope of a house to live in, this winter: He also guiding that some people have taken up some groundless misconstructions of his case; does now declare that he is not clear to stay any longer in that Countrey.'[163] While he declared his intention in August to accept the call of Glendermott, there is no evidence that Tailzeur was installed there, although the failure to record such installations was not unusual. The lack of information is only compounded by the breaking off of the minutes of the Lagan meeting in mid-1681 during the growth in persecution, lest the book be seized by the Prelatical party.[164] In the event, Tailzeur resigned just a couple of years later, in 1683, and returned to Scotland, where he was admitted to the parish of Kinnettles in Forfarshire some time prior to 1689; he was present at the battle of Killiecrankie on 22 July 1689.[165]

The number of presbyterian callings to Ulster increased in the few years prior to the '89. This was undoubtedly facilitated by the general extension of religious toleration by the King, but those who went may at the same time have felt called to work against the encroachment of Catholicism, which similarly flourished during the toleration.

Mr John Darroch, Minister of Glenarm and Cushendall

One Gaelic speaker who transferred from the presbytery of Kintyre to Ireland at this juncture was John Darroch. But the move came at a time which was personally opportune for him inasmuch as a process had already been started against him. A native of Argyll, he had been educated at Glasgow University, licensed by the presbytery of Dunoon and ordained at Kilcalmonell and Kilberry in Argyll in 1669. But he was deprived in 1681, probably because of a failure to subscribe to the Test Act. However, what occurred to him for the next six years is open to question.[166]

Wherever Darroch spent the years between 1681 and 1687, he was back in Southend on 9 November 1687 when a letter was commissioned by the moderator of the presbytery of Kintyre 'to the heretors and others concerned in the parishes of Kilcolmanell and Kilbervie To the intent that they call home Mr John darroch there former minister, (who having deserted prelacy)' had reasserted himself to the presbyterian interest. On 14 December, he agreed to supply the vacancy while they deliberated further. But Darroch's ministry in Kilcalmonell and Kilberry floundered in March 1688 upon notification of the heritors' inability 'to afford a dutiful supplie of maintenance'. And a request from the Lowland congregation of Campbeltown for him to preach 'in such corners of the lowland parish of Campbeltown as lyes next adjacent to the southend' was also refused in April due to unspecified objections from William Hamilton of Briminor. Pushed into a corner, Darroch renounced the call from Southend in an apparent fit of pique, and expressed his intention to leave with his family at the earliest possible convenience, 'declareing that his parteing on the discussing of the foresaids reasons keeps him from a visit he designs to Ireland'.[167]

Darroch asked for certification from the presbytery, which consented to his making a visit out of the country until the next diet of the synod of Argyll at which he was to be in attendance. On 22 May 1688, he also requested a formal suspension of the process against him 'in regard that (as he declares) he is on wing to go to Ireland'.[168] The objections centred round his averred reversion to presbyterianism, but Darroch had been called to subscribe to the Act of Renunciation and Submission – that is, to subscribe to the Test and Succession Acts – which he had done at the last synod. Noting that he had gone to Ireland for a season, on 9 June 1688 the synod of Argyll directed the presbytery of Kintyre 'to proceid to the discussing of the reasons, and objections given in against him at the forme [sic] synod, if he continue within the kuntrey'.[169]

In September 1688, Darroch received a call to Glenarm and Cushendall in County Antrim, which he pursued.[170] His relations with his own congregation of Kilcalmonell and Kilberry were so poor that there was very little incentive for him to stay in Scotland. He also received a call from Ballymena, a parish in the Antrim meeting, in October 1688, whose commissioners sought 'the meeting's concurrence for settling John Darrogh there, & presenting their Call to him, and giving it in to this meeting there being only about six persons who dissent from the said Call'.[171] They were, however, only prepared to take him with the consent of his own presbytery, stating:

> that he is now upon his journey thither to see his family, the meeting will expect that he bring in a full & clear Testimoniall, together with a full & free liberty from the Church of Scotland, in order to his settlement here in Ireland. And if he can obtain this, & return to this country, and be any Sabbath here before our meeting, Then the meeting thinks it fitt to appoint that he may supply Laid and Cushedall one Sabbath & and rest in Glenarm, till he appear before this meeting with the said Testimoniall.[172]

The Glenarm call had been entered before the others, and while the Antrim meeting was technically to consider whether Darroch should accept the call of Glenarm or Ballymena, in the event it only allowed him 'to keep the Calls of Glenarm & Cushendall under his consideration till he appears again before us'.[173]

In February 1689, the synod of Argyll gave an update on Darroch's affairs, reporting that he had come over from Ireland to Kintyre during the last harvest and 'presented to his brethren there a call which he had from the paroch of Glenarm'.[174] Having spent enough time in Ireland to find out the situation, Darroch attended the meeting of the presbytery of Kintyre in October 1688; he 'desired a testificate from them, bearing their consent for him to engadge with the said paroch, for ane Interim untill he have a clearer accesse unto some paroch within the Synod of Argyll'. All endeavours by the presbytery to call him back to his old ministry 'did prove uneffectuall throw want of a competent maintenance'. Furthermore, 'his own old paroch being possessed by a curate was not inviteing him, nor giveing him any encouradgement'; 'the necessities of his familie' were evidently not being met because of the dispute over his stipend.[175]

Seeing that the situation had not improved since the previous May when the presbytery gave Darroch permission to go to Ireland, and considering that 'he hath encouragements offered to him in Ireland', the brethren of the presbytery of Kintyre continued their 'former Consent and allowance given to him to serve in the Gospell within the kingdom of Ireland or elsewhere'.[176] His peers clearly appreciated the problem, with the benefit of their own experience. In February this decision was endorsed by the synod, which granted him certification but restricted him 'both in the acceptance of the said call of Glenarm, or any other call in Ireland, And in the exercise of his ministrie there', which was to depend on the meetings of presbyterian brethren there, and on reservation of the interest which the Kirk and the synod of Argyll had in him.[177]

Darroch returned to Ireland at the end of 1688. The minutes of the Antrim meeting recorded that:

> Mr John Darragh Supply'd Glenarm and Cushendall only since his return from Scotland, and hath brought hither a Testimoniall subscribed by Mr Duncanson and Mr Cunison allowing his continuance in Ireland to serve in the work of the Ministry, with this reservation that the Church of Scotland, and particularly the Presbytery of Kintyre may have access to call him again when Providence opens up a door for his return.

Sent to test the call, another Scottish minister, Mr John Campbell, informed the Antrim meeting in February 1689 that the call was 'unanimous with the proviso therein', and that £24 in maintenance had been pledged.[178] Unfortunately, few details of Darroch's ministry in Ireland survive.[179]

Compelled to return home by the troubles in Revolution Ireland, Darroch was back in his old parish on 2 October 1689, when the synod of Argyll commissioned a letter to the Captain of Skipness and Angus Campbell of Kilberry 'for encourageing Mr John Darroch the present Minister in the mater of his accomodatione and other maters new full'.[180] In November 1689, the

Antrim meeting noted the desire of Mr William Hallyday, commissioner from Glenarm, that they be settled with Gospel ordinances, 'Mr. John Darragh not returning, neither any appearance of it'. However, the meeting found that 'the people are ready to endeavour his return', and gave them permission to do their utmost to achieve it.[181]

But 'being called home by his old parishioners of Kilcollmanell and Kilberrie', as the minutes of the presbytery of Kintyre put it, Darroch did not return to his Irish ministry.[182] Sadly, the financial constraints imposed on Darroch by his old parish had scarcely improved,[183] and by January 1691 he had received a call from John McNeill of Tirfergus (a family with abundant Irish connections) to the parish of Southend.[184] It was refused, but McNeill also declined to take back the call, leaving Darroch to insist on the insertion of his refusal in the presbytery book. Darroch presented his grievances to the presbytery, which met in his home parish of Kilcalmonell, in May 1692, most pressing of which was 'his want of a pastoral relation to the said parish, in regard he never had a Call to from the parishioners, all the relation he had being founded onely upon the presentation & collation which he had, quhill he was under prelacy'.[185] However, Darroch's conforming to 'prelacy' must necessarily have been of a nominal nature, since he did not initially subscribe to the Test Act and, moreover, went as a minister to Ireland where episcopacy was not esteemed in presbyterian communities there. But his ability to speak Irish overrode these other considerations.

This time the presbytery concurred with his grievances, which, besides his inadequate stipend included lack of a church, gleib and manse, declaring that if they were not removed, 'the said Mr John darroch shall be declared transportable'.[186] As good as their word, a month later Darroch was transferred and admitted to Craignish on 8 June 1692. But parochial disagreements continued to dog him well into the eighteenth century. When the synod of Argyll visited Craignish on 28 June 1706, Darroch, 'minister of this place', was checked for not administering the sacrament. He argued (fairly legitimately, perhaps) that the kirk had no roof and that people could have access to the sacrament in other parishes.[187] Although Darroch never returned to Ireland as a minister, he was employed on an ad hoc basis during the summer months as an itinerant evangelist for the remote, mainly Catholic, Gaelic-speaking areas of Scotland until his death on 6 July 1730. He was, for instance, part of a visitation to the Isles during the summer of 1696, and was usually a consultant in any matter pertaining to the welfare of the Gaelic presbyterian community.[188]

But Darroch was not the only presbyterian minister from Argyll in the County of Antrim during the 1680s. Ordained to the parish of Lochgoilhead and Kilmorich in 1683, John Monro went to Ireland in the following year and was placed at Carnmoney in 1685. On 9 June 1688, the synod of Argyll noted the receipt of a letter from Sir Colin Campbell of Ardkinglass showing that 'the paroch of Lochgoyle, and Kilmaglass are to send ane Invitation to Mr John Monro for present in Ireland To return to them as his proper charge And desireing this meetting's concurrence with the said invitation And particularie that a letter be written to the meetting of Antrum in Ireland for looseing him from his present charge there'.[189] In November, James Wylie, an elder at Carnmoney, reported that 'the dealing of the landlords pursuing after rent occasions little done to M., and that in three years they are in arrear, £48'.[190] But the first Jacobite rebellion eventually induced Monro's return to Scotland, where he was readmitted to his old parish sometime in 1689, although he transferred to Rothesay in March 1691.

There was a constant trickle of Gaelic-speaking presbyterians to Ulster during this period, beginning with the arrival of two episcopal non-conformists to the presbyterian regime, and becoming a stream during the heyday of the Ulster army chaplaincy (1642–48). The marked lack of ministers for the presbyterian church in Ireland in the next three decades resulted in a continuing supply of presbyterian ministers from Scotland. A Gaelic-speaking contingent formed a distinct part of this mission. In terms of Gaelic and Irish-speaking ministers (although not of presbyterians ministers in general), the movement was one-way, from the Highlands to Ulster. And although the synod of Moray noted an influx of ministers from Ireland in 1646, there appears to have been only one Irish minister working in the Scottish *Gaidhealtachd* in this period. He did so as a refugee from presbyterial sanction, but as a social rather than a political undesirable, and he may not even have been Gaelic-speaking at that. Throughout this period, the Irish ministry was not sufficiently extensive to cope efficiently with even its English-speaking congregations, let alone run an effective mission in the vernacular. It therefore sought help from its Scottish brethren, showing a willingness to rely on a disproportionately large number of expectants and probationers, which it subsequently ordained within its own bounds. But the Kirk was only particularly concerned to send assistance when it was necessary to stave off political instability in Ireland which might conceivably threaten the presbyterian establishment in Scotland. It therefore gave priority to sending ministers to Ireland during the civil war, even though there were still vacancies in the Highlands and Islands in noted Royalist areas, such as the parish of Kilmallie in Inverness-shire. This parish did not have any reformed services until the advent of Dugald Campbell, minister of Knapdale, in 1651, and even then there was no kirk.[191] On the other hand, the experience in Ireland of ministers like Dugald Campbell not only provided the impetus for missions into neglected and disaffected areas of the Highlands and Islands, but also for translation of the scriptures into Gaelic.

During this period, only one allegedly Gaelic-speaking minister converted to Catholicism, and Ronald MacDonald was a man renowned neither for his integrity nor for a clearly demonstrated Protestant faith. In comparison, this serves to highlight the political significance of the substantial number of ministers cited for collusion with Montrose's force in 1644–45. It suggests that Royalism was not synonymous with Catholicism, as has on occasion been proposed. In the same way, Catholicism was not necessarily synonymous with anti-presbyterianism but can be seen to have been more of a political statement against a culturally alien Lowland government and the expansion of one of its agents, the Protestant Clan Campbell on the western seaboard. After the civil war, however, there is nothing to suggest that those few Highland ministers who went to Ireland did so with the approval of the Kirk. They appear to have done so more as refugees and out of expediency, firstly as Protestant Royalists, secondly as probationers who envisaged greater prospects of a fruitful benefice in Ireland in comparison with a poorly endowed marginal parish in the Highlands, and thirdly (and coterminously) as presbyterian non-conformists to the episcopal régime. Although few in number, the relocation of Gaelic-speaking clerics to Ireland undoubtedly exacerbated the problems of the Kirk in filling vacancies in Gaelic-speaking parishes during the Restoration and post-Revolution periods. Yet apart from the Ulster chaplaincy, this small but notable movement of Highland clerics to Ireland has hitherto been unappreciated, obscured by the comparative abundance of information which survives about Irish Catholic penetration of the Highlands and Islands. It seems less that Highland ministers were going to Ireland to evangelise the Irish than to minister to established Scottish Gaelic-speaking communities, particularly in Donegal and Antrim. Moreover, there was an ironic counterbalance between Catholic and Protestant missions in the two countries: Irish-speaking priests worked in the Highlands and Islands, and Highland ministers took the gospel to Ulster, with the important difference that the faith of the latter was not proscribed but simply non-conformist. But numbers on both missions were only significant when there was also political backing from the state. Thus, while the Irish Catholic mission in the Highlands reached a zenith of ten Irish priests in 1688[192] during James VII's extension of toleration to Catholics, the synod of Argyll sent no fewer than eighteen ministers to Ulster during the civil war.

FOUR

Seducing the People to Popery, 1638–1689

Those who join the Mission should be truly apostolic men thinking nothing of their own convenience, men who have chosen that kind of life and no other as a permanent state.

Prefect William Ballantyne, *Report* (*c.* 1660)

IN THE MAIN, the period 1638–89 is marked by the growth of a secular mission in the Highlands: mission work was increasingly removed from the control of regular orders and placed under the control of a secular mission co-ordinator. The Highland mission became a melting-pot of regular and secular priests. During the uncertainties of the civil war, spiritual succour was taken when and as made available. Catholicism in the Western Isles received a brief fillip from the Irish priests who visited them with Alasdair MacColla. Three priests attended the Royalist troops between 1644 and 1647, as well as a number of Scots Jesuits who joined the forces under command of Montrose as they roved around the country from place to place and battle to battle. But this was an uncommon kind of evangelisation which had only a limited effect on the general population. Then, in 1650, Catholicism in Scotland was boosted by the appointment of the Scots secular, William Leslie, as Scots representative to the Holy See. The immediacy of his presence in Rome greatly benefited the Scottish mission. His only failing was the great antipathy in which he held Jesuits, an antipathy which had consistently dogged the Counter-Reformation Scottish congregation but reached new heights under Leslie. His main aim was the appointment of a secular as bishop for the Scottish mission; in this he conflicted with the Jesuits – then the main arm of organised Catholicism in Scotland – who were keen to protect their privileged position. Yet in spite of this weakness, Leslie was a key player in the reconstruction of the Catholic Church in Scotland. He did more than any other priest to fashion a handful of secular clergy into a mission under a Prefect-Apostolic, and eventually under a Vicar-Apostolic.[1]

Probably under the influence of the Jesuits in *Propaganda Fide*, Innocent X decided against the creation of a Scottish bishop in 1653, although he did agree to making William Ballantyne, a Scottish secular, Prefect-Apostolic. This gave

Ballantyne powers more limited than a Vicar-Apostolic: he had spiritual jurisdiction only, technically over all secular priests on the Scottish mission, but in practice also over those regulars who did not have superiors resident in mission territory. It was mainly an administrative post, concerned with meetings, correspondence, distributing allowances from *Propaganda* and selecting new students for the Scots colleges abroad. Under this arrangement, regular priests of various denominations – Franciscan, Vincentian, Dominican and Barnabite – as well as secular priests worked together as an extended community. Even the Jesuits slipped into *Propaganda*'s orbit when they finally submitted to the authority of the Vicar-Apostolic on 7 February 1701. All of this was an achievement.[2] The tail-end of this period saw the uproar caused by Titus Oates' 'Popish Plot' in August 1678, which exposed a plan to murder Charles II and replace him with his brother, the Catholic Duke of York; the French were to assist an invasion of England to re-establish the Catholic faith there.[3] Although this threw a negative light upon the Catholic community in general, it had few reverberations in the isolated Highlands and Islands other than the distinct religious overtones to the expedition sent into Argyll in 1679 by MacDonell of Glengarry in his attempt to even scores against the Earl of Argyll for the dispossession of MacLean of Duart. After the Popish Plot, Argyll had inveigled a commission from the crown to disarm MacDonell of Glengarry and MacDonald of Keppoch simply on the basis that most of their supporters happened to be Catholic.[4] Having temporarily left the mission for Holland in the late summer of 1678, the Prefect-Apostolic returned the following summer, when the arrival of the Catholic Duke of York boded better times for Catholics.[5] Under James VII, the number of priests on the Highland mission increased manyfold. Even though the toleration proved short-lived, by that time the Highland mission had so firm a foundation that it was able to draw native Scots into the priesthood.

Irish Chaplains with Alasdair MacColla MacDonald

The Franciscan mission in Scotland was formally re-established by decree of *Propaganda Fide* on 22 January 1647. But even during the Bishops' Wars of 1639–40, Scots had continued to flock to Bonamargy in magnitudes of several hundred per year,[6] and Scots continued to be served from Ireland even though the mission had been officially terminated. However, two things seriously impinged upon this work. Firstly, the civil war had spread to Ireland by 1641. Patrick Hegarty informed *Propaganda* in December 1640 that 'because of war between King Charles and the Scots, travel between Scotland and Ireland was forbidden by royal decree, but nevertheless, he received 200 into the church that same year'.[7] Trying to keep a fast hold on the Scottish mission, Hegarty expressed his concern about the chaplains in the predominantly Irish Catholic army raised by the Earl of Strafford, Lord Deputy of Ireland: 'an Irish army is about to go to Scotland to help King Charles, and ... priests who have no jurisdiction from anybody and who have apostatized or have been deprived of office because of their crimes, are to accompany the army as chaplains'. While he may have been referring to priests who had apostatised to join the ranks of the episcopal Church of Ireland, Hegarty had precious little hope of influencing the appointment of chaplains to the Irish army (even had he a papal decree in his favour), though he did ask 'that a rescript be obtained from the pope, obliging every priest, secular or regular, going to Scotland with the army or individually, to apply to him first for approval, unless such a man had been appointed by the pope or by the Congregation to go there'.[8] Although the planned invasion came to nothing, Hegarty's desire to exercise control over the chaplains' ideology (one politically in favour of the native Irish) is readily apparent.[9] Similar factors were at work among the Scottish presbyterian army chaplains in Ireland after 1642.[10] In June 1641, Hegarty told *Propaganda* that little had been achieved on the mission that year due to civil strife; Cornelius Ward had also died and the cardinal had provided two new missionaries.[11] Clearly, the mission was still operational at this point.[12]

The second factor which seriously impinged on the mission was the capture and imprisonment of Patrick Hegarty in the late summer of 1641. Incarcerated for five years, this lengthy period possibly reflects his suspected espionage activities: Hegarty (or one of the other Franciscan missionaries) was probably the Franciscan friar mentioned in a report from Madrid in September 1639 as the exiled Earl of Tyrone's agent in Scotland. Tyrone made secret approaches to the Earl of Argyll around October 1639 for an alliance, for which the same man was undoubtedly his ambassador.[13] Hegarty certainly had the confidence of the leaders of the native Irish rebels. Just before the start of the Irish rebellion in October 1641, Owen Roe O'Neill, nephew of the Earl of Tyrone, wrote from Flanders to his cousin, Sir Phelim O'Neill, and commander of the Irish forces, suggesting that they keep the Covenanters out of Ireland by sending

> one Patrick Heggertie, a fryar, who had spent much time in Scotland, to sollicite for them there, and to putt the Scotts in minde that they weare for the most parte discended from the Irish, and that the Irish never drew any of theire blood, and therefore that they keepe themselves quiet in theire owne countrie, not helping the one parte or the other.

But Sir Phelim was more interested in the support which sympathetic Highlanders might be persuaded to give to the native Irish. In a letter dated 30 October 1641, he asked 'Father Patrick' to 'send word to Scotland to donald Gorme [MacDonald of Sleat] And to the people of Raghline, And everie place in Scotland where yow have freindis, And let them cum hither an we will use them weill'. This letter was probably addressed to Hegarty, but may alternatively have been to Fr. Patrick O'Donnell, a Jesuit identified by the eighteenth-century historian Thomas Carte, to whom Sir Phelim wrote asking him to send Alasdair MacColla to Ireland.[14]

So who were the priests in the Highlands and Islands at this time? In May 1642, the synod of Argyll commissioned a letter to the Marquess of Argyll asking 'that his Lordship would be pleased to concurre with the assembly in wryteing to the Captane of Clan Ronald that he would send the preest commounly resideing in his family to the assembly that ordour may be taken with him'.[15] While this might indicate the presence of an Irish priest in South Uist, it seems just as likely to refer to Ronald MacDonald, the mega-apostate.[16] In addition, a Jesuit (probably Scots) crossed to the north of Scotland from Ireland in 1643; he had 'relatives and connections in the Highlands' and was probably a Gaelic speaker. A Jesuit report for 1644 stated:

> No secure hiding place being discoverable in Scotland, two Fathers formed the resolution of penetrating through the Hebrides into Ireland, but did not succeed in the attempt. One of them, who had been conveyed over from Ireland the year before [1643], had a certain resemblance in his look and his hair to the man of high rank, whom I have just mentioned as having escaped into the Strathearn country, and on this account had great difficulty in escaping the hands of the enemy.[17]

When, on 8 July 1644, a small force of Scots and Irish sailed from Ireland to join Montrose, it was accompanied by three Irish priests. The combined forces were also attended by Scots Jesuits under Fr. James MacBreck.[18] Comprising about 2,000 men in total, the Irish force was formed into three regiments; according to MacBreck 'each regiment had a priest whom they called the *parochus*'.[19] With several priests in attendance, Catholics would have been served sporadically all along the route from Ardnamurchan where the Irish landed in July, east through Lochaber to MacKenzie country in Ross-shire, thence to Badenoch, down the Spey and on to Atholl, where Montrose joined them. But were any of these already Catholic territories? MacKenzie country stretched across Ross-shire from east to west, but by the time Prefect William Ballantyne wrote his report around 1660, the Catholic faith was professed by some of the Clan Munro in Easter Ross 'and in the Gairloch district' of Wester Ross. It was in Atholl that the joint force first became acquainted with the Scottish Jesuits, and there was no suggestion of conflict with the Irish priests. Ballantyne later identified 'some Catholics of the Clan Robertson and some of the Clan Stewart' in the county of Atholl in 1660.[20] After the Royalist victory at Aberdeen in September 1644, the army went to Mar and the Spey in the northern Highlands, where another Jesuit visited the army. From Buchan, Montrose proposed to march to Kintyre to winter, accompanied by one of the Scottish Jesuits. 'The priest accordingly prepared all that would be required to say Mass, with further supplies intended for the Irish priests.'[21] (Places visited by Montrose's Royalist army in 1644 and 1645 in the company of the Irish three priests have been noted in Fig. 4.1. Particular Campbell strongholds already claimed for the Protestants, such as Inveraray, have not been plotted.)

Reinforcing at Badenoch, the army marched through Atholl, where efforts were made to bring the word to any who showed an inclination.[22] But because the Irish really sought a confrontation with the Campbells – 'the fiercest persecutors and ... murderers and assassins of the Catholics, in the north of Ireland and the whole of Scotland'[23] – they proceeded from Breadalbane to Glenorchy and Inveraray. Burning houses and fields before them, they arrived in Lorn where, in December 1644, they camped at Dunstaffnage. By 8 January 1645, the army was again in Lochaber.[24] The two mass stones of Lochaber may date from this period, because this was the second time that the army and its Irish priests had been there in six months. If so, this may have been the MacDonalds of Keppoch's first contact with Catholicism.[25]

There was less opportunity for ministrations when the army engaged in extensive marching: after the battle of Inverlochy, and after the battle of Auldearn in the spring of 1645, the troops endured forced marches from Badenoch to Strathnairn in order to meet the Covenanting forces. Moving eastwards, they ascended Mount Scarsach in the heart of the country. 'The fasts were duly observed, and Mass frequently celebrated, in this land of huntsmen, as if they had been in a Catholic country, and they were attended in addition by numerous Catholics of the Ogilvie clan from Angus, and others who had not been recognised before.' So the Highland peripheries were again plied with Catholicism. And after the Royalist victory at Alford, in Mar, 'the priests ... began to renew their religious ministrations, more particularly among those who had been prevented by sex or inability to bear arms, from making their appearance in camp or on the march'.[26] At this point the Royalist army was reinforced by Highlanders, notably by Alasdair MacColla's levies from Kintyre and the islands, and by a strong regiment from Mull and Jura under Lachlan MacLean of Duart.[27] MacColla's men continued to be served by the Irish priests, but significantly MacLean's were attended by Protestant ministers.[28]

When the army went south, petty jealousies erupted in the Royalist ranks. MacColla's departure with his troops for Kintyre in the summer of 1645 was nevertheless entirely consistent with his commission to occupy Covenanting troops on the western seaboard and prevent them sending reinforcements to Ulster. Half of the Irish force, under Manus O'Cahan, remained with Montrose, who retreated to Atholl after the disaster at Philiphaugh in September 1645; the Jesuits had 'sole charge of all the Catholics, for the Irish priests were either killed, or had gone with Alexander Macdonald, and were living in his territory among the islands'.[29] From this point, the two Royalist

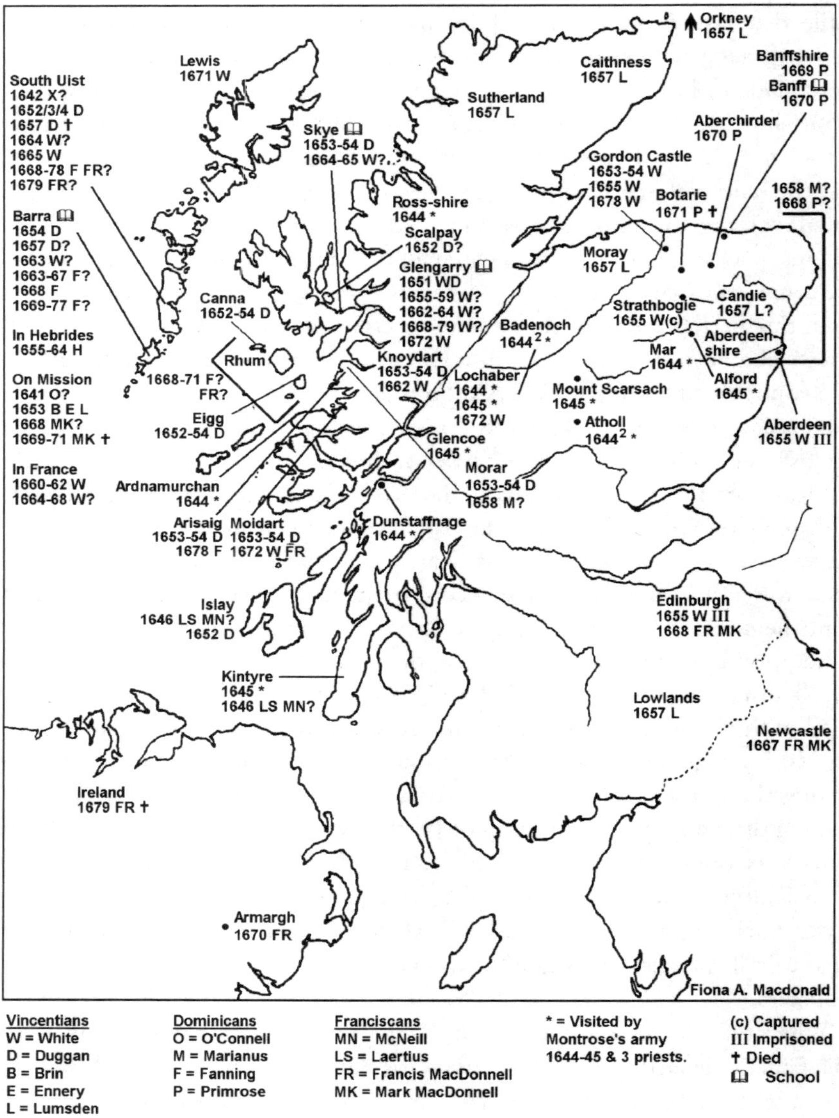

Fig. 4.1. Regular period, 1641–1679: incidence map.

forces in Scotland were physically separated. MacColla maintained a Royalist bridgehead on the western seaboard, waging a private MacDonald war against the Campbells for the next two years.[30] Montrose's campaign ended with his escape to Norway in September 1646.[31] In the same month, the synod of Argyll twice complained to the Commissioners of the General Assembly about the Irish priests in Kintyre. On the first occasion, they moaned that

> with the enemy there ar a number of freiris and seminarie priests, who ar going about Kintyre and some of the Iles, using all diligence and endevour to seduce the people to Poprie; and many not only in Kintyre but also of the adjacent Iles, even of the better sort, already following their wayes, and not only countenancing, but embraceing their superstition.[32]

Containing more or less the same sentiments, the second missive resulted in a representation to the Committee of Estates 'that these men ar come to that hight of insolencie as to professe, that in a short tyme the masse shall be set up there to the open view and beholding of all men, and that this was the end of their comeing into this kingdome'.[33]

The Franciscan mission to the Isles was very closely allied to the political fortunes of the Kintyre MacDonalds and Ulster MacDonnells. Shortly after his release from prison, Hegarty wrote from Waterford in August 1646 that he had four missionaries in mind, apart from himself, to serve in Scotland: John Gormley, Anthony Gearnon (requested from Louvain), Daniel McNeill and Daniel Laertius. The last two were already labouring in Scotland, though he did not say where.[34] Were these the two priests with MacColla in Kintyre (the third having probably been killed at Philiphaugh)? The Franciscan mission continued in Ulster under the protection of the Earl of Antrim, its major financial benefactor, and in Scotland under MacDonald protection on the western seaboard. But the chronological parameters of the official mission seem to have been wholly arbitrary: although the mission officially closed in 1637, Hegarty insisted that his allowance had not been paid since 1631.

Official negotiations to refund the mission had already begun in 1642 when Francesco Scarampi, an Italian sent to prepare the path for Rinuccini (the papal ambassador shortly to be sent to Ireland), had made this recommendation to *Propaganda*. Scarampi, Brian Conny – provincial of the Irish Franciscans – Rinuccini and the Secretary of *Propaganda* corresponded at length, resulting in four Franciscans being chosen to reconstitute the mission to the Highlands. The new staff, conspicuous by their familiarity, were Patrick Brady, Paul O'Neill, Daniel McNeill and Edmund McCann; in effect, there was only one new missionary.[35] Daniel McNeill was certainly in the mission field in August 1646 and was also proposed for the extended mission in January 1647. Daniel Laertius was also on the mission in August 1646 but was not proposed again; perhaps he had returned to Ireland already. In all likelihood, however, they were the two priests with MacColla's force in Kintyre. Restored on 22 January 1647, sadly no details of this mission are extant.[36] With the death of Alasdair MacColla on 13 November 1647 and the coming to power of the radical party in Scotland the following year, did the Franciscans prefer to continue operating from Bonamargy?

Perhaps a clue survives in the southern isles: three brothers Dunbar, from Nerabolls in Islay, arrived at the Scottish Benedictine monastery of Ratisbon in Bavaria in the 1670s. The elder, George (b. 1653), who took vows as Bro. Erhard, arrived in 1674; little information survives about Nicholas, the second brother, other than that he was a Gaelic speaker from the Highlands; while the youngest, George Dunbar, went in 1679, taking vows as Bro. John-Baptist. Although they go unmentioned in the Protestant record, their existence not only confirms that Catholics were being sustained in Islay during the 1650s when the brothers were growing up, but again highlights that area of Islay which used to have links with the monastery of Derry.[37] Did Daniel McNeill stay on in Islay until the 1650s? Certainly one Nicolas Dunbar in Islay – probably the boys' father – is cited in the minutes of the synod of Argyll between 1657 and 1661 as a persistent papist.[38] The Vincentian Fr. Duggan also went to Islay at least once in 1652,[39] apparently the last visit there by Catholic priests during the seventeenth century. But after 1653, when regulars increasingly came under the jurisdiction of the secular mission superior, there is little evidence to show that the priests visited anywhere more southerly than the Moidart and Morar region and Brae Lochaber for the duration of the century.

Laying the Foundation of the Secular Mission, 1653–1680

Secular, as opposed to regular, priests were supposed to be maintained by their own parishes, but where Catholicism was prohibited this was obviously impossible. Sometimes distinguished in Scotland by the appellation 'Mister' (used until the late nineteenth century in preference to 'Father', which was employed only for members of regular orders), Mr was also used in the Catholic record for regular priests who worked on the mission as seculars. Dubbed 'itinerant, free-lance evangelists' by Anson, secular clergy were so few as to be insignificant in Scotland during the early decades of the seventeenth century. Theoretically maintained after 1622 by *Propaganda Fide*, the seculars experienced just the same problems as regulars, with delayed stipends.

There were so few seculars that by 1627 control of three of the four Scots colleges abroad – Douai, Rome and Madrid – had been assumed by the Jesuits. Only Paris, the fourth college, remained in secular hands. It was mainly because of their understandable tendency to defect to the security of religious orders after completing their training that *Propaganda* introduced 'The Mission Oath' in 1625. Thenceforth, any student admitted to the Scottish colleges and sustained by their funds had to promise not to enter a regular order until he had undertaken three years' missionary work in Scotland as a secular priest. The intention was to neutralise the Jesuit influence, which encouraged students to join their order on completion of their studies.[40] But compulsion forged very poor missionaries: Ballantyne stated in 1659 that 'some go on the Mission only to satisfy the obligation of the vow they have taken, and, after they have stayed some time, they go off to get some security in life elsewhere and never think about the Mission again'. He suggested by way of remedy that it was 'of the highest importance that those who join the Mission should be truly apostolic men, thinking nothing of their own convenience, men who have chosen that kind of life and no other as a permanent state'.[41]

It was after Ballantyne's appointment as first Prefect-Apostolic in 1653 that the secular dimension became especially significant in the Highlands and Islands. Certainly, the first documented Irish secular priest came in 1655. But to succeed without the financial and emotional back-up of an order behind them, seculars needed leadership. Based at Gordon Castle, where he had been given refuge by the third Marchioness of Huntly, Ballantyne was in an ideal position to supervise the Highland mission (Gordon Castle served the purpose of headquarters in the north, although it was technically in the Lowlands). All secular priests on the mission were technically in the Prefect-Apostolic's jurisdiction. From 1653, seculars worked together with more enthusiasm throughout Scotland as a whole, especially among the poor. This left the regulars, particularly the Jesuits and the Benedictines (in the Lowlands), more scope to serve the nobility. On the other hand, the Vincentians – 'secular priests under simple vows, not religious in the strict sense', but a regular congregation which aimed to evangelise the poor and convert heathens and heretics – were ideologically suited to missionary work in the Highlands. But did the regulars really accept Ballatyne's authority? In the absence of a resident religious superior of their own, regulars who henceforth came on the mission recognised him as mission superior, with the sole exception of the Jesuits. As a particularly tight-knit organisation with a long-established base of Counter-Reformation in the country, they remained aloof and self-sufficient.[42]

Overall, though, secular and regular priests in the Highlands began increasingly to operate as a homogeneous, quasi-secular unit. As a consequence, the mission endured a minor setback with the imprisonment of Mr Ballantyne and his subsequent exile in France between 1656 and 1660, although Mr Alexander Dunbar (alias Winster or Winchester) acted as Vice-Prefect during his absence. While recuperating in Paris in late 1659, Ballantyne took the opportunity to draw up a report of the state of Catholicism in Scotland.

> In the whole kingdom there are to be found no more than eighteen priests: of these, eight are of the Society of Jesus; seven are secular priests, of whom three

> are Irish, in the Highlands, and four are Scots; together with two Dominicans, and one Capuchin. They are scattered all over the rest of Scotland ... the laity are wont to receive sacraments from any one of them, except the Irish, whose mission is limited to the Highland people (who speak the Irish language).[43]

It is not immediately obvious who the three Irish seculars in the Highlands were, though one was almost definitely Charles Horan. Ballantyne wrote around 1661 that he was the only priest in the Highlands and Islands after the Vincentians left. A native of Elphin diocese in Connacht, Horan was much praised by Ballantyne for his diligence and hard work. A report compiled in 1665 notes his return to Ireland in the previous year, at the age of forty, having spent nine years in the Highlands. This dates Horan's arrival to around 1655. The other two were probably Vincentians just prior to their return to France[44] – Francis White and either Gerald Brin or John Ennery, the remaining member of a pair who had come in 1653. However, when Ballantyne appealed to *Propaganda* shortly afterwards for more priests, specifically asking for people who had previously been in the Highlands, he included among them two priests on the mission who are not mentioned in other sources. Along with Francis White and his brother John, who were Vincentians, he also mentioned one John de Burgh and a MacSweeney. Both appear to have been Irishmen, but whether Vincentians or seculars is not known.[45]

Although Mr Ballantyne resumed his duties in 1660, his imprisonment had taken a serious toll on his health; he subsequently died at Elgin on 2 September. Mr Alexander Dunbar was appointed second Prefect-Apostolic in 1662. By March 1664 he was pleading with Mr Leslie, Scottish agent in Rome, to intercede with *Propaganda* to secure some priests for the Highland mission. The only priest then serving in the Highlands in 1664 was Vincentian Mr White, in Glengarry. Since the Scots colleges were not supplying priests to Scotland, Leslie felt that the only short-term solution was to continue to bring in Irish priests, especially for the Gaelic-speaking areas.[46]

The Vincentians

By the late seventeenth century, a territory which had been almost exclusively a Franciscan domain began to be infiltrated by missionaries from other orders. It was probably as a result of an appeal by MacDonald of Clanranald, who sent to Ireland for more priests in 1651, that *Propaganda* approached the French Lazarists to help in the Highlands and Islands.[47] The Vincentian ethos forged missionaries who were ideal for work in the Highlands. A son of a poor French peasant family, Vincent had been ordained as a priest in 1600. But five years later, while trying to finalise a legacy which he had been left, he was captured by pirates, ending up as a slave in Tunis for two years. In reconverting the last of his three masters from Islam to Christianity, Vincent had acquired his freedom, and although he was later to acquire considerable professional status in France, the joint effect of his humble family origins and his experience as a slave created his drive to help the less fortunate. Hence the Congregation of Priests of the Missions which he later established took a special interest in improving the condition of convicts. His order of the Sisters of Charity drew in women who took vows for a year at a time (with the consent of their husbands or parents), helped care for the sick in their homes or as contract nurses in hospitals such as the Hôtel Dieu in Paris, and looked after foundlings.[48]

In October 1650, Vincent de Paul informed *Propaganda* that two of his priests, Dermot Duggan, a native of Emly, and Francis White from Limerick, had agreed to seek faculties to go as missionaries to Scotland and the Hebrides.[49] Duggan (or de Guy, Gray or Ó Duigin) and White (or le Blanc) set out from Paris and made for Antwerp, where they waited, disguised as merchants, for passage to Scotland. While there, they were befriended by Angus MacDonald of Glengarry, a Highland chief in exile at the court of Charles II. As a Royalist, he too was travelling in disguise.[50] They met more by chance than by organisation,[51] according to Duggan's report of the encounter to de Paul in 1652.

> Having remained a long time in Holland awaiting an opportunity of embarking, God gave us the grace to depart, and we arrived here happily by the favour of the chieftain recently converted, called the Chief of Glengarry, who took us under his protection and showed us so much kindness that words fail me to express it.[52]

After a serious illness delayed his journey to the Hebrides,[53] Duggan left for Uist as instructed. Clanranald, his family and tacksmen met Duggan and were again reconciled to Catholicism, just as they has been under the Franciscans.[54] Indeed, the clan chiefs of all those areas visited by the Franciscans called on Duggan's services.

> [McNeil], Lord of the Isle of Barra, having heard of me, sent a gentleman to beg me to do his island the same service as I had done to the Laird of Clanranald. The Laird of the Isle of Capaga [sic],[55] who is a gentleman of importance, and together with him seven or eight of the gentry of those parts, made me similar requests, whom I shall with God's help satisfy as soon as possible.[56]

Duggan also went to Eigg, Canna and Islay (see Fig. 4.1), where he reconciled 800–900 people, undoubtedly a head-count of those previously sustained by the Franciscans; and the problems of the mission continued in exactly the same vein. 'Money is scarce in these parts and we accept nothing from the people; everything one buys is dear.' Duggan doubtless wished *Propaganda* to understand that he could not rely entirely on the goodwill of chieftains for his needs.

> My poverty is increased because of the fact that I need two men, men I pay. One helps me to row the boat when I go from island to island and to carry the vestments and Mass requisites overland; sometimes it takes me all my strength to cover four or five leagues on foot and on bad roads before saying Mass. I have taught the other man to serve Mass and to help in the teaching of the *Pater*, *Ave*, and *Credo*. If I had money I could buy a small boat and reach other islands, but to accept anything from the people, some of whom are very timid, would hinder the fruits of our labours.[57]

However, he did admit to accepting two crowns for his journey from Lady Clanranald.[58] Duggan's visit to Islay (an island all but abandoned by the end of the Franciscan mission except for a visit by the priests with Alasdair MacColla) had possibly been undertaken on Clanranald's suggestion.[59] (See Fig. 4.1.)

Duggan also made it clear that 'in these islands and throughout all the Highlands there are no priests except Father White and myself'. As had the Franciscans before him, he made attempts to persuade de Paul to send more 'instructors fluent in Gaelic' and able to endure all hardships, pointing out the necessity of an annual pension.[60] Duggan's pleas won a small victory: de Paul sent two more Irish Lazarists, Gerald Brin (possibly O'Brien) and John Ennery. Thomas Lumsden, a Scot originally from Aberdeen, completed the trio, which was approved by *Propaganda* on 1 April 1653 for service on the Highland mission. Lumsden, who did not speak Gaelic, worked mainly with Fr. White on the mainland. Brin and Ennery served in the Hebrides, probably taking over Duggan's mission field when he died in 1657, that is, mainly the Clanranald territories, from which they would make occasional visits to Barra and Skye. But by 1659, they, like all of the Vincentians, had returned to France.[61]

A second mission report survives from April 1654. By then, Duggan had extended his work to the mainland as well. 'The islands I have visited are Uist, Canna, Eigg and Skye and, on the mainland, I have visited the districts of Moydart, Arisaig, Morar, Knoidart and Glengarry.'[62] (See Fig. 4.1.) Duggan seems to have done marginally better than the Franciscans in South Uist, where he claimed that only a couple of people refused his ministrations.

> The island of Uist belongs to two noblemen, one is called the Laird of Clanranald and the other The MacDonald. The part owned by the former has been entirely converted, except for two men who do not want any religion so that they may be able to sin without restraint. A thousand to twelve hundred have been brought back to the Church.[63]

At first sight, this figure of 'a thousand to twelve hundred' might seem no more than a rough population estimate for South Uist at this time. However, Archbishop Oliver Plunkett's report of 2 September 1671 noted a joint population of 12,000 in North and South Uists; it is therefore likely that the population had been larger than 1,200 fifteen years earlier.[64] And the North Uist–South Uist religious divide was already well in place by the mid-seventeenth century. According to Duggan, the Reformation had made quite an inroad in North Uist in the approximately forty years since the arrival of the first minister there.[65]

> Though invited to do so, I have not yet visited the other part of the island which belongs to MacDonald. The resident minister there wanted to carry on a controversy by letter. I answered him and have hopes of good results. The well-to-do people have invited me to go there and the Laird would be very agreeable. I am the more determined to go because the minister is afraid of it and wants to put me off. The two servants they sent me have gone back Catholics by God's grace.[66]

The Vincentians also claimed that the inhabitants of Canna were 'for the most part converted', but only 'some' of those of Eigg.[67] As for Skye, it was ruled by three or four lairds: one part by MacDonald and his mother, another by MacLeod, and a third by 'MacFimine' or MacKinnon of Strath, which was firmly under Protestant rule at this time. 'In the first two mentioned parts a number of families have been converted, but in MacFimine's territory I have made no headway.'[68] Trotternish, then technically held by MacDonald of Sleat, was probably the main Catholic territory in Skye, though it was not mentioned specifically by the Vincentians. However, reconciliations were by no means as wholesale in Skye as in South Uist. This was due to a number of factors: Skye's closer proximity to the mainland; the operations of the presbytery of Skye; and the lack of overt support from the main heritors, MacDonald and MacLeod. But the synod of Argyll was certainly aware of Duggan's presence, having been informed in May 1653 'of a priest that is within the bounds of the presbyterie of Sky, which labours to seduce the people'[69] – the overtly sexual overtones fixing the sheer hideousness of the sin in the fornication-bound presbyterian mentality of the day.

Two years later, in October 1655, the synod of Argyll was 'informed that popery hes not only entered thes bounds by many priests and jesuits come frome Ireland and other places, but also is lyke to spread and increase exceedingly'.[70] It summoned a meeting of all the powerful chieftains to seek redress of these ills. At the next synod in May 1656, the presbytery of Skye continued to complain about the state of several places in the Isles where popery was creeping in through the offices of three seminary priests. Two were named as 'Francis White and Diarmid o Dovegan, who came over sees in companie of the laird of Glengarrie the year 1651'; two Scots were also mentioned.

> Thes preists doe ordinarlie reseid in Uiste, Barra, Mudart, Candort and Arresag where ordinances are not at all, and hes for the most part perverted these bownds and the chief men amongst them, as Captains of Clanrannald elder and

> yonger, McNeill of Barra and M Ien Shemis[71] and Glengaress whole familie, if not himself.[72]

The presbytery of Skye counteracted by sending letters in May 1656 to those in positions of power, particularly 'to Seaforth, Sr James mc Donald, Mc Clowde and others, who hes not countinanced the said priests', to assist it in repressing the infection.[73] Those suspected of harbouring priests were to be summoned, dealt with and eventually excommunicated if inflexible. A letter was commissioned 'to the ministers of Edinburgh requireing of them to procure letteres from the Inglishes [the Cromwellians] to the chief men of thes bounds for banishing thes preists and doing what in them lyes for recovering of thes perverted by them'.[74] In May 1658, the presbytery of Skye sent ministers to these areas under the protection of Sir James MacDonald, who was encouraged to 'use his power for gathering of the people to the ministers abovesaid'.[75]

Duggan's 1654 report throws an interesting light on the meaning behind his use of the word 'conversion'. 'In Moidart, Arisaig, Morar, Knoidart and Glengarry all are converted, or at least resolved to receive instruction when we have an opportunity of visiting each village. There are six or seven thousand people in these parts very far away, difficult to get at on foot and impossible to reach on horseback.' The major problem, however, was in sustaining those susceptible to receiving the faith. He explained that he usually deferred Communion for some time after the general confession (in which the sins of a lifetime were confessed before a person committed to the Catholic faith) 'so that the people may be better instructed and better prepared by a second Confession, and also that they may have a greater desire and appreciation of Holy Communion'.[76] But without the attention of a regular priest, this was little more than conversion in name only.

On Barra, where the inhabitants had kept up a tradition of pilgrimages to Ireland, Duggan found

> a people so devout and anxious to learn that I was astonished. It was enough to teach one child in each village the *Pater*, *Ave* and *Credo*; in two days the whole village knew them – children and adults. I have received all the leading inhabitants into the Church, including the young Laird with his brothers and sisters. There is hope of getting the old Laird on my next journey.[77]

One of Duggan's prizes was a minister's son among the converts, 'whose devotion gives great edification throughout the whole district where he is known'.[78] Since the island was supposed to be served by the minister of Harris,[79] this was presumably the son of John MacPherson.[80] According to Drs Hyndman and Dick, who reported much later, in 1760, on the employment of itinerants and catechists in the Highlands and Islands for the General Assembly, it was during this period that the real damage to the progress of Protestantism in Barra was done. 'In King Charles I's time Herries and Barra were one parish, and the inhabitants were all Protestants; but after the restoration Popish priests got in amongst them, and perverted them; and their then Protestant minister was a man inattentive to his character and duty.'[81] The Vincentian also took the message to the nearby islands of Eriskay and Vatersay.[32]

On 5 May 1657, Duggan wrote what was probably his final missive to the continent, telling his superior that he was preparing to set out on the tenth of that month for Pabba. 'I have not yet told you of this plan of mine fearing that the trouble and danger of it might make you anxious, for it really is a strange and weird place.' De Paul had planned a visit to the Hebrides. In his letter, Duggan begged him not to defer any longer, but warned: 'Take care not to tell the plan to anyone except M. Noeill, for we desire for many reasons to keep it secret.'[83] This was presumably because of the Cromwellian base in Lewis. However, Duggan fell seriously ill after his five years of mission work, and he died in Uist on 17 May. Shortly after Duggan's death, de Paul wrote: 'I have not been fully informed of the fruits of his labours, for one dare not write of religious matters, save only in the most general terms and in code, because of the English who are waging a most cruel persecution against Catholics at present, particularly against priests when they discover them.'[84]

As for Father White, he had remained in Glengarry for some time after Duggan left for the Isles, before moving up towards Inverness. In 1653, Fr. Thomas Lumsden joined him.[85] However, when persecution was stepped up under the Cromwellians, White was arrested in Strathbogie with two other priests.[86] Influence achieved their release after only a few months in captivity in Edinburgh; Fr. White quickly resumed his ministry, although no account remains of his labours between 1655 and 1660. After the Restoration, he returned to Paris. Ballantyne tried to procure a pension from *Propaganda* for him through the papal nuncio in Paris, fearing that 'he may not wish to return to Scotland, as he has no means of support there'.[87] It was agreed to advance Francis White an annual *viaticum*, or pension, enabling him to return to the Highlands in 1662.[88] By June 1664, *Propaganda* recorded that Francis White was the only priest on the Highland mission.[89] He complained bitterly to Fr. Almeras, de Paul's successor: 'You know all I had to do when I had four other priests to help me, but now I work this mission alone. Please tell me how I am to continue ... I have four thousand souls to care for, very dispersed in the islands and other remote places.' Hardly surprising, then, when he wrote that he was only 'able to visit and serve those already converted once every two years. Indeed, there are some far out islands which I have not visited for the past three years.' He had to wait until 17 November 1664 before he was technically granted the necessary missionary faculties. To add insult to injury, his maintenance seems never to have arrived, for he allegedly worked ten years on the mission without any support from *Propaganda*. When in September 1659 Patrick Con, papal nuncio in Paris, wrote to *Propaganda* saying the Scottish missionaries were complaining that they had not received their salaries, he added that the Vincentians in the Highlands were not only paid regularly, but they received far more than the secular clergy.[90] The Lazarist house in France must have sent regular financial support when *Propaganda* failed them.

In 1665, White was operating from Glengarry, as he probably had been since his earliest days in the Highlands. He had even managed to establish a schoolmaster there, Ewan MacAllister, on a salary procured from *Propaganda* by Fr. Almeras, the Vincentian Superior-General. MacAllister regularly received fifty scudi per year. However, the school in Glengarry was not particularly successful. Dunbar wrote in his mission report for 1669–70 that 'the schoolmaster is scarcely tolerated in Glengarry, despite the protection of the lord of that territory; and there is but little hope of position'. MacAllister had previously been schoolmaster in Skye, where he had sixty pupils. (White probably visited the island in 1664 or earlier, if he was also responsible for setting up the Skye school.) MacAllister had been driven from Skye by people hostile to Catholicism – in all probability, the presbytery of Skye. Protestant authority had been strengthened there by the creation in 1662 of a new ecclesiastical jurisdiction, the archdeanery of the Isles (including Skye and the Small Isles), upon the restoration of episcopacy.[91] White had also established a school in Barra which he gave into the care of George Fanning, the Irish Dominican who arrived there in 1663. He also visited Uist in 1665.[92] Like all of the missionaries, White's schedule, which involved him operating in and around his base in Glengarry as well as making occasional trips to the islands, was gruelling, especially since he was still the only priest on the mainland in September 1666.[93] Alexander Dunbar, the second Prefect-Apostolic, made a plea to *Propaganda* for Irish priests, asking particularly for Fr. White's brother, John White. But since he was gravely ill, two Franciscans, Mark and Francis MacDonnell, were sent by *Propaganda* in his stead.[94] White, however, continued with his mission; Dunbar reported in 1669–70 that 'Father White often visits the islands and the lands of Glengarry and all the mountain districts, as far as he is able, though he endures great fatigue and suffering.'[95]

It was undoubtedly the patronage of Glengarry (favoured with the title Lord MacDonell and Aros at the Restoration) that enabled White to carry out such a long, successful mission there. In 1670, Archbishop Plunkett of Armagh revealed in a letter to *Propaganda* that Francis White was maintained by Daniel Arthur, an Irish merchant who lived in London. And in 1671, he was the first priest known to have visited the Protestant Isle of Lewis. Plunkett reported that the landowner of the Isle of 'Lennse', the Earl of Seaforth, had persuaded the Privy Council to let White stay there.[96] After touring the mission in 1672, Alexander Dunbar said that Francis White worked with the Scot Robert Munro in Glengarry and Lochaber during the winter and then transferred to Moidart for the summer.[97] Little of consequence arises concerning Francis White until his death on 7 February 1679.[98] Fortunately there were still Dominicans serving in the mission field.

The Dominican Mission

Only a little information has survived about the Dominicans' mission in the Highlands and Islands. In 1629, the Chapter General (convened in Rome) entrusted the pastoral care of Scotland to the Irish province. The Irish Dominican congregation was then based mainly in Spain under its own Vicar-General; in 1615, another community had been established in Lisbon, and in 1624 a third Dominican community had been established in Louvain for English, Scottish and Irish friars; there was no exclusively Scottish house.[99] In 1633, when the Franciscans were still working in the Highlands, *Propaganda* approved four Dominicans – Fr. Dominic de Burgo and three others – to go on the Scottish mission, on an annual *viaticum* of thirty scudi. They probably never went. *Propaganda* again approved four Irish Dominicans for the mission, on 25 June 1635: in all likelihood they were the same people. They were instructed to go to those Gaelic-speaking parts of the Highlands not already being served by the Franciscans.[100] But, again, there is no evidence that they arrived.

An Irish provincial chapter at Youghal petitioned the Dominican General in 1638 with a view to increasing the numbers entering the order. Perversely, his reply insisted that entrants be restricted because of problems created in other provinces by Irish postulants overseas. As mentioned above, few showed any inclination to return to their native land after protracted study abroad. Recruiting in Ulster was therefore suggested, with the intention of sending friars to Scotland but, according to the General, the result seldom lived up to the ideal. As long as they declined to return to their own country after taking their vows, priests were hardly likely to embrace the harsher conditions on the Scottish mission. Nevertheless, permission was given for receiving Scots to the habit, either in Ulster or in any other province of Ireland within easy access of Scotland, although novices were only to be admitted into communities large enough to sustain the requisite level of regular observance: basic adherence to discipline was absolutely essential on a mission where no ranked superior was resident.[101]

There may also have been Dominicans in Scotland of whom little is known. For example, one Theodore de Pietate O'Connell, who had been studying at the Irish College in Lerida in Spain, was granted an annual allowance of twenty scudi on 14 November 1637 by *Propaganda* and declared a missionary in Scotland. While there is no conclusive proof of his ever having been in Scotland, he wrote to *Propaganda* from London in 1641, indicating that he was unable to go to Scotland because of the hostility between that country and England.

He may even have been heading for the Lowlands, though with a name like O'Connell he was probably an Irish speaker. *Propaganda*'s reply of 12 November 1641 certainly referred to O'Connell as a missionary in Scotland and gave him permission to stay in England until he could safely proceed there. Later, on 23 March 1647, the Master-General gave permission to Fr. John Baptist Fitzgerald to lead a group of five Irish Dominicans to Scotland 'for the propagation of the faith, the comfort of catholics, and the recovery of the convents which our Order had there', as well as to act as Vicar-General over all members of the order in Scotland.[102] However, in June 1647, *Propaganda* then refused to ratify them for the Scottish mission on the grounds that other priests had recently been chosen.[103]

Scots Dominicans within the Irish province were also expected to take their turn in Scotland. Recruits to the Irish province came mainly from the Scots colleges on the continent and were people who had become disillusioned with internal collegiate wranglings or who welcomed the greater security brought by membership of a regular order. This led to some Scots returning to their homeland as missionaries. One such was Fr. Patrick Primrose, who had studied at Edinburgh University. Granted missionary faculties on 20 September 1650 in the three kingdoms of Great Britain, Primrose was a member of the Irish province and the most distinguished member of the Dominican order in Scotland during this period. Initially active in the Lowlands, by 1668 he was working on the peripheries of the Highland mission; he based himself in Banffshire.[104]

Two of Primrose's recruits were closely connected with the Highland mission, which shows his interest in that side of affairs; it would certainly have been easy to co-ordinate Dominican participation from Banffshire. The first of these Dominicans, Fr. George Fanning, was stationed in the Isles; the other is a little more elusive. Fanning was a genuine Irishman and, according to the account of Alexander Leslie (brother of the Scots agent at Rome) of his Highland visitation in 1678, one of three priests from Ireland. He went to the Hebrides in 1663. The Franciscan, Francis MacDonnell, chastised *Propaganda* in a letter from Armagh in July 1671, insisting that 'Father George Fanning also, of the Order of Friars Preachers, would have perished from hunger before now, were it not that he lived with the Laird of Barra. He has not received a sixpence from the Sacred Congregation for the past eight years, although he has laboured much and with great fruit.'[105] (See Fig. 4.1.)

Fanning probably came in answer to a plea for more priests by Mr Dunbar, the Prefect-Apostolic; he stated in 1663 that only Mr White, the Vincentian, and Mr Charles Horan, Irish secular priest, were operating in the *Gaidhealtachd*. Like most on the Highland mission at this time, he pursued a 'more or less free-lance episcopate'.[106] He attended to the needs of the 1,000 Catholics then in Barra at the time, including the MacNeill. But according to

Francis MacDonnell, Fanning's mission was less than officially sanctioned. MacDonnell wrote:

> Father George Fanning, a Dominican, labours here with good results. This father, according to the Procurator of the Mission, has no patents or faculties from the Sacred Congregation. His ground for staying there must be either the privileges of his Order or else because he believes that these people, being as it were abandoned and in extreme necessity of Sacraments, any priest may come to their assistance. This is indeed one of the strongest arguments urged by almost all those working in these British Isles and also in England; and they claim to have a right to continue their functions and their work, all the more as they persuade themselves that recourse to Rome is either impossible or unnecessary, and that the delays of that Court are intolerable.

Both sides (*Propaganda* complaining of lack of communication, and the priest of intolerable delays) had a point. Nevertheless, MacDonnell saw the danger in the mission ground becoming a haven for those escaping the confinements of regular jurisdiction. 'These and similar views are creeping in very fast, and if they are not remedied by giving them Superiors, very few will in time have recourse to the Holy See.'[107]

Gordon's Annual List of missionaries shows three Dominicans on the Scottish mission in 1668. These were probably Primrose, Fanning and a third who appears in the Master-General's records as Vincentius Marianus Scotus, of whom more below.[108] Fanning was in Barra until 1671, and possibly for six years after that.[109] After this, he transferred to Arisaig: when Alexander Leslie reported to *Propaganda* on the state of the faith in Scotland in 1678, he said that the people of Arisaig were very distressed by the death of George Fanning, their priest; they were bitterly disappointed when Leslie did not leave Robert Munro, the Highland secular priest, in his stead. Fanning was active in the *Gaidhealtachd* for fifteen years in all.

The second priest from the Irish province under Primrose' authority was Vincentius Marianus Scotus, whose name suggests that he too was a Scot. The Latinisation has been suggested as 'a pious adaptation of some Scottish name ... to express devotion to Mary. Mair, Murison, Morrison? In the west Highlands the patronymic Mac Gille Mhuire was known – "the son of the servant of Mary". "Marianus" conveys this adequately.' In October 1652, Marianus had written to the Master-General asking to be sent on the mission with Primrose. By 1658 he had achieved his aim. A chalice of his, dated that year, survives in the Catholic church in Morar, Inverness-shire, the inscription revealing that it was for the use of Vincentius Marianus of the Order of Preachers, missionary in Scotland. However, the survival there of his chalice is not conclusive proof that he worked in, or even visited, Morar. When priests left the mission, sometimes their mass ornaments were allocated to others. No further information has come to light about Marianus.[110]

On the death of Primrose, the Dominican mission lost much of its impetus and dynamism, because it had been so fundamentally centred in his personality. In spite of a few Scottish recruits to the order, the Dominican mission base in the north-east seemed to flounder after his death. The Dominican presence was only sustained in the following century by the missionary zeal of a few itinerant Irish Dominicans. But also working on the Highland mission during the last few years of Primrose's life was a second wave of Franciscans.

A Second Franciscan Mission

Propaganda recorded on 20 April 1665 that two Irish Franciscans on their way to Connacht had agreed to become missionaries in the Highlands. As Charles Horan had returned to Ireland in the previous year, this left only one Vincentian on the mainland.[111] Recommended by the Guardian of the Irish Franciscan college of St. Isidore in Rome and the rector of the Scots College in Paris, the Franciscans, brothers Francis and Mark MacDonnell, were authorised to work under the jurisdiction of the Prefect-Apostolic, since their old mission was now defunct. They were approved for the Highland mission on 8 February 1667. Supported by *Propaganda*, Dunbar was to place them wherever he saw fit. After delays in procuring money for their journey, they eventually set out from France in August 1667. Shipwrecked shortly afterwards, they were taken under the wing of John Smithson, an English Franciscan in Newcastle, remaining with him for four months until they were fit to travel to Edinburgh. Bereft of clothing and mission accoutrements, they immediately presented an additional burden on the overstretched resources of the Scottish mission. Dunbar wrote to Rome in March 1668 that Fr. Mark was not yet well enough to go to the Highland mission, but that Fr. Francis would be leaving for it in a week's time.[112]

Further attempts were also made to expand the Highland mission. On 23 January 1668, a full restitution of the Franciscan mission was proposed in *Propaganda*, to include an additional four to six priests under a prefect of their own, who would place them in the most needy districts in a way that would not create conflict with the secular clergy. This proviso had apparently arisen as a result of a complaint to *Propaganda* that Irish Franciscans on the mission had been abusing of their privileges and in disharmony with secular priests; the complainer thought it better that secular priests were sent from France.[113] To whom this referred and from whence it came is difficult to judge, but it is significant in highlighting a topic to which little attention has been paid hitherto. The MacDonnell brothers had not yet arrived in the Highlands. Does this therefore refer to Franciscans operating from Ireland post-1647? Both MacDonnells were in the field by 1669, Francis probably having left for the Hebrides in March 1668. Fr. White, the third priest on the mission, was attempting to find more priests through the agency of his brother Gaspar,

Vicar-Capitular of the diocese of Limerick. Exactly where Fr. Mark laboured is not certain.

On hearing of Oliver Plunkett's appointment as prefect of the Highland Mission, Fr. Francis briefly left his post to see him in Armagh in the summer of 1670.[114] While Plunkett took his responsibility for the mission very seriously, it is apparent that he did not enjoy the confidence of its most important patron, the first Marquess of Antrim (1610–82): of twenty priests he proposed for the mission, the Marquess rejected all of them. This was for a number of reasons. First, Plunkett's treatment of Tories was (understandably) unpopular with the native Irish. Tories were native Irishmen who had been dispossessed at the plantation and lived as wood kern – bandits who eked out a meagre existence in the woods. When news of the plantation had first been divulged, the Irish had quickly understood their fate, realising that they would 'be woodkerne out of necessity, no other means being left to them ... than to live as long as they can by scrambling'.[115] The plantation endorsements of April 1610 had stipulated that land was not to be demised to the native Irish, nor indeed to anyone who refused the oath of Supremacy. The few who did receive land were mainly from the pre-plantation middling classes: local sept leaders who did not command the allegiance of an overlord and therefore did not present a political threat to the English and Scottish undertakers; as native Irish freeholders holding directly of the crown, they were no longer obliged to supply men for the hostings of the greater Gaelic lords.[116] Where the preferred term for such a bandit in the early seventeenth century was wood kern, the word 'Tory' – an anglicisation of the Irish Gaelic meaning 'pursuer, attacker or raider' – came into currency from 1646.[117]

Plunkett obviously sympathised with the dispossessed Gaelic nobility, opening schools in Drogheda to educate their children, but he was none the less committed to reducing the number of them who lived by robbery and violence. Acting as a mediator for the government in August and September 1670, he undertook a mission to persuade the Tories into voluntary exile in France and Belgium (action which resulted in extremely negative reports about him to *Propaganda*).[118] Possibly the second reason for his rejection of so many priests was that Antrim hoped to retain as much control over the Highland mission as he had done in the 1620s and 1630s. That the MacDonnell brothers were related to the MacDonnells of Antrim supports this interpretation. Third, and probably most pertinent, Antrim was aware of the need to exercise political caution in Scotland[119] as well as to protect his position as a planter in Ulster: in choosing to remain in Ulster as a prominent Gaelic landlord, Antrim had indicated his willingness to accept a conforming role.[120]

Although *Propaganda* had expressly ordered the archbishop to visit the Highland mission, Fr. MacDonnell, the Marquess of Antrim and Patrick O'Mulderrig, Vicar-General of Connor, dissuaded him from doing so.[121] In a letter written from Armagh to the secretary of *Propaganda* in July 1671, the reason MacDonnell gave for dissuading the archbishop shows the existence of a more profound political awareness in the Isles than might be expected for a marginal area. MacDonnell pointed out that

> a report had spread of the arrival of the French whom the Scots are said to favour, so that if His Grace, the Primate, were to go there, everyone would think that he had come to prepare the way for the French. It is for this same reason that no missionaries are to be sent there this summer, as the news of their arrival would at once get abroad and they would be cast into prison. For it is proposed to effect the union of the two kingdoms of England and Scotland in one Parliament, to which union the Islesmen are strongly opposed. Now, if the Primate were to visit them, it would at once be said that he came to foster the opposition to this union.[122]

This is a unique Gaelic reference to the manoeuvrings of John Maitland, Duke of Lauderdale, Scottish Secretary and adviser to Charles II, and his curious attempts at a union between Scotland and England – first economic and then all-encompassing – between 1668 and 1670. Neither the King nor Lauderdale appear to have set much store by the prospective union; indeed, the former was engaged in secret negotiations with Louis XIV for a new commercial treaty with France. It was little more than a political gambit.[123]

MacDonnell, of course, made his usual plea for the mission: that native youths be sent to Rome or other seminaries on the continent, and in the meantime more Irish priests would be most helpful. MacDonnell clearly anticipated the arrival of many eager-faced Irishmen, because on 31 August 1671 *Propaganda* renewed missionary faculties for Francis MacDonnell and eight secular priests.[124] Plunkett appended comments of his own to the letter for which MacDonnell was obviously his source; these show that Francis MacDonnell was normally based in Uist. (See Fig. 4.1.) Dunbar reported in a letter of 26 July 1672 that Fr. Francis sometimes worked in Moidart. He was always the more active of the two brothers, perhaps due to having better health. Fr. Mark died towards the end of 1671. When Fr. Francis was forced to retire to a Franciscan convent in Ireland during 1679, ill-health was given as the reason. His retiral was announced to *Propanda* on 30 April 1680, at the same time as the death of Francis White.[125] However, on 6 April 1681 the Protestant record referred to 'preist Francis Mcdonald in Glengerey', suggesting that he had returned despite his alleged bad health.[126] He soon went again: Mr Ryan, then priest on the Highland mission, wrote from Castle Tyre on 23 June 1681 that 'Francis mcdonnell ... is parted most unhappily, god helpe him'.[127] MacDonnell had undoubtedly fled for political reasons: both he and the Scot Robert Munro had joined Lord MacDonell of Glengarry's expedition against Argyll in the early summer of 1679. Dunbar admitted to David Burnet in Paris two months before MacDonnell left the mission that they had joined not as spiritual guides but as fighting officers – Munro as *Capitani* and MacDonnell as *Caballieri* – even though they had been strictly forbidden from doing so by word of mouth and in writing. This presumably explains an unattributed reference to Fr. Francis departing to Ireland 'with shame enough'.[128] It also adds weight to the argument that the political ambitions which the MacDonnells harboured to regain old MacDonald lands in Scotland were tied to a general anti-Campbell policy.

Exactly when Fr. Francis left the mission is not known, although he is last mentioned in Scotland in 1681. In a petition to *Propaganda* in March 1683, he said that he had spent more than twelve years as a missionary in the Highlands of Scotland and hence sought the title 'Father of the Province', which could be given to Franciscans who had done meritorious work over a period of years, set at twelve by Clement IX. The title was granted. Whether because of his relationship to the Earl of Antrim or because of his own innate ambition, MacDonnell applied to *Propaganda* in 1684 to be made a bishop. The petition pointed out that the dioceses of Kilmore, Derry and Down were then vacant (see Fig. 1.1) and that MacDonnell had spent more than fourteen years on the mission. The Earl of Antrim agreed to provide sufficient funds to maintain him as a bishop, but even then the request was refused. Two years later, at the age of fifty-two, MacDonnell again petitioned *Propaganda* for permission to return to the Highlands of Scotland. Having spent many difficult years in that rugged terrain, he wished *Propaganda* to recommend to the Franciscan Father-General that he be made titular provincial of Scotland. On this occasion, *Propaganda* acceded to his requests but referred the matter to Cardinal Howard, Protector of England and Scotland. While MacDonnell was successful, no further details are given, which tends to suggest that either he did not actually return or did so only for a cursory visit.[129]

Dynamic Secularism in the Highlands, 1680–1689

In his 1680 report on the Highland mission, Alexander Leslie particularly recommended that equal faculties be granted to seculars and regulars, because in the prevailing situation many regarded seculars as inferior to regulars. He also asked for more Irish priests for the Lowlands as well as the Highlands.[130] During this period in the Highlands, there were four main areas in the mission field: the Hebrides (mainly South Uist, but also the embryonic Catholic communities of Lewis and Skye), the nearby mainland district of Morar (including Moidart and Arisaig, and possibly Brae Lochaber), the mainland districts of Glengarry and Strathglass, and the more segregated eastern mission (including Glenlivet, Braemar and Strathdon) which had more connections, via Gordon Castle, with the east coast Lowland mission. To a certain extent the first three were interrelated: South Uist and Morar were both Clanranald territories, so they automatically had a certain degree of connection, and missionaries from either tended to serve the intermediary Small Isles of Canna, Rhum and Eigg; similarly, missionaries from Morar always went through Glengarry and Strathglass on their way to the mission assemblies at Gordon Castle. In spite of this, 'Catholics rarely heard Mass oftener than three times a year', according to Leslie.[131]

At the time of Leslie's visitation, only two priests were serving in the Highlands: the Scot Robert Munro and the Irish Franciscan Francis MacDonnell. However before Leslie left Scotland, a secular priest, James MacDonnell, arrived on the mission from Ireland, though he did not stay long.[132] Leslie's report was submitted to *Propaganda* in January 1681; following closely, on 4 March 1681, 'directives were issued covering most of the points raised'.[133] This heralded a period of intense vitality on the Scottish mission, characterised in the Highland sector by an almost exclusively Irish personnel.

Hugh Ryan (or Rian), a clerk regular of the Barnabites in Paris, arrived in the summer of 1680 accompanied by Mr David Burnet, secular priest, who was coming to the mission as Vice-Prefect.[134] On 6 April 1681, the Protestant record refers to 'Father Hugh Orein, another preist, residing in the Chissolme's Country under the notion of a phisician', so Ryan was still in Strathglass at this time, where he had passed the previous winter.[135] Priests at this time frequently assumed other occupational identities in order to shield themselves from detection. In his report to Rome in 1660, for example, William Ballantyne had recommended that 'each missionary might be taught some mechanical craft, or might have some honourable profession; for example, he might be a portrait-painter or a glazier or a watchmaker, or he might be able to profess some knowledge of medicine, and so he would escape the danger of investigation'.[136] On 23 June, Ryan wrote from Castle Tyre to Angus MacDonald, son of Glenaladale, then a student in Paris: 'I am partinge next morneinge to the Eyles, alonge with your uncle Kenloghy who convoyes his married daughter Mary to her owne house in the Eyle of Huist, which will be my first voiage uppon seas in this Countrey.' Ryan had clearly taken as his patrons the MacDonalds of Glenaladale, who were based in Morar.[137] He said that he had nobody to help him but Munro (alias Ratray), but he continued for some years on the mission, probably on the mainland. After attending a meeting at Gordon Castle on 25 April 1687, he thereafter limited his mission to Strathglass, since the increase in Irish priests in the previous few years had enabled him to reduce the area for which he was responsible. Ryan continued his work into the 1690s, but when he and Munro fell ill in the same year, 1687, the Highland mission was in dire need of assistance.[138] (See Fig. 4.2.)

In April 1681, the Protestant record mentions an Irish priest, O'Neill, who is not referred to in the Catholic record but went by the Christian name of

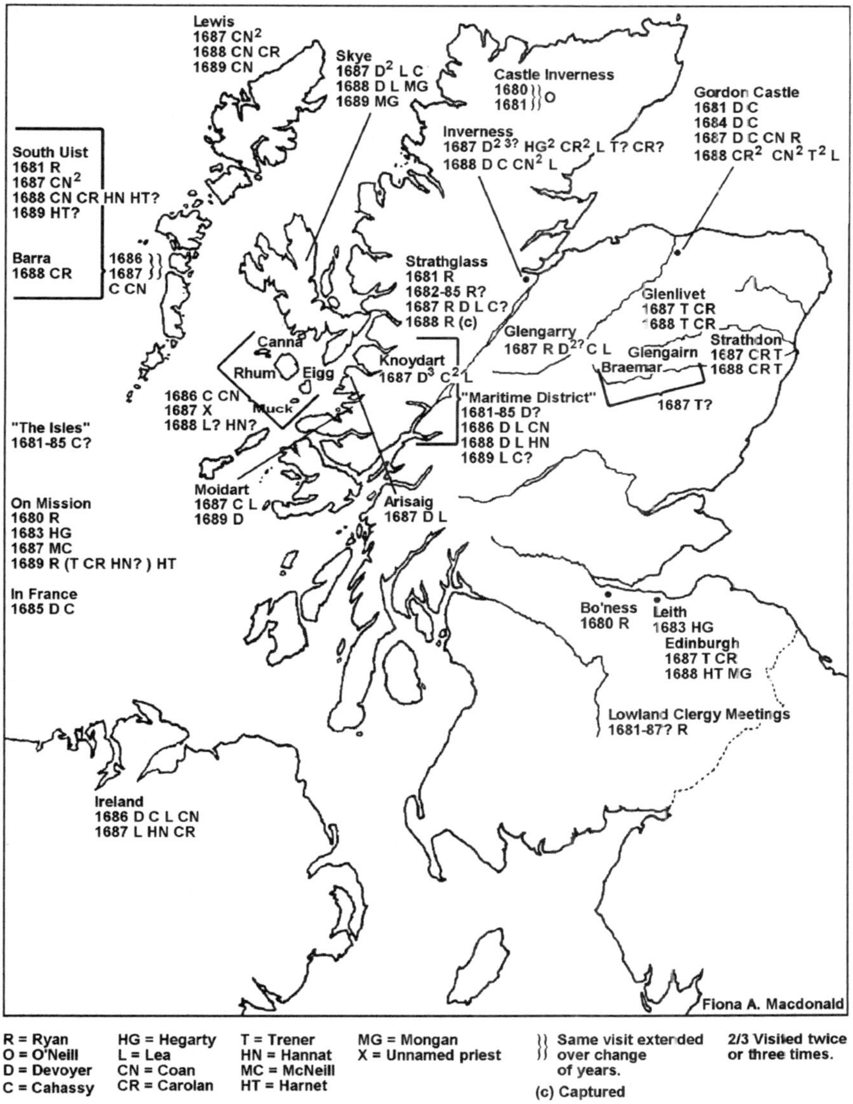

Fig. 4.2. Dynamic secular period, 1680–1689: incidence map.

Alexander; he also came to the mission late in 1680. The presbytery of Inverness noted that 'preist O'Neil, resided in the Castle of Invernes from the 25 of December till Easter last'.[139] Priests were entertained in Castle Inverness under the protection of Sir John Byres of Coates[140] and his wife Lilias Grant, daughter of the Protestant laird of Grant.[141] As governor of the castle, Sir John used his position to protect Catholic priests and laymen. The year 1681 also saw the arrival of another two Irish clergymen who proved long-serving on the Highland mission: Mr James Devoyer (or de Voir) and Mr John Cahassy (Chatty or Cassy).[142] Their services had been procured in Paris by Mr Leslie, who was returning from Rome after delivering the report on his Scottish visitation. Both Vincentians, they were funded by Mr Talon (or Tallon), secretary of Louis XIV's Cabinet at Versailles, who did much to subsidise Irish-speaking missionaries for the Highland mission. 'He could not guarantee their other qualifications, and the extreme need of such and the difficulty of finding them, made it not always possible to be fastidious in employing them. The house of the Lazarists generally furnished the men, and left Monsr. Tallon to furnish the means.'[143] The Vincentians arrived in Scotland in August 1681.[144] They travelled with Leslie to Gordon Castle, and after a brief rest one was sent to the west Highlands and the other to the Islands.

Devoyer and Cahassy remained in Scotland for two years 'serving those poor folk going continualie from toune to toune and from countrie to countrie' before another two priests – 'Mr. hagerty ... an Irish man' and Mr MacDonald, a Scot – were sent to help them. There were now five men on the Highland mission, four Irish and one Scot, though MacDonald died only six months later.[145] Hegarty also came from Paris in 1683 at Talon's behest, accompanied by Mr Angus MacDonald, son of Glenaladale, and Mr Mahon (or MacMahon), an Irish schoolmaster employed in the west, but Hegarty did not tarry long before returning to Ireland.[146] Devoyer and Cahassy had originally promised that they would stay only for three years, but 'the superior of the mission [Leslie] prevailed with us to abyd another yeir while they vold seik some others to supply our places'.[147] This report illustrates how regulars were by then subject to the control of the secular head of the mission: although staffed by many regular priests, the Highland mission was in practice organised more on secular lines. Whether Mahon remained on the mission or not is unknown; one source states that he stayed in the Highlands for another year and then returned with the Vincentians to France. Certainly, the Catholic schools in Barra and Invergarry continued under other teachers.[148]

At the end of their supplementary year, Devoyer and Cahassy holed up in Paris to rest during 1685, but aimed to return. 'Wee intend for Irland nixt spring when wee have provyded some bookes and ornaments for what wee had in scotland belonged to the mission and not to us and health and strenth will serv[e].'[149] They came back to the Highlands (via Edinburgh) in about July

1686, bringing with them two new Irish missionaries, Mr James Lea and Mr Cornelius Coan, who had a doctorate from the Sorbonne. This was the year in which the King asked all Scots priests who were not engaged in foreign colleges to return immediately to the mission, so that during the year 1686–87 there was a pronounced increase in mission personnel. Coan and Lea (his cousin) also appear to have been funded by Talon.[150] Cahassy and Coan had left for Uist and Barra in early November 1686.[151] Devoyer and Lea wrote from Arisaig in February 1687 of 'four other Isles between here and Uist'[152] – probably Canna, Rhum, Muck and Eigg – which were served by the missionaries from Uist. They also identified another unnamed clergyman in the area: 'there is a priest in one of these four who goes to the three others from time to time, mainly in summer'.[153] Was there a predecessor of Mr O'Hara who served in the Small Isles between 1700 and 1708 from a base in Canna?[154] Throughout their careers, Devoyer and Cahassy generally worked from the Morar or maritime regions. Their separation on this occasion was clearly a means of initiating new recruits into the rigours of the Highland mission in the company of two veterans; after that, it was intended that the new men would work together in the Hebrides. Lea and Coan had been intended originally for the Hebridean mission, but the superior's plan failed to materialise because one was emotionally, and the other physically, weak.

Devoyer and Lea not only served the environs of Morar but were invited to Sleat in April 1687. This was possibly the first time since Ward went there in 1637 that priests had been in Sleat – unless Duggan had gone there when he visited the neighbouring Strath Mhic Fhiòngainn in 1652–53.[155] Heading from there to an assembly at Gordon Castle, Mr Lea accompanied Devoyer as far as Strathglass, where 'there had not been a priest for two years',[156] a long time, considering that missionaries had been working in the Highlands for almost seventy years. With Dunbar's permission, Lea left for Ireland in May 1687 to see his parents.[157] Returning at the end of September, he spent a month in Glengarry with Munro and then went on to join Cahassy in Moidart. In Ireland, Lea had obtained the post of dean of Down, and that he returned at all is indicative of his dedication to the mission; Dunbar certainly labelled him 'a good workman'.[158] But called here and there for various ministrations, Cahassy and Lea did not have much opportunity actually to work with each other. Devoyer had gone to Skye around October 1687, but 'instead of 5 or 6 weeks ... was obliged by the storms and other unexpected circumstances to stay there for 4 months'.[159] By March, Lea had taken Devoyer's place in Sleat, but he was too sick to do much.[160] (See Fig. 4.3.)

In Uist, Cahassy and Coan worked 'à nostre maniere ordinaire' until the former was left by himself. In early May 1687, Cahassy spent a couple of weeks serving another three islands nearer the mainland (probably Canna, Rhum and Eigg), where he spent Pentecost. One of the islands had not seen a priest for a

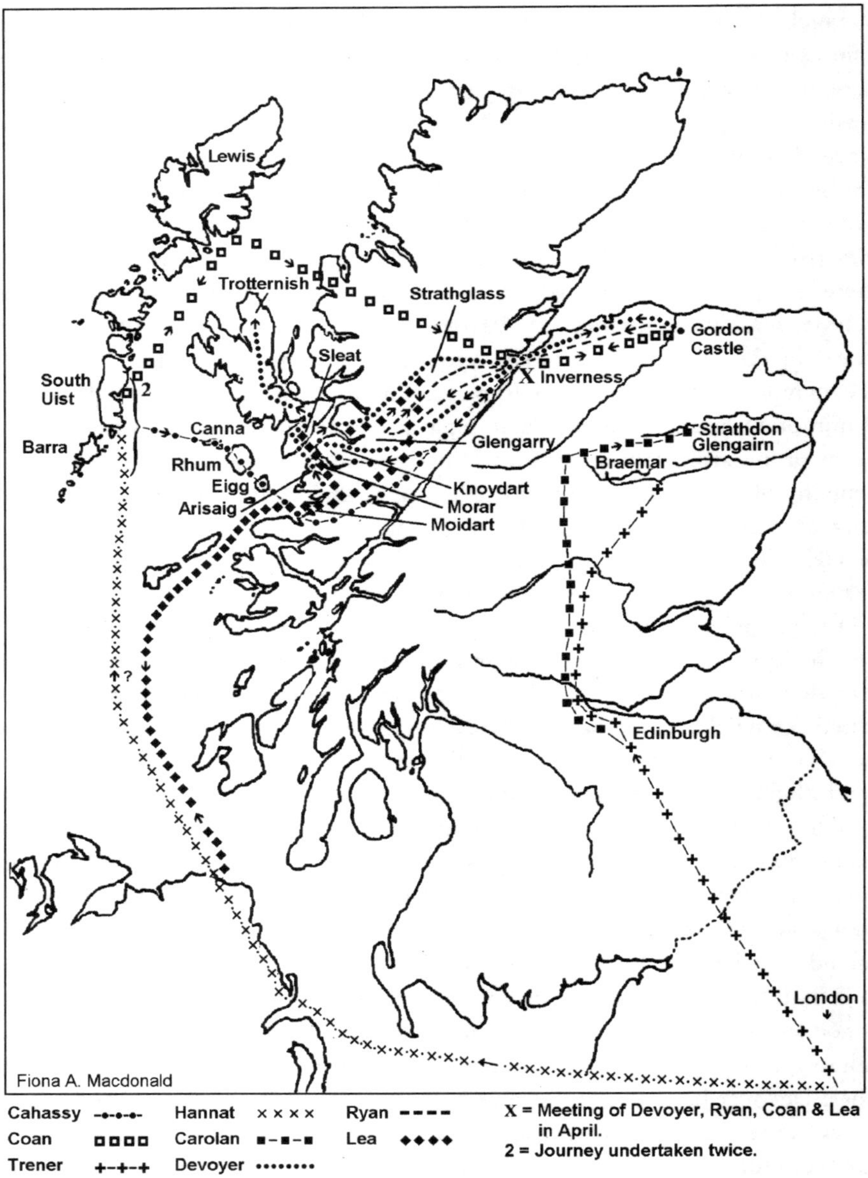

Fig. 4.3. Dynamic secular period, 1687: priests' itineraries.

year, except when the priests themselves had passed through briefly seven months previously.[161] The long-term sustenance of Catholic communities still left a lot to be desired. Having made a beginning in South Uist and Barra, Coan's mission increasingly centred on Lewis where, possibly due to the lack of mature company, he eventually succumbed to the temptations of the flesh and was dismissed. Devoyer had taken him on a tour of the Catholic communities in the Hebrides, because Coan wrote on 3 May 1687 of 'our trip to the Isles',[162] but they had subsequently been invited to Lewis.[163] Devoyer could not justify the time, so he sent Coan there by himself at the end of February without reference to the mission superiors, who were deemed too far away for consultation – yet another indication of the freelance nature of these early missions. He stayed for four or five weeks with George MacKenzie of Kildun, the Earl of Seaforth's uncle; unbelievably it was only the second time since the Reformation that a priest had been to Lewis. Although Kildun is near Dingwall, George MacKenzie spent his later life at Aignish, two miles from Stornoway. His brother Kenneth, third Earl of Seaforth (married to the Catholic daughter of the English Lord Powys), had made him tacksman of extensive lands in the Point district of Lewis. He and his wife subsequently became Catholics when they visited his nephew, the Catholic fourth Earl of Seaforth, in England. Coan's was the only sustained Catholic mission on the island, and Coan was deeply flawed as a priest.[164] Initially, he made some ground: in April 1687, for instance, he pleaded the case of a young man in Lewis who had been studying for the ministry but had since wished to become a priest and have a place in the Scots College in Paris. This was probably Donald (Columba) MacLennan, the son of a skipper, born in Stornoway about 1670. He went on to become one of the first Highland Benedictines.[165] In May, Coan was instructed to return via Lewis to Uist to work with Lea when he came back from Ireland. The most recent mission assembly had encouraged the priests to work together in pairs as much as possible. 'We have found in this regard, and even very necessary, that we come together in pairs to work, in order to have a community.'[166] In this way, priests not only had the necessary companionship of their peers, but they could also help keep their partners on the straight and narrow.

The Irish continued to extend the faith into other Hebridean communities. Devoyer and Cahassy crossed from Morar to Skye in July 1687 with the express purpose of serving 'the very few Catholics who live there among the Protestants, and mainly to talk to a gentleman who it is hoped will be inclined to taste the truths of the Catholic faith'.[167] Subsequent correspondence identifies the area as Trotternish, which most likely makes this man a MacDonald. The 'premier Cadet'[168] of his brother (the laird of two or three townships there), he was probably a brother of Sir Donald MacDonald, third baronet of Sleat, then chief. Indeed, he may have been the Gaelic poet Archibald MacDonald, *an Ciaran Mabach*.[169] The priests certainly thought him of great significance for the continuance of Catholicism in Skye: 'They tell us (and we hope too) that the conversion of this person is like an open door for the conversion of others.'[170] They also spent a few days in Sleat serving other Catholics.[171]

The year 1687 found the mission buckling under a burdensome shortage of labourers. The report of the April mission meeting sent to Cardinal Howard stated that there were only six priests working in the Highlands; these – Cahassy, Devoyer, Ryan, Coan, Munro and Lea – have already been identified.[172] In his August report, Cahassy hoped for the arrival of Mr Hegarty, who had been on the mission in 1683, but he did not come.[173] In September, Coan was in South Uist, complaining of being 'bienfatigué' because of the extent of the Catholic population there, and preparing to winter in Lewis.[174] Owing to the dearth of priests, Devoyer returned to Trotternish by himself in early October 1687, saying to George Gordon at the Chapel Royal in Edinburgh in March 1688: 'There have been two ministers since the pretended Reformation. They have not had any priests since I went.'[175]

Cahassy had been informed by Burnet (dean of the Chapel Royal in Holyrood since 1687) that three new recruits would be coming to the Highland mission from Paris. This was timely assistance: Munro and Ryan were ill, and Cahassy had also been stricken 'by a pulmonary consumption' and was heading for Inverness with Devoyer.[176] Remaining in Moidart in their absence, Mr Lea was not himself in good health. Cahassy added that they were very distressed to see all their Isles uncared for after the departure of Mr Coan for Lewis, especially since the new priests were not expected until Candlemas and Easter 1688.[177] The three new recruits were Carolan, Trener (alias Bayers) and Hannat, of whom only the latter was truly new to the mission.

Carolan and Trener had worked previously in Glenlivet and Strathdon, which were technically in the Lowlands, and they had therefore not been included among the Highland missionaries.[178] After a brief sojourn on the continent, they entered the Highland mission in January 1688 while Hannat went via Ireland and did not reach the mission until the summer.[179] Carolan accompanied Mr Thomas Nicolson, the future bishop, and Mr J. Jameson, a friend and associate of Nicolson's at the seminary in Padua,[180] who were both responding to the King's order for all Scottish priests to return home. Trener, however, came into the country via London in October 1687 with Jacques Hannat.[181] Invited to speak to Lord Melfort, Secretary for Scotland, Hannat and Trener's reception in London amply testifies to the toleration extended to Catholics under James VII.[182] But it was a superficial rather than a grassroots toleration: while recuperating in Inverness in the following year, Cahassy wrote that 'the benefits of the time augment us but the inclination of the people is different. In several Protestant areas we are criticised and censured more severely than ever before. In others we are shown more friendship than hitherto, and more inclination to our religion.'[183]

John Trener and Patrick Carolan, both 'laborious workmen' according to Burnet, initially returned to their Lowland mission.[184] Hannat was in Uist by August 1688, having been 'in the maritime districts and the inner or nearer Isles' in July.[185] Trener was still in Glenlivet and Strathdon in August,[186] but having laboured there with him through the winter and spring, Carolan transferred to the Highland mission in the summer. 'Mr. Carolan has to join with me to go to the Isles,' wrote Coan on 16 June 1688, 'although against his inclination knowing the destitution of the Isles only by account, I will take him to Uist and Barra, among the Catholics we serve there, if it please God, until the month of October.' Coan intended to place Carolan peacefully among the Catholics in Lewis after that, until he found his feet.[187] Another Irish priest, one Alexander McNeill (clearly of Scottish extraction), also came to Scotland around the same time as Nicolson, but not with him. In 1694, he carried several letters to the continent and was referred to by Mr Charles Whytford of the Scots College in Paris as 'one of our Irish missioners lately come from Scotland', though little information of his earlier career there survives.[188]

As the priestly personnel was augmented, mission correspondence reveals distinct signs of discontent amongst the Irish. Mr Devoyer, in particular, reiterated the perennial concern about lack of money, resources and personnel. He also implied dishonourable conduct in the unsealing of a letter, which he had not taken lightly. Needless to say, much of the dissent did concern money. It is difficult to gauge just how much financial responsibility for the missionaries was assumed by Talon and how much by *Propaganda*. Certainly, when Cahassy wrote from Paris in December 1685 he said that *Propaganda* was providing, or supposed to be providing, '50 crounes a yeir for each missioner to the number of 5 that were there But how needful are Missioners in those Countries and how insufficient is 50 crounes a piece yow shal easily understand.'[189] Indeed, there had been no increase in the amount allocated to individual priests for thirty-five years: the ten secular priests working on the Scottish mission in 1650 had also received fifty Roman crowns.[190]

On St. Valentine's Day 1687, Devoyer and Lea tendered information about other benefactors of the mission, effectively showing how piecemeal the financing of the operation was. Though unaddressed, in all likelihood the letter was to Mr Talon. In it, they mentioned other patrons to whom they intended to write: the Princess of Conty, who had helped them already; Reverend Mother Agnes; the Duchess of Vaujau (or Sister Louise in the Carmelite convent in Paris, where Devoyer and another missionary (possibly Lea) had acted as chaplains); and the bishop of Orléans.[191] As usual, the missionaries were hard-pressed for funds. Devoyer wrote in May that Mr Dunbar, 'had no money to send us but 20 escus each'; he had even had to borrow this because he had received nothing from *Propaganda*, nor what he had expected from the 'liberalité du Roy.'[192] Mr Devoyer was entrusted with thirty gold louis (or 149 francs,

10 sols) for the Highland mission, most of which had come from Mr Talon, and another three louis from 'Monsr. L'Abbé des Marais'. He distributed this among the five Highland missionaries (Devoyer, Ryan, Coan, Munro and Lea) then gathered in Inverness; only Mr Cahassy was absent, 'for we are only six in all in the Mountains and Isles'.[193] Coan confirmed in May that they received twenty-five crowns each, but he complained to Talon that although he always hoped to be treated like the others, he feared he had been forgotten.[194] Further correspondence reveals that only Lea was funded by Talon (and only on a temporary basis), though Devoyer had asked him to share the money he received from Talon amongst the other missionaries, namely Ryan and Munro (funded solely by *Propaganda*), and Coan.[195]

There was an increasing clannish solidarity amongst the Irish, at this juncture, and an apparently widening breach between them and their Lowland superiors. Under the stress of constant communication over the minutiae of financial manoeuvring, relations had obviously begun to break down. Devoyer assumed the role of spokesman and broker for the Irish in the Highlands. On 7 March 1688 he assured David Burnet: 'As to the tenn Crowns you speake of, & does not know if M^{r}. Cahassy is to share in them or no. It is a thing I cannot tell also, untill I know from whom, or whence they come.' Untold problems arose over the allocation of Mr Talon's subsidy: 'As to that which Mr. Tallon has sent, I have his letters shewing his will & disposition of the same. He writs he has sent to Mr. Dumbar that little summe in order to be delivered to me, & orders me to passage itt with my brethern.' Possibly after Coan's letter, Mr Talon was more specific about the distribution of the funds he sent. In view of the vast sums he was prepared to spend in setting up a Highland retreat, Devoyer thought this strange but mused philosophically:

> enfin he may dispose of his Charity as he pleases. Our Conscienses can beare us testimony & he also that what ever wee spoke to him touching the Heighland Mission was for the common good therof, & in proofs therof what little thing he has sent last yeare, though in his letter he has appropriated it to three of us only (viz) M^{r}. s Cahassy, Lea & I, it was equally divided amongst us six Missionairs, as their own Recept, which I have sent to Mr. Tallon can testifie.[196]

Devoyer remained anxious to preserve open lines of communication with his superior: he did not suppose that Burnet really thought badly of them, but wrote to him to show his 'indifferences in that matter', believing the money to be best employed for the good of the mission when divided equally among them. This suggests that Talon intended that priests whom he had not agreed to support should no longer be funded by him. However, Devoyer insisted that when he was last in Paris Mr Talon had agreed with him

> that a hundered Crowns att least was needfull for a Missionair in the heighlands ... & uppon that he promissed to do what he could to help us to that

> summe and if the King & he thought otherwise (as you wrote to Mr. Cahassy) it was because nobody did fully represent, unto his Majestie our necessity, nor made Mr. Tallon mindfull of the Relation we left him.

At the time, each missionary received 318 francs a year.[197] In Talon's defence, he fell ill in 1687, which undoubtedly resulted in inattention to the mission, if not changes in his attitude. However, the reduction in his subvention should probably be seen more in political terms: when the Catholic monarch, James VII, was on the throne, support for the Catholic mission was a continuing gesture of solidarity from Versailles but, by the beginning of 1688, rioting in Edinburgh showed that the King was unpopular in Protestant Scotland. Was there any point in continuing to support his régime? Unity among the Catholics in Scotland therefore became all the more imperative. As Cahassy put it in July 1688, 'we well understand that in this time it would be very inappropriate that we or our comerades render ourselves disobedient to their superiors'.[198] Yet, adequate or inadequate, Talon's charity was a major factor in the survival of the Catholic mission to the Highlands.

The financial controversy continued at the April assembly. Dunbar noted complaints from the Irish clergy that their allowance was insufficient to support them. By this time, they received eight crowns per annum each.[199] According to Dunbar, Devoyer and Cahassy were most discontent, so much so that he was 'thinking to licence them home to their own country'. In his opinion, 'Mr. Devoyer is the prettiest man, but the most particular in matters of interest I have known'. And their colleagues were clearly informing on them: Dunbar told Mr Whytford in Paris that both were known to have saved twenty crowns each year out of the fifty they had received in the previous three years in order to create into a fund with which to go to Ireland. Whytford was asked to convey this discreetly to Mr Talon.[200]

Perhaps partly due to prevailing discontent, another meeting was held unusually quickly on 11 June following. Coan, who had arrived at Gordon Castle in May, was summoned by Mr Burnet 'for the purpose of giving him an account of our progress, to bring up our difficulties concerning cases of conscience, and to receive our instructions in order to have a uniformity among ourselves'.[201] Devoyer and Lea had appointed him as their delegate. Coan wrote plainly in a letter to Talon that they were 'also discontent at not having received that money that you had the generosity to send us' (which instead had gone straight to Mr Dunbar), and they had omitted to give him an account of their progress. Coan therefore gave account of them as best he could.[202] These petty squabbles did not imbue Rome, which needed no excuse for withholding funds, with confidence. In August 1688, Burnet informed Mr Leslie in Rome that he had heard how Leslie had borrowed money to pay the missioners for the current half year, 'being that the Congregation would send no money, till they gett more relation firm us of the state of the mission'. Burnet had forwarded the report of their June meeting, but insisted 'if they be not content with that let them send us as many articles by way of Interrogatories of what they desire to know as they think fitt, and I sall have a case to answere them exactly so farre as I can gett information'. How little had changed since the days of the Franciscan mission to the Highlands and Islands. Hugh Ryan, who is seldom mentioned in any correspondence, sided with his fellow Irish missioners over the money issue, however. Burnet wrote to Leslie: 'I beseech you send Mr Hugh Rian his recepts preceeding August 1687 or ane authentick Double of them before a notar for he Denyes me 25 crouns.'[203]

In the year before the Revolution, there were eleven priests on the Highland mission, and a total of twenty-six secular priests altogether in Scotland,[204] showing that by this time the Highlands was almost as well staffed as the Lowlands. An enormous percentage – ten out of eleven of the west Highland missionaries – were Irish, their number having been recently augmented by two new arrivals, Richard Harnet and Anthony Mongan.[205] Burnet's letter listed the places where many of them laboured:

> viz. Mr Coan and Carolan presently in the Lewis. Mr Hannat in Ouist Mr Devoyer in Donalds Countrey about Sleat. Mr Monro in Knoydart Mr Rian in Strathglasse Mr Cahassy somewhat sickly at Invernesse Mr Lea sickly come Downe to Gordon Castle iust now to change and Mr Trener in Glenlivet and Strathdowne and two Irish iust now landed here whom I am very shortly to send to their comerads in those Countreyes.[206]

Added to Burnet's list was Mr Forsyth of the Society of Jesus, who worked 'in Braymarre and thereabouts so there are 12 in all for the Highlands'.[207] Henry Forsyth (Forseu or Forsiter) was a Gaelic-speaking Scot who first trained with the native Irish. Originally a native of Edinburgh born of Protestant parents, he studied humanities at Cashel in Munster under seculars (presumably learning his Irish while there). Converted to Catholicism by Jesuits, he completed his humanities with them, subsequently enrolling on a higher course at the Scots College in Douai, Belgium.[208] When Alexander Leslie left Rome for Scotland in May 1652, he outlined his intention to visit Mechelen, where Forsyth had been sent for his noviceship, before heading to Ostend. 'I will visit Henrie Forsaye, our contriemane now their, ane iouthe of great expectatione, who knowes the Hiland language.' If he is the father mentioned in the Jesuit annual report for 1670 as 'familiar with the Erse language used by the mountaineers of Scotland',[209] then his arrival on the Highland mission can be dated to June of that year. According to the Farquharson Manuscript, Forsyth told Lewis Farquharson, a local laird, that he was working in Glenlivet and Strathavon where, unsure of being betrayed, he made only a few converts. The Jesuit annual report for 1671 claimed that they had infiltrated the Highlands 'in places where the Catholic religion had scarcely been heard of, since the first introduction of heresy, and into which one of our Fathers has for the first time penetrated'. By this time, Fr. Forsyth was probably working further south in Braemar.[210]

There is very little evidence in the extant record which lights upon Harnet, but more survives in relation to Mongan.[211] They arrived together in London in August 1688, coming in answer to the King's edict drafting back to Scotland all missionaries who were then abroad; they were also protégés of Mr Talon. Talon had given the money promised them to Mr Whytford in Paris, who was to forward it to Mr Burnet in an obvious attempt to retain the money in the hands of the mission superiors.[212] Harnet and Mongan had but twenty-four shillings sterling each on arrival in London, much of which was squandered in attendance on the court at Windsor where, according to Mr Dunbar, 'they got not a sixpence of helpe for any of them'.[213] Dunbar advanced them twelve crowns each from their travelling expenses to Scotland, realising that if it had been withdrawn for their salaries they would have had little to live on. Mongan was eventually assigned to the west coast mission, of which Moidart was the hub. By 1691 he was in Skye, sustaining the incipient Catholic community there. Richard Harnet seems to have served in Uist at one stage, and in August 1688 (the month of his arrival), Dunbar expressed his intention to settle an Irish priest in the Enzie district of Banffshire in the hope of creating some Highland scholars there who might ultimately be fit to send to the colleges abroad.[214]

Harnet and Mongan's penniless arrival, in the midst of raging financial controversy, did little to improve the standing of the Irish. In late August, Burnet wrote graphically of the Irishmen's attitude: 'You would wonder at some of our Irishmen's impertinencies, which are sett down in their letters I have beside me. I manifest as little of them as I can for charities cause ... It is manifest they purpose to make bande apart, but for remedy against that I see is not at present.'[215] On 20 September Dunbar warned Whytford: 'Let no more Irish be sent till called for: much less so ill provided as the last two, with not a groat in their pocket, nor a cloak to keep them from the rain, nor ornaments to say mass with and you know we keep no magazine of such things.'[216]

However, the rift between mission personnel was shortly relegated in significance when William of Orange set foot on British soil in November 1688 and James VII fled the country in the following month. The reign of toleration was over; the Edinburgh mob celebrated by unceremoniously sacking the Chapel Royal. In the Highlands, little action was taken against the priests; none were seized except Mr Ryan, and then not until 1696. This is not to say that there were no ramifications for Catholicism in the Highlands. The very fact that no further record of missionary activity exists for five years after the Revolution is sufficient testimony to the circumspection of the times and the near impossibility of sending reports safely.[217] Coan contributed to the upheaval by apostatising and marrying a Lewis woman towards the end of 1688, evidently a daughter of MacKenzie of Kildun who had first invited the priests to the island. Apparently it was a case of personal expediency, but neither was the political situation for Catholics very rosy, King Billy's arrival finally compromising Coan's flimsy faith through fear of an increased risk of seizure. In all of the scandal which surrounded his conduct, Coan's lack of guaranteed funding has never been entered in his defence, mainly because there were many others who continued working under similar hardship. After the assembly in June 1688, he complained to Talon that he was not treated on a par with his other protégés: 'I have had more loss, expense and worry during the last year than all the others, as I have already indicated to you.'[218] Formally suspended by the prefect, Alexander Dunbar, on 22 March 1689, Coan succeeded in alienating both congregation and community where he had worked under trust.[219] The imprisoned Earl of Seaforth was later accused of having had him killed, presumably because he had suffered loss of face and because his family had been instrumental in first inviting Coan to the island. However, Coan was sorely punished for his misdemeanours: falling victim to the islanders' keen sense of natural justice, he spent the next ten years of his life imprisoned, and enduring a catalogue of harrassment, first in Seaforth's castle of Eilean Donan and subsequently on small islands off Lewis, Fladda and North Rona, at the hands of Seaforth and his uncle, MacKenzie of Kildun.[220]

Nor was Coan the only priest to fall by the wayside; as Fr. James Bruce wrote from Ratisbon to Leslie in Rome in 1690, 'It's to be lamented that there are so few labourers in places for the harvest is very great; and the more to be regrated that some of the Irish missioners who have been there have misbehaved extreamly, and given great scandall which has alienat the mynds of the people mightily.' Coan obviously received particular attention, but there were 'bysyds two others who befor some thrie of four yeirs or more played some such lyke trikes'.[221] This would date their games to 1686 or 1687, but there is nothing which personally implicates any of the above-mentioned priests by name.

Results of the Mission

Accounts of the general state of piety of laymen must generally be seen in light of the priests' desire to elicit additional funds from *Propaganda*. On 31 December 1685, Cahassy attempted to manipulate the emotions of the hard-headed Roman administrators, insisting

> there is no people that hath a desyre to be instructed in their Religion more then they, No people comonly more submissive and obedient to church they never speak to a priest but after reseving [receiving] his benediction kneeling befor him it cannot be expressed how much they Rejoyce when a prist comes to the countrie, they come to him from all parts to hear divine service to

> Confesse and Reseav to christn their children ... I cannot tell you how much wee were touched at our departure to see thame weep after us wee are abandoned no bodie will come to us.

This comes but a few lines after his complaining 'how insufficient is that litle pension of the colledg of *Propaganda*'. It truly vexed Cahassy that the Highland mission was more poorly funded than non-European missions, because this restricted the missionaries' work. 'Let him ever be so zealous if he has not withall to be entertained cannot have lyke successe. Wee see many zealous persons goe to Siam and China but they goe provided of all necessars that they be no way troblesome to their prosolites.'[222]

During this period, the mission superior made a start in establishing priests in specific areas so that the consolidation work necessary for Catholicism to flourish properly could begin. Following his visitation of the Highlands and Islands in 1678, Mr Alexander Leslie strongly recommended in his report to *Propaganda* that priests should be assigned to particular stations, although this does not appear to have become a policy until Bishop Nicolson made fixed stations obligatory for priests after 1700.[223] Even though missionaries such as Devoyer and Cahassy worked more or less exclusively in Clanranald territory, they had to move around in order not to become a burden on anyone. This had contrary indications for consolidation.

> Wee have been there 4 yeirs and all this tym wee could not make our residence for one month in one place to instruct them as wee wold wish least wee should be burdensome to them. Many in diverse places offered themselves to become catholikes but having not the tyme to instruct them sufficientlie fearing the great scandall of their eminent relapse wee did allwayes deffer to reseave them.[224]

Inability to sustain the faith was still one of the greatest deficiencies of the mission at this time. Cahassy said that the ultimate aim was to be able to 'stay at least thrie months in one countrie'.[225] Where a local chieftain or laird was particularly sympathetic to the cause, he was sometimes willing to maintain a priest: in South Uist and Glengarry, for example, priests stayed for long periods on extended hospitality.

In the meantime, more attention was given to maximising individual productivity through strict structuring of the priests' timetables. The method employed by Lea and Devoyer in Arisaig was to compile lists of the faithful in each settlement whom they would prepare for the sacrament of penance. They assigned a particular day to each township so that the people could confess without embarrassment, which could not have been avoided if everyone attended together. One day in the week was also set apart for catechising the young, after eight o'clock in the evening when the cattle were enclosed and protected from the Lochaber cattle reivers.[226]

Before reconsidering those areas in which Catholicism was either fortified or reintroduced for the first time since the Reformation, the almost complete extinction of Catholic missionary activity in Argyll and Kintyre by the first Franciscan missionaries should be remembered.[227] Throughout this period, Argyll was maintained as an almost Catholic-free area by vigorous containment of any popery reported to the Kirk. For example, when the synod of Argyll was informed at its meeting at Lochhead in Kintyre on 16 June 1654 'that sevrall persons in the cuntrey conversed with Anna Nc Donald, ane excommunicat papist', it decided 'that no person or persons whatsoever doe converse with any excommunicat person (except such as naturall tyes binds) under the pain of condinge censure, and recomends to the civile magistrat that some civile punishment be inflicted on the contraviners thereof'. Public intimation of the Act the following sabbath probably locates Anna Nc Donald in the Lochhead area itself.[228] Though evidence suggests that such censures were not fully upheld, they doubtless exercised some restriction on behaviour in staunch presbyterian areas.

On only one occasion during this period was it rendered perfectly safe for Irish priests to come to Kintyre, and that was during the civil war under the protection of the Royalist army, when some of the Kintyre folk were said to be embracing their views.[229] The army visited a number of areas. Specifically mentioned was Atholl, which was host to 'a number of gentlemen of some note and consideration, who were Catholics, but had not seen a priest for a long time', and were now admitted to the rites of the church. 'They ... were called Robertson, and formed a numerous party in the neighbourhood.' Significantly, MacBreck's report made clear that 'there is no part of Scotland into which our Fathers have not penetrated, except Argyllshire, and Albany [Breadalbane] which leads to it'.[230] This serves as a yardstick of the extent of Jesuit penetration of the Highlands in the mid-seventeenth century.

But far from a familiarity with Catholicism, much of the evidence shows a lack of extended contact with religion of any kind in many districts. By December 1644, for example, the MacIans of Glencoe – a branch of the MacDonalds – had not yet been visited by Protestantism, and knew only the bare rudiments of Catholic doctrine; that is, they were in religious limbo. 'Not averse to Catholic customs', a man of note among them was even able to repeat 'the Lord's Prayer and the Angelic Salutation in the ancient language of the Scots'. That this was considered such an achievement shows how little they had been exposed to organised religion. While MacBreck may have been correct in stating that 'The Calvinist preachers have never found their way into these parts', he was inaccurate in assuming that 'not one of them was present with the army, in which only Catholic priests were recognised', because several ministers, such as Martin MacIlvory who ministered to MacLean of Duart's troops, were disciplined for fraternising with the Montrose's army.[231] The chief of the MacDonalds of Lochaber (north and south), 'Macranald the Fair', was 'not opposed to orthodox piety', nor were the chiefs of Glengarry and Keppoch, although the Camerons were deemed 'less susceptible to piety'.[232]

On the other hand, the raiding and destruction suffered by Argyll during the Montrose wars can only have entrenched the presbyterianism of the Clan Campbell and made it all the more determined to exterminate Catholicism. The deeply perturbed synod of Argyll stressed to the General Assembly on 10 September 1646 that: 'The suord of the rebells quhilk hes bereft us of our freends, spoiled us of our goods, and burnt out duellings ... cannot parallell the bitternes that the feare of the sorest of all plagues, the removall of the light of the gospell, hes possessed our soules with.'[233] Disciplinary measures were still being pursued by the Kirk in the 1650s.[234] In 1651, the heir to Murdoch MacLean, tenth of Lochbuie, submitted to the synod of Argyll, though his father remained a fairly intransigent Catholic.

Elsewhere in the 1650s, the priests of the Vincentian mission mentioned in their reports how much the Islanders had retained of what the first wave of Franciscan missionaries had taught them. Duggan wrote:

> I have found some of the inhabitants of Uist who called themselves Catholics and had some knowledge of the Sacraments of Penance and the Holy Eucharist. This is due to their having been to Confession formerly to some Fathers of the Order of St. Francis who came here from Ireland, but these people were so little instructed that they did not know how to make the sign of the Cross.[235]

In spite of the hundreds of reconciliations claimed by the Franciscans in South Uist, by 1660 Prefect Ballantyne reported the numbers of Catholics only to be 'more than sixty', among whom was Lady MacNeill, sister of the Earl of Antrim. This was probably a more realistic figure than Francis MacDonnell's estimate of 12,000 in 1671, or that of Cahassy who insisted in 1687 that almost the entire population of South Uist were Catholic.[236] Similarly, the 800–900 people whom Duggan reconciled in Eigg, Canna and Islay in 1652 were apparently 'so ill-instructed in religious matters that there were not fifteen who knew any of the mysteries of faith'.[237] No breakdown is given of the number of souls in each of the three islands, though Ballantyne reported in 1660 that there were 'more than one hundred Catholics' there.[238] Islay takes on significance as the only location south of Ardnamurchan and within Campbell jurisdiction that the Vincentians felt safe to visit by the mid-seventeenth century. All other areas in Argyll and the southern isles had ultimately been abandoned by the first Franciscan missionaries. And Fr. Lumsden informed St. Vincent[239] in 1657 that he had visited the Orkney islands, Caithness, Ross, Moray and Candie, where 'there are but few Catholics', which supports the argument that the Reformation was swiftly and rigorously introduced there.[240] But the major problem during this period was in sustaining the Catholic population where it did exist, and it had clearly not been easy to do this from Ireland.

It is perhaps most appropriate to examine those areas in which Catholicism was established and maintained during this period by quoting directly from the contemporary record. Mr Cahassy wrote on 31 December 1685: 'The catholikes of the highlands are in tuo divers places the one pairt of them in the maine land where all the inhabitants are catholikes and the other part in Iles called hebrides.' He identified seven Catholic areas in the mainland: Strathglass, Glengarry, Moidart, Arisaig, north and south Morar ('moror vic onille' and 'moror vic alester') and Knoydart, which were 'the roughst places that ever man saw some 30 miles, some 20, some 12 distant in great deserts distant one from another'.[241] The missionaries referred to each district as a 'canton' within which there were a number of settlements, which they called 'villages' in French, most probably for Gaelic townships, or *bailtean*. In Arisaig, for instance, they noted twenty-three settlements, each having approximately fifteen communicants other than children.[242] Besides these seven mainland territories, Cahassy said: 'There are six iles whose inhabitants are also catholikes Viz Egge Mouik otherwis Tyreihrane Rumme Canna ouist Barra, some of these are distant from the maine land some 40 leagues some 30 some 20.' In addition, he identified five other little islands 'verie farr in the sea southward to the ile of Barra in everie ile at least a village with so many families': Vatersay, Mingulay, Pabbay, Sandray and Berneray.[243]

How many Catholics were there on the mainland? Cahassy wrote (1685) of his first visit to the Highlands in 1681, and how he was 'conveyed ... all along to the foot of the hylands; wee found therein verie rough and vast countries far distant one from another the matter of seven thousand catholiks, and so much more in the adjacent uest iles of Scotland which they called formerly Hebrides'.[244] Devoyer and Lea specifically singled out the people of Lochaber in 1687 as 'bad neighbours ... people without God and without Religion, they do not scruple to steal all that they can'.[245] The town of Inverness was mainly Protestant; as Fr. MacBreck, the Jesuit, had stated in 1648, the inhabitants 'are ardent Calvinists, having become obstinately imbued with these sentiments by a preacher who was sent here for banishment by King James the Sixth'. According to Cahassy, there was 'only one Catholic family with very few from the neighbouring district who come on some feast days and Sundays and others who come from time to time from our Catholic districts to the fairs and markets'.[246] Nevertheless, when Cahassy was recuperating there from consumption in early 1688, he made three new converts.[247]

The records of the presbyteries of Inverness and Dingwall reveal considerable adherence to Catholicism in Strathglass, the Braes of Glenmoriston and Abertarff. The revival of Catholicism for the first time since the Reformation can be dated in this area to the 1670s.[248] The reintroduction of Catholicism was greatly facilitated here by the conversion of Colin, son of Chisholm of Strathglass, who lived at Knockfin. On 3 July 1677 the elders at Kiltarlity, 'being asked if popery was upon the groweing hand in the over parioch, answered that such as were popish enclyned were in the province of Ross where the Chisolme with his family and dependents were'.[249] Tradition records that Catholic missionaries then in Glengarry heard this and 'two of them repaired immediately to Strathglass'.[250]

In the Moidart region, the majority were allegedly reconciled prior to this period, and certainly the missionaries seldom refer to the number converted.[251] In most of the country around the maritime region, it was as much a question of salvaging the inhabitants from irreligion (even paganism) as of reconciling them to Catholicism. Indeed, on this, the Catholic and presbyterian sources are in accord, one of the few things on which they could agree, apart from the vastness of their parishes. Cahassy insisted on 31 December 1685 that:

> Ma[n]y other of the adjacent countries wold embrace the Catholike Religion if churchmen did frequent them though they bee under the notion of protestants yet treuly they have no Religion at all but are rather infidels then of any sect and commonly they have more difficultie to submite themselves to our christian discipline for to amend themselves of their vices then they have to professe and believ our misteries.

The truth of the matter was that these were almost totally neglected pastures. But reversion to a pre-Christian or quasi-Christian state cannot be equated with savagery. 'They are not as people imagines them so barbarous and wild that they are untractable and therfor Unworthie to be lookit after, but contrary to that they [are] naturally civill and especiallie those of our Vocation and they are endued with a great deal of Natural witt.'[252]

An example of pre-Christian practice was cited by Mr Cahassy from Moidart in 19 September 1687. Like the paganism of the bull sacrifice observed in Ross-shire in the early seventeenth century,[253] Cahassy described a non-Christian form of lay baptism, a recognition ceremony marking the birth of a child in a society without a resident cleric, which was still practised when a priest was not resident, in abuse of the permission that had been extended to them to baptise dying children. Performed by senior members of the community, families uncomfortable with children as yet unbaptised would have them doused at the lochside. 'These old men, not knowing the correct form of baptism make use of a superstitious recitation.'[254] And so the older traditions existed alongside Catholic practice.

But superstitious practices not only affected those areas without a regular Protestant ministry. For example, the session book of Kingarth in Bute noted on 24 April 1649 the appearance of Lachlan M'Kirdy, who confessed 'that he and Alester M'Kaw did use the charme of the ridle in Suthgarachtie for getting of silver that was stolne from him, and that the said Issobell N'Kaw did practise the said charme ane other tyme'. One of these charms, given in full, reveals its provenance in the ubiquitous common folk culture outlined in the *Carmina Gadelica* which was confined neither to Protestant nor Catholic areas.[255]

The main Catholic strongholds in the Isles were Barra and South Uist; Catholic communities here were fairly well sustained – indeed, after the initial work of the Franciscan missionaries they were perhaps the only places consistently sustained. Catholicism here was supported throughout his lengthy chieftainship by Iain Muideartach, twelfth of Clanranald (1618–70), and also, following his conversion by the Franciscans in 1632, by Niall Og MacNeill, sixteenth of Barra.[256] The Franciscans last visited Barra and Uist in 1636, yet it is evident that Catholicism lingered there: in May 1643, the synod of Argyll received intelligence from Mr Martin McPherson about 'two idols keeped by McNeill of Barra in his privat chappell called our Lady and her babe, trimmed up in their apparrell and ornaments'.[257] The island was subsequently served in the 1650s by the Vincentian Fr. Duggan, visited in the mid-1660s by his colleague, Fr. White, and finally achieved its own resident missionaries, George Fanning and Francis MacDonnell, in the late 1660s and the 1670s. As for Uist, Cahassy wrote in June 1687: 'It is a well-populated country and the inhabitants are all Catholic except for the Minister's family who live there, and a few special exalted relatives of whom we have received ten on the last occasion.'[258]

One of the by-products of Clanranald's patronage of the Highland and Island mission was the continuing entrenchment of anti-Campbell attitudes among the missionaries, especially those who worked in Clanranald lands. This attitude, prevalent among most MacDonalds, had two things at its heart: first, the political motivation of the Clan Donald South to regain its lands in Islay and Kintyre (a major factor in MacDonnell of Antrim's support of the mission); and second, those MacDonalds who had fought in the civil war, particularly the MacDonalds of Clanranald, Glengarry and Keppoch, had been reinforced in their hatred of the Campbells. Francis MacDonnell and Robert Munro, who worked as missionaries in South Uist and Glengarry respectively, even went as far as joining Glengarry's expedition against Argyll in 1679 as soldiers. Similarly, after Argyll's rebellion in November 1685, Cahassy, who was based in the Clanranald territories, revelled in

> the Glorious defeat or Rather the miraculous confussion of our hyeland malevolent neybour the arch and hereditarie traytour argyll and the rest of his faction Who were thought to land and lay hands first upon our catholikes being alwayes their mortall enemies not only for his phanatike zeall against the catholike religion (or poperie as he termes it) but also for their descent from those whose losse and misfortune he builded up his vast estate and fortune.[259]

An altogether more quixotic episode was the qualified revitalisation of the faith in Lewis for the first time since the Reformation. Visited in 1671 by the Vincentian Fr. White, with the sanction of the Earl of Seaforth, the island did not see a priest for another sixteen years until the arrival of Mr Coan who, through his disreputable behaviour, probably did as much to promote Calvinism on the island as its three resident ministers. Of Seaforth, Coan wrote in May 1687: 'I have received all his family, and sixty other people.' Valuing his potential to assist the church, Devoyer extolled Seaforth as 'a man with extensive territories and who can raise 1500 men for the King's service'. At the time, he was said to be returning from England to Lewis with two priests for whom he would provide every necessity, but there is no evidence that this came to pass.[260] More interesting was the ministers' change in attitude to Coan who, according to his own evidence, were originally hostile but ended up contesting the principle points of the faith with him, and left content.[261]

In Skye, it is possible to trace two Catholic enclaves: the long-established community in Trotternish, and a young community in Sleat. Having been served by Ward in the final year of the Franciscan mission, the island does not appear to have been served again until it was visited by the Vincentian Dermit Duggan in 1652–53. However, some Catholics must have remained on the island, because the synod of Argyll reported in October 1642 that 'the old Lady mc Cloud and Anguis mc Ferquhar in the yle of Sky are professed papists'.[262] The MacLeods of Dunvegan and Harris – John Mòr, the sixteenth chief (1626–49), Rory Mir, the seventeenth chief (1649–64) and Iain Breac, the eighteenth chief (1664–93); as well as the MacDonalds of Sleat, Sir James Mòr, the ninth chief (1643–78) and Sir Donald, tenth chief (1678–95) – continued to conform outwardly to Protestantism, as had their predecessors.[263] Although the Vincentians maintained their connection with Skye, opposition to Catholicism intensified on the island during this period: Ewan MacAllister, the schoolmaster who transferred to Glengarry in 1665, had previously taught sixty pupils on the island but had been compelled to leave by people hostile to Catholicism. Opposition was undoubtedly fuelled by the presbytery of Skye, but precisely who was responsible for the coercion in this particular case remains unspecified.[264] Even if it had come from MacDonald of Sleat, the clan *fine* surreptitiously supported Catholicism through his bastard brother, Archibald MacDonald, who perpetrated a nocturnal assault on Donald Nicholson, minister of Kilmuir in Trotternish, in August 1667.[265] Regular sustenance of Catholics in Skye was possible only with the growth of the secular mission in the 1680s. The island was served initially from Moidart, mainly by Mr Devoyer and Mr Cahassy, then latterly by Mr Mongan. According to Devoyer, writing on 20 May 1687, 'all are nominally Protestants', but there were also 'about fifty Catholics who are scattered here and there'.[266]

With the arrival of Mr Mongan in August 1688, the mission superior felt able to justify a residentiary in Skye. But in effect, the majority of Skye had been well captured for Protestantism by this time. During Devoyer's visit at the end of 1687, the people came voluntarily to hear the addresses, but they were curiously perturbed by mass and confession, which did not surprise him, 'after the false impressions that the Ministers have made on their Spirits by their sermons full of calumny against the Catholic Church, calling it Idolatrous for the veneration given there to the saints and images which would be easily believed by those who have never heard anything to the contrary'.[267] Yet what Devoyer failed to appreciate was that the people chose to side with the ministers. The small harvest in both Lewis and Skye, where the numbers of Catholics were approximately equal at this time, shows that the Protestants held their ground more than adequately.[268]

The areas of Roman Catholic settlement in the Highlands and Islands as they exist today were more or less codified by the end of the seventeenth century. The most sustained attention during this century was accorded by the missionaries to the Clanranald territories (island and mainland). This was equalled only by that lavished on the MacNeills' isle of Barra and its surrounding islands, and the mainland district of Glengarry. It also seems likely, given the mass stones of Lochaber, that attention was at some point focused on the MacDonalds of Keppoch. Montrose's army certainly billeted amongst them, but there is no evidence that they were visited by the Vincentians. In the early eighteenth century, however, the same priest was responsible for Glengarry and the Braes of Lochaber; this may also have been the case during the seventeenth century.[269]

But even had the Franciscan and Vincentian missions been better supported, it is doubtful whether it could be said that 'there is every reason to suppose that much greater areas, including Skye, Harris, North Uist, Mull, Ardnamurchan and Morvern, would still be Catholic today'.[270] Had MacLeod of Dunvegan and Harris been more openly Catholic, then priests might possibly have been sent to Harris. On the other hand, if they could visit Trotternish in the seventeenth century, what was to prevent them going to Harris (which they did not do)? The main bar was that the Protestant Kirk had simply established itself there earlier. North Uist, too, was firmly Protestant by the time of the Franciscan mission,[271] and there is no reason to assume that it would have reverted to Catholicism just because of its easy accessibility to priests in South Uist. Similarly, Mull had three ministers as early as 1626.[272] There seemed little likelihood of Ardnamurchan and Morvern ever falling to Catholicism because of the latter's proximity to Argyll territory and the former's association with the Campbells. Argyll had gained a royal grant of the barony of Ardnamurchan in March 1610, and it had remained in Campbell hands when he feued it to Donald Campbell of Barbreck-Lochow in 1625 after the revolt there of the MacDonalds.[273]

During the early eighteenth century, attention was focused mainly on consolidating those areas which had already been gained for the Catholic faith and in encouraging a native Scottish priesthood. With such extensive mission work carried out in Clanranald territories in the seventeenth century, it is hardly surprising that many of the indigenous Highland priests bore the name MacDonald. But while this new priesthood was under formation, there was still much scope for Irish aid.

FIVE

Gaelic Presbyterian Co-operation, 1690–1760

> A letter from the Synod of Argile, shewing their readiness to assist us in the pious design of converting the Irish, was read.
>
> General Synod of Ulster, *Records* (1717)

THE IMMEDIATE post-revolutionary period was again characterised by general confusion in the Churches on both sides of the Irish sea. Times of upheaval and instability encouraged a higher degree of geographical mobility amongst the people: just as Scots ministers crossed to Ireland at the Restoration, boosting the presbyterian faith there, so fugitives subsequently fled in the opposite direction when Irish presbyterians were pushed back into Londonderry and Enniskillen and the air smelled of Jacobite victory. In the circumstances, a general meeting of ministers and elders in Scotland – acting as an unofficial General Assembly – requested an authenticated list of ministers and probationers in Ireland, in order to avoid admitting unlicensed persons into vacant parishes. The list, compiled in March 1689, reveals that nearly fifty ministers of Irish congregations had taken refuge in Scotland (although only two of them went to the Highlands).[1] However, by 1689 the Revolution Settlement had restored the presbyterian polity in Scotland, while in Ireland the tide had turned and the victory of Protestants over the Jacobites seemed assured by 1690, and was indeed accomplished in 1691; from this point, the Protestant ascendancy in the established Church of Ireland was dominant politically and economically.[2]

The year 1690 was marked by Irish presbyterians with the erection of the General Synod of Ulster as the Supreme Court of the presbyterian church there. Holding its first meeting in Belfast on 26 September, the General Synod remained its legislative judicatory for a century and a half. Having last met in the capacity of a general meeting in spring 1661 at Ballymena, this shows how closely the fate of their Irish brethren was bound with that of the presbyterian community in Scotland, which had ceased to function as a General Assembly at the Restoration.[3] Although the situation became more tolerable for presbyterians, like Catholics they were still subject to discriminatory legislation throughout this period, 'which, though less stringent, was sufficiently irksome to arouse bitter resentment'.[4] The oath of supremacy was abolished in Ireland towards the end of 1691; it was replaced by oaths of fidelity and allegiance, with which the presbyterians had no quarrel. This development opened the sphere of public employment to them again, although their religion was not yet legally tolerated. Particular bones of contention were that presbyterian marriage was invalid, presbyterians were excluded from teaching in schools, and they often had sites for meeting-houses refused them. None the less, the presbyterian community continued to expand throughout William's reign, especially in the north, the stronghold of Irish presbyterianism. 'From being virtually a hidden, silent community, they became an open community' in the 1690s. 'Their Synod met openly, and they began to take part in public life, quickly increasingly their representation in a number of town corporations (a process that began with James's Declaration of Indulgence) and making efforts to establish congregations outside Ulster.'[5] It became necessary in 1697 to split the five original meetings or presbyteries of the church into two sub-synods, to meet every March and October at Coleraine and Dromore. Similarly, the Antrim presbytery was divided to make the new presbytery of Belfast. By 1702, nine presbyteries and three sub-synods had been created, the third sub-synod meeting being at Monaghan, and the General Synod met annually each summer in Antrim.[6]

Conversely, in the Highlands, it is amazing to see just how little progress presbyterianism made during William's reign. After a period of episcopal government, the presbyterian Kirk returned in 1690 to find it had only a 'slender footing' in areas of Argyll, Easter Ross and parts of Caithness and Sutherland; everywhere else it was strongly opposed. Most were adherents of episcopacy, except in those areas of the west and its adjacent islands which had been reclaimed for Catholicism. Following James VII's 'Third Toleration' in 1687 – which permitted presbyterians to reorganise in Scotland – the first meeting of the synod of Argyll was attended only by those presbyteries under Campbell dominance: Inveraray, Lorn and Kintyre. Highland ministers ousted at the Restoration were often not keen to return to the Highlands when episcopacy was abolished in July 1689, especially when more comfortable livings often fell vacant in the south. Some were also poached by the presbyterian church in Ireland.[7] Presbyterian ministers were scarce anyway, but the problem was compounded by a particular lack of Gaelic speakers. When he was trying to elicit the General Assembly's sanction for a reprinting of the Irish Bible in the 1690s, James Kirkwood, a Scottish episcopalian living in Bedfordshire, stressed that only half of the Highland ministers preached in Gaelic anyway and that the English sermons of the remainder were of little use to the majority of people. Indeed, for at least a decade after the Revolution many episcopal ministers were allowed to remain in their parishes; equally little attention was paid to the encroachments of Catholicism. Two decades after the Revolution, the achievements of the presbyterian Kirk in the Highlands were fewer than they might have been. Many parishes were still far too large: the parish of Ardnamurchan, for instance, had comprised five separate charges in the medieval Church. And few heritors outside the Campbell Pale actually contributed to the minister's manse, glebe or stipend.[8]

In Ireland, Queen Anne's reign brought legislation which compromised the position of the presbyterians.[9] It also heralded a vicious pamphlet war with the episcopalians: between 1709 and 1714 the Rev. William Tisdall, vicar of Belfast, who held a particular grudge against presbyterians, published a deal of damning literature about them. As a result, a number of their supporters in the landowning classes defected to join the Established Church. Nevertheless, conditions were not severe enough to stunt the inexorable growth of the presbyterian church, which in 1708 stood at over 130 congregations. It also engaged in its first mission to the native Irish; although missions in the vernacular had been undertaken by presbyterians before, they had, strictly speaking, been operating under the auspices of the Established Church. Although little of major importance had occurred in this sphere since the work of Bishops Knox and Bedell in the early seventeenth century, Bishop William King of Derry had, more or less of necessity, introduced some Gaelic speakers into his diocese. For a while, he employed two Scottish episcopalian ministers from the Highlands to preach in Gaelic in the barony of Inishowen, mainly to serve Highland Protestant families who had settled there after the Revolution. But it seems not to have lasted long. Patrick McLachlan from Kintyre (mentioned below) was one of the ministers employed by Bishop King. The other was probably one of the many episcopalians who left the Highlands at the Revolution[10] – possibly John Beaton (also mentioned below) who was in Coleraine in 1700. Yet another Highland minister was similarly employed by the Established Church in the northern parts of County Antrim and had some success in converting Catholics there.[11] While these appointments reveal the existence of virtual Highland ghettos in parts of Ulster which obviously required Gaelic-speaking ministers, in general attempts made by the Church of Ireland to convert the native Irish remained as sporadic during the eighteenth century as they had been during the seventeenth. The Established Church concerned itself instead with the pastoral care of those who were already Protestant and with trying to contain expanding presbyterianism.[12]

Unfavourable comparisons have been drawn between the Church of Scotland's attempts to mitigate its Gaelic problem under constant pressure from the grassroots with those of the Church of Ireland under pressure from an anglicised hierarchy.[13] In 1703 and again in 1709, attempts were made, at the convocation of the Church of Ireland, to encourage missionary work among the native Irish. Recommendations were made for instruction of the native Irish in their own tongue, which were reiterated in 1711, although only a few ministers gave serious consideration to implementing the plans. But their example was taken up by the Irish presbyterians who, at their synod in 1710, decided to implement such a scheme themselves. The Ulster Synod also hoped for the 'concurrence of the brethren in Dublin', where there were then five congregations (presbyterianism having expanded in the south of Ireland during the Commonwealth). The thriving presbyterian population in Dublin included many Highlanders.[14] On 1 May 1710, the Dublin presbyterians had established the General Fund 'for the support of religion in and about Dublin and the South of Ireland, by assisting and supporting the Protestant dissenting interest'. The substantial sums of money pledged to it – as much as £7,670 in the early stages – greatly assisted the introduction of the Gospel into the south. But although the presbyterian mission handed out Irish Bibles, Confessions of Faith and Catechisms, various problems with the government over its presbyterian (dissenter) status effectively dampened the project.[15] Only after the '15, when Ulster Protestants sought to unite against a common Catholic Jacobite enemy, did the presbyterian mission to the native Irish really take off. Once again, it was the Dublin brethren (possibly seeking a worthy project for their General Fund) who drew to the attention of the Ulster Synod the mission to the Irish.[16] Three Argyll men – two ministers and a probationer – were to the fore.[17] But although much good work was done, particularly prior to 1720, the ensuing non-subscription controversy effectively diverted energy from it.[18]

The Gaelic-speaking Highlands and Islands was regarded as as much of a mission area as Ireland to the presbyterian Kirk, which in 1694 set up its Commission for the North. In an attempt to utilise those Gaelic speakers who had plumped for comfortable Lowland charges, the General Assembly was empowered in 1696 to send them on a mission to the north, although the scheme remained largely unexpedited. Most of the vacancies in the Lowlands having been supplied by 1704, the Assembly then sought to ameliorate the Highland situation by redeploying half of the bursaries from presbyteries south of the Tay for the maintenance of Gaelic students. Draconian legislation followed in 1708: no Gaelic-speaking minister was to settle in the Lowlands until he had filled a vacancy in the Highlands for at least a year, without receiving a call within that time. Ministers contravening this were deemed liable to enforced translation. Furthermore, congregations and presbyteries could be immensely resolute in their unwillingness to accept a minister who did not speak Gaelic, although dismissal on these grounds was not considered an option by the General Assembly. Although the Kirk encouraged the use of Gaelic in preaching and worship, there was a huge dichotomy between the need to evangelise Gaels in their own language and the Kirk's continued promotion of English as the medium of education.[19] The establishment in 1708 of the Society in Scotland for

Propagating Christian Knowledge (SSPCK), which set up schools in the region, served only to alienate Gaelic further from the realm of formal education.[20] Although the catechism and metrical psalms were available in Scottish Gaelic, society schoolmasters were nevertheless reprimanded if they taught children to read using either these books or the Irish Bible; it was only in 1767, when a Scottish Gaelic New Testament was finally available, that the SSPCK permitted the use of Gaelic as a medium of instruction.[21] But this support came not from a wish to bolster Scottish Gaelic linguistically, but from the realisation that the Highlands could only be effectively civilised and brought to heel if the Gael was won over using his own vernacular.

Possibly the most significant development in Scotland during the early decades of the century was the passing of the Toleration and Patronage Acts in 1712. The former allowed episcopal congregations to meet using the English liturgy, while the latter restored the powers of lay patrons to present to a parish, although the congregation could still dissent from a call. The passing of the Patronage Act laid up great problems for the Kirk, however, which eventually led to the Secession of the 1730s.[22] In the Highlands, the Kirk became increasingly concerned about the inroads made by Catholicism and established the new synod of Glenelg in 1724 in an attempt to tackle the problem more efficiently. The new synod was responsible for the Long Island, Skye, the isles north of Mull, and the presbyteries of Abertarff and Gairloch. It had a difficult remit and was largely unsuccessful in reducing huge parishes or filling vacancies. In the following year, George I instituted an annual grant of £1,000 to the General Assembly, to be used specifically for the reformation of the Highlands and Islands and other areas where Catholicism was prevalent. Administered by the Committee for the Royal Bounty, the money was expended mainly in providing catechists and missionaries.[23]

More generally, this period was dominated by conflict over doctrinal and theological issues. The philosophy of Descartes and the theories of Newton washed through Scotland, as they did throughout Europe, challenging the Calvinist view of the universe on the Godhead, scriptural authority and the immortality of the soul. There was, besides, a good deal of theological controversy over the means of grace and election, as well as fear of the infiltration of Arminianism (which emphasised free will, and limited the grace of God and therefore denied the Calvinist doctrine of predestination).[24] These controversies also reared their heads in Ireland. A basic toleration was extended to Irish presybterians with the passing on 2 November 1719 of 'An Act for exempting the Protestant Dissenters of this kingdom from certain penalties to which they are now subject'. And by another act in the same year, the time during which presbyterians already in office might subscribe to the Test was extended to 25 March 1720. This was the first of many acts of indemnity by which the Test Act was gradually eroded from year to year, until it was finally abolished.[25]

The first rumblings of the non-subscription controversy also began to be heard in the church in the same year. Subscription to the Westminster Confession of Faith as a test of doctrinal orthodoxy had been imposed on those entering the ministry in Ireland in 1698 and 1705, just as it had been reimposed in Scotland at the Revolution. However when an Antrim minister, Mr John Abernethy, preached a sermon to the Belfast Society on 9 December 1719 that was subsequently published as 'Religious Obedience Founded on Personal Persuasion', the title clearly betrayed its non-subscribing tendencies. So-called 'new light' or non-subscribing views held that personal conscience, based on reasoned investigation and not doctrine, was the only way to determine what a man regarded as true and just and in which he had faith. More seriously, it was feared that those who declined to subscribe the Confession of Faith were actually Arians, people who denied the deity of Christ. Ultimately, this free expression of conscience led not only to the creation of two separate Belfast congregations but to the synod's tactical realignment of presbyterial boundaries, so that by 1725 all sixteen non-subscribing ministers and their congregations were consigned to the presbytery of Antrim. In June 1726, that presbytery was eventually excluded from the synod when it became a separate church court.[26]

Gradually the controversy died down, being replaced in the late 1720s by concern over bad harvests, unsatisfactory leases and an increase in tithes to the Church of Ireland. Religious discrimination was one of the main reasons put forward for significant presbyterian emigration from Ulster to North America at this juncture.[27] On 16 June 1730, the synod of Ulster sounded the warning bell: 'It being too evident that the protestant dissenting interest in this kingdom is in a very declining condition, and if proper remedies are not timely applyed, things will in all probability grow worse and worse.' In May of the following year, it was humbly put forward that there should be 'a general meeting of persons delegated from each Presbytery in the Kingdom to think of fit ways and means to revive and strengthen said interest'.[28] The year 1738 saw a major concession, however: presbyterians were given freedom from prosecution for celebrating their form of marriage.[29]

The rest of this period is dwarfed by the patronage issue: the breakaway of the Secession Church in Scotland in 1733 and the formation of the associate presbytery. But although the issue was topical in the Highlands of Scotland, as shown in a minute of the presbytery of Mull in March 1734, the Secession Church did not become a big phenomenon in the Highlands.[30] Nor did the associate presbytery have sufficient members to send probationers to Ireland until 1742; its first congregation at Lylehill, including Belfast and Lisburn, did not obtain a minister until 1746.[31]

The first problem which reared its head in the Highlands during this period with particular implications for religious interrelations was Jacobitism.

The Significance of Jacobitism

In Scotland, Jacobitism was so closely allied with episcopalianism at the Revolution that King William was almost obliged to support the presbyterians. Rather than marking the end of the trouble between the two ecclesiastical groups, conflict only intensified after the Revolution in the reigns of William and Anne. Episcopalians were not deprived of their benefices simply because they were anti-presbyterian, but rather 'because their Jacobitism found its expression in their Episcopacy' and episcopalianism underwrote the doctrine of the divine right of Kings. Obviously not all episcopalians were Jacobites, but episocopalianism had a stronger hold in the Highlands in the immediate post-revolutionary period than presbyterianism, which often led to Highland episcopalians being tarred with the same brush; this whole issue is therefore of particular significance for the Highlands and Islands.[32]

Though King William was keen to include episcopalians in the Settlement, the General Assembly felt otherwise. On 19 May 1693, parliament imposed an oath that meant that before ministers could become members of the Assembly, they had to acknowledge William and Mary as sovereigns, both de jure and de facto.[33] This encouraged yet further division between those episcopalians who took the oath and came under the King's protection and those who did not – the so-called non-jurors – who set their hopes on the restoration of the Stewarts and engaged in correspondence with the exiled court in St. Germain. There were even links between Scottish and English non-jurors, shown particularly by correspondence between Bishop Rose of the main Scottish episcopalian party and Mr Archibald Campbell, a close cousin of the Duke of Argyll's in London. The correspondence ran from at least 1706 to 1715, when the rebellion rendered it too dangerous to continue and links were severed between English and Scottish non-jurors.[34]

Presbyterians in Ireland were affected more by the passing of the Abjuration Oath in 1703, which obliged everyone in civil, military or ecclesiastical office to reject the claim of the pretender – 'James VIII and III' – to the throne. Legal action was taken against four ministers who refused the oath, thus becoming 'non-jurors', because such action effectively branded James as illegitimate. Unfortunately, this cast aspersions of Jacobitism on presbyterians as a whole. In 1704, the passing of the Test Act (appended to an act 'to prevent the further growth popery') similarly required anyone holding office under the crown to take communion in the Church of Ireland within three months of their appointment. Applied to dissenters and Catholics alike, it precipitated the resignation from office of all staunch presbyterians. It caused particular consternation following the French-backed 1708 Jacobite attempt to land the Pretender in Scotland. Owing to Ulster's proximity to Scotland, the militia was called up, but many presbyterians refused to enrol in it. The Test Act caused similar problems at the time of the '15 rebellion.[35] Essentially an English oath (of 1701), the Abjuration Oath did not become an issue in Scotland until 1712, when imposed on ministers by the Toleration Act of the same year with the intention of securing the Protestant succession by keeping Jacobites out of ecclesiastical and civil posts. However, many presbyterians – the so-called 'scruplers' – scrupled to sign it, not only because its Erastian overtones were unacceptable to their Calvinism but because it implied that the Church of Scotland took second place to the Church of England. The oath had to be rephrased in 1719 in a less prejudicial form.[36] Comparing the situations in the two countries: it was mainly the episcopalians in Scotland who suffered from their affilation to Jacobitism, while in Ireland the presbyterians were more tainted by it.

It was not until after the '15 – during which many Ulster presbyterians exempted from prosecution under the Test Act earned the favour of the crown and House of Commons by serving as soldiers – that the presbyterian church in Ireland really felt secure enough to consider a mission to the native Irish.[37] In this respect, a letter from a Mr Henry Maxwell to an unknown correspondent (in the State Papers for Ireland) contains interesting social comment on the dissenting community. Indicating that he was in favour of only partial discrimination against presbyterians, he stated on 9 April 1716:

> It is then surely for the public safety that there should be no law to hinder the protestants of this countrey to unite against our common enemy. The body of our dissenters consist of the middling and meaner sort of people, chiefly in the north, and in the north there are not many of them estated men when compared with those of the Established Church, so that when their disabilities shall be taken off their want of fortune, and interest, will always hinder them from coming into the militia in any invidious or dangerous numbers, so that by the passing that part of the law before you as it relates to the militia we shall be strengthened with their hands without endangering the public peace.[38]

But this concession only went so far: he did not feel the same way about their entry into the army. If the exemption clause was not passed, it 'would be very highly to the prejudice of the king and his service'.[39] Attitudes to the Jacobite threat were markedly different in the Irish and Scottish presbyterian communities. It should be remembered that Ireland participated militarily only in the 1689 rebellion, so although there was concern about Jacobitism in eighteenth-century Ireland, it was not paranoiac. However, it was undoubtedly a factor in the presbyterian attitude towards mission work among native Gaels in both countries.[40] The Kirk, for instance, was very concerned to ensure that even where there was a sizeable Gaelic-speaking population, if the charge was in a garrison town it had to be served by an English-speaking minister.[41] There were of course bilingual ministers whose integrity was thereby impugned.[42]

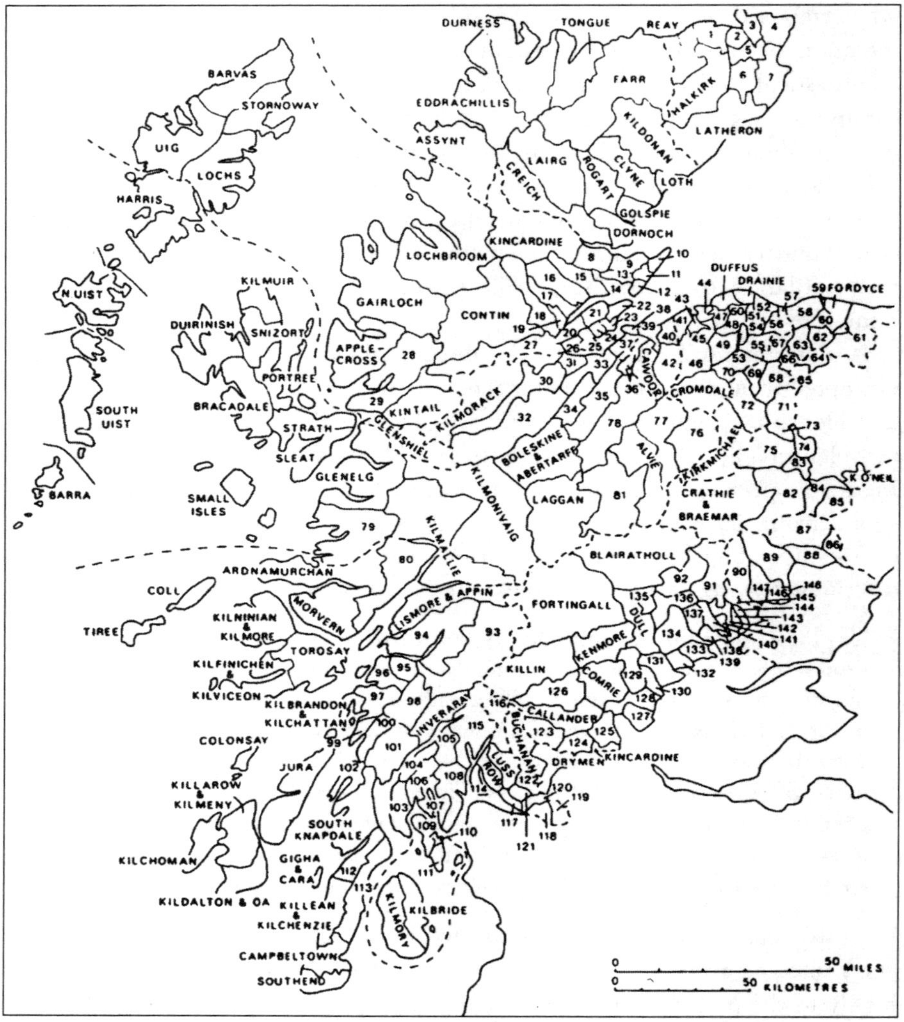

Fig. 5.1. Highland parishes of the eighteenth century.

List of Highland parishes referred by number in Fig. 5.1

Parish name	**No.**	**Parish name**	**No.**	**Parish name**	**No.**
Aberfoyle	123	Edinkillie	46	Logiealmond	132
Aberlour	69	Edzell	86	Logie-Coldstone	83
Abernethy and Kincardine	76	Elgin	48	Logie Easter	13
Aboyne and Glentanar	84	Fearn	11	Logierait	136
Alness	16	Fodderty	18	Monzievaird and Strowan	129
Alves	47	Forres	43	Mortlach	68
Alyth	145	Fowlis Wester	131	Moulin	92
Ardchattan	94	Glass	65	Moy and Dalarossie	78
Ardclach	42	Glenbucket	73	Muckairn	95
Ardersier	38	Glenisla	90	Muthill	128
Ardgour	80	Glenmuick Tullich and		Nairn	39
Ardoch	127	Glengairn	82	New Kilpatrick	119
Arisaig and Moidart	79	Glenorchy and Inishail	93	New Spynie	54
Arrochar	116	Glentrathen	147	Nigg	12
Auchtergaven	133	Grange	62	North Bute	109
Auldearn	40	Inveraven	72	North Knapdale	102
Avoch	24	Inverchaolain	107	Old Kilpatrick	118
Balquhidder	126	Inverness and Bona	33	Olrig	2
Bellie	57	Keith	63	Ordiquhill	61
Bendochy	144	Kilcalmonell	112	Petty	37
Birnie	53	Kilchrenan and Dalavich	98	Port of Menteith	124
Birse	85	Killearnan	26	Rafford	45
Blairgowrie	142	Kilfinan	103	Rathven	58
Boharm	67	Kilmadock	125	Rattry	143
Bonhill	121	Kilmaronock	122	Resolis	21
Botriphinie	66	Kilmartin	100	Rosemarkie	23
Bower	5	Kilmichael Glassary	101	Rosneath	114
Cabrach	71	Kilmodan	106	Rosskeen	15
Cairnie	64	Kilmore and Kilbride	96	Rothes	55
Canisbay	4	Kilmuir Easter	14	Rothesay	110
Caputh	139	Kilninver and Kilmelfort	97	Saddell and Skipness	113
Cardross	117	Kiltarlity and Convinth	30	Speymouth	56
Cortachy and Cloval	89	Kiltearn	17	Spynie	50
Clunie	140	Kingarth	111	St. Andrews Lhanbryd	51
Craignish	99	Kingoldrum	146	Strachur	105
Crieff	130	Kingussie and Insh	81	Stralachlan	104
Cromarty	22	Kinloch	141	Strathdon	75
Croy and Dalcross	36	Kinloss	44	Tain	9
Cullen	59	Kirkhill	31	Tarbat	10
Dallas	49	Kirkmichael (Perthshire)	91	Thurso	1
Daviot and Dunlichity	35	Kirriemuir	148	Towie	74
Deskford	60	Knockando	70	Urray	27
Dingwall	19	Knockbain	25	Urquhart	52
Dores	34	Lethendy	138	Urquhart and	
Dumbarton	120	Lethnot and Navar	88	Glenmoriston	32
Dunkeld and Dowally	137	Little Dunkeld	134	Urquhart and Logie	
Dunnet	3	Lochalsh	29	Wester	20
Dunoon and Kilmun	108	Lochcarron	28	Watten	6
Duthil and Rothiemurchus	77	Lochgoilhead and		Weem	135
Dyke and Moy	41	Kilmorich	115	Wick	7
Edderton	8	Lochlee	87		

After the '15, Jacobite intrigue blossomed in Scotland once again in the mid-1720s, and although the Scottish Jacobite Association was not formed until 1739, the government was still overly protective of the garrison at Fort William, its foothold in the Highlands. On 18 June 1735, the synod of Glenelg noted the petition of the presbytery of Abertarff (made through the Committee for the Royal Bounty), asking 'that one may be sent to Maryburgh[43] to officiate as preacher there who has the Irish language'. Subscribed by 100 heads of families and elders in the area, the elders insisted that some of the names had been forged, with the result that 'little or no regard was to be had to the petition for an Irish preacher from such persons as did subscribe it'.[44] In any case, the synod declined to remove the English-speaking Mr George Anderson, because some of the subscribers were said to be 'communicants with Episcopal nonjurant preachers' – or suspected Jacobites – while other subscribers were known to have little Gaelic anyway. Anderson therefore remained at Kilmallie (see Fig. 5.1), although the synod conceded that 'it should appear altogether necessary ... that ane Irish preacher should be placed in that burgh yet the said Reverend Minister ought to be there also'.[45] But a Gaelic-speaking minister was not installed, and Anderson eventually resigned in 1741.[46]

On the other hand, surviving correspondence from the presbyterian minister of a parish in the Outer Hebrides reveals the ineffectiveness of attempts at establishment control in more peripheral areas. Dated 1750, two letters survive from John MacAulay, minister in South Uist, to David Bruce, Surveyor of the Forfeited Estates in Scotland, then living in London. MacAulay's charge was in inveterate Catholic territory. He wrote from Ormacleit on 2 February 1750: 'The Priests were never more insolent, they are now in Top Spirits, as they have got their Bishop home among them, he is Just now at the Main land of Moidoirt and Arrasaig, adored like a little God!'[47] This alluded to the return of Bishop Hugh MacDonald, first Vicar-Apostolic of the Highland vicariate who, having been imprisoned and exiled for his Jacobite principles in 1746, had returned to Scotland in 1749.[48] MacAulay's next letter, written from nearby Benbecula on 7 February 1750, referred to his having been attacked by the priest 'in a very Odd Manner' and to 'his threatning Blustering Letters'. The letter demonstrates an interesting fugitive connection between Isles and Ulster presbyterians.

> And I can likewise assure you that all the small Protestants in the Island of Benbecula, are so persecuted both on their own account and mine that they are obliged to Transport themselves to Ireland and other Countrys, so that one half of them will not be found here when you come again, few as they were before.[49]

His sarcastic comments also reveal a lack of serious persecution against priests only four years after the rebellion.

> In case the Government shall consult their own Interest so far as to take any Notice of the Priests, I beg leave to Observe that the thing must not only respect

> these two parishes, but likewise, our Neighbouring mainland, Otherwise I will not be safe, I likewise think that it should not be trusted to a rambling officer, for I have known some of them blame the Ministers for the trouble given them, and drunk with the Priests Instead of apprehending them![50]

In truth, the threat from Jacobitism was not considered grave by the mid-century. Even immediately after the Revolution, it was not sufficient to stop the Church of Ireland's pragmatic use of ousted episcopal ministers from the Highlands to preach to communities of Scottish Gaelic settlers and native Irish.

Highland Ministers and Probationers of Irish Congregations

The exodus of Ulster ministers to Scotland at the Revolution meant that the General Synod of Ulster spent most of its time, on reconvening, in recalling its brethren and attempting to fill vacancies.[51] The problem still persisted in June 1694, when the synod approved an overture of the committee ordaining that the presbyteries write again to those ministers who had been called to return to their charges, 'otherwise they are to declare to them that their so staying in Scotland very offensive both to ministers and people, and if they do not return, they will be lookt upon as scandalous persons, and be dealt with as such'.[52] There were only two Ulster ministers who fled to the Highlands at this point: John Darroch from Glenarm and John Monro from Carnmoney, both members of the Antrim meeting. Monro left Ireland before the 'List of Presbyterian Ministers in Ireland' was compiled in March 1689, but Darroch did not leave until the beginning of 1690.[53]

And the visit of at least one Irish clergyman to the Highlands during the 1690s had little to do with the upheavals of Revolution. On 15 July 1697, the presbytery of Kintyre was informed that 'Mr Alexander Campbell a scandalous profligat Curate who for his debauchrie was rejected by his own pairtie in Irland hes Come to the Country and in the parish of Kilberry, hath intruded himselfe on the people Clandestinely marrieing and baptizing contrair to our publick Lawes both Civil & ecclesiastick.' The presbytery determined to write to the elders and gentlemen of this parish warning them neither to meddle with him nor to receive ordinances at his hands.[54] As a curate, Campbell was presumably a member of the Church of Ireland, although the term was also used to denote non-juring episcopalians in Scotland.[55] There may be a possibility that Campbell was a Highland episcopalian who had been ousted at the Revolution, had then fled to Ireland to seek employment with the Established Church (perhaps even as the second, unidentified Highland minister employed by Bishop William King in Derry), and was now returning.[56]

After presbyterianism was restored in Scotland by Act of Parliament of 25 April 1690, it was not simply presbyterian ministers who returned to Ireland after the Revolution, but also a number of episcopal non-conformists who chose to go to congregations where they might be more likely to find vacancies and flocks willing to tolerate their views. Some were deprived and some simply deserted, but the outcome was the same.[57] Alexander Cameron in the presbytery of Kintyre (incumbent in Kilbride in Arran for some years prior to 1688) was deprived and went to Ireland in 1691. He eventually died there between 1715 and 1719.[58] Similarly, John MacLean, in the presbytery of Kintyre, second son of John MacLean of Greshepol in Coll, admitted as parson of Kilmorie in Arran some time before 1688, was ousted shortly afterwards. He attracted influential patronage during his subsequent career in Ireland; minister at Coleraine and Antrim, he was chaplain to Lord Massereene and prebendary of Rosharkin. Married first to a daughter of Lachlan McNeill of Losset, by whom he had several daughters, two sons of his second marriage to a daughter of James Cubbage also carved out ministerial careers for themselves in Ireland: John became minister of Clogher in Ireland and James minister of Rochray. His middle son, Clotworthy, practised medicine in Belfast. The parish of Kilbride (mentioned above) suffered a double loss: moving from Kilmorie, 'the old Archdeacon, McLaine, was subsequently settled at Kilbride. He also afterwards went to Ireland.'[59]

Also ousted from the presbytery of Kintyre at the Revolution was James Campbell who, having received a testimonial for ordination on 5 May 1686, had not long been in the parish of Campbeltown. He, too, went to Ireland, where he died in 1694.[60] However, where episcopal incumbents had many years of service and where the local population was more inclined to episcopacy, as in areas of Ross-shire, they were able to maintain their status without conforming to presbyterianism. But in many parts of Argyll, presbyterianism had, conversely, been too firmly established before the Restoration to allow for this. Yet another minister from the Kintyre presbytery, Patrick McLachlan, incumbent in Kildalton in Islay in 1693, had initially tried to remain in Scotland. He was probably the minister who left Kilchoman in Islay at the Revolution, but he seems to have procured another Islay parish (note that the parishes were not contiguous, and did not constitute a joint charge – see Fig. 5.2 for location). In 1692 he was offered a charge by William King, bishop of Derry, which he left to take up after Whitsunday 1693. Kildalton was declared vacant on 3 August 1693. No fewer than four non-conformers went from the presbytery of Kintyre to Ireland, at least two of whom found employment there.[61]

How did other presbyteries within the synod of Argyll fare? William MacLachlan, in Kilmartin in the presbytery of Inveraray, deserted his charge at the Revolution and was deprived by the Privy Council. Leaving for Ireland some time after 15 August 1690, he eventually died there, though his body was returned to Kilmartin for burial.[62] The problem with John Beaton, minister of Kilninian in the presbytery of Mull (and a member of the famous family of

List of Highland parishes referred to by number in Fig. 5.2

Parish name:	No:	Parish name:	No:
Kilmorich	1	Killimuire	18
Lochgoyl's head	2	Lothgear	19
Stratheurre	3	Killmartin	20
Strathlauchlane	4	Killchrenan and	
Killfinan	5	Dalaich	21
Killmodan	6	Clachandysart in	
Killmune	7	Glenorchie	22
Dunoon	8	Inverary	23
Inverchaolan	9	Craignish	24
Rothesay in Bute	10	Killatan	25
Kingarth in Bute	11	Killbrennan	26
Killchislane and		Killinver	27
Kilmichall	12	Killmelford	28
Saddell and Killean	13	Killmore	29
Killkallumonell		Killbride	30
and Skipnish	14	Ardchattan	31
Kilmarna	15	Appine	32
Kilmichael in		Ardgour	33
Inverlussa and		Elanfinan	34
Killmhivocarnoch	16		
Killmichael in			
Glasrie	17		

NOTE: The list appears to have been compiled as a check for the distributors of the Irish Bible. Thus, some of the recorded names are the names of chapels and churches rather than actual parishes.

Fig. 5.2. Parishes of Argyll and Bute in 1698.

Gaelic physicians), was his entrenched episcopalianism. Beaton had left for Ireland by 22 April 1700, supposedly because of immoral conduct. A graduate of Glasgow University, Beaton became minister in Kilninian in 1668. After the Revolution, like many episcopal ministers, he continued to carry out the duties in his parish and was still there in 1697 when he asked the synod of Argyll to be received into ministerial communion. But his request was rejected. Beaton's position cannot have been ameliorated by his consistent support of the MacLeans (by whom his family had been traditionally employed as physicians) in their struggle against the house of Argyll, which had invaded Mull in 1690. Beaton combined practice as a physician with his ministry, having almost certainly received a training in classical Gaelic medicine from his father, John Beaton of Pennycross, the last *ollamh*, or chief physician, in Mull.[63] Beaton brought with him to Coleraine in County Derry a substantial part of the manuscript collection of the Beatons of Pennycross, which shows that he intended to stay for some time. In 1700, he allowed the Welsh scholar Edward Lhuyd,[64] who described him as a 'poor sojourning clergyman', to view his manuscripts. Beaton eventually returned to Mull for good, dying at Torrelock in the parish of Kilninian in 1714. He may have been there in 1710, because his testament shows that several prominent MacLeans bound themselves to pay annuities to him in that year.[65]

Some perspective on the flight of these six Argyll ministers to Ireland can be gained by looking at the total number of those deprived in this area at the Revolution. In all, twenty-one ministers from Argyll and Bute were either deprived, ousted or fled their parishes.[66] A list of Highland parishes compiled in 1698 gives fifty-six parishes for Argyll and Bute (see Fig. 5.2), so the remaining thirty-five denote a healthier proportion than at a national level, where more than half the country's ministers were deprived. But the same list notes that fourteen of these Highland parishes were vacant, immediately reducing the number of filled charges to forty-two. So the six Highlanders out of forty-two who went to Ireland make a significant proportion of around 13 per cent of non-conformists.[67]

Until the eruption of the non-subscribing controversy, the presbyterian church in Ulster was very eager to accommodate Gaelic-speaking ministers from the Highlands, but after this it became more or less self-sufficient in ministers. At least four, and possibly five (viz. John Wilson) Gaelic-speaking Scots and one probationer went to serve in the presbyterian church in Ireland between 1690 and 1760. (A second probationer also fled there as a fugitive from discipline. He may have undertaken some preaching while there.) To compound the issue, two people from Argyll share the same name of Archibald MacLean: the first of these, discussed immediately below, was a fully fledged minister, while the second, discussed later, was a probationer.

Archibald MacLean, minister, was the son of the Rev. Alexander MacLean of Kilmaglass in Argyll. Born in around 1660, MacLean was licensed in 1684 by the presbytery of Dunoon,[68] and subsequently ordained in Dunoon and Kilmun on 4 February 1685. From then on, he went through a short succession of charges: he resigned from the aforementioned parish in 1686 and was admitted to Lochgoilhead and Kilmorich in 1686, from which he resigned on 6 August 1690. Adhering to presbyterianism at the Revolution, MacLean was admitted into communion by the synod on 16 October 1691 and installed in Kilbride in Arran on 7 July 1692; he resigned in 1698.[69] He was, however, assigned another parish in Islay before he left for Ireland.[70]

MacLean resigned in order to respond to a call from a Tyrone parish, where he was so avidly sought that a representative was sent over to Scotland to request his transportation. Mr Thomas Kennedy, minister of Donaghmore, came with a commission from the parishioners of Omagh which he presented to the presbytery of Kintyre on 23 October 1697. It was subscribed by the elders and several heads of families, empowering him to crave the presbytery's agreement to a call to Mr Archibald MacLean, minister at Kilbride in Arran. But the presbytery were unwilling to commit themselves to an immediate answer until they had visited Mr MacLean's kirk.[71]

The major factor in MacLean's intended transference to Ireland was his general dissatisfaction with the state of affairs in his own parish (as was the case with John Darroch).[72] When the presbytery visited his parish in July 1698, he was admonished for his frequent absences. Though the local heritors and kirk elders declared themselves satisfied with all aspects of his ministry, MacLean did not reciprocate, complaining: 'I have several tymes mett with several Indignities & Injuries from severals of my parishioners particularly some offered Violence to my persone – some defamed me to my nighbours & especially to strangers, some did steal my goods & some destroyed them.' Closely related to many of his parishioners, he felt that he could not easily command their respect. By 22 October 1698, he had requested a move because of his lack of success there.[73]

MacLean then went to Ireland for some months, where in April 1699 he was 'Visiting his father in Law & freinds'.[74] It has always been assumed that at this stage he was declared transportable to Ireland.[75] However, the record of the presbytery of Kintyre shows that he had been serving in the parish of Killarrow in Islay since October 1698 (although this translation has previously gone unnoticed). But by January 1700, MacLean had transferred to Ireland. The parish of Killarrow was therefore declared vacant, 'seing that Mr Archibald McLean thair former minister hes left that Charge'.[76] MacLean was installed in Markethill, Armagh, at some time during 1700.[77] He remained in Ireland for the rest of his life, earning dubious recognition as the first presbyterian minister to suffer prosecution by the ecclesiastical courts of the Church of Ireland for celebrating the presbyterian form of marriage. He was fêted by his contemporaries as 'a man of varied accomplishments and of resolute temper'. Four of his sons were ministers: the Rev. Thomas MacLean in Monaghan (1718–40); the Rev. Archibald MacLean in Banbridge, (1720–40); the Rev. Alexander MacLean in Ballynahinch (1735–42), and in Antrim (1742–59); while the Rev. Daniel MacLean was installed in his father's old charge in Kilbride in Arran in 1704, where he remained until 1720.[78] (For more of MacLean, see the section headed 'Missionaries to the Native Irish', below.)[79]

In the same way as the cultural sympathies of some presbyterian ministers were seen to be tainted with Royalism in the 1640s, similar fears led to the appointment of English-speaking ministers in manifestly Gaelic-speaking areas after the Revolution simply in order to keep the lid upon Jacobitism. Uncompromising presbyterians unable to speak the Gaelic language, and who were therefore not susceptible to Gaelic ideology, were politically desirable in garrison towns. Mr William Brodie, installed by January 1708 as chaplain to Major-General Maitland, governor of the Fort William garrison, is a case in point. Although the presbytery of Lorn objected to his lack of Gaelic 'and no hope that he will acquire it', they were informed 'that the Government had firmly resolved never to call a minister that will make use of Irish, it being the Queen's orders to purge the regiment of all Highland soldiers'. In short, Brodie was considered suitable in every other way. So the synod overruled the presbytery and Brodie was ordained on 9 January 1708. By 1714 he was 'chaplain with Col. Britton's Regiment',[80] with which he went to Ireland via Edinburgh in August 1714, in the impending shadow of the '15 rebellion.[81] Similarly, Robert Baillie was appointed minister in Inverness although he had very little Gaelic, because the General Assembly saw the need for a loyal presbyterian to serve 'the most considerable Post benorth Aberdeen of greatest influence in the Highlands'.[82]

It was more personal expediency that took a Lorn probationer to Ireland in 1714. In January 1713, Mr Archibald McLauchlan was asked to supply Mr James Campbell's parish while he was ill. He failed to do so. The presbytery threatened increasingly serious action in McLauchlan's continued absence. Eventually called to account in August 1713 by formal execution of summons, McLauchlan fled: on 21 October 1713, the presbytery was 'credibly informed that he is gone for Irland'.[83] In May 1714, McLauchlan's case was referred to the synod, which resolved in August that 'the presbytery use all endeavours to be informed if he hath gone to Irland, and if so, to know where he resides, that all meanes may be used to get him back to the country'. Clearly the Kirk was in no position to dismiss outright any probationers who spoke Gaelic.[84] Probably fearful of potential Jacobite proclivities, the synod made the proviso that if he returned he was to be asked 'if he adheres to the present Government of this Church, as he professed and gave under his hand when he was licensed by the presbyterie, And in case he do not adhere to the same, that his licence be declared null which advise the presbyterie resolves to follow.' Two months later, in October 1714, Mr Daniel Morison, minister, said that according to his friends McLauchlan was about to return from Ireland.[85] Unfortunately, subsequent details of his case remain a mystery, because the next presbytery book of Lorn is missing.[86]

After the '15 there was a renewed call for Highland ministers in Ireland. Although there was no direct military involvement in the '15, there was considerable sympathy for the cause in Ulster and other Irish-speaking areas.[87] The presbyterian church therefore made sterling efforts to provide ministers for Irish-speaking communities by formulating its first mission policy for the Irish language. In 1716, a committee was set up for improvement of Irish in the presbyterian church in Ireland. To implement the policy more effectively, the General Synod of Ulster commissioned a letter on 19 June to the synod of Argyll, 'desiring them to send us with all convenient speed a Probationer qualify'd for preaching in Irish; and that they would please to appoint a second Probationer to come afterwards, upon advertisement from the Committee appointed for managing this affair'.[88] It was indeed unlikely that a fully fledged minister would be released from Scotland shortly after a rebellion, when there was still a severe shortage of Gaelic-speaking ministers in the Highlands and Islands. The synod of Argyll had complained only a few years earlier in 1709 that 'at our synodical meetings there are many tymes scarce the face of a good Presbyterie besides a provincial Synod'.[89] Instead, the Ulster synod agreed to defray the travel costs of a probationer from Scotland, ordaining that 'each Presbytery advances him one Guinea'.[90] Thus the session book of Aghadoey in County Derry recorded on 7 January 1717 the 'Charge of bringing Mr m'Lane a probationer to preach in Irish from Scotland 5s Od', the cost being shared among the various kirk sessions.[91] Admission of their financial liability notwithstanding, MacLean later experienced a great deal of difficulty in actually collecting the money. But probationers remained more cost-effective, receiving a lower remuneration than ministers. In an amendment to the quota given for Irish-speaking ministers, on 18 June 1717 the synod agreed that the presbytery which called a minister should judge what to pay him, guided by giving ten shillings as the minimum and twenty shillings maximum. Probationers supplying his congregation during his absence were to have from six and ten shillings, according to the decision of the presbytery which sent them.[92] Irish-speaking probationers, it seems, did not command more.[93]

The synod of Argyll replied to the General Synod of Ulster, stating itself 'much refreshed to hear the pious Zeall of the Reverend Synod of Ulster', and offering its co-operation with them 'in so great and good a designe'. It resolved to send two probationers to Ireland at its earliest convenience, namely Mr Archibald MacLean, then in Mull, recommending that the presbytery of Lorn 'deal with him to Repair to Ireland without loss of tyme', and Mr Daniel

Campbell, who was also to depart when so advised by the presbytery of Kintyre.[94] Within the jurisdiction of the synod of Argyll, it was not merely the threat to presbyterianism which motivated the ministry; potentially, the Campbells had a great deal to lose from native Irish involvement in a successful Jacobite rebellion, because the Irish MacDonnells still claimed hereditary rights to the expropriated lands of the Clan Donald South. In offering its support and co-operation in June 1717, the synod of Argyll was essentially addressing a political threat. The synod of Ulster received a letter from the Argyll synod, 'shewing their readiness to assist us in the pious design of converting the Irish'.[95] By this time, the relationship between the presbyterian church in Ulster and that in Argyll had been close and supportive for well over a century. But as the political threat receded towards the middle of the eighteenth century, very few Scottish presbyterian ministers or probationers transferred to Ulster. Although this probably had more to do with the self-sufficiency of the presbyterian church in Ireland, it is highly significant that there were no further attempts at missionary work to the Irish.

Though Archibald MacLean, probationer, went to Ireland, there is no sign that Daniel Campbell did so. Little concrete evidence remains of MacLean's work there. He appears to have stayed for between one and two years, making a mark only in reference to the immense difficulty he had in extracting his financial remuneration. Back in Scotland by 1718, the General Synod of Ulster received a letter from him in June, 'complaining that he wanted some of the money promist him by the Synod for preaching in Irish within our bounds'.[96] Offending presbyteries were ordered to pay their outstanding dues to his countryman, Mr Patrick Simpson.

Born in Islay, Argyll, in 1682, Patrick Simpson was educated at Glasgow University, from where he graduated MA in 1707. In time-honoured fashion, Simpson went to Ireland as a probationer and was later ordained to the parish of Dundalk in County Louth on 30 December 1713.[97] The reason for his removal to Ireland was clarified some years after the event in letters from Irish presbyterians to the synod of Argyll, when they were taking steps in June 1716 to revitalise their Irish mission. The Ulster synod had not only asked for two probationers to be sent, but also for people able to teach the natives how to read Irish, and for a supply of Irish Bibles.[98] Simpson had been sent by the synod of Argyll to preach in the Irish tongue 'to the poor deluded natives' of Ireland. And it is surely ironic that Irish Bibles were requested from Scotland, to where they had originally been sent from Ireland. This can only argue for the inefficacy of the Church of Ireland's mission policy to the Irish, and for the strength of the relationship between the presbyterian church in Ulster and the Scottish Kirk.

Simpson immediately demonstrated his political integrity by marrying the sister of Malcolm and Archibald McNeill, officers in William III's army.[99] This was possibly just as well, because his doctrine was held in suspicion. At this time, a controversy prevailed in Scotland and Ireland over the dilution of Calvinist orthodoxy as enshrined in the Westminster Confession of Faith, and Simpson was a nephew of the renowned John Simpson, Professor of Divinity at Glasgow University, an unorthodox liberal who was tried before the General Assembly in 1714, 1715 and 1716 for teaching Arminian and Pelagian errors (which denied original sin), before finally being set aside in 1729. Ulster presbyterianism continued to maintain the strong links that it had enjoyed with Glasgow since the early seventeenth century:[100] many of its theology students were trained there since there was no university in the province, and apart from the fact that Ulster presbyterians naturally gravitated towards Glasgow anyway, it had cheaper fees than that bastion of anglicanism, Trinity College, Dublin.[101] Indeed, two leading lights of the Belfast Society, John Abernethy and James Kirkpatrick, had been students of John Simpson's at the University; they continued to correspond with him by letter. Most of the students who afterwards joined the Belfast Society had studied theology under Simpson.[102] In spite, or perhaps because, of this connection, Simpson of Dundalk initially subscribed the Confession, but he joined the non-subscribing party at a later date.[103]

Gaelic and Irish-speaking communities were constantly on the lookout for good ministers. Communications between Ulster and Argyll remained sufficiently close in the early eighteenth century for ministers to be aware generally of what was happening within each other's congregations. So when Patrick Simpson resigned his charge in 1721 on the grounds of inadequate stipend, this quickly became known in the west Highlands. Indeed, it raises an interesting issue: his stipend was not increased even though he could preach in Irish.[104] In theory, preachers in Irish were well remunerated for their labours; in 1710, for instance, they were paid twenty shillings per week.[105] In the event, Simpson was induced to stay on,[106] but this did not prevent the parish of Kilmartin in the presbytery of Inveraray from making an attempt to secure him for their own. On 31 July 1722, Archibald Campbell of Inverliever and Colin Campbell in 'Wiran', commissioners from the parish of Kilmartin, appeared before the presbytery of Inveraray, 'craveing that the presbytery would use their interest with Mr Patrick Simpson Minister of the Gospel at Dundalk in Ireland, now in this countrey of quhom they heard a savory report that he might supply for some sabbaths in their paroch, As also craveing the presbytery would send one of their number to supervise a Call in the said paroch'. Mr John Darroch was appointed to supervise a call from the parish[107] – his Irish connections still being utilised some three decades after he had returned to Scotland at the Revolution.

Although by 2 October 1722 the call to Mr Simpson had been subscribed by the heritors, elders and parishioners of Kilmartin, and various heritors –

Archibald Campbell of Inverliever, Patrick Campbell of Duntroon and Alexander Campbell of Kilmartin – had presented themselves at the presbytery in November to obtain its concurrance, the presbytery had received no answer from Simpson by 5 March 1723. Apparently having no interest in the call,[108] Patrick Simpson remained in Ireland, finally following his conscience in 1726 by leaving the General Synod and joining the non-subscribing presbytery of Antrim. Simpson retired in 1761, forty-eight years after his ordination.[109]

Another Scot included in the early eighteenth-century list of Irish-speaking ministers was John Wilson.[110] Patrick Simpson's predecessor, he had been ordained minister of Dundalk and Carlingford in 1700, but after two years he resigned the first charge and held on to the second, in an obvious rationalisation of parishes.[111] Unfortunately, very little is known of his background. Patrick Simpson was the only one of the missioners in 1716 who preached in Irish on a regular basis, so it may be that Wilson, like others in the group, actually learned his Irish rather than having been a native speaker.

For ministers in Kintyre and surrounding areas of Argyll, calls from Ireland presented a viable alternative to a Highland parish. Presbyterian congregations in Ulster and the sizeable community in Dublin were regarded merely as a peninsula of Scottish presbyterianism. On 27 July 1708, representatives of the Highland congregation of Campbeltown asked the presbytery of Kintyre to declare their parish vacant, 'seeing there was no probability that their former Minister would return to them He being settled elsewhere'. Mr Lauchlan Campbell[112] had resigned on 4 July 1707. The presbytery, however, was constrained by the synod, who refused to declare him transportable. Mr Campbell had gone to Ireland anyway, in July or August 1707. The presbytery was informed that he had been 'admitted and settled in another Congregation in the City of Dublin in Ireland'.[113]

The congregation of Capel Street in Dublin had drafted a call to Lauchlan Campbell – whom 'Many Brethren gave a desirable Character' – to join Mr Iredell, who was minister there. Iredell was himself appointed commissioner to manage the call, which had the support of the synod and the presbytery of Belfast. Campbell was installed in Capel Street by the presbytery of Belfast on 16 September 1707.[114] The Commission of the General Assembly had intervened in the case in the previous month, ordering Campbell to remain within the Church and not to go to Ireland. The only means of relief offered to him by the General Assembly, as yet another minister dissatisfied with his Highland parish, was to transfer to a more northerly parish in the Highlands, an offer which he was not happy to entertain.

A letter on behalf of the Commission assured him:

> such is the Respect they have for you, and desire for your continuing in the church, that they will be ready to use all endeavours in their power, for your

> comfortable setling, and therefore the Commission have ordered me in their Name, to desire you may not leave this Church nor settle in Ireland or any other place without this Church, bot continue with us till the Commisson and you meet and conferre with you.[115]

This, of course, was no special testimony to his personal merit but was altogether consistent with the Kirk's attempts to preserve its caucus of Gaelic-speaking ministers, hence their alleged willingness to relocate him further north. Charges in the north Highlands were notoriously unpopular, because the financial provision of many charges north of Argyll was unsure, while many of the sea-bound western charges suffered infiltration from Catholicism. The Commission's efforts were in any case too late, because Campbell had already flown the nest with the presbytery's blessing.[116] The Highland congregation of Campbeltown was left in the unenviable situation of neither anticipating their former minister's return nor being able to present another call. Again the presbytery took matters into its own hands, insisting that since the General Assembly did not disapprove of Mr Campbell being made transportable, it would declare the parish vacant so that another minister could be called.[117] Mr Campbell's ministration in Dublin did not prove long and fruitful: he eventually returned to his brother's manse in Southend, Kintyre, where he died unmarried on 6 October 1708.[118]

On 31 March 1720, Mr John Campbell in Islay explained his absence from the meetings of the Kintyre presbytery since August 1718 by answering that he was 'necessarily Call'd to Irland, and did what he could before he went off to come to Kintyre & attend the Presbyterie and obtain leave from them to go to Irland, but that he could not get it done'. The rest of his inattendance was blamed on the weather.[119] John Campbell remained a frequent visitor to Ireland: on 11 July 1737, the clerk noted that 'there was no letter wrote to Mr John Campbell in Isla, as he did not hear of his return from Ireland'.[120] Similarly, on 20 April 1737 Mr James Barbour, a missionary from the presbytery of Mull, formally applied for leave to go and see his friends in England and Ireland over the summer quarter, and for a letter to the Committee for the Royal Bounty requesting a locum to supply his charge in his absence. Both requests were granted.[121] Although calls from the Irish often increased in times of political uncertainty, it was often merely social interaction which took ministers from one side of the Irish sea to the other.

The MacCalmans: Ministerial Opportunism

An adultery case incriminating one of the MacCalmans of the hereditary ecclesiastical family from Lorn is a particularly interesting example of cross-channel social interaction among ministerial families, both because of the perspective it throws on mobility during this period and because of the detail in which it is recorded. The protagonists in this adulterous drama were the minister Mr John MacCalman, ex-episcopal minister of Morvern, and Janet MacLean, who fled to Ireland after falling pregnant with his child. Although it was MacLean rather than MacCalman who fled the roost, her flight was engineered on behalf of MacCalman who (supposedly) intended to use his extensive family contacts in Ireland to support MacLean and the child. Deprived of his stipend by Act of Council at the re-establishment of presbyterianism, MacCalman had continued to baptise and marry people 'in planted parishes'. But in January 1706 he had been convicted before the presbytery, which had been 'sufficiently informed of his light behaviour unbeseeming a persone bearing the name of a Minister of the Gospell'.[122]

A fair-sized report on the case fills the minutes of the synod of Argyll for 1708, but the case takes up vast numbers of pages in the records of the presbytery of Lorn. First brought to the attention of the Kirk at a meeting at Kilpatrick in Torosay in Mull on 30 January 1706, Mr Daniel McNeill reported a flagrant scandal of adultery 'upon Mr John McCalman late Episcopal Incumbent at Morvarn, with Janet Nian Alaster vc vc Eohin alias McLean'. MacCalman compeared (appeared) before the kirk session as summoned, but declined it as a lawful judicatory in his case (because he was a minister), at which point he was called before the presbytery.[123] He insisted that his partner in crime should be put under oath first since she was single and he married, but 'this he did, as it seems, because the woman hath fled to Ireland, and cannot be brought present'. It transpired that the details of her flight had been cleverly orchestrated by MacCalman's relatives. Until he was vindicated of the scandal of adultery, MacCalman was suspended by Act of Presbytery.[124]

Following on from the main accusation of adultery on 29 March 1707, two of MacCalman's servant lads added fuel to the fire in giving evidence 'that the said Mr John and his servant Woman More NcLauchlan used to ly together'. In July 1707, the Irish angle to the case came to light when MacCalman was asked by the presbytery 'Whither he had spoken or transacted with one McIlghlais liveing in Irland for the maintainance of the said Jonet NcLean and her child for some tyme, Or if he had imployed any of his relatives or acquaintances in Muvarn to speak or hauf act with the said McIlghlais or NcCalman his spous to the effect forsaid.' MacCalman insisted that he had not. However, too much circumstantial evidence exists for it simply to be an idle fabrication, particularly since the Irishman's wife was called 'NcCalman', and was obviously a kinswoman.[125]

The various testimonies prove beyond reasonable doubt that the MacCalmans had paid for MacLean's removal to Ireland. Indeed, problems only arose when John MacCalman defaulted on his maintenance payments, prompting his kinswoman's husband, one McIlghlais (or Gray) to intervene with the Scottish judiciary. William Inglis, procurator fiscal and writer at

Inveraray, produced a letter before the court addressed to John MacCalman from Archibald MacCalman in Ireland, 'craveing that he would do justice to Archibald McIlghlais and Mary NcCalman his spous in Culraine, who were at considerable expences through their harbouring and intertaining Jonet NcLean and her child upon the said Mr John McCalman his account these four years bygone'. The said letter was used as evidence in a legal action being pursued on their behalf against the three MacCalmans who had transacted with them regarding board and maintainance of the mother and child. McIlghlais insisted that he would already have obtained a decreet against them had it not been for the fact that Alexander Campbell of Cleuchnamacrie (or Clanamacrie)[126] had assured him that the transactors would settle with him financially, as a result of which he had lifted the process.[127] Donald Campbell, bailie of Morvern, had also intervened with Inglis to delay the process against the transactors. And Inglis produced a decreet obtained in the sheriff court in the summer of 1706 by McIlghlais and his wife against Donald MacCalman in 'Ledgrinoch' in Appin and Donald, John and Alexander MacCalman in Ardgour in Morvern, to prove his clients' point. The names of the transactors show the solidarity with which his blood relations stood surety for MacCalman, who clearly operated an extensive network of contacts on both sides of the North Channel.[128]

Various witnesses in the MacCalman affair compeared before the presbytery on 3 September 1707. According to MacCalman's son, Donald, the transactors first met with McIlghlais at Kirktoun after MacLean's initial return from Ireland with her child. Alexander Campbell of Cleuchnamacrie admitted acting for McIlghlais, 'being a kindly man of the family of dunsafnage whereof he is descended'. He also heard McIlghlais acknowledge receipt of £40 from MacCalman, in the presence of his wife, in part payment for MacLean's maintenance, and of a guinea the previous year received in Glasgow. This was confirmed by another witness, Lauchlan McLauran. Although MacCalman completely denied giving McIlghlais money on that count, the evidence of Alexander Stewart, the notary, was incriminating: Stewart had received a note from MacCalman in August 1707, asking him to serve McIlghlais with a discharge from him and his wife to some parties in Ardgour in Morvern (the transactors) of 200 merks contained in a decreet obtained against them.[129] One of the transactors, Alexander McNeill vc Calman, said that he became involved in the affair through McCalman's brother, Nicol MacCalman, but that he 'never doubted but Mr John himself would be careful to send the boording to Irland where the child and its mother were to be, and that he would never let him be troubled on her account of that engagement'. Clearly, he was a poor judge of character. MacLean herself was present at the presbytery meeting of 3 December 1707 at McCalman's request, but denied having had a child.[130]

The evidence of Lauchlan McLauran from Craigdurinish in the parish of

Ardchattan was also incriminating.[131] He deponed that MacLean had stayed for some time in his shieling house in Craigdurinish, with 'a male child with her called Archibald of betuixt three and fyve years of age in appearance'. She had confessed that she was the mother and MacCalman the father. McLauran had asked her if the child was Mr John McCalman's, who was in Scotland, what had made her go to Ireland? She had answered that she went there 'for the safety of his reputation being a persone of such a Character, and likewise for safety of his means'. After this she had gone back to the Wintertown,[132] where she stayed with MacCalman's wife for a week, leaving the child behind when she left. Mrs MacCalman's servant, Fionghual NcLauchlan, had returned the child to McLauran's house for a few days and then, disguising him as a little girl, she had taken him away. By 18 May 1708, concern was being expressed by the synod of Argyll about the whereabouts of the child, and the matter was referred into the hands of the Justice and sheriff depute of Argyll. When MacCalman was obliged to find bail, Fionghual NcLauchlan agreed to give more information to the presbytery of Lorn. She confessed that on her Mistress's order

> shee carryed away that child out of Craigdurinish to Athol, and shee was ordered to leave the child with Mr John's sister who lives there ... And that Mr John's sister directed her to give that child to a poor woman liveing hard by, called Jonet Mcintyre and that shee left the child with that woman accordingly, which woman was a kindly woman of the country of appin being born and bred there.[133]

After the sheriff secured MacCalman because the boy was missing, MacCalman's brother, Duncan Roy MacCalman in Appin, insisted that Janet Macintyre had brought the child back from Atholl to his house.[134] Socially, the case is interesting for the migration patterns it reveals within the MacCalman family, from Appin to Atholl and across to Ireland: it shows evidence of two-way geographic mobility from Argyll in the pre-Clearance era.[135] It also shows that Atholl, like Ireland, was a dumping ground for social unacceptables.

Although MacLean refused to acknowledge her guilt, the presbytery believed her guilty of adultery, and in December 1707 appointed her to do public repentance at four different places: at Ardchattan, then Kilmore, Mull and Morvern. Instead, MacLean withdrew by January 1708 to Kingairloch in Lismore. In May 1708, she had still not done public repentance but had left Kingairloch for Mull, where 'she frequents the Laird of Kingerloch's family, Also at present dwells in Gealasdail in Mull'. On 21 July 1708, the Lorn presbytery decided to enter into a process of excommunication against Janet MacLean, through the ministers of Mull and Morvern. Even more chickens were coming home to roost for MacCalman. Before the Morvern session, Mary Nian Donach vc Ean vc Conachy also admitted that the child she had fathered some years ago on

Duncan McConachy, 'dear foster brother to Mr John McCalman late Episcopal Incumbent at Morvarn', which he had taken as his own and satisfied as a fornicator on that account, was actually John MacCalman's, also conceived while she was his servant.[136]

More than two and a half years after the proceedings against MacCalman had begun, the presbytery clerk was appointed on 13 October 1708 to draw up a libel against him listing all of his misdemeanours. This clarified that MacLean had twice crossed from Ireland since first fleeing there, while a subsequent meeting of the presbytery in March 1709 recorded a third visit, with the child, to Craigdurinish, where MacCalman was staying in August 1708. While MacLean left the day after she arrived, the child remained in Craigdurinish for a week, after which he was subjected to abject humiliation: the child was sent to the ferry at the foot of the Water of Awe and taken across to Morvern, where he was taken up and down the country begging, with each village or township sending someone to accompany him to the next settlement. His mother returned to Appin 'and within a few days finding a boat there bound for Yla, went in that boat in order to go to Irland where shee had been formerly'. The process of excommunication against her, which had proceeded to two public citations, was suspended until her flight was confirmed by the brethren of Islay. Not only was the process against MacCalman to proceed unless he appeared at the next diet, but he was finally deposed, rather than simply suspended, from the ministry.[137]

The threat of excommunication was sufficiently final to break the intransigent MacCalman, who on 28 December 1709 and still under process confessed his adulteries with Janet MacLean and More MacLauchlan, but absolutely denied any carnal dealing with Mary Nian Donach vc Ean vc Conachy. In this case at least, excommunication was effective. Appointed 'to enter on the publick profession of his repentance before the congregations of Ardchattan and Killesbuig kerill [or Muckairn] in sackcloth', MacCalman's public repentance endured for a whole year, for many sabbaths of which he appeared in sackcloth. In December 1710, 'he gave such signes of his serious repentance by many tears, and sensible soul moveing expressiones', that his minister and the session were permitted to receive him when they saw fit.[138] MacLean and her child were never mentioned again.

Another equally infamous minister of a Highland parish during this period also chose Ireland as a refuge. Ordained to the parish of Ardnamurchan on 18 September 1734, Mr Daniel McLachlan soon proved his marked ineptitude for the presbyterian ministry by publishing a 'Scandalous Pamphlet in Defence of Fornication', that cardinal sin of the presbyterian church. Consequent on the disturbance caused by the pamphlet – entitled 'An Essay upon Improving and Adding to the Strength of Great Britain and Ireland by Fornication, justifying the same from Scripture and Reason' – he deserted his parish for Ireland, from where he fled to England without the consent of the presbytery of Mull. In April 1735, the magistrates of Edinburgh, receiving information that the pamphlet justifying fornication was being reprinted in the city, issued their warrant 'for searching all and every of the Printing Houses of this City for the same, and were dispersed, and such of the Sheets as were printed were taken into Custody, and the Printer put under Bail, not to print or publish the same in Time coming, under a severe Penalty'. Enquiries were also made after the author.[139]

In May, the matter was discussed by the Commission of the General Assembly of the Church of Scotland, which ordained the presbytery of Mull to 'proceed against him with the Sentence of summary Excommunication' if McLachlan could be found guilty and convicted.[140] The presbytery replied that it had opposed McLachlan when first called to Ardnamurchan, but that 'after a long Trial and Process, the Libel against him was not proven; so that they did admit and settle him there; but soon after he left that Place, but took Care, upon his Presentation, to obtain a Decreet of three Years Stipend, tho' he did not officiate but about a Month in the Parish after his admission'.[141] In the same month, the presbytery resolved 'That no more of what is allowed for Pious Uses, go to support a Man who seem [sic] to Covet the Sacred office of the Ministry, merely for the sake of filthy lucre'. McLachlan, who clearly made a killing on his pamphlet, was therefore deprived. On 13 June 1735, the presbytery formally drew up a libel against him, a copy of which was sent to him in London, charging him not only with writing the pamphlet but also with neglecting and forsaking his ministerial duties in travelling abroad to Edinburgh, Glasgow and other places in Scotland, Ireland and England. Shortly afterwards McLachlan was imprisoned, a punishment which induced a renunciation and recantation of the pamphlet and 'all the pernicious Opinions and Principles therein Contained' in front of the bishop of Rochester. Upon his release, he emigrated to Jamaica.[142] William Ferguson suggested that McLachlan was probably an episcopalian who reluctantly found his way into the Establishment in seeking a living. In this context, his lurid tract has been seen as 'a satire on the presbyterian obsession with the subject of sexual immorality', a genre apparently not familiar to his contemporary presbyterian critics.[143]

However, those who thought they could routinely escape Kirk discipline simply by fleeing to Ireland were sorely mistaken. There was relatively close contact and co-operation between the two presbyterian communities in Scotland and Ireland, so that censure could be, and was, imposed across borders.

Presbyterian Co-operation

Although Ulster remained a favourite refuge for delinquents from the west of Scotland, the close ties between the presbyterian communities in Antrim and Kintyre often blew their cover. On 27 November 1716, for instance, the presbytery of Kintyre noted 'that Agnes Bruce a single woman in this congregation is with child to one Henry Ker a Shoemaker in Ballimenoch [Ballymena] in Ireland and a married man which neither she nor any in the place [knew] when he came here first nor for sometime thereafter'. However, since the presbytery was fortunate enough to know the offender's place of residence in Ireland, it was able to follow the case through. In January 1717, the moderator was appointed to write to the minister of Ballymena in Antrim 'acquainting him of the said Henry Ker's falling into the said sin and that he deal with him to repair to this place to give satisfaction'. In a similar case heard before the presbytery of Kintyre in October 1721, involving Edward Armor and Elizabeth Stewart, Stewart was enjoined to stay in Campbeltown until the process was finalised and to appear before the next meeting of the kirk session. Instead, 'she went off to Irland, and now resides in the parish of Dundalk there' (the most southerly tip of Ulster). Taking the matter in hand, the presbytery wrote to Mr Patrick Simson, presbyterian minister there, 'to use his influence to obliege the said Elizabeth Stewart to repair to this place, to which they had gotten a return'. However, there being little sign of her compearance, the session referred the entire process to the presbytery.[144]

Although there are a few examples of presbyteries in Ireland writing to their Scottish counterparts, in general communication was conducted more at synodal level. One exception to this is noted in the record of the kirk session of Kilmory, in Arran. On 23 December 1708, the brethren received a letter from Mr McCracken, minister of Lisburn in the south of Antrim, with regard to 'Kathren Duncanson's deserting her husband & the session's course thair with'. He sought information about the said Kathren, then resident in Kilmory, even though she was 'spouse to one Duncan Mcninch for present living at Lysburn in Irland, who after she had lived in the forsaid place with her said husband for the space of a whole year, afterwards deserted him', and in spite of many invitations to return from her husband, and others, refused to do so. Finding her in obvious breach of her marriage vows, the session insisted that she be persuaded to return to her husband, but 'if she shall be found to refuse, They Appoynt the Minister to make publick Intimation of the Matter from the pulpit', forbidding anyone in the parish from harbouring her or giving her service or charity. Finally, the session threatened to apply to the civil magistrate 'to punish her as a perjured & disorderly person', but is is clear, from the frequency of such citations, that the civil authority, then as now, had no real power in these fundamentally domestic cases.[145]

The incidence of citations for irregular marriage, i.e. where the banns had not been proclaimed properly for three weeks in a row, or indeed not proclaimed at all, shows it to have been a general problem in Ireland and Scotland. It was possibly more of a problem in the Gaelic-speaking areas, where presbyterian clergy had to compete with itinerant priests or with priests just across the channel in Ireland who were prepared to marry Highland visitors on the spot. Certainly, on 16 October 1702 the synod of Argyll recommended to the moderator 'ane master John Darroch to give in a list of Irish curats, as baptizes and marries irregularely, within there bounds, to the Justiciars and to addresse him, to take loyall methods, with such persons, and curats for marrying'.[146] Legislation against irregular marriage could also be used as a means of controlling the influx of politically suspect persons, few of whom were under greater suspicion than Irish Catholics. This was particularly so in the year of rebellion, 1745, when, just as the civil authority exercised more stringent controls over the west-coast fishing fleets, so the Kirk paid greater attention to the act concerning clandestine marriages.[147] On 19 March 1745, taking into their consideration the frequency of clandestine marriages within their jurisdiction, the brethren of the presbytery of Lorn signified their firm resolution 'to do all in their power to prevent such pernicious practices in their Bounds'.[148]

Nor were marriages celebrated by episcopalians (who had not openly conformed at the Revolution) automatically ratified by the civil authority. On 15 May 1708, the synod of Argyll considered evidence in the alleged marriage of Mr John McKinnie and Catherine Clerk from the parish of Kilmaglash in the presbytery of Dunoon. McKinnie produced a certificate subscribed by a Mr John Ross 'and he being asked how he knew that the said pretended Mr. Ross was a minister or in any capacity to mary him with the said woman, he answered that he was weel acquainted with him and knew him to be the archbishop of St Andrews' Chaplain, and that he was going to the Kingdome of Ireland'. Not only is this evidence for the continuing movement of episcopalians to Ireland,[149] but it is a later example of the longstanding connection between ministers from St. Andrews and Ireland apparent from the early seventeenth century.[150] Although 'the said Master John was once Reputed a minister', the synod was suspicious of him; clearly, he had not been a presbyterian.[151] The matter was referred to the next synod. McKinnie and Clerk were instructed to ratify their marriage civilly, under pain of process as fornicators. They presumably succeeded in satisfying the synod in some way, because there is no further reference to them.

An important aspect of a kirk session's work was in providing testimonials when people relocated. These certificates of transference, requested when people moved congregations, took the form of personal histories (sometimes from infancy), which indicated whether the person concerned was free from discipline or not.[152] Such testimonials are mentioned in the early eighteenth-century record in both Ireland and Scotland, showing that this form of vetting was not yet dead within the presbyterian community in Ireland, even if Highlanders fled there in the hope of avoiding discipline. For instance, on 20 February 1701 the parish of Larne and Kilwaughter in Antrim 'produced a testimonial of one Cathren Murtach from Arran dated the 9th of May 1693 signed by Mr Archibald M'Clane Minister and by Patrick Hamiltone, John Stewart elder and James Hamilton elder'.[153] Suspicions were always aroused when strangers appeared with a child. The following example, dated 9 December 1722, in the records of the same parish, shows what could happen in the absence of a testimonial (the surname is suggestive of a native of Bute): 'After prayer the Session came to consideration of one Matt Stewart who had a child to be baptised and having no certificate from Scotland where he formerly resided. Resolves the child should be presented by a Sponsor and have Baptism administered upon the parents' promise of bringing a Certificate.'[154]

The insistence on testimonials from a person's previous parish was enforced just as stringently in Scotland. On 12 November 1712, the Rothesay session discussed a request from Robert Wallace, a young man born in the parish of Ballintoy in Ireland and now living in the Rothesay parish, who 'presented a testificate of his good behaviour there [Ballintoy] and the paper being somewhat lacerate and worn desired it might be recorded here that he might have access to a new testificate if he should happen to remove again'. This was an indication of the value generally laid on such a document, which the session underwrote by acceding to his request. The tenor of his testimonial is notable as an example of its type. 'These are to certify that the bearer, Robert Wallace, was born in the parish of Ballentoy where he has almost constantly lived hitherto and has behaved himself modestly as becoming one of his age without any kind of reproach, as witnesseth my hand, August 1st, 1712, *Sic subscribitur*, JOHN MARTIN.'[155] Yet (illiteracy notwithstanding), it must have been relatively easy to counterfeit such documents, and equally difficult to insist upon their production in times of military and political disturbance.

Shared Resources

Ireland and Scotland not only shared a pool of presbyterian ministers and certain members of their congregations, but also literary resources, composed in a stylised Irish that the scholars of both communities could readily understand but which was not so accessible to ordinary people. In Scotland, work to bring the Bible to Highlanders in vernacular Gaelic began in earnest in the late seventeenth century. In this, they were far behind the Irish: Nehemiah Donellan had published Walsh and Kearney's translation of the New Testament in 1603. In contrast, the first New Testament in vernacular Gaelic did not appear until 1767.[156] Similarly, the work of William Bedell,[157] bishop of Kilmore, ensured that a start was made on a translation of the Old Testament in Irish, although this labour of love was not completed until 1686, some forty-four years after his death. Both these testaments were in Irish as opposed to Roman script. Highlanders did not get an Old Testament in Scots Gaelic until 1801, while the first fully combined Gaelic Bible did not appear until 1826.[158] Just how much the Protestant community felt threatened by the Catholics in Ireland is revealed in Dr Andrew Sall's complaint to the Hon. Robert Boyle, son of the Earl of Cork – both of whom were involved in the printing of Irish scriptures – that he had incurred a good deal of ill-will, as well as threats, for his work.[159]

In Scotland, the man mainly responsible for the translation of the scriptures into classical common Gaelic was the episcopal minister the Rev. Robert Kirk of Aberfoyle, who had translated the first complete metrical psalter into common classical Gaelic, and was thus not unsuited for the task.[160] The dedication of Kirk's Psalter to Lord John Murray, Marquess of Atholl, stated that the work was intended:

> For assisting of our sagacious Scottish Irish people in their public or private Devotions; specially, seeing experience tells us that this their maternal Tongue either in Ireland or Scotland, is not easily abolisht by the contiguity and commixture of another language, which no doubt is well understood by the present worthy and Laborious Translators of the Holy Bible in Irish.[161]

Even if they were not in the preferred vernacular, scriptures in the classical language were a valuable joint resource for both Irish and Scottish Gaelic speakers, being more easily understood – with a little help from the minister – than scriptures in English.

One of the most frequent excuses given for the delay in furnishing scriptures in Scottish Gaelic was the alleged illiteracy of the Gaelic-speaking Highlanders. Certainly, there were very few schools in the Highlands and Islands before the last two decades of the seventeenth century, and when more schools were established in the eighteenth century the declared aim of most, other than the Catholic schools, was the extirpation of the Gaelic language.[162] But although there are no figures for levels of general literacy among the laity in the Highlands during this period, literacy in common classical Gaelic would have been fairly common among the clan *fine* and literati. The oral transmission of literary culture, which has had a long history in the *Gaidhealtachd*, clearly played a significant role in promoting the spread of Protestantism before the scriptures were published in vernacular Gaelic,[163] but this strong oral culture was supported and nurtured by an equally important scribal tradition whose extent before the eighteenth century has often been underestimated.[164] The most likely cause for delay was the general prejudice perpetrated against the

Gaelic language by the Lowland government. The Established Church did little to improve the situation by its ambivalent attitude to Gaelic, and in the Highlands and Islands much was therefore dependent on the support of the various presbyteries and synods. Fortunately, the synod of Argyll had taken a positive approach to the translation of devotional material into Gaelic since the superintendence of John Carswell (and especially from the early seventeenth century) because many of their ministers used Gaelic in their services. Indeed they had no choice: it was often the only language of their parishioners.[165]

However, two other protagonists played important roles in relaying the first Gaelic scriptures to Highlanders: the Rev. James Kirkwood, an exiled Scottish episcopalian in England, and the Hon. Robert Boyle, son of the Earl of Cork, mentioned above. Born in Dunbar, Kirkwood was not a Gaelic speaker, but his first ministerial appointment was as chaplain to Sir John Campbell of Glenorchy, Earl of Caithness. After that he held two Lowland parishes, then, after being ousted from the parish of Minto for refusing the Test Act in November 1681, he appears to have travelled in England and Ireland. It was this visit to Ireland which seems to have deepened in him a resolve to provide scriptures in a language that Highlanders could understand. But it was the acquaintance he made of Robert Boyle during this time which allowed him to carry through his initiative, because Boyle had the financial resources to give practical shape to Kirkwood's desire. Soon after gaining the living of the rectory of Astwick in Bedfordshire in March 1684, Kirkwood put his plan into action. Having recently reprinted Bedell's Irish Bible and Donellan's New Testament in Irish type at his own expense, Boyle offered to provide copies of the quarto Old Testaments to be sent to Scotland 'to see what reception they might meet with there'. A total of 207 Bibles, or one for each parish, arrived in Edinburgh in July 1688, into the charge of Colin Campbell of Carwhin, writer to the signet. But the management of their distribution devolved entirely upon Robert Kirk.[166]

A friend of Kirkwood's, Kirk was corresponding with him at the time about a catechism produced by the Rev. Lawrence Charteris, presbyterian minister and Professor of Divinity at Edinburgh University, which had been translated into Gaelic by Sir Hugh Campbell of Cawdor. The Highland *fine* therefore involved themselves in making the scriptures more accessible in ways other than merely financial. Although the catechism was corrected and reworked by Kirk, it was Sir Hugh Campbell who attended the printing of 3,000 copies in London, financed once again by the benevolence of Boyle. While Kirk took great pains to establish that the Bibles he distributed were the property of the parish itself, Carwhin subsequently allowed many of them to be alienated for personal use.[167] However, Kirk is best remembered for implementation of his grand scheme that the Bible should be printed not in Irish but in Roman script and freely distributed, so that the minister might have an informed audience. He managed to fund the scheme through the generosity of Robert Boyle and other

English benefactors, such as Dr Stillingfleet, bishop-elect of Worcester who, in spite of his reservations gave ten guineas. Some Scots also helped: the Countess of Cassillis and Gairntully, for instance, gave £10 sterling. Kirk transcribed Bedell's and Donellan's Testaments in just over a year and took the manuscript to London for printing in the summer of 1689. By 1 April 1690 the Bibles were printed, the run extending to 3,000 Bibles, 1,000 Testaments and 3,000 Catechisms. Unfortunately, Kirk died in May 1692, before the final distribution was completed in 1706.[168] Noting the receipt of its kirk Bible and others for use of the congregation, Kingarth Kirk Session minuted on 26 July 1696:

> About this time was given (by donation of the honourable, pious and learned Robert Boyle, son to the Earle of Corck, etc., in Ireland, a principall member of the Royall Societie, an big Irish Bible in the proper character bestowed on the parish Church of Kingarth in Bute to continue there as a Church Bible for the use of the present minister and for the behoof of all the ministers who shall succeed him in that parish), as also twentie small Irish bibles in the Romane Character for the use of the parishioners.[169]

Kirkwood continued to further the use of the Irish Bible in Scotland after Kirk's death. Particularly insistent that it be used in schools, as the most effective method of evangelisation, he published in 1697 his 'Answer to the Objection against Printing the Bible in Irish, as being Prejudicial to the Design of Extirpating the Irish Language out of the Highlands of Scotland'. When in 1703 a projected reprinting of the Irish Bible was opposed by George Meldrum, a member of the Highland libraries committee, he was forceful in his counter-attack. Meldrum pointed out, with a certain validity, that the Irish translation was little understood, but Kirkwood argued that there were equally as many words used in Argyll and the Isles which were 'not vulgarly known nor used in other counties', as indeed many words in the English Bible were no longer used in the contemporary vernacular.[170]

Devotional texts in Scottish Gaelic also travelled in the other direction. When, by 7 August 1722, the Confession of Faith and Larger Catechism had still not been published, 'and ... there is a Generall expectation from the highlands of Scotland and many in Ireland, that the printing thereof might be expede without loss of time', the synod of Argyll appointed Mr Duncan Campbell, minister of Kilchrenan, to go to Edinburgh to attend the press for that end.[171]

The SPCK also operated in Ireland (as well as England), and members of the Society in Scotland (the SSPCK) were well aware of the developments across the North Channel.[172] The record clearly shows that the Society sought to emulate the success of Irish manufacturers and industry in the Highlands of Scotland. From its formation in 1708, much of the Society's Scottish work was carried out in the Highlands, for which the economic changes wrought in areas of Ulster served as a useful example for improvement. Since the time of the plantation many fertile areas of Ulster had been significantly improved agriculturally and industrially, and its ports attracted business from Britain, the continent and America. Its economy was far more buoyant than that of the Highlands. A surviving manuscript states that the Society 'did encourage Our Nighbours in Ireland and attempt to follow our Example, with an addition to imploy their Schollars in Manufacture Agricultur and Industry, which is most necessary in Sco'land as well as thair'. It also outlines the Society's intention to pursue the ends of its new charter (as advertised in the newspapers), hence the presbyteries had been approached to persuade the heritors and other influential people in their bounds, 'to Deale with them to Contribute and give their assistance and Concurrence in so good a work, as we find is done in Ireland'. They admitted, however, that the only encouragement given in Scotland was that offered by the Duke of Gordon, who had given them land in Lochaber. This is probably Cosmo George, the third Duke of Gordon and the first duke to be raised a Protestant, which therefore dates the document to some time after 1728, when he succeeded his father.[173] The presbyteries were asked to acquaint the Society on what ground heritors would either feu or lease land, how much and on what terms, and what assistance they would give in furnishing houses and appropriate accommodation for these purposes. The heritors in Ireland gave land either in perpetuity or on long leases, 'for Agriculture, sowing Flax, and Gardening, And for Manufacture, and many thair, give annuall support to this Excellent designe'.[174] But the response had not been immediate: this was the third letter asking the presbyteries for a list of those heritors prepared to assist in erecting schools and facilitating manufacture and improvement.[175]

Not only was there interaction between members of the SSPCK in Scotland and Ireland, but also mutual support in the religious life of presbyterian communities, although this was extended largely by Highlanders to the presbyterians in Ulster rather than the other way round.

Missionaries to the Native Irish

Around half the congregations in the Dublin presbytery had firm links with the Ulster synod at the end of the seventeenth century, although the presbytery was not officially connected to it. Missionary work among the Irish-speaking population was frequently discussed in correspondence. In July 1699, it was drawn to the General Synod's attention that the Dublin brethren

> had a mind to visit the Upper Country, by Preaching, & therefore judged it would be convenient that this Synod would appoint one or two of their number to preach in the Irish Tongue to go along with 'em, or any they shall appoint for this Work, so that, while they from Dublin are preaching to the British, the Person or Persons sent by this Synod may be exercised in preaching among the

Irish.[176]

Approving the suggestion, the presbytery of Tyrone was appointed to second Mr Archibald MacLean for a while to Dublin when called by the ministers there. His charges were to be met out of the *Regium Donum*. In the event he was not called, but this Argyll-born minister was obviously considered one of the best Irish preachers of his day.[177] It is equally evident that the presbyterian church in Ulster had as big a problem in finding ministers to evangelise the native Irish and Highland Scots. Even at this late juncture, it was partly reliant on attracting Gaelic speakers from Scotland.

The name of Mr Archibald MacLean, minister of Markethill, is continually linked with missionary efforts to preach to the native Irish. Broaching the subject at length in an overture of 21 June 1710, the synod recognised 'the earnest Desire of all true Protestants that the Ghospel may be propogated in its Purity, and particularly that the Papists may be converted'. However, appreciating that desire alone was insufficient, the synod resolved to accompany it with 'Suitable Endeavours', by employing some ministers to preach in Irish. It had expressed such intentions for some time, 'but the Smallness of our Number, and especially of such as understood the Irish Tongue, has in a great Measure obstructed the Execution of it – at least confin'd it much more than we desir'd'. It was now in a better position to undertake such work, having a number of men in its midst who understood Irish: 'Mr McClane, Mr McGrigor, Mr Humpry Thompson, Mr Samuel Dunlop, Mr John Wilson, Mr Archibald Boyd, Ministers, with Mr Higginbothom, Mr Plunket, Mr John Dunlop, Probationers'.[178]

A certain strategy had to be adopted for such missionary work. The missionaries would be sent out in groups of two, a minister and a probationer together, the synod ensuring that the minister's charge was supplied in his absence. Bibles, Confessions of Faith and Catechisms were to be supplied for the purpose, all of which were then available in Irish. Each pair would work among the Irish for three months at a salary of twenty shillings per week; ministers were encouraged to use their interest to obtain a fund for this good work, which it was hoped the Dublin brethren would also support. And every presbytery was to 'endavour to obtain Irish hopefull Youths, who may be educated in our Way, thereby they may be usefull for obtaining this Desireable End'.[179]

After this, missionary work amongst the Irish is not mentioned again until 19 June 1716. On this occasion the initiative came from the presbytery of Dublin, who wrote to the synod earnestly entreating them 'to joyn them in the use of all proper means for the conversion of the Irish Papists'. The synod concurred. Those ministers who had the Irish language were listed again, but a great deal of work was apparently necessary before all of them reached the requisite standard for preaching. Several new ministers and probationers were appended – 'Mr Charles Lyle, nigh to Straban ... Mr Robert Thompson of Belturbet, Ministers, and Mr Robert Stuart in Tyrone Presbytery, Mr Samuel Irwin in Monahan Presbytery, Probationers' – as well as Mr Patrick Simpson at Dundalk, the only minister to be included amongst those who 'have oft preacht in Irish'. Patrick Simpson, like MacLean, was an Argyll man. It is surely telling that out of the three who were said to have preached a great deal in Irish, two were Highlanders while the third was the Irishman Mr James McGregor of Aghadoey in Derry, who was clearly of Scottish descent and had been licensed by the Route presbytery, an area of marked Highland settlement.[180] This points to the survival of thriving Scottish Gaelic communities in Ulster. Certainly in existence in the 1690s, when the Church of Ireland had employed some ousted Scottish episcopalians to preach in Ulster, these communities clearly remained unassimilated by the second decade of the eighteenth century.

Perhaps due to the '15 rebellion in the previous year, activity was to be well planned and co-ordinated on this occasion. A committee of nine brethren was appointed, mainly composed of English speakers, other than Samuel Dunlop of Letterkenny in Donegal and Mr Humphrey Thompson of Ballybay in Monaghan, who were to meet with ministers from Dublin at Newry and at Dungannon in Armagh when they had discussed the matter. In addition, those brethren who were enjoined to improve their Irish would be formed into two societies for that purpose: the first was to meet at Dungiven and the second (of which both Mr MacLean and Mr Simpson were members) at Armagh, at least once every two months.[181]

Enthusiasm for the Irish Language Societies did not run deep. The Dungiven Society failed to meet again after its first appointment, other than in the person of Mr Higginbotham. As for the Armagh Society, Mr MacLean, minister, had not been alerted to its first meeting, but he preached before them when it met a second time. After that, it too failed to keep any more meetings. However, some progress was made on an individual level (where most necessary), the Armagh Society reporting that 'Mr Samuel Dunlop has improv'd so much in the Irish Language, that he can now preach in it. Mr Lynd and Mr Strawbride can read it. Mr Higginbotham has preacht oft in Irish since the Synod.' Thus, in spite of the logistics of convening such meetings, the synod's Irish Committee decided that the two Irish societies be continued – to meet in August, in Derry and Armagh. Thereafter they were to meet quarterly, but by 29 June 1720 they still had not done so.[182]

At the same synod, Patrick Simpson was appointed to preach in Irish in Dublin for three months, returning once a month to supply his own congregation. McGregor, Higginbotham and MacLean, probably being less in need of practice, were appointed to preach in Irish in such places as the presbytery deemed it most necessary, for which they were to receive twenty shillings a week. It was also ordered 'that a Charity School be set up at Dundalk for teaching to read Irish, and that each of our Presbyteries give twenty shillings towards it'. This was Simpson's parish, although no firm evidence is given that he was the teacher there. However, when the synod ordered the printing of the Catechism in Irish in June 1716, 'with a little short Irish Grammer of a leaf or two subjoyn'd to it', Simpson was to see it to press in Dublin. Every minister had to subscribe and pay for thirty copies of this book. By June 1717, Simpson reported that the grammar had been finished with assistance from an Irishman, there being significant differences by this time between vernacular Irish and Scottish Gaelic, but that 'because it was some time before it could be got well translated', the Irish Catechism had not yet been printed.[183]

The Ulster synod of June 1717 ordained Archibald MacLean, former minister of Kilmaglass in Argyll, to 'preach in part of the County of Ardmagh, Monahan, and Tyrone, at Benburb, Dungennan, Stewarton, Cookestown, and Minterbirn, Kinaird, VeniCash, LoghGall, Kedy, and Monahan town'. His release was to be agreed with his own presbytery, ensuring that his own congregation was supplied. As for Mr Simpson, he was 'to preach in any place of the County of Downe where he may have an Irish congregation and audience; in any part of the County of Ardmagh not allotted to Mr Macclane; as also in part of the County of Monaghan'. It is obvious from these huge allocations how much of the burden of Irish preaching was assigned to these Highlanders. But they did at least receive back-up: the synod specified that 'the Ministers in whose congregations the Irish sermons are to be should carefully visit the Irish after such sermons, in order to promote their conversion'.[184]

The other Archibald MacLean, Argyll probationer, must have arrived some time after June 1716, for he was not present at the synod. He had been engaged as an itinerant preacher, under the direction of a committee of the synod (other presbyterians who spoke Irish had particular districts assigned to them).[185] Unfortunately, the official record is rather more concerned with the deficiencies in contributions to his stipend than in giving much information about the areas in which he preached: in June of 1717, Convoy, Derry and Monaghan had 'not paid their Quota to Mr Archbald Macclane, Probationer from Argyle'. MacLean was not happy: he asked the synod for testimonials because he intended to return to his own country. After discussion, the synod proposed that 'endeavours be us'd to keep Mr Macclane, Probationer, in the Countrey, in order to his preaching among the Irish', but it was not a unanimous decision: some were of the opinion that MacLean could be spared, since there were now several with the ability to speak Irish. However, it was eventually agreed that MacLean would receive £40 a year, to be paid quarterly, and that he would take responsibility for arranging his own accommodation: 'By this means the people where he goes, and himself, will be more easy.'[186] To this end, the

General Synod of Ulster wrote to the synod of Argyll signifying that MacLean had 'acquitted himself every way to their great satisfaction', and asking it not to hinder him if he chose to stay in Ulster until the following summer. Mr Dugald Campbell, junior, was to reply to the synod of Ulster 'to signify this Synod's readiness to give all the assistance they can to them in so good a work',[187] while Mr James Getty was to write to MacLean to clarify his own inclination in the matter. MacLean stayed in Ireland for another year but had returned to Scotland by the summer of 1718.[188]

Every effort was made to improve the rate of conversion among the native Irish. For instance, the synod made moves in June 1717 to reduce the size of the two frontier presbyteries which contained the largest number of Irish-speaking Catholics. These presbyteries suffered from having large disparately scattered congregations in which the ministers found it hard to fulfil missionary obligations made for them by the presbytery in addition to their normal parish load. A similar situation was found in many Highland parishes. In just the same way as the Scottish Kirk subdivided some of its more unwieldy presbyteries, like the Outer Hebrides or the Long Island in 1742, or had created new jurisdictions like the synod of Glenelg in 1724, the Ulster synod divided the presbytery of Monaghan into the presbyteries of Augher and Longford, and Convoy into the presbyteries of Strabane and Letterkenny. Unfortunately, the former two had to be expediently reunited after six years, probably because subdivision did not necessarily ensure more ministers.[189]

By June 1718, missionary endeavours by the presbytery of Antrim were bearing fruit 'amongst the Irish Papists of Killilagh and Killmakevat'. No precise location is given for this evangelising – most of which was the work by Mr Abernethy – so 'Killilagh' may refer either to Killelagh in County Londonderry, Killyleagh in County Down, or possibly, since the work was undertaken in conjuction with the presbytery of Dublin, to Killelagh in County Clare. There is a Kilmakevoge in Kilkenny in Leinster.[190] However, out of 'concern for the welfare of their souls, and, for their further encouragement', the synod appointed Archibald MacLean and Patrick Simpson, Irish-speaking ministers, to go and consolidate Mr Abernethy's conversions, which they did. James McGregor, however, left Londonderry for the richer pastures of Boston in the summer of 1718, his parish being in debt to him to the sum of £80, and his contribution was lost to the missionary programme.[191] The presbytery of Dublin and the synod of Ulster continued to co-operate with each other in missionary work. In June 1717, the synod had asked the presbytery of Dublin to share in some of the essential costs of the mission. Two years later, in June 1719, the presbytery made an overture to the synod regarding the supply, in their own language, of preachers to the Highlanders and Irish in Dublin. The Highlanders also sent a commission to Mr McNeill (probably Archibald McNeill in Dundalk), and others he might recommend, to prosecute their petition. The synod approved the petition and decided to do all it could to encourage the plans, 'having an account of fifty pounds per annum bequeath'd by Dr Williams for the Encouragment of an Irish Preacher, and fifty pound sent by Mr Reynolds and Mr Evans, Ministers in London, which fifty pound is now in Dublin, besides considerable sums expected for the same use'.[192]

Mr Simpson was one of three ministers subsequently sent to Dublin, where they were to spend three months, in turn, preaching in Irish to the Highlanders and any who felt inclined to join them. All four appointments were fulfilled by 21 June 1720. Four of the Dublin ministers were to aid progress by meeting 'with other dissenting Ministers in Dublin, and other Gentlemen that are willing to engage in this work, in a Society, to prepare a place and make what other provision is necessary to begin the said preaching in Irish the first Lords's day in August'. By 29 June 1720 it was noted: 'The Society for preparing what is necessary for the preaching in Irish have a commodious place for these preachings.' The good work continued: the synod received a second petition from 'the Highlanders and Irish Papists who attend the preaching of the Gospel in Irish in and about the City of Dublin', about the very good prospect of winning souls. The same trio of ministers was again seconded to Dublin.[193]

The extent of the Irish Church's dependence on Scottish presbyterian and episcopalian settlers is one of the most salient features of the period before 1720. If not outrightly hostile, the climate during the Restoration period was sufficiently intolerant of presbyterianism to push some ministers across to Ireland, while the period after the Revolution saw a similar transfer of Scottish episcopalians there. Most of the traffic in Gaelic speakers was one-way, from Scotland to Ireland. Yet the situation was still markedly different in Ireland than in Scotland, because presbyterians had the status of dissenters. Although the Church of Ireland might be castigated for insufficient attention to the promotion of an Irish-speaking mission to the native Irish, the presbyterian church there compared pretty favourably. Why was this? It was mainly due to the close links it maintained with the Scottish Kirk, which was making distinct efforts to improve a similar situation in its own house. The dearth of accomplished Irish speakers in the presbyterian church in Ireland was caused by a combination of factors: the large numbers of Lowland presbyterians in the Ulster church, the scarcity of competent Irish-speaking ministers in either country, and the lower conversion rate among the native Irish simply because the presbyterian church did not have legal status in Ireland. But perhaps it is more significant that Highland ministers went to Ireland at all, given the profound problems which the Kirk had in addressing its own inadequacies in the Highlands and Islands. On the other hand, there is almost negligible movement of ministers from Ireland to Scotland, except those who were of Highland origin in the first place.

During the last four decades of the period 1690–1760, this fruitful source of ministerial movements completely dried up. Ministers only crossed to Ireland in social capacities. This reflects a self-suffiency in the Irish presbyterian church, which was by then more or less able to supply its own congregations, while a degree of toleration extended by the Irish establishment permitted it to expand. Up to and including the early part of the period under consideration, the presbyterian church in Ulster was still seen as an offshoot of the mother Church in Scotland. Many members of the Ulster synod had been educated in Scottish universities and were licentiates of the Kirk; they had been prepared to follow the same system of discipline and government. Until the early eighteenth century, the Irish branch of the church concurred with the doctrinal views of the Church in Scotland and showed no apparent digression from the constitutional principles of presbyterianism as practised in Scotland.[194] However, by the end of this period the presbyterian church in Ireland had come of age, its umbilical cord with Scotland well and truly severed.

During the early eighteenth century, particularly after the '15 rebellion, the Kirk began to make a concerted effort to deal with the problem of Catholic infiltration in certain areas of the Highlands and Islands. It attempted, not entirely successfully, to plant ministers in vacant parishes bordering on Catholic districts, as well as sending missionaries north into Catholic districts during the summer months.[195] But a comparison of the numbers of Protestant ministers who went as missionaries to Ireland during this period – six episcopalians and five or six presbyterians – compares unfavourably with the numbers of Irish priests in the Highlands during the same time; between 1690 and 1760 there were at least thirty-one Irish Catholic missionaries working in the Highlands and Islands, as well as an unnamed lay Capuchin in 1695 who in all probability was also Irish. That is, there were nearly three times as many Catholic priests in Scotland as there were Protestant ministers in Ireland; a few may have gone unrecorded on both sides. By the end of the period, the Kirk was beginning to reap the fruit of its effort in the Highlands and Islands. Especially after the '45, it was better supported by the civil authorities, and it continued its own efforts to settle Gaelic-speaking ministers there. By 1760, the Kirk no longer felt so threatened by the Catholic community; while it had not been eradicated, it was certainly left more to its own devices.[196]

SIX

Fishers of Herring and the Priesthood of Aaron, 1690–1760

Little instructed and not very zealous.
Propaganda Archives (early eighteenth century)

JAMES VII's abdication and the ensuing Jacobite rebellion of 1689 seriously circumscribed mission activities. The main difficulty for the missionaries was the severing of lines of communication; their stipends were delayed at the best of times. When David Burnet, former dean of the Chapel Royal, wrote in May 1690 to William Leslie, the Scots agent in Rome, he told him that 'wee borrowed as long as wee could get people that would lend us but our credit for that point is exhausted, the countrey extremely poor for want of comerce, and the being harassed be the souldiors wee can get no more to borrow'. Food was very scarce: when Burnet passed through Badenoch, Lochaber and Mull on his way to Ireland, he was unable to buy even a stone of butter or cheese to sustain him on his journey. Nevertheless, in spite of all the difficulties, a number of Irish priests continued their work on the Highland mission, not scrupling to use Jacobitism to fire their communities with enthusiasm, and urging them not to take the Oath of Allegiance.[1]

Arguably the most important development for Catholicism in this period was the appointment in August 1694 of Mr Thomas Nicolson as Vicar-Apostolic or missionary bishop to Scotland. This gave Scottish Catholics their first fully fledged bishop in ninety-one years. He was styled 'Vicar-Apostolic' because he acted basically as a delegate of the Pope. Though Roman Canon Law no longer had the weight of the civil authority behind it, the judgements of the Vicar-Apostolic were accepted as spiritual law by his clerical subordinates and by good Catholics. He could ordain and confirm, but decisions over marriages held no legal sanction in the country and could be overturned by the presbyterian clergy. However, because of the prevailing post-Revolutionary attitude, it was two and a half years before the titular bishop of Peristachium was able to take up his new position. The situation became less tense for Catholics with the signing on 20 September 1697 of the treaty of Ryswick by France, England,

Spain and Holland, because fears of a French-backed restoration were allayed by France's recognition of William's sovereignty. But things were decidedly less favourable under the presbyterian regime, and at the same time the mission also suffered the ill-effects of the famine of the 1690s.[2] In order to cope with the situation, Bishop Nicolson drew up a series of disciplinary regulations in 1700 which held the mission on a tighter rein. After approval by *Propaganda*, these were given to the clergy in 1706 and remained as guidelines until 1780.[3] The submission of the Jesuits to the authority of the secular bishop on 7 February 1701 was equally significant. Still working in the Highlands and its peripheries[4] by this time, the Jesuits no longer operated exclusively from the houses of patrons (a change in modus operandi which undoubtedly facilitated their submission).[5]

As if to counter this new Catholic solidarity, a presbyterian drive began in the Highlands with the foundation of The Society in Scotland for Propagating Christian Knowledge on 18 August 1708. Well over fifty Protestant schools had been established by the second decade of the eighteenth century. Anti-Catholic work was also supported by George I's gift in 1723 of an annual sum of £1,000 sterling – the Royal Bounty – to promote Protestantism in the Highlands; the Royal Bounty Committee was formed in the following year to administer it. The Kirk was also prompted in 1724 to reduce the extensive charge of the synod of Argyll by establishing a new synod of Glenelg, which took parishes from the synods of Argyll and Ross. In spite of all this, the work of the Established Church and the SSPCK progressed in the Highland districts only in direct proportion to the support given by local landlords and heritors. Hence Protestant schools were not founded in the major Catholic enclaves of South Uist, the Small Isles, Glengarry, Knoydart and North Morar and Fort Augustus until 1774.[6] A presbyterian manuscript of 1718 showing 'The State of Lochaber and the Countries bordering on it with respect to popery' confirms that in the Braes of Lochaber, Glengarry, Knoydart, both Morars, Moidart and Arisaig 'thair is no Schooll in all the bounds'.[7]

Numbers of missionaries in the Highlands waxed and waned according to the political climate as well as personal and financial circumstances. The anti-Catholic climate continued to prevail under Queen Anne, although the proclamation of the penal laws in 1702, 1704 and 1705 was designed mainly to disarm support for Jacobitism.[8] Nevertheless, the political mood and the deaths of many mission veterans combined to reduce the number of priests to only four in 1705, no more than those on the original Franciscan mission. To ameliorate this situation and in view of Nicolson's advancing age, a coadjutor, James Gordon, was consecrated on 11 April 1708, to give the mission a second bishop. Persecution of Catholics increased, particularly at times of Jacobite plotting and unrest. If somewhat exaggerated, the connection between Catholicism and Jacobitism was not totally unfounded: the secular priest James

Carnegie (alias Hall) for one, was in close communication with the Old Pretender. In 1714, the first seminary in Scotland since the Reformation was opened on Loch Morar, but fear of the political face of Catholicism conspired to close it after the '15. Bishop Nicolson was also captured after the rising, in March 1716, but managed to escape. On his death in 1718, Bishop Gordon succeeded as second Vicar-Apostolic, and because he too was in poor health, he was also given a coadjutor in 1720 in the form of the aged loyal Jacobite John Wallace. However, closet Jacobites plotted with abandon during the 1720s, resulting in small bands of military troops, encouraged by bounties, roaming about the Highlands in 1726 hunting for priests. The Royal Bounty Committee began work at the same time, increasing Protestant missionary activity in the Highlands. To counter this presbyterian encroachment, the bishops recommended the appointment of a specifically Gaelic-speaking Vicar-Apostolic.[9]

In preparation for the new bishop, the Scottish mission was divided into two vicariates in 1727: the Highlands and the Lowlands. (See Fig. 6.1.) Engineered mainly on the basis of linguistic division, Gaelic-speaking Glenlivet and Strathavon were nevertheless retained in the Lowland vicariate because Gordon's seminary at Scalan was in Glenlivet. Hugh MacDonald, a son of MacDonald of Morar, was consecrated as the first bishop of the Highlands in 1731. On Wallace's death in 1733, Colin Campbell, a younger son of the family of Lochnell, fully expected to be appointed as coadjutor, but because relations between him and Bishop Gordon had begun to break down, he was passed over. Due to this personal grudge, Campbell became instrumental in hurling accusations of Jansenism at Gordon and sowing discontent among Highland missionaries. Not only was the priests' perennial discontent over lack of funds ripe for exploitation, but inter-clan rivalry exacerbated the whole situation. It flared up into one of the biggest conflicts of the eighteenth century mission.[10]

Dynamic Secularism, 1690–1715

In the immediate aftermath of the Revolution, Mr Burnet, the vice-prefect, sent a general overview of the mission to Mr Talon, who was still one of its main benefactors. Writing from Dublin on 20 June 1690, where Dunbar had sent him to greet James VII in his name and to report on the Scottish Catholic mission,[11] Burnet gave an account of all the priests on the Highland mission. Passing through the Highlands on his way to Dublin, Mongan had told him that Devoyer, Cahassy, Hannat and Harnet were beavering away on the mainland, their health and strength much diminished by inadequate nourishment. The enemy blocked all communication with the Lowlands. However, Carolan was well and living in the Isle of Barra, Ryan was in the Isle of Eigg, and Trener was in that part of his mission field closest to the Lowlands, probably

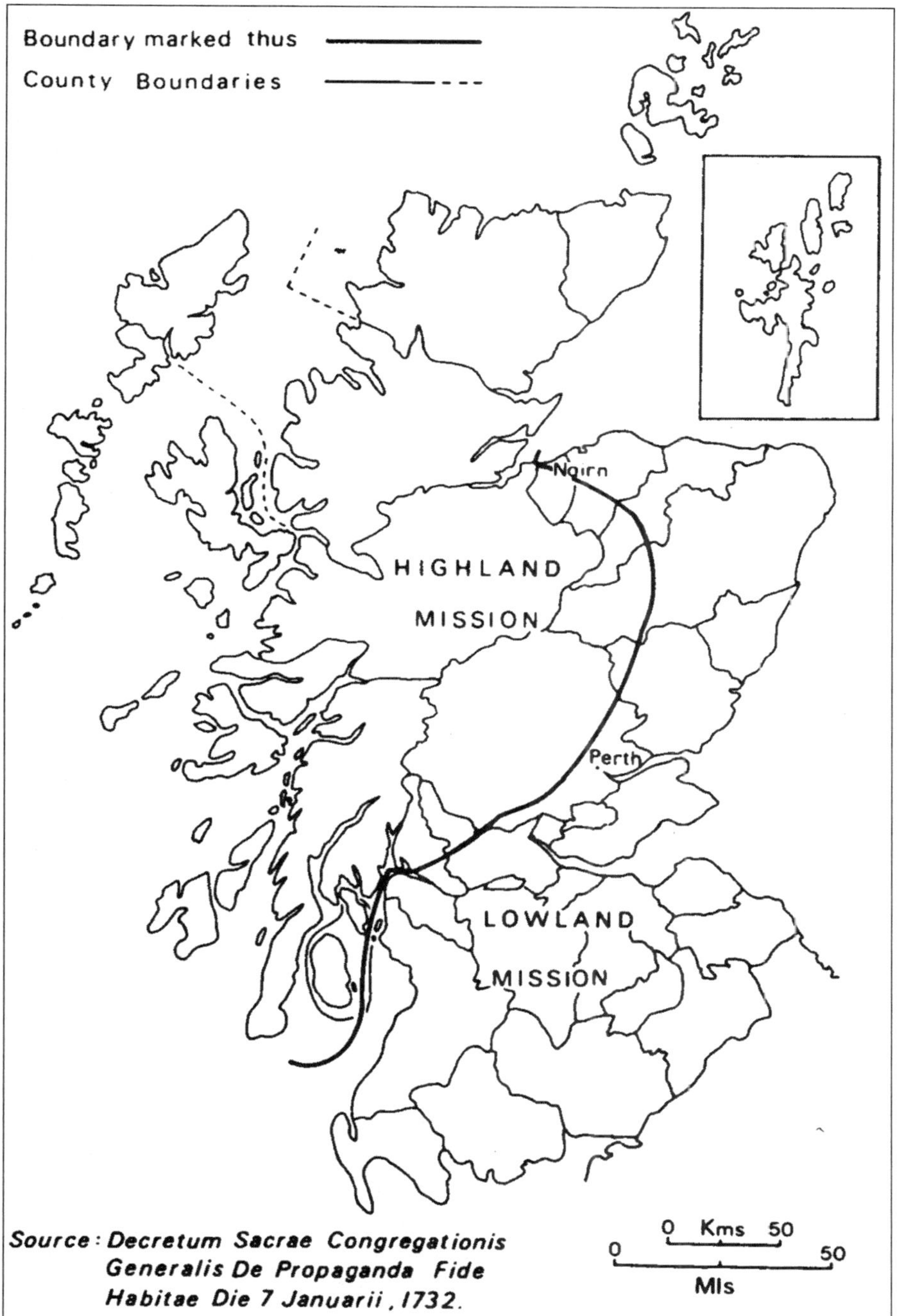

Fig. 6.1. The Catholic *Gaidhealtachd*, 1732.

Braemar.[12] It was now more than twenty months since Coan had apostatised and married the daughter of a man of rank whom he had previously debauched, to everyone's great scandal.[13]

The King granted Burnet permission to go to Paris to try and secure support for his brethren on the Scottish mission.[14] A letter to William Leslie, Scots agent in Rome, showed that Burnet had clearly been aiming for the Holy See, but he was called back early to the mission and therefore his design of seeing Leslie 'and exposing our missions caise to our patrones is broken of'. But he urged Leslie to plead the case 'to any who may be touched with compassione and moved to yeeld us Releef' that the King's generosity had encouraged them to augment their number to twenty-seven. Although the King's order of 1686 had encouraged all Scottish priests on the continent to return to Scotland, the unstated implication is that in the changed circumstances, the mission could not afford to sustain so many. That the Highlands was something of a missionary backwater with a high turnover in personnel only served to compound the issue. Burnet mentioned nine missionaries in the Highlands: eight Irishmen and Robert Munro, the Scot.[15]

Writing to William Leslie at some time in the year of Revolution, Fr. James Bruce in Ratisbon illumined the way in which the Irish comported themselves on the mission. All of his information came from one 'Mcclealand born in the lewes' who had been in Ratisbon.[16] He also mentioned Cornelius Coan, the memory of whose flagrant scandal kept the grapevine buzzing throughout the long years of his apostasy. Mongan and Cahassy referred in June 1691 to 'The fatal fall of one of our comerades', laying the blame firmly on the moderacy of their superiors who had listened to his excuses and his promises of performing miracles on the mission. Even the Protestants were horrified by his conduct.[17] But the synod of Argyll championed Coan's cause, more as a stick with which to beat the Catholic faith than because it had any true insight into his character.[18] The concluding episodes in the Cornelius Coan story only came to light in the last few years of the century.

A direct order from Seaforth put Coan behind bars. Already compromised by a parliamentary decreet for the return of a bond, as well as large arrears of feu-rents in Lewis, knowledge of Coan's ill-treatment at his hand only threatened to compromise Kenneth MacKenzie, fourth Earl of Seaforth, further. An avid Jacobite, Seaforth was not released from prison until 1697.[19] In the same year, the Privy Council sent Lieutenant Walkingshaw to the Outer Hebrides to investigate Coan's imprisonment. He was guarded by the MacLennans, tacksmen of Little Bernera, but he was moved before the party arrived there.[20] (See Fig. 6.2.) The synod of Argyll's account of the affair in June 1697 confirms the presence of other priests in the vicinity: Mr John McLauran reported that he had spoken to the King's Advocate 'anent liberating D. Cornelius O Coan and apprehending Patrick O kerulan and Richard

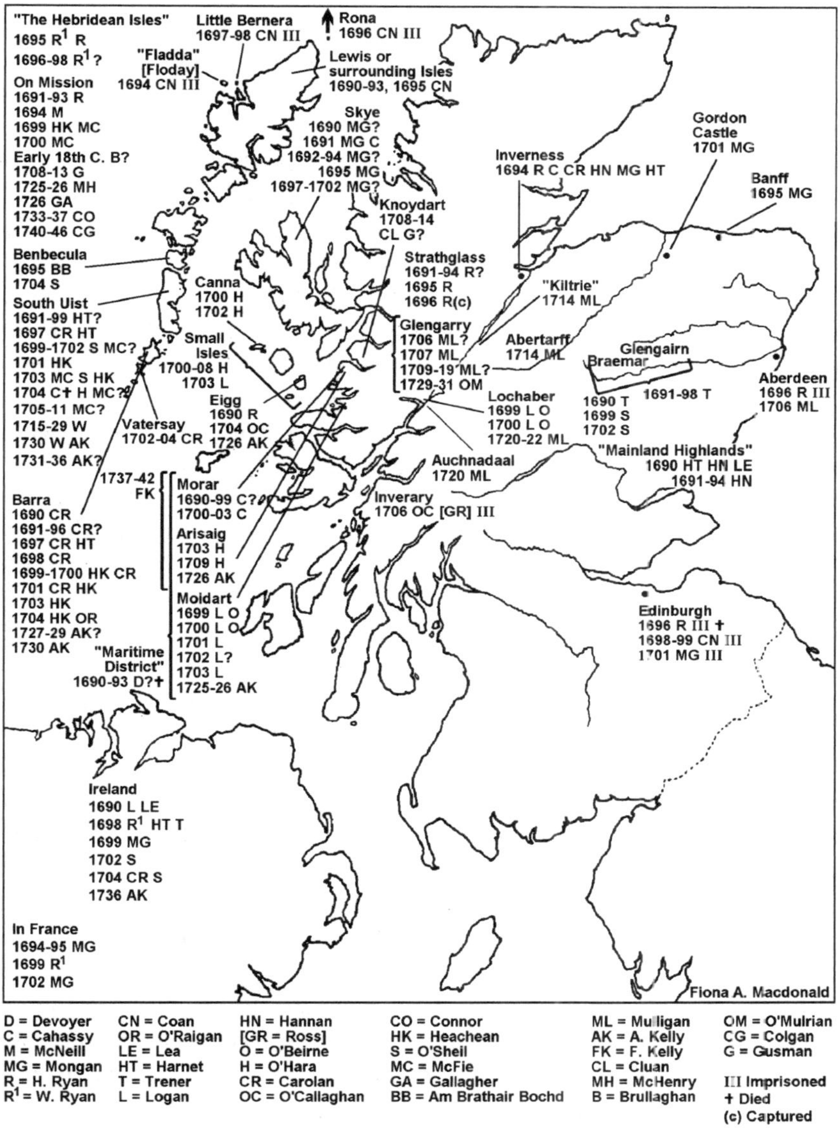

Fig. 6.2. Secular period, 1690–1760: incidence map.

Arnot Jesuits in Barra and South Uist'.[21] There was also trouble in Skye, whose presbyters spoke of writing to Sir Donald McDonald 'to compesce [compass] tumult in his bounds, which obstructed the brethren of Sky there Supplying the vacancies there'. Under instruction from the Lord Advocate, Colonel Hill, governor of Fort William, apprehended some priests, whom he sent down to Edinburgh. In the meantime, the Lord Advocate laid down a plan for liberating Coan.[22]

Seaforth was ordered to produce Coan and his keeper before the Privy Council in September 1697. Failing to comply, Seaforth concocted a story and simply added to his unpopularity by starting a riot in Chanonry against one of his creditors. He was ordered south in February 1698, although he was released on bail. On 19 May 1698, the clerk to the synod of Argyll was appointed to memorialise the Council on Coan's miserable condition and to suggest methods for his liberation. It also requested that Brigadier Maitland, who replaced Hill as governor of Fort William early in 1698, be asked to secure trafficking Jesuits in the bounds of the synod. When Seaforth appeared before the Council without Coan in July 1698, he was imprisoned in Edinburgh Castle. In the following month, Coan was offered by Lady Seaforth as a sop for her husband's release. On 7 June 1699, a letter of thanks from Coan was presented to the synod, thanking members for their 'paines and diligence in procureing his liberatione'. In spite of his wife's valiant efforts, Seaforth was not released until March 1700 when no proof could be found to link him with the riot in 1697. The government eventually became disillusioned with Coan, who initially declared himself willing to testify against Seaforth but was evasive when questioned. He was also consigned to the Castle and then banished.[23]

Correspondence from the mission does not pick up until a year after the Revolutionary upheavals. In June 1691, Mongan and Cahassy took the opportunity to send a letter by Mr Talon from a Jacobite ship which had docked at the Isle of Skye. Their Jacobitism shines forth: the missionaries stated that 'we have never been more necessary in these countries here than since the troubles, as much for affirming our poor Catholics in their faith as for encouraging them to hold firm for the King while awaiting His Majesty's help'.[24]

Financial considerations continued to dominate. In 1694, the missionaries received an allowance of only twenty-five crowns a year, but because of the special circumstances of rebellion, 'they must of necessity spend more then ever they did befor, because they dare not stay with catholiques that have means to gie them a piece of meat least they be aprehended with them, and Imprisoned'. No increase in the lump sum allocated to the Scottish mission – 500 crowns a year – had been made since 1650.[25] At the same time, there had been a reduction in what they had come to expect from their clerical brethren in France because 'the vast allowance the clergy of france has given the king hinders them from giving us one farthing of charity as I expected'.[26] Appended to the end of a letter to Mr Talon, written sometime after August 1694, are the names of most of the Irish priests on the Highland mission, six in all. Probably compiled at one of the annual meetings at Gordon Castle, it was signed by Ryan, Cahassy, Mongan, Hannat, Carolan and Harnet; only Devoyer and Trener were absent.[27]

Little support had been forthcoming from Talon since the Revolution. The Irish missionaries made a (literary) pretence of taking the blame on themselves: they had obviously been remiss in not informing him of their immense need nor of the condition of the Highland Catholics. However, they expressed themselves happy to hear that he was alive and continuing to give generously as before. They informed him of the demise of Mr Devoyer after a six-month illness: 'we have suffered a great loss by the death of the very worthy Mr. Devoyer who God called to himself to crown (as we hope) his exemplary life. He died on the 20th August last.' This fixes Devoyer's death in August 1693.[28] Two years later, Mr Talon himself was dead.[29]

In general, however, the Scottish superiors and the Paris College remained far from satisfied with the Irish. On 13 June 1695, Louis Innes, principal of the Scots College in Paris, informed William Leslie in Rome that he 'had sent home two Irish missionaries,[30] and a schoolmaster, who have cost pains enough and great expenses, near twice as much as so many of our own would have done'. In his opinion, 'we will never be well served in that country till we have of our own'; and this would not be achieved until Leslie had managed to secure *viatica*, or allowances, for them and pensions for schools in the Highlands.[31] In the year 1695–96, persecution against Catholics accused of conspiring against King William directly impinged upon the Highland mission. In May 1695, Ryan had gone herring fishing in the Hebrides – undoubtedly a Highland slant on the biblical 'fishers of men' – where 'another of the same trade' was working. The country was scoured for priests. Robert Munro and Hugh Ryan were taken prisoner in Strathglass in late 1695 or early 1696, Ryan being the second of only three Irish priests ever seized on the Highland mission.[32] They were kept first in Aberdeen and then in Edinburgh. Munro was eventually banished to Flanders, leaving Ryan 'in a dying condition at Edinburgh' where he lingered before finally expiring in the November.[33] The penal laws were re-enacted and enforced in Ireland and Scotland by a Williamite government wary of a French-backed Jacobite invasion of Ireland. The Catholic clergy, who openly sympathised with James VII and II, were particularly suspect. The first act of the parliamentary session of 1697 banished all Catholic clergy exercising ecclesiastical jurisdiction (bishops and regular clergy). Regulars who were more dependent on the Pope's authority were regarded as a greater menace than seculars, because they held greater sway over the people and were regarded as more irreconcilable to the government. From the beginning of 1698, arrangements were made for the transportation of those clergy affected by the act. About 700 regulars seem to have left, many afforded government passages to the continent,[34] although some went to the Highlands instead. A supporting act was drafted in Ireland in 1698 entitled 'An Act for the more speedy reducing of Ireland to conform to the Established Church', which enforced attendance at Protestant churches on all Catholics, punishable by loss of estate. In Scotland, a proclamation was passed on 4 March 'anent seminary Priests, Jesuits, and trafficking Papists', confirming all previous penal laws against Catholics. However, no Highland clergy were seized on this occasion.[35] Indeed, the contention that the ensuing persecution of Catholics 'was the worst yet known' in the Highlands is validated only by the virtual absence of persecution hitherto.[36]

En route to Rome in the summer of 1698 where he was being sent to assist William Leslie, the aged Scots agent John Irvine (alias Cuttlebrae) reported from Paris in September that there were ten missioners in the Highlands, eight of whom were Irish.[37] In the following year, a large injection of Irish personnel – in the form of six Irish Franciscans – arrived on the mission. This third wave of Franciscans must have come to make good the losses of the previous year. Three of them crossed from houses in France: James O'Shiel, Anthony Logan and a priest called O'Beirne, about whom little is known,[38] while the other three – Charles O'Hara, William Heachean (or Hachen/Hackeen) and Colin McFie – were fleeing the persecution in Ireland.[39] But the tone of a letter from Louis Innes in June 1699 indicated that he was reluctant to send any more Irish to the mission: 'As to these two Irish marchands, I am not much for encouraging those of that nation any further than necessity requires: but I think these must go.' They were going firstly because the King wished them to go and had given them *viatica*. Secondly, Innes was also concerned that Mr Trener's mission in Braemar and Glengairn be supplied. Thirdly, he had learned from recent correspondence with Rome that the mission allowance would be doubled in the next two years, allowing them to augment their number. Mr Strachan, Jesuit, concurred with Innes about the poor state of these Irishmen. He wrote in March 1701 of a priest called Nisbet who was 'much afflicted that those who were last adjoined to the company, are so weak every way, and so raw and void of improvements necessary for trade'.[40]

Bishop Nicolson's report of 1700 was no more encouraging. Referring to the Irishmen who had come in the last decade of the seventeenth century, he said: 'The other Irish priests were of the order of St. Francis like Messrs. O'Shiel and Logan who came from France, whom sheer necessity compelled us to use.' Apparently, the main factor mitigating against the success of the Irish priests as missionaries was

> the harshness of the life that it is necessary to lead in this country, and above all the difficulty of travelling there, so frightened the people who were not at all accustomed to it that they scarcely knew any more how to find Irish priests who wanted to come; only having, in effect, the natives of the country who

> could serve there with the most success and bear the toils, because the air and the land are natural to them.[41]

One of these new Irish missionaries, James O'Shiel was placed by Nicolson in Braemar. O'Shiel hailed from a respectable family in the diocese of Down and would therefore have been familiar with Scottish settlers. He had completed his higher study in Rome and then taught in Prague before being sent by his superiors to Ireland where he presided as guardian over the mission until 1698. In that year, the regulars were proscribed in Ireland; O'Shiel fled to France, from where he volunteered for the Highland mission.[42] However, his alleged educational achievement conflicts with some less favourable comments about him.[43] A late eighteenth-century report, compiled from many original sources, states that within two or three months he had converted sixty people,

> but in a short time a Jesuit came to that country and told him he had been sent thither by his Superiors, and that the station belonged to him; and as the Irishman was a stranger in the country, he easily drove him from the station; and yet the Jesuit did not know a word of the Erse, which was the only language used there at the time, and was consequently unfit for the country.

Although the bishop is said to have confirmed O'Shiel in his post, the people's fervour for conversion had apparently been cooled by the arrival of a military garrison in the area, and by intimidation from the ministers. Curiously, the conflict with the Jesuit occurred after the Jesuits had supposedly yielded to the secular mission superior. The problem says little for mission organisation and co-ordination. But there was no confrontation; Fr. O'Shiel was simply removed to South Uist, where he was serving in 1700.[44]

The only surviving account from an Irish missionary in the post-revolutionary decade is a letter from William Ryan to Louis Innes at the Scots College.[45] Dated 13 September 1699, Ryan, who came on the mission in 1695, stated that he retired from his 'laborious employ, to change climate, in order I should receive physic'. He was staying in the parish of O'Gonally, County Clare, near Captain Symon Gordon, and did not have hopes of returning. Any letters were to be directed to Master Robert Hannan, merchant and factor in Limerick. He mentioned his comrade, Mr Mongan, who anticipated his return, which suggests that Ryan had been working in the Moidart, Skye, and Small Isles region. Mr Cahassy was still alive, but weak and infirm, and 'although he cannot run the hills, yet he cannot be idle there'. One of the monks who had fled Ireland because of the 1698 Act was keeping Harnet's place, and the other was tending Carolan's mission because he was unwell. He asked Innes to further the bearer of the letter, Peter Hogan, 'in hopes the Lord would give him a vocation to help the mission hereafter'. But if Hogan ever joined the Highland mission, no trace remains of him.[46] Mr Mongan, on the other hand, was to prove one of the longest-serving Irish missionaries. (For the areas in which the priests served, see Fig. 6.2.)

Mr Mongan, First Resident Missionary in Skye

Mongan was the most prolific mission correspondent for the period from the Revolution to the Union, which is an indication of his seniority. Nothing is known of his origins in Ireland, although his name suggests that he may have been descended from one of three septs of Ó Mongáin in Limerick, north Connacht and County Tyrone. The sept in Termonomogan, County Tyrone, was an *erenagh* family (lay lords holding church property) called Mongan in preference to the variant Mangan. Similarly, the family in north Connacht was sometimes known as Mongan. Towards the end of 1694, he was sent to Paris to give an account of the condition and requirements of the mission. In December, he drew attention to the problem of the long-term sustenance of the Catholic community in a letter to William Leslie in Rome. The priests' work was admirable but not enduring. In his opinion, only the provision of Catholic schools would have long-term benefits in establishing a permanent clergy in the Highlands and Islands, but they would need adequate funding and proper management.[47] Louis Innes stressed to Leslie that one of the main reasons for sending Mongan on the mission in the first place had been to set up a school, so when he got back to Scotland Mongan was to see that one was established, 'being a good humanist and designed for that seven years ago when first sent'.[48]

In May 1695, Mongan wrote from Camphere in the Netherlands to Louis Innes saying that he was 'going to the North to order the affairs of my master the son of My lord Tarbat'.[49] He was setting sail for Scotland with several others in a vessel which he intended to disembark just sixteen miles from Castle Gordon. Daniel Ryan was going as a 'palfernier' or groom, and the other Mr Ryan was 'un pescheur D'harangs' – literally 'a fisher of herring' (a metaphorical 'fisher of men') – who was making for the Hebridean Isles, where he had a brother in the same job. This identifies him as Hugh Ryan's brother, William.[50] Although he feared detection by the Scottish Consul in Rotterdam, he was going to the Highlands none the less, disguised as a sailor.[51] Mongan was passionate about the Highlanders' plight – 'the memory of their state makes me shed tears and I believe that you would need to be harder than a rock to not be affected'. He was one of the few ever to ask Innes not for money but for prayers,[52] and he so conducted his service on Skye that he was created provicar of the Isles in 1700; Mr Munro received the same honour on the mainland. Each was expected to relieve the bishop of some of the regional burden of mission responsibility.

Anti-Irish allegations continued, blowing up on this occasion in the form of slanderous attacks against Mongan himself. Columba MacLennan, the

Wurzburg Benedictine serving in Knoydart, circulated malicious rumours about him which he accredited to Louis Innes: Mongan was labelled contentious and accused of having embezzled a considerable sum of money. When he eventually heard the rumours, Anthony Mongan wrote to Innes on 26 May 1699 in a letter which is a poignant indication of some of the psychological difficulties under which the missionaries laboured.[53] He had incurred the 'common displeasure of Camerades' by a false rumour which was circulating that he had defrauded the mission of the 3,000 livres he had received in France from Innes. Money (or rather the lack of it) was still the main bone of contention among the missionaries. Mongan insisted, shrewdly, that the truth of the matter was known neither by Innes nor those in Ireland, since none of them were actually in the Highlands and Islands. He asked Innes to counter the rumour against him by taking testimonies from his brethren and his superiors.[54]

Fortunately, the malicious stories against Mongan received little credence. Mongan's letter was sent to the principal's brother, Thomas Innes in Glenlivet, to be forwarded. He assured his sibling that MacLennan was a 'mauvais esprit' or bad influence. MacLennan had no love of Hibernians in general: he 'endeavoured to ruin the Irishmen's credit in the west' and was under threat of dismissal. Thomas added that it was necessary to pacify Mongan (he 'must be managed'). Mongan was held in esteem, whereas MacLennan's behaviour had merely cheated them all. It was a view shared in writing some years later by Bishop Gordon, who wrote of his visitation of the Highlands in 1709: 'The worst I saw there was Don McLennan, whom I began to smell out before, but now have found him to be quite naught, and therefore we must part with him: and I believe 'twill be next spring.'[55] However, the acute shortage of missionaries precluded MacLennan's removal at this point. On the other hand, Mongan – praised as the 'best and painfullest of our Highland labourers' – was still working in April 1701 but was contemplating leaving the mission. O'Shiel, then in South Uist, was thought best able to replace him.[56]

In a letter of 27 May 1701 to Louis Innes, Mongan referred to Nicolson's visit to the Highlands and Islands in the previous summer of which he had sent a report, according to the bishop's instructions. Nicolson had not had time to investigate everything because he did not understand the native language, so Mongan was given the job because there was no area in the Isles or mainland whose inhabitants he did not know by name and face or by conduct and conscience, having by this time spent more than thirteen years among them. Mongan's letter also supports the above-mentioned statements about the general inadequacy of missionaries: 'It is true that there are some regulars just now, but in truth, these, with the exception of one or two, are scarcely fit to serve.' Indeed, he insisted that 'if some good clerics are not soon sent to help them, I fear that things will not go so well'.[57] He pleaded with Mr Innes for 'temporal' assistance, urgently requesting some honest clerics.[58]

Shortly afterwards, in June 1701, Mongan was the first priest since Ryan to be arrested. Mongan's mission was clearly winning converts. The synod of Argyll referred on 12 June to one 'Lauchlen Mac bheartich vic finguon [MacKinnon]' in 'I sean uachdarach, Scalpa', an island off Skye, who 'Did beatt and blood Mr Martin Macpherson'. The Skye brethren were ordered to hand in a list of abettors of priests, prelates and Jesuits, and on 16 June 1701 the synod commissioned a letter to Brigadier Maitland about apprehending the priests and suppressing the Catholic schools in Moidart and Arisaig. On 16 October, the synod thanked the commander 'for apprehending a priest the last summer' – obviously Mongan. He was further exhorted to proceed to suppress trafficking Jesuits in the Isles and to seize Mr Panton, the popish schoolmaster in Arisaig.[59] Maitland sent Mongan to Edinburgh in the hope of securing the 500-merk bounty then offered for captured Catholic priests. And because the Treasury delayed payment of the commander's due premium, the presbyterian ministers themselves collected a sum to reward him and to encourage others. Mongan was eventually banished under pain of death for re-entry.[60] The increasing number of soldiers stationed in the Highlands, especially when Jacobite plotting was on the increase, imposed a greater vigilance on most Highland priests.

As for Mongan, his difficulties continued in exile. His correspondence reveals how difficult it was for priests to work on the mission without the spiritual and financial support to which they felt they were entitled. In July 1703, now doubtless even more disinclined to return to the rigours of the mission after his imprisonment, he wrote from Ponguin in France to the principal's brother in Paris stating that the reason he had left the mission was because he felt 'abandoned by those in whom I had the greatest Confidence'. He had not anticipated such poor treatment after fourteen or fifteen years on the mission. Not only he, but all of his fellow Irish missionaries, appear to have been maligned at Rome: 'It shal appear to my most sensible grief how much the wel disposd people of the highlands wil be loosers when they'l have no more the assistance of these Irishmen so much cry'd down, and misrepresented.'[61] This reads ironically in view of the opinions expressed by Mongan himself about the lack of good clerics (but he did not specifically say that these were Irish). However, he insisted that Innes well knew 'of the little fruit don amongst them by the two only natifs who are Missioners amongst 'em. I don't name them you know them well.' They were presumably MacLennan and Munro, and this is a clear indication of the continuing extent of Irish manning of the mission.[62]

In a plaintive and incriminatory letter to Thomas Innes on 19 November 1703, Mongan accused him of indifference. Although he wished to return to the Highlands, considering 'what had befallen me, how I was dealt with', he had decided to accept the premier cure of the city of Chartres, which he had been offered by the bishop there. Reflecting on the inner satisfaction he had enjoyed among the corporeal miseries endured in the Highlands, he observed that in France, conversely, there was plenty on the outside but nothing but dolour on the inside, a theme to which he returned two years later.[63] According to Mongan, one of the most serious flaws of the Highland mission was its failure to produce native priests, but this was not because of lack of effort. He wrote to Innes in December 1703 that he was 'heartily sorry and Concerned for the frequent disappointments you met with in your Contry youth after so much pains and expences about them'; he, for one, was 'not a stranger to Their temper and genius'.[64] In 1700, Bishop Nicholson mentioned a school at 'Kagroch' attended by over thirty children of the best gentlemen in the Highlands. There were also schools in South Uist and in Barra: in fact, there were two on Barra, one of which was at Kiessimul, where MacNeill of Barra resided and whose schoolmaster in 1704 was George Nicol, while the Uist school was taught at Clanranald's house in South Uist.[65] Even so, the Highlands were failing to produce enough priests.

Again, on 12 April 1704, Mongan referred to his sadness about the insufficiency of Highland students, mentioning specifically a Neil Beaton who had been under his care on the mission.[66] Four months later, Mongan received a letter from Beaton 'intimating his final resolution or rather dissolution, which is occasioned not by any pretence of insufficiency butt by the pernicious impressions he has received from bad examples and suggestions in such and like other Cases'. The thwarted Beaton clearly intended to join the army:[67] Mongan told Innes to advise him to return home, which was far less dangerous than throwing himself amongst soldiers. Still corresponding with Innes in 1705, Mongan gently chastised him in April for sending no news about his friends in the Highlands, especially asking about 'what Irish Churchmen (if there be any) that serves amongst them'. He understood that Mr Cahassy had died and wished to know for certain. By 21 November 1705, he was expressing hope that the pre-Union political infighting would divert attention from Catholics, that 'the project of ruining the catholick interest in Scotland will be lett aside dureing the difference between the Scots and English which I'm afraid is not so much fomented as I wou'd wish, and consequently the English penny and policy shal prevail against the honest party'.[68]

Innes finally deigned to reply to Mongan on 25 November 1705, informing him that Mr Cahassy had indeed died. In Mongan's opinion, he had been the only worthy missionary left in the Highlands, whose people 'have never suffer'd more detriment then by that holy churchmans death, whose only shadow as I may say so was sufficient to edify the poor people, and keep in and force the very church men to their duty'.[69] Of the other missionaries, he was not so charitable: 'some leaves it, that mission, for to com to their one [own] ends and interest, and som other go there indeed by the same motifs.' He suggested that better methods be taken to examine and encourage churchmen who were more appropriate for those places, for 'when those are onely sent there of late who are not onely useless but very improper for better regulated contrys, no wonder if so many disorders falls out which if not prevented will I fear me occasion the loss of those once so well instructed people'. Contemporary reports in the *Propaganda* Archives concur with him in finding the Irish missionaries in the Highlands too 'little instructed and not very zealous'.[70] But Mongan's ardour for the Highland mission remained intense: 'I look upon scotland as my contry haveing abandonned ease and interest & friends & relations to serve there.'[71]

Bishop Nicolson's Visitation of the Highlands, 1700

The year 1700, just prior to Mongan's departure into exile, was one of intense activity for Nicolson, who at one of the mission meetings at Gordon Castle formulated a strict set of regulations for his priests to follow. From May to August of that year he also made an extensive tour of the Highlands and Islands mission to acquire first-hand knowledge of its condition. The tour went westwards from Preshome, down the Great Glen to Morar, where the party embarked for all the islands, travelling via the Small Isles to South Uist, Benbecula and Barra. They then returned across the Minch in an open boat through Morar, Knoydart and Glengarry and back to Banffshire.[72] An account of the visitation survives in French, giving details of the priests serving in each area. There were two Irishmen – Cahassy and Mongan – in Morar, when the visitation arrived at the Isle of 'Bath', or Eilean Ban on Loch Morar on 13 June 1700. After taking some decisions with Mr Cahassy, 'whose infirmity obliged him to stay on the island', Mr Ratray (alias Munro) and several other priests, the bishop sent them all back to their people except Mr Mongan and Mr MacLennan, whom he decided to take to the isles 'to serve as interpreters and to help with the functions'.[73]

On 21 June 1700 the visitation came to Canna, where all of the inhabitants were Catholic and about one hundred of whom were confirmed. 'They were served by Mr. Charles Hara under the direction of Mr. Mongan who goes there from time to time and to the neighbouring isles.'[74] On 23 June they reached South Uist, where it was implied that priests like the miserable Mr Coan were responsible for all the reproachful conduct that had occurred in that region and Benbecula: 'nearly all the scandals occurred through the lack of good workers, and those amongst them who were not, gave themselves up to more freedom by the distance that they were from the superiors'.[75] The reality was that many of the missionaries in the Isles operated as freelance evangelists, outside the authority of their superiors.

Surprisingly, given the size of the Catholic community there, the report pointed out that Uist had been without a proper priest for the previous two years.[76] The position had been filled intermittently 'by some who came and went and a Franciscan monk banished from Ireland who seemed a good enough man, but not having sufficient letters Mr. Osheil was sent there, being prescribed the most appropriate rules to remedy the disorders and to put everything back on a good footing under the direction of Mr. Mongan, provicar'.[77] The question of creating native priests was topical at this time, but Highland students were a less popular choice than Lowlanders for the continental colleges. According to Mr John Irvine, writing from Rome in April 1701, the main problem was that the 'vyne irritats ther sicklish braine'.[78] O'Shiel earned high accolades in Uist, which was the largest Catholic community on the mission. Barra was also served by a refugee from Ireland, the report noting that 'we only have one of the Franciscans banished from Ireland to put there, waiting until God would provide for it'. There were also another six inhabited isles near Barra which had chapels, of which Vatersay was the biggest.[79] Yet however transitory the stays of the Irish priests on the mission, the total inability of the Scots colleges on the continent to provide even inadequate native priests stands as a far greater indictment.

The appearance of so many new priests in the previous few years had not gone unnoticed by the Protestants. In October 1700, after Nicolson's visit, the presbytery of Islay informed the synod of Argyll that 'there are severall priests come from Ireland to the northern Isles perverting the people, and that there is one Mcinaish now in their presbyterie professing his repentance for deludeing the people of Saint Kilda, and alledging that John the Baptist useallie appeared to him'.[80] The reference to the priests is quite clear. The report may be suggesting that this Mcinnes was a deluded convert of theirs who had tried to pervert the people of St. Kilda prior to the island's first sustained encounter with Protestantism in 1710. Before this, the minister of Harris, John Campbell, visited the island in 1697 accompanied by Martin Martin.[81] The second edition of Martin's *A Description of the Western Islands of Scotland* (1716) revealed that Mcinnes' first name was Roderick. According to Martin he could not read, but 'obtruded a false Religion upon the credulous People, which he pretended to have receiv'd from St. John the Baptist'. He allegedly communicated with the Baptist on a hill which he designated as sacred, the upshot being that if a beast ate grass on the hill it had to be killed and immediately eaten, but always (as might be expected) in the company of Mcinnes. The religion which he professed appears to have been some debased form of Catholicism, because he taught the people of St. Kilda that they each had a tutelar saint in heaven to intercede for them whose feast days were to be strictly observed. He also taught the women a hymn that he claimed the Virgin Mary had relayed directly to him. At the minister's arrival on the island in 1697, however, Roderick made a public recantation of his imposture. The presence of a Catholic on St. Kilda was clearly felt to be a threat to the growing presbyterian communities of Lewis and Harris. Therefore when the party left the island, Roderick was taken to Harris with them and – ironically – ended up living in Skye, probably the strongest Protestant community in the Islands.[82]

Since the Highlands and Islands were so far away from Preshome, Nicolson's base in the Enzie district of Banffshire, two provicars had been appointed in 1700, as mentioned previously: Mr Munro for the Scots, 'and for the Irish Mr. Mongan who has the capacity and talents with several years' experience in the mountains'.[83] The bishop had bestowed more faculties and authority upon them and had granted them the dispensation of weighty cases, which the lesser capacity of some of the missionaries hindered him from giving to them all. They also had visitation rights within their own region, under the instruction that they should send the bishop a written report every six months giving an account of their charges.[84]

A significant achievement by this time was the allocation of fixed stations to all the clergy missioners, which addressed one of the main deficiencies of the mission in the late seventeenth century. The pockets of Catholics which had been created could thereby be more efficiently sustained. In a report written in around 1702, Mr James Gordon, priest in the Enzie, gave an update on the service stations of the Irish priests. He divided the priests into two main sections: 'Benedictines and Franciscans', and 'clergymen'.[85] There were five Irish Franciscans, three from Ireland and two who had been sent for from France by the bishop. Fr. Heachean was still stationed in Barra, Frs. McFie and O'Shiel in Uist, and Frs. Logan and O'Hara in Moidart and Arisaig, who also served the Small Isles. The point was stressed that these regulars had no superior other than the bishop and were dependent on him like the secular clergy – a clear attempt to define the secular nature of their appointment. But the mission still relied to a certain extent on the independent finance of the regulars. For instance, while the five Franciscans received allowances from the mission, only two of the Benedictines did. The two Irish clergymen were identified as Mr John Cahassy in Morar and Patrick Carolan on the island of Vatersay near Barra. (See Fig. 6.2.) Gordon also stated that in order for Fr. O'Hara to be able to devote himself entirely to the Small Isles, the bishop was planning to promote Mr Peter Fraser to Holy Orders. According to him, the priests still depended on the nobility for help, protection and the ability to work unhindered. Missionaries were expected to convene once or twice a year to report to the bishop.[86] Even though they operated more as seculars, the mission was still very dependent on regular clergy. In 1705, Gordon recorded eight priests in the Highlands and one in Gaelic-speaking Deeside, only one of whom was technically a secular.[87]

Just four years after Nicolson's visitation of the Highlands and Islands, a pretended plot claimed in 1704 that Jacobites and Catholics intended to bring about a revolution in favour of James VIII, the Old Pretender, which led to a stepping up of the persecution against Catholics. By March, when the General Assembly met in Edinburgh, the persecution was at its height. Mr Munro was seized for the second time by a party of soldiers in Glengarry. Owing to the infirmity of old age, Munro could neither walk nor straddle a horse and so was thrown athwart the horse and taken to the dungeon of Glengarry Castle. He died within three days. The General Assembly, in an address to the Queen supplicating the suppression of popery, made mention of the daily growth of Catholicism and the infinite number of priests in the north and the Highlands. It estimated that there were six priests to one minister in those areas, which was a gross exaggeration. Two of the Irish Franciscans are said to have left the mission and returned to Ireland.[88] One of these was Carolan, who had been ill in Vatersay for some time. The other may have been O'Shiel, last heard of in Benbecula in 1704. O'Shiel went on to greater things in his native country. Dr MacMahon, bishop of Clogher, reported to *Propaganda* in 1713 that he had worked for ten years as a secular priest in his native Down. In 1707, he was made bishop of Down and Connor.[89]

With the death of Cahassy in the same year, this inexorable falling away in personnel represented a crisis for the mission. Bishop Nicolson sent to Ireland and the continent for help, because although some youths had been sent to the Scots colleges in Paris and Rome since his appointment, the majority of them had not stayed the course. Thomas and Louis Innes wrote in November 1704 to James Gordon in Rome, telling him to stress the dire need for staff on the mission: 'I say the *extreme* want, for by all the letters from Scotland it appears that the want is most extreme in the highlands especially, all the Irish being gone and the places they were formerly in abandoned.'[90] In order to support Bishop Nicolson on a mission beset with problems, James Gordon was appointed coadjutor in July 1705 under the title bishop of Nicopolis. It proved difficult to set up and sustain Catholic schools, but the most pressing need was for missionaries. The Rev. James Thompson reported for the same year: 'The Bishop some time before had procured from France and Ireland, Irish priests and friars, at a great expense, for the Highlands. Two of these friars soon left the country; a third, who stayed some time longer, soon followed them.'[91] Presumably these were the Franciscans acquired by Nicolson in 1699. The early leavers were probably O'Beirne and Logan; the other is even less certain – possibly Heachean or O'Shiel? The mission was in such a precarious state of decline that the missionaries themselves were said to have entertained thoughts that it might fail.[92]

New Irish Personnel

An account among the General Assembly papers presents the Protestant view of the Irish on the early eighteenth-century Highland mission. This account, easily dated from internal evidence to 1704, appears to have been compiled with a view to facilitating the capture of these priests.[93] 'Old father Casey' is portrayed as 'a Grand promoter of the popish interest', permanently resident on an island (Eilean Ban) in Loch Morar where there was 'but one boat upon the Loch which waits upon the preists service'.[94] MacLennan, the Scot, was still in Arisaig and Knoydart. The presence of a third priest, Fr. Patrick O'Callaghan, survives in none of the Catholic sources: resident on the island of Eigg, he usually said mass 'in the dwelling-house of one Lachlane mcDonal vic lachlane'. O'Callaghan, identified as middle-aged, had obviously come to Eigg at some time since Nicolson's visit in the summer of 1700;[95] his alias was Thomas Campbell and he had been apprehended with an assistant, George Ross (alias MacDonald), on 5 January 1706 when attempting to enter the country from Ireland. They must have aroused suspicion in some way, because even in their mission stations priests generally dressed in ordinary Highland attire 'and armour', except when performing services, so that their office was not readily distinguishable.[96] Ross had probably assumed a medical alter ego by way of disguise, because he was found with a recipe for curing corns by means of boiled roots, lilies and roasted black snails on his person. He was tried before the justice depute of Argyll on 15 January 1706 on suspicion of being a trafficking priest.[97]

James O'Shiel who had been sent after his débâcle in Braemar to South Uist was by this time in nearby Benbecula. Colin McFie lived for the most part at Ormacleit in South Uist, where he was personal chaplain to MacDonald of Clanranald. He was said to be 'a lustie bodied black haired young man'.[98] Although McFie or 'McOvie' was an Irish Franciscan, he may have had connections with Colonsay – the original home of the MacPhies, or Lochaber – where there were MacOvies associated with the Camerons of Lochiel, at the west end of Locharkaig.[99] Heachean, referred to simply as 'father William', had been in Barra since the 'distraction' of the priest there – Patrick Carolan – before him. According to the report, Carolan 'fell out upon the back of some difference betwixt him and the laird of Bara anent a soum of money which he alledgeth he had given the laird and which the laird denieth. And only continuing since in that distemper he remains now confined in ane Island of Barra called Water shaw [Vatersay].' Another priest, by the name of O'Raigan, who also goes unmentioned in Catholic correspondence, was said to officiate with Fr. William in Barra.[100] Nothing was said of O'Hara, although he was apparently at Cahassy's deathbed in September 1704.[101] (See Fig. 6.2.) Mr Angus MacDonald, episcopal encumbent in South Uist, also came under attack for fraternising with the Irish priests, because he 'carries very laxly keeping frequent and familiar converse with the preists who are daylie perverting the few who are protestant in his paroch'. The natural Jacobite inclination of many episcopalian ministers, significant numbers of whom were suffered to remain in their charges after the

Revolution because of a lack of presbyterian clergy in the Highlands, was always a matter of suspicion for the Kirk.[102] In June 1706, the synod of Argyll recommended that the presbytery of Skye 'look more after the Popish Bounds within their Presbyterie, and that they take more inspection of the Long Island, and of the Episcopal Incumbents as to their doctrine and Discipline and attendance on their Charge, and to make report'.[103]

Although a native priesthood began slowly to establish itself, Irish priests continued to be recruited in the early eighteenth century to supply the shortfall. Fr. Peter Mulligan, Irish Augustinian, was persuaded to go on the Highland mission by Mr James Gordon when he was in Rome for his consecration as coadjutor at the beginning of 1706. The pair travelled via Holland from Paris, arriving in Aberdeen in July. The year 1706 was a quiet one for the mission, which experienced little in the way of persecution. Mulligan quickly took on the alias MacDonald, by which he more often appears in contemporary records. A presbyterian document dating from about 1710 states that 'Mr Peter Mcdonald constantly resides at abertarph and Glengary'.[104] Nor had Bishop Gordon been idle in France: he had persuaded two Irish Dominicans, Peter Cluan and John Gusman, from the convent of St. Clemente at Rome, to come on the mission;[105] he informed William Leslie in June 1706 that 'we have seen their obedience from their General which gives them licence to go to Ireland, but does not restrain them to it only and we know that their General's inclination is that his Religious who are fitt for missions, help such as are most destitute'.[106]

About the same time, a Dominican priest called Bourke also showed interest in the Highland mission. In a letter dated around 1706, a Fr. Bourk informed William Leslie that his namesake, Mr Bourke, had left the previous Wednesday. He asked Leslie to recommend him to the Duke of Perth.[107] This may be the Fr. Redmond Bourke who stated in 1706 that two religious of his order – 'Frs. Peter Colman and John Gusmane' – had recently arrived from Rome to serve on the Scottish mission. His unidentified correspondent had told him that he wished to find more recruits from the same order. Bourke dutifully offered himself: 'if you please sir to furnish me with a little money, as you was pleased to furnish the two aforsaid religious men mentioned, I will in the name of God vinter my life to serve christians with all discretion imaginable for not onely I speake Irish and English but yett I speake Spanish and frinch'. He added, by way of a curriculum vitae, that he had preached for twelve years in Ireland in the Irish language and had made conversions in the north of Ireland, 'that is to say, near Sligoe and in those places adiacent to the County of farmanaugh which is partly in the nort of Irland'.[108] He obviously regarded this a sufficient training ground for the Highlands. However, in a letter of 26 March 1707 Patrick Cusack, superior of the Community of the Just at Nantes, informed the principal of the Scots College that Bourke had been asked to defer his resolution until the spring, which he had done.[109] It also confirmed that he was a good preacher. But if Bourke ever reached the mission, his presence on it has gone unrecorded. Another priest who showed interest in the mission but probably never arrived was Mr John O'Niel. In January 1713, he wrote from Prague to an unidentified correspondent stating that he was awaiting clearance of his *viaticum* from Rome. He also said that he was a fully fledged Master of Arts, an indication perhaps that the period of employing ill-qualified Irish priests was over.[110]

Although the attempt to re-establish a Dominican presence in Scotland had fallen into abeyance after the death of Patrick Primrose,[111] a number of Dominicans subsequently came to work as seculars on the mission. Apart from those already mentioned, Fr. Dominic Brullaghan (or Bradley), one of a handful of eighteenth-century friars who undertook occasional visits to Scotland, probably worked in the Highlands as well. A strolling friar from Coleraine priory, Brullaghan was the brother of the bishop of Derry, Dr Patrick Brullaghan. Mainly evangelising the areas around Derry in the early eighteenth century, he was known in Irish, in the Highlands and Coleraine, as 'An Brathair Bán'.[112] He is renowned for his book on missionary practice in Britain, which stressed the different ways in which priests worked in various areas. Missionaries in Scotland, he insisted, were not likely to be assigned to any particular district, but worked where they could to advance 'the glory of God, the Catholic faith and the salvation of souls', a statement which qualifies Gordon's account of 1702, above, and tends to suggest that not all priests had yet been assigned to fixed stations. Even if things had greatly improved since the seventeenth century, priests on the Highlands and Islands mission still expected to travel a good deal more than their Irish contemporaries.[113]

In 1707, the year of parliamentary union with England, Bishop Gordon decided, as had Bishop Nicolson before him, to undertake a tour of the Highland mission. He set out on 5 June accompanied by Mr Daglish (or Douglas), a deacon from Rome who spoke Erse and later on the trip was ordained as a priest at Borrodale in Knoydart on 25 July. The route this time was from Banffshire through Glenlivet, Badenoch and Glengarry to Knoydart. The party also went to Eigg, Rhum, South Uist, Barra, Vatersay, Benbecula and Canna before returning once again to Knoydart. From here they went to Strathglass, Lochaber, Badenoch and on to the east coast.[114] A list of 1707, which notes the location of missionaries in the Highlands, was probably compiled as a result of Gordon's tour. It is particularly useful because it establishes the missionaries by denomination and number in specific districts, making it possible to match priests of known denomination. For instance, there was a Jesuit in Strathglass, an Augustinian in Glengarry, a Benedictine in the Knoydart and Isle of Skye area, a Franciscan in the Isles of Canna, Eigg and Rhum and another Franciscan in the Morar area, a secular priest in Arisaig, and two Franciscans each in Uist and Barra.[115]

Understandably, after the French-backed Jacobite attempt of 1708, Catholics again came under close surveillance and soldiers were garrisoned around the country. In 1709, the SSPCK, a powerful agent of anti-Catholicism, also began to open Protestant schools in the Highlands.[116] Persecution increased as prominent Catholics were summoned before circuit courts, while ministers pursued the lower echelons. Nevertheless, converts continued to be attracted to the Catholic church, particularly in Strathbogie, Glenlivet, Strathaven, Braemar, Strathglass and Glengarry,[117] although a number of those converted in Glenlivet and Strathaven left the church under continuous pressure from ministers and JPs. However, a spirit of moderation prevailed between 1711 and 1714, during which priests reaped good harvests in Lochaber, Glengarry, Strathglass, the Enzie and Strathbogie.[118] At least some were people who had reconverted to Catholicism after a period of episcopalianism. A presbyterian document of May 1714 said: 'In the Countreys of Glenlivet & Strathaven in the presbytery of Aberlour, priests are very Insolent & busie, and have seduced some to apostatize, and others who had renounced popery are now fallen back to their former delusions.'[119] Furthermore, the significant inclination towards Jacobitism in many episcopalian communities cannot be overlooked either as a factor in their conversion or as a reason for inciting presbyterian fears.

Indeed, after the Union a good case has been made for a shift from the Catholicism in which the Gaelic identity had taken root in the early seventeenth century to non-juring episcopalianism as the cultural and ideological medium in which Gaelic identity was mainly founded. By 1707, eighteen of the fifty main clans were non-juring episcopalians, while as many again were at least partly committed to episcopaliansim; on the other hand, no more than six of them were predominantly committed to Catholicism.[120] And this is hardly surprising after 150 years of Protestant polity. This ideological shift had occurred more rapidly after the civil war of the 1640s as the political and military links between Gaels across the North Channel declined markedly. The cultural integrity of the *Gaidhealtachd mòr* had been strained and impugned by the advance of the Reformation in Scotland in comparison with extensive resistance to it in Ireland.[121] During the Restoration, episcopalianism established a firm hold in the Highlands. All it took was a refusal to abjure the Stuarts at the Revolution to add that distinctive element of political resistance to the cultural medium. In many ways the Royalism of the mid-seventeenth century simply transmuted into the Jacobitism of the eighteenth century; non-juring episcopalians were as much a target of the Protestant establishment during the Jacobite period as the Catholics.

At this point, several of the Irish had also grown personally discontented with life on the mission and were threatening to leave. In July 1713, Bishop Gordon wrote to Thomas Innes in Paris: 'When I was in West I persuaded M. Mulig. (who brings in prodigious numbers) and the two Doms to stay one year more.' Although the two Dominicans – Cluan and Gusman – probably left in the following year, Mulligan was persuaded to stay and did not finally leave the mission until 1722. A Protestant account of 1714 referred to him living in Abertarff or sometimes in Glengarry, and keeping mass in MacDonald of Kiltrie's house. (See Fig. 6.2.) But he was discontented in his work. Bishop Gordon wrote of him in October 1717: 'I have great difficulty to keep the laborer I brought home with me, who is one of the most usefullest, though he does not please me so well as at first.'[122] Indeed, he was not well pleased with many of the missionaries in the west.

None the less, to the presbyterians it seemed as if the Highlands was crawling with Catholic priests, and certainly Nicolson and Gordon felt secure enough to open a seminary on Loch Morar. Its opening in this staunchly Catholic MacDonald country was significant not only in religious terms, but because it added fuel to the fire of presbyterian political paranoia. The threat presented to presbyterianism by popish priests and Jesuits in Scotland was expressed in an anti-papal pamphlet written in December 1713. Identifying the main areas in which Catholicism had the ascendancy, the pamphlet also said that there were

> 6 or 7 Priests in the Bounds of the Presbytery of Skay, and some about Lochaber, and Bounds of the Presbytery of Lorn, and many more who are traveling through the Country, suspected to be Priests and Missionaries from Rome, going under borrowed Names, and pretend to be in other Imployments, and severals of the rest are Blood Relations to Families of good Note in the Places they most haunt.[123]

Once again, priests were operating as far south as Lorn, something they had not done since the early seventeenth century. But this is less likely to have been in the jurisdiction of the synod of Argyll than in those parishes which were eventually separated from the presbytery of Lorn in May 1724 to constitute the presbytery of Abertarff within the synod of Glenelg – Boleskine and Abertarff, Kilmallie, Kilmonivaig and Glenelg.[124]

Irish Priests and the Growth of a Native Priesthood

Although presbyterian sources show that the Kirk was perturbed by the increase in Catholicism in the Highlands and Islands, particularly before the '15 rebellion, the synod of Argyll made no mention of trafficking priests between 16 October 1701 and 8 June 1720 (although there are occasional references to 'popery'). On 8 June 1720 the synod of Argyll broke its silence, appointing a representation to the Commission of Assembly regarding the lamentable circumstances of several parishes within their bounds because of the growth of popery, particularly mentioning the Braes of Lochaber and the 'great number of trafficking priests that are of late come in, besides these who were in the Countrey formerly'. It alluded especially to Fr. Peter MacDonald or Mulligan, who had moved from Glengarry to permanent residence in Lochaber, and Mr Gregor McGregor who had filled his place in Glengarry.[125] This fresh presbyterian assault on Catholicism appears to have been made in response to an influx of personnel which had probably resulted in defections among the episcopalian, non-juring ranks. The native Scots contingent was also growing: there were eight Scots priests in the Highland Vicariate in 1733, and eleven by 1743.[126] In comparison, there were only two Irish priests on the mission in the same decade.

Who were the new personnel? In July 1722, Bishop Gordon expressed his desire to retain Mulligan, although Mulligan in his turn was not pleased with 'Rob. the Recollect' and (it was said) would gladly be rid of him.[127] This unidentified Franciscan (Recollect) was probably a short-term Irish worker who soon left the mission. In August 1725, Niel McFie wrote from Rome to Thomas Innes, vice-principal of the Scots College in Paris, asking him to send 'Father Galagher an Irish fryar to our mission'. The Capuchin came on good recommendation: 'He has a good stock of learning, especially what's requisite for our mission, and knows the Irish tongue better then any in the Convent.'[128] But the lack of endurance apparent in some of the Irish missionaries in the previous century was still in evidence. In another letter to Thomas Innes in November 1725, McFie stated:

> I know full well that there's a great difference to be suppos'd still betuixt the passing assistence of strangers and the affectionate zeal of our countrey people in order to support or propagate the catholick religion in these parts; for I have known some Irish there who skipt of for Ireland as soon as they mette with some hardships which a missioner in these parts must necessarily expect, and so left the countrey in a miserable condition, there being no other missionars nigh hand at that time to prevent the disorders that ensued.[129]

Much of this was due to the mission oath. But McFie's comments had arisen directly from Innes' negative reaction to his recommendation of the Irish friar Gallagher, who nevertheless had received clearance for the mission by February 1726. Convinced that he would prove equal to his recommendation, McFie expressed his sadness that the mission still had to be supplied with foreigners at all.[130]

The Rev. John Thompson's account for 1725 stated: 'Two Irish priests also came to the Mission this year from France, the one a Dominican and the other a Recollect; which proved a very seasonable relief in the present circumstances.' These were the Dominican Bernhard McHenry and the Franciscan Anthony Kelly.[131] On 2 February 1726, Anthony Kelly set out for the Isles. By the 21st of the same month, Brother Kelly (as he signed himself) had established himself in Eigg. Writing to James Gordon in Edinburgh, he boasted that unlike the others he was 'able to undergo tolerably the Highland mission as to the bodily labour'. His only request was to be allowed to wear the habit (Eigg was, after all, more isolated than the mainland), and almost uniquely among the missionaries he did not ask for ready cash – 'as for mony I pray you nominate none for me I only desire an alms of Cloaths'.[132] But Bishop Gordon did not set great store by his modesty, referring to him as 'very simple and not having great prudence'.[133] The presbyterian record referred to him in June of the same year as one of five priests allowed to reside in the countries of Moidart, Morar and Arisaig.[134] By 1728 Kelly was serving in Barra, where he remained in 1730.[135] (See Fig. 6.2.) Kelly, it seems, had an alcohol problem: Gordon wrote in November 1729 of 'his old inclinations of wronging himself with drink'.[136] But Bishop Hugh MacDonald thought more highly of him, writing a stunning testimony of his worth when Kelly was eventually recalled by the superiors of his order in 1736: 'If poor Anthony Kelly should come back, I would willingly dispense with all the rest.' He described him to *Propaganda* as 'a most worthy and apostolic man who was on this mission for many years and did an immense amount of good'.[137]

The year 1726 was financially fruitful for the Scottish mission which, as a result of accounts sent to Rome in the previous year about persecution of Catholics, was granted an extraordinary subsidy of 500 crowns by *Propaganda*, enabling the mission to procure more hands.[138] In areas such as Glengarry, Catholics had increased threefold and persecution was said to be the worst encountered in 160 years, although this may reveal a concealed defection to Catholicism by Jacobite episcopalians following their persecution (and decline) after the 1715 rebellion. The persecution was also linked to fear of post-Union economic unrest inflamed by Jacobites: after attending to meal riots in Glasgow in 1726, military units were sent to the Highlands to arrest Catholic missionaries.[139]

Ostensibly aimed at containment of the simmering Jacobite threat by enabling easier penetration of hotbeds of political disaffection, General Wade began his programme of military road building in the Highlands in 1725, opening up glens and passes which had previously been accessible only by drove roads and dirt tracks. Although they have been seen retrospectively as rather limited in scope, Wade's roads were undoubtedly an improvement on travel at the time. Between 1725 and 1736, 250 miles of road were constructed on four routes: on the south side of Loch Ness from Inverness to Fort William; between Inverness and Dunkeld through Drumochter Pass; from Fort Augustus to Dalwhinnie through the Pass of Corrieyairack; and between Dalnacardoch and Crieff via Tummel Bridge. The Highlanders' criticism of the roads was telling: it was generally felt that the roads opened up the country to strangers and to attack, as well as undermining the attachment of clansmen to their chieftains

– although according to Wade they saw them as good for transporting merchandise. In this sense, Wade's roads presented a threat – even if a limited one at this stage – to Catholic communities, in making them more accessible to government troops, but understandably this only steeled government resolve to continue funding them, a hardening of resolve which was given further impetus by the '45 rebellion.[140]

In the meantime, the use of 'foreigners' to man the mission was beginning to decline under a burgeoning of native priests. Two Irish friars left the mission in 1729, probably Gallagher and McHenry; one died and the other returned to Ireland for health reasons. Kelly remained on the mission until 1736, but Gordon wrote to France for replacements for the friars.[141] However, a cousin of Kelly's came on the mission in the year after he left. In November 1737, Mr George (James) Gordon wrote from the seminary at Scalan to George Gordon at Mortlach, saying that 'the Irish Franciscan lately come over, called F: Francis Kelly (a cousin of the pious Franciscan F: Anthony Kelly at present a provincial of his order in Ireland,) is setled in Mr Lesly's place in Arasaig and Clanranald's Moror'.[142] A third Kelly, with the Christian name of Peter, was cited for reputed fabrication about the Scottish mission in a note dated October 1738.[143] Fr. Michael O'Mulrian (or Ryan) an Irish Dominican, arrived in about July 1729 and was sent to serve in Glengarry.[144] On 21 February 1730, Mr Carnegie (alias Mr Hall), secular priest and Jacobite agent,[145] wrote from Paris to the Scots agent in Rome of a potential recruit to the Highland mission:

> We have got here a priest born in Ireland of Scotch parents, he past his philosophy and divinity with applause at Edinburgh and Glasgow, and was to be a presbyterian minister, but becoming a Catholick he returned to Ireland, not to his parents who are bigot presbyterians, but to the Catholick Bishop of Dublain who ordained him, and put him to serve in a Chapel in that town, but he thought he would do better to come here and improve himself, and then go to the highlands, so we give him here all the encouragement we can.[146]

Although the priest is not named, it is impossible to ignore the immense similarities between this and the case of John Campbell, below, which would adequately explain Campbell's deployment to a Scots college.

The Scottish mission had been divided into Highland and Lowland vicariates in July 1727, but it was not until the consecration of Bishop Hugh MacDonald, titular bishop of Diana, on 18 October 1731 that the Highlands received its own bishop. MacDonald was the first indigenously trained priest there since the Reformation.[147] The extent of his geographical remit was outlined on 25 March 1735 by Mr Patrick Leith, an Edinburgh-based priest, who wrote: 'Bishop Mcdonald has got under his Charge all the midle *highland Countries* such as your two Strathdown and Glenlivet, Glengirn Braemar, and wherever the Erse is the current language. And the Jesuits in those places are *ordered to send* him as soon as possible, the exact number of their hearers.'[148] The other contender proposed for the position of Highland bishop was Irish – a Dominican called Ryan, undoubtedly the O'Mulrian who came on the mission in 1729. But after almost a century of relatively indifferent direction from Ireland, it had clearly been decided that a native Scot could deal with the task more efficiently.[149] When MacDonald took office, he regarded it as a serious problem that, apart from a few seculars, most of his missionaries were Scots or Irish religious who had no real obligation to the mission other than their own commitment. And rigours and hardships soon wore down personal enthusiasm. The opening of the seminary on Loch Morar was an attempt to remedy this; it was also by far the easiest way to retain students' fluency in Gaelic. In August 1733, Hugh MacDonald lamented to Mr William Stuart at Hamburg the lack of mission workers who spoke Gaelic: 'You'l easily observe how necessary it's that any students there who had any thing of the Highland language should endeavour to keep it, and lickwise that I should be informed when you have any vacancy, because necessity requires that for a time, those who have our language should be sent to the Colledge.'[150] Like the Established Kirk, the Catholic church experienced great difficulty in recruiting enough Gaelic-speaking personnel.

Four years later, in June 1737, missionaries Colin Campbell and John Tyrie were still lamenting the insufficiency of priests in the Highlands. In the north and Highlands alike, the gentry and the common people were said to so revere the Catholic faith that wherever a missionary stayed he soon brought many to the faith. This only increased the load on the small number of priests who already attended the Catholic population.

> But this is so evident in the Highlands that whole countreys have often demanded earnestly Missioners to instruct them in the Catholick faith, yet so feu are the Missioners that none coud be sent them, since the feu that are, cannot sufficiently serve them who are already Catholicke because of the roughness of the Countreys, and the Catholicks living much despersed and in several different Isles, which occasions that every Missioner can scarcely visit all his flock once in two years.[151]

Campbell and Tyrie were major protagonists in the main conflict manifesting itself on the mission in the early eighteenth century – the Jansenist controversy. Jansenism was a particularly harsh form of Catholicism whose doctrine was much akin to Calvinism in terms of strict morality, asceticism and its narrow views on determination. In its most severe form it limited the grace of God and the possibility of salvation to practising Catholics. The Scots College in Paris became very Jansenist in outlook, but accusations of Jansenism in Scotland – given that it denied free will and could therefore easily be tainted with association with the presbyterian doctrine of predestination – were particularly dangerous in Scotland. It was also a cause for consternation among the Jesuits who, after they had surrendered to secular authority in 1701, made complaints of Jansenism against four seculars, including Robert Munro, in 1702 and again in 1724–25.[152] Jansenism (or more correctly the threat of it) really began to impinge upon the mission in the late 1720s; Irish priests on the mission were implicated in the controversy, too, which reached its height in the 1730s. Those in connection with the Scots College in France were on their guard. On 5 July 1729, James Carnegie, procurator of the Scots College, wrote to Edinburgh expressing fears about Michael O'Mulrian, whom Bishop Gordon had accepted with a view to replacing the Benedictine Gregor McGregor and whose complaints of Jansenism against the bishop were gathering force. O'Mulrian had begun to show his true colours as soon as he came to Edinburgh, declaring himself a sworn enemy of the French because of their Jansenism. Ironically, the Irish replacement for McGregor was as vehemently anti-Jansenist as himself. Carnegie saw anti-Jansenists under the bed: 'Our people have got it, both Bishops and Priests, that Mr. Ryan the Dominican that cam from your parts and is gone lately to the highlands is to stay but a short time there as a spy over Bishops and Clergy, and then is to go to Ireland to be Bishope, in the mean time he is to observe if he sees anything of Jansenism.' He went on to say that 'if many such come amongst us we will soon go to ruin'.[153] And indeed the anti-Jansenists went on to wreak havoc on the mission in the next few years.

The high point of the controversy came in 1733 when Colin Campbell succeeded in persuading Bishop Gordon, senior Vicar-Apostolic, to elicit subscriptions to the papal bull *Unigenitus* of 1713 which had condemned the main tenets of Jansenism. A formulary was drawn up for all missionaries to sign which not only repudiated Jansenism but also Baianism, at the same time as subscribing to *Unigenitus*. Significantly, all but one of the Scottish clergy signed it.[154] But those who accused Bishop James Gordon of Jansenism – the above-mentioned Scots Colin Campbell and John Tyrie as well as Gregor McGregor, who first laid written charges against the bishop – used such malicious accusations as ways of giving vent to their own discontent. Appointed pro-vicar in 1728, Colin Campbell's particular grievance was in subsequently having been passed over for the position of first Highland Vicar-Apostolic in 1731, and again for coadjutor in 1735. He had the support of Bishop Gordon, who felt that Campbell, as a kinsman of the Duke of Argyll, would have evened up the overwhelming hierarchical bias in favour of MacDonalds on the mission, who by the turn of the eighteenth century had already earned themselves the nickname 'the priesthood of Aaron'.[155] But the fact that the Clan Campbell had stood on the government side in the '15 rebellion was enough to militate against his being chosen. Tyrie's support for the campaign similarly stemmed from a desire to escape his marginal station in the Highlands. The Jesuits and

Scots Benedictines also threw in their support – the former in an attempt to thwart the dominance of seculars, the latter in an attempt to divert some of *Propaganda*'s funds to its own priests.

Campbell and Tyrie masqueraded as champions of the poverty-stricken mission and went by the name of the 'Pilgrims' after 1735 as a result of a commission by Bishop MacDonald to present the Highland missionaries' grievances to *Propaganda*. The main grievance in the Highlands remained the lack of money: the priests received only twenty-eight crowns a year in 1737, which in reality was so little that 'some are forced to leave small debts behind them when they dye, which is some kind of reflexion upon Religion'. Campbell and Tyrie used this discontent to their own advantage.[156] In particular, they demanded a more equitable division of Scottish mission funds according to actual financial need, because Highland priests travelled far greater distances between the communities they served than priests in the Lowlands and therefore required more funding.[157]

In June 1737, the Pilgrims wrote a memorial to James VIII and III, the Old Pretender, referring to the death of Mr William Stuart, 'who for these many years bygone was Procurator of our Clergy Mission' or Scottish agent in Rome. Stuart had an interesting Highland–Irish heritage: the memorial stated 'all what Bishop Gordon and the Missioners of Scotland knou about him, is that he was born in Ireland of Scots parents', studied at Prague in Bohemia and spent some time in Scotland after the Revolution. Ordained in Rome in 1694, he had accompanied Bishop Nicolson to Scotland after his consecration, arriving in England in early 1696 before proceeding to Scotland in 1697. After a year in Scotland Stuart was sent to Rome with William Leslie, and through his influence he was made 'superior of the Convertits'. In 1703, he succeeded Mr James Gordon as agent for the Scots clergy mission. 'He was indeed originally descended of Stuart of Appin but neither that family or any other can [instruct] his being their nigh Relation, nor was he ever heard by any of us who studied in the Scots Colledge and were in some respect under his direction, speak of his Relations, further than that he was a Scots Highlander.' Apparently he had forgotten how to speak his native language, although he still understood it.[158] The Pilgrims' memorial petitioned that Stuart's effects should go to support a missionary in Scotland, since he had died intestate.[159] Their action is consistent with resolutions laid down by them on 14 April 1735, in a scroll entitled *Instructions for Mr. John Tyrie*. Allegedly a consensus of Highland priests who met in the Isle of Morar, the document was actually forged by Tyrie but serves nevertheless as a useful indicator of their grievances, significant amongst which was a demand for a greater say in the management of the mission's funds. They particularly wished for assurance that they would receive a fair share of any legacies bequeathed to the mission.[160]

Investigations into the shortcomings of Scots missionaries extended as far as

Ireland. In 1740, the archbishop of Armagh received assorted letters from colleges in Italy, Alexander Lawson, catechist at the hospital for the converted in Borga, and Peter Grant, agent for Muria, concerning a student by the name of John Campbell at the Scots College in Rome. Born in Ireland of Scottish parents, Campbell had converted from Calvinism, arriving in Rome in 1738. His attendance at the Scots College there, when he could easily have attended an Irish one, shows the extent to which the Ulster Scot identified with his roots. Duplicity was suspected in the drawing up of Campbell's testimonials. The Principal of Ireland claimed in a letter to Sir Thomas Sheridan, former tutor of the Young Pretender (and later one of the 'seven men of Moidart'), that the extent of his correspondence with Campbell had been to provide a commendation in Latin with his seal attached. He claimed that a letter produced in his name was a forgery. A later report on Campbell stated that he had been dismissed from the Scots College in Rome for persistent obstinacy after the second-year theology class.[161]

Between 1729 and 1742 there were never more than two Irish priests on the mission in any one year, so it is difficult to speak in terms of a specifically Irish attitude towards Jansenism. What can be said is that O'Mulrian, the one Irish priest on record for his anti-Jansenist stance, was summarily dealt with by the bishop. Ordered from the mission in October 1731 on suspicion of a crime against chastity, it is likely that this was merely an excuse to implement his removal, given that complaints had been made about his anti-Jansenist stance since 1729.[162]

Catholicism was practised with extreme caution in the Highlands between 1745 and 1760. As might be expected, Catholics were particularly vulnerable in the aftermath of the '45 rebellion. In 1747, a pamphlet laboriously entitled 'A letter to the Most Noble Thomas, Duke of Newcastle, on the Dangers arising from Popery and disaffection, occasioned by the Seizing of certain papers in a Popish Chapel in the North-West Highlands of Scotland' and addressed to the Secretary of State was published anonymously in London. Printed in the pamphlet was a 'List of the Popish Missionaries, in the Lowlands and Highlands of Scotland, as they stood Anno 1740'. Only two of the twenty-five missionaries identified were Irish: Francis Kelly and Dominic Colgan.[163] The writer insisted that amidst this bunch of papists – cruel and barbarous thieves, murderers and traitors, who constituted a standing army for the Pretender – 'McDonalds more especially, will be found a great body of relentless Foes to the Protestant Names'.[164]

Although more Highlanders were taking orders by the mid-eighteenth century, the desire for Irish mission workers persisted, especially just after the '45. Bishop MacDonald wrote from Edinburgh to Monsr. L'Abbé Grant at the Scots College in Paris in May 1755, saying that he had two hopeful apprentices ready to send to him who were having difficulty in finding ships to take them.

He commented: 'It's true in the present situation it were better they should be of any other name than McDonalds as that name is more obnoxious to the Government than any other', but lamented that unfortunately 'the most of our westerns are of that suspected Clan'. Not having been out in the last two rebellions, the Irish were under less suspicion, 'therefore it wou'd be of great use, if you cou'd find some good Irish Labourers there who wou'd have the charity to com to our assistance, since they might expect more tolleration than our owne people, as we are credablly informed'.[165] He reiterated his request in 1756,[166] in the February of which year he was himself tried before the high court of justiciary in Edinburgh, indicted of being a 'trafficking Papist ... together with his refusing to purge himself of Popery', and ordered to depart the kingdom[167] – a final ironic justification of the Irish whom the Scottish superiors had been so long trying to replace with indigenous clergy.

Irish Contribution to the Highland Mission

Although this book is specifically concerned with the contribution of Irish priests in the Highlands, it is only possible to arrive at a meaningful assessment of their work when seen as part of the overall pattern of conversion during this period. Whereas discussion of the seventeenth-century mission is almost coterminous with the contribution of the Irish missionaries, by the early eighteenth century native dominance had been established in the priesthood. The following account, therefore, places the Irish contribution within a context of the general expansion of Catholicism at this time, and of the presbyterian campaign to limit it.

In the two decades after the Revolution, the contribution made by Irish priests to the Highland mission was still considerable. A total of twenty-one Irish priests worked on the mission in the two decades between 1690 and 1710. However, from 1711 until 1746, when the last of the Irish priests on the mission left for the continent, only another eight Irish priests came to work in the Highlands.[168]

Although the Irish presence on the mission was declining, Bishop Nicolson admitted that the codification of practice laid down in his statutes of 1700 was influenced by Catholic practice in Ireland, notably the introduction of the idea of public penitence for scandalous crimes like fornication. It had been abolished by rulings in several of the Scottish Catholic mission assemblies about twenty years previously because it was considered contrary to modesty, humanity and the common practice of the church. The practice had continued, however, because the Protestants used it; the fact that the Catholics did not do so became yet another reason for invective and calumny, as if there were no need for Catholics to obtain pardon or to confess crimes.[169] In the post-Reformation Catholic congregation, the sanction was often applied, as in the Protestant

Kirk, for sexual offences or marriage by a minister. The penitent was called to the altar or made to stand up in the gathering. The practice continued to be used, according to the draft of the statutes, for fear 'lest the discipline of the Church seem too lax, if penitents are received back on easier conditions among Catholics than they would find among heretics'. But Nicolson's purported origin of the practice was inaccurate: public penitence had in fact been practised in the medieval Church and was merely adopted by the Protestants.[170]

The other contribution made by the Irish to the Highland mission was in the provision of Catholic education. Catholic schools were considered to be one of the major instruments in attracting Highlanders to the faith and possibly to the priesthood; in Bishop Nicolson's report, their absence was identified as one of the main reasons for the lack of continuity of Catholicism in the Highlands. Therefore, the sons of chiefs and tacksmen had to attend Protestant schools, where as well as learning their letters they learned hatred for and an aversion to Catholicism.[171] Although a school had been kept by a Scot called Cheyn for more than twenty years, it had been taken over by a series of Irishmen, but according to Nicolson's report they had done little of value and were not particularly motivated to succeed. This had merely led the Catholic authorities to believe that there were many difficulties involved in running schools in the Highlands. While those actually on the mission were said to have experienced the contrary, the fact that the schools did not initially produce an abundance of youths for the priesthood easily accounts for these views.[172]

But when the Catholic *fine* took matters into their own hands and imported Catholic schoolmasters from Ireland, this also became a matter for their harrassment. In October 1704, the synod of Argyll noted that 'there is a popish Schoolmaster in Lochbuy's house appoints the moderatur to address the Irishe pepil of the shir, to take loyal methods, with Lochbuy, and the said schoolmaster; as accords of the Law'.[173] Lochbuie eventually felt sufficiently constrained by the power of the Kirk to concur with whatever its wishes were, but he took his time, possibly while pressure was brought to bear on him. The presbytery of Lorn reported in March 1706 'that Lochbuy hath dismissed the popish schoolmaster that was in his bounds, and that he is gone for Ireland', but this proved to be but a ploy; the schoolmaster had simply transferred his services to another Highland gentleman. On 4 March 1707, the presbytery was informed that 'hew o donill who was a popish schoolmaster sometyme at Lochbuy, is harboured by Alexander McLauchlan in Coll teaching his children'. Once again the Kirk sprang into action, appointing the moderator of the presbytery to write to McLauchlan 'to put him a Way from that employment of teaching his children, and to shew him his hazard if he refuses to do it'. The fear of Kirk censure was strong enough to goad McLauchlan into action: in May 1708, it was reported that 'Alexander McLauchlan in Coll hath put away from him hew O donill the popish Schoolmaster, and hath taken another protestant boy in his stede.'[174] The force of Protestantism was already too strong within the bounds of the synod of Argyll. Martin Martin had said of Mull in 1695: 'the Inhabitants are all Protestants, except two or three, who are Roman Catholicks', and those were mainly to be found in Lochbuie's territory. This was because the greater part of the island of Mull had fallen to Argyll in the 1670s, and he had used his powers as heritable justiciary to seize the estates of the indebted Sir John MacLean of Duart. But Martin Martin's wholesale fervour for Protestantism must be questioned in light of a report by the synod of Argyll in 1720 which showed that about a third of the population of the Isle of Rhum were Catholic in 1720,[175] when he had insisted in 1695 that they were all Protestant.[176]

Reconciliation and Expansion

Consolidating Catholic gains was not merely a case of sustaining those areas which had been reclaimed during the seventeenth century, but of stimulating the spiritual interest of the inhabitants in a few inaccessible areas where previously there had been little religion at all but which had been taken under the Catholic wing by the eighteenth century. These areas did not always become entrenched hotbeds of Catholicism; that was dependent on the residence of a priest. For example, although the MacDonalds of Keppoch of the Braes of Lochaber were said by the Royalists not to be averse to orthodox piety in the 1640s, they were derided by Devoyer and Lea in 1687 as people without God and without religion because of their continuous cattle reiving. Clearly, little had been done to establish the true spirit of Catholicism in Lochaber in the forty-three years since the Royalists made a brief stay there. Fr. White visited the area briefly in 1672, but it did not receive the sustained attention it needed until the early eighteenth century. The work of evangelisation was begun in earnest by the Irish Dominican Peter Cluan, who served Glengarry and Lochaber by turns between 1708 and about 1714. In July 1712, the presbytery of Lorn reported that 'popery is full increasing, and particularly in the Braes of Lochaber'. Presbyterian neglect had provided a window of opportunity for the priests: when members of the presbytery had visited Lochaber the previous sabbath, they received only one child, which was three nights old, to be baptised because a minister had not been there for a quarter of a year. Therefore, all the rest had taken their children to the priest for baptism, 'who takes the parrats obliged to conforme to his way before he give them that benefit'. The areas in which the General Assembly was petitioned to erect schools – in Lochaber, at Castle Tirim for the Moidart region, and in the Isle of Mull – readily identifies those areas 'overgrown with popery'.[177] Mull had joined the list of endangered regions since Martin Martin's day.

In June 1720 the synod of Argyll sent a representation to the General

Assembly, stating that when the parish of Kilmonivaig (which included the Braes of Lochaber) was planted with Protestant settlers, there had been only four families which professed the popish religion. But recently, since February 1720, about 400 people had converted, including the followers, relations and dependants of the lairds of Glengarry and Keppoch where the Irish Augustinian, Peter Mulligan (alias MacDonald), had taken up residence. This accords with the generally irreligious state of Lochaber in the late seventeenth century and dates the advent of significant Catholicism in the area to the early decades of the eighteenth century. Mulligan also ventured into Auchnadaal, about four miles from the garrison town of Fort William, where he publicly invited the people of the town to hear him and he converted some families.[178] To prevent the growth of popery in Lochaber, the synod recommended the speedy planting of the parish of Kilmonivaig and that Mr Archibald Campbell, probationer, be settled there.[179] But Campbell was said to be unwilling to take up the appointment because of the low stipend and lack of a manse, kirk or preaching house. He was eventually settled there on the express condition that if the grievances were not removed within three years, he would then be transportable.[180]

Among others, Mulligan was also responsible for evangelising the nearby Badenoch where, according to a Royal Bounty Committee memorial of 10 May 1726, 'Popery has of late made great progress'. Catholicism was promoted there by the Dukes of Gordon, who held land in area and whose followers came mainly from the MacKintoshes, MacPhersons and Farquharsons who formed the Clan Chattan. The Duke at this time – Alexander, second of Gordon – was a Catholic, although his son was raised a Protestant. Mulligan apparently held the position of bailie of regality to the Duke in Lochaber and the surrounding country and, according to the Protestant memorial, used the tactics of coercion to gain converts by 'Threatning the Heads of Families with the Duke's Displeasure'. The Duke had assisted the work of conversion by charging 'a great many Protestant Families to remove from their possessions. And this to make way for some of the Popish McDonalds in the Braes of Lochaber.' The memorial also confirmed the synod's report of 1720 that hundreds had been converted in the area: in recent years about 300 had apostatised, so that by 1726 there were 'about Six hundred Papists in the parish of Kilmanivaig where there were few within these twenty years'.[181]

But in spite of the level of conversion in Lochaber, Badenoch and nearby Glencoe, there was an element of pragmatism in some of the people there, who were prepared to use either faith to their own ends. Conversion continued apace, with the minister of Lismore, Appin and Glencoe complaining on 27 March 1729 'that some Effectual Course is not taken with the New Apostates to popery in that Country'.[182] However, the acceptance of Catholicism by the people of Glencoe was to a certain extent an anti-Establishment gesture after the massacre of 1692. Archibald Campbell, who went on to be minister of

Glenorchy and Inishail in 1731, was prepared to make minor concessions. The presbytery of Lorn reported in October 1730 that when MacDonald of Keppoch was marrying the daughter of Robert Stewart of Appin, Keppoch did not have time to stay and hear the banns pronounced, so Stewart had asked Campbell to marry them without having them read. Campbell had refused, until Keppoch threatened to invite a Catholic priest to solemnise the marriage instead.[183]

Presbyterian Counter-Attack

The growth of Catholicism in the Highlands was constantly restricted by pressure applied by internal agents. With the exception of the conversion of Sir Duncan Campbell of Auchinbreck to Catholicism in the late 1690s, the Campbells pursued a policy of rigorous containment of Catholicism within the bounds of the synod of Argyll, to which the first Irish priests had confined their mission. For instance, on 12 June 1701 an address was commissioned to Mr John Campbell, justiciar depute and brother of the Earl of Argyll, asking him to execute the penal laws against Catholics in Skye. With Anthony Mongan then permanently stationed in Skye, Catholicism was on the increase there.[184] In May 1701, and having recently been appointed provicar of the Isles, Mongan wrote of the good foundation that the Highland people of the mission had in religious instruction, having had 'the good fortune to be instructed by clerics equally knowledgeable and zealous as Messrs. White, Horan, Devoyer, etc'. They had, he said, an intense faith and desire to be Catholic, and God had made 'true children of Abraham of these people who were formerly for the most part stones and rocks'. However, the good missionaries who had taught them were for the most part dead or had returned to their own country; the few who were left behind were broken with age and sickness.[185] Catholics continued to be kept under close surveillance by the synod of Argyll. In June 1706, it had an address drawn up to the justice depute of Argyll 'to cause summond all the popish gentlemen within their bounds and within the Duke of Argyle's Jurisdiction to Compear befor him at Inveraray to give in Securitie that they intertaine no priests in their bounds or houses and that they oblidge themselves to send in their children to Inveraray to School to be educated protestants.'[186]

On May Day 1729, a letter from Mr Patrick Leith outlined the nature of sanctions used against Catholics. It shows that though Protestant domination of Argyll was unquestionable, it was not exclusive.

> Within these 2 or three days I had accounts from Inveraray that the poor papists are hardly dealt with in Argyleshire. They are but very few & 'tis resolved to keep them so. They are warned to remove from their tacks & ane Gentleman after having refus'd to consent to his removal, was by a Warrant taken up a traficking papist, (when he design'd to come to Edinburgh to suspend a Decreet

> given out against him for his removal as a habite & repute papist) & put in the tolbooth of Inveraray. I got a Memorial sent him of Instructions how he ought to do, with a Petition to be given in for his Liberation to the Justiciary Lords now on their Grant in that Country what effect it will have, God knows. Warrants (as the persecuted Gentleman writes me) are out against Colin or any others may happen to be in that Countrey: but I suppose no body will be in danger that way, tho' good people must be very much discouraged, when so used every where.[187]

The Colin referred to by Leith was probably Colin Campbell, one of the 'Pilgrim' protagonists of the forthcoming Jansenist controversy. Second son of the Lochnell family and kinsman of the Duke of Argyll, Campbell had an extensive network of connections in Argyll, which he used after his conversion to bring Catholicism back to an area which the Irish missionaries had largely abandoned a century earlier in 1629.[188]

Campbell has been credited with a final attempt at Catholic expansion in the early eighteenth century by nearly succeeding in extending the Catholic enclave to Mull.[189] Lamenting the unmanageable size of his parish in a representation to the synod of Argyll on 9 August 1728, Mr James Stevenson, minister of Ardnamurchan (which included Sunart, Moidart, Arisaig and Morar), pointed out that Colin's brothers, Alexander Campbell of Ardslignish and James Campbell of Eriska and his whole family, had apostatised to popery in 1727. This conversion had resulted in twenty-four families of Protestants being removed from Ardslignish, Camisnakell and Gortnafarn in Ardnamurchan, which were instead planted with Catholic tenants and servants. Additional Catholic servants had been brought in from Moidart, Arisaig and Morar, and no Protestants were allowed into the family. Moreover, 'Alexander Campbell of Ardslignish and James Campbell of Eriska ... brought one Bishop Gordon from the north, Master Coline Campbell and Hugh MacDonald priests, and Entertained them in their Family'.[190] Campbell and his brothers went to Mull, where Colin established his mission headquarters, but Colin eventually relocated to Ardnamurchan with his converts, where they could be more easily sustained by Catholic priests in the nearby maritime region. Stevenson readily admitted in the representation that even at this stage of the eighteenth century the Reformation had 'never had a footing' in Moidart, Arisaig, Morar, Kinlochmoidart and 'Bellfinla'. James Campbell went on to train for the priesthood, later returning to Lorn, from where the Lochnell family originated. Twenty years later, in 1747, Mr John McVean, minister of Lorn, identified Mr James Campbell, brother of Sir Duncan Campbell of Lochnell, as one of the few Catholics in his parish.[191]

Their elder brother, Sir Duncan Campbell of Lochnell, proprietor of Ardnamurchan and Sunart, remained resolutely loyal to the government but, in tolerating their presence on his land, did so possibly with a view to protecting the family inheritance. In his report, Stevenson said that Lochnell assisted him by enforcing discipline and discouraging priests, punishing anyone who harboured them on his property. He especially 'would not allow any within Ardnamurchine or Shunart to marry any popish wives'. But between the introduction of Catholics, and 300 miners and other workmen who had come to work in Murray of Stanhope's lead mine, many of the old Protestant parishioners (some 200 in number in Sunart) had felt compelled to remove themselves; they had gone to Lorn, Mull and other places, and people friendly to neither the Kirk nor the government had been put in their place. Although Stanhope was very civil he did not uphold the Establishment, so that 'The Minister hes no Civil Magistrat to Strengthen his hand in that Countrie as formerly he had in the Exercise of Discipline, notwithstanding of a great deal of prophanness that is Committed there.' Since his advent, nine or ten young MacDonalds, Camerons and Stewarts had married Catholics in the previous year and had brought them to Ardnamurchan. Each had also brought two or three Catholic servants with them. Lochnell was therefore earnestly entreated to use his authority to thwart the bad consequences resulting from the perversion of his brothers, while the synod of Argyll threatened 'for their own vindication and to Show their Endeavors to prevent the Encroachments of popery upon the shire of Argyll ... to print the whole of this affair if a stop be not speedily put to such Encroachments upon the shire of Argyll'.[192]

The partial tendency to Catholicism within the Lochnell family has been explained by their being related through marriage to the MacDonalds of Glencoe.[193] It has been a subject of debate whether the latter were actually Catholic or episcopalian during the late seventeenth century and they may, indeed, have adhered to both faiths (neither of which had the fortune of being in favour with the government).[194] That there was at least a Catholic interest in Glencoe is indisputable. Just three years after Stevenson's representation, in July 1731, the presbytery of Lorn noted a petition from Mr Archibald Campbell, minister of Glenorchy and Inishail, who stated 'that since he had come from home he was told a Priest had been sent for to Baptise some Children in Glenco, Therfor beg'd the Presbytery wou'd allow him to return with all possible Dispatch to prevent this Incursion which the Presbytery considering the said Mr Archibald was allowed to repair home forthwith'.[195]

In south Argyll, the presbytery of Dunoon took umbrage in March 1714 at paying the quarter centesimal[196] which the General Assembly was asking to defray the costs of sending missionaries to the popish bounds. It sent its own missions to Moidart, Ardnamurchan and Glengarry and thought it hard, therefore, to have to pay for other places, especially when the General Assembly totally neglected the Catholic regions of Argyll.[197] This was hardly because the borders of Dunoon were not under threat from popery: the parish of Rothesay in Bute, which had strong connections with Antrim in Ulster, was within this presbytery.[198] Indeed, a Royal Bounty memorial about popery, dated 10 May 1729, particularly highlighted the bounds of the presbytery of Dunoon, amongst others, as an area where popery most prevailed.[199] But other than this, Catholics in Argyll were generally a declining and much coerced minority. When the Committee of the General Assembly enquired about the state of popery in Kintyre, the presbytery there replied in November 1735 that 'there are no papists in their Bounds but vagrant persons, some of whom Comply and some return to their own Country'.[200] The implication is that many of them were visiting Irish vagrants or labourers from elsewhere in the west Highlands moving to Ireland via Kintyre.

The Kirk was also relatively successful in keeping Catholicism at bay in the Isle of Lewis. The two episcopal ministers there had conformed at the Revolution. One of them, Kenneth Morrison, minister of Stornoway, was instrumental in helping to establish presbyterianism there and in reducing the influence of MacKenzie of Kildun, who had first brought Irish priests to the island in the late 1680s. None the less, Frances, the younger Countess of Seaforth, was still being pursued before the Privy Council in 1704 at the instance of the Earl of Cromarty and Lord Justice Clerk (two close kinsmen of her son, the fifth Earl), and the Queen's Advocate, for sending the young Seaforth abroad to be raised a Catholic.[201] Neither Bishop Nicolson nor Bishop Gordon went to Lewis on their Highland visitations because of the ascendancy which the presbyterian Church enjoyed there,[202] but a Royal Bounty report of about 1737 shows that the presbyterians still did not regard Lewis as an exclusively Protestant territory. Although the scandalous Irish priest Cornelius Coan had done little to promote Catholicism there in the late seventeenth century,[203] the impetus had reverted to the indigenous MacKenzies. Formerly there had been no Catholics on the island except those under the protection of MacKenzie of Kildun, but one of his sons, having had a Catholic education abroad, was expected home shortly in orders, and it was feared that 'popery is beginning to encrease in this Island'. This priest was one of the sons of Colin MacKenzie of Kildun and grandson of the George MacKenzie who had first invited the priests to Lewis in the previous century. Both of Colin's sons, George and Alexander, entered the College at Douai in April 1729 and later joined the Jesuits at Nancy. They were clearly deemed unacceptable, because George was dismissed after his ordination and Alexander prior to his, which makes it more likely that it is George who is referred to here.[204] The number of papists on Lewis was precisely fourteen, but there was no one to exercise jurisdiction in that area nearer than Ross.[205] The island's Jacobite disaffection and the subversive influence of MacKenzie of Kildun were both mentioned in an undated document, probably written in the 1750s. MacKenzie, technically substitute to the sheriff depute of Ross, was chastised for never holding a court. Employed as factor to Lord Fortrose, he was stated to be 'a very improper and bad Man' who had recently fortified himself with three pieces of brass cannon that had belonged to the Earl of Seaforth in the 1715 rebellion. Equally heinously, it stated that 'He encourages, and harbours, The Popish Priests, and exercises great Tyranny, and Oppression over the Poor People there; takes upon Him to make Orders, and set Fines, in a most arbitrary manner; and it does not appear that any other Authority is exerted there.'[206] This is significant not only in documenting the existence of priests in Lewis in the mid-eighteenth century, but also in revealing a lingering Catholicism in the island, if only among the retainers of MacKenzie of Kildun.

Organised mission activity into staunch Catholic areas had been undertaken within the bounds of the synod of Argyll since 1690 (and after 1724, within the Synod of Glenelg), and more particularly after the founding of the SSPCK in 1708. When the episcopal minister in South Uist had refused to conform to presbyterianism at the Revolution, a presbyterian minister, Angus MacDonald, was entered there in 1689. But he made no converts outside of his small congregation;[207] the majority still adhered to the priest, who in that year was the Irishman Jacques Hannat. A presbyterian report written in about 1737 showed that the Kirk was making a little headway: there was an SSPCK school in South Uist by this time, as well as a catechist. There were also some Protestant wadsetters.[208] All of this was assisted by the fact that the Lady Clanranald was herself a Protestant.[209]

The presbyterians also tried to infiltrate other Clanranald territories. In 1725, the Committee for the Reformation of the Highlands and Islands sent Mr Daniel of Bracadale and Mr Kenneth Beaton of Kilmuir to the Small Isles. 'They had good success in Rum But little access to do any good in the other three Islands, Because of the Influence of the Popish Heretors and their Priests upon the poor People.'[210] The main influence in these islands was the Catholic heritor of Canna and Eigg, MacDonald of Clanranald. In spite of Clanranald's protection Protestantism advanced minimally on the islands between 1725 and 1736, when the Irish priest Anthony Kelly worked there. In 1695, all of the inhabitants of Eigg were allegedly Roman Catholics, 'except one Woman, that is a Protestant'.[211] The Catholic–Protestant ratio of these islands was given again in presbyterian documents of June 1720 and August 1728. By 1720, the situation on Eigg had changed little: the 400 dependants of Clanranald were 'all Roman Catholicks, except the Baillie and two servants, and are all encouraged chiefly by Allan McDonald Laird of Morhir who lives there'. By 1728, the population of the island had fallen to 340 catechisable persons, among whom there were sixteen Protestants (so the presbyterian mission of 1728 had resulted in a handful of converts). That the Kirk did not make greater headway can be laid at Clanranald's door. In 1720, the 120 inhabitants of the Isle of Canna were 'friends and dependants of the Clanranalds'.[212] Eight years later, the population numbered 236 catechisable people, all but sixteen of them

Catholic. On Muck in the same year there were fifty Catholics, dependants of the arch-Catholic MacDonald of Clanranald and of MacLean of Muck, a cadet branch of the MacLeans of Duart. By 1728, there were sixty Protestants and sixty-eight Catholics on Muck. However, significant headway was made on Rhum, where the heritor, MacLean of Coll, was Protestant. Of the one hundred people on the island in 1720, only a third were said to 'have been alwayes popish', but the priests had recently converted eighteen souls, notwithstanding the Laird of Coll's endeavours to the contrary. However, just eight years later all 152 inhabitants of the island were Protestant, except for six women.[213]

Nearby Barra, wallowing in the protective shade of Catholic South Uist, was relatively impervious to the advances of Protestantism. In 1695, MacNeill of Barra and his followers were all Roman Catholics, 'one only excepted, viz. Murdock Mackneil; and it may perhaps be thought no small Virtue in him to adhere to the Protestant Communion, considering the Disadvantages he labours under by the want of his Chief 's Favour, which is much lessen'd, for being a Heretick, as they call him'.[214] The aforementioned presbyterian report of about 1737 refers to the settlement of a minister in Barra three years previously; the SSPCK and the Committee for the Reformation of the Highlands and Islands also maintained a schoolmaster and catechist there. These were probably under the protection of the wife of Roderick MacNeill of Barra who, along with one of her daughters, adhered to the Protestant faith. But their Protestantism was badly received by the islanders: according to the report, they 'are necessitate to leave this Family, by reason of the bad treatment they meet therein'.[215] This shows the extent to which the islanders of Barra identified culturally and ideologically with Catholicism.

Although relatively little appears to have been achieved by Protestant attempts to quash Catholicism in the Hebrides, even there things may not have been as optimistic as painted by Catholic commentators. A flagrantly anti-Catholic document dating from 1704 highlighted the complaints of the dependants of the lairds of Glengarry, old and young, the captain of Clanranald, and the people of Barra, Morar and Benbecula, at paying maintenance for the priests. There was undoubtedly an ulterior motive in claiming these dues for presbyterian ministers. Nevertheless, such evidence must be taken into account because any exaction on a people who by all accounts lived very frugally must have been an encumbrance. The poor people were said to groan about the exaction, 'and complain ... to such protestants as happine now and then to come amongst them, under hatches declaring unto such that they would rather want the service than to bear the burden and insolencie of their preists'.[216]

But not all Protestants took a paranoiac attitude to the existence of Catholics within Scotland. A Protestant report entitled 'State of Popery in Scotland, 1713–1737' made the usual points about 'popery' and Jacobitism, and the intrusion of episcopal ministers into northern parishes, but it also brought a certain sense of proportion to the issue.

> Yet, after all, the Interest of popery and Jacobitism in Scotland, does not appear to be so universall in Scotland as formerly. For by the Reports from presbyteries and Lists of Papists sent to the Commission, we have no account of papists from any of the Number of 964 parishes in Scotland, Except about 30, and in some of them, very few, according to a more particular list of them herewith given in.

It concluded, therefore,

> that popery is not growing in Scotland, but has decreased, Except in those places, where the heretors are popish, and Priests and Emissaries of Rome are resett and Encouraged, and where there are none in Authority to support and protect such as incline to favour the Protestant Ministers and other Missionaries, but the people left to the Arbitrary Will of Papists.[217]

In essence, this was probably a fair assessment of the situation. Those areas especially singled out come as no surprise: Barra, South Uist, Eigg, Muck, Canna, Knoydart and Morar. Many stubborn non-juring congregations, evident in the early years covered by the report, were retrieved by the removal of Jacobite episcopalian ministers 'because of their accession to the Rebellion in the year 1715'.[218] But when the report was written around 1737, the Establishment was not fearful of Jacobite insurgence; the Protestants had ample funding for missionaries to the Catholic districts, and the Catholic congregation itself was much weakened by infighting over the Jansenist controversy. At long last, the presbyterian Kirk had begun to make its mark in the Highlands and was far more at ease.

The State of Catholicism by the End of the Period

In May 1729, the Royal Bounty Committee helpfully identified the 'wide parishes' of the presbyteries of Dunoon, Lorn, Kintyre, Skye, Long Island, Gairloch, Abertarff, Dingwall, Dunblane, Dumbarton and some parts of the Highlands of Angus and Mearns as those 'Places where Popery prevails most'. The Highland parishes of Criech and Kildonan in Sutherland, Kincardine and Contin in Ross-shire, Glenmoriston, Kiltarlity and Kilmorack in Inverness-shire, Lismore, Appin and Glencoe in Argyll, and Braemar in Aberdeenshire were mentioned in a second (less severely affected) category. (See Fig. 5.1.) The second group were to be considered for missionary assistance only after those in the first 'where there is great Ignorance and Superstition, and which do much need the Means of Knowledge'.[219] These were more or less those areas in which pockets of Catholicism had been established in the Highlands and Islands during the seventeenth and the early eighteenth centuries. It remains only to give a final indication of the size of those Catholic communities established, which will be done with reference to a Privy Council document compiled in 1698 and entitled 'A list of Papists in the Highlands'; Dr Alexander Webster's census of Scotland in 1755, which was one of the earliest in Europe; the report of Drs Hyndman and Dick, appointed by the General Assembly in 1760 to visit those places in the Highlands and Islands where itinerants and catechists were employed; and Bishop Hugh MacDonald's report on the Highland Vicariate in 1764, at the very end of the period. However, the different bias and intentions of these sources must be taken into account: on the one hand, there was the wish to access the funds deployed against the spread of Jacobitism, on the other, the need to justify the mission to *Propaganda*. The aim here is not to arrive at a definitive number of Catholics in the Highlands and Islands in 1760, but broadly to identify where there were substantial communities or otherwise.[220] In some cases, these figures have been additionally compared with interim figures given by the synod of Argyll in 1720 and by the Royal Bounty Committee in 1737.[221]

In Kintyre, there was never more than a token number of Catholics. The peninsula was never mentioned in the copious Catholic mission reports of the time. Such Catholicism as existed was probably confined to the lower social orders rather than to the mainly presbyterian gentry. For instance, on 1 August 1694 Effie nc a Chlerigh from Kilchenzie parish in Kintyre was cited before the presbytery for fornication, where she was found to be of the popish profession. Perhaps the most pertinent question to ask is where her faith had been instilled and sustained, because her name is indigenous to Kintyre. The most likely possibility is that she was mobile as a domestic, either in Ireland or in north Argyll, although according to Webster a considerable number of papists came to Campbeltown in the fishing season.[222] Similar mobility, either as a servant or a fisherman, probably accounted for John MacLean, 'a papist from Muidard', who was cited before the presbytery of Kintyre by the minister of the Highland congregation of Campbeltown in December 1722.[223] Indeed, vagrant Irish Catholics who came across on the ferry, and imported Catholic domestics, probably perturbed the authorities in Kintyre more than any local growth in Catholicism.

The Establishment's concern about popery in the presbytery of Lorn, especially in the joint parish of Appin and Lismore, as well as Glencoe was not particularly valid either. The Catholicism alleged in these areas by presbyterian reports did not attract anything other than a cursory mention in Catholic mission reports.[224] Neither were any of these areas mentioned in the Privy Council's list of 1698 or in Bishop Hugh MacDonald's report of 1764.[225] In 1760, Hyndman and Dick noted 900 souls in Lismore and 2,860 in Appin and Ardsheil, Glencoe and Kingairloch, and no papists among them, although 'not above a fourth part of the inhabitants understand a sermon in English'.[226]

But the bounds of the presbytery of Skye were an altogether different matter.[227] Sleat and Trotternish – the two areas in the isle of Skye which had been inclined to Catholicism in the seventeenth century – show a marked decline in adherence over the period. In 1698, the Privy Council noted only fourteen Catholics in Sir Donald MacDonald of Sleat's territories. Although Devoyer had claimed in 1687 that there were between fifty and sixty Catholics in Skye, the island had not actually been visited by a priest since it had been abandoned, under pressure from the presbyterians, by the Vincentians in the early 1660s. So this figure scarcely represents a mature Catholic community.[228] Even by the beginning of Mongan's residency on Skye between 1688 and 1702, the death-knell had already been sounded for Catholicism on Skye, though it lingered on a few decades more. From 1722, going over the sea to Skye became a more hazardous undertaking for missionaries, since the narrow crossing at Kyle Rhea was henceforth guarded by a barracks at Bernera, at the lower end of Glenelg.[229] It is therefore no surprise to find Skye absent from Bishop MacDonald's report in 1764. Hyndman and Dick mentioned only two papists in a catechisable population of 1,300 in the parish of Kilmuir, 'which are not natives of the isle of Sky'; and of 1,400 souls in the parish of Sleat, all were Protestant 'except one person, who came from the mainland'.[230] However, the presbytery of Skye also took in the Small Isles, where the containment of Catholicism on the Isles of Muck and Rhum, at the hands of presbyterian proprietors, had followed a similar pattern. In 1698, there were only four Catholics on MacLean of Coll's Isle of Muck; Rhum was not even mentioned. But the synod of Argyll's representation on the state of popery in 1720 noted a phenominal increase of Catholics on Muck and Rhum since 1698.[231] Even allowing for some exaggeration by the synod, which was greatly perturbed by the extent of Catholicism in its bounds, it would seem that a Catholic counter-attack had indeed been waged there, more particularly on Muck. Although Hyndman and Dicks' estimate of twenty-two, and MacDonald's figure of twenty-four, Catholics in both islands in 1764 showed a net increase in conversions to Catholicism over the period, like Skye these islands had essentially been lost to presbyterianism by 1760. The islands of Eigg and Canna, on the other hand, remained Catholic preserves throughout. The number of Catholics grew in Eigg from 200 in 1698 to 394 in 1760 (or a more conservative estimate of 350, according to MacDonald in 1764), and in Canna from 110 in 1698 to 276 in 1760 (or, once again, a more conservative figure of 250 in 1764), while Webster gave the figure of 582 papists in the Small Isles as a whole in 1755.[232]

When the Royal Bounty Committee made its report in 1729, the presbytery of the Long Island consisted of South and North Uists, Barra, Harris, Berneray, St. Kilda and Lewis.[233] The southern part of the presbytery – Barra and its associated isles and the parish of South Uist, including Benbecula – formed the major Catholic enclave of the Outer Hebrides. The Catholic populations of Barra, South Uist and Benbecula under the protection of their Catholic landowners MacNeill of Barra, MacDonald of Clanranald and Ronald MacDonald of Benbecula were cited at 440, 1,100 and 200 souls respectively in 1698. Over half a century later, in 1755, the number of papists in Barra was given as 1,100; in 1760, Hyndman and Dick recorded 1,020 papists in Barra (and only 80 Protestants), and although by 1764 some of the Barra gentry had turned Protestant, the Catholic population had almost tripled from the end of the seventeenth century to 1,200 souls. In 1755, the Catholic population of South Uist and Benbecula was collectively estimated at 2,040; in 1760, the joint Catholic population of South Uist, Benbecula and Eriskay was said to be 1,850 (and only 250 Protestants); and by 1764, this had risen to 2,503. The parish of Harris, including Berneray, under MacLeod of MacLeod, remained a Catholic-free zone, receiving no mention in the 1698 list or the 1764 report. And in 1737 there was 'no account of any professed Papists thairin', while in 1760, there were no papists among the 2,000 souls in the entire parish of Harris, including the islands of Bernaray, Pabbay and Scalpay, although 'there are few who understand a sermon in English'.[234] St. Kilda, on the other hand, was almost totally devoid of religion; having been toyed with by a quasi-Catholic renegade in the last decade of the seventeenth century, it was eventually claimed for presbyterianism in the early eighteenth century.[235] Catholicism in Lewis was negligible in 1698, when there were said to be only five Catholics in the Earl of Seaforth's territory. And although the presbyterian authorities were never complacent about their position, Catholicism in Lewis was not really an issue by the end of the period. Hyndman and Dick reported in 1760 that 'there are no Papists in the whole country of Lewis', which then had a population of 4,800 souls and four presbyterian catechists – but this was probably not, strictly speaking, true, given the clutch of Catholics at Aignish, near Stornoway.[236]

However, Catholicism was rife in the Inverness-shire division of the presbytery of Gairloch, which took in the joint parish of Glenelg and Knoydart. The Catholic community here grew from 260 in 1698 to nearly 500 in 1728, and it stood at 827 in 1755; the population of Knoydart, North Morar and Glenelg was estimated at between 1,560 and 1,660 souls in 1760, and was estimated conservatively at 1,400 (including North Morar) in 1764. However, in the staunchly presbyterian country of Ross-shire, where the presbyteries of Gairloch and Dingwall held sway, only fifteen Catholics were noted in the Privy Council list in 1698. In 1755, according to Webster, there were but a score of Catholics in Ross-shire but, surprisingly, only three in Kintail, even though the synod of Glenelg had reported twenty-eight years earlier, in July 1727, that the Jesuit Alexander MacRae was 'making Incursions into the Parishes of Lochalsh and Kintail, where he preaches publicly to considerable numbers'.[237] Hyndman and Dick noted only one papist in a population of 3,000 catechisable persons in the parish of Contin, one popish family in the parish of Glenshiel and Letterfern, and none whatsoever in the parishes of Lochbroom, Gairloch,

Applecross, Lochcarron, Lochalsh and Kintail. Ross-shire was not mentioned at all in 1764.[238] Also covering part of Inverness-shire, the presbytery of Dingwall included part of the Catholic community of Strathglass: the parishes of Kilmorack and Kiltarlity were in the presbyteries of Dingwall and Moray respectively.[239] In 1698, there were thirty-six Catholics in Inverness and Fochabers, to the east.[240] The Royal Bounty Committee noted in June 1726 that a third of the 1,700-strong population of Kilmorack was Catholic – that is, about 560 souls – while there were 400 Catholics among the 1,000 catechisable persons in Kiltarlity. Webster gave almost exactly the same figures in 1755, recording 564 papists in Kilmorack and 402 in Kiltarlity. In 1760 there were upwards of 2,000 souls in Kilmorack, of whom 300 were papists, and 1,000 souls in Kiltarlity, of whom 300 were papists 'and live in that part of Strathglass which belongs to this parish'. Hyndman and Dick noted in addition that 'a great part of the forefeited estate of Lord Lovat lies in these parishes'. In 1764, the number of Catholics in Strathglass was precisely 1,321, 'according to the most careful count'. In the parish of Urquhart and Glenmoriston, to the south, there were fifty-five Catholics in 1737.[241]

But the most inviolable Catholic enclaves on the mainland were in the bounds of the presbytery of Abertarff. The vast parish of Kilmonivaig, which encompassed parts of Glengarry and Lochaber, came within this presbytery, with the remainder falling in the parish of Laggan in the presbytery of Dunkeld.[242] Similarly, it included the Catholic communities in the parishes of Kilmallie, Abertarff and Boleskine, and Arisaig, including Moidart and South Morar – an area known in Gaelic, for fairly obvious reasons, as 'Morar bheannaichte' (blessèd Morar).[243] In 1698, the presbyterians estimated that there were 680 Catholics in Glengarry, the huge number of 1,300 in Badenoch and only thirty in Protestant Lochaber. Indeed, the conversion of Lochaber took place mainly in the early eighteenth century: 300 allegedly converted between 1722 and 1726. In 1720 the synod of Argyll's representation stated that in Glengarry, where Mr Gregor McGregor had taken over from Peter Mulligan, the people were 'Generally all Popish, extending of above the number of seven hundered persons'.[244] Webster put the number of Catholics in the parish of Kilmonivaig at 1,400 in 1755, including another 130 in the parish of Laggan. Although Lauchlan Macbean was catechist in Kilmallie and Kilmonivaig, two popish priests resided in the bounds of these parishes in 1760, which were the 'object of particular attention' due to the 1,600 Catholics in a population of only 2,500 catechisable persons in Kilmonivaig. Regarded as the most important mission in the Highland Vicariate, Glengarry was home to 1,400 Catholics by 1764, and 1,270 more in the Braes of Lochaber and the Braes of Badenoch.[245] Around Fort William, the synod of Argyll estimated that seventy converts were made in the parish of Kilmallie in 1720. But the faith did not easily flourish so close to a military garrison: Webster noted only twenty papists in Kilmallie in 1755;

Hyndman and Dick noted only twenty or thirty Catholics in Kilmallie in 1760 in a population of some 3,300. In Boleskine and Abertarff, the area around Fort Augustus, there were reputedly 250 Catholics in 1737, a figure which had almost doubled to 428 in Boleskine alone by 1755.[246] In 1698, the Catholic population of Morar was estimated at 200, but no separate figure was given for Moidart. The representation of 1720 gave the figure of 900 Catholics in the parish of Islandfinan, which included Moidart, Arisaig and Morar, all friends and dependants of the captain of Clanranald. Webster cited 2,300 papists in the parish of Ardnamurchan, which in 1755 encompassed the districts of Moidart, Ardnamurchan and Sunart, Arisaig and Morar. Although Hyndman and Dick insisted that there were no papists in Ardnamurchan itself – where 'a good number of people ... understand a sermon in English; the reason of which is, their having had a company of miners from the low countries, so long settled amongst them' – only two families in Moidart professed the Protestant religion in a population of 500 souls, only four people in Arisaig in a similar population of Catholics, only four in Sunart out of 443 souls, and only one among 300 Catholic souls in South Morar. By 1764, Bishop MacDonald recorded 817 Catholics in Moidart, Arisaig and South Morar, and a further seventy-seven scattered in nearby Protestant areas. Finally, the Aberdeenshire district of Glencairn, technically in the Lowlands, was included with Braemar in the Highland Vicariate because it was Gaelic-speaking. Braemar had sixty Catholics in 1698, Crathie and Braemar jointly had 684 by 1755, 700 in 1760, and about 900 in 1764, with a further 612 in Glencairn.[247]

The Irish had undeniably made a huge contribution to the Highland mission, not only in the period from 1690 to 1760 but from the beginning of the Counter-Reformation in the Highlands in the early seventeenth century, when Irish priests had unilaterally supplied the mission. Even the presbyterians recognised their dedication and determination. Drs Hyndman and Dick wrote in 1760 that:

> The priests of this communion are numerous and active; and although their salaries be small, yet the advantage of a foreign education, which they receive from a public fund, and the influence which their politic religion gives them over the minds of the people, have contributed to check the progress of the reformation, and at some periods to gain proselytes to their own church. In countries so ill supplied with Protestant ministers, and with schools for the instruction of the youth, where so little good seed, of any kind is sown, is it to be wondered, that the enemy should sew his tares, and that these should bring forth a plentiful increase?[248]

Their rejuvenation of Catholicism in the Highlands and Islands, which had gathered momentum and come to fruition in the final decades of the seventeenth century, resulted in the creation of a native Scottish clergy to staff the mission. Though it is difficult to gauge its extent, there was also an element of rivalry between the Scots and Irish on the mission. It had been apparent in the 1680s but became more pronounced after the appointment of Bishop Nicolson as Vicar-Apostolic in 1694, when the native secular element came into the ascendant. Irish priests coming to the mission for the first time were frequently said to be substandard. Although this may have been true in some cases, it is obvious that the Scots wished to establish their superiority on the Highland mission. Both of these factors combined with political considerations to reduce the number of Irish priests in the Highlands. There were eight Irish priests on the Highland mission in the year of Revolution, but by 1760 – after the upheavals of rebellion and its aftermath – there were none. However, this compares favourably with the number of Gaelic-speaking ministers (episcopalian and presbyterian) then in Ireland at the same time, of which there were three in 1690. In 1690, the full impact of the Revolution had not yet been felt; moreover, the number of priests had uncharacteristically swelled as a result of the King's edict of 1686 which ordered all available priests from the continent back to Scotland. It would perhaps be fairer to compare the situation in 1700, by which time there were four ministers serving in Ireland (two others having taken refuge there and died). In the same year, there were nine Irish priests in the Highlands and Islands, two of whom were incapacitated by illness. Moreover, although the number of Irish priests on the mission between 1720 and 1746 rarely exceeded two, by comparison no presbyterian ministers transferred permanently to Ireland during the same period. Rivalry and jealousy was also the root of the Jansenist controversy in the Highlands, arguably the biggest problem to hit the mission in the eighteenth century. Having lost his bid to become Vicar-Apostolic in the Highlands in 1731 as well as a later battle to become coadjutor in the Lowlands, Colin Campbell vented his spleen not only on the mission hierarchy and the superiors of the Scots College in Paris but on any missionaries who had not supported him. What little can be discerned of the Irish stand on this issue suggests that, as a marginalised minority, they were mainly anti-Jansenist in stance.

As for the Kirk, it was largely resigned to the existence of pockets of Catholicism within its Highland and Island bounds by the mid-eighteenth century, although it still worked hard to keep the Campbell Pale free from papist contagion. The last allusion made in the Protestant record to trafficking priests before the year 1760 was on 14 April 1756, in reference to the districts of Ardnamurchan and Sunart which lay exposed to the incursions of trafficking priests because the parish was without a minister: 'Encroachments were lately attempted particularly in the Neighbourhood of Lochsheil.'[249] There is, however, no evidence to suggest that any of these priests were Irish, because in spite of Bishop MacDonald's pleas for Irish clerics after the '45 rebellion, Dominic Colgan appears to have been the last Irishman to work on the mission in this period, and he left Scotland with the Pretender in 1746.

Epilogue

I have shown in this book how Scottish and Irish Gaels had a profound effect on each other's religious development in the century and a half after the Reformation. The contribution made by Highland ministers in spreading and nurturing an embryonic reformed faith among the native Irish predates the better-publicised activity of Irish Franciscans in seventeenth-century Scotland and (though the numbers involved were relatively few) was highly significant historically. None the less, other than the emphasis on the significance of the role of military chaplains in Ulster during the civil war of the 1640s, their contribution has not been accorded the importance it deserves. Similarly, Irish priests almost single-handedly brought Catholicism back to the Highlands and Islands of Scotland in the seventeenth century, after the last traces of the Catholic faith were swept away in the late sixteenth century. Although the work of the Irish Franciscan mission to the Highlands and Islands between 1619 and 1646 is very well known, the contribution of the numerous priests – regular and secular – who worked there after the civil war is less well appreciated.

It must be concluded that the greatest pan-Gaelic co-operation in the religious sphere, in both Protestant and Catholic terms, occurred in the seventeenth century. Though the number of ministers and priests involved was relatively small, their contribution to each other's religious heritage was enormous, revealing the vital importance of religion as a political force for each denomination. However, after the civil war little trace remained of the strong political relationship that had existed between the Gaels during the mid-seventeenth century. In Ireland, the Protestant religion had by this time been so thoroughly associated with an invading, foreign authority that most native Irish were inexorably drawn to the one authority which opposed it – the Catholic church – whereas in Scotland the reformed faith had made reasonable headway even in the Highlands. Under these circumstances, it became increasingly difficult to maintain a common ideology of Gaelic resistance which had been grounded mainly in a common Catholic faith (though examples of it none the less persist into the next century). The early eighteenth century marks an even sharper break with the past: at this point, the ecclesiastical links between the two began to tail off, so that the most vigorous links persisting between Irish and Scottish Gaels were socio-economic and cultural.

As I discussed in Chapter 1, Scots ministers who were presbyterian in tendency experienced no crisis of conscience in serving in the Church of Ireland in the decades after the Reformation because, though episcopal, it had a Calvinist tone, so in Ulster many of the early bishops were Scots. The 'prescopalianism' of these early Highland ministers reinforced the Calvinist tradition in Ulster. Little attempt was made there to impose the Act of Uniformity or to use of the Book of Common Prayer. The value of Scottish Gaelic-speaking ministers in Irish-speaking areas of Ulster, particularly in the early seventeenth century when so few Irish-speakers were conforming to Protestantism and the educational standard of those who did was low, should not be underestimated. The Scots had university degrees, whereas a university education was not made compulsory even by the presbyterian church in Ulster until 1691.[1] Not only did they understand the language of the natives, they also played a useful part in bolstering the morale of Scots who settled there during the plantation, as well as that of the communities established earlier in Donegal and Antrim. Considering that there were only nineteen ministers serving in the Isles in 1626, the three Gaelic-speaking ministers known to have entered the Church of Ireland before 1622 made up a significant percentage of the personnel available to the Kirk for serving in its own parishes.

Far more striking is the exclusive connection of all the early Gaelic-speaking Protestant ministers in Ulster with Donegal, especially with the diocese of Raphoe. This pleads for revision of Michael Perceval-Maxwell's explanation for the existence of substantial numbers of Campbells in Donegal in the early seventeenth century: that they were probably Campbells from Ayr rather than Argyll Campbells.[2] Certainly this is the easiest assumption, but it is probably far from accurate. If these Campbells were predominantly Lowlanders, why was there a need to furnish them with Gaelic-speaking ministers? On the contrary, the evidence argues for distinct communities of Highland Campbells from Argyll who sought the spiritual sustenance of ministers from among their own kin and who intermarried with Highlanders. None the less, the plantation of Ulster did introduce a distinct Lowland element into the equation of Scoto-Irish relations, resulting in the allocation of an entirely different set of values to all aspects of Gaelic interaction. The drafting-in of Andrew Knox, the ex-bishop of the Isles, to co-ordinate the Protestant evangelisation of the area tends to suggest that his previous experience in the Highlands and Islands – a position which he continued to hold concurrently for a while – was regarded as a valuable in-post training. The presence of Campbells in numerous proportions in Donegal argues not only for an earlier settlement during the mercenary period (which makes their dispersion over a larger area by the early seventeenth century more understandable) but, more importantly, implies a noteworthy Highland presence – if not first-generation – on the plantation lands in Donegal. The explanation is more likely to be found in the fact that the Earls of Argyll were the main suppliers of mercenaries to the O'Neills of Tyrone and

O'Donnells of Tirconnell, both of whom, in the sixteenth century, paid an annual pension to the house of Argyll to ensure a ready supply of redshanks.

Migration to Ulster slowed in the 1620s as the opportunities for new settlement in the plantation passed, and though it increased again in the 1630s, it was never as enthusiastic as in the first decade. Hence, as outlined in Chapters 2 and 3, the number of Gaelic-speaking Scots entering the Church of Ireland before the civil war was almost negligible. However, the promulgation of the National Covenant of 1638 resulted in a significant deepening of the political and religious connections between Highland and Ulster presbyterians. To avoid taking the Black Oath, which forced them to deny the Covenant and pledge loyalty to Charles I, some Highland presbyterians fled from Ulster back to Argyll. And on the outbreak of the Irish rising in October 1641, many more refugees crossed the North Channel to Argyll and Bute as well as to Lowland areas. Indeed, they so strained the local mechanisms of poor relief that the Privy Council passed legislation to relieve them at the national level. The Campbells of Argyll in particular saw it as essential to send out ministers with the Scottish troops who were drafted to Ulster in 1642, in order to maintain the Protestant faith among the settlers.

After all, Ulster was the Royalist front line into Argyll, and the Campbells therefore had to defend it militarily at all costs. The presbyterian pulpit was considered the first line of defence against Royalism in the 1640s. It was the chaplains with Argyll's regiment, under the command of Campbell of Auchinbreck, who set up the army presbytery at Carrickfergus in June 1642; presbyterianism was also widely supported among the Scottish settler population in Ulster. There was a constant flow of Gaelic-speaking chaplains to Ulster between 1642 and 1648, which put a strain on the communities at home. The synod of Argyll sent no fewer than eighteen ministers to Ulster in this period, which can have done little to promote presbyterian solidarity in the Highlands and Islands. It also gave more scope to some of the ministers left behind to collaborate with the Royalists under the leadership of the Marquess of Montrose and Alasdair MacColla MacDonald. Their activities refute the claims tendered by Protestant contemporaries (and some secondary commentators today) that Royalism was the exclusive preserve of Highland papists in alliance with the savage Irish.

The Gaelic expression of Catholicism, on the other hand, had a distinctly continental flavour and was marked by a nostalgia for which the Gaels became later renowned only after clearance and famine, when they were in permanent exile from the old countries. Emigration of Catholics to the continent, in order to preserve a faith which was proscribed in both countries, was a shared aspect of Irish and Scottish Gaelic communities in the early seventeenth century. Gaels went abroad not only to further their general education, engage in commercial enterprise or fight as mercenaries in the armies of almost every European state but, from the late sixteenth century, they also went to train for the priesthood, although Scottish Gaels were less successful in finding seminary places than the Irish because of a bias against them on the part of the Lowlanders who ran the Scots Colleges. The very proscription of Catholicism had an important side-effect: among clans who still valued the traditional Gaelic values of kinship and its military defence, of extended communal living and its hospitality ethic, it caused Catholicism to be equated with the Golden Age of Gaelic chieftainship. While Scots and Irish Gaels did not exactly make common cause in this, they did so ideologically, and to a limited extent practically, through their Royalism and Jacobitism. That Golden Age stood for autonomy of the kin group, power, self-direction and a relatively stable socio-political and economic system that was distinctively Gaelic. For these clans, Protestantism smacked of the centralist values of the nation–state. And while there were always some traditional kin groups who were prepared to go with the flow of power for fame, fortune, glory and aggrandisement, in reality most clans – including the Campbells of Argyll – had to make a choice when the outcome was not apparent.

Traditional Irish society, more so than Scottish, looked to Catholic Europe to bolster a fairly localised sense of Gaelic identity. Counter-Reformation ideas filtered to Ireland through the Irish clerics and scholars exiled on the continent, who formulated most Irish nationalist ideology. Although it was nowhere near as extensive as the Catholic regrouping that occurred in Ireland, a few Scots regulars based on the continent made occasional trips to the Highlands in the late sixteenth and early seventeenth centuries, but those Scots Jesuits who returned to the north-east of Scotland in 1582 mainly confined their work to the east coast and the peripheries of the central Highlands. However, the significance of the contact between Hugh O'Neill and the Earl of Huntly during the Ulster rebellion of the 1590s, the presence of Scottish Jesuits in O'Neill's camp, and the lines of communication which both had open to Spain have generally been underestimated in Scottish historiography. When the Catholic archbishop of Armagh, Peter Lombard (1601–25), assumed the nominal headship of the Highlands and Islands of Scotland, he saw the necessity in sending a number of Irish-speaking priests on short trips to the southern isles. But traces of only one of these remain – a Jesuit from Cork who made at least three visits to Kintyre and the southern isles.

Gaelic resistance to the alien Protestant governments was intellectually honed and morally reinforced by the dynamics of the Counter-Reformation. It is not insignificant, for example, that all the prominent confederate commanders during the civil war of the 1640s had fought as soldiers on the continent.[3] In the Highlands, too, MacDonald of Clanranald also attempted to galvanise the military might of the Counter-Reformation in 1626, to enhance his personal status in Scotland. Though his letter to the Pope stressed the links between the Scottish and Irish Gaelic chieftains and the willingness of each to proceed against their Calvinist oppressors, Clanranald was probably motivated more by the political encroachments of central government on the western seaboard than by religious issues. By that time, the lands of four clans had been appropriated, the last of which, in 1624, belonged to his near neighbours, the MacIains of Ardnamurchan.

In Scotland, those clan chiefs who chose to go with Edinburgh did so largely at the expense of the traditional relationship between chief and tenants, inevitably entering into more commercial relationships with their people. The chieftainly system had begun inexorably to decay in any case. Nevertheless, under growing pressure from central government, with their autonomy increasingly constrained and their political hands tied, those chieftains who had had an extensive powerbase – like the Clan Donald South – but chose not to become government agents often dreamed – at home, and in displaced Gaelic communities on the continent – of how things used to be. Their kin, the MacDonnells of Antrim, were one of the few élite families who managed, at least for a while, to combine a strong Catholic faith with loyalty to the Dublin government.

The role of Sir Randal MacDonnell, first Earl of Antrim, in supporting and protecting the Irish Franciscan missionaries who worked in the Highlands and Islands between 1619 and 1637 is of major importance. His motives were not exclusively spiritual, since he undoubtedly saw his involvement as an opportunity to extend his political influence in the west of Scotland by reviving contacts which would support his historic claim to the lands of the expropriated Clan Donald South. Certainly, in the 1620s the Franciscans concentrated their evangelical efforts in Kintyre and Islay and the surrounding islands. It was only after 1630, when the vigorous opposition of the Kirk in Argyll and the southern Isles became too dangerous to justify their working further south, that they confined themselves to the lands of the MacDonalds of Clanranald – South Uist, the Small Isles and Moidart. Though the Franciscans laboured under tremendous disadvantage and were constantly taxed by their small numbers (there were never more than five priests on the mission) in comparison with the extent of the territory they covered, the retention of Catholicism in many of the areas visited by these Franciscans is a testimony to the labour expended by so few exceptional Irish-speaking missionaries. Through their work, Catholicism was reintroduced to pockets of the Highlands and Islands, from Benbecula in the Outer Hebrides to Moidart in Inverness-shire.

Equally dedicated were the two Irish Vincentians who came to the Highland mission in 1652 – one serving on the mainland and one in the isles – and the Dominican who served in the Hebrides between 1663 and 1676. But from the mid-century, regular priests working as missionaries in the Highlands were subject to the Prefect-Apostolic, the secular head of the mission. The

Franciscans also kept alive their commitment to the Highlands through the MacDonnell brothers who arrived in 1668. A testament to the rigours of life as a Highland missionary, one brother died within four years, while the other left the mission under taint of political scandal in 1681. The persistence of the Catholic faith in the Highlands and Islands was less a by-product of strong social and cultural links with Ireland sustained from a previous period than of the dynamism of a few unique individuals entirely committed to their faith. The number of Irish priests in the Highlands peaked in 1687–88 under the Catholic monarch James VII, who encouraged Catholic priests on the continent to return to Scotland.

The deployment of Irish regulars to the Highland mission throughout the seventeenth century should therefore not be seen simply as an attempt to restore the Catholic faith to a marginal area of Scotland but as an extended arm of the Counter-Reformation – a far more complex beast, with immense socio-political and cultural significance. It was an arm which the MacDonnells of Antrim employed, in a circumscribed way, for their own ends. In many senses, those Scottish clans who chose to adhere to Catholicism did so to make a statement against the politics and culture of the Edinburgh government: rejection of Protestantism entailed an implicit rejection of the Establishment. Thus it was no coincidence that until the early nineteenth century the Counter-Reformation was more successful in the Highlands than in the Lowlands,[4] though after the Union of 1707 a bigger statement was made by adherence to non-juring episcopalianism. In spite of sterling efforts, the Kirk – battling against enormous odds at the outset of its own mission to the Highlands – was unable to fill benefices over vast geographical areas. This inevitably left open a window of opportunity for the clandestine reintroduction of Catholicism to those parts. And as I demonstrated in Chapters 2 and 4, it was almost exclusively Irish priests who by the end of the seventeenth century had reclaimed for Catholicism those areas of the Highlands and Islands which persist as Roman Catholic communities today.

At the same time, during the late seventeenth century, presbyterian ministers continued to be pulled across to Irish parishes, as I discussed in Chapter 3, though in markedly fewer numbers than in the 1640s. After significant entrenchment of presbyterianism during the civil war, the power of the envigorated presbyterian community in Ulster was seen as a threat to be managed by both the Scottish and Irish governments. Certainly, the Duke of Lauderdale exercised a more conciliatory policy towards the presbyterians during his rule in Scotland (as expressed in the first and second indulgences), and a similar policy was pursued in Ulster by Sir Arthur Forbes, marshal of the army in Ireland, who was responsible for instituting the *regium donum*.

The spate of migration to Ireland by Gaelic-speaking episcopal non-conformists between 1688 and 1700 was a phenomenon precipitated by the

Revolution. In the 1690s, the presbyterian pulpit functioned again – as it had fifty years earlier – as a first line against Jacobitism (Royalism). Those most clearly seen to be breaching it were deprived; some went to Ulster to minister to Gaelic-speaking Highland communities, where fear of their Jacobitism was outweighed by the dearth of Gaelic speakers. And although a handful of episcopal ministers continued to operate in the Highlands well into the eighteenth century, the flight of seven non-conforming ministers at the Revolution was still a loss that the Kirk could ill afford. Between the Revolution and the beginning of the non-subscribing controversy in Ireland, four or five ministers and a probationer entered the presbyterian church in Ulster; another probationer fled there from ecclesiastical discipline. At the same time, presbyterian dissenters in Ulster were experiencing a degree of assimilation into the wider Protestant community, which ultimately led to a decline in links with the old community in Scotland. Although there was concern about the reaction of Ulster Scots to the Union of 1707, by 1715 the presbyterians had ceased to embody an independent political interest, because they had rejected the sacramental test imposed on them in 1704 and entered the militia to defend the Protestant succession.[5] Their unified stance against a common Jacobite enemy encouraged them to pursue a Gaelic-speaking mission to the native Irish and Highland Scots in Dublin. As I explained in Chapter 5, this mission was mainly staffed by Highlanders.

Publication of the Irish Bible in Roman rather than Irish script, and its distribution, with assistance from the Hon. Robert Boyle, son of the Earl of Cork, to Gaelic-speaking Scots in the last decade of the seventeenth century, has been well documented in secondary literature.[6] Yet the infiltration of the north of Ireland by Highland ministers who did so much to nurture an embryonic Protestant faith predates this and has never been accorded the weight it merits. However, the defection of Gaelic-speaking ministers to Ulster merely exacerbated the immense problems the Kirk already had in furnishing the requisite number of ministers for the Highlands and Islands. The difficulties experienced by the Kirk in this respect have already been outlined in William Ferguson's article 'The Problems of the Established Church in the West Highlands and Islands in the Eighteenth Century' (1969). Those few probationers drawn across to Ireland in the early eighteenth century appear to have preferred to assume dissenting status in Ulster rather than take the chance of being assigned an unpopular parish in an area such as Lochaber. This was in marked distinction to the way in which Irish Catholic missionaries operated on the Highland mission; one of the major difficulties was in their constant movement from community to community in order to take the faith to as many people as possible. The eventual assignment of priests to fixed locations was largely contingent on the natural growth of the native priesthood.

This study has also made a particular addition to knowledge of the survival of specific pockets of Catholicism in the Highlands and Islands. Far from having been utterly extinguished at the end of the seventeenth century, after Cornelius Coan's lapse from the priesthood the Royal Bounty Committee expressed its fear of the growth of popery in Lewis in 1737, referring to a fourteen-strong group of Catholics, and priests were still being harboured there in the 1750s.

As I indicated in Chapter 6, the native priesthood began to assume the burdens of its own mission in the early eighteenth century, so that by 1733 there were only two Irish priests on the Highland mission. Native Highland priests may have consolidated gains made for the faith in the late seventeenth and early eighteenth centuries, but a firm foundation had earlier been laid almost exclusively by Irish regulars.

This book has, I hope, explained the importance of the Gaels in each other's religious heritage. Each faith had specific achievements and limited success in the prosecution of its overall aims: although the reformed faith was effectively established across broad areas of the Highlands and Islands by the mid-eighteenth century, relatively impregnable geographical pockets of Catholicism persisted, and although the Counter-Reformation made much greater headway in Ireland by allying itself with native Irish resistance to the English government, there was a substantial and politically powerful Protestant faction to which members of the former paid lip-service when it suited them.[7] Each faith has grown and consolidated further, but it has not always learned to live with the other.

Notes

Notes to Introduction

1. The classic discussion of this subject is G. A. Hayes-McCoy, *Scots Mercenary Forces in Ireland, 1565–1603* (Dublin and London, 1937).
2. Rev. George Hill, *An Historical Account of The MacDonnells of Antrim: Including Notices of Some Other Septs, Irish and Scottish* (Belfast, 1873, reprint Shannon 1980), p. 21.
3. Rev. John MacInnes, 'West Highland Sea Power in the Middle Ages', *TGSI*, 48, (1972–74), pp. 518–56.
4. Jane Dawson, 'The Gaidhealtachd and the emergence of the Scottish Highlands', in Brendan Bradshaw and Peter Roberts (eds.), *British Consciousness and Identity: The Making of Britain, 1533–1707* (Cambridge, 1998), pp. 279–81.
5. *A New History of Ireland*, II, p. 320; Edward J. Cowan, 'Fishers in Drumlie Waters: Clanship and Campbell Expansion in the Time of Gilleasbuig Gruamach', *TGSI*, 54, (1984–86), p. 276.
6. For its place in Irish Gaelic society, see K. Simms, 'Guesting and feasting in Gaelic Ireland', *Journal of the Royal Society of Antiquaries of Ireland*, 108 (1978), pp. 67–100. And for a general discussion of the pressures on clanship at this time, see T. M. Devine, *Clanship to Crofters' War: The Social Transformation of the Scottish Highlands* (Manchester, 1994), pp. 1–18.
7. E. Knott, *The Bardic Poems of Tadhg Dall Ó Huiginn*, I, II, Irish Texts Society, 22, 23 (London, 1922 and 1926), pp. 272, 181.
8. A. I. Macinnes, 'Scottish Gaeldom, 1638–1651: The Vernacular Response to the Covenanting Dynamic', in John Dwyer, Roger A. Mason and Alexander Murdoch (eds.), *New Perspectives on the Politics and Culture of Early Modern Scotland* (Edinburgh, 1982), p. 64. For all these issues, also see *idem*, 'Crown, Clans and *Fine*: The "Civilising" of Scottish Gaeldom, 1587–1603', *Northern Scotland*, 13 (1993), pp. 31–55.
9. Ronald Black, 'A Manuscript of Cathal Mac Muireadhaigh', *Celtica*, 10 (1973), pp. 195, 202–03.
10. See, for instance, Eric Cregeen, 'The Changing Role of the House of Argyll in the Scottish Highlands', in N. T. Phillipson and R. Mitchison (eds.), *Scotland in the Age of Improvement* (Edinburgh, 1970), pp. 5–23, and Robert A. Dodgshon, *From Chiefs to Landlords: Social and Economic Change in the Western Highlands and Islands, c. 1493–1820* (Edinburgh, 1998).

11. For views on the increasing taste of the Gaelic élite for Lowland life and luxury goods, see Frances J. Shaw, *The Northern and Western Islands of Scotland: Their Economy And society in The Seventeenth Century* (Edinburgh, 1980).
12. L. M. Cullen and T. C. Smout, *Comparative Aspects of Scottish and Irish Economic and Social History 1600–1900* (Edinburgh, 1977).
13. T. M. Devine and D. Dickson, *Ireland and Scotland 1600–1850. Parallels and Contrasts in Economic and Social History, 1600–1900* (Edinburgh, 1983).
14. R. Mitchison and P. Roebuck (eds.), *Economy and Society in Scotland and Ireland, 1500–1939* (Edinburgh, 1988).
15. S. J. Conolly, R. A. Houston, and R. J. Morris (eds.), *Conflict, Identity and Economic Development: Ireland and Scotland, 1660–1939* (Preston, 1995).
16. David Stevenson, *Scottish Covenanters and Irish Confederates* (Belfast, 1981); *idem*, *Revolution and Counter-Revolution in Scotland, 1644–1651* (London, 1977); *idem*, *The Scottish Revolution, 1637–1644* (Newton Abbot, 1973); and specifically from a Highland perspective in *idem*, *Alasdair MacColla and the Highland Problem in the Seventeenth Century* (Edinburgh, 1980).
17. Jane H. Ohlemeyer, *Civil War and Restoration in the Three Stuart Kingdoms: The Career of Randal MacDonnell, Marquis of Antrim, 1609–1683* (Cambridge, 1993).
18. Derick Thomson, 'The MacMhuirich Bardic family', *TGSI*, 43 (1966), pp. 276–304; *idem*, 'The Poetry of Niall MacMhuirich', *TGSI*, 46 (1970), pp. 281–307; *idem*, 'Niall Mòr MacMhuirich', *TGSI*, 49 (1977), pp. 9–25; *idem*, 'Three Seventeenth Century Bardic Poets: Niall Mòr, Cathal and Niall MacMhuirich', in A. J. Aitken, M. P. McDiarmid and D. S. Thomson (eds.), *Bards and Makars* (Glasgow, 1977), pp. 221–46.
19. Ronald Black, 'Poems by Maol Domhnaigh Ó Muirgheasáin', I, II, III, *Scottish Gaelic Studies*, 12 (1976), pp. 194–208; 13 pt. 1 (1978), pp. 46–55; 13 pt. 2 (1981), pp. 289–301.
20. John Bannerman, *The Beatons: A Medical Kindred in the Classical Gaelic Tradition* (Edinburgh, 1986).
21. An organisation whose purpose was to propagate the faith in newly discovered lands, reconcile schismatic oriental churches and also take some responsibility for countries such as Scotland which had lapsed into heresy.
22. Cathaldus Giblin, *The Irish Franciscan Mission to Scotland, 1619–1646. Documents from Roman Archives* (Dublin, 1964).
23. See *ibid.*; Cathaldus Giblin, 'The Mission to the Highlands and the Isles *c.* 1670', *Franciscan College Annual* (MultyFarnham, 1954), pp. 7–20.
24. James Kirk, 'The Kirk and the Highlands at the Reformation', *Northern Scotland*, 7, no. 1 (1986), p. 1.
25. F. G. Thompson, 'The Folklore Elements in 'Carmina Gadelica', *TGSI*, 44 (1967), pp. 229, 239–40.
26. Alexander Carmichael, *Carmina*

Gadelica (Edinburgh, 1940), III, p. 118.

27. Alan Ford, 'The Protestant Reformation in Ireland', in Ciaran Brady and Raymond Gillespie (eds.), *Natives and Newcomers: Essays on the Making of Irish Colonial Society, 1534–1641* (Dublin, 1986), p. 72.
28. See Chapter 1, section headed 'Effect of the Plantation of Ulster on Religious Connections'.
29. PRONI D1759/1A/1 & 2, Presbytery of Antrim, 1654–1658, 1671–1691.
30. PRONI D1759/1E/1 & 2, Presbytery of Lagan, 1672–1679, 1679–1695. As noted in Chapter 1 below, 'prescopalian' is a word coined to describe Scots employed in the Church of Ireland who cherished presbyterianism within an episcopal fold. Rev. Professor A. F. Scott Pearson, 'Puritan and Presbyterian Settlements in Ireland, 1560–1660', II, (Belfast, 1948), p. 582.
31. According to Edward Furgol, only slightly more than one in ten Scottish Kirk Session records survive. Edward Mackie Furgol, 'The Religious Aspects of the Scottish Covenanting Armies, 1639–1651' (DPhil dissertation, University of Oxford, 1982), p. 162.
32. Duncan C. Mactavish (ed.), *Minutes of the Synod of Argyll, 1639–1651*, SHS, 3rd series, 37 (Edinburgh, 1943); Duncan C. Mactavish (ed.), *Minutes of the Synod of Argyll, 1652–1661*, SHS, 3rd series, 38 (Edinburgh, 1944); NAS CH2/557/3–7, Synod book of Argyll, 1687–1700, 1701–1707, 1708–1727, 1728–1755, 1756–1775.
33. Mactavish, *Minutes of the Synod of Argyll, 1639–1651*, p. xii.
34. NAS CH2/1153/1–4, Presbytery books of Kintyre, 1655–1706, 1707–1723, 1723–1748, 1749–1794.
35. Anson, *Underground Catholicism*, p. 77.
36. *IFM*, p. 74.
37. D. O. Blundell, *The Catholic Highlands of Scotland. The Western Highlands and Islands*, II (Edinburgh, 1917), p. 3.
38. *IFM*, p. xii.

Notes to Chapter 1: Gaelic Attitudes to Religion, 1560–*c*.1619

1. *A New History of Ireland*, III, pp. 56, 61.
2. Mícheál Mac Craith, 'The Gaelic reaction to the Reformation', in S. Ellis and S. Barber (eds.), *Conquest and Union: Fashioning a British State, 1485–1725* (London, 1995), p. 140.
3. Alan Ford, 'The Protestant Reformation in Ireland', in Ciaran Brady and Raymond Gillespie (eds.), *Natives and Newcomers: Essays on the Making of Irish Colonial Society, 1534–1641* (Dublin, 1986), pp. 50–51.
4. Ford, 'Reformation in Ireland', pp. 51–53.
5. Michael Perceval-Maxwell, 'The Ulster Plantation: Scotland's First Colonial Venture', *Scottish Colloquium Proceedings*, 2 (Guelph, 1969), p. 13.
6. Ford, 'Reformation in Ireland', pp. 52–55, 57–58.
7. K. Bottigheimer, 'The Failure of the Reformation in Ireland: Une

Question Bien Posée', *The Journal of Ecclesiastical History*, 36 (1985), p. 197.

8. *A New History of Ireland,* III, pp. 103–09, 190; Colm Lennon, 'The Counter-Reformation in Ireland, 1542–1641', in Brady and Gillespie (eds.), *Natives and Newcomers*, p. 85.
9. Lennon, 'Counter-Reformation in Ireland', pp. 76–77, 87; Bottigheimer, 'The Failure of the Reformation in Ireland', p. 198.
10. Bottigheimer, 'The Failure of the Reformation in Ireland', p. 198.
11. Ford, 'Reformation in Ireland', pp. 59–61.
12. Christine Johnston, *Developments in the Roman Catholic Church in Scotland, 1789–1829* (Edinburgh, 1983), p. 33; Michael Lynch, *Scotland: A New History* (London, 1992), p. 197.
13. D. E. R. Watt, *Fasti Ecclesiae Scoticanae Medii Aevi ad Annum 1638* (Edinburgh, 1969), pp. 205–07, 209, 227–28; James Kirk, 'The Kirk and the Highlands at the Reformation', *Northern Scotland*, 7 (1986), p. 10; *idem*, 'John Carswell, Superintendent of Argyll', in *idem*, *Patterns of Reform: Continuity and Change in the Reformation Kirk* (Edinburgh, 1989), pp. 284–85; *idem*, 'The Jacobean Church in the Highlands, 1567–1625', in Loraine MacLean of Dochgarroch (ed.), *The Seventeenth Century in the Highlands* (Inverness, 1986), pp. 29, 38, 43.
14. Kirk, 'The Jacobean Church', pp. 29, 43; Watt, *Fasti,* pp. 270, 61; E. B. Fryde, D. E. Greenway, S. Porter, and I. Roy (eds.), *Handbook of British Chronology*, 3rd edition (London, 1986), p. 319; Kirk, 'The Kirk and the Highlands at the Reformation', pp. 10–11; David Laing (ed.), *The Miscellany of the Wodrow Society*, I (Edinburgh, 1844), p. 335. See section headed 'Effect of the Plantation of Ulster on Religious Connections', below .
15. Gordon Donaldson, *Scotland, James V to James VII* (Edinburgh, 1971), p. 111.
16. See section headed 'Catholic Conformers and Protestant Reformers', below.
17. Margaret H. B. Sanderson, 'Catholic Recusancy in Scotland in the Sixteenth Century', *Innes Review*, 21 (1970), pp. 88–89. In addition there were four deprivations in Roxburghshire and Fife.
18. See Chapter 2, 'The Franciscan Mission to the Highlands and Islands, 1619–1637', for details.
19. J. L. Campbell, 'The Catholic Church in the Hebrides: 1560–1760', *The Tablet*, 206, no. 6032 (31 December 1955), p. 655.
20. J. L. Campbell, 'The Catholic Church', p. 655.
21. Kirk, 'The Jacobean Church', pp. 47, 38.
22. One of these financial series has recently been published in its entirety: see James Kirk, *The Books of Assumption of Thirds Benefices: Scottish Ecclesiastical Rentals at the Reformation*, Records of Social and Economic History, New Series, 21 (Oxford, 1995).
23. 'The Kirk and the Highlands at the Reformation', pp. 1, 17–18; Rev. John MacInnes, 'Baptism in the Highlands', *RSCHS*, 13 (1959), p. 4; Hew Scott *et al.* (eds.), *Fasti Ecclesiae Scoticanae*, 10 vols.

(Edinburgh, 1915–1981), IV, pp. 2, 5, 8, 13, 15, 22, 27, 28, 81, 86, 91, 98, 100, 96, 88, 30, 36, 94, 44.

24. See John Carswell, below. The synod of Argyll, comprising the presbyteries of Dunoon, Kinloch, Inveraray, Kilmore and Skye, was not erected until 18 December 1638. *Fasti*, IV, p. 1. See Fig. 3.1 for the extent of the jurisdiction of the synod of Argyll.
25. *Fasti*, VII, p. 205.
26. See below.
27. 'A Description of the Westerne Iles of Scotland called Hybrides. Compyled by Mr. Donald Monro Deane of the Iles. 1549', *MacFarlane's Geographical Collections*, III, SHS, 53 (1908), p. 300. See the four parishes of Lewis in Fig. 5.1.
28. 'The Kirk and the Highlands at the Reformation', pp. 7, 12–13, 15–16, for references to the provision of benefices in Ross; Kirk, 'The Jacobean Church', p. 35; Laing, *Miscellany*, p. 334. Frances Shaw, 'Sources of the History of the Seventeenth Century in the Highlands', in Loraine MacLean of Dochgarroch (ed.), *The Seventeenth Century in the Highlands* (Inverness, 1986), p. 18.
29. *Fasti*, VII, pp. 1, 4, 8, 10, 14, 17, 18, 21, 25, 30, 32, 36, 38, 39, 41, 46, 49, 51, 53, 56, 58, 60, 62, 65, 70, 74, 144, 146, 151, 154, 156, 159, for Caithness; *Fasti*, VII, pp. 77, 79, 81, 83, 86, 89, 92, 95, 97, 101, 106, 113, 116, 118, 121, 125, 128, 132, 135, 138, 140.
30. MacInnes, 'Baptism in the Highlands', p. 4. Bruce was Moderator of the General Assembly which met on 6 February 1588 to consider the means of defence against the threatened invasion of the Spanish Armada. Moderator again in May 1592, Bruce was a very skilled preacher, but he fell out of favour with the King in 1596 when (with others) he opposed James's prelatic tendencies and was banished from Edinburgh. Ordered to leave Edinburgh again, in August 1600 over the Gowrie Conspiracy, Bruce was prohibited from preaching anywhere in Scotland on pain of death. From 1605 to 1609 he was confined to Inverness, where he is said to have met harsh treatment from Lord Enzie, but his preaching was appreciated by many of his friends and others besides. He was banished to Inverness a second time in 1620, remaining there until 1624, but since he was ill and weak it is doubtful if his impact there was in any way comparable to what he achieved on the earlier visit. *Fasti*, I, pp. 54–55.
31. For more on this, see Chapter 5.
32. Kirk, 'John Carswell', pp. 282–83.
33. Sanderson, 'Catholic Recusancy in Scotland in the Sixteenth Century', p. 103. Some converts to Protestantism were clearly made at the expense of Catholicism: in 1587 there had been a complaint in the General Assembly that in Ross 'there is a great coldness amongst all, both gentlemen and commons ... since the Jesuits had liberty to pass through the country in the time of the earl of Huntly's lieutenancy'. *Ibid.*, p. 97.
34. See Chapter 2.
35. *RPCS*, 1616–1619, pp. 467–68.
36. Robert Pitcairn, *Ancient Criminial Trials in Scotland, 1609–1615*, 3, pt. 1, Maitland Club (Edinburgh, 1832), pp. 26–27; Donald Gregory, *The History of the Western*

Highlands and Isles of Scotland, from A.D. 1493 to A.D. 1625 (London and Glasgow, 2nd edition, 1881), pp. 386–88; *RPCS*, 1616–1619, pp. 467–68, 507–08.

37. R. L. Thomson (ed.), collected by the late Angus Matheson, *Foirm na h-urrnuidheadh; John Carswell's Gaelic Translation of the Book of Common Order*, Scottish Gaelic Texts Society (Edinburgh, 1970), p. 10.
38. John Bannerman, 'Literacy in the Highlands', in Ian B. Cowan and Duncan Shaw (eds.), *The Renaissance and Reformation in Scotland* (Edinburgh, 1983), pp. 214, 216, 218, 221, 228–29, 234–35.
39. Bannerman, 'Literacy in the Highlands', p. 234.
40. For more on devotional material in Gaelic, see section headed 'The Jesuit Missions', below, and Chapter 5, 'Shared Resources'.
41. Terence P. McCaughey, 'Protestantism and Scottish Highland Culture', in James P. Mackey (ed.), *An Introduction to Celtic Christianity* (Edinburgh, 1989), p. 176.
42. Donald Meek, 'The Gaelic Bible', in David F. Wright (ed.), *The Bible in Scottish Life and Literature* (Edinburgh, 1988), p. 9.
43. Thomson, *Foirm na h-urrnuidheadh*, pp. 12, 179–80.
44. McCaughey, 'Protestantism and Scottish Highland Culture', p. 175.
45. Kirk, 'John Carswell', pp. 294–95.
46. Sanderson, 'Catholic Recusancy in Scotland in the Sixteenth Century', p. 106.
47. Kirk, 'John Carswell', pp. 280, 293; *idem*, 'The Kirk and the Highlands at the Reformation', p. 18.
48. *Minutes of the Synod of Argyll*, I; *Minutes of the Synod of Argyll*, II; NAS CH2/557/3–6, Proceedings of the Synod of Argyll, 1687–1755; NAS CH1/5/51, Royal Bounty Records 1725–1730.
49. Ian B. Cowan, *The Parishes of Medieval Scotland*, Scottish Record Society, 93 (Edinburgh, 1967), p. 198.
50. J. B. Craven (ed.), *Records of the Dioceses of Argyll and the Isles, 1560–1860* (Kirkwall, 1907), 'Report by Thomas Knox, Bishop of the Isles, of the State of his Diocese, 1626', p. 47; *Fasti*, IV, p. 119; Nicholas Maclean-Bristol, *Warriors and Priests: The History of the Clan Maclean, 1300–1570* (East Linton, 1995), p. 141; MacInnes, 'Baptism in the Highlands', p. 5.
51. *Fasti*, VII, pp. 70, 111, 119.
52. J. R. N. MacPhail (ed.), *Highland Papers*, IV, SHS, 3rd series, 22 (Edinburgh, 1934), pp. 226–27.
53. Craven, 'Report by Thomas Knox', p. 49.
54. *Fasti*, VII, p. 174. The island of Muck formed part of the parish of Eigg, while Rhum formed part of the parish of Canna. In the sixteenth century, the three parishes of Eigg, Canna and Strath or Strathswordale in Skye had been united.
55. Cosmo Innes, James B. Brichan, *et al.* (eds.), *Origines Parochiales Scotiae* (henceforth *OPS*), 3 vols. (Edinburgh, 1850–1855), II, pt. 1, Dioceses of Argyll and the Isles (Edinburgh, 1854), pp. 358, 377. See next page.
56. *Fasti*, VII, pp. 166, 168.
57. 'A Description of the Westerne Iles of Scotland called Hybrides', p. 281.
58. Iona Club, *Collectanea de Rebus*

Albanicis (Edinburgh, 1847), p. 13. The obligation is recorded in the General Register of Deeds, 19, on 16 June 1581.

59. He does not appear in the revised *Fasti*.
60. *Fasti*, VII, p.171.
61. David McRoberts and Alexander Boyle, 'A Hebridean Cisiojanus', *Innes Review*, 21, no. 2 (1970), pp. 108–10; William O'Sullivan, 'An Irish cisiojanus', *Collectanea Hibernica*, 29 (1988), p. 8.
62. J. L. Campbell, *Canna – The Story of a Hebridean Island* (Oxford, 1984), pp. 56–57; Kirk, 'The Jacobean Church', p. 39.
63. *Fasti*, VII, p. 194. It seems likely that John MacKinnon was the minister of Bracadale in Skye. See Chapter 2, section headed 'The Advancing Tide of Protestantism'. Thus the first resident minister of South Uist was not appointed until some time before 6 May 1642.
64. For further discussion, see Chapter 2, section headed 'Problems, Difficulties and Extenuating Circumstances'.
65. A company of Lowlanders licensed to promote fishing in Lewis, the Fife Adventurers had abandoned Stornoway by 1610, leaving their patent with MacKenzie of Seaforth. John R. Elder, *The Royal Fishery Companies of the Seventeenth Century* (Glasgow, 1912), p. 31.
66. *Fasti*, VII, pp. 189–91, 199, 205, 207–08; Kirk, 'The Jacobean Church', p. 38; *Collectanea de Rebus Albanicis*, pp. 6–8; I. F. Grant, *The MacLeods: The History of a Clan* (Edinburgh, 1981), pp. 195, 206.
67. Donaldson, *Scotland*, p. 152; M. H. B. Sanderson, 'Roman Catholic Recusancy 1560–1603', in Peter McNeill and Ranald Nicolson (eds.), *An Historical Atlas of Scotland* (St. Andrews, 1975), p. 89.
68. Donaldson, *Scotland*, pp. 146–47.
69. For instance, in the diocese of the Isles at the end of the fifteenth and early sixteenth centuries, eight churches were appropriated to the bishop of the Isles, thirteen to the abbey of Iona, two to the nunnery of Iona, two to the priory of Oronsay, one to the Chapel Royal in Stirling, and another to the collegiate church of Restalrig. Nineteen or twenty churches remained unappropriated, 'which included all four parish churches in Lewis, all three in Islay, six or seven in Skye, two in Uist and one each in Barra, Eigg, Gigha and Harris [which] were exempted not because their teinds were undesirable but because of their very remoteness from the claims of appropriating institutions'. The situation was similar in the diocese of Argyll. Fourteen churches were unappropriated, eight of them in Morvern where there was no religious institution to appropriate them. Ian B. Cowan, 'The Medieval Church in Argyll and the Isles', *RSCHS*, 20 (1980), p. 26.
70. *Collectanea de Rebus Albanicis*, p. 13.
71. *RPCS*, 1607–1610, pp. 26–27.
72. Handfasting was mainly practised among the élite of the clan, apparently in order to ensure lineal succession. It was a contract by which a man and woman agreed to live together for a year and a day. If the woman proved fertile within that period, the marriage was legalised even though there

had been no ceremony. If there was no sign of issue, both parties were at liberty to handfast with or marry others. Frank Adam, *The Clans, Septs and Regiments of the Scottish Highlands* (Edinburgh and London, 1934), p. 29.

73. *RPCS*, 1616–1619, p. 777.
74. Campbell, *Canna*, p. 47.
75. James Gordon was the fifth son of the fourth Earl of Gordon and an uncle of the sixth Earl of Huntly. Donald MacLean, *The Counter-Reformation in Scotland, 1560–1930* (London, 1931), pp. 30, 62–63.
76. A. and A. MacDonald, *Clan Donald*, 3 vols. (Inverness, 1896, 1900, 1904), II, p. 759. It might be questioned, though there is no definite corroborative evidence, whether any priests had visited Skye by the late 1580s because MacLeod of Dunvegan's name was included in a list appointing various lairds to expel Jesuit priests, beggars and malefactors from the country as part of the precautions surrounding the Armada scare. Grant, *The MacLeods*, p. 180.
77. Lynch, *Scotland*, p. 198.
78. Campbell, *Canna*, p. 47.
79. On this topic see W. D. H. Sellar, 'Marriage, Divorce and Concubinage in Gaelic Scotland', *TGSI*, 51 (1978–80), pp. 464–93.
80. J. Bain *et al.* (eds.), *Calendar of State Papers Relating to Scotland and Mary, Queen of Scots, 1547–1603*, 13 vols. (Edinburgh, 1898–1969), 1595–1597, p. 203. Campbell's 'Observations' are also published in Joseph Robertson (ed.), 'Observations of Mr Dioness Campbell, Deane of Limerick, on the West Isles of Scotland. A.D. 1596', in *Miscellany of the Maitland Club*, IV, pt. 1 (Glasgow, 1847), pp. 35–57.
81. MacPhail, *Highland Papers, IV*, p. 227.
82. MacPhail, *Highland Papers, IV*, pp. 226–27.
83. James VI and I, *Basilicon Doron 1599* (Menston, 1969 facsimile reprint), pp. 42–43, 49–50, 52.
84. See section headed 'The Jesuit Missions', below.
85. *CSPI*, 1574–85, pp. 92–93.
86. M. Perceval-Maxwell, *The Scottish Migration to Ulster in the Reign of James I* (London, 1973), p. 2.
87. The renegade priest and redshank, John Eldar, a native of Caithness, explained to Henry VIII *c.* 1543 the term redshank when used of Highland mercenaries: 'Moreover ... they call us in Scotland Reddshankes, and in your Grace's dominion of England roghe footide Scottis' because in both summer and winter, except when the frost was most vehement, they always went "bair leggide and bair footide".' *Collectanea de Rebus Albanicis*, pp. 23–24, 26, 28.
88. *CSPS*, 1595–1597, pp. 186, 198–99.
89. *CSPS*, 1597–1603, pt. 2, pp. 668, 778; Sir James Balfour Paul, *The Scots Peerage*, 9 vols. (Edinburgh, 1904–1914), I, p. 349.
90. *CSPI*, 1599–1600, p. 360; *CSPI*, 1600–1601, p. 352.
91. A. F. Scott Pearson, 'Puritan and Presbyterian Settlements in Ireland 1560–1660', I (unpublished typescript, Belfast, 1948), p. 135; Perceval-Maxwell, *Scottish Migration to Ulster*, p. 255.
92. Ford, 'Reformation in Ireland', p. 54, quoting Public Record Office (London), State Papers, 63/222/111.

iii.

93. Bottigheimer, 'The Failure of the Reformation in Ireland', pp. 201–03.
94. Scott Pearson, 'Puritan and Presbyterian Settlements in Ireland 1560–1660', I, p. 136; *Handbook of British Chronology*, p. 381.
95. Perceval-Maxwell, *Scottish Migration to Ulster*, pp. 255–58; David Stevenson, *Alasdair MacColla and the Highland Problem in the Seventeenth Century* (Edinburgh, 1980), p. 38.
96. *A New History of Ireland*, III, pp. 139–40.
97. Ford, 'Reformation in Ireland', pp. 61–62, quoting M. C. Griffith (ed.), *Irish Patent Rolls of James I* (Dublin, 1966), p. 471.
98. Ford, 'Reformation in Ireland', p. 63.
99. Scott Pearson, 'Puritan and Presbyterian Settlements in Ireland, 1560–1660', I, p. 136.
100. Perceval-Maxwell, *Scottish Migration to Ulster*, pp. 255–56, p. 253 note.
101. For which see Chapter 2, 'The Franciscan Mission to the Highlands and Islands, 1619–1637'.
102. The first instance I have found of 'Scottish Gallic' is on 5 August 1751 in the records of the Synod of Argyll. NAS CH2/557/6, Synod Book of Argyll, 1728–1755, fol. 315. Yet a contrary piece of evidence occurring earlier (in Scotland itself) must be pointed out in reference to Donald Munro, who conformed to Protestantism and became the first incumbent of Kiltearn and Lemlair in Ross-shire. Although an initial complaint had been made about his ineptitude in 1564, there was an additional complaint on 5 July 1570 that he was 'not prompt in the Scottish tongue'. This presumably meant that he could not communicate with Lowland ministers – in Easter Ross, for example – in Scots, rather than that he could not speak Gaelic. *Fasti*, VII, p. 40.
103. Perceval-Maxwell, *Scottish Migration to Ulster*, p. 253 note.
104. Scott Pearson, 'Puritan and Presbyterian Settlements in Ireland, 1560–1660', I, p. 81.
105. However, the Catholic John Campbell of Irvine (see below), is also thought to have attended Glasgow University.
106. A. F. O'D. Alexander (ed.), 'The O'Kane Papers', pt. II, Bishop Montgomery's Survey of the Bishoprics of Derry, Raphoe and Clogher, *Analecta Hibernica*, 12 (1943), p. 102.
107. Alexander, 'The O'Kane papers', pp. 103–04.
108. Alexander, 'The O'Kane papers', p. 105. Campbell's appointment was made during the period (1571–1604) when the See was unfilled by the crown. *Handbook of British Chronology*, p. 382.
109. I am grateful to Professor Archibald Duncan for pointing this out.
110. Iain Murray Bishop, 'The Education of Ulster Students at Glasgow University during the Eighteenth Century' (unpublished MA thesis, Queen's University, Belfast, 1987), pp. 18–19. The school was later referred to by the Rev. John Livingstone, who graduated MA from Glasgow in 1621.
111. Perceval-Maxwell, *Scottish Migration to Ulster*, pp. 24, 47, 50, 256–57; Timothy Paul Joseph

McCall, 'The Gaelic Background to the Settlement of Antrim and Down 1580–1641' (unpublished MA dissertation, Queen's University, Belfast, 1983), p. 63; Ernest Raymond Gillespie, 'East Ulster in the Early Seventeenth Century: A Colonial Economy and Society' (PhD thesis, Trinity College Dublin, 1982), pp. 5, 83–84. See the now published *idem*, *Colonial Ulster: The Settlement of East Ulster, 1600–1641* (Cork, 1985). Braidstane is 'Stane' in the parish of Irvine. *Registrum Secreti Sigilli Regum Scotorum,* VII, 1575–1580, 77. Stane Castle, NS3339.

112. Scott Pearson, 'Puritan and Presbyterian Settlements in Ireland, 1560–1660', II, p. 497, quoting *CSPI*, 1608–10, p. 444, no. 748.

113. For details, see Perceval-Maxwell, *Scottish Migration to Ulster*, pp. 259–60; Scott Pearson, 'Puritan and Presbyterian Settlements in Ireland 1560– 1660', II, pp. 500–01.

114. Scott Pearson, 'Puritan and Presbyterian Settlements in Ireland, 1560–1660', II, p. 502; A. F. Scott Pearson, 'Alumni of St. Andrews and the Settlement of Ulster', *UJA*, 3rd series, 14 (1951), p. 7; H. R. Trevor-Roper, *Archbishop Laud, 1573–1645* (London, 2nd edition, 1962), pp. 29, 238–241.

115. Scott Pearson, 'Puritan and Presbyterian Settlements in Ireland 1560–1660', II, pp. 582–83; *Handbook of British Chronology*, p. 379. For greater detail, see Chapter 2, section headed 'The Advancing Tide of Protestantism'.

116. Perceval-Maxwell, *Scottish Migration to Ulster*, pp. 260–01, quoting *CSPI*, 1611–14, pp. 149, 315, *CSPI*, 1615–25, p. 3; Scott Pearson, 'Puritan and Presbyterian Settlements in Ireland, 1560–1660', II, pp. 498–500.

117. See 'Introduction'. His son, Mr Timothy Pont, minister of Dunnet in Caithness, a mathematician, geographer and Lord of Session, was successful in an application for a grant of land in the Ulster plantation; on 25 July 1609 he received a Crown grant of 2,000 acres for an outlay of £400. This is one of the few grants ever made to a resident in the north of Scotland, but it should also be made clear that Dunnet was one of a group of English-speaking parishes in the north of Caithness and, though north of the Highland line, it was not culturally or linguistically part of the *Gaidhealtachd* (see Fig. 2.1). Timothy, the eldest son of Robert Pont (the former minister of St. Cuthbert's in Edinburgh) had retained influential Lowland connections. Perceval-Maxwell, *Scottish Migration to Ulster*, p. 95; C. W. J. Withers, 'The Highland Parishes in 1698: An Examination of Sources for the Definition of the Gaidhealtachd', *Scottish Studies*, 24 (1980), pp. 79, 85; *Fasti*, VII, p. 119.

118. Denization was the process by which settlers became denizens or were admitted to the rights of a citizen of Ireland (and England).

119. J. M. Barkley, 'Some Scottish Bishops and Ministers in the Irish Church, 1605–35', in Duncan Shaw (ed.), *Reformation and Revolution*, Essays presented to The Very Reverend Principal Emeritus Hugh Watt (Edinburgh, 1967), p. 152; Scott Pearson, 'Alumni of St. Andrews and the Settlement of Ulster', p. 12. Note

that Pont does not appear in the Visitation Roll of 1622, for which see Chapter 2, section headed 'The Advancing Tide of Protestantism'. This perhaps indicates that he was technically working outwith the fold of the Church but under the protection of Knox.

120. For more on whom see Chapter 3, section headed 'Mr Dugald Campbell', in connection with his namesake cousin from Argyll.

121. Scott Pearson, 'Alumni of St. Andrews and the Settlement of Ulster', p. 12. A student of that name matriculated at St. Andrews at the same time as Adair (St. Salvator's, 1593), then dean of Raphoe, graduating MA in 1597. 'Another Dugald Campbell took his M.A. at Glasgow in the same year as Bishop Knox (1579). Which was the minister of Conwal it is not easy to determine.' Although geography makes it more likely that Campbell went to Glasgow University, he was still alive in 1653, possibly even in 1657 (see Chapter 3), when he would then have been 98. While this was not impossible, it is perhaps more likely that he graduated from St. Andrews in 1597. As such, he probably formed part of a whole group of St. Andrews graduates who figure prominently amongst the earliest clerical settlers in Ulster.

122. Scott Pearson, 'Puritan and Presbyterian Settlements in Ireland, 1560–1660', II, p. 504.

123. Sanderson, 'Roman Catholic Recusancy 1560–1603', p. 89; *RPCS*, 1625–1627, p. cxvii; Kirk, 'The Kirk and the Highlands at the Reformation', pp. 4–5, 8–9, 11.

124. Niall MacMhuirich, the writer of the history, got this date wrong: John Moydartach died ten years later in 1584. Hugh Montgomery-Massingberd (editorial director), *Burke's Genealogical and Heraldic History of the Landed Gentry*, 18th edition, 3 (London, 1972), p. 568.

125. Kilmory in Arisaig already had a church in 1506 before John Moydartach became chief, therefore his church was presumably a new one. Archdeacon Monro noted that there was a parish church in Kildonan in Eigg in 1549. *OPS*, II, pp. 200, 335.

126. Alexander Cameron, *Reliquiae Celticae*, II (Inverness, 1894), pp. 170–71. This volume contains the Gaelic text and an English translation of 'The Book of Clanranald', pp. 138–309. One of John Moydartach's namesakes was buried in the chapel almost a century later. 'Anno domini 1670 an bhliadhna do theasda Eoin muideordach anéirisgáigh anuibhisd 7 do cuiredh achorp an Thogh mór.' (1670 [was] the year in which John Moydartach (son of Donald) died at Eriskay, in Uist, and his body was interred in Howmore.) *Ibid*., pp. 206–07.

127. See Chapter 6, section headed 'Presbyterian Counter-Attack'.

128. *CSPI*, 1574–1585, p. cxvi.

129. J. L. Campbell, 'The MacNeils of Barra and the Irish Franciscans', *Innes Review*, 5 (1954), p. 34.

130. See Chapter 4, section headed 'The Vincentians'.

131. Campbell, *Canna*, p. 44.

132. Ian B. Cowan and David E. Easson, *Medieval Religious Houses, Scotland* (London and New York, 2nd edition, 1976), pp. 22–23.

133. *Collectanea de Rebus Albanicis*, pp. 1–4, 15–18.
134. Maclean-Bristol, *Warriors and Priests*, pp. 154–55.
135. Neither this form nor anything close to it appears in William Grant and David D. Murison, *The Scottish National Dictionary* (Edinburgh, 1956), or in Sir William A. Craigie, *A Dictionary of the Older Scottish Tongue* (Chicago and London, 1937), but it would seem to have the sense of 'coyne' – that is *coinnmheadh*, or tribute levied in the form of billeting.
136. 'Gerig' is not noted in Grant and Murison, *The Scottish National Dictionary*, or Craigie, *A Dictionary of the Older Scottish Tongue*. I am not clear what it means – possibly jury service or galley service?
137. *Collectanea de Rebus Albanicis*, pp. 1–4, 15–18.
138. *Collectanea de Rebus Albanicis*, p. 161.
139. *RPCS*, 1625–1627, pp. cxxxii–iv; Allan I. Macinnes, 'The Origin and Organisation of the Covenanting Movement during the Reign of Charles I, with a Particular Reference to the West of Scotland', 2 vols. (PhD thesis, University of Glasgow, 1987), I, pp. 13–16.
140. It should be noted that further attempts were made to regain the church lands feued to MacLean of Duart in the sixteenth century under Charles I's revocation of Church property gifted to laymen since 1540. MacLean had since lost Islay and Jura to the Campbells, but the Kirk had been attempting to regain Iona without success since 1612. In 1635 the King wrote to Sir Lachlan MacLean commanding that 'furthwith you restore unto the Bishop (of the Isles) the absolute possession of the said Island (Iona) without further hearing or delay'. Nicholas MacLean-Bristol, 'The MacLeans from 1560–1707: A Re-appraisal', in Loraine MacLean of Dochgarroch (ed.), *The Seventeenth Century in the Highlands* (Inverness, 1986), pp. 81–82.
141. *Collectanea de Rebus Albanicis*, pp. 161–79, quoting *Registrum Magni Sigilli*, lib. 37, no. 130. The original reads: 'AC ETIAM quinque mercatas terrarum de Narrabolsadh cum pertinentibus jacentes in dicta Insula de Ylay, finibus lie ruidis nuncupatis ejusdem infra Vicecomitatum predictum olim ad prefatum monasterium Derrense attintentes.' (And also five merklands of Narrabolsadh with pertinents lying on the said island of Islay, with the borders of the same called the Rhinns within the aforesaid sheriffdom, formerly pertaining to the aforesaid monastery of Derry.) I am indebted to Dr. John Durkan for this translation. The former link with the monastery of Derry did not necessarily impute religious ties between Islay and Derry but is undoubtedly further evidence of secularisation of Kirk lands. The reddendo payable from Narrabolsadh was 'sixty ells or yards of cloth – white, black, and grey respectively' (or a money conversion at 8d a yard) – presumably for monks' habits. *Collectanea de Rebus Albanicis*, pp. 173 n., 179. The Derry link is further ratified in the next century, for which see J. R. N. MacPhail

(ed.), *Highland Papers I, 1337–1680*, SHS, 2nd series, 5 (Edinburgh, 1914), 'Papers relating to the MacLeans of Duart, 1670–1680', pp. 251–52. A lavatorial explanation of how the abbey came to hold the land in the first place is given in a memorandum dated 16 April 1659, which refers to the lands of MacLean of Duart. 'As for that roume in Ila pertaining to the Abacie of Derie our Scheanachies or as Buchannane calls them Senetiones doe affirme that the same was mortified to the Abacie of Derrie in Ireland by M'Donald of Ila For ane untymeous fart he did let go, This I bot tell you by the way.' J. R. N. MacPhail (ed.), *Highland Papers III, 1662–1677*, SHS, 2nd series, 20 (Edinburgh, 1920), p. 67 n. While amusing, this anecdote smacks of the poetic satire of the *seanchaidh*, who would be well aware of the longstanding feud between the MacLeans and MacDonalds over the Rhinns of Islay. It was probably written to humiliate the MacDonalds further (because it is hard to imagine that MacLean would not have been man enough or covetous enough to brazen it out).

142. See the account of the Minims, below.
143. See the section headed 'The Jesuit Missions', below.
144. *CSPI*, 1574–1585, p. 175.
145. About 2,000 Scots were massacred the next day at Ardnarea by the English.
146. *CSPI*, 1586–1588, p. 178.
147. One of these O'Haras was named in May 1589 by the Lord Deputy, who stated that the Sheriff of Roscommon had 'taken Tymolter Oge O'Hara, a good subject (who was guide against the Scots of Ardnary)'. *CSPI*, 1588–1592, p. 196.
148. *Calendar of Scottish Papers, 1595–1597*, p. 204; MacLean-Bristol, 'The MacLeans from 1560–1707', p. 80.
149. Loraine MacLean of Dochgarroch (ed.), *The Seventeenth Century in the Highlands* (Inverness, 1986), pp. 79–81.
150. John Durkan, 'Catholic Survival in the West of Scotland', *St. Peter's College Magazine*, 21, no. 82 (1954), pp. 89–90.
151. Durkan, 'Catholic Survival in the West of Scotland', pp. 90–91.
152. As a contracter open to the best bidder, Donald Gormeson of Sleat even received enquiries from Queen Elizabeth in 1570 requesting mercenaries for English service. Her ire had been aroused by the dispatch by the fifth Earl of Argyll of 700 mercenaries to the Irish rebels; a messenger was sent to Sleat to score a retaliatory point: she seems never to have hired them. *CSPI*, 1563–1569, p. 349. Also see section headed 'The Jesuit Missions', below.
153. John Durkan, 'The Career of John Brown, Minim', *Innes Review*, 21, pt 2 (1970), pp. 165–66. Baird hailed from Auchmeddan, near Fraserburgh; in 1609 he had moved from Lyons to Dieppe in order to be nearer Scotland. Maitland probably came in contact with the Minims in Antwerp in 1614; as the grandson of Sir William Maitland of Lethington, secretary to Queen Mary, he was very much a Lowlander. Thomas Robertson, his brother Andrew and their parents

were exiles from Scotland for their faith. Thomas was in the Paris province and spent much time in Calais tending to visitors by way of mass and confession. Many of them were Scots, but he also spoke Italian and French. *Ibid.*, pp. 163, 165.

154. Durkan, 'The Career of John Brown', p. 166.
155. Durkan, 'The Career of John Brown', pp. 163, 166–67.
156. Durkan, 'The Career of John Brown', pp. 167–68.
157. M. V. Hay, *The Blairs Papers, 1603–60* (London and Edinburgh, 1929), p. 72.
158. Sanderson, 'Catholic Recusancy in Scotland in the Sixteenth Century', p. 95.
159. D. MacLean, *Counter-Reformation in Scotland*, pp. 94–95.
160. *CSPI*, 1601–1603, pp. lxxv–vi, 338–42.
161. D. MacLean, *Counter-Reformation in Scotland*, p. 95.
162. See Chapter 4, note 18.
163. D. MacLean, *Counter-Reformation in Scotland*, pp. 64–65; *CSPI*, 1586–1588, p. 7; *Handbook of British Chronology*, p. 415. In 1599 all Scottish priests were put under the jurisdiction of George Blackwell, an English secular priest, though the Jesuits of both England and Scotland paid him lip-service only. D. MacLean, p. 87. This connection between the north of Scotland and the diocese of Armagh continued, especially in the *Gaidhealtachd*, well into the seventeenth century when Oliver Plunkett, appointed archbishop of Armagh in 1669, was designated superior of the mission to the Isles. Cathaldus Giblin, 'St. Oliver Plunkett, Francis MacDonnell, O.F.M., and the Mission to the Hebrides', *Collectanea Hibernica*, 17 (1974–1975), pp. 69–71.
164. *CSPI*, 1586–1588, p. 10.
165. Hiram Morgan, 'The End of Gaelic Ulster: A Thematic Interpretation of Events between 1534 and 1610', *Irish Historical Studies*, 26 (1988), pp. 27–28; *Handbook of British Chronology*, p. 423.
166. *CSPS*, 1595–1597, p. 210.
167. This is probably why he resigned the chiefship to Hugh O'Neill in 1594, a year before he died. *CSPI*, 1592–1596, pp. 116, 145; *A New History of Ireland*, III, p. 117.
168. *CSPS*, 1589–1593, pp. 250, 252, 264–66, 284.
169. Rev. Edmund Hogan S. J., *Distinguished Irishmen of the Sixteenth Century*, 1st series (London, 1894), p. 353.
170. Donal F. Cregan, 'The Social and Cultural Background of a Counter-Reformation Episcopate, 1618–60', in A. Cosgrove and D. McCartney (eds.), *Studies in Irish History Presented to R. Dudley Edwards* (Dublin, 1979), pp. 107, 109. Cregan points out that though they may have held differing political opinions, there was also a cultural unity between the two groups.
171. Nicholas Canny, 'The Formation of the Irish Mind: Religion, Politics and Gaelic Irish Literature, 1580–1750', *Past and Present*, no. 95 (May 1982), p. 95.
172. Canny, 'Formation of the Irish Mind', p. 97.
173. Cregan, 'Counter-Reformation Episcopate', pp. 103–04.
174. Séathrún Céitinn (Geoffrey Keating) from Tipperary in Munster was of Old English

derivation.

175. Canny, 'Formation of the Irish Mind', p. 100; *A New History of Ireland*, III, p. 531.
176. Canny, 'Formation of the Irish Mind', pp. 95–96; *A New History of Ireland*, III, p. 534.
177. Canny, 'Formation of the Irish Mind', pp. 95–97.
178. See Chapter 4.
179. Hogan, *Distinguished Irishmen*, p. 462.
180. *Handbook of British Chronology*, p. 415.
181. Hogan, *Distinguished Irishmen*, pp. 467–68; H. Concannon, 'Irish Missions to Scotland in Penal Days', *The Irish Ecclesiastical Record*, 5th series, 14 (1919), p. 397.
182. Hogan, *Distinguished Irishmen*, pp. 472–73.
183. Concannon, 'Irish Missions to Scotland', p. 402.
184. Hogan, *Distinguished Irishmen*, p. 473.
185. Hogan, *Distinguished Irishmen*, p. 478; Cathaldus Giblin, 'Francis MacDonnell, O.F.M., Son of the First Earl of Antrim (d. 1636)', *Seanchas Ardmhacha*, 8 (1975–76), p. 51.
186. *IFM*, p. 20.
187. See Chapter 2, 'The Franciscan Mission to the Highlands and Islands, 1619–1637'.
188. The Puritan Laird of Callaton is presumably Campbell of Cawdor, often referred to contemporarily as Caddell (of which 'Callaton' is probably a variant). Cawdor acquired Islay in 1614 and doubtless Texa with it, though he was not converted to Catholicism until 1624. See Chapter 2, section headed 'Cultivating the Scottish *Fine*'.
189. Hogan, *Distinguished Irishmen*, pp. 493–94.
190. At the time of Munro, dean of the Isles' report in 1549, Gigha was possessed by the Clan Donald, though he intimated that the old thane of Gigha should have been laird of the same. Sir Arthur Mitchell and James T. Clark (eds.), *MacFarlane's Geographical Collections*, III, SHS, 1st series, 53 (Edinburgh, 1908), 'A Description of the Westerne Iles of Scotland called Hybrides. Compyled by Mr. Donald Monro Deane of the Iles. 1549', pp. 265–66. The island appears to have been repurchased by the MacNeills during the reign of Charles I. I. F. Grant, *The Social and Economic Development of Scotland before 1603* (Edinburgh, 1930), p. 488.
191. There is nothing ressembling 'Cuin' anywhere off the coast of Arran. The one-inch to one-mile ordnance survey indicates two islands off the coast of Arran, both at about two miles' distance: the Holy Island and Pladda. It therefore remains a mystery which island is referred to here.
192. Hogan, *Distinguished Irishmen*, pp. 494–95.
193. Rev. Sean Mac Guaire, 'Ireland and the Catholic Hebrides', *The Irish Ecclesiastical Record*, 5th series, 42 (1933), p. 358. At this time there was, of course, no Duke of Argyll. This presumably refers to the seventh Earl before he converted to Catholicism in 1618.
194. The narrative is originally from Cardinal Moran's *Life of the Most Rev. Oliver Plunkett*, itself based on a Jesuit *Relatio* published in *Spicilegium Ossoriense*, II, p. 54.
195. Concannon, 'Irish Missions to

Scotland', pp. 403–04.
196. Concannon, 'Irish Missions to Scotland', p. 404.
197. Monro, 'A Description of the Westerne Iles of Scotland called Hybrides', p. 291.
198. *Fasti*, VII, p. 192.

Notes to Chapter 2: The Franciscan Mission to the Highlands and Islands, 1619–1637

1. James Kirk, 'The Jacobean Church in the Highlands, 1567–1625', in Loraine MacLean of Dochgarroch (ed.), *The Seventeenth Century in the Highlands* (Inverness, 1986), p. 47.
2. 'Report by Thomas Knox, Bishop of the Isles, of the State of his Diocese, 1626', in J. B. Craven (ed.), *Records of the Dioceses of Argyll and the Isles, 1560–1860* (Kirkwall, 1907), pp. 46–49.
3. James Kirk, 'The Kirk and the Highlands at the Reformation', *Northern Scotland*, 7, no. 1 (1986), pp. 1–22.
4. Anson, *Underground Catholicism*, p. 20.
5. Allan Macinnes, 'Catholic Recusancy and the Penal Laws, 1603–1707', *RSCHS*, 23, pt. 1 (1987), pp. 30–31.
6. Anson, *Underground Catholicism*, p. 28.
7. Macinnes, 'Catholic Recusancy', p. 31.
8. For instance, on 9 September 1656 Murdo M'Conill vic Wurchie vic Conill vic Allister in Torritan and Donald Smyth in Applecross were to be summoned 'for sacrificeing of beasts upon the 25 August, as also in poureing of milk upon hills as oblationes'. The practice was still current in 1678 when, on 6 August, Hector MacKenzie in Mellan in the parish of Gairloch, and John Murdoch and Duncan, his sons, and Kenneth, his grandson, were all summoned before the presbytery of Dingwall 'for sacrificing a bull in ane heathenish manner in the island of St Ruffus, for the recovering of the health of Cristan MacKenzie, spouse to the said Hector'. *Fasti*, VII, pp. 160, 146. See also William Mackay (ed.), *Records of the Presbyteries of Inverness and Dingwall, 1643–1688*, SHS, 1st series, 24 (Edinburgh, 1896).
9. Anson, *Underground Catholicism*, p. 18. For an account which emphasises the significance of bulls as the supreme sacrificial animal, see Michael Rice, *The Power of the Bull* (London, 1997).
10. See J. L. Campbell, *Canna – The Story of a Hebridean Island* (Oxford, 1984.)
11. Macinnes, 'Catholic Recusancy', p. 30.
12. Scotland had to wait another seventy years for hers – see introduction to Chapter 6.
13. Anson, *Underground Catholicism*, pp. 8, 9, 11.
14. As mentioned in Chapter 1, the people of Barra made a pilgrimage by sea to Croagh Patrick in Mayo in 1593. W. C. Mackenzie, *The Highlands and Isles of Scotland* (Edinburgh and London, 1937), p. 193.
15. That is, the Protestant bishop of the Isles.
16. *IFM*, pp. vii–viii, quoting J. R. N. MacPhail (ed.), *Highland*

Papers, III, SHS, 2nd series, 20 (Edinburgh, 1920), pp. 185–86. Also see Chapter 1, section headed 'The Jesuit Missions'.

17. David Stevenson, *Scottish Covenanters and Irish Confederates* (Belfast, 1981), p. 5; *idem*, *Alasdair MacColla and the Highland Problem in the Seventeenth Century* (Edinburgh, 1980), pp. 50–52.
18. Stevenson, *Scottish Covenanters and Irish Confederates*, pp. 6, 8. For the Kintyre negotiations, see PRONI D2977/5/1/4, Antrim papers. I am indebted to the staff of the Public Record Office, Belfast, for allowing me to view four boxes of unclassified material in the Antrim Papers. Particularly pertinent is an unclassified box labelled 'Early Correspondence and Vouchers' which includes an envelope enscribed 'Kintyre papers', and in Envelope 4, a manuscript headed: 'Ane Naration of the bargaine betwixt the Earle of Antrim and the Lord of Kintyre for the land of Kintyre and Jura'.
19. Anson, *Underground Catholicism*, p. 42.
20. Stevenson, *Scottish Covenanters and Irish Confederates*, pp. 13–14.
21. Anson, *Underground Catholicism*, p. 18.
22. Some studies specifically elucidate the Gaelic contribution. See, for instance, Timothy Paul Joseph McCall, 'The Gaelic background to the settlement of Antrim and Down, 1580–1641' (unpublished MA thesis, Queen's University, Belfast, 1983).
23. For some indication of Highland settlement in the Glens of Antrim, see Brian Samuel Turner, 'Distributional aspects of family name study illustrated in the Glens of Antrim' (unpublished PhD dissertation, Queen's University, Belfast, 1974).
24. See Chapter 1, section headed 'Catholic Conformers and Protestant Reformers', for a breakdown of the benefices filled in the diocese of Argyll after the Reformation.
25. *Fasti*, IV, pp. 57, 59, 64, 48, 66; Cosmo Innes, James B. Brichan and others (eds.), *Origines parochiales Scotiae*, 3 vols. (Edinburgh, 1850–55), II, pt. 1 (Dioceses of Argyll and the Isles), p. 12. This parish went on to become the Gaelic section of the parish of Campbeltown when it was divided in 1655.
26. *Fasti*, IV, pp. 116, 105.
27. *Fasti*, IV, pp. 105, 134, 129, 136, 133, 126, 131; *Fasti*, VII, p. 149.
28. Robert Clyde, *From Rebel to Hero: The Image of the Highlander, 1745–1830* (East Linton, 1995), p. 89.
29. *Fasti*, IV, pp. 178, 186–87, 145–47.
30. *Fasti*, VII, pp. 166, 168, 171, 174, 176. Given the geographical proximity, the surname McColgan of 1632 may represent a naturalisation of the Irish name O'Colgan documented earlier.
31. MacDonald of Clanranald was in possession of Canna in 1593, but John MacLeod (probably of Dunvegan) was said to be possessor when the bishop of the Isles wrote his report in 1626, though there is no confirmation of this possession. It was also Clanranald who intervened on the Franciscan Ward's behalf in the summer of 1625 when Neil MacKinnon, minister of Sleat, came with soldiers to capture him.

Campbell, *Canna*, pp. 63, 56.

32. *Fasti*, VII, pp. 182, 174.
33. See below, section headed 'The Franciscan Mission to the Highlands and Islands'.
34. See Chapter 1, section headed 'Catholic Conformers and Protestant Reformers – Malcolm MacPherson.
35. For whom see *ibid.*
36. *Fasti*, VII, pp. 185, 188, 191, 194, 199, 208.
37. *Presbyterian Church in Ireland*, I, pp. 92–94.
38. Michael Perceval-Maxwell, 'The Ulster Plantation: Scotland's First Colonial Venture', *Scottish Colloquium Proceedings*, 2 (Guelph, 1969), p. 14.
39. K. Bottigheimer, 'The Failure of the Reformation in Ireland: Une Question Bien Posée', *The Journal of Ecclesiastical History*, 36 (1985), p. 200.
40. A. F. Scott Pearson, 'Puritan and Presbyterian Settlements in Ireland, 1560–1660', 2 vols. (unpublished typescript, Belfast, 1948), I, p. 503; Sister Phil Kilroy, 'Bishops and Ministers in Ulster during the Primacy of Ussher, 1625–1656', *Seanchas Ardmhacha*, 8, no. 2 (1977), pp. 287, 295–96; Perceval-Maxwell, The Ulster Plantation: Scotland's First Colonial Venture', p. 14.
41. See Chapter 1, section headed 'Effect of the Plantation of Ulster on Religious Connections'.
42. Both Pearson and Perceval-Maxwell confound an easy understanding of the situation by referring to 'Irish reading ministers' and 'reading ministers in Irish' respectively, which tends to accord readers a status confusing to the Scottish researcher. This has been elucidated by Alan Ford, who indicates that reading ministers were 'clergy who could not preach, but merely read the service book to their parishioners'. In the early seventeenth century, they tended to form an inferior stratum beneath the emigrant settler preachers who had degrees. Alan Ford, 'The Protestant Reformation in Ireland', in *Natives and Newcomers: Essays on the Making of Irish Colonial Society, 1534–1641* (Dublin, 1986), pp. 54, 63.
43. A. F. Scott Pearson, 'Alumni of St. Andrews and the Settlement of Ulster', *UJA*, 3rd series, 14 (1951), p. 12. There were Rosses who graduated MA in 1578, 1579 or 1606 and matriculated in 1611. Possible dates for a John Ross at St. Andrews are MA in 1599 or matriculation in 1612; once again it is difficult to come to a decision as to which one he was.
44. See Chapter 1, section headed 'Effect of the Plantation of Ulster on Religious Connections'.
45. Scott Pearson, 'Puritan and Presbyterian Settlements in Ireland, 1560–1660', I, pp. 502–03, 583.
46. Ford, 'Reformation in Ireland', p. 64; Perceval-Maxwell, 'The Ulster Plantation: Scotland's First Colonial Venture', p. 13.
47. Bottigheimer, 'The Failure of the Reformation in Ireland', p. 203.
48. Michael Perceval-Maxwell, *The Scottish Migration to Ulster in the Reign of James I* (London, 1973), p. 261.
49. See Chapter 3, section headed 'Highland Ministers in Ireland'.
50. Perceval-Maxwell, *Scottish Migration to Ulster*, p. 272; J. M. Barkley, 'Some Scottish

Bishops and Ministers in the Irish Church, 1605–35', in Duncan Shaw (ed.), *Reformation and Revolution. Essays presented to The Very Revd Principal Emeritus Hugh Watt* (Edinburgh, 1967), p. 150.

51. See Chapter 1, section headed 'Effect of the Plantation of Ulster on Religious Connections'.
52. Barkley, 'Scottish Bishops and Ministers', p. 153.
53. Phil Kilroy, 'Radical Religion in Ireland, 1641–1660', in Jane H. Ohlmeyer (ed.), *Ireland from Independence to Occupation 1641–1660* (Cambridge, 1995), p. 203. In 1641, after Wentworth fell from power, the presbyterians of Ulster utterly rejected the Established Church as reformed by the Convocation of 1634. (*Ibid.*, pp. 203–04.)
54. Barkley, 'Scottish Bishops and Ministers', p. 141.
55. S. G. E. Lythe, *The Economy of Scotland in its European Setting, 1550–1625* (Edinburgh and London, 1960), pp. 68–69.
56. *Fasti*, VII, pp. 11, 74.
57. Sir James Balfour Paul (ed.), *The Scots Peerage*, 9 vols. (Edinburgh, 1904–1914), 8, p. 346. For Cluny see below, section headed 'The Franciscan Mission to the Highlands and Islands'.
58. Sir William Fraser, *The Sutherland Book*, 3 vols. (Edinburgh, 1892), I, p. 207.
59. Fraser, *The Sutherland Book*, II (Edinburgh, 1892), p. 154. He had offered the estates to his nephew, the Earl, and appeared to have had considerable debts, but complained at harsh and unnatural treatment by him – 'My going north hes hinderit me mutch, and I have done no goode, bot spent my meinis and my tyme iyedillie, for I culd get nothing done with my brother sone, the earll.'
60. Fraser, *The Sutherland Book*, I, p. 207; II, pp. 155, 164; Balfour Paul, *The Scots Peerage*, 8, p. 346. He wrote again to his brother on 23 May 1636 when he still appeared to have been in possession of his land of Navidale, asking him to speak to one William Dick concerning his debts, 'and show him he salbe compleitlie payit off me, principall and interest, at Lambes when I go to Iyrland'. Earlier comments suggest that his brother, too, had contacts in Ireland, for he wrote to him: 'As to that bissines of my Lord of Ormonthis I can wryt nothing of it wntill I go to Irland and try maters as they go. Nather can I end anything wntill my Lord of Thirles be in Iyrland.' His brother was to send letters either to Monaghan or Clones, where Sir John Wishart would inform him where to direct them, for Sir Alexander now lived in 'Cluincalge', land formerly held by Sir John Wishart. *Ibid.*, II, pp. 155, 164.
61. This is given as initials only.
62. Perceval-Maxwell, *Scottish Migration to Ulster*, p. 272.
63. *CSPI*, 1625–32, p. 512. Deposition of Thomas Plunkett, reclaimed from popery, before the bishop of Derry, 4 January 1630.
64. Edmund Hogan (ed.), *The Description of Ireland, and The State thereof as it is at this present In Anno 1598* (Dublin, 1878), p. 27.
65. Perceval-Maxwell, *Scottish Migration to Ulster*, p. 68.
66. R. J. Hunter, 'Ulster Plantation Towns 1609–41', in David

Harkness and Mary O'Dowd (eds.), *The Town in Ireland*, Historical Studies, 13 (1979), p. 60.

67. Kilroy, 'Bishops and Ministers in Ulster', p. 291.
68. *IFM*, p. ix.
69. Donald Gregory, *The History of the Western Highlands and Isles of Scotland from A.D. 1493 to A.D. 1625* (Edinburgh, London and Dublin, 1836), pp. 339–41.
70. Campbell, *Canna*, pp. 53–54.
71. *IFM*, p. ix.
72. See Nicholas Canny, 'The Formation of the Irish Mind: Religion, Politics and Gaelic Irish Literature, 1580–1750', *Past and Present*, no. 95 (1982), pp. 94–104.
73. In effect, this mission was a subsidiary of the Franciscan mission to Scotland; it had begun in 1612 with the arrival of Fr. John Ogilvie in the Lowlands, a Franciscan who lived in the Irish College of St. Anthony in Louvain. Note that this Ogilvie is distinct from the John Ogilvie, Scottish Jesuit, who was martyred in Scotland in 1613. See *IFM*, p. 1, which makes the distinction.
74. *IFM*, pp. 4–5. Nothing more is known about Stuart's relatives or of his origin.
75. *IFM*, pp. ix, 19.
76. *IFM*, p. x, 4. Unfortunately none of the official reports for this first stage of the Franciscan mission has survived; such information as exists has been gleaned from other letters in the Archives of the *Congregazione de Propaganda Fide*.
77. Gregory, *History of the Western Highlands*, pp. 401–02.
78. See Chapter 5, section headed 'Catholic Conformers and Protestant Reformers', in relation to the diocese of Argyll.
79. *IFM*, p. x.
80. *IFM*, pp. 59, 98, 101, xi.
81. Literally 'noble men'.
82. *IFM*, p. 62. Cornelius Ward wrote that he set out from the Ross of Mull after a visit to MacLean of Lochbuie in 1625 with two attendants, who had presumably been provided by Lochbuie.
83. They continued to refer to the necessity of the mission being terminated if they did not receive their allowances, but this was in a vain attempt to provide themselves with some financial security.
84. *IFM*, p. 26.
85. *IFM*, p. 24.
86. Stevenson, *Alasdair MacColla*, pp. 51, 53.
87. *IFM*, p. 14.
88. For an account of this voyage, see R. Black, 'Colla Ciotach', *TGSI*, 48 (1972–74), pp. 201–43.
89. Campbell, *Canna*, pp. 52–53.
90. Stevenson, *Alasdair MacColla*, pp. 31, 38, 40, 49.
91. *IFM*, pp. 51, 125.
92. Campbell, *Canna*, pp. 56–57, 62, 56; Kirk, 'The Jacobean Church in the Highlands', p. 31; I. F. Grant, *The MacLeods: The History of a Clan* (Edinburgh, 1981), pp. 94–95, 221–22.
93. Kirk, 'The Jacobean Church in the Highlands', pp. 31, 47.
94. The bishop of Ross cited the children of Donnald Neilsoun MacLeod of Assynt, on the west coast of Sutherland, as under suspicion of being corrupted in their religion by remaining in their father's company (though the MacLeods of Assynt were an offshoot of the MacLeods of Lewis rather than Harris). *RPCS*, 1629–1630, p. 246; Grant, p. 148.

95. Grant, *The MacLeods*, p. 238.
96. *RPCS*, 1630–1632, p. 176. As there had been scaremongering on MacDonald of Clanranald's lands, similarly the minister stated that the Sunday prior to the complaint, Murdoch MacLean and some of his accomplices, all armed with swords and other weapons, had come to his kirk (which of the two is unspecified) where he was about to preach and 'thrust him to the doores, locked the same, and vowed if he found him there againe he sould doe worse turne to him'. However, this initial antagonism between MacIlvory and MacLean was later rectified because MacIlvory joined the Royalist MacLean to minister to his troops when he fought with Montrose in 1645. See Chapter 3, section headed 'Scottish Ministerial Collaborators'.
97. Clanranald was one of the chiefs answerable to the Privy Council for the Clan Iain, and when in the summer of 1625 the Clan Iain pirates were pursued from Skye by MacLeod of Harris (also answerable for them), they had taken refuge with Clanranald in Moidart. With the arrival of Lord Lorne many of them were killed or banished, and those who remained identified themselves with the Clanranald and were never again encountered as a separate clan. Gregory, *History of the Western Highlands*, pp. 410–11.
98. Gregory, *History of the Western Highlands*, pp. 410–11.
99. Campbell, *Canna*, p. 58.
100. Campbell, *Canna*, p. 58.
101. Campbell, *Canna*, p. 59.
102. *IFM*, pp. 53–54.
103. *IFM*, p. 80.
104. I am indebted to Professor Allan Macinnes for this point, who made an in-depth study of these records for his article 'Catholic Recusancy and the Penal Laws, 1603–1707', *RSCHS*, 23, pt. 1 (1987), pp. 27–63.
105. *IFM*, p. 79.
106. *IFM*, p. 123.
107. *RPCS*, 1625–1627, p. 389.
108. Benignus Millett, OFM, 'Catalogue of Irish material in Fourteen Volumes of the *Scritture Originali Riferite nelle Congregazioni Generali* in *Propaganda* Archives', *Collectanea Hibernica*, 11 (1967), p. 10.
109. *RPCS*, 1625–1627, pp. 377–78.
110. *RPCS*, 1629–1630, pp. 177–79. The direct influence of the family as Catholics ended with his alleged lunacy. John Campbell of Cawdor (1596–1654) took ill in 1638 and apparently could not be cured. In 1639 he was declared unfit to manage his estates for eighteen months, and his brother, Colin, was declared Tutor-at-Law. John Campbell, 'the fiar', was declared a lunatic and spent his last years in Islay. Hugh, the eldest son of Tutor Colin, became the next laird. C. Innes (ed.), *The Book of the Thanes of Cawdor*, The Spalding Club, 30 (Edinburgh, 1859), pp. xxxi–xxix. While John Campbell may indeed have had lunatic tendencies, his official declaration in 1639 when the house of Argyll faced a Royalist attack from Ireland cannot be seen as other than politically motivated.
111. *IFM*, p. 56; Gregory, *History of the Western Highlands*, p. 410. For references to the Clan Iain's piracy at this time, see the letters of Sir John Campbell, fourth of Cawdor,

to Thomas Hamilton, Lord Binning, first Earl of Melrose, Scottish Secretary, and to John Erskine, 19th Earl of Mar, Lord High Treasurer of Scotland, in 1625. NLS Ms. 3134 II, 102, Yule collection.

112. *IFM*, pp. 69, 72, 76, 83; J. L. Campbell, 'North and South Uist and Barra in Prefect Ballantine's Report', *Innes Review*, 9 (1958), p. 215.
113. *IFM*, pp. 62–63, 67. This comment is sigificant because it refutes the above assertion that only the east coast élite had truck with court circles. See the beginning of this chapter.
114. See John L. Campbell, 'The Letter Sent by Iain Muideartach, Twelfth Chief of Clanranald, to Pope Urban VIII, in 1626', *Innes Review*, 4 (1955), pp. 110–16.
115. *IFM*, p. 81.
116. *IFM*, p. 159. It is as well to note, however, that this Clery is a relation of Cornelius Ward, which he mentions in a letter from Madrid on 1 July 1634. While not invalidating him as a witness, the historian must be aware of his interest in the writing of testimonials. *IFM*, p. 164.
117. The surname is a variant of MacClure, most common in Galloway, which would tend to suggest that he came from one of the more southerly islands, perhaps Arran. The forename Louis further suggests a possible identification with the McLewises – Gaelic MacLughaidh – or MacCloys of Arran.
118. *IFM*, p. 160; George F. Black, *The Surnames of Scotland* (New York, 1946), pp. 450, 471–72. This makes it unlikely that Macallea was one of a number of families from Sleat who took the English name Maclure, but was one whose name derived in Gaelic from MacGille dheóradha, a variant of Dewar. Indeed, the Franciscans do not appear to have visited Sleat until 1636. See Fig. 2.4.
119. *IFM*, pp. 160–61.
120. *Memoirs of Scottish Catholics*, I, pp. 129–30.
121. Sir Alexander was probably the son of Sir Thomas Gordon of Cluny, who was fiar of Cluny in 1581 and whose daughter married in 1618. If this is so, Sir Alexander Gordon would be fourth of Cluny, following Alexander of Strathoun, the second son of the third Earl of Huntly, the progenitor (1), John Gordon, his brother (2) and Sir Thomas Gordon (3). Balfour Paul, *The Scots Peerage*, 4, p. 533; 2, pp. 9, 12; 1, p. 199.
122. A wadset was a medieval mortgage of heritable property.
123. *RPCS*, 1630–1632, p. 391. Sir Alexander Gordon secured for himself a disposition of his brother's estate to the prejudice of the latter's creditors, who included William Leslie of Ryhill. Sir Alexander's estate of 7,000 merks was all in his brother's hands on a wadset of Ryhill's farm. Sir Alexander's brother was evicted from his estate by the Earl of Mar, who disponed it to Cluny. Cluny very craftily forced him to grant the lands redeemable for payment of a smaller sum, but notwithstanding the lands were apprised from him by his brother's creditors as his cautioner. Ryhill petitioned the Privy Council in 1631 for protection as cautioner to his brother, the Laird of Wardes,

having been unjustly excluded from a protection purchased from the crown by Cluny for himself, his brother and some friends, to the endangerment of Ryhill's estate. The petitioner was granted protection. *Ibid.*, pp. 391–92.

124. *IFM*, p. xii. Giblin notes that 'Sutherland in the Northern Highlands was Patrick Brady's centre of activity, and except for one or two short visits to the isles or to Ireland his entire eighteen years as a missionary seem to have been spent there.'
125. *IFM*, p. 106.
126. *IFM*, p. 55. For Catholic use of 'the north' see, for instance, Donald MacLean, *The Counter-Reformation in Scotland 1560–1930* (London, 1931), p. 109.
127. MacLean, *Counter-Reformation in Scotland*, p. 109.
128. *IFM*, p. 180; E. B. Fryde, D. E. Greenway, S. Porter and I. Roy, *Handbook of British Chronology* (London, 3rd edition, 1986), p. 424.
129. Stevenson, *Alasdair MacColla*, pp. 68–72.
130. *IFM*, pp. 92–93.
131. *IFM*, p. 86.
132. See earlier section headed 'The Advancing Tide of Protestantism'.
133. For an account of the friary, see Francis Joseph Bigger, *The Ancient Friary of Bun-na-Margie* (Belfast, 1898).
134. Rev. George Hill, *An Historical Account of The MacDonnells of Antrim* (Belfast, 1976), p. 231.
135. See Chapter 1, section headed 'The Jesuit Missions'.
136. *IFM*, pp. 81, 120.
137. *IFM*, pp. 105–06, 120, 111. The more significant among those converted were said to be a minister and 'an Englishman, named Thomas Norton, who is brother-in-law to the earl of Antrim'. Sir Randal MacDonnell was second Earl of Antrim at this time. Hill makes no mention of a Norton in *The MacDonnells of Antrim*, but only names five of the six daughters of the first Earl of Antrim and their husbands. Norton may have been the husband of the sixth. Hill, *MacDonnells of Antrim*, pp. 247–50.
138. *IFM*, p. 178. Similarly, Cornelius Ward wrote to Cardinal Barberini in Madrid on the 16 September 1634 requesting, among other things, that they 'be given faculties to accept other Franciscans who are willing to go on the mission'. p. 168.
139. *IFM*, p. 111.
140. *IFM*, p. 117.
141. *IFM*, p. 129.
142. Macinnes, 'Catholic Recusancy', pp. 43–44.
143. *IFM*, pp. 101, 111.
144. Cathaldus Giblin, OFM, 'Francis MacDonnell, O.F.M., Son of the First Earl of Antrim (d. 1636)', *Seanchas Ardmhacha*, 8 (1976), p. 46.
145. Giblin, 'Francis MacDonnell', pp. 46–47, 51.
146. Stevenson, *Alasdair MacColla*, p. 38. Among their petitions in 1629, the missionaries mentioned that the Earl of Antrim had not allowed his son to go on the mission 'for political reasons'. *IFM*, p. 111.
147. Stevenson, *Scottish Covenanters and Irish Confederates*, pp. 5–22.
148. Giblin, 'Francis MacDonnell', pp. 51–52.
149. Giblin, 'Francis MacDonnell',

p. 48.

150. Giblin, 'Francis MacDonnell', p. 49. MacDonnell himself was not unaware of these machinations. In 1628, he requested that *Propaganda* itself appoint him to work in Scotland so that no Irish Franciscan could prevent his going to that country or have the power to recall him once he had joined the mission. *Ibid.*, pp. 49, 51.

151. MacDonnell had crossed to Ireland by November 1628 to await his transfer to the Scottish mission, but instead had had to adjust to a friar's life in Ireland. He had not long been in Ireland when he was suggested for the Catholic bishopric of Clogher or Derry, but even with the support of the Irish Primate and his father the petitions came to nought. *IFM*, pp. 50, 52; Rev. James O'Laverty, *The Bishops of Down and Connor*, V (Dublin, 1895), pp. 417–18.

152. These pockets will be examined in the next section.

153. *IFM*, pp. 66, 95.

154. *IFM*, pp. 96, 111.

155. By 1637 their request seems to have been realised. *IFM*, p. 177.

156. *IFM*, p. xiii.

157. *IFM*, p. xiii. In March 1626 O'Neill and Hegarty were in Dublin for holy oils and other requisites. *IFM*, p. 77.

158. *IFM*, p. 114. In November 1629 Ward was told that he could apply for those faculties customarily granted to missionaries labouring in England. *IFM*, pp. 118–19. However, this still failed to come to grips with the problem, which was that these faculties could only work where there was a bishop (or the equivalent) as in England.

159. *IFM*, p. 166.

160. Although the priests carried with them travelling sets of all the requisites, i.e. 'a chalice, chasuble, alb, missal, etc., for saying mass; a ritual for administering the sacraments; three or four books of controversy, and a bible', the mission reports reveal that the missionaries often ran out of communion wafer and wine. *IFM*, pp. 29.

161. *IFM*, p. 56.

162. Similarly, it was stated that 'the Franciscan who laboured for some years in the Hebrides before Hegarty could not say mass for the whole of Lent because he had no wine, and Hegarty himself had to send his attendant from the Hebrides to the Scottish Lowlands to procure wine'. *IFM*, p. 35.

163. *IFM*, p. 22.

164. Giblin, 'Francis MacDonnell', p. 48.

165. *IFM*, p. 78.

166. *IFM*, p. 114.

167. *IFM*, pp. 69, 72.

168. *IFM*, pp. 92–93. The conversion list of Patrick Hegarty, dated 13 June 1625, is printed in *IFM*, pp. 37–45.

169. *A New History of Ireland*, III, pp. 617–28. Significantly, the College of Alcalá in Spain was founded by Count Jorge de Paz y Sylveira, whose mother was a MacDonnell from Antrim; thus the college was founded exclusively for Ulstermen. *Ibid.*, pp. 618, 627–28.

170. *A New History of Ireland*, III, p. 629.

171. *IFM*, pp. 100, 94, 127, 170; Giblin, 'Francis MacDonnell', p. 51.

172. D. Maclean, 'Catholicism in the Highlands and Isles, 1560–1680',

Innes Review, 3 (1952), p. 7.

173. *IFM*, p. 90.

174. Although this man had sufficiently impressed the nuncio in Belgium to provide him with letters of commendation, on his arrival in Douai 'three candidates from the English-speaking parts of Scotland were admitted to the college in preference to him'. *IFM*, pp. 90, 97. MacDonald subsequently proved to be a most notorious religious turncoat whom few men of any perception would have admitted to any college. Peter Anson, a commentator on modern Catholic ecclesiastical history, is inclined to believe that MacDonald did have integrity. He states that MacDonald was captured twice, once with Ward in London in 1630 and a second time in 1642 when he was taken to Edinburgh, where 'he convinced the authorities that he had been coerced into becoming a priest, which was untrue, and so he was allowed to go back to the Hebrides. Part of the teinds of Snizort in Skye were granted to him for maintenance.' This, however, is a very optimistic view of his character. It seems far more likely that he was a subsidised Highland opportunist. Anson also identifies him as the son of the chief of Clanranald, though this seems to have opened no doors for him, and though the Franciscans refer to him as a man of status, they do not specify this connection. Anson, *Underground Catholicism*, p. 24.

175. *IFM*, pp. 117, 150, 127.

176. *IFM*, p. 151.

177. Anson, *Underground Catholicism*, pp. 15, 48.

178. 'They are to take care not to give the impression that they seek temporal gain . . . the missionaries are to show they have no interest in acquiring earthly gain or riches, but that they value poverty above all things.' *IFM*, pp. 24–26.

179. *IFM*, p. 96.

180. *IFM*, 174. For John MacKinnon, see above, section headed 'The Advancing Tide of Protestantism'.

181. *IFM*, p. 47.

182. O'Laverty, *Bishops of Down and Connor*, p. 423.

183. *IFM*, pp. xiii, 102, 59, 31.

184. Giblin, 'Francis MacDonnell', p. 48.

185. *IFM*, pp. 138–39, 140, 142.

186. *IFM*, pp. 175, 178.

187. Allan I. Macinnes, 'The Origin and Organisation of the Covenanting Movement during the Reign of Charles I, with a Particular Reference to the West of Scotland', 2 vols. (PhD thesis, Glasgow, 1987), I, p. 1; Gordon Donaldson, *Scotland James V – James VII* (Edinburgh, 1971), p. 310.

188. *IFM*, p. 178.

189. See the biography, Jane H. Ohlmeyer, *Civil War and Restoration in the Three Stuart Kingdoms: The Career of Randal MacDonnell, Marquis of Antrim, 1609–1683* (Cambridge, 1993).

190. O'Laverty, *Bishops of Down and Connor*, pp. 428–29.

191. *IFM*, p. 180. In this letter, Hegarty detailed the fate of those who had worked longest on the Scottish mission. Edmund McCann, of the first-stage missionaries, could not work any more because he broke his leg in prison in Scotland. He was then living in the friary of Armagh, fifty miles from the Scottish coast. Paul O'Neill,

Patrick Brady and Cornelius Ward were advanced in years and worn out by their exertions on the mission and lived in the friaries of Monaghan, Cavan and Donegal respectively.

192. *IFM*, p. 181.
193. *IFM*, p. 81.
194. *IFM*, p. 90.
195. *IFM*, pp. 68, 172.
196. Rev. John MacInnes, 'Gaelic Religious Poetry, 1650–1850', *RSCHS*, 10 (1950), p. 33.
197. Derick S. Thomson (ed.), *The Companion to Gaelic Scotland* (Oxford, 1983), p. 36.
198. *IFM*, pp. 175, 122. Donald MacDonald's clan background is unknown, but writing from Colonsay it must be presumed that he was a member of the Clan Donald South. It should be remembered that Sir James MacDonald of that clan and Alasdair MacDonald of Keppoch escaped to Spain after the Islay rebellion of 1615. Therefore, if not a member of the former clan, he is likely to have been a Keppoch MacDonald.
199. *IFM*, pp. 108, 69. It may be that this was the only thing akin to the ceremonial attached to military mobilisation – very much at the heart of militarist Gaelic society. Ward was forced to reason with them, pointing out that this was not necessary.
200. *IFM*, pp. 32–33.
201. *IFM*, pp. xi, 18.
202. Certainly, the ninth Earl of Argyll claimed that the resistance by the MacLeans of Duart to his expropriation of their chief in 1679 (in satisfaction of vast private debts) was a Scottish extension of the Popish Plot. This appears to have been based on the premise that two of the clans who opposed expropriation were allegedly Catholic, that is, the MacDonalds of Glengarry and of Keppoch. Macinnes, 'Catholic Recusancy', p. 55. However, the claim may have gained weight from the fact that there was some survival of Catholicism amongst the other Mull MacLeans, the MacLeans of Lochbuie. MacLean of Lochbuie's citation before the presbytery of Lorn in 1704, for the employment of a Catholic schoolmaster in his house, may show how a limited Catholicism was sustained in Mull. NAS CH2/557/4, Synod of Argyll, 1701–1707, fols. 113, 119.
203. *IFM*, pp. 55, 122, 33. No indication is given as to where he said mass.
204. Though the sanction did not appear to work with Cawdor, see Chapter 5, section headed 'The MacCalmans: Ministerial Opportunism', for the effect of excommunication on the life and subsequent career of the Rev. Duncan MacCalman.
205. *IFM*, p. 125. The attempt on Ward was made in Colonsay, which had been technically in Campbell hands since March 1610 when it was included in a grant to Argyll of the barony of Ardnamurchan, and was subsequently feued to Cawdor in 1614. Lord Lorne also received the feudal superiority of Oronsay in 1629. Stevenson, *Alasdair MacColla*, pp. 35, 52.
206. Stevenson, *Alasdair MacColla*, pp. 53–54.
207. *IFM*, pp. 94, 48.

Notes to Chapter 3: The Entrenchment of Gaelic Presbyterianism, 1637–1689

1. James Kirk, *Patterns of Reform* (Edinburgh, 1989), p. 70. Protestantism, including both episcopal and presbyterian strains, was characterised by emphasis on the preaching of the gospel, particularly in the vernacular language, the importance of the teachings of the Bible, and the exclusive mediation of Christ. In addition, the Scottish reformers believed that it was through faith that believers were raised heavenwards to receive what Christ offered in the sacrament, rejecting Roman doctrines of transubstantiation and Lutheran belief in consubstantiation. In terms of ecclesiastical organisation, they adopted a form of church government which at congregational level was entrusted to a consistory of one or more ministers and a number of elected elders and deacons, as financial officers. All of these were essentially Calvinist features. Kirk, *Reform*, pp. xii, 74, 78.
2. Kirk, *Reform*, pp. 80–88, xx–xxii. Presbyterians believed that the church should be governed not by bishops or superintendents but by committees of ministers or presbyteries; similarly, the General Assembly should consist only of ecclesiastical personnel (including elders but no nobles, lairds or burgesses). Gordon Donaldson, *Scotland James V to James VII* (Edinburgh, 1971), p. 149; Kirk, *Reform*, p. 85.
3. Kirk, *Reform*, pp. 344, 356–57, 361, 429–30, 435; Donaldson, *Scotland*, p. 181.
4. Ultimately the movement proved too strong to quell, and a statute of 1592 authorised a presbyterian system which had effectively been operating since 1586. Donaldson, *Scotland*, pp. 198–99.
5. After receiving financial endowment in 1606 and status as permanent moderators of Synods in 1607, the bishops' jurisdiction was eventually restored in 1609 and 1610. Kirk, *Reform*, p. 430.
6. See Chapter 1, section headed 'Effect of the Plantation of Ulster on Religious Connections', and Chapter 2, section headed 'The Advancing Tide of Protestantism'.
7. Donaldson, *Scotland*, pp. 208–10.
8. Allan I. Macinnes, *Charles I and the Making of the Covenanting Movement, 1625–1641* (Edinburgh, 1991), pp. 56–57; Donaldson, *Scotland*, pp. 296–311.
9. Edward Mackie Furgol, *The Religious Aspects of the Scottish Covenanting Armies, 1639–1651* (DPhil dissertation, University of Oxford, 1982), pp. 3, 17, 22–23, and see the subsequently published Edward M. Furgol, *A Regimental History of the Covenanting Armies, 1639–1651* (Edinburgh, 1990). Donaldson, *Scotland*, pp. 314, 331, 333–34; J. C. Beckett, *The Making of Modern Ireland, 1603–1923* (London, 1969), p. 75; James Seaton Reid, *The History of the Presbyterian Church in Ireland*, 3 vols. (1837), II, pp. 245–49; *Fasti*, VII, pp. 49, 355; David Stevenson, *Alasdair MacColla and the Highland Problem in the Seventeenth Century* (Edinburgh, 1980), pp. 120–21.

10. Phil Kilroy, 'Radical Religion in Ireland, 1641–1660', in Jane H. Ohlmeyer (ed.), *Ireland from Independence to Occupation, 1641–1660* (Cambridge, 1995), p. 202.
11. Donaldson, *Scotland*, p. 340; *Presbyterian Church in Ireland*, II (1937), pp. 170–74. In Ireland, Belfast presbyterians drafted a document known as the 'Representation', which protested against both the execution and 'the insolent and presumptuous practices of that sectarian army in England', and subsequently sent it to parliament. *Presbyterian Church in Ireland*, II, p. 174.
12. The Engagement was a secret agreement drawn up by three Scottish Commissioners and the King.
13. Beckett, *Making of Modern Ireland*, pp. 101–03; Kilroy, 'Radical Religion in Ireland', pp. 202–03, 206. Julia Buckroyd, *Church and State in Scotland, 1660–1681* (Edinburgh, 1980), pp. 2, 7–9; *Fasti*, VII, p. 116.
14. A. C. Anderson, *The Story of the Presbyterian Church in Ireland* (Newcastle, Co. Down, 1965), pp. 45–46; *Presbyterian Church in Ireland*, II (1837), pp. 236–38.
15. F. D. Dow, *Cromwellian Scotland, 1651–1660* (Edinburgh, 1979), p. 80.
16. Donaldson, *Scotland*, p. 346; Buckroyd, *Church and State*, pp. 10–11.
17. Anderson, *Story of the Presbyterian Church*, p. 46; *Presbyterian Church in Ireland*, II (1837), p. 288; Beckett, *Making of Modern Ireland*, p. 114.
18. *Presbyterian Church in Ireland*, II (1837), pp. 292–96, 318–24, 497, 499; Anderson, *Story of the Presbyterian Church*, pp. 46–47; Buckroyd, *Church and State*, pp. 12, 15.
19. This policy had been evident from the early seventeenth century with the banishment of Robert Bruce of Kinnaird to Inverness. See Chapter 5, section headed 'Catholic Conformers and Protestant Reformers'.
20. Kilroy, 'Radical Religion in Ireland', pp. 216–17. The establishment was still intimidated by the presbyterians' kinship connections in Scotland, and by their militarism: in 1656, Major Morgan, an enemy of presbyterianism, stated: 'In the north, the Scotch keep up an interest distinct in garb and all formalities; and are able to raise 40,000 fighting men at any time.' *Presbyterian Church in Ireland*, II (1837), p. 308 n.
21. Anderson, *Story of the Presbyterian Church*, pp. 48–49; Buckroyd, *Church and State*, pp. 3–4, 20, 33–34; Donaldson, *Scotland*, pp. 362–63, 365; *Presbyterian Church in Ireland*, II (1837), pp. 337, 350–54.
22. Buckroyd, *Church and State*, pp. 124–25; Donaldson, *Scotland*, pp. 369–71.
23. On 7 October 1663 it became necessary for the Scottish Estates to legislate against these 'many seditious and turbulent persons, Ministers and others in the Kingdom of Ireland' not complying with the Government there and who 'were coming over, expecting shelter here'. British Library Add. Ms. 23120, Lauderdale Papers, miscellaneous correspondence, 8, fol. 112,

September to December 1663, Proclamations against Ministers Coming from Ireland, 1663. But to date, none of these ministers is known to have gone to the Highlands or to have been Gaelic-speaking.

24. Anderson, *Story of the Presbyterian Church*, pp. 50–51.
25. Alick Morrison, 'Early Harris Estate Papers, 1679–1703', *TGSI*, 51 (1981), p. 95.
26. Buckroyd, *Church and State*, pp. 136, 6; Donaldson, *Scotland*, pp. 379–80; Anderson, *Story of the Presbyterian Church*, p. 51.
27. Stevenson, *Alasdair MacColla*, pp. 67–68.
28. James Seaton Reid, *The Presbyterian Church in Ireland*, 3 vols. (Belfast, 2nd edition, 1867), I, pp. 273–74, p. 311 n.
29. A. F. Mitchell and J. Christie (eds.), *General Assembly Commission Records, I, 1646–47*, SHS, 1st series, 11 (Edinburgh, 1892), pp. 70–71.
30. Mitchell and Christie, *General Assembly Commission Records, I, 1646–47*, p. 323.
31. *Minutes of the Synod of Argyll*, I, pp. 37, 88–89.
32. Case studies of those disciplined for complicity follow later in this chapter. See below, section headed 'Scottish Ministerial Collaborators'.
33. *Minutes of the Synod of Argyll*, I, p. 92.
34. Furgol, *Scottish Covenanting Armies*, pp. 249–50.
35. David Stevenson, *Scottish Covenanters and Irish Confederates* (Belfast, 1981), p. 61.
36. Also see below, section headed 'Highland Ministers in Ireland'.
37. See Chapter 4, section headed 'Irish Chaplains with Alasdair MacColla MacDonald'.
38. *Minutes of the Synod of Argyll*, I, p. 100.
39. Duncan MacCalman is the likely father of the infamous John MacCalman, minister in Morvern, who had ample connection with Ireland. See Chapter 5, section headed 'The MacCalmans: Ministerial Opportunism'.
40. *Fasti*, IV, p. 105. This is in marked contrast to the treatment of the earlier incumbent of the parish. See Donald Omey in Chapter 2, section headed 'The Advancing Tide of Protestantism'.
41. *Minutes of the Synod of Argyll*, I, p. xiii; Derick Thomson, 'Gaelic Learned Orders and Literati', *Scottish Studies*, 12 (1968), pp. 67–68.
42. *Minutes of the Synod of Argyll*, I, p. 171.
43. See Chapter 1, section headed 'Catholic Conformers and Protestant Reformers'.
44. On this, see Mitchell and Christie, *General Assembly Commission Records, I, 1646–47*, p. 38.
45. *Minutes of the Synod of Argyll*, II, pp. xx, xxi, 121.
46. *Minutes of the Synod of Argyll*, II, p. 122. It should be noted that in the previous decade, some time after October 1642 (date unspecified), Archibald MacQueen, minister of Snizort and Uig, was deposed for the great sin of conducting the marriage ceremony of MacDonald of Clanranald, though this was reponed before 28 October 1657. *Fasti*, VII, p. 179.
47. *Minutes of the Synod of Argyll*, II, pp. xxii.
48. *Fasti*, IV, pp. 70, 73; Stevenson,

Alasdair MacColla, p. 221; Alexander Cameron, *Reliquiae Celticae*, II (Inverness, 1894), pp. 202–03. Although no connection is noted in the *Fasti*, it seems more than probable (in the absence of any evidence to the contrary) that this is the father of his namesake, John Darroch, minister of Kilcalmonell and Kilberry, who served briefly in Glenarm in Ireland in the 1680s before returning to his own parish and subsequently translating to Craignish. For the son, see the final section of this chapter, headed 'Mr John Darroch, Minister of Glenarm and Cushendall'. One of Archibald MacAllister's two spells away from Islay seems to have been spent at Kilberry. For which see below, section headed 'Mr Dugald Campbell'.

49. *Fasti*, IV, p. 119.
50. *Minutes of the Synod of Argyll*, I, p. 120.
51. *Minutes of the Synod of Argyll*, I, p. 120.
52. *Fasti*, IV, p. 114.
53. See also Murdo MacKenzie of Achilty in Wester Ross, who in 1651 'drew consolation from the fact that Charles II in exile would be protected from the "barbarous flock" who had gained a position of political dominance "by hatred and deceit"', and who is probably one and the same. Allan Macinnes, 'The Vernacular Response to the Covenanting Dynamic', in John Dwyer, Roger A. Mason and Alexander Murdoch (eds.), *New Perspectives on the Politics and Culture of Early Modern Scotland* (Edinburgh, 1982), p. 83.
54. Mitchell and Christie, *General Assembly Commission Records*, *I*, *1646–1647*, pp. 68, 265. After 1649, other ministers were deposed in the more northerly parishes for subscribing Montrose's articles but were not directly associated with the Montrose–MacColla Royalist campaign of 1644–47. These included David Monro from the parish of Latheron, presbytery of Dornoch, and more pertinently, the entire presbytery of Caithness, except William Smyth. For such a sin of omission, the latter was taken to Thurso, put on board ship and towed for two miles, where he eventually lay in irons until Montrose was executed in May 1650. Those who were deposed in around 1650 from the presbytery of Caithness for compliance with Montrose include a namesake, William Smith, from the parish of Dunnet, John Smart, minister of Wick, probably David Allardyce from the parish of Olrig, John Munro of Reay, and William Abernethy, minister of Thurso. *Fasti*, VII, pp. 92, 113, 119, 129, 132, 136. This hearty identification with the Royalists perhaps reflects the general attitude of the area – few men were raised in northern Scotland for the Covenanters – although Captain George Gordon, brother of the fourteenth Earl of Sutherland, raised a company in Sutherland for the Earl of Leven. Stevenson, *Scottish Covenanters and Irish Confederates*, p. 75.
55. *Fasti*, IV, p. 23. See the final paragraph of the study of Mr Dugald Campbell, below, for further reference to Cameron.
56. He has been referred to previously in Chapter 2, section headed 'Problems, Difficulties and

Extenuating Circumstances'.

57. *Minutes of the Synod of Argyll*, I, pp. 69, 71. It is interesting to note Argyll's tacit compliance in the cases of MacCalman and MacDonald.
58. *Minutes of the Synod of Argyll*, I, p. 72.
59. See Chapter 2, note 174, although he may have stayed there for a trial. According to the Catholic record, Ranald MacDonald resided at the Irish College in Louvain for some months in January 1627. *IFM*, p. 104.
60. *IFM*, pp. 174–75, 104.
61. He may even have been in communication with the Irish Franciscan missionaries whose mission to the Highlands and Islands had been officially renewed in 1647, though no records of the mission remain. He may possibly have known Daniel McNeill if the surname suggests connections with Barra and South Uist (rather than Cowal, Knapdale and Kintyre).
62. *Minutes of the Synod of Argyll*, I, pp. 74, 172, 185. As always, when they had little means of effecting a change the matter was to be left in the hands of the Marquess of Argyll, as Justice of the region, who was to be written to.
63. Mitchell and Christie, *General Assembly Commission Records, I, 1646–47*, p. 38.
64. For which see Chapter 2, section headed 'The Advancing Tide of Protestantism'.
65. A. F. Mitchell and J. Christie, *General Assembly Commission Records, II, 1648–49*, SHS, 1st series, 25 (Edinburgh, 1896), pp. 275–76.
66. *Minutes of the Synod of Argyll*, I, p. 153 n.
67. See Chapter 1, section headed 'Effect of the Plantation of Ulster on Religious Connections', particularly George Montgomery's survey of the bishoprics of Derry and Raphoe.
68. A. F. Scott Pearson, 'Puritan and Presbyterian Settlements in Ireland, 1560–1660', 2 vols. (unpublished typescript, Belfast, 1948), I, pp. 80–81.
69. On 24 April 1649, when the Kingarth session ordained Janet Crawford to satisfy for her fornication with '—— M'Kamy', it was revealed that 'The man is dwelling in the rout in Irland and the minister is desyred to wryt to Mr. Jeremiah O'Cronie about him, quhilk was accordingly done'. Henry Paton (ed.), *The Session Book of Kingarth, 1641–1703* (Edinburgh, 1932), p. 9.
70. *Minutes of the Synod of Argyll*, I, p. 153.
71. Ker graduated in 1646. Scott Pearson, 'Puritan and Presbyterian Settlements in Ireland, 1560–1660', I, p. 84.
72. Mitchell and Christie, *General Assembly Commission Records, II, 1648–1649*, pp. 275–76.
73. Mitchell and Christie, *General Assembly Commission Records, II, 1648–1649*, p. 277, notes. They asked for advice from the General Assembly and for affirmation 'whither or not those things, which we object against in your Representation, be all true'.
74. Mitchell and Christie, *General Assembly Commission Records, II, 1648–1649*, pp. 278–79, p. 279 n; Kilroy, 'Radical Religion in Ireland', p. 205. Though the Assembly upheld the presbytery's censure, it deemed 'that the

grounds and way of their dissenting from yow have bein unsufficient'. The ministers were 'authorized againe to exercise their Ministry', but the Assembly urged a closing of ranks against 'the enemies' (the malignants or those who opposed the Covenants). The Assembly also thought extremely ill of the public divulgence by the two ministers of the grounds of the presbytery's complaint against them: 'These papers had been communicated to the commanders of the Commonwealth's forces in Down and Antrim, and were ultimately published in London, with the view of shewing "the pitifull slavery they lie under where a presbytery is established"'.

75. But O'Quinn's sterling work of evangelisation in the Gaelic language was eventually praised retrospectively by the synod of Ulster on 21 June 1710. *Records of the General Synod of Ulster*, I, p. 211. Both Ker and O'Quinn were restored as ministers about 1652, and like many others at this juncture subsequently took their salaries from the Protectorate. O'Quinn was first appointed on 30 March 1654 at £40 sterling per annum. It is, however, an estimation of his worth as an Irish missionary that he appeared on another list for 1654, as well as the list for 1655, at the grossly inflated salary of £100. O'Quinn's ministry in Billy, in the precinct of Belfast, was continually interrupted by his mission work to the south and west of Ireland. In 1654 he was sent to Athy, Connacht and Athlone and Loughrea to preach. On 23 October 1657, in the records of the Inquisition taken at Antrim, he is described as 'Mr Jeremy Quinn, a preaching minister in salary'. He died on 31 January 1658. Scott Pearson, 'Puritan and Presbyterian settlements in Ireland, 1560–1660', I, pp. 82–84, p. 82 n.

76. Kilroy, 'Radical Religion in Ireland', p. 205.

77. *Presbyterian Church in Ireland*, II (1837), pp. 272–75, and for the list of names, *Presbyterian Church in Ireland*, II (1837) appendix No. 13, pp. 492–96. However, a Highland origin cannot necessarily be imputed for some of these names. MacClee, for instance, may represent either the MacLeays of Easter and Wester Ross and Argyll, the McOnleas of Lunga, Rothesay and Islay or the MacLeas of Banffshire. Similarly, Macilroy is an old surname in Ballantrae, Ayrshire and in Ayr, but it is also found in Rothesay in Bute, Perth and Inverness. Macclellans hail from Galloway, but also from Morar in Inverness-shire, and Aberfeldy in Perthshire. Ferguson is found in Atholl, but also in Aberdeenshire and Ayrshire. And it is difficult to know the derivation of M'Kerger, though it could conceivably be Macerchar (MacKerchar and other variations) from 'Mac Fhearachair', 'son of Farochar', a name found in Kintyre in Argyll, and in Glenorchy, Inverness and Moray. The nearest to the form M'Kerger is M'Kerquhar, which appears in Caithness in 1662. George F. Black, *The Surnames of Scotland* (New York, 1946), pp. 533–36, 514–15, 470, 260, 490–91.

78. Kilroy, 'Radical Religion in Ireland', p. 205.

79. NAS CH2/1153/1, Presbytery of Kintyre, fol. 22. This was to be announced publicly to the congregation.
80. Black, *Surnames of Scotland*, pp. 694, 562. Originally Macintoshes descended from Richard Macintosh, MacRitchies appeared in Glenshee in the late sixteenth century; and some have been connected with the parishes of Clunie and Caputh in Perthshire since 1683.
81. Stevenson, *Scottish Covenanters and Irish Confederates*, p. 20.
82. *Fasti*, VII, pp. 49, 355. Translating from Suddie after a year, his place was taken by the Royalist sympathiser Murdo MacKenzie, for whom see above and below. This establishes Suddie, like Ardnamurchan, as a peripheral repository for politically suspect ministers.
83. Furgol, *Scottish Covenanting Armies*, pp. 73, 323, 326–27, 335. From 1642 to 1644 the army was quartered in a 'coastal crescent' stretching from Limavady, to the south-west of Coleraine, to the Lecale, south of Strangford Lough, with outlying representations at Dungannon, in Tyrone, Mountjoy, in Armagh, and Newry in Down. The outposts were abandoned in the winter of 1643–44. *Ibid.*, p. 324.
84. Furgol, *Scottish Covenanting Armies*, pp. 328–29.
85. Mitchell and Christie, *General Assembly Commission Records, I, 1646–47*, p. 33.
86. Furgol, *Scottish Covenanting Armies*, pp. 329–30. The presbytery even went as far as to depose Church of Ireland clergy, indicating not only the extent of their power, but the way in which presbyterian clergy could be brought in and kirk sessions established.
87. Stevenson, *Scottish Covenanters and Irish Confederates*, p. 31; Furgol, *Scottish Covenanting Armies*, pp. 83, 100–01, 39. It was Gustavus Adolphus in Sweden who blueprinted the concept of the Godly army and recognised that ministers from the same area as a regiment could best inspire them. Leven, having fought under him, drew on this ideology. But where Adolphus had recommended two chaplains per regiment, the Covenanters found it difficult enough to supply one (although it must be said that no Covenanter army, from 1639 to 1651, ever took to the field without a chaplain). Furgol, *Scottish Covenanting Armies*, pp. 83, 85.
88. Alexander Fraser, *North Knapdale in the Seventeenth and Eighteenth Centuries* (Oban, 1964), p. 117.
89. The precise calculation is 5.4 months.
90. Furgol, *Scottish Covenanting Armies*, pp. 94, 108, 112.
91. *Minutes of the Synod of Argyll*, I, pp. 43, 66, 90–91.
92. *Minutes of the Synod of Argyll*, I, p. 36.
93. *Minutes of the Synod of Argyll*, I, pp. 43, 66, 90–91. Mr MacCallum, Campbell's relief, also remained in Ireland at least a year, because the synod provided for the bi-monthly services at his kirk in May 1644.
94. Fraser, *North Knapdale*, p. 107, quoting J. R. N. Macphail (ed.), *Highland Papers, IV*, SHS, 3rd series, 22 (Edinburgh, 1934), p. 68.
95. Fraser, *North Knapdale*, p. 107, quoting J. R. N. Macphail (ed.),

Highland Papers, II, SHS, 2nd series, 12 (Edinburgh, 1916), p. 217; *Fasti*, IV, p. 15.

96. Indeed, prior to his visit to Ireland he had, in 1640, accompanied a similar Argyll expedition to the North, possibly witnessing the harrying of Badenoch, Lochaber and Rannoch and the burning of the House of Airlie, when Argyll ravaged the lands of the Earl of Atholl and the Farquharsons during the Second Bishops' War. Fraser, *North Knapdale*, p. 113.
97. Scott Pearson, 'Puritan and Presbyterian Settlements in Ireland, 1560–1660', I, pp. 45, 86, 91.
98. See Chapter 1, section headed 'Effect of the Plantation of Ulster on Religious Connections', and Chapter 2, section headed 'The Advancing Tide of Protestantism'. Note that the one possible Highland appointment in the bishopric of Derry appears to have been of an absentee.
99. Scott Pearson, 'Puritan and Presbyterian Settlements in Ireland, 1560–1660', I, pp. 73–75; Furgol, *Scottish Covenanting Armies*, p. 331.
100. That is, licensed to minister, but without a charge.
101. For more on the Stewarts of Ballintoy, see the Rev. George Hill, *The Stewarts of Ballintoy (with notices of other families in the district in the seventeenth century)* (Ballycastle, 1976 reprint).
102. Archibald Stewart may have been holding out for an uncompromising presbyterian. Scott Pearson, 'Puritan and Presbyterian settlements in Ireland, 1560–1660', I, p. 77. McNeill, on the other hand, seems to have been protecting himself: he was probably the 'Daniel MacNeile', minister in Ballycastle, in receipt of a salary of £80 sterling salary from the Commonwealth in 1655, and was almost definitely the 'Daniel M'Neale' who by 12 September 1661 was vicar of Billy, Culfeightrin and Loughguile. *Presbyterian Church in Ireland*, II (1837), p. 354 n., appendix no. 14, p. 499.
103. Mitchell and Christie, *General Assembly Commission Records, I*, 1646–47, p. 203.
104. *Minutes of the Synod of Argyll*, I, p. 118.
105. The 'continent' simply refers to the mainland Highlands. It was only a short journey from Islay to Knapdale.
106. Mitchell and Christie, *Minutes of the Synod of Argyll*, I, p. 123.
107. Stevenson, *Alasdair MacColla*, p. 40; *IFM*, pp. 53–54.
108. David Stevenson, *Revolution and Counter-Revolution in Scotland, 1644–1651* (London, 1977), p. 24; David Stevenson, *The Scottish Revolution, 1637–1644* (Newton Abbot, 1973), p. 26.
109. Allan I. Macinnes, 'Scottish Gaeldom, 1638–1651: The Vernacular Response to the Covenanting Dynamic', in John Dwyer, Roger A. Mason and Alexander Murdoch (eds.), *New Perspectives on the Politics and Culture of Early Modern Scotland* (Edinburgh, 1982), p. 83. Only among the Clan Donald South and the MacDonalds of Clanranald (though not of Sleat) had anti-presbyterianism become associated with Catholicism by this time, because under the episcopal direction of the Church (1610–37) most of the other Highland clans

had acquired a semblance of Protestantism.

110. Hence MacColla returned to the western seaboard in the summer of 1645, motivated by hatred of the Campbells – though MacLachlan, the minister of Islay, was not compelled to flee until the summer of 1648, possibly when the full extent of the demise of the Clan Donald South as a territorial clan was realised.

111. Furgol, *Scottish Covenanting Armies*, p. 211, quoting Cosmo Innes (ed.), *The Book of the Thanes of Cawdor*, Spalding Club, 30 (Edinburgh, 1859), p. 286.

112. Stevenson, *Scottish Covenanters and Irish Confederates*, p. 237.

113. Furgol, *Scottish Covenanting Armies*, p. 321, and also refer to Chapter 1, section headed 'Effect of the Plantation of Ulster on Religious Connections', and Chapter 2, section headed 'The Advancing Tide of Protestantism'.

114. A. F. Scott Pearson, 'Alumni of St. Andrews and the Settlement of Ulster', *UJA*, 3rd series, 14 (1951), p. 12; Scott Pearson, 'Puritan and Presbyterian settlements in Ireland, 1560–1660', II, p. 503; Rev. David Stewart, 'The History of the Presbyterian Settlements in Ireland 1641–1760' (unpublished typescript, Belfast, 1948), p. 74 n. Dugald Campbell, the parson, was introduced as parson of the parish of Conwal, in Donegal, in 1615, though he appears to have been in Ireland since September 1611 when ordained in the diocese of Raphoe. The parish church in Conwal was ruined, and a new one was built at Letterkenny in the same parish. But note that Stewart's footnote (quoting as sources the Visitation of Raphoe, 1622, the transactions of the Synod of Argyll, and the Minutes of Lagan Meeting) is exceptionally inaccurate and tries to piece together several bits of disparate information on different people – the parson of Letterkenny, his cousin Dugald who attended Argyll's regiment, as well as the former's son Duncan – as if they referred to the same person, stating in justification that this Campbell was 'called variously Dugald and Duncan'.

115. Fraser, *North Knapdale*, pp. 116, 128, quoting Macphail, *Highland Papers, IV*, p. 69.

116. John Lindsay had three sons by the parson's eldest daughter, two of whom (Dugald, minister of Glenorchy, and Colin, minister of Kilbrandon) continued to promote presbyterianism within Argyll.

117. Several of his wife's Scottish Campbell relations were also involved in this mammoth task. See below.

118. *Fasti*, IV, pp. 91–92, 49.

119. *Minutes of the Synod of Argyll*, II, p. 37. Having been in Ireland since 1611, Campbell would probably have been in his late sixties, possibly even his early seventies, by this point and seems to have decided to retire permanently to Scotland.

120. *Minutes of the Synod of Argyll*, II, p. 152.

121. Fraser, *North Knapdale*, pp. 122–27. The translation is thought to have been completed by 1662, but the manuscript seems to have disappeared. Campbell was also given the book of Ecclesiastes to translate when plans were underway to translate the bible into Gaelic, but whatever work he

did on this task it was not done by 1689.

122. *Presbyterian Church in Ireland*, II (1837), appendix, p. 497, extracts from 'The Civil Establishment of the Commonwealth for Ireland for the year 1655'.

123. See above, under the section headed 'Scottish Ministerial Collaborators'.

124. The Duke of Ormond, previous lord lieutenant of Ireland, was the leader (with Clanricard) of the Irish royalist adherents to the Stuarts.

125. Ormond's secretary, and heir of Tulske in County Roscommon.

126. T. C. Barnard, 'The Protestant Interest, 1641–1660', in Jane H. Ohlmeyer (ed.), *Ireland from Independence to Occupation* (Cambridge, 1995), p. 230.

127. Scott Pearson, 'Puritan and Presbyterian settlements in Ireland, 1560–1660', I, pp. 45–47. Jeremy O'Quinn, parish minister of Billy, was also a part of this Cromwellian vernacular missionary drive. In 1655, he was part of a mission to Connacht and Clare with James Wallace of Urney; Wallace conducted the preaching in English and O'Quinn in Irish.

128. Kilroy, 'Radical Religion in Ireland', p. 206.

129. NAS CH2/111/2, Presbytery of Dunoon, 1639–1686, fol. 148. Johnston does not appear as a minister in the *Fasti*; he was perhaps a kirk elder.

130. NAS CH2/111/2, fol. 165. Mr Patrick Stewart was a minister charged with swearing and sabbath-breaking. *Ibid.*, fol. 187.

131. PRONI D1759/1A/1, Presbytery of Antrim, 1654–1658, fols. 175–76.

132. See the rest of this chapter and Chapter 5, section headed 'Highland Ministers and Probationers of Irish Congregations'.

133. *Minutes of the Synod of Argyll*, II, p. 145.

134. PRONI D1759/1A/1, fol. 165.

135. The connection with the parson is indicated by a marginal addition by the twentieth-century copyist (of the Minutes of the Laggan Meeting) of an extract from the *Minutes of the Synod of Argyll*, relating to the parson.

136. PRONI D1759/1E/1, fol. 98.

137. For which, see Chapter 2, section headed 'The Advancing Tide of Protestantism'.

138. PRONI D1759/1E/1 fols. 140, 154, 168; *Irish Fasti*, p. 81.

139. *Presbyterian Church in Ireland*, II (1837), appendix no. 19, p. 516 n; PRONI D1759/1E/1, fol. 171.

140. Curiously, this reference is given in Francis H. Groome, *Ordnance Gazeteer of Scotland*, 6 vols. (London, Edinburgh and Glasgow, 1882–85), IV, p. 388.

141. PRONI D1759/1E/1 fols. 170, 172–73, 178, 183. A fellow minister was required 'to visit Fermanagh and to try that people's willingness in reference to their Call to Mr James Tailzour, and what encouragement they will give for this effect'.

142. PRONI D1759/1E/1, fols. 192–93.

143. PRONI D1759/1E/1, fol. 194.

144. PRONI D1759/1E/1, fol. 198. Salaries in Ireland were paid (as might be expected) in pounds sterling.

145. This perhaps refers to inadequate accommodation or an inability to get the necessary finance together because on 1 September 1675 a

letter was read from James Tailzeur, 'shewing that the people of Fermanagh cannot get his affairs so soon dispatched as the Meeting desired & expected; but that after a few days more time, they will get all things relating to his return to us, dispatched'. PRONI D1759/1E/1, fol. 195.

146. PRONI D1759/1E/1 fols. 198–99; Presbyterian Historical Society of Ireland, *A History of Congregations of the Presbyterian Church in Ireland, 1610–1982* (Belfast, 1982), p. 471.
147. PRONI D1759/1E/1, fols. 203, 245. Tailzeur was still in Scotland on 4 April 1676, and though Rule had returned from Scotland by 11 July 1676, there is no indication that Tailzeur was with him. *Ibid.*, fol. 241.
148. *Presbyterian Church in Ireland*, II (1837), appendix, pp. 515–17.
149. Beckett, *Making of Modern Ireland*, p. 133.
150. The reasons for the holding of the fast are not specified.
151. One of these was Robert Campbell, who had been ordained to Ray or Raymoghy in County Donegal in 1671. If he left Ireland after his release from prison (like William Trail), the question arises of what he was doing for a number of years afterwards, since he was not admitted to the parish of Rosneath on the Gareloch, in the Firth of Clyde, until 3 December 1689. And he probably spoke Gaelic, as there was a sizeable community of Highland Campbells there, because the Earl of Argyll maintained the Castle of Rosneath. *Fasti*, VII, p. 527; Stevenson, Alasdair MacColla, p. 52.
152. *Presbyterian Church in Ireland*, II (1837), pp. 421–25; Historical Manuscripts Commission, *Report on the Manuscripts of the Marquis of Ormonde K.P., Preserved at the Castle, Kilkenny*, II (London, 1899), pp. 219–20. Mr Trail became minister of Borthwick, in the Borders.
153. PRONI D1759/1E/1, fols. 292–93, 303.
154. PRONI D1759/1E/1, fols. 309–10, 319.
155. *Presbyterian Church in Ireland*, II (1837), appendix, p. 516 n.
156. PRONI D1759/1E/2, pp. 21–22.
157. PRONI D1759/1E/2, pp. 44–45, 53, 56–57, 65, 84.
158. PRONI D1759/1E/2, p. 50.
159. PRONI D1759/1E/2, p. 58.
160. PRONI D1759/1E/2, pp. 65–67.
161. Donaldson, *Scotland*, p. 371; *Presbyterian Church in Ireland*, II (1837), appendix, p. 516 n.
162. See, for instance, on this issue, A. L. Wyman, 'The Surgeoness: The Female Practitioner of Surgery, 1400–1800', *Medical History*, 28 (1984), pp. 22–41; M. Lochhead, *The Scots Household in the Eighteenth Century* (Edinburgh, 1948), pp. 332–41.
163. PRONI D1759/1E/2, pp. 69–70.
164. PRONI D1759/1E/2, p. 103. The minutes of the Lagan meeting resume in December 1690.
165. Presbyterian Historical Society, *History of Congregations*, pp. 471, 501–02; *Irish Fasti*, p. 81. Tailzeur died in 1694.
166. *Irish Fasti*, p. 61; Donaldson, *Scotland*, pp. 379–80. It has been suggested that Darroch might have been in Ireland, but the evidence is inconclusive. The Scottish *Fasti*, IV, p. 58, states that he 'Had

charge of a Presbyterian congregation at Glenarm in Ireland; returned at the Toleration, and was present at the erection of the Synod 29th Sept, and of Presbytery 9th November 1687'. But no corroborating evidence has been found to support his being in Ireland prior to 1688. Moreover, neither the *Fasti of the Irish Presbyterian Church*, p. 61, nor the *History of Congregations of the Presbyterian Church in Ireland*, p. 500, has any information on his being in there prior to 1688. The minister of Glenarm (1674 to 1685) was the Rev. John Anderson; the Rev. Hugh Crawford was called there in July 1686. *Ibid.*, pp. 499–500.

167. NAS CH2/1153/1, Presbytery of Kintyre, fols. 35–36.
168. NAS CH2/1153/1, fols. 36–37.
169. NAS CH2/557/3, Synod of Argyll, fol. 6.
170. *Irish Fasti*, p. 61.
171. PRONI D1759/1A/2, Minutes of the Antrim meeting, 1671–1691, fol. 397.
172. PRONI D1759/1A/2, fol. 398.
173. PRONI D1759/1A/2, fol. 398.
174. NAS CH2/557/3, Synod of Argyll, fol. 10.
175. NAS CH2/557/3, fol. 10; NAS CH2/1153/1, fols. 37–38.
176. NAS CH2/1153/1, fol. 38.
177. NAS CH2/557/3, fol. 10.
178. PRONI D1759/1A/2, fols. 413, 416. The proportional breakdown of payment was recorded thus: 'Cushendall promises a fourth part of Stipend further upon their being supply'd every fourth day, or more, if every third day; wherein the meeting acquiesces for the present, as likewise Mr. Darragh: The bonds of which payment they promise to renew every year during his incumbency.' *Ibid.*, fol. 417.
179. PRONI D1759/1A/2, fols. 417, 419. Little is known other than that he was designated in February to supply Antrim for one sabbath, and that he was excused from the March sederunt.
180. NAS CH2/557/3, fol. 16; Presbyterian Historical Society, *History of Congregations*, p. 500.
181. PRONI D1759/1A/2, fol. 425.
182. NAS CH2/1153/1, fol. 38. Indeed, Darroch's presence brought the number of ministers in the bounds of the presbytery up to three, so that 'the meeting is put in a greater capacitie to acte in the capacitie of a fixed presbyterie'.
183. NAS CH2/557/3, fol. 45. On 9 October 1690, owing to the burden of all his children, he was to receive '£60 Scots for keeping Wiliam Darroch his son att schoole'.
184. See Donald Gregory, *History of the Western Highlands and Islands of Scotland from A.D. 1493 to A.D. 1625* (Edinburgh, 1836), pp. 423–25; A. I. B. Stewart, 'Lachlan McNeill Buidhe', *The Scottish Genealogist*, 34, no. 4 (Dec. 1987), pp. 380–83; A. I. B. Stewart, 'Some Descendants of Lachlan McNeill Buidhe', *The Scottish Genealogist*, 34, no. 4 (Dec. 1987), pp. 377–79; and for the Irish branch of the family, PRONI T1071, Pedigree of Col. James Graham Robert Douglas McNeill C.B. and of the McNeills of Faughart, Cushendun, Gallochelly and Colonsay.
185. NAS CH2/1153/1, fol. 41.
186. NAS CH2/1153/1, fol. 42. Subsequently the parish presented

a formal call to Darroch (which had been one of his main grievances), but it was only signed by the laird of Loup, Kilberry and John dow MacAllister. Skipness, for example, would not sign unless Darroch gave a service in the church formerly proposed by his father, but Darroch had indicated that the parish was too large for such an undertaking. The presbytery insisted that it be signed by more heritors and as many of the common people as possible. NAS CH2/1153/1, fol. 43.

187. *Fasti*, IV, p. 3; NAS CH2/557/4, fol. 211.
188. NAS CH2/557/3, Synod of Argyll, fol. 753.
189. NAS CH2/557/3, fol. 6.
190. *Fasti*, IV, p. 37.
191. *Fasti*, IV, p. 134.
192. See Chapter 4.

Notes to Chapter 4: Seducing the People to Popery, 1638–1689

1. Anson, *Underground Catholicism*, pp. 47–48, 50.
2. Anson, *Underground Catholicism*, pp. 52, 54, 100.
3. Rev. Breifne Walker, 'Blessed Oliver Plunkett and the Popish Plot in Ireland', *The Irish Ecclesiastical Record*, 5th series, 109 (1968), p. 327.
4. The very Rev. Duncan Canon MacLean, 'Mr. Robert Munro, Secular Priest, 1671–1704', *St. Peter's College Magazine*, 20, no. 77 (1951), p. 51. The general disturbance caused by the Popish Plot also caused some backlash against Highland presbyterian communities in Donegal. See Chapter 3, section headed 'Mr James Tailzeur, First Minister of Enniskillen'.
5. Anson, *Underground Catholicism*, pp. 77–78.
6. David Stevenson, 'The Irish Franciscan Mission to Scotland and the Irish Rebellion of 1641', *Innes Review*, 30 (1979), p. 54.
7. *IFM*, p. 180. At this time, he was still asking *Propaganda* for his allowance for the previous nine years.
8. *IFM*, p. 181.
9. Stevenson, 'The Irish Franciscan Mission to Scotland and the Irish Rebellion of 1641', p. 55.
10. See Chapter 3, section headed 'Highland Ministers in Ireland'.
11. *IFM*, p. 183.
12. *IFM*, p. 185.
13. Timothy Paul Joseph McCall, 'The Gaelic Background to the Settlement of Antrim and Down, 1580–1641' (unpublished MA thesis, Queen's University, Belfast, 1983), p. 126; David Stevenson, *Scottish Covenanters and Irish Confederates* (Belfast, 1981), p. 90.
14. Stevenson, 'The Irish Franciscan Mission to Scotland and the Irish Rebellion of 1641', pp. 55–57, 61. For earlier Jesuit activity, see Chapter 1, section headed 'The Jesuit Missions'.
15. *Minutes of the Synod of Argyll*, I, p. 37.
16. For whom see Chapter 3, section headed 'Scottish Ministerial Collaborators'.
17. *Memoirs of Scottish Catholics*, I, p. 268. The Jesuit of Highland extraction 'succeeded in obtaining the good will of his relatives and connections in the Highlands, who said it was much to be regretted,

that a man of high character and learning should not be able to find a convenient home in his native land, and devote his powers to the service of his country and his nation'. The three Jesuits in the north of Scotland were Fr. John Smith, Fr. William Grant and Fr. Andrew Leslie. Of these, Fr. William Grant was the most likely to have been of Highland origin. Certainly a William Grant of Conglass, in the north-east Highlands, was excommunicated later in October 1668 and may represent the fruit of earlier work in that area. *Ibid.*, I, pp. 232, 268, 313; II, p. 395.

18. A. Roberts, 'The "Irishes" in Scotland, 1644–1647', *The Glynns*, 14 (1986), p. 41. MacBreck wrote that Montrose allowed the Jesuit priests free scope in the exercise of their functions. *Memoirs of Scottish Catholics*, I, p. 266.
19. Stevenson, *Scottish Covenanters and Irish Confederates*, p. 173; *Memoirs of Scottish Catholics*, I, p. 281.
20. *Memoirs of Scottish Catholics*, I, p. 291; Rev. W. J. Anderson, 'Narratives of the Scottish Reformation IV Prefect Ballentine's Report, *circa* 1660. Part 2', *Innes Review*, 8 (1957), pp. 109–10.
21. *Memoirs of Scottish Catholics*, I, p. 298.
22. See below, section headed 'Results of the Mission'.
23. *Memoirs of Scottish Catholics*, I, p. 306.
24. For MacBreck's report on the religious state of the MacIan family in Glencoe, see below, section headed 'Results of the Mission'.
25. Most churches dating from the medieval period were either in use as Protestant churches or were in a state of ruin, so mass tended to be celebrated in the open air. Celebration of open-air mass in the vicinity of a boulder or rock – the mass stone or *clach na h-aifrinn* – used as a natural altar, probably derived as a practice from Ireland. That the priests travelling with the army were Irish is consistent with the dating of two extant mass stones in Lochaber to this period, though it is always possible that the stones date from a later period. A. MacDonell and D. McRoberts, 'The Mass Stones of Lochaber', *Innes Review*, 17 (1966), pp. 71–72.
26. *Memoirs of Scottish Catholics*, I, pp. 334, 341, 344.
27. Murdoch MacLean, tenth of Lochbuie, on the contrary, seems to have remained firmly committed to Catholicism during this period, though his heir Lachlan nominally submitted to the synod of Argyll in 1651.
28. See Chapter 3, section headed 'Scottish Ministerial Collaborators'.
29. *Memoirs of Scottish Catholics*, I, p. 355; Allan I. Macinnes, 'The Vernacular Response to the Covenanting Dynamic', in John Dwyer, Roger A. Mason and Alexander Murdoch (eds.), *New Perspectives on the Politics and Culture of Early Modern Scotland* (Edinburgh, 1982), p. 81.
30. Macinnes, 'Vernacular Response', p. 84.
31. Roberts, 'The "Irishes" in Scotland', p. 40; L. Duggan, 'The Irish Brigade with Montrose', *The Irish Ecclesiastical Record*, 5th

series, 89 (1958), pp. 251–52.

32. A. F. Mitchell and J. Christie (eds.), *General Assembly Commission Records, I, 1646–1647*, SHS, 2nd series, 11 (Edinburgh, 1892), p. 67.
33. Mitchell and Christie, *General Assembly Commission Records, I, 1646–1647*, pp. 70–71.
34. *IFM*, p. 187.
35. See Chapter 2, section headed 'The Franciscan Mission to the Highlands and Islands'.
36. *IFM*, p. xiv.
37. For Nerabolls, see Chapter 1, section headed 'The Catholic Counter-Attack'.
38. Rev. Dom. Mark Dilworth, OSB, 'Benedictine Monks of Ratisbon and Wurzburg in the 17th and 18th Centuries: Émigres from the Highlands of Scotland', *TGSI*, 44 (1964–66), pp. 97–99; Anson, *Underground Catholicism*, p. 16. Both Nicholas and George Dunbar later appeared on the Scottish mission (neither on the Highland mission), except briefly during the Revolution when Nicholas took refuge with the King's party in the Highland hills. Dilworth, 'Benedictine Monks', pp. 98–99.
39. Rev. Seán MacGuaire, 'Ireland and the Catholic Hebrides', *The Irish Ecclesiastical Record*, 5th series, 42 (1933), p. 360.
40. Anson, *Underground Catholicism*, pp. 15–16. 'It was not until well after the middle of the nineteenth century that secular priests in England began to be addressed as "Father", a custom introduced apparently from Ireland. In Scotland, the secular clergy continued to be addressed as "Mr." until after the restoration of the hierarchy in 1878.' *Ibid.*, p. 12 n.
41. Anderson, 'Ballentine's Report', p. 114.
42. Anson, *Underground Catholicism*, pp. 54–55, 62, p. 57 n.
43. Anderson, 'Ballentine's Report', pp. 100, 111. The published report is dated *c.* 1660. There is a section entitled: 'On the Chief Families of the Kingdom who Profess the Catholic Faith', which as the Rev. Anderson has pointed out is 'essentially a list of houses where itinerant missionaries could safely visit, where they not be betrayed, rather than a census of persons in full communion with the Holy See', though there was, perhaps, little difference between the two at the time. *Ibid.*, pp. 112–13.
44. Cathaldus Giblin, 'The Mission to the Highlands and Isles *c.* 1670', *Franciscan College Annual* (Multyfarnham, 1954), p. 12. For the Vincentians, see below.
45. Giblin, 'The Mission to the Highlands and the Isles *c.* 1670', p. 12 n. Note that Horan, a secular, is mentioned immediately after them. The original reads: 'et Joannes Borgo, Maksuini, et Horano'. Either of these could conceivably also have been one of the three Irish working on the Highland mission in 1659.
46. Anson, *Underground Catholicism*, pp. 67, 69.
47. MacGuaire, 'Ireland and the Catholic Hebrides', pp. 358–59.
48. Vern L. Bullough and Bonnie Bullough, *The Care of the Sick: The Emergence of Modern Nursing* (London, 1979), pp. 60–62.
49. Mary Purcell, *The Story of the Vincentians* (Dublin, 1973), p. 42. He was of the opinion that their knowledge of Gaelic made them

best equipped for the mission. However, some of the notes to the chapter on the Vincentians in Scotland are inaccurate, e.g. note 31.

50. Purcell, *Vincentians*, p. 44; Stevenson, *Scottish Covenanters and Irish Confederates*, p. 189. In September 1647, Angus Og MacDonell of Glengarry had accompanied Antrim to Ireland to fight with Owen Roe O'Neill (though few of his clansmen appear to have accompanied him). Annie M. MacKenzie (ed.), *Orain Iain Luim*, The Scottish Gaelic Texts Society (Edinburgh, 1973), p. 250.

51. Dom Odo Blundell, *The Catholic Highlands of Scotland*, 2 vols., *I, The Central Highlands*, *II, The Western Highlands and Islands* (Edinburgh and London, 1909 and 1917), II, p. 160.

52. D. O. Blundell, 'St. Vincent of Paul and the Highlands of Scotland', *Dublin Review*, 149, (1911), p. 305. Some other accounts – notably Gordon's Annual List of Scottish priests on the mission – give the misinformation that the priests were brought from Spain by MacDonell of Glengarry. Rev. J. F. S. Gordon, *Journal and Appendix to Scotichronicon and Monasticon*, 4 vols. (Glasgow, 1867), I, p. 627. But inaccuracies and incompleteness notwithstanding, the list is an invaluable initial guide to missionaries in the Highlands and Islands during this period. The exact date of their arrival, 1 March 1651, can be taken from an autograph on the title page of a book – Tirinus' *Commentaries on the Scriptures* – still preserved in Scottish archives. Purcell, *Vincentians*, pp. 43–44.

53. Duggan used this experience to make a plea to de Paul for doctors to come on the mission to act jointly as healers and missionaries, for there were no doctors within a ninety-mile radius. Purcell, *Vincentians*, p. 46.

54. Blundell's interpretation of their understanding of 'conversion' is worth quoting. He writes: 'Throughout these accounts of the missionary labours in the Highlands and islands, when it is said that so many persons were "converted", this must be understood of their being granted the grace of the Sacraments which hitherto they had never had any opportunity of receiving, and of acquiring correct instruction in place of the erroneous ideas which the absence of proper teachers had allowed to grow up amongst them.' Blundell, 'St. Vincent of Paul and the Highlands of Scotland', p. 308. Also see *IFM*, p. xii, for Giblin's view of what was meant by the word 'conversion'.

55. Blundell, 'St. Vincent of Paul and the Highlands of Scotland', p. 306. Blundell does not offer a modern transcription for this word. Purcell's translation simply substitutes 'the Lord of another island'. MacGuaire, 'Ireland and the Catholic Hebrides', p. 360. And there is nothing in modern ordnance survey maps which approximates to it. It might be a Latin variant of 'Scalpay' (off the Isle of Skye near Pabay), or possibly 'Calfa', an isle near the coast of Mull. James T. Clark (ed.), *MacFarlane's Geographical*

Collections, III, SHS, 1st series, 53 (Edinburgh, 1908), p. 279.
56. Blundell, 'St. Vincent of Paul and the Highlands of Scotland', p. 306.
57. Purcell, *Vincentians*, p. 47; Blundell, 'St. Vincent of Paul and the Highlands of Scotland', p. 307.
58. Blundell, 'St. Vincent of Paul and the Highlands of Scotland', p. 307.
59. Clanranald had landed on Islay in the previous decade. For which, see Chapter 2, section headed 'Achievements of the Mission'.
60. Blundell, 'St. Vincent of Paul and the Highlands of Scotland', p. 307.
61. Giblin, 'The Mission to the Highlands and the Isles *c.* 1670', p. 12. White was in Paris by September 1660. The Vincentians' financial backing from Paris failed in 1661.
62. MacGuaire, 'Ireland and the Catholic Hebrides', p. 361.
63. MacGuaire, 'Ireland and the Catholic Hebrides', p. 361
64. Giblin, 'The Mission to the Highlands and the Isles *c.* 1670', p. 18.
65. The first noted minister was John MacKinnon who was rector in 1633, although he may not have been resident. The next minister was Martin MacPherson, who was admitted before 6 May 1642. *Fasti*, VII, p. 194.
66. MacGuaire, 'Ireland and the Catholic Hebrides', p. 361.
67. Eigg, which has survived to the present century almost totally Catholic, received continuous attention from the end of the seventeenth century. It was served by Hugh Ryan in 1690, William O'Hara from 1699 and Anthony Kelly from 1726. See Chapter 6.
68. MacGuaire, 'Ireland and the Catholic Hebrides', p. 361.
69. *Minutes of the Synod of Argyll*, II, p. 27.
70. *Minutes of the Synod of Argyll*, II, p. 109.
71. This is possibly Domhnall MacIain 'Ic Sheumais – grandson of James MacDonald of Castle Camus (late tutor to Donald Gorm Mòr) – mentioned just before he died in the early 1650s. He had been born in his mother's native district of Moidart, but brought up at Castle Camus. A. and A. MacDonald, *Clan Donald*, 3 vols. (Inverness, 1896, 1900, 1904), III, pp. 500–03.
72. *Minutes of the Synod of Argyll*, II, pp. 121–22. Candort = Knoydart.
73. *Minutes of the Synod of Argyll*, II, p. 122. The Captains of Clanranald, elder and younger, were in a state of excommunication.
74. *Minutes of the Synod of Argyll*, II, p. 122.
75. *Minutes of the Synod of Argyll*, II, p. 170.
76. MacGuaire, 'Ireland and the Catholic Hebrides', pp. 361–62.
77. MacGuaire, 'Ireland and the Catholic Hebrides', p. 362.
78. MacGuaire, 'Ireland and the Catholic Hebrides', p. 362. Duggan's labours in Barra are commemorated by a mountain pass – *Bealach a' Dhugain*, and also in South Uist by an old graveyard – *Cladh a' Ghùgain*. *Ibid.*, p. 362; Purcell, *Vincentians*, p. 49.
79. See introduction to Chapter 2.
80. *Fasti*, VII, p. 189.
81. *The Scots Magazine*, 28 (1766), p. 514.
82. MacGuaire, 'Ireland and the Catholic Hebrides', p. 363.
83. MacGuaire, 'Ireland and the Catholic Hebrides', p. 364.

84. Purcell, *Vincentians*, p. 51. Duggan's tomb is in the old church at Kilvanan. Michael Barrett, OSB of Fort Augustus Abbey, *Sidelights on Scottish History* (Edinburgh, 1918), p. 169 n. However in May 1658, the synod of Argyll referred to seminary priests in South Uist and Barra. Who were these? Certainly, Horan was in the Hebrides in 1657, or this may refer to Brin and Ennery. For whom, see above, section headed 'Laying the Foundation of the Secular Mission, 1653–1680'; *Minutes of the Synod of Argyll*, II, p. 170.
85. Purcell, *Vincentians*, p. 49. Thomas Lumsden was with White during the summer of 1654. He was still on the mission in the autumn of 1657 when he wrote to de Paul about his work in the Orkneys, Moray, Ross, Sutherland, 'Candie', Caithness and the Lowlands. *Ibid.*, pp. 49–51.
86. Blundell, 'St. Vincent of Paul and the Highlands of Scotland', pp. 310–11.
87. Purcell, *Vincentians*, pp. 50, 52.
88. Purcell, *Vincentians*, p. 53.
89. Cathaldus Giblin, 'The 'Acta' of *Propaganda* Archives and the Scottish Mission 1623–1670', *Innes Review*, 5 (1954), p. 64 n. Horan probably operated in the Isles and in any case returned to Ireland in 1664. The Dominican, Fr. George Fanning, seems to have come in about 1663, but he was probably in Barra.
90. Purcell, *Vincentians*, pp. 51–53.
91. Purcell, *Vincentians*, pp. 54–55, 58; Donald MacLean, 'Roman Catholicism in Scotland in the Reign of Charles II,' *RSCHS*, 3 (1929), p. 49. Dunbar wrote in his mission report of 1669–70 that 'the schoolmaster is scarcely tolerated in Glengarry, despite the protection of the lord of that territory; and there is but little hope of position'.
92. Purcell, *Vincentians*, p. 56.
93. Giblin, 'The 'Acta' of *Propaganda* Archives', p. 67 n.
94. Purcell, *Vincentians*, pp. 56–57. For the Franciscans, see below.
95. Purcell, *Vincentians*, p. 58.
96. It is very interesting that Seaforth was given permission to let him stay, but it must be remembered that Scotland was now in its period of episcopal government, and it might have been concluded that Lewis was a peripheral enough area. However, it should be noted that there is no mention of White in the relevant Privy Council volume, that is in *RPCS*, 1669–72.
97. Giblin, 'The Mission to the Highlands and the Isles *c.* 1670', p. 19.
98. David McRoberts, 'The Death of Father Francis White', *Innes Review*, 17 (1966), pp. 186–88; Purcell, *Vincentians*, pp. 59–61. In a document of *c.* 1678 (noted by Lord Fountainhall in his *Historical Notices*), White is much maligned: he is accused of having debauched the wife of the Captain of Clanranald, her husband returning to find them 'together in some unchast posture; wheiron he immediately caused lead out the Priest to his utter gate and hing him over it'. The story is generally regarded as an unsubstantiated piece of anti-Catholic propaganda, issued at a time when the Paisley witch-hunt and the Titus Oates plot of 1678 encouraged such behaviour, because all surviving

reports of White are favourable. McRoberts, 'Father Francis White', pp. 186–88.

99. Anthony Ross, 'Dominicans and Scotland in the Seventeenth Century', *Innes Review*, 23 (1972), p. 45.
100. D. C. Pochin Mould, *The Irish Dominicans. The Friars Preachers in the History of Catholic Ireland* (Dublin, 1957), p. 154.
101. Ross, 'Dominicans and Scotland', p. 46.
102. Ross, 'Dominicans and Scotland', pp. 46–47.
103. Pochin Mould, *Irish Dominicans*, p. 154. This refers to the official revival of the Franciscan mission to the Highlands in January 1647. The seventeenth century was particularly marked by rivalry between the Irish Dominicans and Franciscans; *Propaganda* may not have wished to see competition developing between the two in such a troublesome and impoverished area. Ross, 'Dominicans and Scotland', p. 46.
104. Ross, 'Dominicans and Scotland', pp. 44–59. Primrose died in 1670.
105. Blundell, *The Catholic Highlands of Scotland*, II, pp. 10, 17.
106. Anson, *Underground Catholicism*, p. 71.
107. Blundell, *The Catholic Highlands of Scotland*, II, p. 8.
108. Ross, 'Dominicans and Scotland', p. 52.
109. Giblin, 'The Mission to the Highlands and the Isles, *c.* 1670', p. 20; Anson, *Underground Catholicism*, p. 87 n. He was probably the unnamed Dominican who David Burnet, then vice-principal of the Scots College in Paris, mentioned as working in the Isles in a letter to Rome in May 1677.
110. Ross, 'Dominicans and Scotland', pp. 52–54.
111. See above, section headed 'Laying the Foundation of the Secular Mission, 1653–1680'.
112. Giblin, 'The Mission to the Highlands and the Isles', pp. 13–15.
113. The complaint could either have arisen from the Jesuits attempting to undermine any other authority in the north of Scotland, or possibly from the Dominicans, or from the secular authority itself through William Leslie, Scots agent at Rome.
114. Giblin, 'The Mission to the Highlands and the Isles *c.* 1670', p. 16.
115. Robert J. Hunter, 'The Ulster Plantation in the Counties of Armagh and Cavan 1608–41' (unpublished MLitt dissertation, Trinity College, Dublin, 1968), p. 77.
116. For those native Irish who did receive land in the plantation, see *A New History of Ireland*, III, pp. 201–02. For others of the Irish élite who did not either take to the woods or flee to the continent but conformed to the government's view of their future, there was a paltry living to be had as small tenant farmers on fairly unproductive pieces of land. Many who were children at the beginning of the plantation were by 1670 said to have been old men in freize coats, farming the small scraps of land which had been given to their fathers, reliant for their support on the kindness of retainers and friends who were mindful of their former status. Rev. George Hill, *An Historical*

Account of the Plantation in Ulster (Belfast, 1877), p. 349.

117. T. W. Moody, 'Redmond O'Hanlon', *Belfast Natural History Society Proclamations*, 2nd series, I (1937), pp. 17, 19, 21. For further discussion of the term Tory, see Allan I. Macinnes, 'Notes and Comments – the first Scottish Tories?', *SHR*, 67 (1988), pp. 56–66, on the anonymous poem 'An Cobhernandoir' (The Help of the Tories), which is a castigation of the Engagement or 'Band' of 1648 – an attempt by the Scottish nobility to rescue the King from captivity in return for a trial period of presbyterianism in England – from a Royalist standpoint. Also see Alison Ann Whyte, 'Scottish Gaelic Folksong 1500–1800' (unpublished BLitt dissertation, University of Glasgow, 1971), pp. 205–07, who first connected this song with the Engagement of 1648.
118. Twenty-one members of the principal families of O'Neill, MacDonnell and O'Hagan lived as Tories in his diocese in the counties of Tyrone and Armagh. Rev. Breifne Walker, 'Blessed Oliver Plunkett and the Popish Plot in Ireland', *The Irish Ecclesiastical Record*, 5th series, 109 (1968), p. 322.
119. Cathaldus Giblin, OFM, 'St. Oliver Plunkett, Francis MacDonnell, O.F.M. and the Mission to the Hebrides', *Collectanea Hibernica*, 17 (1974–75), pp. 73, 82; Walker, 'Blessed Oliver Plunkett', p. 321.
120. Gretchen M. MacMillan, *State, Society and Authority in Ireland: The Foundations of the Modern State* (Dublin, 1993), p. 45.
121. Giblin, 'The Mission to the Highlands and the Isles *c.* 1670', p. 17; Giblin, 'St. Oliver Plunkett', p. 72. But the appointment of Oliver Plunkett, newly designated archbishop of Armagh, as prefect of the Highland mission, was doubtless in anticipation of the expansion of the mission.
122. MacGuaire, 'Ireland and the Catholic Hebrides', p. 493.
123. William Ferguson, *Scotland's Relations with England: A Survey to 1707* (Edinburgh, 1977), pp. 147, 152–56.
124. MacGuaire, 'Ireland and the Catholic Hebrides', p. 493; Giblin, 'The Mission to the Highlands and the Isles *c.* 1670', p. 18.
125. Giblin, 'The Mission to the Highlands and the Isles *c.* 1670', pp. 19–20.
126. William Mackay (ed.), *Records of the presbyteries of Inverness and Dingwall, 1643–1688*, SHS, 1st series, 24 (Edinburgh, 1896), p. 100.
127. SCA BL1/72/9, Blairs Letters, Scottish Mission Correspondence 1627–1694.
128. Giblin, 'St. Oliver Plunkett', p. 81; MacLean, 'Mr. Robert Munro, Secular Priest, 1671–1704', p. 51; Very Rev. Alexander Canon MacWilliam, 'A Highland Mission: Strathglass, 1671–1777', *Innes Review*, 24 (1973), p. 84. In September 1678, Munro was in the Isles with an Irish priest, 'Mr Drein', who has not yet been identified. 'A Highland Mission', p. 84. However, this is possibly a mistranscription for 'O Rein' or O'Ryan, which might suggest that Hugh Ryan visited the mission two years before his arrival in 1680, or the presence of another Irish

priest.

129. Giblin, 'St. Oliver Plunkett', pp. 81–82.
130. Anson, *Underground Catholicism*, p. 76.
131. James Darragh, 'The Catholic Population of Scotland since the Year 1680', *Innes Review*, 4, No. 1 (Spring 1953), p. 52.
132. Giblin, 'The Mission to the Highlands and the Isles *c.* 1670,' p. 20. There are no further references to James MacDonnell, nor does he appear in Gordon's Annual List.
133. Anson, *Underground Catholicism*, p. 77.
134. SCA CC1/8–15, Canon William Clapperton, 'Memoirs of Missionary Priests', revised and transcribed by the very Rev. George Canon Wilson, pp. 271–72.
135. Mackay, *Presbyteries of Inverness and Dingwall*, p. 100.
136. Anderson, 'Ballentine's Report', pp. 112–13.
137. SCA BL1/72/9.
138. Clapperton, 'Memoirs', p. 273.
139. Mackay, *Presbyteries of Inverness and Dingwall*, p. 100; MacWilliam, 'Strathglass, 1671–1777', pp. 82–83.
140. Coates is near Edinburgh.
141. Coates and his wife probably converted to Catholicism in the early 1670s. They were certainly placed under process of excommunication, on 28 May 1670, along with Robert Munro 'for obstinacie, defection, and apostacie form the doctrine and ordinances of the Church of Scotland'. Munro, the Scots priest who served Strathglass, was also their chaplain. Mackay, *Presbyteries of Inverness and Dingwall*, pp. 3, xxxv.
142. Cahassy also refers to him as 'Mr Voyer' in SCA BL1/90/1, fol. 1.
143. Clapperton, 'Memoirs', pp. 287, 301, 640, 638. Clues to Devoyer and Cahassy's denomination can be taken from Clapperton in his various references to Mr Talon; they received an allowance of eighty crowns a year from Saint-Lazare, paid through the agency of Talon. Purcell, *Vincentians*, p. 61. Devoyer and Cahassy knew each other on arrival, and continued to work closely together until Devoyer's death. But it is most unlikely, as indicated in Wendy Doran's list, that Devoyer was a Jesuit. Wendy J. Doran, 'Bishop Thomas Nicolson and the Roman Catholic Mission to Scotland, 1694–1718' (unpublished MLitt dissertation, Glasgow, 1986), p. 147. Most Jesuits worked on the north-eastern periphery of the Highlands, and most were Scots.
144. Originally intending for Ireland, in November 1685 they decided 'not to goe in the conjuncture of the pretended and invented popish plot; and that our prelate was not pleased with any of our vocation for going in that conjuncture'. SCA BL1/90/1. This copy letter is unaddressed, but Clapperton identifies the original recipient as Don Gulielmo Everard, chaplain to Cardinal Norfolk, which is corroborated by evidence within the letter.
145. SCA BL1/90/1. Note that Blundell in his *The Catholic Highlands of Scotland*, II, quoting Mr Thomson's notes (SCA) misdates their arrival to 1687. Although Hegarty's return was expected during this year, there is no evidence to suggest that he did. See below.

146. Clapperton, 'Memoirs', p. 330; SCA BL1/77/8.
147. Doran, 'Bishop Thomas Nicolson and the Roman Catholic Mission to Scotland 1694–1718', pp. 135, 137.
148. Clapperton, 'Memoirs', p. 321. However, Clapperton does not cite a source letter for this information.
149. SCA BL1/90/1.
150. SCA BL1/100/2; Donald MacLean, *The Counter-Reformation in Scotland 1560–1930* (London, 1931), p. 308. For the year 1687, Gordon's Annual List notes that Mr Thomas Nicolson (future bishop) and Mr J. Jameson arrived in December, and that 'with them came four Irish Churchmen, one of whom was called Coan'. The one specified name is clearly an inaccuracy, since Coan had been on the mission since the latter half of 1686.
151. SCA BL1/104/11, fol. 1; Clapperton, 'Memoirs', p. 300. Clapperton dates this letter 24 February 1687, but the manuscript shows that it was written on the 14th. As Clapperton shows, Gordon's Annual List is therefore in error in stating that Lea and Coan came at the end of 1687. By that time they had been on the mission for over a year.
152. Note that all translation from the French in the Blairs papers is my own. It aims to give a reasonably accurate but not fine prose translation. For those interested, the original French is to be found in the notes to Chapters 8 and 10 of my PhD thesis: Fiona Anne Macdonald, 'Ireland and Scotland: Historical Perspectives on the Gaelic Dimension, 1560–1760, 2 vols. (unpublished PhD dissertation, University of Glasgow, 1994), I and II.
153. SCA BL1/104/11, fol. 1.
154. See Chapter 6, section headed 'Bishop Nicolson's Visitation of the Highlands, 1700'.
155. For which see Chapter 2, section headed 'The Advancing Tide of Protestantism'.
156. SCA BL1/100/5. See also SCA BL1/104/11, fol. 1. Ryan must therefore have been elsewhere, possibly in Glengarry.
157. SCA BL1/100/5.
158. SCA BL1/99/1. Note that Clapperton, p. 313, transcribes this 22 November 1687, while the manuscript clearly reads '12'. Mr Lea had been installed dean of Down ('Doune') by papal brief, a post obtained through the influence of friends in Rome and the Primate of Ireland. The deanery (considered, along with Derry and Raphoe, one of the most valuable in the established Church in the early eighteenth century) had four parishes attached to it, but with the Primate's permission Lea was allowed to stay in Scotland. *A New History of Ireland*, IV, p. 85. For dioceses, see Fig. 1.1. His promotion was conditional on taking the degree of Doctor of Theology. A petition was made to Rome for the appointment 'to last as long as can be conveniently arranged'. (I owe this this translation from the Latin to Dr John Durkan.) Mr Lea promised to share the financial benefits of his office, which the Vicar-General would not permit him to draw on himself, with the mission. Clapperton, 'Memoirs', pp. 311–12. Note that Lea does not

appear as dean of Down in Henry Cotton's *Fasti Ecclesiae Hibernicae: The Succession of the Prelates and Members of the Cathedral Bodies in Ireland* (Dublin, 1845–50), III, p. 227, which was still held in 1687 by John McNeale, prebendary of Effin in the cathedral of Limerick, who had been installed on 15 February 1683. So Lea was probably an appointee of James VII.

159. SCA BL1/110/1.
160. SCA BL1/110/1.
161. SCA BL1/100/6. On the last occasion, they had spent a night there baptising children.
162. SCA BL1/100/2.
163. SCA BL1/100/2.
164. SCA BL1/100/6, BL1/100/5; Paul Hopkins, *Glencoe and the End of the Highland War* (Edinburgh, 1986), pp. 105, 534; MacWilliam, 'Strathglass, 1671–1777', p. 100. Fr. White had visited Lewis in 1671. See section headed 'The Vincentians', above.
165. Mark Dilworth, 'Notes: The Blind Harper and Catholicism', *Innes Review*, 22 (1971), p. 113. However, when he eventually came on the Highland mission he caused a great deal of contention and was very unpopular. See Chapter 6, section headed 'Mr Mongan, First Resident Missionary in Skye'.
166. SCA BL1/100/5.
167. SCA BL/100/7. Recapping on their achievements in 1687, Cahassy wrote on 18 July that it was 'a protestant District where there were only 5 or 6 Catholics'. SCA BL1/110/1.
168. The 'premier' or eldest cadet was the second son of the chief; younger sons of the chief also became *ceann-tighean* or heads of the houses into which the clan was divided. From them, at various points, derived the *sliochdan*, the distinctive branches or septs into which a clan divided, and who were identified by a progenitor (e.g. *sliochd Iain*).
169. Alasdair Roberts, 'Highland Catholicism at the Margin: Skye, Lewis and Ardnamurchan' (unpublished typescript), see section on Skye. I am grateful to Alasdair for sending me a copy of this paper. There had been feuding between MacLeod of Dunvegan and Harris and MacDonald of Sleat over Trotternish from the early sixteenth century. It was ultimately granted to MacDonald of Sleat in 1614, who had occupied it since 1540, though a considerable MacLeod presence appears to have remained. I. F. Grant, *The MacLeods: The History of a Clan, 1200–1956* (Edinburgh, 1981), pp. 95, 221–22.
170. Donald J. MacDonald of Castleton, *Clan Donald* (Loanhead, 1978), p. 402; SCA BL/100/7.
171. SCA BL/100/7.
172. Anson, *Underground Catholicism*, p. 80. This meeting took place in the aftermath of James VII's extension of tolerance to Catholics, and clearly aimed to review their activity within more lenient parameters.
173. SCA BL1/99/2. Blundell, *The Catholic Highlands of Scotland*, I, p. 174, quoting Thomson, notes (SCA), erroneously states that Hegarty did come back on the mission. But he took 'a Canon's post in Ireland' instead. SCA

BL1/99/1.

174. SCA BL1/99/2; SCA BL1/99/1. He was back in Uist in March. SCA BL1/110/12.

175. SCA BL1/110/13. Note that the *Fasti* identifies three possible ministers in Trotternish from 1662. The first of these, Farquhar M'Lennan (minister in 1662), was probably not there long enough to have made an impression on posterity. Within a year he had transferred to Strath in Skye. The other ministers were Donald Nicolson, admitted about 1663 and was probably outed after the Revolution in 1697, and Dugald MacPherson (presumably the son of Martin MacPherson, minister of Duirinish), who appears to have been styled minister during the previous incumbent's ministry in 1670. *Fasti*, VII, pp. 182, 171, 168.

176. SCA BL1/99/1. Cahassy reported to Burnet in March 1688 that they had been residing, since they came north at the beginning of the year, in a change house, which was not up to their expectations. 'Wee got there but the bare walls of a Chamber the Glasses of the windows broken, no bedds, chairs or Commoditie whatsomever', a state of affairs which was, indeed, hardly likely to cure a man of consumption. SCA BL1/110/12.

177. SCA BL1/110/1.

178. Anson, *Underground Catholicism*, p. 80.

179. SCA BL1/110/1.

180. Wendy Doran, 'Bishop Thomas Nicolson: First Vicar-Apostolic, 1695–1718', *Innes Review*, 39, no. 2 (1988), pp. 112–13, quoting letter Nicolson to Charles Whytford, Le Havre, 11 November 1687.

181. Clapperton, 'Memoirs', p. 332. Blundell, probably mistakenly, assumes Carolan to have been a Franciscan, since a Franciscan was left in Barra by Bishop Nicolson in 1700; by deduction from Gordon's Annual List, which has Heachean and Carolan serving in Barra, he assumes this was Carolan rather than Heachean. Blundell, *The Catholic Highlands of Scotland*, II, p. 18. For various reasons – see Chapter 6, section headed 'Bishop Nicolson's Visitation of the Highlands, 1700' – it is far more likely to have been Heachean.

182. SCA BL1/101/13.

183. The letter is not addressed, but he wrote to 'Notre Cher patron', that is, Mr Talon.

184. SCA BL1/118/14; Doran, 'Bishop Thomas Nicolson', *Innes Review*, p. 116. Note that Burnet included Glenlivet and Strathdon among the Highland areas, for to all intents and purposes they were to him, since they were Gaelic-speaking. Yet as Cahassy wrote in July 1688, the 'stations' where Carolan was working until the summer were 'close to the stations of our Lowland colleagues, and well removed from ours'. SCA BL1/110/1.

185. SCA BL1/110/1. He probably went via the mainland to receive instructions from his seniors.

186. SCA BL1/110/1; Clapperton, 'Memoirs', p. 314.

187. SCA BL1/110/3.

188. Clapperton, 'Memoirs', pp. 335–36.

189. SCA BL1/90/2.

190. Doran, 'Bishop Thomas Nicolson and the Roman Catholic Mission to Scotland, 1694–1718', pp. 135, 137.

191. SCA BL1/104/11, fols. 2, 3;

Clapperton, 'Memoirs', p. 304.

192. SCA BL1/100/5.

193. SCA BL1/100/5. Note that Clapperton, 'Memoirs', p. 307, is in error here; he states that all six were present except Lea. The original manuscript shows otherwise.

194. SCA BL1/100/2.

195. SCA BL1/100/5. The same Christian charity had been extended to Lea, who had similarly received 25 crowns of the pension from Rome like the others.

196. SCA BL1/110/12. After recovering from illness at the end of 1687, Mr Talon asked the Scottish superiors to brief him on the likely expense of a retreat for the Highland missionaries. Irish views were taken through Mr Cahassy. With a Catholic monarch on the throne, a Highland retreat became a possibility because it was no longer necessary for missionaries to retire to France to recuperate. Their plans were ultimately relayed to Mr Talon through Mr Louis Innes and Charles Whytford in Paris in a document entitled 'Memoire de ce qu'il faut pour l'establissement d'une maison pour servir de retraite aux Missionairs des Montagnes d'Escosse', dated 1687. SCA SM2/17/5. It suggests two possible locations: either Inverness or the Duke of Gordon's country. Inverness was rejected because most of the inhabitants were Protestant, potentially exposing priests to criticism and censure both physical and spiritual (hardly in accordance with the ideals of retreat); rent was exorbitant at 30 crowns per annum for three rooms; and lastly, 'if we buy a house or have one built there is a danger of losing it at the first change in public affairs'. A house in the Duke of Gordon's country would be far more convenient (if further from the Highlands), with the advantage that nearly all the surrounding countryside was Catholic in affiliation. Furthermore, the missioners had already bought a piece of ground there with a house, identified as Walkerdale, to which three extra rooms could easily be added. Clapperton, 'Memoirs', p. 315; SCA BL1/99/1.

197. SCA BL1/110/12.

198. SCA BL1/110/1.

199. Priests in the Lowlands still received the old rate of 50 crowns per year, though they could supplement that sum more easily.

200. Clapperton, 'Memoirs', pp. 317–18. Letter from Dunbar to Mr Whytford, dated 19 April 1688.

201. SCA BL1/110/3.

202. SCA BL1/110/3.

203. SCA BL1/118/16.

204. SCA BL1/118/16.

205. The ten were Ryan, Cahassy, Devoyer, Coan, Carolan, Hannat, Lea, Trener and the two new missionaries Harnet and Mongan.

206. SCA BL1/118/16.

207. SCA BL1/118/16.

208. Douai was in Belgium until 1667 when it became French.

209. At this time 'Erse' was a term used for both the Irish and Scottish Gaelic tongues.

210. Pochin Mould, *Irish Dominicans*, p. 272; M. V. Hay, *The Blairs Papers 1603–60* (London and Edinburgh, 1929), p. 151; the Very Rev. Alexander Canon MacWilliam, 'The Jesuit Mission in Upper Deeside 1671–1737', *Innes Review*, 23 (1972), pp. 24–25;

Memoirs of Scottish Catholics, II, pp. 120, 127.

211. I am grateful to the Rev. Mark Dilworth who suggested that the name 'Morgan' as it appears in Butte's index of the Blairs Letters (SCA) and the earlier Gordon's list was probably the Irish surname 'Mongan'. The clear signature on many of the original letters proves it to be Mongan.
212. Mr Talon had promised them 200 livres each, but had in effect only given them 135 livres. The balance was to be used to buy clothes and arms. Clapperton, 'Memoirs', p. 638.
213. Clapperton, 'Memoirs', p. 638. Dunbar's letter is dated 13 September 1688.
214. Clapperton, 'Memoirs', pp. 636, 639–40, 321. Mongan's subsequent missionary career is discussed in Chapter 6, section headed 'Mr Mongan, First Resident Missionary in Skye', as a result of the revitalisation of the record a few years after the Jacobite rebellion.
215. Clapperton, 'Memoirs', pp. 319–20.
216. Clapperton, 'Memoirs', p. 239.
217. Though a letter was slipped out from Skye in 1691.
218. SCA BL1/110/3.
219. SCA BL1/120/13. A transcription of the Latin, noting him as 'Natione Hybernum' is given in Clapperton, 'Memoirs', p. 331.
220. Hopkins, *Glencoe*, p. 105. The next part of Coan's story is taken up in Chapter 6, section headed 'Dynamic Secularism, 1690–1715', where it chronologically belongs.
221. SCA BL1/90/2, fol. 3.
222. SCA BL1/90/2, fol. 3.
223. Duncan Canon MacLean, 'Catholicism in the Highlands and Isles 1560–1680', *Innes Review*, 3 (1952), p. 12.
224. SCA BL1/90/2, fol. 3.
225. SCA BL1/90/2, fols. 2, 3.
226. SCA BL1/104/11, fol. 2.
227. For specific information see Chapter 2, section headed 'Achievements of the Mission'.
228. *Minutes of the Synod of Argyll*, II, p. 69.
229. See above, section headed 'Irish chaplains with Alasdair MacColla MacDonald'.
230. *Memoirs of Scottish Catholics*, I, pp. 300–04.
231. See Chapter 3, section headed 'Scottish Ministerial Collaborators'.
232. Forbes Leith, *Memoirs or Scottish Catholics, I*, pp. 317, 319.
233. Mitchell and Christie, *General Assembly Commission Records, 1646–47*, p. 67.
234. For instance, one Lauchlan McCawish appeared in front of the synod of Argyll in May 1650 for having been married to More NcNeill by a priest when the Royalists were in Kintyre. The excuse he gave was 'that he durst not mary that woman openly, for feare that old Sanay [Archibald MacDonald of Sanda] should hinder the same, who had intention to mary the woman upon one of his own kind'. The synod decided to let the marriage stand, but the couple were obliged to repent openly in the kirk of Lochhead for the scandal of having been married by a priest. *Minutes of the Synod of Argyll*, I, p. 162.
235. MacGuaire, 'Ireland and the Catholic Hebrides', p. 360.
236. Anderson, 'Ballentine's Report', p. 110. Ballantyne was inaccurate in stating that South Uist belonged

to Sir James MacDonald. He was presumably mixing Donald MacDonald of Clanranald with Sir James MacDonald of Sleat. MacDonald, *Clan Donald* (1978), p. 288.

237. MacGuaire, 'Ireland and the Catholic Hebrides', p. 360.
238. Anderson, 'Ballentine's Report', p. 111.
239. St Vincent de Paul (*c.* 1580–1660) was a French priest acclaimed for his organised philanthropic work. His care of the poor in Paris and his general piety inspired a revival in French Catholicism. In 1625, he founded an order of secular priests to undertake work in rural areas, which became the Congregation of the Mission, the Vincentians or Lazarists.
240. MacLean, 'Roman Catholicism in Scotland in the Reign of Charles II', pp.50–51. Identification of 'Candie' is problematic. There is a 'Candy' just below Strathbogie (OS 1:500000 NO7980), which is near the southern border of his mission, perhaps a possibility. All the other places visited by Lumsden appear to be substantial geographical areas or counties.
241. SCA BL1/90/2, fol. 2.
242. SCA BL1/104/11, fol. 2. Note that Clapperton, 'Memoirs', p. 302, records twenty-five villages in Arisaig, but the manuscript clearly has 'vingt trois' (23).
243. SCA BL1/104/11, fol. 3.
244. SCA BL1/90/1.
245. SCA BL1/104/11, fol. 2.
246. See Chapter 1, section headed 'Catholic Conformers and Protestant Reformers'.
247. SCA BL1/110/1.
248. Mackay, *Presbyteries of Inverness and Dingwall*, p. xxiv. Thomas Chisholm, Laird of Strathglass, had continued to adhere to his Catholic faith, being summoned to court and imprisoned in 1579. There had been some Jesuit activity in Strathglass between 1580 and 1600, although their retiral from the district shortly afterwards was probably caused by the conversion of Thomas Chisholm's descendants to the Protestant faith (the Jesuits always preferred to operate under protection). The Vincentians, White and Duggan, also visited Glengarry in the 1650s, and White again in 1672. See Fig. 4.1. These dates accord with the tradition of the inhabitants, recorded in the first decade of this century, that 'the interval between 1660 and 1680 is the date of the revival of the Catholic faith in Strathglass'. Blundell, *The Catholic Highlands of Scotland*, I, pp. 191–93.
249. Mackay, *Presbyteries of Inverness and Dingwall*, p. 77.
250. Blundell, *The Catholic Highlands of Scotland*, I, pp. 193–94. According to Blundell, those priests opened two stations: 'the one in the remote locality near Knockfin, where a humble chapel must have been built, as the place to this day is called *Achada-na-h-eaglais* (the Church field), the other about the centre of the district, at a place called Clachan Comar'. The priests can be identified as Munro and Ryan, who continued to labour in and around Strathglass for the rest of their time on the mission. 'Bishop Thomas Nicolson and the Roman Catholic Mission to Scotland, 1694–1718', Appendix 1, p. 147. In 1679, the region's Catholics are

mentioned at length, for which see Mackay, *Presbyteries of Inverness and Dingwall*, pp. 329, 90–92. On the other hand, a Royal Bounty memorial of 1726 insisted that there were only seven Catholics in the three regions of Stratherrick, Strathglass and the Airds as late as 1703. MacLean, 'Roman Catholicism in Scotland in the Reign of Charles II', p. 51. This would appear to be merely Protestant wishful thinking. It is difficult to align this with the Catholic tally of 640 Catholics noted in Strathglass in 1709, during Bishop Gordon's visitation. MacWilliam, 'Strathglass, 1671–1777', p. 89.

251. SCA BL1/99/1. For those few reconciled, see SCA BL1/99/1 and SCA BL1/110/1.

252. SCA BL1/90/2, fol. 3.

253. See Chapter 2, note 8.

254. SCA BL1/99/2. During the ceremony, they would mix salt in the water and put the child in a nanny-goat's skin. With the mother or father outside the door, the old man, holding the child in the door portal, would ask the mother from which illness she wished to protect the child by the baptism, and which particular fortune she wished for it. 'Having received his reply He throws the water over the child saying I baptise you for your father and mother, for your spouse and new child, for all your relations and friends, and I secure and preserve you from such illnesses and misfortune etc.' SCA BL1/1/99/2. Note that Cahassy did not mention that a goat was sacrificed to obtain the skin.

255. Henry Paton (ed.), *The Session Book of Kingarth, 1641–1703* (Edinburgh, 1932), pp. 13, 15, 20. On 17 March 1650, in Kingarth session, Archibald M'Neill confessed the use of a Gaelic charm, confessing 'that he maks thes charme in tallow and applyes the same to horses for a wristed legg'. *Ibid.*, p. 20.

256. J. L. Campbell, 'The Catholic Church in the Hebrides: 1560–1760', *The Tablet*, 206, no. 6032, (December 1955), p. 656; also see Chapter 2.

257. *Minutes of the Synod of Argyll*, I, p. 68.

258. SCA BL1/100/6. Uist was also a base from which to visit various other islands, especially in the summer.

259. SCA BL1/90/1, fol. 2.

260. SCA BL1/100/5.

261. SCA BL1/100/2.

262. *Minutes of the Synod of Argyll*, I, p. 60.

263. Campbell, 'The Catholic Church in the Hebrides: 1560–1760', p. 656.

264. Purcell, *Vincentians*, p. 54.

265. Allan I. Macinnes, 'Catholic Recusancy and the Penal Laws, 1603–1707', *RSCHS*, 23, pt. 1 (1987), p. 57.

266. SCA BL1/100/5. Another ten presented themselves to receive the faith while the missionaries were there.

267. SCA BL1/110/13. All the well-versed, anti-Catholic arguments were put forward, for example, that in France and Rome they worshipped images like little Gods and that they made more of the Virgin and the saints than Jesus Christ.

268. Those converted in Skye are referred to in SCA BL1/100/7 and

BL1/110/1.

269. See Chapter 6, section headed 'Reconcilation and Expansion'.
270. Campbell, 'The Catholic Church in the Hebrides: 1560–1760', p. 656.
271. See Chapter 2, section headed 'Hobnobbing with the Ulster Élite'.
272. See Chapter 1, section headed 'Catholic Conformers and Protestant Reformers'.
273. Stevenson, *Alasdair MacColla*, pp. 35, 49. Although it seemed unlikely that Ardnamurchan would fall to Catholicism, nevertheless see Chapter 6, section headed 'Presbyterian Counter-Attack', for Colin Campbell's subsequent introduction of Catholic converts to the area.

Notes to Chapter 5: Gaelic Presbyterian Co-operation, 1690–1760

1. *Presbyterian Church in Ireland*, II (1837), pp. 464–65. For the list of ministers, see Appendix no. XX, pp. 519–20.
2. William Ferguson, *Scotland 1689 to the Present* (Edinburgh, 1968), The Edinburgh History of Scotland, IV, pp. 103, 107; J. C. Beckett, *The Making of Modern Ireland, 1603–1923* (London, 1969), pp. 149–52, 157.
3. *Presbyterian Church in Ireland*, III (1853), pp. 13–14; *Irish Fasti*, p. 87.
4. *A New History of Ireland*, IV, p. 101.
5. Peter Brooke, *Ulster Presbyterianism: The Historical Perspective, 1610–1970* (Belfast, 1994), pp. 61–62.
6. *Presbyterian Church in Ireland*, III (1853), pp. 21–24, 66, 90–91; A. C. Anderson, *The Story of the Presbyterian Church in Ireland* (Newcastle, Co. Down, 1965), p. 52; *A New History of Ireland*, IV, p. 101.
7. See Chapter 3, section headed 'Highland Ministers in Ireland'.
8. William Ferguson, 'The Problems of the Established Church in the West Highlands and Islands in the Eighteenth Century', *RSCHS*, 17 (1969), pp. 16–21; Victor E. Durkacz, 'The Church of Scotland's Eighteenth-Century Attitudes to Gaelic Preaching', *SGS*, 13, pt. 2 (1981), p. 146.
9. See below, section headed 'The Significance of Jacobitism'.
10. See below, section headed 'Highland Ministers and Probationers of Irish Congregations'.
11. *Presbyterian Church in Ireland*, III (1853), pp. 92–103, 131–32, 138; Anderson, *Story of the Presbyterian Church*, pp. 57–61.
12. John Walsh, Colin Haydon and Stephen Taylor (eds.), *The Church of England, c. 1689–c. 1833: From Toleration to Tractarianism* (Cambridge, 1993), p. 15.
13. Durkacz, 'The Church of Scotland's Eighteenth-Century Attitudes to Gaelic Preaching', p. 154.
14. Highlanders undoubtedly first settled there in trading and commercial capacities. There was also a significant illegal dimension to these trading activities, for which see Fiona A. Macdonald, 'Perspectives on the Running of Contraband Cargoes between

Ireland and the Scottish Highlands in the Mid-Eighteenth Century', *SGS*, 17, Special volume, Festschrift for Professor D. S. Thomson, pp. 221–38.

15. *Presbyterian Church in Ireland*, III (1853), pp. 138–41; Anderson, *Story of the Presbyterian Church*, pp. 61–62.
16. *Presbyterian Church in Ireland*, III (1853), p. 209. The background to the presbytery of Dublin is that in 1696 a union was effected between the presbyterian and independent congregations of Leinster and Munster leading to the formation of the presbytery of Munster. Presbyterian ministers in Dublin linked with this presbytery to form the 'southern association'. Some Dublin ministers were members both of the southern association as well as the Synod of Ulster. By 1716, there were six presbyterian congregations in Dublin, which can be placed in two divisions: the Capel Street, Plunket Street and Usher's Quay congregations were distinctive as part of the synod of Ulster, under the charge of the presbytery of Belfast; the Wood Street, New Row and Cook Street congregations, on the other hand, though nominally presbyterian (and meeting as a presbytery) were basically independents. Although all the Dublin ministers convened at a meeting which they called a presbytery, it was more an association or 'ministerial conference', because it did not seek to exercise presbyterial authority over its members. During the non-subscription controversy, in 1726, the above-mentioned independent congregations joined with six other dissenting congregations in towns in the South to form the presbytery of Dublin (later the southern presbytery of Dublin), which was, however, more congregational in bent than presbyterian. The subscribing ministers of the South, on the other hand, established the presbytery of Dublin, under the jurisdiction of the synod of Ulster. *Presbyterian Church in Ireland*, III (1853), pp. 209, 237 n.; *A New History of Ireland*, IV, p. 99. For a more extensive history, see Clarke H. Irwin, *A History of Presbyterianism in Dublin and the South and West of Ireland* (London, 1890).
17. See below, section headed 'Missionaries to the Native Irish'.
18. *Presbyterian Church in Ireland*, III (1853), p. 215.
19. Durkacz, 'The Church of Scotland's Eighteenth-Century Attitudes to Gaelic Preaching', pp. 147–50, 153.
20. C. W. J. Withers, *Gaelic Scotland: The Transformation of a Culture Region* (London and New York, 1988), p. 136.
21. Kenneth M. MacKinnon, 'The School in Gaelic Scotland: Some Historical and Sociological Perspectives and Suggestions', *TGSI*, 47 (1971–72), pp. 374–91.
22. Ferguson, *Scotland 1689 to the Present*, pp. 110–11, 121–22.
23. Ferguson, 'The Problems of the Established Church', p. 22–23.
24. Ferguson, *Scotland 1689 to the Present*, pp. 113–14.
25. *Presbyterian Church in Ireland*, III (1853), pp. 230–31; Anderson, *Story of the Presbyterian Church*, p. 64.
26. *Presbyterian Church in Ireland*, III (1853), pp. 239–40, 248–327;

Anderson, *Story of the Presbyterian Church*, pp. 65–67; *A New History of Ireland*, IV, p. 103. A similar situation occurred in Dublin, for which see note 16, above.

27. Anderson, *Story of the Presbyterian Church*, p. 67; *A New History of Ireland*, IV, p. 102.
28. *Records of the General Synod of Ulster*, II, p. 157.
29. Anderson, *Story of the Presbyterian Church*, p. 67.
30. NAS CH2/273/1, Mull presbytery, 1729–1762, fol. 40. The presbytery was sympathetic to Erskine's view, advising its commissioners: ''Tis our Advice you side the most Moderate Party, with respect to Mr Erskin's Affair; as it is our Opinion, That if he be Chargeable with Nothing, but Defending the Rights of the Christian People, in the Choice of their Pastor, he ought to be treated with all Tenderness & Charity, by such as Differ from him and his adherents.'
31. Anderson, *Story of the Presbyterian Church*, p. 71. For the spread of Secession to Ulster, see Robert Allen, 'Scottish Ecclesiastical Influence upon Irish Presbyterianism' (unpublished MA dissertation, Queen's University, Belfast, 1940), pp. 87–180.
32. Rev. D. H. Whiteford, 'Jacobitism as a Factor in Presbyterian Episcopalian Relationships in Scotland, 1689–90', pt. 1, *RSCHS*, 16 (1966–68), pp. 137–39; Ferguson, *Scotland 1689 to the Present*, p. 102; Ferguson, 'The problems of the Established Church', p. 18.
33. Andrew L. Drummond and James Bulloch, *The Scottish Church, 1688–1843* (Edinburgh, 1973), p. 16.
34. Rev. D. H. Whiteford, 'Jacobitism as a Factor in Presbyterian Episcopalian Relationships in Scotland, 1689–1714', pt. II, *RSCHS*, 16 (1966–68), pp. 188, 193–94, 201.
35. *Presbyterian Church in Ireland*, III (1853), pp. 123–24.
36. Ferguson, *Scotland 1689 to the Present*, p. 119.
37. *Presbyterian Church in Ireland*, III (1853), pp. 203–04. The Establishment was anxious at this time, to secure both the loyalty and the numerical strength of the presbyterians; it passed resolutions in the Commons which exempted those who had taken a commission in the army or militia from prosecution under the Test Act, even though the Test Act was not itself repealed until 1780.
38. PRONI T448, Transcripts of State Papers for Ireland, fol. 280.
39. PRONI T448, Transcripts of State Papers for Ireland, fol. 281.
40. See below, section headed 'Missionaries to the Native Irish'.
41. See below, the case of Mr William Brodie, section headed 'Highland Ministers and Probationers of Irish Congregations'.
42. As shown in Chapter 3, it was assumed that those ministers who spoke Gaelic were not only culturally assimilated to the Gaelic cause, but were one step nearer to being politically disaffected. An obvious example is Mr James Stewart, Gaelic-speaking minister of Kingarth in Bute, who was reported by the presbytery of Dunoon in April 1746. At the time of the '45 rebellion, Stewart said things which were regarded as

politically suspect. According to the evidence, when he read the 'Commission's Seasonable Warning and Exhortation' regarding the rebellion, he attempted to modify it with his own comments, calling for moderation. He had apparently said 'That there was much more noise made of Robberies and Disturbances they were making than he believed to be true', and also that 'there was a great noise made that they were to bring in Popery amongst us but he thought they were in no Danger at this time Nor did he think it in a king's power to do so'. The presbytery's decision to consult the General Assembly on the matter with a view to proceeding to a formal libel against him, indicates the extent of their fear. On 10 June 1746, Stewart was suspended 'from the Exercise of all the parts of the Ministerial Office'. But it was short-lived; he was later restored and chosen as moderator on 12 November 1751. NAS CH2/111/5, Presbytery of Dunoon, 1737–1761, fols. 92, 94, 97, 99, 153.

43. Maryburgh later became Fort William.
44. NAS CH2/568/1, Minutes of the Synod of Glenelg, 1725–1749, fols. 148–49. For 'Irish preacher' read Gaelic-speaking preacher.
45. NAS CH2/568/1, fol. 150.
46. *Fasti*, IV, p. 130.
47. British Library (henceforth BL) Add. Ms. 35,447, Hardwicke Papers, XCIX, fol. 151.
48. Anson, *Underground Catholicism*, p. 150.
49. BL Add. Ms. 35,447, fol. 153. On abandoning Catholicism in the eighteenth century, although the Clanranalds were not personally hostile to their Catholic tenants, their factors artfully supplanted and ejected them, replacing them with Protestants from North Uist, Skye and Harris, while the Catholics were expatriated. Rev. J. F. S. Gordon, *Journal and Appendix to the Scotichronicon and Monasticon*, I (Glasgow, 1847), p. 626. It would therefore appear that most of these settlers were from the Isles.
50. BL Add. Ms. 35,447, fol. 153.
51. *Presbyterian Church in Ireland*, III (1853), p. 15; *Records of the General Synod of Ulster*, I, p. 5. See, for example, the entry for 30 September 1691.
52. *Records of the General Synod of Ulster*, I, p. 13.
53. *Presbyterian Church in Ireland*, II (1837), Appendix, no. XX, pp. 519–20.
54. NAS CH2/1153/1, Presbytery of Kintyre, 1655–1706, fol. 68.
55. Ferguson, 'The Problems of the Established Church', pp. 18–19.
56. Alexander Campbell of Stonefield, former minister of Kilmore and Kilbride in Lorn, a Gaelic speaker who had been involved in the translation of the Psalms into Gaelic in the 1670s, would appear to be the most likely candidate in such a case. A non-juror, he was deprived at the Revolution for not praying to William and Mary (though the *Fasti*, unfortunately, gives no indication that he went to Ireland on his deprivation). *Fasti*, IV, p. 94.
57. *Fasti*, IV, p. 23. Some of these ministers were actually assisted in their flight to Ireland. On 13 June 1696, for instance, the Faculty of Advocates considered 'a petitione

given in to the Faculty by Mr John Park sometyme minister at Carriden that the petitioner being to goe to Ireland where he is hopefull to obtain freedome to preach the gospell and haveing nothing to support him in his intended journey nor to maintain his wife and numerous family and therfor begging the Faculty would extend some of their charity for his releife, the Dean and Faculty allow the petitioner £30 for his reliefe and ordain their thesaurer to make payment to him therof'. John MacPherson Pinkerton (ed.), *The Minute Book of the Faculty of Advocates I, 1661–1712*, Stair Society, 31 (Edinburgh, 1976), p. 169.

58. *Fasti*, IV, p. 56.
59. *Fasti*, IV, p. 62; J. B. Craven (ed.), *Records of the Dioceses of Argyll and the Isles, 1560–1860* (Kirkwall, 1907), pp. 151, 166.
60. *Fasti*, IV, pp. 49–50.
61. *Fasti*, IV, p. 75; Craven, *Dioceses of Argyll and the Isles*, p. 151.
62. *Fasti*, IV, p. 13.
63. John Bannerman, *The Beatons, a Medical Kindred in the Classical Gaelic Tradition* (Edinburgh, 1986), pp. 36–38, 127; *Fasti*, IV, p. 114.
64. For an account of Lhuyd in the neighbouring Scottish Highlands, see J. L. Campbell and Derick Thomson, *Edward Lhuyd in the Scottish Highlands, 1699–1700* (Oxford, 1963).
65. Bannerman, *The Beatons*, p. 38.
66. *Fasti*, IV, pp. 2, 6, 9, 13, 23, 29, 31, 40, 50, 56, 58, 60, 62, 73, 92, 94, 96, 106, 112, 117, 119. Owing to the severe shortage of ministers in the Highlands, however, there were a number like William Campbell, minister of North Knapdale, who later conformed and was accepted by the less radical presbytery of Perth, and Dugald Lindsay who retained his charge till 1728 though he never conformed to presbyterianism. *Fasti*, IV, pp. 16, 86. In Argyll, all but three ministers were interrupted in their tenure but some subsequently recovered their charges. Andrew L. Drummond and James Bulloch, *The Scottish Church 1688–1843* (Edinburgh, 1973), p. 8.
67. C. W. J. Withers, 'The Highland Parishes in 1698: An Examination of Sources for the Definition of the Gaidhealtachd', *Scottish Studies*, 24 (1980), pp. 68–69; Gordon Donaldson, *Scotland James V to James VII* (Edinburgh, 1971), p. 366. In calculating these fifty-six parishes, joint charges have been noted as one parish (and not separately as they were for the distribution of the Bible for which this list was compiled). This is therefore an accurate representation of the number of charges at this time.
68. *Fasti*, IV, p. 56; *Irish Fasti*, p. 116.
69. *Irish Fasti*, p. 116; *Fasti*, IV, p. 56.
70. NAS CH2/1153/1, fol. 94.
71. NAS CH2/1153/1, fol. 70.
72. See Chapter 3, section headed 'Mr John Darroch, Minister of Glenarm and Cushendall'.
73. NAS CH2/1153/1, fols. 78–79, 82, 84.
74. NAS CH2/1153/1, fol. 86.
75. *Fasti*, IV, p. 56.
76. NAS CH2/1153/1, fol. 94.
77. *Irish Fasti*, p. 116. MacLean is the first noted presbyterian minister of the Markethill presbyterian congregation, though there had

been presbyterian families there since 1607, when eighteen Scottish families settled under the protection of Mr Henry Acheson who had a grant of a thousand acres. Some of the early ministers between 1607 and 1634 were probably prescopalians. Note, however, that the Irish spelling of the name was MacLaine. Presbyterian Historical Society of Ireland, *A History of Congregations in the Presbyterian Church in Ireland, 1610–1982* (Belfast, 1982), p. 635.

78. In addition, one of his daughters married the Rev. John Menogh, minister at Magherally, Ireland, and another, the Rev. Robert Milling, minister of the Scots Kirk of Leyden from 1702 to 1710, at the Hague. *Irish Fasti*, p. 116. Like the family of Dugald Campbell of Letterkenny (see Chapter 1, section headed 'Effect of the Plantation of Ulster on Religious Connections, and Chapter 3, section headed 'Mr Dugald Campbell'), the dynasty of Archibald MacLean constituted, in itself, a new ecclesiastical dynasty.
79. See below, section headed 'Missionaries to the Native Irish'.
80. *Fasti*, IV, pp. 129–30.
81. NAS CH2/557/5, Synod of Argyll, 1708–1727, fols. 156, 163.
82. Withers, *Gaelic Scotland*, p. 137.
83. NAS CH2/984/2, Lorn presbytery, 1707–1714, fols. 305, 307, 313, 316, 321–22, 329.
84. The case of Francis MacDonnell or Macdonald, later, in 1743, is another in point. A former priest in the Kinlochmoidart region and probably guilty of an incestuous relationship with his sister Catherine, the Establishment was nevertheless prepared (most unusually) to overlook his horrendous sexual crimes and welcome him into the fold as a Royal Bounty missionary in nearby Strontian. His familiarity with Catholic controversy, his unparallelled knowledge of the area and his ability to speak Gaelic obviously outweighed his fundamental sins against Christianity. Even the presbyterian Kirk had its price. Ferguson, 'The Problems of the Established Church', pp. 25–28.
85. NAS CH2/984/2, fols. 347, 354–55, 358.
86. The next book of the presbytery of Lorn begins in 1729.
87. See, for instance, Hector MacDonnell, 'Jacobitism and the Third and Fourth Earls of Antrim', *The Glynns*, 13 (1985), pp. 50–54; F. J. McLynn, 'Ireland and the Jacobite Rising of 1745', *Irish Sword*, 13 (1982), pp. 339–52.
88. Mr Alexander Sinclair and Captain Malcolm McNeill (brother-in-law of Patrick Simpson, minister of Dundalk) were appointed to write the letter. For McNeill, see below. Presbyterian Church in Ireland, *General Synod of Ulster, 1691–1720*, p. 403.
89. Ferguson, 'The Problems of the Established Church', p. 21.
90. *Records of the General Synod of Ulster*, I, p. 403.
91. J. M. Barkley, 'The History of the Ruling Eldership in Irish Presbyterianism', 2 vols. (unpublished MA dissertation, Queen's University, Belfast, 1952), II, p. 166. This includes appendix extracts from Old Session Minute Books.
92. *Records of the General Synod of*

Ulster, I, p. 441.
93. See Patrick Simpson, below.
94. NAS CH2/557/5, Synod of Argyll, 1708–1727, fols. 196–97.
95. *Records of the General Synod of Ulster*, I, p. 422.
96. *Records of the General Synod of Ulster*, I, p. 457.
97. *Irish Fasti*, p. 121.
98. NAS National Register of Archives, Argyll Survey, I, 28, bundle 547.
99. These two brothers were very active members of the Dundalk congregation. According to the Presbyterian Historical Society's *Congregations*, they were ancestors of Sir John McNeill, an engineer who came from Scotland towards the end of the seventeenth century, who built his house on the site of the old manse occupied by his kinsman, the Rev. Patrick Simpson. However, according to the manuscript pedigree of the McNeills, they were related to, rather than being ancestors of, John McNeill. Archibald was his full brother, and Malcolm a half-brother from his father's second marriage. The only sister in the pedigree whose marriage is not stipulated is Elizabeth McNeill who, therefore, must have married Simpson. PRONI T1071, Pedigree of Col. James Graham Robert Douglas MacNeill, CB., and of the McNeills of Faughart, Cushendun, Gallochelly and Colonsay, descendants of the McNeills of Gigha and Taynish. Archibald McNeill was instrumental in the building of the old presbyterian church in Dundalk (the second church erected there for presbyterians). Equally philanthropic, his brother Malcolm built a presbyterian church at Ballyscanlon, 3½ miles from Dundalk. Presbyterian Historical Society, *History of Congregations*, p. 452. Thus, the contribution made by the descendants of the McNeills of Kintyre to the presbyterian community in Ulster was very significant. On this, see, for instance, Randal McDonnell, 'The McNeills of Cushendun and the McNeiles of Ballycastle', *The Glynns*, 1 (1979), pp. 21–24.
100. See Chapter 1, section headed 'Catholic Conformers and Protestant Reformers'.
101. For the continuing importance of the university of Glasgow to Ulster students, see Iain M. Bishop, 'The Education of Ulster Students at Glasgow University during the Eighteenth Century' (unpublished MA dissertation, Queen's University Belfast, 1987).
102. A. L. Drummond and J. Bulloch, *The Scottish Church, 1688–1843* (Edinburgh, 1973), pp. 31–34; *Presbyterian Church in Ireland*, III (1853), pp. 237, 405.
103. *Presbyterian Church in Ireland*, III (1853), pp. 297, 298 notes. He was responsible at the Synod of 1724, for instance, for taking shorthand notes on the case of Thomas Nevin, a non-subcriber accused of Arianism, to which the Synod tried, unsuccessfully, to put a stop. Arianism or Unitarianism was the assertion of the unity of the Godhead rather than the Trinity. These notes were eventually used by Nevin to write a 300-page account of the proceedings.
104. Presbyterian Historical Society, *History of Congregations*, p. 451.
105. For further details see below,

section headed 'Missionaries to the Native Irish'.

106. *Irish Fasti*, p. 121.

107. NAS CH2/190/2, Presbytery of Inveraray, 1691–1702, fol. 89.

108. NAS CH2/190/2, fols. 90, 93, 98.

109. Presbyterian Historical Society, *History of Congregations*, p. 451; Presbyterian Historical Society Record card index, Belfast. He died twenty years later, in November 1781, at the grand age of ninety-nine and was buried at Ballymascanlan.

110. *Records of the General Synod of Ulster*, I, p. 211. See below, section headed 'Missionaries to the Native Irish'.

111. Presbyterian Historical Society, *History of Congregations*, p. 451.

112. Campbell was the son of John Campbell of Kildaloig, chamberlain of Kintyre, who was a great friend and correspondent of Wodrow, the minister and historian. *Irish Fasti*, p. 92.

113. NAS CH2/1153/2, Presbytery of Kintyre, 1707–1723, fol. 53; *Irish Fasti*, p. 92.

114. *Records of the General Synod of Ulster*, I, pp. 131, 144. Note that there is a discrepancy here with the *Irish Fasti*, p. 92 which records that he was installed at Capel St., Rutland Square, on 10 September 1707. The discrepancy perhaps arises from an original mistranscription of '10' and '16', or more probably from the Scottish *Fasti* which also records the 10th.

115. NAS CH1/2/26/2, General Assembly Papers, fol. 181.

116. NAS CH1/2/27/2, fols. 155–56 is a letter from P. Campbell, moderator of the presbytery of Kintyre, from Campbeltown on 4 June 1707, to the Commission, defending the presbytery's action in making ministers transportable within the Synod of Argyll.

117. NAS CH2/1153/2, fol. 53.

118. *Irish Fasti*, p. 92. There is some controversy over the place of death. *Congregations in the Presbyterian Church in Ireland*, p. 427, records that he died in Dublin in October 1708, but, he was undoubtedly buried in Kintyre where his tombstone lies, so his body may have been returned after death.

119. NAS CH2/1153/2, fol. 280.

120. NAS CH2/1153/3, Presbytery of Kintyre, 1724–1748, fols. 159, 207.

121. NAS CH2/273/1, Mull Presbytery, 1729–1762, fol. 61. Barbour had been ordained missionary in Strontian on 27 May 1730. Having declined calls to Torosay in Mull and Kilmallie in the presbytery of Abertarff in 1731 and 1733, he finally accepted the call of the parish of Morvern in 1742. *Fasti*, IV, p. 117.

122. NAS CH2/984/2, Lorn Presbytery, 1707–1714, fol. 56.

123. Ministers could be tried only by the presbytery. MacCalman might also have refuted the session as an episcopalian (but then there is little reason for him later complying with the presbytery).

124. NAS CH2/984/2, fols. 55–56.

125. NAS CH2/984/2, fols. 96, 101.

126. The manuscript has 'Clifnamabrie'.

127. Major Sir Duncan Campbell of Barcaldine and Glenure, *The Clan Campbell*, 8 vols. (Edinburgh, 1916), IV, p. 43. This was a branch of the Campbells of Dunstaffnage, from which the branches of Combie and Ederline on Loch Awe

are descended.

128. NAS CH2/984/2, fols. 102–03, 109.

129. NAS CH2/984/2, fols. 108–09, 132, 135. Gray is the anglicisation of McIlghlais; *glas* means grey/blue.

130. NAS CH2/984/2, fols. 123, 130.

131. A grassy islet in Loch Etive, opposite the coast of Bonawe in the parish of Ardchattan, Argyll, called Duirinnis or Duirnish would seem the most likely location. Francis H. Groome, *Ordnance Gazeteer of Scotland*, 6 vols. (London, 1882–85), II, p. 382.

132. At this time, Highland society was essentially a pastoral economy in which seasonal population movement was associated with the transfer of cattle to the upland pastures. In the summer, there was movement to the shieling or the *baile samhraidh* (summer town), and in the winter, to the more permanent occupation, the *baile geamhraidh* (winter town). For a study of the shieling in the central Highlands, see Albert Bil, *The Shieling 1600–1840: The Case of the Central Scottish Highlands* (Edinburgh, 1990).

133. NAS CH2/984/2, fol. 159

134. NAS CH2/984/2, fols. 123, 130–32; NAS CH2/557/5, Synod of Argyll, 1708–1727, fols. 34, 36.

135. For an argument against the widely held conception that clan society was static and immobile before the mid-eighteenth century, see Allan I. Macinnes, 'Social Mobility in Medieval and Early Modern Scottish Gaeldom: The Controvertible Evidence', *TGSI*, 58 (1992–94), pp. 371–405.

136. NAS CH2/984/2, fols. 134–35, 143, 151, 153, 159.

137. NAS CH2/984/2, fols. 159, 170, 181.

138. NAS CH2/984/2, fols. 210, 213, 239.

139. *The Edinburgh Evening Courant*, 17 to 21 April 1735, p. 4.

140. *The Edinburgh Evening Courant*, 20 to 22 May 1735, p. 4.

141. *The Edinburgh Evening Courant*, 27 to 29 May 1735, p. 3.

142. NAS CH2/273/1, Mull presbytery, fols. 51–53, 62; *The Edinburgh Evening Courant*, 13 to 17 November 1735, p. 4.

143. Ferguson, 'The Problems of the Established Church', p. 25.

144. NAS CH2/1153/2, Presbytery of Kintyre, 1707–1723, fols. 186, 188–89, 313.

145. NAS CH2/214/1, Kilmory Kirk Session, 1718–1723, fol. 83.

146. NAS CH2/557/4, Synod of Argyll, 1701–1707, fol. 45.

147. In that year, the burgh records of Campbeltown recorded an embargo on all shipping in the harbour 'in consequence of an order from the Lord Justice Clerk to the Honourable Commissioners of the Customs'. Argyll and Bute District Archives BC/1/2, Burgh Records of Campbeltown, 28 September 1739 – 29 September 1767, fol. 31.

148. NAS CH2/984/3, Lorn presbytery, 1729–1771, fol. 164.

149. See above, section headed 'Highland Ministers and Probationers of Irish Congregations'.

150. See Chapter 1, section headed 'Effect of the Plantation of Ulster on Religious Connections'.

151. NAS CH2/557/5, Synod of Argyll, 1707–1727, fol. 31.

152. Barkley, 'Ruling Eldership in Irish Presbyterianism', I, p. iii.

153. Barkley, 'Ruling Eldership in Irish Presbyterianism', II, Appendices –

'Extracts from the old Session Minute-Books' (extract from the Larne and Kilwaughter session book, 1699–1701), p. 121.

154. Barkley, 'Ruling Eldership in Irish Presbyterianism', II (extract from the Larne and Kilwaughter session book, 1720–1826), p. 131.

155. Henry Paton (ed.), *Rothesay Parish Records. The Session Book of Rothesay, 1658–1750* (Edinburgh, 1931), p. 285. For use of testimonials as indicators of mobility in the Lowlands in seventeenth- and eighteenth-century Scotland, see R. Houston, 'Geographical Mobility in Scotland, 1652–1811: The Evidence of Testimonials', *Journal of Historical Geography*, 11, 4 (1985), pp. 379–94.

156. Rev. D. MacLean, 'The Life and Literary Labours of the Rev. Robert Kirk of Aberfoyle', *TGSI*, 31 (1922–24), p. 337.

157. See Chapter 2, section headed 'The Advancing Tide of Protestantism'.

158. MacLean, 'Robert Kirk of Aberfoyle', p. 337.

159. Victor Durkacz, 'The Source of the Language Problem in Scottish Education, 1688–1709', *SHR*, 57 (1978), p. 29.

160. The synod of Argyll had produced the First Fifty Psalms of David in 1659, but Kirk was the first to complete all 150 psalms. However, Kirk's work was limited by his use of both the classical language and Irish orthography, and was less understandable than the synod of Argyll's publication, in 1694, of the remaining 100 psalms, which were in the vernacular. MacLean, 'Robert Kirk of Aberfoyle', p. 334.

161. MacLean, 'Robert Kirk of Aberfoyle', p. 335.

162. Donald W. MacKenzie, 'The Worthy Translator – How the Scottish Gaels Got the Scriptures in Their Own Tongue', *TGSI*, 57 (1990–92), pp. 174–75.

163. Jane Dawson, 'Calvinism and the Gaidhealtachd in Scotland', in A. Pettegree, A. Duke and G. Lewis (eds.), *Calvinism in Europe 1540–1620* (Cambridge, 1994), pp. 234–38.

164. John Bannerman, 'Literacy in the Highlands', in Ian B. Cowan and Duncan Shaw (eds.), *The Renaissance and Reformation in Scotland* (Edinburgh, 1983), p. 224.

165. Donald Meek, 'The Gaelic Bible', in David F. Wright (ed.), *The Bible in Scottish Life and Literature* (Edinburgh, 1988), pp. 10–11.

166. MacLean, 'Robert Kirk of Aberfoyle', pp. 338–40.

167. MacLean, 'Robert Kirk of Aberfoyle', pp. 339, 342. Only 108 can be traced to parishes.

168. MacLean, 'Robert Kirk of Aberfoyle', pp. 347, 350, 352, 355–56.

169. Henry Paton (ed.), *The Session Book of Kingarth, 1641–1750* (Edinburgh, 1932), pp. 186–87.

170. Durkacz, 'The Source of the Language Problem in Scottish Education', pp. 33–34.

171. NAS CH2/557/5, Synod of Argyll, 1708–1727, fol. 286.

172. Indeed in December 1738 Hannibal Hall, a Dublin surgeon, left £100 sterling to the Scottish rather than the Irish branch of the Society. NAS GD95/10/148, SSPCK Records. As late as this, the two presbyterian communities were still supporting each other's missionary endeavours.

173. Sir James Balfour Paul, *The Scots Peerage*, 9 vols. (Edinburgh,

1904–1911), IV, p. 551.

174. NAS GD95/10/153, SSPCK Records.

175. NAS GD95/10/152 is docketed 'Plans for Manufacture'. Probably a list of the sites which the Society hoped to develop, it mentions 'Lewes at Stornoway, Skye portrie or Danevagan, Glenelg, Maryburgh, Fort Augustus, Brae Mar, Blair Atholl, Cairston in orkney and Kirkmichall'.

176. *Records of the General Synod of Ulster*, I, p. 38.

177. *Records of the General Synod of Ulster*, I, pp. 38, 42; *Irish Fasti*, p. 116.

178. *Records of the General Synod of Ulster*, I, p. 211. MacLean, as already mentioned, was of Highland origin. James McGregor was Irish. Humphrey Thompson was educated at Glasgow and ordained in Ireland, but no information is given about his place of origin. *Irish Fasti*, pp. 115, 122. He is listed on 10 December 1695 in Glasgow University matriculation records as the theological student 'Humphredus Thomson Scoto-Hibernus (pastor de Balybay in Hibernia)'. He was probably also the Humphredus Thomson noted in the fourth class in humanities in 1688, since most theology students did an Arts degree before proceeding to theology. Cosmo Innes (ed.), *Munimenta alme Universitatis Glasguensis: Records of the University of Glasgow from its Foundation till 1727*, 4 vols., Maitland Club, 72 (Glasgow, 1854), III, pp. 244, 146. John Dunlop was Irish. John Wilson was born somewhere in Scotland, educated at Glasgow and Edinburgh, and, conceivably, might have been Highland. Archibald Boyd was Irish (but sounds of Scottish origin) and like McGregor, had been licensed by the Route presbytery. Robert Higginbotham was born in Co. Antrim, Patrick Plunket was an Irish convert from the Roman Catholic church and John Dunlop was from Co. Donegal. *Irish Fasti*, pp. 95, 124, 90, 105, 119.

179. *Records of the General Synod of Ulster*, I, pp. 211–12.

180. *Records of the General Synod of Ulster*, I, pp. 401–02; *Irish Fasti*, p. 115.

181. *Records of the General Synod of Ulster*, I, p. 403.

182. *Records of the General Synod of Ulster*, I, pp. 421, 439, 541.

183. *Records of the General Synod of Ulster*, I, pp. 403, 422.

184. Those Ulster ministers capable of preaching in Irish were also assigned missionary work, but only Mr McGregor seems to have carried a burden as large as the Scots, being assigned the 'County of Derry, Antrim, and part of Tyrone, Mahera, Dawsons Bridg, Coah, and Monymore'. *Records of the General Synod of Ulster*, I, p. 440.

185. *Presbyterian Church in Ireland*, III, 1853, pp. 210–11.

186. *Records of the General Synod of Ulster*, I, pp. 422, 440, 447.

187. CH2/557/5, Synod of Argyll, 1708–1727, fols. 204–05. The letter was received on 8 August 1717.

188. *Records of the General Synod of Ulster*, I, pp. 447, 457.

189. *Presbyterian Church in Ireland*, III (1853), p. 211; Ferguson, 'The Problems of the Established Church', p. 23.

190. General Register Office, Ireland, *The Census of Ireland for the Year 1851* (Dublin, 1852), pp. 934, 936.
191. Charles Knowles Bolton, *Scotch Irish Pioneers in Ulster and America* (Baltimore, 1967), pp. 106–07.
192. *Records of the General Synod of Ulster*, I, pp. 461, 440, 497.
193. *Records of the General Synod of Ulster*, I, pp. 521, 497, 540–41, 534.
194. *Presbyterian Church in Ireland*, III (1853), p. 234.
195. Noel MacDonald Wilby, 'The "Encreasce of Popery" in the Highlands, 1714–1747', *Innes Review*, 17 (1966), p. 101.
196. Ferguson, 'The Problems of the Established Church', p. 28.

Notes to Chapter 6: Fishers of Herring and the Priesthood of Aaron, 1690–1760

1. SCA BL1/129/6, Blairs Letters, Scottish Mission Correspondence 1627–1694; Paul Hopkins, *Glencoe and the End of the Highland War* (Edinburgh, 1986), pp. 301, 465.
2. T. C. Smout, 'Famine and Famine-Relief in Scotland', in L. M. Cullen and T. C. Smout (eds.), *Comparative Aspects of Scottish and Irish Economic and Social History, 1600–1900* (Edinburgh, 1977), p. 22.
3. Anson, *Underground Catholicism*, pp. 9, 91, 94–95, 97, 99, 105–06. Nicolson's statutes laid down strict codes of fasting, indicated who was allowed to be present at mass, stipulated the duration of the period of instruction before receipt into the church, sanctioned the practice of public penitence, permitted arms to be carried for self-defence, and warned of familiarity with women as well as the dangers of joining in field sports. Wendy J. Doran, 'Bishop Thomas Nicolson and the Roman Catholic Mission to Scotland, 1694–1718' (unpublished MLitt dissertation, Glasgow University, 1986), p. 132.
4. For areas of their earlier operation see Chapter 4, sections headed 'Irish Chaplains with Alasdair MacColla MacDonald', and 'Dynamic Secularism in the Highlands, 1680–1689'.
5. Anson, *Underground Catholicism*, p. 111; Doran, 'Bishop Thomas Nicolson and the Roman Catholic Mission to Scotland, 1694–1718', pp. 94, 114. Bishop Gordon professed himself pleased with the obedience of the Jesuits in May 1709. They appear, however, not to have shared the mission funds but to have continued to receive allowances from their order in France as well as some of the nobility in Scotland. They also still received their faculties directly from their superiors. Nevertheless, the difficulties did not evaporate overnight. The seculars often made complaints about Jesuit laxity, accusing them of immorality, drunkenness and overexpenditure, while the Jesuits accused them, in return, of Jansenism. In particular, William Leslie, Scots agent in Rome for the early part of this period, was rampantly anti-Jesuit.
6. Mary McHugh, 'The Religious Condition of the Highlands and Islands in the Mid-Eighteenth Century', *Innes Review*, 35, no. 1

(1984), pp. 12–13; Alasdair Roberts, 'Gregor McGregor (1681–1740) and the Highland Problem in the Scottish Catholic Mission', *Innes Review*, 39, no. 2 (1988), p. 94; *Fasti*, VII, p. 144.

7. Noel MacDonald Wilby, 'The "Encreasce of Popery" in the Highlands, 1714–1747', *Innes Review*, 17 (1966), p. 105. Nothing was said of schools on Canna, Eigg or South Uist, which were also mentioned.
8. A. Macinnes, 'Catholic Recusancy and the Penal Laws, 1603–1707', *RSCHS*, 23, pt. 1 (1987), pp. 61–62. For a summary of the penal laws against Catholics from 1581, see 'An abridgement of all the Laws against Papists', *The Scots Magazine*, 40 (1778), pp. 513–17.
9. Anson, *Underground Catholicism*, pp. 102, 104, 109–16, pp. 109–10, 122–24 notes; Christine Johnson, *Developments in the Roman Catholic Church in Scotland, 1789–1829* (Edinburgh, 1983), p. 40.
10. Roberts, 'Gregor McGregor', p. 82; Johnson, *Roman Catholic Church in Scotland*, pp. 38, 42, 54. Note that the first three Highland bishops were MacDonalds, all of whom were closely related to clan chiefs.
11. SCA BL1/129/11.
12. Note that this agrees with the information given by the Rev. John Thompson compiled from original sources in the eighteenth century. However, Thompson states that by the end of 1689 several missionaries had been apprehended, but none of the Highland missionaries were imprisoned. *Memoirs of Scottish Catholics*, II, p. 148.
13. SCA BL1/129/11.
14. SCA BL1/129/13.
15. He also said that 'Mr Lea ane Irish man, went to Irland for hes health'.
16. McLellan is probably the convert made by Coan. He is usually referred to as Columba McLellan or MacLennan, and his name at birth was Donald. A Benedictine from Wurzburg, he ultimately went on the mission in 1698 and appears to have been rampantly anti-Irish.
17. SCA CC1/8–15, Canon William Clapperton, 'Memoirs of Missionary Priests', p. 640.
18. In much the same way, they were to champion the cause of Francis MacDonnell, priest in Moidart, in the following century, who apostatised to Protestantism and became a minister, mainly because of the gross scandal of his alleged incest with his sister. See Chapter 5, note 84.
19. Hopkins, *Glencoe and the End of the Highland War*, p. 465. Also see Chapter 4.
20. William Matheson, *An Clarsair Dall: The Blind Harper*, The Scottish Gaelic Texts Society, 12 (Edinburgh, 1970), p. 220; Hopkins, *Glencoe and the End of the Highland War*, p. 465.
21. NAS CH2/557/3, Synod of Argyll, 1687–1700, fol. 761. The last two are O'Carolan and Harnet.
22. NAS CH2/557/3, fol. 761.
23. NAS CH2/557/3, fols. 787, 812; Hopkins, *Glencoe and the End of the Highland War*, pp. 459, 465–66; NAS PC1/53, Registrum Secreti Concilii Acta, June 1703 – April 1707, fol. 56.
24. SCA BL1/140/15.

25. Doran, 'Bishop Thomas Nicolson and the Roman Catholic Mission to Scotland, 1694–1718', p. 135.
26. SCA BL1/129/13.
27. The Rev. John Thompson stated in his account for this year that there were seven Irish priests (excluding Trener who worked in Braemar and Glengairn) on the Highland mission. *Memoirs of Scottish Catholics*, II, p. 169. Very little can be traced of his work in the Highlands. Clapperton, 'Memoirs', p. 636.
28. SCA BL1/180/9. Devoyer died of a chest infection and rawness of stomach caused by tiredness, study and poor food.
29. Clapperton, 'Memoirs', p. 647.
30. Mongan and Ryan.
31. Clapperton, 'Memoirs', pp. 645–46. Born in Aberdeenshire in 1651, the son of James Innes of Drumgask and the eldest of six brothers, Louis Innes was the principal of the Scots College in Paris between 1682 and 1714. After James VII fled the country in 1689, Innes was his special confidant. Anson, *Underground Catholicism*, p. 85 n.
32. Mr John Munro, ex-minister of Glenarm and Carnmoney, reported to the synod of Argyll on 10 October 1695 that he had addressed the King's commissioner, secretary and advocate in Edinburgh in the summer of 1694 about the trafficking of Jesuits in the isles and 'gave in an order to Collonel Hill, to apprehend the said Jesuits and to send them in prisoners to Edinburgh'. NAS CH2/557/3, fol. 139. He carried out similar anti-Catholic work in the Highlands to Darroch. For the other Irish priests captured, see Chapter 4, section headed 'The Vincentians' for Fr. White who was seized in 1655; and later in this chapter, section headed 'Mr Mongan, First Resident Missionary in Skye', who was seized in 1701.
33. Clapperton, 'Memoirs', pp. 273–74.
34. J. G. Simms ed. D. W. Hayton and Gerard O'Brien, *War and Politics in Ireland, 1649–1730* (London and Ronceverte, 1986), pp. 235, 248.
35. *Memoirs of Scottish Catholics*, II, pp. 171–72, 175–77.
36. Macinnes, 'Catholic Recusancy', p. 61.
37. Doran, 'Bishop Thomas Nicolson and the Roman Catholic Mission to Scotland, 1694–1718', p. 53; Anson, *Underground Catholicism*, pp. 96–97. Moreover, Irvine may have known before he left Scotland that two of them left for Ireland in June 1698.
38. Rev. J. F. S. Gordon, *Journal and Appendix to Scotichronicon and Monasticon*, 4 vols. (Glasgow, 1867), I, p. 629. The annual list of priests which this contains is cited as Gordon's Annual List.
39. Note that Clapperton, 'Memoirs', p. 337, states that O'Hara's Christian name was William. The primary sources suggest otherwise. Nicolson's report (1700) clearly states that his name was Charles, while a Protestant source of 1706 calls him Patrick. For this source, see the reference in note 97 below.
40. Clapperton, 'Memoirs', p. 650.
41. SCA SM3/1/2, Scottish Mission 1695–1732, Bishop Nicolson's Visitation of the Highlands, 1700, p. 21.
42. Rev. James O'Laverty, *The Bishops of Down and Connor*

(Dublin, 1895), p. 511.

43. See above, Bishop Nicolson's report that they were compelled to use him and Logan.

44. Rev. Alexander Canon MacWilliam, 'The Jesuit Mission in Upper Deeside, 1671–1737', *Innes Review*, 23 (1972), pp. 31–32. This eighteenth century report, entitled *Some Account of the State of Religion and of the Mission in Scotland since the Reformation*, was written by John Thomson when he was Scottish agent in Rome in 1782.

45. Clapperton, 'Memoirs', p. 1088, implies that this is Louis Innes (though the address 'tres digne pretre' was more usually afforded to his brother Thomas).

46. Clapperton, 'Memoirs', pp. 1087–90. Attention has been drawn to Ryan's naievety in assuming that Innes, who lived at the exiled Jacobite court of St. Germains, could procure him a pass from King William, because Ryan feared being in the very anti-Catholic climate in Ireland without it.

47. Edward MacLysaght, *The Surnames of Ireland* (Shannon, 1969), pp. 15, 156, 164; *Memoirs of Scottish Catholics*, II, p. 170; Clapperton, 'Memoirs', pp. 641–42. Leith states that he was sent abroad in 1695, but many of the dates in this source tend to be a year out of chronology (usually a year later).

48. Doran, 'Bishop Thomas Nicolson and the Roman Catholic Mission to Scotland, 1694–1718', p. 51.

49. SCA BL2/9/10, Blairs Letters, Scottish Mission Correspondence 1627–1694. The spot sixteen miles from Gordon Castle was probably Banff. Clapperton, 'Memoirs', p. 646.

50. These trades were obviously mission codes.

51. SCA BL2/9/10.

52. SCA BL2/9/10.

53. SCA BL2/61/2.

54. SCA BL2/61/2.

55. Clapperton, 'Memoirs', p. 648.

56. Clapperton, 'Memoirs', p. 649; SCA BL 2/70/10.

57. SCA BL2/70/11.

58. SCA BL2/70/11.

59. NAS CH2/557/4, Synod of Argyll, 1701–1707, fols. 8–9, 13 & 21. The transcription of 'Panton' is not absolutely certain.

60. *Memoirs of Scottish Catholics*, II, p. 185; Clapperton, 'Memoirs', p. 651.

61. SCA BL2/89/8.

62. SCA BL2/89/8.

63. SCA BL2/89/8; SCA BL2/89/10. He was still insisting in November 1705 that he 'had more inward satisfaction in the most horrid penury I suffered in the highlands then I have hear in my abundance of wheat and wine'. SCA BL2/121/9.

64. SCA BL2/89/11.

65. SCA SM3/1/2, Bishop Nicolson's Visitation of the Highlands, 1700, p. 7; *Memoirs of Scottish Catholics*, II, p. 187; NAS CH1/2/29/6, General Assembly Papers, fol. 569.

66. SCA BL2/105/3.

67. SCA BL2/105/3.

68. SCA BL2/121/9.

69. SCA BL2/121/10.

70. Doran, 'Bishop Thomas Nicolson and the Roman Catholic Mission to Scotland, 1694–1718', p. 50, quoting National Library of Ireland, Archive della Sacra Congregazione di Propaganda

Fide, Scozia, Scriture Riferite nei Congressi, ii (1701–1760), 5666–67. The extract is not dated but clearly belongs somewhere in the period between 1701 and 1718.

71. SCA BL2/121/10. This marks the end of Mongan's extant correspondence, after which he seems to disappear. On 8 March 1706, Louis Innes wrote that he had failed to get any news of him, although he had expended time and money in doing so. Clapperton, 'Memoirs', p. 661.
72. Anson, *Underground Catholicism*, pp. 99–100.
73. SCA SM3/1/2, p. 7.
74. SCA SM3/1/2, p. 12. Canna is written 'Connay' in the ms.
75. SCA SM3/1/2, p. 14.
76. SCA SM3/1/2, p. 14.
77. SCA SM3/1/2, p. 15.
78. SCA BL2/70/5. He asked an unidentified correspondent at the Scots College in Paris to discuss with the principal 'if it be expedient in tymes comeing to send hither young highlanders, or rather if it be not surer to keeppe the highlanders in your College at Paris, and send up low Countreymen when called for'. SCA BL2/70/3.
79. SCA SM3/1/2, p. 15. These islands are referred to in Chapter 4, section headed 'Results of the Mission'.
80. NAS CH2/557/3, Synod of Argyll, 1687–1700, fol. 873.
81. *Fasti*, VII, pp. 192–93.
82. Martin Martin, *A Description of the Western Islands of Scotland* (Edinburgh, 1987, facsimile reprint of 2nd edition of 1716), pp. 288–89.
83. SCA SM3/1/2, p. 29; Anson, *Underground Catholicism*, p. 95.
84. SCA SM3/1/2, p. 29. The Rev. John Thompson's report for 1701 mentions twenty-five priests in all on the Scottish mission. The Irish priests were stationed as follows: 'Messrs O'Sheil and M'Phie in Uist; Messrs Carolan and Heachean in Barra, but Mr Carolan was *non agendo*; Mr Hara in the little isles Eigg, Rum, and Canna; Mr Cahassy in Morar; Mr Laggan [Logan] in Moidart.' *Memoirs of Scottish Catholics*, II, p. 187.
85. *Memoirs of Scottish Catholics*, II, pp. 213–14. This may have been Thompson's division.
86. *Memoirs of Scottish Catholics*, II, pp. 213–14.
87. Johnson, *Roman Catholic Church in Scotland*, p. 38.
88. *Memoirs of Scottish Catholics*, II, p. 218.
89. Rev. James O'Laverty, *The Bishops of Down and Connor* (Dublin, 1895), pp. 511–14.
90. Roberts, 'Gregor McGregor', p. 83.
91. *Memoirs of Scottish Catholics*, II, pp. 219–23.
92. *Memoirs of Scottish Catholics*, II, p. 224.
93. NAS CH1/2/29/6, fol. 569. The information which accurately dates the document is that Fr. 'Casey' is still alive. Cahassy died in September 1704.
94. The document specifies that 'the Island where he dwells is centring between other two Islands which stand upon the west end of the loch pointing towards the sea within the distance of a mile to a known harbour called Buninstuagh which is about 30 miles northwestward from our Garrison'. This is Eilean Ban (NM6992) or the Isle of 'Bath'

(probably mis-transcribed from the original ms.) mentioned in Nicolson's report. NAS CH1/2/29/6, fol. 569; Anson, *Underground Catholicism*, p. 128; *The Ordnance Survey Gazetteer of Great Britain, 1:50,000* (London and Basingstoke, 1987), p. 252.

95. NAS CH1/2/29/6, fol. 569.
96. Clapperton, 'Memoirs', p. 329.
97. NAS Argyll Survey, NRA(S)/1209, bundle 65. 'Rose' is a variant of Ross. For a full exposition of their case, see Fiona A. Macdonald, 'Irish Priests in the Highlands: Judicial Evidence from Argyll', *Innes Review*, 45 (1995), pp. 15–33; and Errata, *Innes Review*, 46 (1995), p. 165.
98. NAS CH1/2/29/6 fol. 569. O'Shiel is named here as a Jesuit, but both Clapperton and Gordon cite him as a Franciscan. The lack of discrimination with which Protestants used the term 'Jesuit' probably accounts for this.
99. George F. Black, *The Surnames of Scotland* (New York, 1989 reprint), p. 493; Andrew Lang, *The Highlands of Scotland in 1750* (Edinburgh and London, 1898), pp. 89, 166.
100. NAS CH1/2/29/6, fol. 569. Note that the name O'Raigan, the Irish of which is Ó Réagain or, more commonly, Ó Riagain, is connected with the counties of Waterford, Clare, Cork and Leix. Edward MacLysaght, *The Surnames of Ireland* (Shannon, 1969), p. 188.
101. Clapperton, 'Memoirs', p. 329. For more information on O'Hara, see the article mentioned in note 97, above.
102. See Chapter 5, section headed 'The Significance of Jacobitism'.
103. NAS CH2/557/4, Synod of Argyll, 1701–1707, fol. 174.
104. NAS CH1/2/29/6, General Assembly papers, fols. 554–55, List of Catholic Priests in Scotland. The document is not dated, but most others in the volume are from around 1710.
105. *Memoirs of Scottish Catholics*, II, pp. 225, 228.
106. Doran, 'Bishop Thomas Nicolson and the Roman Catholic Mission to Scotland, 1694–1718', p. 890.
107. SCA BL2/123/5. A nineteenth-century endorsement dates the letter to about 1706.
108. SCA BL2/123/6.
109. SCA BL2/142/1.
110. SCA BL2/185/12.
111. See Chapter 4, section headed 'The Dominican Mission'.
112. Clapperton, 'Memoirs', p. 329.
113. D. C. Pochin Mould, *The Irish Dominicans. The Friars Preachers in the History of Catholic Ireland* (Dublin, 1957), pp. 179, 242; A. Ross, 'Dominicans and Scotland in the Seventeenth Century', *Innes Review*, 23 (1972), pp. 58–59, 63.
114. *Memoirs of Scottish Catholics*, II, pp. 229–36; Anson, *Underground Catholicism*, pp. 110–11.
115. SCA SM3/12/10. The entry next to Arisaig is 'sacedos de Ilen', that is, 'priest of the Isles'. Projected identities are: Strathglass – Mr Alexander MacRae (alias John Forbes); Glengarry – Peter Mulligan; Knoydart – Columba MacLennan; Small Isles – Patrick O'Callaghan?; Morar – ?; Arisaig – Peter Fraser?; Uist – Colin McFie; Barra – William Heachean?
116. Andrew L. Drummond and James Bulloch, *The Scottish Church, 1688–1843* (Edinburgh, 1973), p. 143.

117. *Memoirs of Scottish Catholics*, II, pp. 238–49.
118. *Memoirs of Scottish Catholics*, II, pp. 264, 265, 269, 277–78.
119. Noel MacDonald Wilby, 'The "Encreasce of Popery" in the Highlands, 1714–1747', *Innes Review*, 17 (1966), p. 92.
120. Allan I. Macinnes, *Clanship, Commerce and the House of Stuart, 1603–1788* (East Linton, 1996), p. 176.
121. Mícheál Mac Craith, 'The Gaelic Reaction to the Reformation', in S. Ellis and S. Barber (eds.), *Conquest and Union: Fashioning a British State, 1485–1725* (London, 1995), p. 161.
122. Roberts, 'Gregor McGregor', pp. 90, 93. 'Kiltrie' is the modern 'Coiltry' (NH3506) on the east bank of the river Oich, south of Fort Augustus. *Ordnance Survey Gazetteer*, p. 175. Given the geographical proximity, MacDonald may have been related to the MacDonnells of Glengarry.
123. SCA SM3/25, 'Popery Reviving, or an Account of the Growth of Popery and the Insolence of Papists and Jacobites in Scotland in a Letter from a Gentleman in Edinburgh to his Friend in the Country'.
124. *Fasti*, VII, p. 144; IV, pp. 126, 134, 136.
125. NAS CH2/557/4, Synod of Argyll, 1701–1707, fol. 257. Further aspects of this representation are discussed in the last few sections of this chapter.
126. F. Forbes and W. J. Anderson, 'Clergy Lists of the Highland District, 1732–1828', *Innes Review*, 17 (1966), pp. 135, 140.
127. SCA BL2/242/8.
128. SCA BL2/277/7.
129. SCA BL2/277/8.
130. SCA BL2/289/1.
131. *Memoirs of Scottish Catholics*, II, p. 302.
132. SCA BL2/288/4.
133. Roberts, 'Gregor McGregor', p. 99.
134. NAS CH1/5/51, Royal Bounty Records, 1725–1730, fol. 75.
135. Annual List, p. 633.
136. Roberts, 'Gregor McGregor', p. 99.
137. Sean MacGuaire, 'Ireland and the Catholic Hebrides', *The Irish Ecclesiastical Record*, 5th series, 42 (1933), p. 497.
138. *Memoirs of Scottish Catholics*, II, pp. 303–04.
139. Roberts, 'Gregor McGregor', p. 97; William Ferguson, *Scotland 1689 to the Present* (Edinburgh, 1968), p. 115. These riots followed the Shawfield malt tax riots of 1725. William Shand in Morar was arrested, but none of the Irish priests.
140. A. R. B. Haldane, *New Ways through the Glens: Highland Road, Bridge and Canal Makers of the Early Nineteenth Century* (Newton Abbot, 1973), pp. 4–5, 7, 9,
141. *Memoirs of Scottish Catholics*, II, p. 314.
142. SCA BL3/29/9, Blairs Letters, Scottish Mission Correspondence, 1733–1788.
143. Archives of Propaganda Fide, SC 2, Scritture riferite nei Congressi, Scozia, 1701–1760, fol. 260. I am grateful to Prof. Allan Macinnes for allowing me to view his ms. handlist and notes on these papers.
144. SCA BL2/320/12; Gordon, Annual List, p. 633.
145. Carnegie worked on the Scottish mission between 1700 and 1729. He retired to France in 1729. Anson, *Underground Catholicism*,

p. 109 n.

146. SCA BL2/327/4.

147. Anson, *Underground Catholicism*, p. 127. Hugh MacDonald was the son of the Laird of Morar, had been baptised by Mongan, and had attended the island school on the Loch. Gordon, *Journal and Appendix to Scotichronicon and Monasticon*, p. 584.

148. SCA BL3/17/10. The italics are contemporary. For more on Leith, see James F. McMillan, 'Jansenists and anti-Jansenists in Eighteenth Century Scotland: The Unigenitus Quarrels on the Scottish Catholic Mission, 1732–1746', *Innes Review*, 39, no. 1 (1988), p. 20.

149. Roberts, 'Gregor McGregor', p. 96.

150. SCA BL3/6/4.

151. SCA BL3/29/2.

152. Anson, *Underground Catholicism*, pp. 131–32; Brian M. Halloran, *The Scots College, Paris, 1603–1792* (Edinburgh, 1997), pp. 102–05, 107. Chapter 7, pp. 102–48, is detailed discussion of the Jansenist controversy as it affected the Scots College in Paris,

153. Roberts, 'Gregor McGregor', p. 99; Anson, *Underground Catholicism*, p. 109 and p. 109 n.

154. McMillan, 'Jansenists and anti-Jansenists', p. 13; Anson, *Underground Catholicism*, p. 132. Baianism preceded and influenced Jansenism, advancing new doctrines of grace and justification, particularly concerning the fall of man. Baius held that the first sin destroyed intrinsic human nature.

155. Bruce Lenman, *The Jacobite Risings in Britain, 1689–1746* (London, 1980), p. 228. For an account of the kin-based tactics of the MacDonalds of Clan Ranald, see James A. Stewart Jr., 'The Clan Ranald and Catholic Missionary Successes, 1715–1745', *Innes Review*, 45 (1994), pp. 29–46.

156. Roberts, 'Gregor McGregor', p. 82; SCA BL3/29/2; McMillan, 'Jansenists and anti-Jansenists', pp. 25, 27, 30, 33, 38; Anson, *Underground Catholicism*, p. 131.

157. Halloran, *The Scots College, Paris*, p. 108.

158. SCA BL3/29/2; Anson, *Underground Catholicism*, pp. 94, 103, 128, 136.

159. SCA BL3/29/2.

160. McMillan, 'Jansenists and anti-Jansenists', p. 38.

161. Archives of Propaganda Fide, Congregazione Particolari, 87, di Scozia et Ingliterra, 1737–41, fols. 378–89; *A New History of Ireland*, IV, p. 635.

162. See Gordon's Annual List, p. 633.

163. SCA SM4/38/5, Scottish Mission 1733–1788, Printed broadsheets and pamphlets 1746–48; Clapperton, 'Memoirs', p. 2885. The Annual List, which finishes in the year 1741, is continued by Clapperton in his 'Memoirs', pp. 2884 and following, until the year 1800.

164. Anson, *Underground Catholicism*, p. 147 and n.

165. SCA BL3/121/4.

166. SCA BL3/125/5.

167. 'The Trial of Hugh Macdonald, a Popish Bishop', *The Scots Magazine*, 18 (1756), p. 100.

168. Furthermore, there was a gap of seventeen years between Frs. Cluan and Gusman who came on the mission in 1708, and the first in a final wave of Irish missionaries, Anthony Kelly, who came in 1725.

169. SCA SM3/1/2, 'Bishop Nicolson's Visitation of the Highlands, 1700',

p. 24.
170. Anson, *Underground Catholicism*, p. 106.
171. SCA SM3/1/2, p. 20.
172. SCA SM3/1/2, p. 22.
173. NAS CH2/557/4, Synod of Argyll, 1701–1707, fol. 113.
174. NAS CH2/984/2, Presbytery of Lorn, 1707–1714, fols. 62–63, 147, 152.
175. See below.
176. Martin, *Description of the Western Islands*, pp. 255, 276; I. F. Grant and Hugh Cheape, *Periods in Highland History* (London, 1987), p. 140.
177. Pochin Mould, *Irish Dominicans*, p. 242; Anson, *Underground Catholicism*, p. 104; NAS CH2/984/2, fols. 279–80.
178. NAS CH2/557/5, Synod of Argyll, 1708–1727, fol. 257.
179. This is probably the minister of Glenorchy and Inishail, mentioned below.
180. NAS CH2/557/5, fols. 257–58.
181. CH1/5/51, Royal Bounty Records, 1725–1730, fol. 75; David Stevenson, *Alasdair MacColla and the Highland Problem in the Seventeenth Century* (Edinburgh, 1980), pp. 72, 116; *idem*, *The Scottish Revolution* (Newton Abbot, 1973), pp. 197–99; Sir James Balfour Paul, *The Scots Peerage*, 9 vols. (Edinburgh, 1904–1911), IV, p. 551.
182. NAS CH1/5/51, fol. 430.
183. NAS CH2/984/3, Presbytery of Lorn, 1729–1771, fol. 17.
184. Hopkins, *Glencoe and the End of the Highland War*, p. 465; NAS CH2/557/4, Synod of Argyll, 1701–1707, fols. 8–9.
185. SCA BL2/70/11; Clapperton, 'Memoirs', p. 647.
186. NAS CH2/557/4, fol. 146.
187. SCA BL2/324/6.
188. See Chapter 2, section headed 'Achievements of the Mission'.
189. Roberts, 'Gregor McGregor', p. 95.
190. NAS CH2/557/6, Synod of Argyll, 1728–1755, fols. 9–10.
191. NAS CH2/984/3, Presbytery of Lorn, 1729–1771, fol. 190; McMillan, 'Jansenists and anti-Jansenists', p. 27.
192. NAS CH2/984/3, fols. 9–11; NAS CH2/557/6, Synod of Argyll, 1728–1755, fols. 9–10.
193. Roberts, 'Gregor McGregor', p. 95.
194. See W. Ferguson, 'Religion and the Massacre of Glencoe', *SHR*, 46 (1967), pp. 82–67; *SHR*, 47 (1968), pp. 203–09; J. Prebble, 'Religion and the Massacre of Glencoe', *SHR*, 46 (1967), pp. 185–88.
195. NAS CH2/984/3, Presbytery of Lorn, 1729–1771, fol. 36; *Fasti*, IV, p. 87.
196. Presumably a hundredth levy on the parish of Dunoon and Kilmun (parishes were subdivided into quarters for administrative purposes, particularly in terms of poor relief).
197. NAS CH2/111/4, Presbytery of Dunoon, fol. 130.
198. See, for instance, Rev. George Hill, *The Stewarts of Ballintoy (with notices of other families in the district in the seventeenth century)* (Ballycastle, 1976 reprint).
199. NAS CH1/5/51, Royal Bounty Records, 1725–1730, fol. 80.
200. NAS CH2/1153/3, Presbytery of Kintyre, 1723–1748, fol. 140.
201. NAS PC1/53, Registrum Secreti Concilii Acta June 1703 – April 1707, fol. 154. The Countess' swingeing retort to the recommendation that a new process be raised against her is a masterpiece of its kind: 'if his

friends who persue for his Returne will Imploy the lyke pains for the preservation of his Estate That soe he may have the petitioners Joynture Its probable his Returne might be easie. But to order his returne without ane fond for his provisione Is ane inconsistant hardshipe whiche the petitioners looking in his face and he in hers berailling each others' callamities will not supplie.'

202. Doran, 'Bishop Thomas Nicolson and the Roman Catholic Mission to Scotland, 1694–1718', p. 73. For MacKenzie of Kildun, see Chapter 4, section headed 'Dynamic Secularism in the Highlands, 1680–1689'.
203. See Chapter 4, section headed 'Dynamic Secularism in the Highlands, 1680–1689', and the first section of this chapter.
204. Very Rev. Alexander Canon MacWilliam, 'A Highland Mission: Strathglass, 1671–1777', *Innes Review*, 24 (1973), p. 100.
205. NAS CH1/5/51/119, fol. 7. This presumably refers to the ecclesiastical jurisdiction of the synod of Ross, parts of which were geographically closer to Lewis than the synod of Glenelg, which Lewis had been a part of since 1724.
206. NLS Ms. 5127, Erskine Murray Papers, fol. 157. The manuscript postdates the '45 rebellion, which is referred to in distinction to the '15.
207. Doran, 'Bishop Thomas Nicolson and the Roman Catholic Mission to Scotland, 1694–1718', p. 73.
208. The wadsetter was the creditor to whom lands were conveyed, by feu-contract, in a medieval mortgage of heritable property known as a wadset. A conditional clause provided for redemption of the lands by the reverser or debtor upon payment of a specified sum of money. The wadsetter technically remained in possession of the land until the lands were recovered by repayment.
209. NAS CH1/5/51/119, fols. 6–7.
210. NAS CH1/5/51, fol. 99.
211. Martin, *Description of the Western Islands*, p. 279.
212. NAS CH2/557/5, fols. 257–58.
213. NAS CH1/5/51, fols. 344–5; NAS CH2/557/5, fol. 257.
214. Martin, *Description of the Western Islands*, p. 99.
215. NAS CH1/5/51/119, fol. 6.
216. NAS CH1/2/29/6/569, General Assembly papers.
217. NAS CH1/5/51/119, Royal Bounty Records, 1725–1730, 'State of Popery in Scotland 1713–1737', fol. 5.
218. NAS CH1/5/51/119, Royal Bounty Records, 1725–1730, fol. 2.
219. NAS CH1/5/51, fol. 80.
220. For in-depth comparisons on this subject see McHugh, 'Religious Condition of the Highlands and Islands', pp. 12–20; James Darragh, 'The Catholic Population of Scotland since the Year 1680', *Innes Review*, 4, no. 1 (1953), pp. 49–59.
221. Those areas discussed do not include the bounds of the presbytery of Dunoon which was visited but once by the Franciscan, Ward, in 1629; the Highlands of Angus and Mearns or the parishes of Criech, Kildonan and Kincardine, which were dominated initially by the Jesuits and later by native clergy; or the Highland parishes of the presbyteries of Dunblane or Dumbarton, which

were never visited by Irish priests.

222. NAS CH2/1153/1, Presbytery of Kintyre, 1655–1704, fols. 57–58; James Gray Kyd (ed.), *Scottish Population Statistics, including Webster's Analysis of Population, 1755*, SHS, 3rd series, 44 (Edinburgh, 1952), p. 33 n.
223. NAS CH2/1153/2, fol. 347.
224. Attention has been drawn to a letter from the Irish priest Anthony Mongan to William Leslie on 13 December 1694, which alleged that the MacDonalds of Glencoe were Catholic martyrs because they were found with rosaries and other signs of the Catholic religion on them. Hopkins, *Glencoe and the End of the Highland War*, p. 75 citing SCA BL1/108; *Memoirs of Scottish Catholics*, II, p. 170. This was undoubtedly Jacobite propaganda. A. I. Macinnes, 'The Massacre of Glencoe', *The Historian*, 35 (1992), pp. 16–18.
225. *Fasti*, IV, pp. 80, 84; Donald MacLean, *The Counter-Reformation in Scotland, 1560–1930* (London, 1931), p. 153; Anson, *Underground Catholicism*, pp. 158–62.
226. 'The Report of Drs Hyndman, Dick, &c. appointed by the general assembly 1760 to visit the Highlands and Islands, and the places where Itinerants and Catechists are employed', *The Scots Magazine*, 28 (1766), p. 460.
227. *Fasti*, VII, p. 176.
228. See Chapter 4, section headed 'Dynamic Secularism in the Highlands, 1680–1689'.
229. Haldane, *New Ways through the Glens*, p. 10.
230. 'Report', *The Scots Magazine*, 28 (1766), pp. 517–18.
231. See above, section headed 'Presbyterian Counter-Attack'.
232. MacLean, *Counter-Reformation in Scotland*, p. 153; 'Report', *The Scots Magazine*, 28 (1766), p. 513; Anson, *Underground Catholicism*, pp. 158–62; Kyd, *Scottish Population Statistics*, p. 33.
233. In 1742, the presbytery was divided into the presbytery of Uist, including Harris and all the islands to the south, with the territory to the north accruing to the new presbytery of Lewis. *Fasti*, VII, p. 199.
234. MacLean, *Counter-Reformation in Scotland*, p. 153; Kyd, *Scottish Population Statistics*, pp. 59–60; 'Report', *The Scots Magazine*, 28 (1766), pp. 513–14; Anson, *Underground Catholicism*, pp. 158–162; NAS CH1/5/51/119, fol. 7.
235. See above, section headed 'Bishop Nicolson's Visitation of the Highlands, 1700'; *Fasti*, VII, p. 193.
236. MacLean, *Counter-Reformation in Scotland*, p. 153; Anson, *Underground Catholicism*, pp. 158–62; 'Report', *The Scots Magazine*, 28 (1766), p. 515.
237. For a fuller discussion of the Catholic community of Kintail, see Alasdair Roberts, 'Catholic Kintail: A Marginal Community', *TGSI*, 58 (1992–94), pp. 123–35.
238. MacLean, *Counter-Reformation in Scotland*, pp. 153–54; NAS CH1/5/51, fol. 305; Kyd, *Scottish Population Statistics*, p. 61; NAS CH2/568/1, Minutes of the Synod of Glenelg, 7 July 1725 to 24 June 1749, fol. 27; 'Report', *The Scots Magazine*, 28 (1766), pp. 516–18; Anson, *Underground Catholicism*, pp. 158–62.

239. *Fasti*, VII, p. 38; VI, p. 468.
240. The figure 530 has been crossed through in the manuscript and would seem more like the number expected if Strathglass had been included.
241. MacLean, *Counter-Reformation in Scotland*, p. 154; NAS CH1/5/51, fol. 76; Kyd, *Scottish Population Statistics*, p. 60; Anson, *Underground Catholicism*, p. 162; NAS CH1/5/51/119, fol. 11; 'Report', *The Scots Magazine*, 28 (1766), p. 519.
242. McHugh, 'Religious Condition of the Highlands and Islands', p. 15.
243. *Fasti*, IV, pp. 126–37; C. W. J. Withers, 'The Highland Parishes in 1698: An Examination of Sources for the Definition of the Gaidhealtachd', *Scottish Studies*, 24 (1980), p. 78.
244. NAS CH2/557/5, fol. 257.
245. MacLean, *Counter-Reformation in Scotland*, p. 154, NAS CH1/5/51, fol. 75; Kyd, *Scottish Population Statistics*, p. 33; 'Report', *The Scots Magazine*, 28 (1766), p. 460; Anson, *Underground Catholicism*, p. 162.
246. See above, section headed 'Reconciliation and Expansion'; NAS CH1/5/51/119, fol. 12; Kyd, pp. 59–60; 'Report', *The Scots Magazine*, 28 (1766), p. 460.
247. MacLean, *Counter-Reformation in Scotland*, pp. 153–54; NAS CH2/557/5, fol. 257; Kyd, *Scottish Population Statistics*, pp. 33, 51; 'Report', *The Scots Magazine*, 28 (1766), pp. 461, 575; Anson, *Underground Catholicism*, pp. 160, 162.
248. 'Report', *The Scots Magazine*, 28 (1766), p. 576.
249. NAS CH2/273/1, Mull Presbytery, 1729–1762, fol. 211.

Notes to Epilogue

1. Iain M. Bishop, ' The Education of Ulster Students at Glasgow University during the Eighteenth Century' (unpublished MA dissertation, Queen's University, Belfast, 1987), p. 29, quoting The General Assembly of the Presbyterian Church in Ireland, *Records of the General Synod of Ulster, I, 1691–1720* (Belfast, 1890), p. 6. However, the fact that the resolution was reiterated in 1702 shows that it had difficulty in implementing it.
2. M. Perceval-Maxwell, *The Scottish Migration to Ulster in the Reign of James I* (London, 1973), p. 288.
3. *A New History of Ireland*, III, pp. ii–iii.
4. Rev. Mark Dilworth, 'The Counter-Reformation in Scotland: A Select Critical Bibliography,' *RSCHS*, 22 (1984), pp. 91–92.
5. J. C. Beckett, *The Making of Modern Ireland, 1603–1923* (London, 1969), p. 45; Daniel Szechi and David Hayton, 'John Bull's Other Kingdoms: The English Government of Scotland and Ireland', in Clyve Jones (ed.), *Britain in the First Age of Party, 1680–1750* (London and Ronceverte, 1987), p. 270.
6. See Victor Durkacz, 'The Source of the Language Problem in Scottish Education, 1688–1709', *SHR*, 57 (1978), pp. 28–39; *idem*, 'The Church of Scotland's Eighteenth-Century Attitudes to Gaelic Preaching', *SGS*, 13, part 2 (1981),

pp. 145–58.

7. There is clearly a great deal of scope for further work in a similar direction for both denominations. In particular, the appearance of a modern, thematic and well-researched history of the Counter-Reformation in the Highlands and Islands to replace old and now inadequate texts is long overdue.

Bibliography

Unpublished Primary Sources

Argyll and Bute District Archives, Lochgilphead
BC/1/2, Campbeltown Burgh Records, 28 September 1739 to 29 September 1767.

British Library, London
Add. Ms. 23120, Lauderdale Papers, miscellaneous correspondence, 8.
Add. Ms. 35, 447, Hardwicke Papers, XCIX, fol. 151.

National Archives of Scotland, Edinburgh
National Register of Archives (Scot)/1209, Argyll Survey I and II.
GD220/5/453/11, Montrose Manuscripts.
GD95/10, SSPCK Records.
PC1/53, Registrum Secreti Concilii Acta, June 1703–April 1707.
Church Records
CH1/5/51, Royal Bounty Records, 1725–1730.
CH1/2/26–27, General Assembly Papers, 1707–1708.
CH2/111/1–5, Presbytery records of Dunoon, 1639–1686; 1689–1707; 1707–1716; 1737–1761.
CH2/190/1–3, Inveraray Presbytery records, 1691–1702; 1715–1744; 1745–1763.
CH2/214/1, Kilmory (Arran) Kirk Session records, 1718–1723.
CH2/273/1, Mull Presbytery records, 1729–1762.
CH2/557/3–8, Synod books of Argyll, 1687–1700; 1701–1707; 1708–1727; 1728–1755; 1756–1775.
CH2/568/1, Minutes of the Synod of Glenelg, 1725–1749.
CH2/984/1–3, Lorn Presbytery records, 1651–1681; 1704–1715; 1729–1771.
CH2/1153/1–4, Presbytery books of Kintyre, 1655–1706; 1707–1723; 1723–1748; 1749–1794.

National Library of Scotland, Edinburgh
Ms. 5127, Erskine Murray Papers.
Ms. 3134 i, ii, Yule Collection.

Public Record Office of Northern Ireland, Belfast
D2977/5/1/4, Antrim papers.
T1071, Pedigree of Col. James Graham Robert Douglas MacNeill, CB, and of the McNeills of Faughart, Cushendun, Gallochelly and Colonsay, descendants of the McNeills of Gigha and Taynish.

T448, Copies of State Papers for Ireland.
T812, Pedigree of the MacDonald family of Glencoe, Scotland and Drumbohena, County Fermanagh.
Church Records
D1759/1A/1–2, Presbytery of Antrim, 1654–1658; 1671–1691.
D1759/1E/1–2, Presbytery of Lagan, 1672–1679; 1679–1695.
D1759/2A/13, Route Presbytery, 1701–1705.

Scottish Catholic Archives, Columba House, Edinburgh
BL1, Blairs Letters, Scottish mission correspondence 1627–1694.
BL2, Blairs Letters, Scottish mission correspondence 1695–1732.
BL3, Blairs Letters, Scottish mission correspondence 1733–1788.
SM2, Scottish Mission 1604–1694.
SM3/1/2, Scottish Mission 1695–1732, Bishop Nicolson's Visitation of the Highlands, 1700.
SM4/38, Scottish Mission 1733–1788, Printed broadsheets and pamphlets 1746–48.

Printed Primary Sources

State Papers
Bain, J. *et al.* (eds.), *Calendar of State Papers Relating to Scotland and Mary, Queen of Scots*, 1547–1603, 13 vols. (Edinburgh, 1898–1969), vol. XII.
Hamilton, H. Claude, *et al.* (eds.), *Calendar of State Papers Relating to Ireland*, 1509–1670, 30 vols. (London, 1860–1910), vols. III, IV, V, VI, VII, VIII, IX, X, XI, XVI, XVII.
Brown, P. Hume and D. Masson (eds.), *The Register of the Privy Council of Scotland*, 1625–1660, 2nd series, 8 vols. (Edinburgh, 1899–1908), vols. I, III, IV.
Burton, J. H. and D. Masson (eds.), *The Register of the Privy Council of Scotland*, 1545–1625, 1st series, 14 vols. (Edinburgh, 1877–1898), vols. VIII, XI.
Donaldson, G. *et al.* (eds.), *Registrum Secreti Sigilli Regum Scotorum*, 8 vols., 1488–1584 (Edinburgh, 1908–1982), vol. VII.
General Register Office, Ireland, *The Census of Ireland for the Year 1851*, 3 vols. (Dublin, 1852–1856).

Printed Surveys and Descriptions
Alexander, A. F. O'D. (ed.), 'The O'Kane Papers', pt. II, Bishop Montgomery's Survey of the Bishoprics of Derry, Raphoe and Clogher, *Analecta Hibernica*, 12 (1943), pp. 67–127.
Butler, Rev. Richard (ed.), *A Treatice of Ireland; by John Dymmok*, Irish Archaeological Society, II (Dublin, 1842).
Hogan, Edmund (ed.), *The Description of Ireland and the State Thereof as it is at This Present in Anno 1598* (Dublin, 1878).
Hore, Herbert F. (ed.), 'Marshal Bagenal's Description of Ulster, Anno 1586', *UJA*, 1st series, 7 (July 1854), pp. 137–60.
Knox, Thomas, 'Report by Thomas Knox, Bishop of the Isles, of the State of his Diocese, 1626', in J. B. Craven (ed.), *Records of the Dioceses of Argyll and the Isles, 1560–1860* (Kirkwall, 1907), pp. 46–49.

Monro, Donald, 'A Description of the Westerne Iles of Scotland called Hybrides. Compyled by Mr. Donald Monro Deane of the Iles. 1549', in Sir Arthur Mitchell and James T. Clark (eds.), *MacFarlane's Geographical Collections*, III, SHS, 53 (1908), pp. 262–302.

Newspapers and Periodicals

'An Abridgement of All the Laws against Papists', *The Scots Magazine*, 40 (1778), pp. 513–17.

The Edinburgh Evening Courant, 17 to 21 April 1735; 20 to 22 May 1735; 27 to 29 May 1735; 13 to 17 November 1735.

'The Trial of Hugh Macdonald, a Popish Bishop', *The Scots Magazine*, 18 (1756), p. 100.

'The Report of Drs Hyndman, Dick, &c. Appointed by the General Assembly 1760 to Visit the Highlands and Islands, and the Places where Itinerants and Catechists are Employed', *The Scots Magazine*, 18 (1756), pp. 457–63; 513–20; 573–78; 680–88.

Books

Cameron, Alexander, *Reliquiae Celticae*, 2 vols., (Inverness, 1892–94), II.

Carmichael, Alexander, *Carmina Gadelica* (Edinburgh, 1940), III.

Christie, James (ed.), *General Assembly Commission Records: III, 1650–52*, SHS, 1st series, 58 (Edinburgh, 1909).

Clark, James T. (ed.), *MacFarlane's Geographical Collections*, III, SHS, 1st series, 53 (Edinburgh, 1908).

Craven, J. B. (ed.), *Records of the Dioceses of Argyll and the Isles, 1560–1860* (Kirkwall, 1907).

Forbes Leith, W., *Memoirs of Scottish Catholics during the XVII and XVIIIth Centuries*, I and II, 1627–1649 and 1647–1793 (London, 1909).

General Register Office, Ireland, *Census of Ireland for the Year 1851*, 3 vols. (Dublin, 1852–1856), pts I, III.

Giblin, Cathaldus, *The Irish Franciscan Mission to Scotland, 1619–1646. Documents from Roman Archives* (Dublin, 1964).

Hay, M. V., *The Blairs Papers, 1603–60* (London and Edinburgh, 1929).

Innes, C. (ed.), *The Book of the Thanes of Cawdor*, The Spalding Club, 30 (Edinburgh, 1859).

Innes, Cosmo (ed.), *Munimenta alme Universitatis Glasguensis: Records of the University of Glasgow from its Foundation till 1727*, 4 vols., Maitland Club, 72 (Glasgow, 1854), III.

Iona Club, *Collectanea de Rebus Albanicis* (Edinburgh, 1847).

James VI and I, *Basilicon Doron 1599* (Menston, 1969 facsimile reprint).

Knott, E., *The Bardic Poems of Tadhg Dall Ó Huiginn*, I and II, Irish Texts Society, 22 and 23 (London, 1922 and 1926).

Kyd, James Gray (ed.), *Scottish Population Statistics, Including Webster's Analysis of Population, 1755*, SHS, 3rd series, 44 (Edinburgh, 1952).

Laing, David (ed.), *The Miscellany of the Wodrow Society* (Edinburgh, 1844), I.

Mackay, William (ed.), *Records of the Presbyteries of Inverness and Dingwall, 1643–1688*, SHS, 1st series, 24 (Edinburgh, 1896).

MacKenzie, Annie, M. (ed.). *Orain Iain Luim*, The Scottish Gaelic Texts Society (Edinburgh, 1973).
MacPhail, J. R. N. (ed.), *Highland Papers I, 1337–1680*, SHS, 2nd series, 5 (Edinburgh, 1914).
MacPhail, J. R. N. (ed.), *Highland Papers III*, 1662–1677, SHS, 2nd series, 20 (Edinburgh, 1920).
MacPhail, J. R. N. (ed.), *Highland Papers IV*, 1296–1752, SHS, 3rd series, 22 (Edinburgh, 1934).
Mactavish, Duncan C. (ed.), *Minutes of the Synod of Argyll, 1639–1651*, SHS, 3rd series, 37 (Edinburgh, 1943).
Mactavish, Duncan C. (ed.), *Minutes of the Synod of Argyll, 1652–1661*, SHS, 3rd series, 38 (Edinburgh, 1944).
Martin, Martin, *A Description of the Western Islands of Scotland* (Edinburgh, 1987, facsimile of 2nd edition 1716).
Matheson, William, *An Clarsair Dall: The Blind Harper*, The Scottish Gaelic Texts Society, 12 (Edinburgh, 1970).
Mitchell, A. F. and J. Christie (eds.), *General Assembly Commission Records: I, 1646–47*, SHS, 1st series, 11 (Edinburgh, 1892).
Mitchell, A. F. and J. Christie (eds.), *General Assembly Commission Records: II, 1648–1649*, SHS, 1st series, 25 (Edinburgh, 1896).
Mitchell, Sir Arthur and James T. Clark (eds.), *MacFarlane's Geographical Collections*, III, SHS, 1st series, 53 (Edinburgh, 1908).
Paton, Henry (ed.), *Rothesay Parish Records. The Session Book of Rothesay, 1658–1750* (Edinburgh, 1931).
Paton, Henry (ed.), *The Session Book of Kingarth, 1641–1703* (Edinburgh, 1932).
Pinkerton, John MacPherson (ed.), *The Minute Book of the Faculty of Advocates I, 1661–1712*, Stair Society, 31 (Edinburgh, 1976).
Pitcairn, Robert, *Ancient Criminal Trials in Scotland, 1609–1615*, 3, pt. 1, Maitland Club (Edinburgh, 1832).
The General Assembly of the Presbyterian Church in Ireland, *Records of the General Synod of Ulster: I, 1691–1720; II, 1721–1777* (Belfast, 1890 and 1897).
Thomson, R. L. (ed.), collected by the late Angus Matheson, *Foirm na h-urrnuid-headh: John Carswell's Gaelic Translation of the Book of Common Order*, Scottish Gaelic Texts Society (Edinburgh, 1970).

Articles

Anderson, Rev. William James, 'Narratives of the Scottish Reformation IV. Prefect Ballentine's Report, circa 1660. Part 2', *Innes Review*, 8, no. 1 (1957), pp. 99–129.
Black, Ronald, 'A Manuscript of Cathal Mac Muireadhaigh', *Celtica*, 10 (1973), pp. 193–209.
Black, Ronald, 'Poems by Maol Domhnaigh Ó Muirgheasáin', I, II and III, *Scottish Gaelic Studies*, 12 (1976), pp. 194–208; 13 pt. 1 (1978), pp. 46–55; and 13 pt. 2 (1981), pp. 289–301.
Campbell, John L., 'The Letter Sent by Iain Muideartach, Twelfth Chief of Clanranald, to Pope Urban VIII, in 1626', *Innes Review*, 4 (1955), pp. 110–16.

Robertson, Joseph (ed.), 'Observations of Mr Dioness Campbell, Deane of Limerick, on the West Isles of Scotland. A.D. 1596', in *Miscellany of the Maitland Club*, IV, pt. 1 (Glasgow, 1847), pp. 35–57.

Secondary Works

Books

Adam, Frank, *The Clans, Septs and Regiments of the Scottish Highlands* (Edinburgh and London, 1934).

Anderson, A. C. *The Story of the Presbyterian Church in Ireland* (Newcastle, Co. Down, 1965).

Anson, Peter F., *Underground Catholicism in Scotland, 1622–1878* (Montrose, 1970).

Balfour Paul, Sir James (ed.), *The Scots Peerage*, 9 vols. (Edinburgh, 1904–1914).

Bannerman, John, *The Beatons, A Medical Kindred in the Classical Gaelic Tradition* (Edinburgh, 1986).

Barrett, Michael, OSB, *Sidelights on Scottish History* (Edinburgh, 1918).

Beckett, J. C., *The Making of Modern Ireland, 1603–1923* (London, 1969).

Bigger, Francis Joseph, *The Ancient Friary of Bun-na-Margie* (Belfast, 1898).

Bil, Albert, *The Shieling 1600–1840: The Case of the Central Scottish Highlands* (Edinburgh, 1990).

Black, George F., *The Surnames of Scotland* (New York, 1946 and 1989 reprint).

Blundell, D. O., OSB, *The Catholic Highlands of Scotland: I, The Central Highlands; II, The Western Highlands and Islands* (Edinburgh and London, 1909 and 1917).

Bolton, Charles Knowles, *Scotch Irish Pioneers in Ulster and America* (Baltimore, 1967).

Brooke, Peter, *Ulster Presbyterianism: The Historical Perspective, 1610–1970* (Belfast, 1994).

Buckroyd, Julia, *Church and State in Scotland, 1660–1681* (Edinburgh, 1980).

Campbell, Major Sir Duncan, of Barcaldine and Glenure, *The Clan Campbell*, 8 vols. (Edinburgh, 1916), IV.

Campbell, J. L., *Canna – The Story of a Hebridean Island* (Oxford, 1984).

Campbell, J. L. and Derick Thomson, *Edward Lhuyd in the Scottish Highlands 1699–1700* (Oxford, 1963).

Clyde, Robert, *From Rebel to Hero: The Image of the Highlander, 1745–1830* (East Linton, 1995).

Conolly, S. J., R. A. Houston and R. J. Morris (eds.), *Conflict, Identity and Economic Development: Ireland and Scotland, 1660–1939* (Preston, 1995).

Cosgrove, Art (ed.), *A New History of Ireland: II, Medieval Ireland 1169–1534* (Oxford, 1987)

Cotton, Henry, *Fasti Ecclesiae Hibernicae: The Succession of the Prelates and Members of the Cathedral Bodies in Ireland*, 4 vols. (Dublin, 1845–50), III.

Cowan, Ian B., *The Parishes of Medieval Scotland*, Scottish Record Society, 93 (Edinburgh, 1967).

Craigie, Sir William A., *A Dictionary of the Older Scottish Tongue* (Chicago and London, 1937).

Cullen, L. M. and T. C. Smout (eds.), *Comparative Aspects of Scottish and Irish Economic and Social History, 1600–1900* (Edinburgh, 1977).

Devine, T. M., *Clanship to Crofters' War: The Social Transformation of the Scottish Highlands* (Manchester, 1994).
Devine, T. M. and D. Dickson, *Ireland and Scotland, 1600–1850. Parallels and Contrasts in Economic and Social History, 1600–1900* (Edinburgh, 1983).
Donaldson, Gordon, *Scotland: James V to James VII* (Edinburgh, 1971), The Edinburgh History of Scotland, III.
Dow, F. D., *Cromwellian Scotland, 1651–1660* (Edinburgh, 1979).
Drummond, Andrew L. and James Bulloch, *The Scottish Church, 1688–1843* (Edinburgh, 1973).
Dudley Edwards, Ruth, with Bridget Hourican, *An Atlas of Irish History,* (London, 3rd edition, 2005).
Dwyer, John, Roger A. Mason and Alexander Murdoch (eds.), *New Perspectives on the Politics and Culture of Early Modern Scotland* (Edinburgh, 1982).
Elder, John R., *The Royal Fishery Companies of the Seventeenth Century* (Glasgow, 1912).
Ferguson, William, *Scotland 1689 to the Present* (Edinburgh, 1968), The Edinburgh History of Scotland, IV.
Ferguson, William, *Scotland's Relations with England: A Survey to 1707* (Edinburgh, 1977).
Fraser, Alexander, *North Knapdale in the Seventeenth and Eighteenth Centuries* (Oban, 1964).
Fraser, Sir William, *The Sutherland Book*, 3 vols. (Edinburgh 1892), I, II.
E. B. Fryde, D. E. Greenway, S. Porter and I. Roy (eds.), *Handbook of British Chronology*, (London, 3rd edition, 1986).
Giblin, Cathaldus, OFM, 'Catalogue of Material of Irish Interest in the Collection Nunziatura di Fiandra, Vatican Archives, Part 1, vols. 1–50', *Collectanea Hibernica*, 1 (Dublin and London, 1958).
Gordon, Rev. J. F. S., *Journal and Appendix to Scotichronicon and Monasticon*, 4 vols. (Glasgow, 1847), I.
Grant, I. F., *The MacLeods: The History of a Clan, 1200–1956* (Edinburgh, 1981).
Grant, I. F., *The Social and Economic Development of Scotland before 1603* (Edinburgh, 1930).
Grant, I. F. and Hugh Cheape, *Periods in Highland History* (London, 1987).
Grant, William and David Murison, *The Scottish National Dictionary* (Edinburgh, 1956).
Gregory, Donald, *The History of the Western Highlands and Isles of Scotland from A.D. 1493 to A.D. 1625* (Edinburgh, London and Dublin, 1836).
Groome, Francis H., *Ordnance Gazeteer of Scotland: A Survey of Scottish Topography, Statistical, Biographical and Historical*, 6 vols. (London, 1882–85).
Haldane, A. R. B., *New Ways through the Glens: Highland Road, Bridge and Canal Makers of the Early Nineteenth Century* (Newton Abbot, 1973).
Halloran, Brian M., *The Scots College, Paris, 1603–1792* (Edinburgh. 1997).
Hayes-McCoy, *Scots Mercenary Forces in Ireland, 1565–1603* (Dublin and London, 1937).
Hill, Rev. George, *An Historical Account of The MacDonnells of Antrim* (Belfast, 1976 reprint).
Hill, Rev. George, *An Historical Account of the Plantation in Ulster* (Belfast, 1877).

Hill, Rev. George, *The Stewarts of Ballintoy (with notices of other families in the district in the seventeenth century)* (Ballycastle, 1976 reprint).
Historical Manuscripts Commisson, *Report on the Manuscripts of the Marquis of Ormonde K.P., Preserved at the Castle, Kilkenny*, II (London, 1899).
Hogan, Rev. Edmund, SJ, *Distinguished Irishmen of the Sixteenth Century*, 1st series (London, 1894).
Hopkins, Paul, *Glencoe and the End of the Highland War* (Edinburgh, 1986).
Innes, Cosmo, James B. Brichan, *et al.* (eds.), *Origines Parochiales Scotiae*, 3 vols. (Edinburgh, 1850–55), II, pt. 1, Dioceses of Argyll and the Isles (Edinburgh, 1854).
Irwin, Clarke H., *A History of Presbyterianism in Dublin and the South and West of Ireland* (London, 1890).
Johnson, Christine, *Developments in the Roman Catholic Church in Scotland, 1789–1829* (Edinburgh, 1983).
Kirk, James, *Patterns of Reform* (Edinburgh, 1989).
Kirk, James, *The Books of Assumption of Thirds Benefices: Scottish Ecclesiastical Rentals at the Reformation*, Records of Social and Economic History, New Series, 21 (Oxford, 1995).
Lenman, Bruce, *The Jacobite Risings in Britain, 1689–1746* (London, 1980).
Lochhead, M., *The Scots Household in the Eighteenth Century* (Edinburgh, 1948).
Lynch, Michael, *Scotland: A New History* (London, 1992).
Lythe, S. G. E., *The Economy of Scotland in its European Setting, 1550–1625* (Edinburgh and London, 1960).
McConnell, Rev. James and Rev. S. G. McConnell, *Fasti of the Irish Presbyterian Church* (Belfast, 1937–1950, reprinted from *The Genealogists' Magazine*, September and December 1936).
MacDonald, A. and A., *Clan Donald*, 3 vols. (Inverness, 1896, 1900 and 1904).
MacDonald, A. M. (ed.), *Chambers's Etymological English Dictionary* (Edinburgh and London, 1967).
MacDonald, Donald J., of Castleton, *Clan Donald* (Edinburgh, 1978).
Macinnes, Allan I., *Clanship, Commerce and the House of Stuart, 1603–1788* (East Linton, 1996).
MacKenzie, W. C., *The Highlands and Isles of Scotland* (Edinburgh and London, 1937).
MacLean, Donald, *The Counter-Reformation in Scotland, 1560–1930* (London, 1931).
MacLean, Loraine, of Dochgarroch (ed.), *The Seventeenth Century in the Highlands* (Inverness, 1986).
MacLysaght, Edward, *The Surnames of Ireland* (Dublin, 1980).
Maclean-Bristol, Nicholas, *Warriors and Priests: The History of the Clan Maclean, 1300–1570* (East Linton, 1995).
Mitchison, R. and P. Roebuck (eds.), *Economy and Society in Scotland and Ireland, 1500–1939* (Edinburgh, 1988).
Montgomery-Massingberd, Hugh (editorial director), *Burke's Genealogical and Heraldic History of the Landed Gentry*, 18th edition, 3 vols (London, 1965–72), 3.
Moody, T. W., F. X. Martin and F. J. Byrne (eds.), *A New History of Ireland: III, Early Modern Ireland, 1534–1691* (Oxford, 1976).
Moody, T. W. and W. E. Vaughan (eds.), *A New History of Ireland: IV, Eighteenth-Century Ireland, 1691–1800* (Oxford, 1986).

Moody, T. W., F. X. Martin and F. J. Byrne (eds.), *A New History of Ireland: IX, Maps, Genealogies, Lists* (Oxford, 1984).
Ohlmeyer, Jane, H., *Civil War and Restoration in the Three Stuart Kingdoms: The Career of Randal MacDonnell, Marquis of Antrim, 1609–1683* (Cambridge, 1993).
O'Laverty, James, *The Bishops of Down and Connor*, 5 vols. (Dublin, 1878–95), V.
Perceval-Maxwell, M., *The Scottish Migration to Ulster in the Reign of James I* (London, 1973).
Pochin Mould, Daphne D. C., *The Irish Dominicans. The Friars Preachers in the History of Catholic Ireland* (Dublin, 1957).
Presbyterian Historical Society of Ireland, *A History of Congregations in the Presbyterian Church in Ireland, 1610–1982* (Belfast, 1982).
Purcell, Mary, *The Story of the Vincentians* (Dublin, 1973).
Reid, James Seaton, *History of the Presbyterian Church in Ireland*, 3 vols. (Belfast, 1st edition, 1837 and 2nd edition, 1867).
Rice, Michael, *The Power of the Bull* (London, 1997).
Scott, Hew *et al.* (eds.), *Fasti Ecclesiae Scoticanae*, 10 vols. (Edinburgh, 1915–1981), I, IV, VII.
Shaw, Frances J., *The Northern and Western Islands of Scotland: Their Economy and Society in the Seventeenth Century* (Edinburgh, 1980).
Simms, J. G., D. W. Hayton and Gerard O'Brien (eds.), *War and Politics in Ireland, 1649–1730* (London and Ronceverte, 1986).
Stevenson, David, *Alasdair MacColla and the Highland Problem in the Seventeenth Century* (Edinburgh, 1980).
Stevenson, David, *Revolution and Counter-Revolution in Scotland, 1644–1651* (London, 1977).
Stevenson, David, *Scottish Covenanters and Irish Confederates* (Belfast, 1981).
Stevenson, David, *The Scottish Revolution, 1637–1644* (Newton Abbot, 1973).
Stevenson, David and Wendy (eds.), *Scottish Texts and Calendars. An Analytical Guide to Serial Publications*, SHS, 4th series, 23 (Edinburgh, 1987).
The Ordnance Survey Gazetteer of Great Britain, 1:50,000 (London and Basingstoke, 1987).
Thomson, Derick, S. (ed.), *The Companion to Gaelic Scotland* (Oxford, 1983).
Trevor-Roper, H. R., *Archbishop Laud, 1573–1645* (London, 2nd edition, 1962).
Walsh, John, Colin Haydon and Stephen Taylor (eds.), *The Church of England, c. 1689–c. 1833: From Toleration to Tractarianism* (Cambridge, 1993).
Watt, D. E. R., *Fasti Ecclesiae Scoticanae Medii Aevi ad Annum 1638* (Edinburgh, 1969).
Withers, C. W. J., *Gaelic Scotland: The Transformation of a Culture Region* (London and New York, 1988).

Articles

Bannerman, John, 'Literacy in the Highlands', in Ian B. Cowan and Duncan Shaw (eds.), *The Renaissance and Reformation in Scotland* (Edinburgh, 1983), pp. 214–35.
Barkley, J. M., 'Some Scottish Bishops and Ministers in the Irish Church, 1605–35', in Duncan Shaw (ed.), *Reformation and Revolution*, essays presented to The Very Reverend Principal Emeritus Hugh Watt (Edinburgh, 1967), pp. 141–59.

Barnard, T. C., 'The Protestant Interest, 1641–1660', in Jane H. Ohlmeyer (ed.), *Ireland from Independence to Occupation* (Cambridge, 1995), pp. 218–40.
Black, Ronald, 'Colla Ciotach', *TGSI*, 48 (1972–74), pp. 201–43.
Blundell, D. O., 'St. Vincent of Paul and the Highlands of Scotland', *Dublin Review*, 149 (July and October 1911), pp. 304–20.
Bottigheimer, K., 'The Failure of the Reformation in Ireland: Une Question Bien Posée', *The Journal of Ecclesiastical History*, 36 (1985), pp. 196–207.
Campbell, J. L., 'North and South Uist in Prefect Ballantine's Report', *Innes Review*, 9 (1958), pp. 214–15.
Campbell, J. L., 'The Catholic Church in the Hebrides: 1560–1760', *The Tablet*, 206, no. 6032 (31 December 1955), pp. 655–57.
Campbell, J. L., 'The MacNeils of Barra and the Irish Franciscans', *Innes Review*, 5 (1954), pp. 33–38.
Campbell, R. H., 'The Influence of Religion on Economic Growth in Scotland in the Eighteenth Century', in T. M. Devine and David Dickson, *Ireland and Scotland, 1600–1850* (Edinburgh, 1983), pp. 220–34.
Canny, Nicholas P., 'The Formation of the Irish Mind: Religion, Politics and Gaelic Irish Literature, 1580–1750', *Past and Present*, 95 (May 1982), pp. 91–116.
Concannon, H., 'Irish Missions to Scotland in Penal Days', *The Irish Ecclesiastical Record*, 5th series, 14 (1919), pp. 395–409.
Cowan, Edward J., 'Fishers in Drumlie Waters: Clanship and Campbell Expansion in the Time of Gilleasbuig Gruamach', *TGSI*, 54 (1984–1986), pp. 269–312.
Cowan, Ian B., 'The Medieval Church in Argyll and the Isles', *RSCHS*, 20 (1980), pp. 15–29.
Cregan, Donal F., 'The Social and Cultural Background of a Counter-Reformation Episcopate, 1618–60', in A. Cosgrove and D. McCartney (eds.), *Studies in Irish History Presented to R. Dudley Edwards* (Dublin, 1979), pp. 38–84.
Cregeen, Eric, 'The Changing Role of the House of Argyll in the Scottish Highlands', in N. T. Phillipson and R. Mitchison (eds.), *Scotland in the Age of Improvement* (Edinburgh, 1970), pp. 5–23.
Darragh, James, 'The Catholic Population of Scotland since the Year 1680', *Innes Review*, 4, no. 1 (1953), pp. 49–59.
Dawson, Jane, 'Calvinism and the Gaidhealtachd in Scotland', in A. Pettegree, A. Duke and G. Lewis (eds.), *Calvinism in Europe, 1540–1620* (Cambridge, 1994), pp. 231–53.
Dawson, Jane, 'The Gaidhealtachd and the Emergence of the Scottish Highlands', in Brendan Bradshaw and Peter Roberts (eds.), *British Consciousness and Identity: The Making of Britain, 1533–1707* (Cambridge, 1998), pp. 259–300.
Dilworth, Rev. Dom. Mark, 'Benedictine Monks of Ratisbon and Wurzburg in the Seventeenth and Eighteenth Centuries: Emigrés from the Highlands of Scotland', *TGSI*, 44 (1964–1966), pp. 94–110.
Dilworth, Rev. Mark, 'The Counter-Reformation in Scotland: A Select Bibliography', *RSCHS*, 22 (1984), pp. 85–100.
Dilworth, Mark, 'Notes: The Blind Harper and Catholicism', *Innes Review*, 22 (1971), pp. 113–14.
Dilworth, Mark, 'The Scottish Mission in 1688–1689', *Innes Review*, 20 (1969), pp. 68–79.

Doran, Wendy, 'Bishop Thomas Nicolson: First Vicar-Apostolic, 1695–1718', *Innes Review*, 39, no. 2 (1988), pp. 109–32.

Duggan, Lucy, 'The Irish Brigade with Montrose', *Irish Ecclesiastical Record*, 5th series, 89 (1958), pp. 171–84, 246–58.

Durkacz, Victor E., 'The Church of Scotland's Eighteenth-Century Attitudes to Gaelic Preaching', *SGS*, 13, part 2 (1981), pp. 145–58.

Durkacz, Victor, 'The Source of the Language Problem in Scottish Education, 1688–1709', *SHR*, 57 (1978), pp. 28–39.

Durkan, John, 'Catholic Survival in the West of Scotland', pp. 87–91, *St. Peter's College Magazine*, 21, no. 82 (June 1954), pp. 87–91.

Ferguson, W., 'Religion and the Massacre of Glencoe', *SHR*, 46 (1967), pp. 82–87; and *SHR*, 47 (1968), pp. 203–09.

Ferguson, William, 'The Problems of the Established Church in the West Highlands and Islands in the Eighteenth Century', *RSCHS*, 17 (1969), pp. 15–31.

Forbes, F. and W. J. Anderson, 'Clergy Lists of the Highland District, 1732–1828', *Innes Review*, 17 (1966), pp. 129–84.

Ford, Alan, 'The Protestant Reformation in Ireland', in Ciaran Brady and Raymond Gillespie (eds.), *Natives and Newcomers: Essays on the Making of Irish Colonial Society, 1534–1641* (Dublin, 1986), pp. 50–74.

Giblin, Cathaldus, OFM, 'Francis MacDonnell, O.F.M., Son of the First Earl of Antrim (d. 1636)', *Seanchas Ardmhacha*, 8 (1975–1976), pp. 44–54.

Giblin, Cathaldus, OFM, 'St. Oliver Plunkett, Francis MacDonnell, O.F.M. and the Mission to the Hebrides', *Collectanea Hibernica*, 17 (1974–1975), pp. 64–102.

Giblin, Rev. Cathaldus, OFM, 'The "Acta" of Propaganda Archives and the Scottish Mission, 1623–1670', *Innes Review*, 5 (1954), pp. 39–76.

Giblin, Father Cathaldus, OFM, 'The Mission to the Highlands and the Isles *c.* 1670', *Franciscan College Annual* (Multyfarnham, 1954), pp. 7–20.

Houston, R., 'Geographical mobility in Scotland, 1652–1811: The Evidence of Testimonials', *Journal of Historical Geography*, 11, 4 (1985), pp. 379–94.

Kilroy, Sister Phil, 'Bishops and Ministers in Ulster during the Primacy of Ussher, 1625–1656', *Seanchas Ardmhacha*, 8, no. 2 (1977), pp. 284–98.

Kilroy, Phil, 'Radical Religion in Ireland, 1641–1660', in Jane H. Ohlmeyer (ed.), *Ireland from Independence to Occupation, 1641–1660* (Cambridge, 1995), pp. 201–17.

Kirk, James, 'John Carswell, Superintendent of Argyll', in *Patterns of Reform: Continuity and Change in the Reformation Kirk* (Edinburgh, 1989), pp. 280–304.

Kirk, James, 'The Jacobean Church in the Highlands, 1567–1625', in Loraine MacLean of Dochgarroch (ed.), *The Seventeenth Century in the Highlands* (Inverness, 1986), pp. 24–51.

Kirk, James, 'The Kirk and the Highlands at the Reformation', *Northern Scotland*, 7, no. 1 (1986), pp. 1–22.

Lennon, Colm, 'The Counter-Reformation in Ireland, 1542–1641', in Ciaran Brady and Raymond Gillespie (eds.), *Natives and Newcomers: Essays on the Making of Irish Colonial Society, 1534–1641* (Dublin, 1986), pp. 75–92.

McCaughey, Terence P., 'Protestantism and Scottish Highland Culture', in James P. Mackey (ed.), *An Introduction to Celtic Christianity* (Edinburgh, 1989), pp. 172–205.

MacCraith, Mícheál, 'The Gaelic Reaction to the Reformation', in S. Ellis and S. Barber (eds.), *Conquest and Union: Fashioning a British State, 1485–1725* (London, 1995), pp. 139–61.

Macdonald, Fiona A., 'Irish Priests in the Highlands: Judicial Evidence from Argyll', *Innes Review*, 45 (1995), pp. 15–33; and Errata, *Innes Review*, 46 (1995), p. 165.

Macdonald, Fiona A., 'Perspectives on the Running of Contraband Cargoes between Ireland and the Scottish Highlands in the Mid-Eighteenth Century', in Donald MacAulay, James Gleasure and Colm Ó Baoill (eds.), *SGS*, 17, Special Volume, Festschrift for Professor D. S. Thomson, pp. 221–38.

MacDonell, A. and D. McRoberts, 'The Mass Stones of Lochaber', *Innes Review*, 17 (1966), pp. 71–81.

MacDonnell, Hector, 'Jacobitism and the Third and Fourth Earls of Antrim', *The Glynns*, 13 (1985), pp. 50–54.

McDonnell, Randal, 'The McNeills of Cushendun and the McNeiles of Ballycastle', *The Glynns*, 1 (1979), pp. 21–24.

MacGuaire, Rev. Sean, CSSR, 'Ireland and the Catholic Hebrides', *The Irish Ecclesiastical Record*, 5th series, 42 (1933), pp. 345–64, 488–507.

McHugh, Mary, 'The Religious Condition of the Highlands and Islands in the Mid-Eighteenth Century', *Innes Review*, 35, no. 1 (1984), pp. 12–22.

Macinnes, Allan I., 'Catholic Recusancy and the Penal Laws, 1603–1707', *RSCHS*, 23, pt. 1 (1987), pp. 27–63.

Macinnes, Allan I., 'Crown, Clans and *Fine*: The "Civilising" of Scottish Gaeldom, 1587–1603', *Northern Scotland*, 13 (1993), pp. 31–55.

Macinnes, Allan I., 'Notes and Comments – The First Scottish Tories?' *SHR*, 67, pt. 1, no. 183 (1988), pp. 56–66.

Macinnes, Allan, I., 'Scottish Gaeldom, 1638–1651: The Vernacular Response to the Covenanting Dynamic', in John Dwyer, Roger A. Mason and Alexander Murdoch (eds.), *New Perspectives on the Politics and Culture of Early Modern Scotland* (Edinburgh, 1982), pp. 59–94.

Macinnes, Allan I., 'Social Mobility in Medieval and Early Modern Scottish Gaeldom: The Controvertible Evidence', *TGSI*, 58 (1992–1994), pp. 371–405.

Macinnes, Allan I., 'The Massacre of Glencoe', *The Historian*, 35 (1992), pp. 16–18.

MacInnes, Rev. John, 'Baptism in the Highlands', *RSCHS*, 13 (1959), pp. 1– 24.

MacInnes, Rev. John, 'Gaelic Religious Poetry, 1650–1850', *RSCHS*, 10 (1950), pp. 31–53.

MacInnes, Rev. John, 'West Highland Sea Power in the Middle Ages', *TGSI*, 48 (1972–1974), pp. 518–56.

MacKenzie, Donald W., 'The Worthy Translator – How the Scottish Gaels Got the Scriptures in Their Own Tongue', *TGSI*, 57 (1990–1992), pp. 168–202.

MacKinnon, Kenneth M., 'The School in Gaelic Scotland: Some Historical and Sociological Perspectives and Suggestions', *TGSI*, 47 (1971–1972), pp. 374–91.

MacLean, Rev. D., 'The Life and Literary Labours of the Rev. Robert Kirk of Aberfoyle', *TGSI*, 31 (1922–24), pp. 328–66.

MacLean, very Rev. Duncan Canon, 'Catholicism in the Highlands and Isles, 1560–1680', *Innes Review*, 3 (1952), pp. 5–13.

MacLean, very Rev. Duncan Canon, 'Mr. Robert Munro, Secular Priest, 1671–1704', *St. Peter's College Magazine*, 20, no. 77 (1951), p. 50.

MacLean, Rev. Robert Donald, 'Roman Catholicism in Scotland in the Reign of Charles II', *RSCHS*, 3 (1929), pp. 43–54.

MacLean-Bristol, Nicholas, 'The MacLeans from 1560–1707: A Re-appraisal', in Loraine MacLean of Dochgarroch (ed.), *The Seventeenth Century in the Highlands* (Inverness, 1986), pp. 70–88.

McLynn, F. J., 'Ireland and the Jacobite Rising of 1745', *Irish Sword*, 13. (1982), pp. 339–52.

MacLysaght, Edward, *The Surnames of Ireland* (Shannon, 1969).

MacMillan, Gretchen M., *State, Society and Authority in Ireland: The Foundations of the Modern State* (Dublin, 1993).

McMillan, James F., 'Jansenists and anti-Jansenists in Eighteenth Century Scotland: The *Unigenitus* Quarrels on the Scottish Catholic Mission, 1732–1746', *Innes Review*, 39, no. 1 (1988), pp. 12–45.

Macpherson, Alan G. 'An old Highland Genealogy and the Evolution of a Scottish Clan', *Scottish Studies*, 10 (1966), pp. 1–43.

McRoberts, David, 'The Death of Father Francis White', *Innes Review*, 17 (1966), pp. 186–88.

McRoberts, David and Alexander Boyle, 'A Hebridean Cisioganus', *Innes Review*, 21, no. 2 (1970), pp. 108–23.

MacWilliam, very Rev. Alexander Canon, 'A Highland Mission: Strathglass, 1671–1777', *Innes Review*, 24 (1973), pp. 75–102.

MacWilliam, very Rev. Alexander Canon, 'The Jesuit Mission in Upper Deeside, 1671–1737', *Innes Review*, 23 (1972), pp. 22–39.

Meek, Donald, 'The Gaelic Bible', in David F. Wright (ed.), *The Bible in Scottish Life and Literature* (Edinburgh, 1988), pp. 9–23.

Millet, Benignus, OFM, 'Catalogue of Irish Material in Fourteen Volumes of the *Scritture Originalie Riferite Nelle Congregazioni Generali* in Propaganda Archives', *Collectanea Hibernica*, 10 (1967), pp. 7–59.

Moody, T. W., 'Redmond O'Hanlon', *Belfast Natural History Society Proclamations*, 2nd series, I (1937), pp. 17–33.

Morgan, Hiram, 'The End of Gaelic Ulster: A Thematic Interpretation of Events between 1534 & 1610', *Irish Historical Studies*, 26 (1988), pp. 8–32.

Morrison, Alick, 'Early Harris Estate Papers, 1679–1703', *TGSI*, 51 (1978–1980), pp. 81–172.

O'Sullivan, William, 'An Irish *Cisiojanus*', *Collectanea Hibernica*, 29 (1988), pp. 7–13.

Perceval-Maxwell, Michael, 'The Ulster Plantation: Scotland's First Colonial Venture', *Scottish Colloquium Proceedings*, 2 (Guelph, 1969), pp. 1–19.

Prebble, J., 'Religion and the Massacre of Glencoe', *SHR*, 46 (1967), pp. 185–88.

Roberts, Alasdair, 'Catholic Kintail: A Marginal Community', *TGSI*, 58 (1992–1994), pp. 123–35.

Roberts, Alasdair, 'Gregor McGregor (1681–1740) and the Highland Problem in the Scottish Catholic Mission', *Innes Review*, 39, no. 2 (1988), pp. 81–108.

Roberts, Alasdair, 'Highland Catholicism at the Margin: Skye, Lewis and Ardnamurchan', unpublished typescript.

Roberts, Alasdair, 'The "Irishes" in Scotland, 1644–1647', *The Glynns*, 14 (1986), pp. 34–43.

Ross, Anthony, 'Dominicans and Scotland in the Seventeenth Century', *Innes Review*, 23 (1972), pp. 40–75.

Sanderson, Margaret H. B., 'Catholic Recusancy in Scotland in the Sixteenth Century', *Innes Review*, 21 (1970), pp. 87–107.

Sanderson, M. H. B., 'Roman Catholic Recusancy, 1560–1603', in Peter McNeill and Ranald Nicolson (eds.), *An Historical Atlas of Scotland* (St. Andrews, 1975), pp. 89–90.

Scott Pearson, Professor A. F., 'Alumni of St. Andrews and the Settlement of Ulster', *UJA*, 3rd series, 14 (1951), pp. 7–14.

Sellar, W. D. H., 'Marriage, Divorce and Concubinage in Gaelic Scotland', *TGSI*, 51 (1978–1980), pp. 464–93.

Simms, K., 'Guesting and Feasting in Gaelic Ireland', *Journal of the Royal Society of Antiquaries of Ireland*, 108 (1978), pp. 67–100.

Smout, T. C., 'Famine and Famine-Relief in Scotland', in L. M. Cullen and T. C. Smout (eds.), *Comparative Aspects of Scottish and Irish Economic and Social History, 1600–1900* (Edinburgh, 1977), pp. 21–31.

Stevenson, David, 'The Irish Franciscan Mission to Scotland and the Irish Rebellion of 1641', *Innes Review*, 30 (1979), pp. 54–61.

Stewart, A. I. B., 'Lachlan McNeill Buidhe', *The Scottish Genealogist*, 34, no. 4 (December 1987), pp. 380–83.

Stewart, A. I. B., 'Some Descendants of Lachlan McNeill Buidhe', *The Scottish Genealogist*, 34, no. 4 (December 1987), pp. 377–79.

Stewart, James A., Jr., 'The Clan Ranald and Catholic Missionary Successes, 1715–1745', *Innes Review*, 45 (1994), pp. 29–46.

Szechi, Daniel and David Hayton, 'John Bull's Other Kingdoms: The English Government of Scotland and Ireland', in Clyve Jones (ed.), *Britain in the First Age of Party, 1680–1750* (London and Ronceverte, 1987), pp. 241–80.

Thomson, Derick, 'Niall Mòr MacMhuirich', *TGSI*, 49 (1977), pp. 9–25.

Thomson, Derick, 'The MacMhuirich Bardic Family', *TGSI*, 43 (1966), pp. 276–304.

Thomson, Derick, 'The Poetry of Niall MacMhuirich', *TGSI*, 46 (1970), pp. 281–307.

Thomson, Derick, 'Three Seventeenth Century Bardic Poets: Niall Mòr, Cathal and Niall MacMhuirich', in A. J. Aitken, M. P. McDiarmid and D. S. Thomson (eds.), *Bards and Makars* (Glasgow, 1977), pp. 221–46.

Thompson, F. G., 'The Folklore Elements in "Carmina Gadelica"', *TGSI*, 44 (1967), pp. 226–55.

Walker, Rev. Breifne, 'Blessed Oliver Plunkett and the Popish Plot in Ireland', *The Irish Ecclesiastical Record*, 5th series, 109 (1968), pp. 313–30.

Whiteford, Rev. D. H., 'Jacobitism as a Factor in Presbyterian Episcopalian Relationships in Scotland, 1689–90', *RSCHS*, 16 (1966–1968), pt. I, pp. 129–49, pt. II, pp. 185–201.

Wilby, Noel MacDonald, 'The "Encreasce of Popery" in the Highlands, 1714–1747', *Innes Review*, 17 (1966), pp. 91–115.

Withers, C. W. J., 'The Highland Parishes in 1698: An Examination of Sources for the Definition of the Gaidhealtachd', *Scottish Studies*, 24 (1980), pp. 63–88.

Wyman, A. L., 'The Surgeoness: The Female Practitioner of Surgery, 1400–1800', *Medical History*, 28 (1984), pp. 22–41.

Unpublished Secondary Material

Theses

Allen, Robert, 'Scottish Ecclesiastical Influence upon Irish Presbyterianism' (unpublished MA dissertation, Queen's University, Belfast, 1940).

Barkley, J. M., 'The History of the Ruling Eldership in Irish Presbyterianism', 2 vols. (unpublished MA dissertation, Queen's University, Belfast, 1952).

Bishop, Iain Murray, 'The Education of Ulster Students at Glasgow University during the Eighteenth Century' (unpublished MA dissertation, Queen's University, Belfast, 1987).

Doran, Wendy J., 'Bishop Thomas Nicolson and the Roman Catholic Mission to Scotland, 1694–1718' (unpublished MLitt dissertation, Glasgow University, 1986).

Furgol, Edward Mackie, 'The Religious Aspects of the Scottish Covenanting Armies, 1639–1651' (PhD dissertation, Oxford University, 1982). See the published Furgol, Edward M., *A Regimental History of the Covenanting Armies, 1639–1651* (Edinburgh, 1990).

Gillespie, Ernest Raymond, 'East Ulster in the Early Seventeenth Century: A Colonial Economy and Society' (PhD dissertation, Trinity College Dublin, 1982). See the published Gillespie, R., *Colonial Ulster: The Settlement of East Ulster, 1600–1641* (Cork, 1985).

Hunter, Robert J., 'The Ulster Plantation in the Counties of Armagh and Cavan, 1608–41' (unpublished MLitt dissertation, Trinity College, Dublin, 1968).

McCall, Timothy Paul Joseph, 'The Gaelic Background to the Settlement of Antrim and Down, 1580–1641' (unpublished MA dissertation, Queen's University, Belfast, 1983).

Macdonald, Fiona Anne, 'Ireland and Scotland: Historical Perspectives on the Gaelic Dimension, 1560–1760', 2 vols. (unpublished PhD dissertation, University of Glasgow, 1994), I, II.

Macinnes, Allan Iain, 'The Origin and Organisation of the Covenanting Movement during the Reign of Charles I, with a Particular Reference to the West of Scotland', 2 vols. (PhD dissertation, Glasgow University, 1987), I, II. See the published Macinnes, A. I., *Charles I and the Making of the Covenanting Movement, 1625–1641* (Edinburgh, 1991).

Turner, Brian Samuel, 'Distributional Aspects of Family Name Study Illustrated in the Glens of Antrim' (unpublished PhD dissertation, Queen's University, Belfast, 1974).

Whyte, Alison, 'Scottish Gaelic Folksong, 1500–1800' (unpublished BLitt dissertation, University of Glasgow, 1971).

Unpublished Scripts

Presbyterian Historical Society, Belfast

Record index of individuals.

Scott Pearson, Rev. A. F., 'Puritan and Presbyterian Settlements in Ireland, 1560–1660', 2 vols. (unpublished typescript, Belfast, 1948), I, II.

Stewart, Rev. David, 'The History of the Presbyterian Settlements in Ireland, 1641–1760' (unpublished typescript, Belfast, 1948).

Scottish Catholic Archives, Columba House, Edinburgh

CC1/8–15, Canon William Clapperton, 'Memoirs of Missionary Priests', revised and transcribed by the very Rev. George Canon Wilson.

Scottish History Department, University of Glasgow

Macinnes, Allan I., Handlist and Notes from Congregazione Particolari (CP) 87, di Scozia et Ingliterra, vol. 89, 1737–41, and Scritture riferite nei Congressi (SC) 2, Scozia, vol. 2, 1701–1760, in the Archivio del Palazzo di Propaganda Fide, Rome.

Index